Making Morality Work

Making Morality Work

Holly M. Smith

OXFORD
UNIVERSITY PRESS

OXFORD
UNIVERSITY PRESS

Great Clarendon Street, Oxford, OX2 6DP,
United Kingdom

Oxford University Press is a department of the University of Oxford.
It furthers the University's objective of excellence in research, scholarship,
and education by publishing worldwide. Oxford is a registered trade mark of
Oxford University Press in the UK and in certain other countries

First Edition published in 2018

Published in the United States of America by Oxford University Press
198 Madison Avenue, New York, NY 10016, United States of America

British Library Cataloguing in Publication Data
Data available

Library of Congress Control Number: 2017956293

ISBN 978–0–19–956008–0

For Alvin,
Raphe, and Sidra

Contents

Acknowledgments

Moral philosophers propose ethical theories that provide comprehensive accounts of what kinds of actions are right and wrong. Typically such theories (just like their counterpart moral codes in everyday morality) make heavy *informational* demands on those governed by them: one needs substantial information in order to identify one's best option by the lights of such a theory. But people suffer from imperfect information: they labor under false beliefs, or they are ignorant or uncertain about the consequences and circumstances of their possible actions. Dating back over many years, my puzzlement about how moral theories should deal with these impediments to decision-making first found published expression in a 1983 article on culpable ignorance. Since then I have returned again and again to a cluster of closely related questions about the epistemic problem for morality. The publications reporting my deliberations finally became so interconnected that I realized only a book-length treatment would suffice. This book is the product of that conclusion.

No author is an island. One needs assistance and support of many kinds, and I have been most fortunate in this regard. Extremely generous institutional support has been forthcoming for various phases of this project: the Minnie Cumnock Blodgett Endowed Postgraduate Fellowship from the American Association of University Women; the hospitality of the Center for Advanced Study in the Behavioral Sciences (as a non-Fellow); sabbatical and other research leaves from the University of Michigan, the University of Illinois at Chicago Circle, the University of Arizona, and Rutgers, The State University of New Jersey; a Fellowship for Independent Study from the National Endowment for the Humanities; a Visiting Fellowship at the School of Philosophy, Research School of the Social Sciences, The Australian National University; and a Visiting Scholar appointment at the University of California, Berkeley. The Carl and Lily Pforzheimer Foundation Fellowship at the National Humanities Center provided a wonderful venue for concentrated focus on the manuscript, enlivened by wide-ranging conversations with the other Fellows, and supported by a superb staff of research librarians and the expert editorial assistance of Karen Carroll.

I am especially grateful to Walter Sinnott-Armstrong for organizing and hosting a 2009 workshop at Dartmouth College on the book manuscript in its initial stage, and to the other participants in the workshop—Julia Driver, Peter Graham, Carey Heckman, Mark Timmons, and Michael J. Zimmerman—all of whom dedicated an amazing amount of time and philosophical acumen to probing my arguments.

Papers emerging from this project were presented in too many venues over the years to enumerate here, but I continue to be grateful for the insightful feedback I received from these audiences. Various aspects of the project (not all of which found their way into the final book manuscript) have been published in a series of papers over the years;[1] I appreciate the referees for these papers whose comments invariably improved the final versions.

Along the way discussions with a number of individuals about the questions addressed in the book have been of immense value. Many of these conversations happened too long ago for me to retrieve the names of all the interlocutors, but among those with whom I debated these issues in recent years the following deserve special mention and thanks: Douglas Blair, John Carroll, Janice Dowell, Andy Egan, Fred Feldman and also attendees in his Spring 2010 moral philosophy seminar, Nancy Gamburd, Thomas Hurka, Douglas Husak, Frank Jackson, the participants in my 2008 graduate seminar (particularly Timothy Campbell, Pavel Davydov, Preston Greene, Angela Harper, Nicholas Laskowski, Zachary Miller, and Jennifer Wang), and especially the participants in my 2015 graduate seminar (Ben Bronner, Nate Flores, Anders Herlitz, Atina Knowles, Eli Shupe, and Philip Swenson). In the final stages Eli Shupe valiantly leapt into the breach on Chapter 14 when a temporary visual impairment disrupted my ability to put it into final form, while Rochel (Roxy) Moskowitz labored long and effectively to impose order on the reference section.

Finally, I would like to thank Peter Momtchiloff for providing unflagging and patient editorial advice and encouragement, and two anonymous Oxford University Press readers for producing multiple pages of closely-spaced and even more closely-reasoned comments on the manuscript that led to what I hope are considerable improvements.

My children Raphael Goldman and Sidra Goldman-Mellor and my husband Alvin Goldman have lived with this project for as long as I have, and never failed to supply encouragement, advice, and welcome distractions. I am grateful to them all.

Holly M. Smith

April 2017

[1] "Culpable Ignorance," *The Philosophical Review* 92 (October 1983): 543–71; "Making Moral Decisions," *Noûs* 22 (March 1988): 89–108; "Deciding How To Decide: Is There a Regress Problem?" in Michael Bacharach and Susan Hurley, eds., 194–219. *Essays in the Foundations of Decision Theory*, 194–219 (Oxford: Basil Blackwell, 1991); "Subjective Rightness," *Social Philosophy and Policy* 27 (Summer 2010): 64–110; "Measuring the Consequences of Rules," *Utilitas* 22 (December 2010): 413–33; "The Prospective View of Obligation," *Journal of Ethics and Social Philosophy* (February 2011) (<http://www.jesp.org/>); "The Moral Clout of Reasonable Beliefs," in Mark Timmons, ed., *Oxford Studies in Normative Ethics*, Vol. 1, 1–25 (Oxford: Oxford University Press, 2011); "Using Moral Principles to Guide Decisions," *Philosophical Issues* 22 (2012): 369–86; "The Subjective Moral Duty to Inform Oneself before Acting," *Ethics* 125 (October 2014): 1–28; "Review of Michael Zimmerman, *Ignorance and Morality*," *Mind* 125 (2016): 935–42; and "Tracing Cases of Culpable Ignorance," in Rik Peels, ed., *Perspectives on Ignorance from Moral and Social Philosophy*, 95–119 (New York: Routledge, 2016). Note that some of these publications appeared under the name "Holly S. Goldman," while most of them appeared under the name "Holly M. Smith."

1

Introduction

On July 2, 1881, President James A. Garfield was shot twice by Charles A. Guiteau. The first bullet grazed Garfield's arm, but the second struck him in the right side of the back and lodged deep in the body. Although no one expected Garfield to live through the night, he lingered on his deathbed for eighty days. At the time, without the benefit of modern diagnostics, Garfield's doctors could not determine the location of the second bullet. The lead physician came to believe the bullet was lodged on the right side of Garfield's body. At least a dozen medical experts probed the president's wound, often with unsterilized metal instruments or bare hands. Believing that the bullet might have pierced his intestines, Garfield's doctors did him a disservice by strictly limiting his solid food intake. The president lost over 100 pounds from July to September. At the autopsy, it became evident that the bullet had pierced Garfield's vertebra but missed his spinal cord, had not struck any vital organs, arteries, or veins, and had come to rest in fatty tissues on the left side of the president's back. Historians agree that massive infection, which resulted from unsterile practices, contributed to Garfield's death. Dr. Ira Rutkow, a professor of surgery and medical historian, said, "Garfield had such a nonlethal wound ... the doctors basically starved him to death." Guiteau, hanged on June 30, 1882, repeatedly criticized Garfield's doctors, suggesting that they were the ones who had killed the president. "I just shot him," Guiteau said.[1]

Garfield's doctors rightly understood their chief duty to be saving the president's life. However, hampered by lack of understanding of the importance of sterile procedures, by the false belief that limiting his food intake would protect him, and by uncertainty about the bullet's location, in fact their efforts led to his death. What are the implications of this kind of situation for morality? On one view, the primary role of a morality's *theory of right conduct*—its tool for evaluating actions—is to explain the moral status of actions by providing an account of the features that make actions right or wrong. A full-blown moral system contains, among other components, a complete account of these features. This account might be viewed as a *moral theory*: it is (roughly) comparable to a scientific theory that sets out the factors governing the state of a given type of physical system. Thus the gas laws tell us that the temperature of a body of gas

---

[1] Schaffer (2006). My account is taken almost verbatim from this article. However, in order to provide a brief but clear account, I have elided and transposed passages, and added transitions, which are here unmarked.

depends on its volume and pressure. Similarly, a moral theory tells us that the rightness or wrongness of an action depends on such features as the rights honored or violated by the action, the values of the consequences the action produces, the promises the action fulfills or breaches, and so forth.

The gas laws, like all scientific theories, can be true and illuminating even though it may be impossible, at least in particular cases, to ascertain what the pressure and temperature of a given body of gas are.[2] But is the same thing true in morality? Can a proposed moral theory be both true and illuminating even though it may be impossible, either in general or in some particular cases, to ascertain whether concrete actions have the characteristics stated by the theory as determining their moral status? Many philosophers would say "no." They insist that a moral theory must successfully play *two* primary roles: a *theoretical role*, in which it provides a correct account of the features that make actions right or wrong, and a *practical role*, in which the theory helps a person choose which actions to perform and which not.[3] Indeed, some philosophers go further by holding that the *only* role of moral theories is a practical one: their use in guiding decision-making.[4]

If moral theories must serve a practical role—as their only role, or as one of their two leading roles—this suggests that their user-friendliness as decision-guides provides a crucial test for the adequacy of any proposed moral theory. On this view, if a moral theory cannot be used successfully to guide decisions, it must be rejected as inadequate. The view of Garfield's physicians that they had a duty to save the president's life would have to be rejected, since they lacked the information necessary to carry out this duty. Such a rejection could be extremely broad: if there is even a single person who cannot use the theory on one occasion, the theory is deemed inadequate in general. Or the rejection could be extremely narrow: if there is someone who cannot use the theory on a single occasion, then the theory is merely inadequate for that person on that occasion.

The claimed theoretical and practical roles of a moral system are closely linked. Indeed, they are so closely linked that many discussions did not even distinguish

---

[2] The view that scientific theories articulate what is true without catering to our ability to use them is seen by some philosophers as a naïve view. For somewhat different views about scientific theories, see recent work on the role of idealization in formulating scientific theories, for example Cartwright (1983) and (1989), and McMullin (1985). McMullin describes "Galilean idealization" as "the practice of introducing distortions into theories with the goal of simplifying theories in order to make them computationally tractable." This quotation and above references are from Weisberg (2007). More discussion is available in Godfrey-Smith (2009).

[3] One of many examples is provided by Mark Timmons, who states in (2002), p. 3, that "There are two fundamental aims of moral theory: one practical, and the other theoretical." Another clear statement is given by Väyrynen (2006): "We can distinguish two motivations for constructing ethical theories. One is *practical*: we might want an ethical theory to guide action. Another is *theoretical* and, specifically, *explanatory*: we might want an ethical theory to explain why certain actions are right and others wrong" (p. 291).

[4] For examples, see Narveson's statement (1967), p. 112, that "…the purpose of ethics is to guide action"; and Gibbard (1990), p. 43.

these roles until relatively recently.[5] But it is not at all clear that what enables a moral principle to fulfill one role automatically equips it to fulfill the other role. In particular, as the example of President Garfield's faulty medical care shows, when we attempt to choose an action by reference to the factors that we believe would make our action right, a variety of *cognitive impediments* may stand in our way.

Brief reflection about the kinds of cognitive impediments that might prevent us from straightforwardly using a moral principle to successfully make decisions suggests many potential problems. A moral principle might be unintelligible: it might involve difficult concepts or a baroque structure that cannot be understood by many agents. Or on some occasions agents may labor under false beliefs about the relevant facts about their circumstances, beliefs that cause them to draw erroneous conclusions about what is morally required or forbidden by the principle. The physicians' belief that the bullet had pierced Garfield's intestines is an example of this kind of error. Or agents may be uncertain what the facts of their situation are, so they are unable to draw any conclusions at all about what actions the principle implies would be right or wrong. The physicians' uncertainty about the exact location of the bullet is an example of this form of uncertainty. Or agents may suffer from computational constraints: they may lack time or intellectual capacity to think the problem through, acquire relevant information, or calculate what would be best according to the principle. And of course agents may also suffer from cognitive deficiencies regarding *morality itself*: they may be uncertain or in error about what the correct moral theory is.

These deficiencies affect us as profoundly as they affected President Garfield's physicians in 1881. A Catholic doctor trying to apply the Doctrine of Double Effect to a difficult obstetrical case may realize he doesn't understand the Doctrine well enough to apply it to his decision. Soldiers in contemporary conflicts shoot innocent civilians whom they falsely believe to be suicide bombers. Political leaders are torn between supporting and opposing a proposed stimulus plan because they are uncertain whether it would effectively rescue the faltering economy. Airplane pilots dealing with sudden flight emergencies may not have sufficient time to calculate the best corrective measure to take. People disagree, often violently, about the moral permissibility of abortion or of writings denigrating religion, while many are unsure whether it is wrong to kill animals for food.

It is a commonplace among philosophers that attempts to follow act utilitarianism founder on the shoals of our inability to accurately predict the consequences of our actions on the general welfare. But deontological theories are equally subject to limitations on our knowledge, since the relevant *circumstances* or *nature* of an action—quite apart from its consequences—may also be difficult for the agent to ascertain accurately. Deontological theories may forbid killing the innocent, committing adultery,

---

[5] For a discussion of the mistakes this conflation has led to, see the ground-breaking discussion by E. Bales (1971). In (1986) Pettit and Brennan discuss a theory they label "standard consequentialism" which assumes that "the function which determines which is the right decision is also the function which ought to be applied in decision-making; it serves at once to evaluate options, and to select them" (p. 438).

convicting innocent defendants, stealing, lying, failing to compensate those whom one has unjustifiably harmed, and so forth. But any given agent may be mistaken or uncertain as to whether a possible killing victim is innocent, whether the person with whom she has sexual relations is married, whether a defendant is guilty of the crime, whether an item of property belongs to her or to someone else, whether her statement will mislead her intended audience, or whether a given level of compensation covers the loss.

The responses advocated by moral theorists who have addressed the issue of human cognitive limitations impeding moral decision-making tend to fall into three distinct categories.[6]

First, some theorists hold that these problems are not problems with the moral theories, but rather problems *in us*: we are the ones lacking (for example, lacking adequate nonmoral knowledge), and we should devote our efforts to improving ourselves so that we can use the correct moral principles. On this view, the sole role of a moral theory is to provide a theoretical account of right and wrong. Its correctness in this role is unaffected by its adequacy or inadequacy for use by limited human beings as a practical decision-guide. The *content* of the correct moral theory is not determined by how well or poorly it plays a practical role. I shall call this response the "Austere Response," since it maintains that purely theoretical considerations dictate the content of the theory, and refuses to bow to pressure to improve the theory's workability as a practical decision-guide.

Second, some theorists hold that a moral theory must be capable both of providing a theoretical account of right and wrong, *and also* of providing a practical guide to decision-making. On this view a moral theory's inadequacy as a practical decision-guide—arising from the cognitive failings of the decision makers themselves—shows that the theory is inadequate not only as a decision-guide but also as a theoretical account of right and wrong. The solution of these theorists is to replace the inadequate theory with a new theory, perhaps similar in normative spirit, which can serve successfully in both roles. I shall call this response the "Pragmatic Response." It accepts the claim that the usability of a moral theory for making decisions provides a constraint on its correctness as a theoretical account of right and wrong.

Third, still other theorists hold that a moral theory must indeed be usable both as a theoretical account and also as a decision-guide, but claim that the theory need not be

---

[6] The question whether the correctness of a proposed moral theory is constrained by agents' cognitive capacities to ascertain what it prescribes in particular cases has its parallels in other domains of philosophy. Peacocke (1999), p. 1, labels this "the problem of reconciliation," and describes it as follows: "We have to reconcile a plausible account of what is involved in the truth of statements of a given kind with a credible account of how we can know those statements, when we know them." Peacocke cites, as examples, modal truths, truths about the intentional contents of our own mental states, and truths about the past (pp. 3–5). His own solution appears to most closely resemble what I call the "Pragmatic Response" in the text below. In philosophy of science certain theorists maintain that it is a constraint on laws of nature that they be "epistemically accessible." For discussion, see J. Cohen and C. Callendar (2009). Similar debates arise in epistemology. For example, A. Goldman (1978) argues that "epistemic advice or rules must be capable of being followed" (p. 513). I am grateful to Jason Stanley for pointing out discussions of this broader set of issues.

directly usable. Instead, on their view, the moral theory is established as the correct account of right and wrong purely by reference to considerations that do not include its practical usability. Once established as the correct account, the theory (if not directly usable itself to make decisions) can be supplemented by auxiliary decision-guides that are themselves directly usable by agents in making their decisions. Such a theory accepts a division of labor between the portion of the theory that offers a purely theoretical account of right and wrong and the portion of the theory that offers practical guidance. I shall call this response the "Hybrid Response." It does not try to combine, unaltered, all the elements of the Austere and Pragmatic views. However, it tries to capture the Austere theme that pragmatic considerations cannot affect the truth or falsity of a theory, together with the Pragmatic theme that usability is a crucial attribute for any acceptable moral theory. An important task for the Hybrid theorist is to link the correct account of right and wrong to decision-guides that are appropriate for agents trying to make decisions by indirect reference to the correct theoretical account.

This book focuses on issues raised for morality by the fact that we, who are asked (and ask ourselves) to do what morality requires, and who are judged by our success or failure in this endeavor, are epistemically limited agents who must contend with false beliefs, uncertainty, ignorance, and intellectual limitations in trying to ascertain and do what is right. The inquiry can be seen as a branch of the debate between "ideal" and "non-ideal" theory, a debate in which some participants advocate developing moral theories that idealize away the imperfections (in this case, epistemic imperfections) which burden the subjects addressed by the theory, while other participants argue that such imperfections must be taken into account even in the foundational formulation of the theory.[7] The book has three main projects. The first project is to examine the three types of responses to agents' cognitive limitations as moral decision makers, and in particular to their limited or faulty grasp of the nonmoral circumstances affecting the moral status of their possible actions. The difficult problem of agents' imperfect grasp of the correct moral principles will not be directly addressed in this book, although it will crop up in unexpected ways. The book's second project is to develop far more detailed versions of the Pragmatic and Hybrid approaches than have hitherto been offered so that we can see more clearly what they can and cannot accomplish as responses to the problem of cognitive limitations. The third project of the book is to argue for a version of the Hybrid Response as the best response to the problem of cognitive limitations: a response that adopts the Austere insistence that a moral theory's correctness as a theoretical account of right-making features does not depend on its capacity to lead decision makers aright, but also adopts the Pragmatic insistence that a moral theory must provide guidance to decision makers.

I will interpret the various responses to agents' cognitive weaknesses as proposals about what the *content* of morality must be. Along the way we will need to look

---

[7] The contemporary debate between ideal and non-ideal theory traces back most visibly to Rawls (1971), and has been much discussed since then, primarily in debates about political rather than moral theory.

more carefully at a number of questions. What is the rationale for the demand that moral theories be usable for making practical decisions? What kinds of cognitive limitations impede the usability of a moral theory? What is it for a principle to be usable for an agent in making decisions? How strong is the demand for practical usability? Is it met if most agents can use the theory, or if normal agents can use it, or only if all agents can use it? How should the demand for practical usability in a moral theory be balanced against other considerations in assessing the theory? Should the Hybrid approach supplement the governing moral theory with a single all-purpose decision-guide or with a multiplicity of guides? What is the content of the proposed supplementary decision-guide(s)? What makes them appropriate to the governing account of right and wrong in Hybrid theories? In the context of the Hybrid Response, should we draw a distinction between acts that are "objectively right" and those that are "subjectively right," and if so, how should we characterize it? What is the nature of our duty to acquire information before deciding how to act? Since questions about the wisdom of agents' decisions are linked to questions about their blameworthiness for acting as they do, we will also need to deepen our understanding of the conditions under which a person is to blame for what she does or chooses.

Although most current debates on the issues I have identified focus on morality as having two possible roles—a role as a theoretical account of right and wrong, and a role as a practical decision-guide—it is important not to lose sight of the fact that morality has many other roles as well. For example, we use morality's theory of right conduct not just when we are deciding what we ourselves should do, but also when we are advising others what they should do. We also use morality's theory of right conduct when there is no occasion for decision or advice: for example, when we are assessing our own past actions or the past actions of others. Of central importance is the fact that we use the theory of right conduct when we are judging whether individuals (perhaps ourselves) are blameworthy or praiseworthy for their actions. In assessing how our cognitive limitations should be taken into account in determining the correct moral theory, we must keep in mind these other roles as well, and ensure that our answers maintain an appropriate place for all of them. My primary focus, however, will be on the two principal roles that morality plays.

As we have seen, this book focuses on issues raised for morality by the fact that as decision makers we are often cognitively deficient (or "constrained," as psychologists often say). Recent philosophical discussion has also focused on issues raised for morality by the fact that we are often motivationally defective: even when we believe that morality may require some self-sacrificing act from us, we may not be able to muster sufficient motivation to perform that act. Utilitarianism, for example, is sometimes rejected as a theoretical account of right and wrong because it is seen as too motivationally demanding on normal human agents. Moral theorists have adopted various responses to the fact of our motivational deficiencies. These responses often parallel, in form and sometimes in substance, those adopted by theorists concerned solely with our cognitive limitations.[8] There may be important and illuminating parallels between the constraints that should be placed on morality by our cognitive limitations and the constraints that should be placed on morality by our motivational limitations. Unfortunately there will not be space in this book to explore these potential parallels, a project that must be left for another occasion.

Before beginning, it is worthwhile commenting on several background issues. First, the issues raised for morality by our cognitive deficiencies are ones that are similarly raised for many other normative systems for assessing and guiding activities, such as legal systems, principles of prudence, codes of military conduct and professional ethics, rules of social etiquette, duties of religious observance, norms of assertion, and principles of belief formation. To keep exposition brief, I shall confine my attention to morality, although the lessons learned along the way may often be applicable to these other systems as well. On the other hand, I shall feel free to draw liberally on suggestions that have been made in other fields, such as economics and psychology, when they seem relevant to the moral case.

Second, many moral philosophers do not find it congenial to think of morality as involving principles or rules, but rather as involving "reasons" or "considerations" which must be balanced against each other. Particularists take an extreme view of this sort, arguing that the significance and weight of these considerations vary from one context to another, so that morality cannot involve general principles.[9] But whether one invokes principles or considerations as the way in which morality should be expressed, it is equally vulnerable to the difficulties raised by our epistemic deficiencies as decision makers. In developing my theory I shall normally utilize the language of principles and rules. Having a uniform approach to this question makes exposition simpler. But it is also true that framing our questions in terms of principles and rules, rather than in other terms, enforces a certain level of precision that is salutary for understanding the issues. Further, it highlights certain structural questions that might otherwise be less visible. However, it should be possible for defenders of different views about the logical structure of morality to translate the arguments and conclusions of this book into locutions that will fit more comfortably within their paradigm. It is apparent that virtue ethicists must face the same issues about cognitive limitations in developing their theories; they, too, are invited to translate the findings in the book into their own framework.

Related views are held by a second category of moral philosophers who deny that we make our moral decisions by reference to principles. These philosophers are inspired by research on concepts by cognitive scientists suggesting that the content of an ordinary concept (such as the concept of a table or a knife) cannot be captured by a principle stating necessary and sufficient conditions for an item's falling under that

---

[8] For classic discussions, see B. Williams (1973), Hardin (1988), Kagan (1989), and Scheffler (1982) and (1992), as well as many earlier discussions of rule utilitarianism.

[9] Perhaps the most prominent expositor of Particularism is Dancy (2013).

concept. Instead the content of the concept is captured by a mental representation of the concept that consists of a "prototype" or an "exemplar." A *prototype* (for example, the prototype of a table) is an abstraction constructed from particular members of the category to which an agent has been exposed, and represents the universal concept through specific features most common to instances falling under the concept. Thus the prototype "table" used by an agent might include features such as having four legs, being made of wood, and standing three feet high. The agent would judge whether a new item is a table by how many of the core features possessed by the prototypical table are possessed by the candidate in question; none of these features may be necessary. According to exemplar theories, the agent constructs a set of *exemplars*, or individual instances, of the category, based on her experience with instances that are so classified. To determine whether a new item belongs to the category in question, the agent determines how similar the new item is to a set of exemplars of that category. Thus an agent might include doves, robins, and chickens as exemplars of the category "bird." When asked to decide whether penguins should be categorized as birds, the agent evaluates the similarity of penguins to these exemplars.[10]

These cognitive science-based views about mental representation can be deployed in the field of morality by claiming that an agent's moral code is mentally represented by her, not as a set of rules or principles providing necessary and sufficient conditions for having a given moral status, but rather as a set of prototypes or exemplars of right and wrong action. To make a decision, then, the agent would not derive a prescription from moral rules, but rather try to act in ways that closely match the relevant prototype or set of exemplars.[11]

But these views, too, must somehow incorporate the fact that moral decisions are often made in conditions in which the agent has limited or imperfect information about her situation. Hence proponents of these positions must contend with the same problems arising from human cognitive limitations as the ones that must be contended with by proponents of moral principles as the basis for decision-making. Rather than trying at every point to translate my arguments and conclusions into the terminology appropriate to the prototypes and exemplars views, I instead invite these theorists to consider how my conclusions would best fit within their framework.[12]

---

[10] For a general philosophical discussion of the treatment of concepts in contemporary cognitive science, see Machery (2009).

[11] The exemplar view, of course, bears an interesting resemblance to contemporary injunctions to decide what to do by asking what an ideal figure such as Jesus, or Buddha, or Mohammed would do. Note that this procedure could itself be stated as a rule ("Do what most closely matches the exemplars") so it is not clear that it genuinely eliminates the idea that making moral decisions relies on reference to rules or principles.

[12] For a clear discussion of the prototypes-and-exemplars view of moral decision-making, see McKeever and Ridge (2006), pp. 215–22. McKeever and Ridge argue cogently that even if we use prototypes and exemplars to represent our moral beliefs, there is still both room and need for the use of moral principles to guide and shape these forms of mental representation.

Still other moral philosophers and psychologists argue that our emotional responses drive our moral judgments and decisions. See, for example, Greene (2008) and Haidt (2001). It would be natural for such theorists to deny any significant role for rules in moral decision-making.

Third, rapid advances in empirical fields studying how human beings make decisions, both moral decisions and decisions outside morality, will provide valuable insights, for example about our psychological limitations, about the kinds of tools we have devised for overcoming or working within them, and about the extent to which our decision-making should be seen as rational or irrational.

Finally, precisely how one wants to approach the issues I have described will be determined, at least to some extent, by one's view about the foundations of morality, where the possible views span an enormous range that includes (for example) the view that moral principles are necessarily true by virtue of their concepts, the view that moral theories express natural facts, the view that morality emanates from the requirements of practical reason, the view that moral principles derive from principles of rationality holding for all rational beings, the view that morality is the product of human evolution, the view that morality is a set of commands for human beings issued by a deity, and the view that moral systems are the constructions, real or ideal, of human beings working jointly to meet their social and environmental needs. One strategy for confronting the questions addressed in this book would be to adopt one of these positions and then approach the issues raised by our limited cognitive powers from the perspective of the favored position. I shall not adopt this strategy, but rather try to put forward arguments that will be cogent whichever of these points of view one takes about the foundations of morality. Partly this is because the issues in which I am interested can arise whatever one's view is about the fundamental nature of morality, and I wish to provide an examination of them that will be useful to parties of all persuasions. Partly this is because I think deliberating about the issue of human limitations may throw indirect, but important, light on the question of the nature and foundation of morality. Doubtless there are hazards in attempting to provide arguments that rest on no meta-ethical foundation but will nonetheless be found illuminating by all parties to these debates. Doubtless I shall not always succeed. Nonetheless, this is one of the aims of the project.

The plan of the book is as follows. In Chapter 2 I develop the concept, crucial for our project, of using a moral principle to guide decisions. In Chapter 3 I describe in richer detail the impediments that may exist to using a given principle for this purpose, characterize the three main approaches to the problem of epistemic barriers to usability, and set out the rationales that theorists have offered for requiring that a moral principle be usable in decision-making. In Chapters 4 through 7 I describe various ways in which theorists have tried to develop the Pragmatic approach to epistemic limitations, and argue that each of these has fatal problems. In Chapters 8 through 11, I discuss the virtues as well as the limitations of the Austere approach, and introduce the Hybrid approach. Chapters 12 and 13 are devoted to developing the Hybrid approach in the light of the emergence of several severe barriers to its success, and to analyzing how much it can ultimately achieve. Since I believe that the Hybrid approach is the most successful one, in many ways Chapters 10, 11, 12, and 13 are the heart of the book. Chapter 14 reviews the ground covered and summarizes my conclusions.

As the argument progresses I often propose more or less formal accounts or definitions of crucial concepts. Ultimately I reject and replace some of these, while others are left standing. For ease of reference, all are assembled in the Appendix at the end of the book. I have no illusions that even the ones remaining standing in the end will ultimately survive further critical scrutiny, including my own. However, attempting to articulate these ideas precisely is worthwhile because it is the best way to illuminate the issues raised by trying to pin down the relevant ideas. I offer these accounts in the spirit of promoting continued inquiry.

One last point: this book attempts to find a moral system that will enable even severely epistemically challenged moral agents, including children and the cognitively impaired, to use it to make decisions. Regrettably the discussion in this book is itself complex, and hardly accessible to all these agents. Perhaps I can take solace in the fact that even young children can grasp enough of the laws of physics to navigate their physical world successfully, even though it takes an advanced degree in physics to fully understand the proof that these laws are correct. Similarly, epistemically limited moral agents should be able to grasp the relevant principles of the correct moral theory well enough to navigate their moral world, even though it takes someone with a sophisticated background in philosophy to apprehend the full theory, or to understand what makes these principles correct.

With these initial matters in hand, let us turn to a more detailed introduction to our question.

2

Using Moral Principles to Guide Decisions

The function of moral principles is to guide conduct.[1]

Many people believe that one of morality's essential functions—perhaps its most important function—is to serve as a guide for individuals who wish to choose their course of action in light of moral considerations.[2] For a moral principle to serve as such a guide, it must not only set out the types of features that make an action right or wrong, but it must also be usable by human beings, with all their limitations, in selecting an action to perform under the conditions in which they must make such choices.

Let us call the requirement that an acceptable moral principle must be usable for guiding decisions the "Usability Demand". To understand the Usability Demand, and to assess whether or not to endorse it, one needs an account of what it is for a theory to be action-guiding in a practically usable way. Little work has been done to articulate the relevant notion of usability. This chapter aims to provide such an account. In the course of developing this account, I will argue that we need to distinguish between a *core* and an *extended* sense of having the ability to use a principle to guide conduct. Philosophers advocating the importance of a principle's usability must choose which of these two senses provides the appropriate criterion for moral principles. We will consider that question in succeeding chapters.

2.1 Using Moral Principles to Guide Conduct

What is involved in guiding one's behavior by reference to a moral principle?[3] As Kant pointed out long ago, simply behaving in conformity with a principle does not

[1] Hare (1965), p. 1.
[2] A significant portion of the material in this chapter was originally published in H. Smith (2012). As indicated in subsequent notes, this article itself followed earlier work of mine.
[3] There is a massive contemporary literature on rule-following starting with Saul Kripke's discussion of Wittgenstein's puzzles about rule-following (Kripke 1982). This literature focuses primarily on what counts as following one rule *rather than another*, where an adequate account must (a) account for the possibility of objective error in following the rule, (b) account for the infinite character of rules, and in particular the fact that a rule may theoretically require action under circumstances in which no human agent could ever

guarantee that you have used it for guidance.[4] You order chicken rather than pork at a restaurant, thus conforming to the Levitican law prohibiting consumption of any animal that parts the hoof but fails to chew the cud. But if you are wholly unaware of this law, you have hardly used it for guidance. Nor does knowledge of what the law requires, together with conformity of behavior, show that you have guided your action by it. You might be aware of the dietary law but completely unmoved by it; your only concern in ordering your dinner is to avoid high cholesterol foods. The concurrence between the biblical command and the avoidance of cholesterol is purely coincidental. These considerations suggest that we may say roughly, then, that a principle is *usable* by an agent for making a decision just in case it is true that if the agent wanted all-things-considered to act in conformity with the principle, the agent would choose an act out of her desire to conform to the principle and a belief that the act does conform. Thus suppose Susan decides to signal a lane change because she desires to follow the highway code, and believes that the highway code requires lane changes to be signaled. She has used the code to make her decision.

2.2   Two Different Kinds of Usability

We need to make this notion of a principle's being usable by an agent more precise. To see what is needed, let us first examine the barriers that might prevent a person from using a principle to guide her decision. We have already seen that there could be several. For example, the principle itself may suffer from defects in content that prevent its practical use. Thus a principle might incorporate concepts that on closer examination turn out to be incoherent. It is often claimed, for example, that act utilitarianism requires a concept of "utility" that makes it possible to compare the utility of one person with that of another person, and that this concept is incoherent or can be given no operational meaning. Or a principle may be so vague, or ambiguous, that it leaves the moral status of some actions indeterminate. Consider a principle which states that killing persons is wrong, but fails to clarify whether human fetuses are included among "persons," or leaves it indeterminate whether fetuses between eighteen and twenty-two weeks qualify as persons. No one can use this principle (isolated from other information) in deciding whether it is wrong to obtain the abortion of a nineteen-week-old fetus, since no one can tell whether or not abortions are prohibited by it. Similarly, a single principle (or several principles jointly) might, when applied to a given situation, deliver inconsistent assessments that an agent both ought to do A and ought not to do A.[5] Or a principle might prescribe, as the only permissible choice in a

---

find herself, and (c) account for the fact that an agent following a rule can justify her action by referring to the rule. (See Hindriks (2004), p. 67.) Although these issues are related to those in the present chapter, they are largely orthogonal to our present concerns, so I shall not try to address them.

[4] Kant (1959), pp. 13–16.

[5] In some cases the inconsistent prescriptions (derivable using various principles of deontic logic) may arise from tragic situations, for example a situation in which both the son and the daughter of the agent are

given situation, a type of action that is not available. Thus a principle which requires an employer to hire the job candidate who has better qualifications than any other would be useless in a hiring situation in which there are two equally well-qualified candidates, each of whom is superior to all the remaining candidates. Some of the barriers just described not only prevent the principles affected by them from being used to make the relevant decisions, but they also undermine the principles' adequacy as theoretical accounts of right and wrong. For example, suppose a moral code includes two principles, "It is all-things-considered wrong to kill a human being," and "It is all-things-considered obligatory to kill one's sister when she has dishonored the family through sexual contact outside of marriage." This moral code delivers inconsistent evaluations of a brother's act of killing his sister for a sexual transgression because it evaluates the killing as both wrong and obligatory. Such a code is flawed *both* as a theory *and* as a practical guide. Moreover, its defects as a practical guide flow directly from its defects as a theoretical account of right and wrong—even an omniscient agent could not apply such a code in making decisions. Clearly the appropriate response to a code that is flawed in the ways just described is to revise the code to make it more acceptable as a theoretical account.

But even a principle (or code) that exhibits none of these flaws *qua* theory may still be unusable for actual decision-making. To see how this can arise, let us first return to our account of what it is for a principle to be usable for making a decision: we said that, roughly speaking, a principle is usable by an agent for making a decision just in case it is true that if the agent wanted all-things-considered to act in conformity with the principle, the agent would choose an act out of her desire to conform to the principle and a belief that the act does conform.

Even this rough account is too simple, since it is ambiguous between two different possibilities. Consider John, who wants to follow the principle "Give an anniversary card to one's spouse today if, and only if, today is one's wedding anniversary." John believes that today is his wedding anniversary, and by reference to this principle, decides to give his wife a card. However, John is mistaken: the anniversary is next week. There is an obvious sense in which he has *not* regulated his decision in accordance with his principle—but another obvious sense in which his decision clearly *has* been guided by it. Reflecting on this case, we may draw a distinction between having the ability in the *core* sense to use a principle to guide one's decision, and having the ability in the *extended* sense to use a principle to guide one's decision. Thus we can say, roughly speaking, that an agent is able to use a principle in the *core* sense just in case he would derive a prescription for action from the principle if he wanted all-things-considered

---

in peril and the agent has a duty to rescue each of them, but rescuing either one would necessitate allowing the other to die. These situations are regarded as "moral dilemmas," and some, but not all, moral philosophers hold that it is acceptable for a moral principle to deliver inconsistent evaluations in genuine moral dilemmas. On their view, such a principle might be flawed as a practical guide but not as a theory of right and wrong. For a careful discussion of how to characterize "moral dilemmas," see Sinnott-Armstrong (1988), Chapter 1, and for a general discussion of approaches to moral dilemmas, see McConnell (2010).

to do so. (In this book I shall use the term "prescription for action" with unusual breadth so that it can refer to a prescription to perform some act as obligatory—but also refer to a *pro*scription not to perform some act as wrong, or a *permission* to perform some act as morally optional.)[6] By contrast, an agent is able to use a principle in the *extended* sense just in case he would derive a prescription for action from the principle if he wanted all-things-considered to do so, and the action for which he would derive a prescription is one that he would be able to perform, and also one that would conform to the principle.[7] Thus John, who decides to give his wife an anniversary card, is able to use his principle in the core sense, since he is able to derive a prescription from his principle. However, he is not able to use it in the extended sense, since the action for which he derives the prescription is not one that conforms to the principle. By contrast, Seth wants to follow the same principle, knows that his anniversary is indeed today, and so decides to give his wife a card. Seth has the ability to use this principle in both the core sense and in the extended sense.

Thus we should distinguish between a principle's being usable as a core or as an extended decision-guide by a given agent, depending on which of these abilities the agent has with respect to the principle. Any agent who has either kind of ability is able to derive a prescription from the principle (and in consequence can use that principle in deciding what to do). A chief part of what distinguishes an agent who has the ability to use a principle merely in the core sense from an agent who has the ability to use a principle in the extended sense is that the latter agent, but not the former, has *true* beliefs about what action is prescribed by the principle: if he follows through by performing the action he believes is prescribed, he will act in a way that conforms to the principle.

Of course, merely *having the core or extended ability* to derive a prescription from a principle does not imply that one actually derives any prescription, since one might not exercise that ability. When a person *exercises her core ability* to use some principle P as a decision-guide, she wants to derive a prescription from P, and this desire leads to her deriving such a prescription.[8] When a person *exercises her extended ability* to use some principle as a decision-guide, she wants to derive a prescription for action from P, and this desire leads her to derive a prescription for an action which she can perform

---

[6] In ordinary conversation, to say that an act is obligatory is not to say precisely the same thing as to say that it ought to be done all-things-considered. Obligatory acts are a narrower class than acts that ought to be done (it can be true that I ought to donate to famine relief efforts without it being true that I have an obligation to do so), and an obligation (say, to repay my debt) is normally understood as holding even though all-things-considered it ought not to be satisfied because some conflicting moral consideration outweighs it, whereas what ought to be done all-things-considered cannot be outweighed by any conflicting moral consideration. Regrettably English does not provide a common noun for acts that ought to be done, so for stylistic reasons I shall normally use the term "obligation" for an act that ought to be done, and will refer to such acts as "obligatory." "Duties" are much like "obligations" in these respects.

[7] See H. Smith (1988), pp. 91–2, and also (2010a) for earlier discussions of a closely related distinction.

[8] A more precise characterizing of "exercising an ability" would stipulate that the desire leads to the derivation via a non-deviant path. Since issues about deviant paths (or deviant causal chains) are irrelevant to our main concerns, I shall not try to incorporate this condition in this or subsequent definitions.

and which would actually conform to P. Even exercising the core or extended ability to use a principle as a decision-guide does not necessarily involve the agent's actually choosing to perform, or actually performing, the action whose prescription she derives. Exercising either ability simply involves the agent's deriving a prescription from the principle for an action. She might derive a prescription from the principle but fail to follow through, either because she has no allegiance to the principle (she notices that the Levitican dietary law forbids consuming the pork chop in front of her, but cares nothing about this), or because her conflicting interests outweigh her allegiance to the principle (although she is an observant Jew, the pork chop is too tempting to pass up), or even because she is distracted before she can act, say by a waiter shouting "Fire!" before she takes the intended bite. Nonetheless having the extended ability to use a principle as a guide is a distinctly stronger ability than merely having the core ability to use the principle as a guide. In the case of extended ability to use a principle, there are constraints on the nature of the act whose prescription the agent derives: it must be one that the agent could perform, and it must be such that it would actually conform to the principle in question if the agent were to perform it. By contrast, in the case of having the core ability to use a principle, the act whose prescription the agent derives might be one she could not perform (perhaps she has been struck with sudden paralysis, or is mistaken in believing she can bench-press seventy-five pounds), or it might not comply with the principle (for example, from the principle that one must pay one's debts, she derives a prescription to send a check to her creditor and dispatches a check, but the check is lost in the mail so she fails to pay her debt).

2.3 Immediately Helpful Descriptions

To fully clarify the concept of a principle's being usable for making decisions, still more work needs to be done. In an obvious sense an agent often can derive "a prescription" from a principle, even though the agent cannot derive a prescription from that principle for any action under what Bales calls "an immediately helpful description."[9] Thus someone who has no idea what the consequences would be of her various alternatives can still derive a "prescription" from act utilitarianism—she can derive the prescription "Perform the act that would maximize utility." In terms of actually using the principle to guide action, this is no help if she can't identify which act this is.[10] To deal with this problem we need a more complicated definition of what it is to be able to use a normative principle. Definitions 2.1 and 2.2 outline a strategy for dealing with this problem. I will start by defining what it is for an agent to have the ability in the core sense to

---

[9] E. Bales (1971), p. 261.
[10] As Piller (2007), p. 53, points out, "Karl Kraus once said 'Whenever you are in doubt about what to do, simply do the right thing'. There is something funny about giving advice like this… 'Simply do the right thing!' sounds like advice, but it cannot play the role of advice because if the agent knew which action was right, no advice would be needed. Useful advice would need to help the agent to recognize which of his options… would be right."

directly use a principle as a decision-guide, and then use this account to define what it is for a moral principle to be directly usable in the core sense. Later I will introduce an account of "ability in the extended sense" on the same model.[11] These definitions are phrased in terms of "direct use" because we will subsequently need a concept of "indirect use."

Definition 2.1.   Ability in the core sense to directly use a moral principle to decide what to do: An agent S is able in the core sense at t_i to directly use moral principle P to decide at t_i what to do at t_j *if and only if*:

(A)   there is some (perhaps complex) feature F such that P prescribes actions that have feature F, in virtue of their having F,

(B)   S believes at t_i of some act-type A that S could perform A (in the epistemic sense) at t_j,

(C)   S believes at t_i that if she performed A at t_j, act A would have F, and

(D)   if and because S believed at t_i that P prescribes actions that have feature F, in virtue of their having F, and if and because S wanted all-things-considered at t_i to derive a prescription from principle P at t_i for an act performable at t_j, then her beliefs[12] together with this desire would lead S to derive a prescription at t_i for A from P in virtue of her belief that it has F.[13]

---

[11]   Formal definitions will be labeled to indicate the chapter in which they first appear and their order of appearance within that chapter. Thus the first definition in Chapter 2 is Definition 2.1. All formal principles and definitions are collected for easy reference in the Appendix. Page numbers are in the General Index.

[12]   We should understand "her beliefs" to refer to the beliefs described in clauses (B) and (C), but for simplicity I will not include this qualification.

[13]   The forerunner to this definition was originally introduced in H. Smith (2010a), pp. 101–2, and subsequently developed in H. Smith (2012).

For completeness we would also need to state specific variants of Definition 2.1 setting out whether the "prescribed" acts are obligatory, forbidden, or permissible.

In this and subsequent contexts I understand "want" in a very broad sense, so that it includes not just ordinary desires (e.g., the desire to have an ice cream), but also moral motivations (e.g., respect for duty).

In certain cases whether or not an agent would do something if she wanted to depends on *how much* she would want to do it. Normally, for example, I would not lift the front end of my small car even if I wanted all-things-considered to do so. But if my child were being crushed by the car, I might want *hard enough* to lift the car that I would do so (in such cases special physiological factors kick in). In most cases whether or not an agent can apply a moral principle to her decision does not depend on phenomena of this sort, so we do not need to accommodate them in this definition.

We can distinguish between (a) an agent who has (say) the general ability to play the piano, but has no specific ability to play the piano right now, since there is no piano available, and (b) an agent who has the specific ability right now to play, since a piano is right in front of her. Similarly an agent might have the general ability to use a principle in the core sense, but not have the specific ability right now to do so, since she doesn't believe of any act that it has F. Definition 2.1 focuses on the latter sort of specific ability.

Under another heading, consider someone who is standing in front of her locked toolshed. The key to the shed is 50 yards away in her kitchen. Does she have the ability to unlock the shed? Since she doesn't have the key in hand, at t_i she does not have the ability to unlock the shed at t_i. However, there is a clear sense in which she has the ability at t_i to unlock the shed at later time t_n, since if she wanted at t_i to unlock the shed at t_n, she would go back to the kitchen, retrieve the key, and unlock the shed at t_n. Similarly, if a person does not believe at t_i that act A has F, she does not have the ability (on Definition 2.1) to use principle P at t_i. However, she may have the ability at t_i to use principle P at later time t_n, if it is true that she could acquire the relevant information between t_i and t_n, and if she acquired the information

Several questions about this definition are worth addressing immediately. It might be argued that the usability of a moral principle depends, not only on the extent to which agents possess the nonmoral beliefs necessary to apply that principle, but also on the extent to which they are (or could be) motivated to follow it.[14] It is certainly true that many moral theorists have criticized optimizing act utilitarianism on grounds that it demands more sacrifices from agents than most people are prepared to accept. For example, it is often said that utilitarianism requires people to devote most of their personal resources to alleviating the suffering of impoverished populations or those caught in humanitarian crises, and that most of us balk at such a demand.[15] However, lack of motivation to follow a principle does not affect a person's ability to use the principle in the normal sense, any more than lack of motivation to do so affects a person's ability to use the can-opener in his kitchen drawer. It would not be appropriate, then, to incorporate motivation into the definition as a factor affecting our ability to use a principle. However, it is true that a moral theorist, in considering which moral principle is overall best, may wish to balance the usability of candidate principles against people's capacities to be motivated by them, capacities that depend partly on their inborn interests and partly on motives they have acquired through social learning. The most easily used principle may not be the most motivating one.[16] This point will be discussed further in Chapter 6, when we explore the non-ideal Pragmatic approach.

This definition is not meant to address issues of whether or not the agent has free will. There are many contexts in which we need a notion of "ability" that assumes nothing about freedom of will. For example, I can judge whether or not I have the ability to lift the 150 pound weight in front of me (I do not, but the bodybuilder next to me in the gym does) without having to determine whether or not I have free will. Ascertaining

---

between t_i and t_n, she would then come to believe that A has F in time to derive a prescription from P at t_n. Of course, if she acquired the information by t_n, then she would also count under Definition 2.1 as having the ability at t_n to use P at t_n.

In Definition 2.1 and later definitions, "time t_i" refers to a very short interval of time, just long enough for an agent who so desires to derive a prescription "A is obligatory/right/wrong" from the belief that principle P prescribes actions having F as obligatory/right/wrong and the belief that act A has F.

A question I shall not try to address is whether an agent who truly believes that she *might* do A if she tries to do A counts as having the ability to do A (think of a basketball player who believes that she might make a free throw if she tries, is not fully confident of this, but succeeds in making the basket).

Definition 2.1 defines an *epistemic* ability (to be explained in the text below) to use a principle as a decision-guide, since the agent's ability depends in part on her having the beliefs described in clauses (B) and (C). Although one could define a parallel *non-epistemic* ability to use a principle, the notion of epistemic ability is the most fruitful one for the purposes of our general inquiry.

Definition 2.1 and its allied definitions all use subjunctive conditionals to define the concept of "ability." An assortment of serious problems for such definitions has been raised in the literature. Since these problems are not germane to our immediate concerns, I shall not try to address them. For a good substantive review of these issues, see Maier (2011).

[14] This view is urged by one of the anonymous referees of the Press.

[15] For discussion, see Kagan (1989), Mulgan (2001), L. Murphy (2000), Scheffler (1982), Singer (1979), and Unger (1996).

[16] The autonomous referee emphasizes the importance of balancing these considerations. Peter Singer (1972), p. 237, has noted how culturally-based expectations influence what is motivationally possible.

whether or not an agent has the ability to use a moral principle in decision-making is often one of those contexts, so we do not need to build in conditions meant to assure such freedom.[17]

With Definition 2.1 in hand, we can also define its correlate, a principle's core usability as an action-guide:

Definition 2.2.   Core usability as an action-guide: A moral principle P is directly usable in the **core** sense by an agent S to decide at t_i what to do at t_j *if and only if* S is able in the core sense at t_i to directly use principle P as a guide to decide at t_i what to do at t_j.

Thus suppose principle P prescribes carrying out one's job responsibilities, and Sally's job responsibilities include opening the safe. Sally believes that she could open the safe, and also believes that her opening the safe would carry out her job responsibilities. If Sally believed that P prescribes carrying out one's job responsibilities and she wanted to derive a prescription from P for an act performable at t, then her beliefs together with this desire would lead her to derive a prescription to open the safe. Principle P is usable by Sally, in the core sense, as a decision-guide. This is true even though Sally may be mistaken that she can open the safe (the combination has been changed), or mistaken that opening the safe would carry out her job responsibilities (this responsibility has been assigned to another employee). Still, Sally *can make a decision* by reference to P: she can choose to do what she believes P requires.

It may seem that this definition doesn't succeed in solving Bales' problem of ensuring that an agent can derive a prescription from P in terms of an act under an "immediately helpful description." For suppose a different agent, Molly, believes that P requires her to carry out her job responsibilities, but she has no idea what those responsibilities are, or that they require her to open the safe, or even what the combination to the safe is. We would want to say that P is not usable by Molly even in the core sense. Still, it looks as though Definition 2.1 implies that Molly *does* have the ability to use principle P (so that P is usable by her), because she believes that there is some act-type (namely, *carrying out her job responsibilities*) that she can perform, and she believes that if she carries out her job responsibilities, her doing so will have feature F, namely the feature of carrying out her job responsibilities. Hence she can derive a prescription from P to carry out her job responsibilities. But this gets her nowhere, since she doesn't know more specifically what her job responsibilities require.

Fortunately Definition 2.1 avoids this unwanted implication, because it requires, via clause (B), that Molly believes at t_i of some act-type A that she could perform A *in the epistemic sense* at t_j. To see why the unwanted implication is avoided, we need to explain what it is to have the ability to perform an act in the epistemic sense of ability.

---

[17]   Even if S met Definition 2.1, on some views S would not count as being free to use principle P if he had a psychological horror of using P that would prevent him from wanting to derive a prescription from it. Since our concern is with epistemic barriers to usability, rather than motivational ones, there is no need to address this kind of issue in Definition 2.1.

The distinction between being able in the epistemic sense to do something, and being able in the non-epistemic sense to do something, is meant to capture the difference between Alice, who is able in the epistemic sense to turn on the light (she is standing in front of the light switch and correctly believes that the switch is connected to the light and would turn the light on if flipped), and Alan, who is able in the non-epistemic sense but not in the epistemic sense to turn on the light (Alan is also standing in front of the light switch and has the physical ability to flip it, but since he believes that *this* switch is the one connected to the fan, he would not flip it if he wanted to turn on the light).[18]

Here is a characterization of epistemic ability, based on Alvin Goldman's definition of this idea:

Definition 2.3.   Epistemic ability to perform an act: S has the epistemic ability at t_i to perform act A at t_j *if and only if*:

(A)   there is a basic act-type A* which S truly believes at t_i to be a basic act-type for her at t_j,

(B)   S truly believes at t_i that she is (or will be) in standard conditions with respect to A* at t_j, and

(C)   either

(1)   S truly believes at t_i that A* = A, or

(2)   S truly believes at t_i that there is a set of conditions C* obtaining at t_j such that her doing A* would generate her doing A at t_j.[19]

Sally has the epistemic ability to carry out her job responsibilities because (1) there is a basic act-type, namely *moving her fingers in ways XYZ*, which she truly believes to be a basic act-type for her, and (2) she further truly believes that she will be in standard conditions with respect to moving her fingers in ways XYZ, and (3) she further truly

---

[18] There may be an additional complication to spelling out the notion of *epistemic ability to do A* that I shall not try to address. This complication is raised by the following kind of case. Consider Alex, who, like Alice and Alan, is standing in front of a light switch which he has the non-epistemic ability to flip. However, Alex's identical twin Max is also standing in the room in front of a switch—the switch for an exhaust fan. Alex and Max are standing in a room full of mirrors which create many images of individuals standing in front of switches. The mirrors are arranged in such a way that Alex cannot tell which images are images of him and which images are of Max. Alex can only guide his action by looking in the mirrors. Although Alex knows he is standing in front of the light switch, he may lack the epistemic ability to turn on the light, because he lacks the ability to *identify himself*. A thorough definition of *epistemic ability* might need to incorporate some treatment of what the literature calls "self-locating beliefs," but I shall not attempt this. For a survey discussion of self-locating beliefs, see Kriegel (2007). I am grateful to Alvin Goldman for pointing out this issue.

[19] A. Goldman (1970), p. 203. This definition is formulated in terms of a "fine grained" theory about the individuation of actions of the kind Goldman advocates in (1970). "Act-types" are special kinds of properties that an agent may exemplify. *Moving one's finger* would be a basic act-type (for most people), while *pulling the trigger* would be a non-basic act-type whose exemplification would be generated by (or grounded in) a person's moving his finger when his finger is positioned on a gun's trigger. Roughly speaking, a person is in standard conditions with respect to an act property just in case (a) there are no external physical constraints making it physically impossible for the person to exemplify the property, and (b) if the property involves a change into some state Z, then the person is not already in Z. See A. Goldman (1970), pp. 64–5.

believes that if she moves her fingers in ways XYZ, this would generate her opening the safe, and this in turn would generate her carrying out her job responsibilities. In short, she knows *how* to carry out her job responsibilities, and she is physically able to do what she knows how to do. Of course most agents wouldn't have the technical concepts used in Definition 2.3. However, I will regard such an agent as satisfying clause (B) in Definition 2.1 so long as she can represent the content of Definition 2.3 in her own terms. For example, Sally believes she has the relevant epistemic ability because she correctly believes that she knows how to open the safe and so how to perform her job responsibilities.

By contrast Molly does not have the epistemic ability to carry out her job responsibilities. It is true of Molly that (1) there is a basic act-type, namely *moving her fingers in ways XYZ*, which she truly believes to be a basic act-type for her, and (2) she further truly believes that she will be in standard conditions with respect to moving her fingers in ways XYZ. However, it is *false* that (3) she truly believes that if she moves her fingers in ways XYZ, this would generate her opening the safe, and this in turn would generate her carrying out her job responsibilities. Of course Molly believes that carrying out her job responsibilities will carry out her job responsibilities. But there is no *basic act* which she truly believes will generate her carrying out her job responsibilities. Because she does not know how to do this, she can't get started.[20]

For this reason Molly fails to satisfy clauses (B) and (C) of Definition 2.1 for ability in the core sense to use a moral principle as a decision-guide. Molly does not believe of any relevant act-type A both that she could perform A (in the epistemic sense) and that A would have the right-making feature F identified by principle P, namely *carrying out her job responsibilities*. Thus inclusion in Definition 2.1 of the requirement that an agent believes she has the epistemic ability to perform an action that would fulfill the principle's prescription enables Definition 2.1 to ascribe ability to use a principle to an agent only when the agent, as Bales puts it, possesses an "immediately helpful description" of an action prescribed by the principle. Molly does not count as having the ability, in the core sense, to use her moral principle as a decision-guide, and for similar reasons an agent who can derive from utilitarianism the prescription to maximize utility, but who doesn't know which concrete act would do this, does not count as someone who has the ability, in the core sense, to use utilitarianism as a decision-guide.

Notice one implication of this definition. Suppose a trustworthy moral sage informs Randy that there's a moral principle called "The Categorical Imperative," and, without explaining the content of the Categorical Imperative, states that the Imperative requires him to tell the truth to his sister about their mother's deteriorating health. Randy is then in a position to state that the Categorical Imperative requires him tell the

---

[20] Note that having the epistemic ability to perform an action requires the agent to have certain true beliefs. However, she can believe herself to have that epistemic ability, even though in actuality she does not have the requisite true beliefs.

truth to his sister. But does he have the ability in the core sense to use the Categorical Imperative as a decision-guide? Definition 2.1 implies that he may not have this ability, even though he may know what the Categorical Imperative prescribes on this occasion. For all that has been said so far, Randy doesn't believe that if he told the truth to his sister, that act would have the crucial feature F in virtue of which the Categorical Imperative deems his act to be right, namely *being in accord with a maxim which he could at the same time will that it become a universal law*. Suppose he doesn't have this belief. Then Randy does not have the ability to use the Categorical Imperative because he fails to satisfy clause (C) of the definition: he doesn't believe that if he told the truth to his sister, that act would be in accord with a maxim which he could at the same time will that it become a universal law. And since he does not believe that his act has this feature, he also fails to satisfy clause (D) of Definition 2.1. Although I suspect our concept of "having the ability to directly use a moral principle as a decision-guide" is somewhat uncertain in its treatment of cases like that of Randy, I find it most plausible on the whole to accept this implication of Definition 2.1, and to say that Randy does not have this ability because he does not believe about any action of his that it has the relevant property F.

Having spelled out a definition of what it is to have the ability in the core sense to use a moral principle as a decision-guide, let us now define what it is for an agent to be able in the *extended* sense to use a moral principle. This definition builds on Definition 2.1 by crucially strengthening clauses (B) and (C) to stipulate that the agent's beliefs are true.

Definition 2.4.   Ability in the extended sense to directly use a moral principle to decide what to do: An agent S is able in the extended sense at t_i to directly use moral principle P to decide at t_i what to do at t_j *if and only if:*

(A)   there is some (perhaps complex) feature F such that P prescribes actions that have feature F, in virtue of their having F,

(B)   S *truly* believes at t_i of some act-type A that she could perform A (in the epistemic sense) at t_j,

(C)   S *truly* believes at t_i that if she performed act A at t_j, act A would have F, and

(D)   if and because S believed at t_i that P prescribes actions that have feature F, in virtue of their having F, and if and because S wanted all-things-considered at t_i to derive a prescription from principle P at t_i for an act performable at t_j, then her beliefs[21] together with this desire would lead S to derive a prescription at t_i for A from P in virtue of her belief that it has F.[22]

---

[21] Again, we should understand "her beliefs" to refer to the beliefs described in clauses (B) and (C), but for simplicity I will not include this qualification.

[22] There is a possible Gettier-like anomaly allowed by Definition 2.4. Suppose principle P states "A is obligatory if and only if A has F," where F = G or H. Perhaps F is *treating one's children appropriately in one's will*, and G = *leaving one's estate to those among one's children who have honored their parents* while H = *disowning those among one's children who have failed to honor their parents*. Fred believes that his act A (signing a certain document) has G, and is able to derive a prescription for A from principle P in virtue of his belief that A has G and therefore has F. However, A does not have G, although it does have H (imagine

Given this definition, we can also define its correlate, a principle's extended usability as an action-guide:

Definition 2.5.   Extended usability as an action-guide: A moral principle P is directly usable in the **extended** sense by an agent S to decide at t_i what to do at t_j *if and only if* S is able in the extended sense at t_i to directly use principle P as a guide to decide at t_i what to do at t_j.

Thus, as in the first safe-opening case, suppose P prescribes carrying out one's job responsibilities and Sally's job responsibilities include opening the safe. Let's imagine that Sally truly believes that she could open the safe, and also truly believes that her opening the safe would carry out her job responsibilities. Moreover, if Sally believed that P prescribes carrying out one's job responsibilities and she wanted to derive a prescription from P for an act performable at t, then her beliefs together with this desire would lead her to derive a prescription to open the safe. It follows that principle P is directly usable in the extended sense by Sally as a decision-guide. If she proceeded to derive a prescription and to carry it out, she would succeed in doing what principle P requires her to do. Because P is usable by Sally in the extended sense, we can infer that she is not mistaken either about whether she can open the safe, or about whether it is her job responsibility to open the safe. Because her beliefs about the situation are true, she can both derive a prescription from P and also carry out what P actually requires of her. A third agent Polly, who is in the same situation as Sally, and who has the same beliefs that Sally does, but whose beliefs are false—say, she falsely believes that dialing 60–89–35 will open the safe—qualifies as someone who can use P in the core sense as a decision-guide, but she does not qualify as someone who can use P in the extended sense. She fails to satisfy clause (C) of Definition 2.4.

An agent who satisfies Definition 2.4 necessarily also satisfies Definition 2.1: that is, if an agent is able in the extended sense to use a principle as a decision-guide, she is also able to use it in the core sense. This is what we would expect. But of course the reverse implication doesn't hold: an agent (such as Polly) who can use a principle in the core sense may not be able to use that principle in the extended sense. This, too, is what we would expect.

No doubt Definitions 2.1, 2.2, 2.3, 2.4, and 2.5 need further refinement. On the other hand, some readers may feel—paying heed to Judith Jarvis Thomson's (perhaps tongue-in-cheek) advice never to pay out more arguments than one has to,[23] that it would be better to leave these concepts at an intuitive level, rather than attempting to pin

---

that Fred is being defrauded, since unbeknownst to him, signing the document actually disowns Fred's son—but also imagine that his son has dishonored Fred behind his back). Thus A does have F, and would conform to principle P, although not in virtue of the precise underlying feature Fred believes it to have. Under Definition 2.4, Fred would still count as having the ability in the extended sense to use P as a decision-guide, even though this ability rests on the accident of A's possessing a feature that Fred does not believe A has. I shall not attempt to revise Definition 2.4 to avoid this kind of case.

[23] Thomson (1971), p. 48.

them down as these definitions attempt to do. However, my hope is that the definitions will be sufficiently accurate for our purposes, and contain enough details to force us to see, as we proceed, the nature of some of the issues that must be resolved in determining what is required for a moral principle to meet the Usability Demand.

Given these definitions of what it is for a moral principle to be usable by an agent in either the core or extended sense, the advocate of the Usability Demand must decide whether to interpret the Demand as a requirement for core or extended usability. Interpreted merely as a requirement for *core* usability, the Demand stipulates only that agents have beliefs that would enable them to derive prescriptions from the principle in question. These beliefs may be erroneous (as in Polly's case), but the principle will still count as usable by such an agent. Interpreted as a requirement for *extended* usability, the Demand stipulates not only that agents have relevant beliefs, but also that these beliefs be *true*, and so enable them to derive accurate prescriptions from the principle in question. On this interpretation of the Usability Demand, agents must have relevant, accurate beliefs about any potential action for which they might try to derive guidance from the principle. This is obviously a much stronger requirement, and one that will be met by many fewer principles. Advocates of the Usability Demand have not always been clear about which version of the Demand they wish to defend. Considerations supporting the two versions may derive from different sources. For example, one virtue of the core-usability version is that it endorses a moral principle if it enables agents to identify acts they believe the principle prescribes: it does not leave them in the dark about what choice to make if they want to make a moral choice. The extended-usability version, on the other hand, has an additional virtue: it both enables agents to identify acts they believe the principle prescribes, and it also ensures that if they choose to carry out that action, their action will actually conform to the principle. A moral theorist who is primarily interested in the interior lives of agents may be content with mere core-usability, while a moral theorist who is primarily interested in securing actual right conduct from agents may need to adopt extended-usability instead.

2.4 Issues and Implications

Several issues and implications of these definitions are worth remarking before we move on.

2.4.1 The time and scope of a principle's usability

Definitions 2.2 and 2.5 characterize a moral principle's usability by an individual agent at some specific time t_i. Proponents of the Usability Demand may tend to assume (implicitly or explicitly) that an acceptable moral principle must be usable as a decision-guide by all moral agents on all occasions on which they have the opportunity to make a moral decision covered by that principle. However, there are weaker possible versions of the Demand: it could require that the principle be usable by the majority of agents, or by each agent on the majority of occasions, or by each agent who has investigated the situation as thoroughly as he ought to have done, and so forth. Whichever version of the Demand is adopted, Definitions 2.2 and 2.5 can be adapted for stating it.

2.4.2 Moral ignorance or uncertainty

Definitions 2.1 and 2.4 require the agent S to have certain beliefs about the nonmoral nature of her options. But what do they imply for cases in which P requires act A in virtue of its having feature F, and S believes of A that it has F, but S lacks complete or accurate information about principle P itself? Let us look first at cases of moral ignorance in which S is unaware of principle P, or unaware or uncertain what kinds of actions it prescribes. For example, an agent might never have heard of utilitarianism, or might be aware of utilitarianism merely as the moral theory that Bentham and Mill advocated, but not know what the content of the principle is, and so not be aware of the kinds of actions utilitarianism prescribes (that is, those that maximize utility). Assuming that clauses (A), (B), and (C) are met, Definition 2.1 implies that such an agent is nonetheless able to use P, since it is true of her that *if* she believed P prescribes actions having F, and if she wanted to derive a prescription from P, she would derive a prescription for A. This seems to be an appropriate feature of one important sense of the term "able to use." A parallel use of "ability" is our saying that S (who knows how to iron) is able to use the iron in the closet of her hotel room, even though she is unaware of the existence of the iron. If she *were* aware of the iron and wanted to use it, she would do so. This S contrasts with a different agent S* who, because her recently-broken arm is in a cast, is unable to use the iron, since even if she were aware of the iron she would be physically unable to wield it. In expressing this sense of "ability to use," in effect Definitions 2.1 and 2.4 do not countenance these sorts of ignorance or uncertainty as barriers to the use of a moral principle to guide decisions.

Clearly there is another sense of "able to use" that would deny S has the ability to use an iron of whose existence she is unaware, and would also deny that S can use a moral principle with which she is unfamiliar. But this sense does not seem pertinent to the concerns that motivate the Usability Demand. Theorists who accept the Usability Demand are trying to ascertain which moral principles are correct. It would be putting the cart before the horse for them to hold that a moral principle's correctness depends on whether or not agents are *already* familiar with it. Instead they should be prepared to identify the correct principle independently of the degree to which people are already aware of that principle. Once such a principle is found, its advocates can choose to promulgate it. But if our definitions of usability required prior familiarity with the principle and its crucial concepts, theorists' freedom to select the best principle would be held hostage to the current state of moral information among moral agents, and it would appear that no moral progress might be made.

A second kind of moral ignorance involves an agent who is aware of the content and requirements of moral principle P, but is not aware—or even denies—that principle P is correct. Definitions 2.1 and 2.4 correctly do not countenance this sort of ignorance or error as a barrier to an agent's *ability to use principle P*. An agent who believes P is incorrect may nonetheless be able to derive a prescription from P, just as a commuter may have the ability to take the 1:10 train for New York, even though she believes the 1:10 is not the best train for her to take.

Here again, there is another sense of "ability" according to which this second kind of morally ignorant agent lacks a relevant ability. For example, one might hold that the crucial question is not whether an agent has the ability to use a given moral principle, but whether she has the ability to *do the right thing*. Arguably an agent has this ability if and only if (a) she truly believes of some act A that A conforms to P, (b) she truly believes that P is correct, and (c) if she wanted to do the right thing, then in virtue of these beliefs she would choose to perform A.[24] This is indeed an important kind of ability. It implies that an agent only has the ability to do the right thing if she knows which moral principles are correct. Thus the ability to do the right thing could be seen as an amalgam of two kinds of abilities: the ability to know which moral principles are correct, and the ability to derive prescriptions from those principles when decisions are needed. Regrettably I can offer no insights into the nature of our ability to know which moral principles are correct. Hence I shall have to leave that inquiry to others, and focus solely on the question of when an agent has the ability to use a moral principle. Since my account is intended to work for correct principles as well as incorrect ones, it is a crucial part of the project of defining the circumstances under which agents have the ability to do the right thing. It will also be valuable for theorists who may be mistaken about which moral principle is correct, but are interested in ascertaining whether or not their favored principle is usable.

The upshot is that in accepting these definitions of a moral principle's usability, I am setting aside standard problems of *moral* ignorance, error, or uncertainty as barriers to the usability of a principle. My focus is on the effect of an agent's cognitive shortcomings about nonmoral matters, not on her cognitive deficiencies about moral matters per se. However, developments in later chapters will show that the line between these two kinds of ignorance is less clear-cut than it may appear at first glance.

2.4.3 Beliefs and credences

The third issue arises because our definitions are phrased in terms of an agent's *beliefs*, not in terms of her *credences*, where an agent's credence is her degree of belief or subjective probability (which may fall anywhere from 0 to 1.0) for some proposition. Thus the definitions imply that an agent lacks the ability to use her moral principle if,

---

[24] Thanks to an anonymous reader for the Press for pointing out the importance of this kind of ability, and for proposing a variant of this definition.

for example, she has some moderately high degree of belief that, say, her opening the safe would carry out her job responsibilities, but does not fully believe or feel certain about this matter. Of course most agents must make decisions in light of less-than-certain credences, so this feature of the definitions entails that agents are often unable to use standard moral principles in making their decisions. This—perhaps startling—implication of the definitions is correct. An agent who merely has a moderately high degree of belief that her opening the safe would carry out her job responsibilities does *not* thereby have the ability to use a principle requiring her to carry out her job responsibilities.[25] Of course, she *does* have the ability to use a different principle such as P*, which prescribes performing an act if it is highly likely to carry out her job responsibilities. What this suggests is that a Pragmatic advocate of the Usability Demand may wish to abandon P in favor of P* or some similar less epistemically demanding variant on P. Indeed, many Usability Demand supporters have recommended exactly this. The kinds of epistemic deficiency that stand in the way of an agent's being able to use certain moral principles include not only failure to have any relevant belief about nonmoral matters, and failure to have relevant true beliefs, but also failure to have sufficient *certainty* to draw the required conclusions.

2.4.4 Unconscious beliefs

The definitions do not address the question of whether the agent's relevant beliefs can be *unconscious*. Suppose, for example, that Sally no longer consciously believes that her dialing 70–89–35 (the correct combination) would open the safe; possibly she could not restore this belief to consciousness even if she tried. She has been opening the safe for so long that when she wants to open it, she simply goes to the safe and goes through the appropriate motions, guided by an unconscious belief that dialing 70–89–35 would open the safe. Even though this belief is unconscious, does she count as having the ability to use P as a core or an extended decision-guide? In this case it certainly seems as though she should count as being able to use P, since if she wanted to carry out her job responsibilities, she would fulfill this duty by opening the safe. Her unconscious beliefs would play the appropriate causal role in her deriving a prescription from P if she wanted to, even though those beliefs are unconscious. The question

---

[25] Clearly there are many levels of credence (for example, credence in the proposition that A has F) at which an agent is unable to derive a prescription from P, although the agent could certainly derive a *conditional* prescription to the effect that *if* A has F, *then* P prescribes A. But the question of whether there is some threshold level of credence below 1.0 (say, 0.9) such that at that level of credence or above, the agent could—or should—derive an *unconditional* prescription from P is a knotty issue, closely tied to the difficult epistemic question of whether there are levels of credence below 1.0 that nonetheless count as "full belief," and also to the question of what the epistemic standards are for forming justified beliefs. I shall not try to address these questions here. One might argue that a form of "pragmatic encroachment" affects the answer to this question: perhaps it is legitimate to derive an unconditional prescription from P when one has a lower level of credence, so long as the stakes are quite low, but it is only legitimate to derive a prescription from P when one has a very high level of credence if the stakes are very high. On pragmatic encroachment, see Stanley (2005) and Fantl and McGrath (2009).

about unconscious beliefs is one that will rear its head again and that deserves more extended scrutiny than I can give it, but I will assume that unconscious beliefs *can* satisfy clauses (B), (C), and (D) in Definitions 2.1 and 2.4. There may also be cases in which they cannot, since the unconscious beliefs in question would not lead to the required derivation of a prescription.[26]

2.4.5 Occurrent versus dispositional beliefs

Clauses (B) and (C) of Definitions 2.1 and 2.4 refer to the agent's belief about some act-type A that she could perform A (in the epistemic sense) at t_j, and her belief that if she performed A at t_j, A would have F. But must these beliefs be occurrent beliefs, or can they be merely dispositional beliefs or dispositions to believe? Clearly occurrent beliefs would satisfy these clauses, and constitute the central case. Nonetheless we may wish to acknowledge that there are cases in which an agent qualifies as able at t_i to use a principle P even though at t_i itself her attention is not focused on the relevant propositions—so long as, were she to want to derive a prescription from P, she would immediately come to have the relevant beliefs. Robert Audi helpfully distinguishes between dispositional beliefs and dispositions to believe in part by pointing out that a person with a dispositional belief has already formed that belief (although she may have to retrieve it from memory), while a person who merely has a disposition to believe has not already formed the belief, but has a disposition to form the belief once the question is posed. A disposition to believe is, as Audi puts it, one step further away from availability in reasoning.[27] Thus a person who has memorized her father's phone number (but is not thinking actively about it) has a dispositional belief that the phone number is 634–8128. By contrast, a person who has never addressed the question before nonetheless has a disposition to believe that 6,348,128 is an even number. When we ask what kind of belief is necessary to count as having the ability to use a moral principle, the key point is how long it would take the person to retrieve or form the belief once she wanted to derive a prescription from the principle. There are many cases in which a person has already formed a belief, but nonetheless it would take her quite a while to retrieve it from memory. Similarly there are many cases in which a person has a disposition to believe something (for example, an obscure logical implication of something she occurrently believes) but it would take quite a while for her to form that belief once she asked herself the question. But there are other cases in which a person who has a disposition to believe something (such as whether a given number is odd or even) would come to believe it immediately on posing the question. What is important for the person's ability to use a moral principle is that the person would come immediately to have the relevant belief if she

---

[26] For sample discussions on the role of unconscious beliefs in reasoning and morality, see Audi (1994), p. 425; Haji (1998), pp. 156–60 and 232–4; King and Carruthers (2012); Levy (2014); and Shepherd (2015). Much of the emerging discussion has focused on the question of how unconscious beliefs affect an agent's responsibility for what she does.

[27] Audi (1994).

wanted to use the principle. Since this could happen whether she has a dispositional belief or a disposition to believe, I shall place no further restriction on the kind of belief required to satisfy clauses (B) and (C). The intended interpretation of clause (D) is that someone who has evidence at t_i that would justify her in believing that act A has F does not have the ability at t_i itself to use principle P if it would take her a while to infer that A has F from her evidence. She may, of course, come to have that ability after making the required inference.

2.4.6 Mental representation of a moral principle

There is a related question of how the decision maker would have to mentally represent a moral principle in order to qualify as having the ability to use that principle to make a decision and actually exercise that ability. Clearly, actually using a principle involves some kind of mental activity. But it is possible that this activity takes different forms, depending on how the principle itself is mentally represented by the decision maker. A decision maker may explicitly represent the principle as the content of a conscious propositional attitude: for example, a belief that the principle is correct, or a desire to follow a principle having that content. Or a decision maker may only subscribe to the principle in the sense that she is disposed under certain circumstances to follow a mental procedure that involves unconscious representation of the principle, of which she may never be aware. Thus advocates of dual-process theory in psychology hold that decisions are generally made in either of two ways: either using what is some-times called "System 1" decision-making, which involves an automatic, quick, relatively effortless process, in which the agent often has no conscious awareness of the stimulus to the decision, and no conscious access to the nature and content of the process, or "System 2" decision-making, which involves a relatively slow, deliberate, effortful conscious representation of the decision and the factors to be considered in making it.[28] Thus a new employee who refers to printed instructions for closing out the cash register at the end of the day represents those instructions to himself in explicit propositional form and uses a System 2 process to decide what steps to take in closing the register. By the end of the month the employee has become so well acquainted with this process that he carries it out swiftly and automatically, without conscious thought about the steps that need to be taken. He now uses a System 1 process to close out the register. Nonetheless it appears appropriate to describe the experienced employee, like the novice employee, as following a certain rule in deciding what to do. Some System 1 decisions are made, not on the basis of procedures consciously learned through long experience (as in the case of the cashier), but rather on the basis of a process in which the agent never becomes aware of the content of what she learns—what features of the situation actually lead her to make her decision. Thus young children learn to use their

---

[28] For accessible descriptions of System 1 and System 2 processes, see Evans and Frankish (2009) and Kahneman (2011). For an updated description, which ascribes greater information-sensitivity and updating capacity to System 1, see Railton (2014).

native language correctly, usually without any teacher articulating the grammatical rules they must follow. It is certainly natural to describe such learners as deciding how to express an idea in spoken language by reference to rules or principles, even though they could not articulate the rules. Other System 1 decisions are made on the basis of procedures that may be hard-wired into the human brain (for example, jumping back in fear when unexpectedly seeing a snake). It is less obvious that we should interpret these hard-wired decisions as ones in which the decision maker "follows a rule."

The question of whether individuals make moral decisions by using rules or in some other non-rule-based manner is one with a long history. Philosophers such as Kant hold that moral decision-making involves invoking rules or principles, while other philosophers, such as Aristotle, see moral decision-making as based on rich experience that is not reducible to the following of rules.[29] This controversy has reappeared in contemporary form as a debate among philosophers and psychologists who utilize findings from cognitive research to support their views. Some argue that moral decision-making is based on rules, albeit unconscious ones.[30] Others argue that moral learning and decision-making involves broad pattern-based associative learning capacities that encode information whose richness and context sensitivity far exceeds the information that could be represented by linguistically framed rules or principles.[31] Still others argue that sophisticated moral learning requires both pattern-based associative learning capacities *and* the capacity to deploy linguistically-based rules, rules that make possible the kind of complex pattern-based learning that also underlies moral expertise.[32] Finally, many argue that reasoning cannot be understood as proceeding by reference to explicitly represented rules, for then it would necessarily involve an infinite regress. For example, the agent who, using modus ponens, deduces "Q" from "P" and "If P then Q" would also have to mentally represent the rule of modus ponens, and then further have to represent a higher level rule by which "Q" can be deduced, using modus ponens, from "P" and "If P then Q," and so on. These theorists argue that following a rule does not need to involve mentally representing a rule, but may rather involve having a special kind of mental disposition.[33]

Whether abstract moral information is represented as rules and principles, or as special dispositions, or in some other fashion in the brain, it is nonetheless true that people will often lack sufficient (or sufficiently accurate) information about the nonmoral circumstances in which they act to directly connect their moral with their nonmoral beliefs in order to deliver a clear-cut and correct recommendation. For purposes of

---

[29] Aristotle (1941) and Kant (1956) and (1959).

[30] One prominent contemporary view assimilates our knowledge and use of moral rules to our knowledge and application of linguistic rules. We may be masters of using linguistic rules, without being conscious of their content or even their existence. Similarly, it is argued, we may be masters of using moral rules, without being conscious of their content. See, for example, Dwyer (2009); Hauser (2006); Mikhail (2007); and Roeder and Harman (2010).

[31] This characterization is from Clark (2000). Theorists who hold this view include Churchland (1996); Dreyfus and Dreyfus (1990); and Flanagan (1996).

[32] Clark (2000).   [33] See, for example, Broome (2014).

this book, it will simplify our project to conceive of moral decision makers, in our central cases, as individuals who utilize moral principles as explicitly represented objects of propositional attitudes. People may sometimes (perhaps usually) make moral decisions by using moral principles that are only available to them as mental procedures whose content they never, or never accurately, represent to themselves. But we will be able to answer our questions in this book most clearly if we focus, at least for the most part, on cases in which the agent consciously entertains some moral principle in propositional form. We can subsequently extend our findings to cases in which the agent represents the principle in some other way.

2.4.7 Decision procedures

One final note on the ability to use a moral principle: some philosophers, following Bales, have characterized a moral principle as usable by an agent to make a decision only if there is a "decision procedure" that enables the agent to derive a prescription from the theory. In a variant on the Aristotelian-inspired rejection of moral rules, Bales and some subsequent philosophers seem to have assumed that such a "decision procedure" is actually a "mechanical sequence of operations" that the agent could perform in order to arrive at an "overall moral verdict about the action in question."[34] But a closer examination of what they have in mind by a "mechanical sequence of operations" suggests that the operations in question are operations by which the agent *informs herself about the nonmoral* but morally relevant aspects of her choices: operations by which she discovers what the consequences of her choices would be, what the past and present circumstances of her proposed actions are, and so forth.[35] And many philosophers object to the idea that there can be any such "mechanical operations"—they note that agents must often call on delicate human skills such as capacity to detect the psychological states of those around them, imagination about the outcomes of certain actions, ability to predict how things will turn out, judgment about how people would react to being treated in certain ways, and so forth. These philosophers value the exercise of such human skills, and balk at any depiction of applying a moral principle that side-steps exercise of these skills in favor of a more mechanical use of modus ponens.[36] We should acknowledge that gathering nonmoral information relevant to a moral decision can be a sophisticated and complex procedure, apparently not reducible to any purely "mechanical" operations. However, once this information is gathered, the agent can use it, together with a moral principle, to use modus ponens to infer that a given action is prescribed by his moral principle.

---

[34] These quotations are from Scheffler (1992), pp. 39–40.

[35] In their discussion of a demand for "algorithmic decision-procedures," McKeever and Ridge (2006) seem to join in this view on p. 11.

[36] See Scheffler (1992), pp. 38–48. However, we may be kidding ourselves about how special and non-mechanical these human skills are. Recently researchers developed a mechanical computer model that can judge a subject's personality more accurately than the person's own friends and family can—using nothing but the subject's Facebook activity. See Quenqua (2015).

Of course many moral philosophers have claimed that sophisticated non-mechanical procedures must also be used in the more narrowly moral aspects of deliberation about what to do. Thus W. D. Ross, and following him Particularists and virtue ethicists, have emphasized the need to weigh or balance conflicting moral considerations in deciding what ought to be done all-things-considered. And they have insisted there is no mechanical way of doing this.[37] But if, at the end of the day, the decision maker arrives at a conclusion that some option ought all-things-considered to be done, he has derived a prescription from his moral theory. For such theories, there will always be a feature F of the act in virtue of which it ought all-things-considered to be done— a feature such as *satisfies the highest net number of prima facie duties*, or *has the greatest favorable balance of moral considerations*. The role of this feature can be expressed in a moral principle, and the usability of such a theory to make decisions still fits under Definitions 2.2 and 2.5.

2.5 Summary

In this chapter I have argued that we must distinguish between the core and the extended sense in which a principle is usable. I then developed formal definitions for an agent's ability in both the core and extended senses to use a moral principle as a decision-guide, and for the core and extended usability of a moral principle to make decisions. These definitions enable us to deal with Bales' challenge concerning an "immediately helpful description" of an act. However, for most purposes it will be sufficient for us to use the shorter, less formal definitions of an agent's being able to use a principle in the core or extended sense, namely, an agent is able to directly use a principle in the core sense for deciding what to do just in case he would directly derive a prescription for action from the principle if he wanted all-things-considered to do so, and an agent is able to directly use a principle in the extended sense for deciding what to do just in case he would directly derive a prescription for action from the principle if he wanted all-things-considered to do so, and the action for which he would derive a prescription is one that he would be able to perform and that would

---

[37] Again, we may be deceiving ourselves about the ineffable complexity of such judgment processes. Some contemporary research on human decision-making strongly suggests that we actually employ fairly conceptually simple rules in arriving at decisions, even though the process of doing so may feel complex to the decision maker herself. See Gigerenzer (2008a), pp. 12–15. The research described focused on English magistrates making bail decisions on defendants (Dhami (2001), (2003); Dhami and Ayton (2001)). The magistrates were required to make such decisions by taking into account the nature and seriousness of the offense, the character, community ties, and bail record of the defendant, the strength of the prosecution case, the likely sentence if convicted, and any other factor that appeared to be relevant (Gigerenzer (2008a), p. 12). Magistrates reported variously that in making these decisions they thoroughly examined all the evidence; that the decision involved an "enormous weight of balancing information, together with our experience and training;" and claimed that "the decisions of magistrates are indeed complex, each case is an 'individual case' " (Gigerenzer (2008a), p. 14). Despite their views about how they reasoned, analysis showed that in 95 percent of all decisions, the magistrates essentially made their decisions using a very simple algorithm.

conform to the principle. For brevity I shall sometimes use these informal definitions. A chief project that emerges from this chapter is to determine whether champions of the Usability Demand should require a moral code to be usable in the extended sense, or should rest content with mere core usability. We will take this up in later chapters.

In Chapter 3, however, we will turn to a more detailed look at the kinds of cognitive deficiencies that can prevent an agent from using a moral principle to make her decision.

3

Impediments to Usability
Error, Ignorance, and Uncertainty

We don't know much about the world, and much of our information is wrong.[1]

In Chapter 2 we introduced the Usability Demand—the demand that an acceptable moral principle must be usable for guiding decisions. We also brought into clearer focus the concept of a moral principle's being usable for guiding decisions, and found it helpful to distinguish between two senses of a principle's being usable by an agent. In the core sense, a principle is usable when the agent can derive a prescription from it. By contrast, a principle is usable in the extended sense when the agent can derive a prescription from it, and moreover the action for which she would derive a prescription is one that she would be able to perform and that would actually conform to the principle. In this chapter we will look more closely at the kinds of cognitive and informational deficits that can impede an agent from using a moral principle.

3.1 The Theoretical and Practical Domains of a Moral Principle

Let us call the *theoretical domain* of a moral principle all the actual and possible acts to which it ascribes deontic status (where "deontic status" would include any of the types of moral status specially ascribable to acts, such as being right, obligatory, wrong, permissible, just, unjust, and supererogatory, or being prima facie right, and obligatory[2]). Different moral principles have different theoretical domains. A principle prohibiting lying has a relatively small theoretical domain, since it only assigns moral status (being wrong) to actual and possible acts of lying. Act utilitarianism, by contrast, has

---

[1] Brooks (2015).

[2] Some philosophers use "blameworthy" and "praiseworthy" as types of moral status that an action may have. In my conception, these types of moral status are attributed in the first instance to *agents* for the acts they perform and the psychological states in which they perform them. On this view, "blameworthiness" and "praiseworthiness" are attributed to acts only by extension. Hence I do not include them in this list of types of deontic status. There is a debate about whether being supererogatory belongs in the same deontic category as being right, or belongs in the same category as praiseworthy, or constitutes some amalgam between the two types.

a very large theoretical domain, since it ascribes moral status to all actual and possible acts.[3] Let us further call the *practical domain* of a principle every actual and possible act with respect to which the principle can be used by the act's potential agent for guiding decisions (including decisions based on an assessment of the act as morally permissible).[4]

For a supporter of the Usability Demand it is plausible to think that a moral principle's practical domain ought to approach its theoretical domain as closely as possible, and indeed ought to match its theoretical domain exactly. For such a supporter, it is surely plausible to hold that if a person is subject to the mandate that she acts according to a given moral principle, then it ought to be the case that she can effectively choose what to do by reference to that principle. A principle which meets this ideal may be said to be *universally usable*.[5] Such a principle could be used for making a decision, not necessarily with respect to *every* action, but with respect to every action *that it evaluates*. This ideal, although rarely articulated explicitly, seems to be implicitly assumed in many discussions of moral principles as decision-guides. Representative expressions of it may be found in Rawls, Castañeda, and Narveson.

[P]rinciples are to be universal in application…I assume that [everyone] can understand these principles and use them in his deliberations.[6]

Morality is…a complex system of norms…that are *universal*, in that they apply to all persons; [and] *pervasive*, in that they apply to every moment of each person's life; [and] *practical*, in that they purport to constitute an effective guidance to action….[7]

…we must be able to see what the principle we are examining says about each case it is intended to cover.[8]

---

[3]   Similarly, some religions aspire to provide "a complete program for human life" (Hubbard, 2016).

[4]   Our distinction between the core and extended usability of a principle implies that we would need to distinguish the "core practical domain" from the "extended practical domain" of a principle. The distinction between the theoretical and practical domains of a principle was originally introduced, using slightly different terminology, in H. Smith (1988), pp. 91–3. It is further discussed in H. Smith (2010a), pp. 100–2.

[5]   Notice that the universal usability of a principle with a small theoretical range (like "Marrying one's brother is wrong") will not require that *every* agent, on every occasion, be able to make her decision by reference to it, since many agents' actions will never be evaluated by the principle.

[6]   Rawls (1971), p. 132.

[7]   Castañeda (1974), pp. 15–16. Note that Castañeda's requirements for morality's usability are stronger than my own, because he is referring to an entire moral system, rather than to a single principle only (which might constitute only part of a moral system). Many theorists have a concept of morality as being far less intrusive than the one suggested by Castañeda's words, but we should note that a morality might be universal and pervasive in his sense while telling us, for most of our acts, merely that they are morally permissible, rather than that one or the other act is required.

[8]   Narveson (1967), p. 38. An apparent demand for universal usability is also articulated by Hudson (1989), pp. 222 and 227. Similar assumptions are discernible behind the statements of a number of moral philosophers: Sidgwick (1907), p. 5, states that the practical role of morality is its only role ("moral has a practical aim: we desire knowledge of right conduct in order to act on it"; Prichard (1968) claims that ordinary thought holds that there can be no particular duty that is not recognized as such by the person obligated to do it; and Jackson (1991), p. 467, states that ethical theories are theories about what to *do*, and that guides to actions must in some appropriate sense be "present" to the agent's mind, so that he can move from theory to action.

Like most theorists, these three do not draw the distinction between core and extended usability, so it is impossible to tell which kind of usability they require of a moral theory. Other theorists are explicit in rejecting the demand for universal usability and limiting the demand to a subset of agents or occasions for decision. Thus Väyrynen states that a moral theory need only be usable on the "occasions the agent is *likely* to encounter" (my emphasis), and stipulates that a theory need only be usable by cognitively "normal" moral agents who act under idealized conditions and who have met their duty to acquire relevant information.[9] However, the acceptance of such limitations appears to arise from an implicit acknowledgment of the impracticality of requiring a moral theory to be usable by all agents on all occasions. No reason is given to defend such limitations as preferable on the ground that a moral theory with limited usability is theoretically equal or superior to one with broader usability. Indeed, Väyrynen states explicitly that an ethical theory is better to the extent that it provides adequate moral guidance.[10] Neither he nor others argue that it is less important for cognitively impaired moral agents to be able to use their moral theory than it is for agents with average or superior cognitive abilities. Thus the idea of universal usability emerges as the ideal for any theorist who advocates the importance of usability at all, even if that theorist concedes that the ideal may be unattainable for practical reasons. It is difficult to see how one could defend limiting this ideal except for such considerations.

This kind of demand for usability is not restricted to the realm of ethics or political theory. "Operational epistemology," a parallel ideal for epistemology, has been articulated by Timothy Williamson, who describes it as providing a method for believing what is true:

Operational epistemology ... is the attempt to provide enquirers with methods such that one is, at least in principle, always in a position to know whether one is complying with them.... We should do epistemology in a first-personal way... [and] provide enquirers with guidance that they can actually use, in whatever situation they find themselves.[11]

The ideal that a moral principle should be universally usable is a naturally compelling one. We will consider its rationale more carefully later in this chapter, but for now we can note at least one intuitively obvious source of its attractiveness. It seems clear that any tool falls short of perfection if it cannot be used on every task that calls for it. A computer keyboard with keys too small to be manipulated by large hands is less perfect than one with keys that fit any user's hands. If a moral principle, meant to function as an action-guide—that is, as a tool for decision-making—can be used for only *some* decisions within its theoretical domain, or can only be used by a limited number of moral agents, then it is a less perfect tool than a principle which can be used by *all* agents and for *all* such decisions. One of our questions, then, must be whether moral

---

[9] Väyrynen (2006), pp. 294, 296, and 299–300.   [10] Väyrynen (2006), p. 292.
[11] Williamson (2008), pp. 277–8. (In this quotation I have slightly changed the order of his remarks in order to enhance clarity.) Williamson argues that operational epistemology in this sense is impossible.

principles are "meant" to be used as action-guides in this way. But we should acknowledge how strong the demand for universal usability is. Although philosophical ethics tends to focus on the moral decisions of rational, alert, and well-informed adults, the range of agents who are subject to moral demands is much wider than this. Children, at least by a certain stage of development, are subject to moral demands, although the nature of the demands on them may be different from the nature of the demands on adults.[12] Cognitively impaired individuals, at least if they have certain minimum capacities, are subject to moral demands: a person with a moderate case of Down syndrome can act wrongly, just as can a normally endowed individual. Even normally endowed individuals may be multi-tasking, sleepy, jet-lagged, moderately drunk, or under the mild influence of drugs or stimulants—all conditions that interfere with the individual's ability to use a moral principle in making a decision, even though his actions are subject to moral evaluation.[13] When the action of any of these agents is judged right or wrong by some moral principle, then the demand for universal usability requires that the agent be able to use that principle in making his decision what to do.

3.2   The Impact of Cognitive Limitations on our Ability to Use Moral Principles in Making Decisions: Let Us Count the Ways

Given the intuitive appeal of the ideal of universal usability, let us inquire whether or not traditional moral principles satisfy it.[14] By "traditional" moral principles I shall mean both the standard moral principles commonly discussed by philosophers, such as traditional consequentialist and deontological principles, and also moral precepts invoked in everyday life, including rules from informal codes as well as from formal codes such as the Ten Commandments, codes of professional ethics, and school honor

---

[12] See Franklin-Hall (2013) for discussion and references.

[13] Some individuals are so drunk or drugged as to be completely unconscious or out of control. They cannot make moral decisions, but then their "actions" are not subject to moral evaluation, except possibly as the upshots of earlier decisions they may have made (e.g., the decision to go on a drinking binge). Clearly it is no defect in a principle that it cannot be applied by someone in one of these extreme conditions. Thanks to Nicholas Sturgeon for pressing me on such cases.

[14] Note one immediate issue. Although an individual act-token, if it takes place at all, only takes place at a given time, there are many earlier times at which a decision might or does take place whether or not to perform that action. Indeed, there might be a sequence of actual decisions if the agent vacillates back and forth on what to do, or perhaps keeps reaffirming to herself that she will actually do the act when the time comes. From the point of view of the Usability Demand, there are clear attractions to requiring that a principle be usable on *each* occasion on which the agent might consider whether or not to perform the action. However, such a requirement may seem impossible to satisfy. A much weaker requirement would only insist that there be at least one occasion—perhaps long in advance of the time for action—on which the principle is usable. However, since this stance seems far too lax, the following discussion will assume that the demand for universal usability is a more restricted demand, namely that the principle is usable on the final occasion for decision. For discussion of the issues raised by an agent's ability to choose an action in advance of the time it would be performed, see H. Goldman (1976) and (1978) and H. Smith (2011).

codes.[15] Even setting aside problems of usability arising from the theoretical deficiencies canvassed in Chapter 2 from which moral principles may suffer, little reflection suffices to convince us that the traditional moral principles fail the test of universal usability because of problems arising from our epistemic deficiencies as decision makers. Although these deficiencies may take many forms, eight major types of cognitive impediments are the most salient.

3.2.1 *The problem of unintelligibility*

First, the agent may, by reason of her cognitive limitations, be *unable to understand* the principle in question: to grasp some of its crucial concepts (whether these are evaluative, formal, or empirical), or to comprehend the overall structure of the principle.[16] Kant, for example, advocated a principle we might state as "An act is permissible if and only if it is done in accordance with a maxim by which you can at the same time will that it should become a universal law."[17] Generations of philosophy instructors can testify that not every undergraduate is readily capable of understanding this precept; those who do not are certainly not in a position to apply it themselves in making personal decisions. Of course such a baffled undergraduate might procure assistance in applying the principle, and might come to believe, under the guidance of her philosophy professor, that (say) cheating on an organic chemistry exam would involve performing an action whose maxim she could not will as a universal law. However, such advisors may not always be readily available. And if no such authority comes to her assistance, the undergraduate cannot use this principle to make any decisions.

Most of the moral principles with which we are most familiar are—probably not accidentally—stated in a manner lending itself to the comprehension of the average person even without recourse to an advisor. However, this is not true of all attractive principles, and even those that are readily graspable by the average person may be beyond the capacities of cognitively less well-endowed agents who nonetheless face a variety of moral choices and have moral duties.[18] And some principles may involve

---

[15] Of course there are many "non-traditional" moral theories, many (but not all) of which include principles that take a "subjective" form (such as "Do nothing you believe may be a killing of someone" or "Maximize subjective expected utility"). I do not include here non-traditional theories that have been proposed precisely to secure usability, because we first need to see whether and how the traditional theories fail before we can see what kind of non-traditional theory might serve this role more successfully.

[16] Rawls (1980), p. 561, holds that a moral conception's "first principles cannot be so complex that they cannot be generally understood," and Carlson (2002), p. 72, argues that a person is unable to use a moral theory unless the person is able to understand the theory.

[17] Kant (1959), p. 39.

[18] There is a deep issue of establishing the point at which an agent's limited cognitive (or emotional, or self-governance) endowments place her outside the scope of morality, not in the sense that we need not care how we treat her, but rather in the sense that she herself is not subject to moral imperatives. (See Schapiro (1999) for related discussion.) This issue is complicated by the fact that there is a graded continuum here: an agent may not be able to understand principle P, but would be able to understand some related but simpler principle P*. If we think P is the correct account of morality, do we conclude this agent is not subject to moral demands, even though she could understand and follow P*?

concepts or structures that are even outside the grasp of cognitively superior agents, although there might be reasons to think such principles capture the moral truth.

An agent who cannot understand a given moral principle well enough to derive prescriptions from it (and who has no source of information to help her overcome this deficit) is an agent for whom that principle is not usable either in the extended or in the core sense, since she fails to satisfy clause (C) of Definitions 2.1 and 2.4: she doesn't believe of any action that it has the feature(s) required by the principle.

3.2.2 The problem of error regarding nonmoral facts

The second impediment to usability is raised by the *problem of error regarding nonmoral facts*.[19] This problem afflicts an agent who can reason in the requisite manner, that is, who can derive a prescription for action from his or her moral principle. But some nonmoral factual premise the agent would invoke, in order to derive a prescription for an act, is false, and the conclusion would often be false as well.[20] The act the agent believes has F does not have F; hence his inference that the act would be prescribed by the principle would usually be erroneous. Consider a state governor who wants to follow utilitarianism in deciding whether to balance the state budget by raising taxes or by cutting state spending. The governor believes, falsely, that cutting spending would maximize the general welfare, and so proposes a budget reducing state expenditures. But he is mistaken: in fact only the policy of raising taxes would maximize welfare and satisfy utilitarianism. The governor's decision is in error. Utilitarianism is usable by the governor in the core sense for this decision, since he can derive a prescription from it. However, it is not usable in the *extended* sense, because he fails to satisfy clause (C) in Definition 2.4—his belief that reducing state expenditures would maximize welfare is false, not true as clause (C) requires.

In this case the governor would derive a false conclusion. In other cases an agent's conclusion might, by accident, be correct, even though his factual premise is incorrect. Here is an example of an "accidental success" case: S believes (falsely) that if he performed act A, A would keep a promise, and S also believes that principle P prescribes acts of promise-keeping. For this reason S performs A. However, act A actually does *not* keep his promise, but it does involve telling the truth. Luckily for S, another

---

[19] I shall use the term "moral fact" to refer to facts involving the moral status of some being or event, and use the term "nonmoral fact" to refer to any other kind of fact. Thus moral facts would include the facts that normal adults have a right to life, and that witnesses have a moral duty not to lie under oath. Nonmoral facts would include facts about the natural world, human psychology, and theological or metaphysical matters. Nonmoral facts, in this usage, would also include normative facts about other nonmoral realms, such as law, prudence, epistemology, or rationality broadly construed. Philosophers who deny the existence of moral "facts" should translate this distinction into their favored terminology. For brevity I will typically use the unmodified term "fact" to refer only to nonmoral facts.

[20] Again, some philosophers hold that moral statements, such as "It would be morally right to raise taxes," are not truth-apt, so that it is misleading to describe the agent's "conclusion" as "false." Nothing in the present argument seems to turn on this issue. Hence philosophers of this persuasion should substitute their favored terms for "true" and "false" in such locutions. I will hold to common usage which often ascribes truth or falsity to such moral statements.

principle Q of the same code requires acts that involve telling the truth, although S is unaware of Q. Principle Q is more stringent than P, so S ought to do A, just as S believes. Thus in performing A, S has managed accidentally to do what is morally right, even though S's ground for concluding that A is right is mistaken.[21] But many cases in which S would choose A from a false belief that A has some specific property prescribed by principle P are cases in which S arrives at a mistaken conclusion about the moral status of his act.

The problem of nonmoral error has commonly been noted in connection with consequentialist principles such as utilitarianism, but deontological principles are often felt to be immune to it.[22] As was pointed out in Chapter 1, this is a mistake: an agent may easily be mistaken about the properties of a proposed action that are relevant to its deontological status. For example, a judge may try to follow a retributive principle requiring him to impose penalties that are proportional to the gravity of offenders' crimes. He sentences an offender to three years in the penitentiary, but since he has overestimated the severity of the damage suffered by the offender's victim, the penalty is not proportional to the gravity of the crime. Similarly an agent can be mistaken about such matters as whether the statement he proposes to make will deceive his audience, whether an object he proposes to remove from the locker room belongs to him or to another person, whether he has caused an injury or deprivation that he ought to remedy, whether he has made a promise to someone or what the content of the promise was, whether the law requires him to avoid performing a certain act, whether a prospective sexual partner has genuinely consented to sexual intercourse, and so forth. Non-consequentialist moral principles, just like consequentialist ones, can easily be subject to the problem of nonmoral error.

Of course, principles subject to the problem of nonmoral error may still be usable in the *core* sense, because an agent hampered by false beliefs about his circumstances may still be able to derive a prescription from such a principle. However, these principles are not usable in the *extended* sense, and invoking them would not (except by accident) lead such an agent to perform the act actually prescribed by his moral code.

3.2.3 *The problem of uncertainty about nonmoral facts*

The third problem created by our cognitive deficiencies is the *problem of uncertainty about nonmoral facts*. This problem arises when an agent is beleaguered by uncertainty regarding the nonmoral facts necessary for deriving a prescription from the principle in question. In terms of Definitions 2.1 and 2.4 of ability to use a moral principle as a core or extended guide, the agent believes that her principle prescribes acts having

---

[21] One difference between this case and the "Gettier-type" case described in footnote 19 in Chapter 2 is that in the Chapter 2 case the agent truly believes his act has the relevant right-making property F (being G or H) and chooses his act for this reason, whereas in this case the agent does not choose the act for a right-making property that it actually has.

[22] See discussion of this in Pettit (2003), p. 99. Lenman (2000) provides a take-no-prisoners account of the ways in which consequentialism is subject to the problems of nonmoral error and uncertainty.

feature F, but she is uncertain whether any act-type she could perform has F. Thus if she tried to use her principle in deciding what to do, she would be uncertain which (if any) known option would satisfy the principle. Her uncertainty about the relevant nonmoral facts might be uncertainty which known option would have F, or alternatively her uncertainty might be whether she has the ability to perform a given act, although she believes that if she did perform it, it would have F. For an example of the first kind of case, consider an individual who believes she ought to keep her promises, and who has promised her elderly mother (who cannot get to a telephone) to pick up something at the grocery store. Once the agent is in the store, she is uncertain whether she promised to buy milk or bread. She doesn't have enough money to buy both. This agent knows what her options are—buying milk or buying bread—but she is uncertain which option would satisfy her principle of keeping her promises. She can derive no guidance—even core guidance—from her principle about what to do. She satisfies clause (B) of Definition 2.1, but fails to satisfy clause (C). As we noted before, she might believe of each of her options that it has a certain probability of carrying out her promise, but this does not rescue her from her dilemma. She might believe there is a 70 percent chance she promised to get milk, and a 30 percent chance she promised to get bread. Still, her principle requires her to actually *keep her promise*. It does not require her (for example) to *do something that will maximize the chance of keeping her promise*, or to *try to keep her promise*. Her uncertainty prevents her from deriving any prescription directly from the principle to which she has allegiance. In everyday thinking we tend to move so readily from a principle that one ought to keep one's promises to an allied principle that (for example) one ought to maximize the chance of keeping one's promise that we don't even notice that we have shifted the principle we have used for direct guidance. Nonetheless we have shifted—perhaps unwittingly adopting a Hybrid approach to the problem of uncertainty—and we must be strict about which principle is being directly used if we are to determine how moral codes ought to handle the limits on decision makers' knowledge.

For an example of the second kind of case (uncertainty whether one can perform the relevant act), consider a lifeguard who wants to follow standard utilitarianism, that is, the form of objective utilitarianism which evaluates acts in light of their actual consequences, not in light of their expected consequences. He believes (correctly) that swimming out to save a drowning swimmer, Felicity, would have greater utility than throwing a life preserver to her. However, given the strength of the tides, the lifeguard is uncertain whether he can successfully swim out to Felicity and bring her back to shore. The lifeguard believes of his putative option—swimming out to save Felicity—that *if* he could carry it out, doing so would maximize utility, but he is uncertain whether it is a genuine option for him. Hence the lifeguard can derive no guidance—even core guidance—from utilitarianism, because although he believes that if he swam out and saved Felicity his doing so would maximize utility, his uncertainty means that he does not fully believe that he can swim out and save her. He satisfies clause (C) of Definition 2.1, but fails to satisfy clause (B). In this case too, the lifeguard's ability to assign some probability (say, 80 percent) to his being able to swim out to save the swimmer does not extricate him from the problem of uncertainty about nonmoral facts. His principle tells him to *maximize utility*, not (say) to *maximize the chance of maximizing utility*, or to *try to maximize utility*. He cannot use the principle he wants to apply, since our definition of a moral principle's usability requires that the decision maker be able to infer what that principle prescribes—not what it *may* prescribe, or what it *probably* prescribes.[23]

In these cases of nonmoral uncertainty, the agents in question cannot use their moral principles either in the core or the extended sense: neither agent can choose an action that he or she believes conforms to the favored principle, and even if one of these agents somehow chooses an action to perform, it will not be one that he or she fully believes satisfies the favored principle.

At this point we can see that an agent who is subject to the problem of unintelligibility with regard to some moral principle is blocked from using that principle in much the same way she would be if she were subject to the problem of uncertainty regarding nonmoral facts. The agent who doesn't understand a principle doesn't believe that it assesses an act as right if and only if it has some property F. Hence she is unable to derive a prescription from the principle because she doesn't believe of any act that it would have the feature that is required by the principle. Similarly an agent who is uncertain for empirical reasons which act has F is likewise unable to derive a prescription. Both agents fail to satisfy clause (C). This suggests that both types of cognitive limitation should be approached in the same general way in any attempt to remedy them.

3.2.4 The problem of ignorance of nonmoral facts

The fourth problem created by our cognitive deficiencies is the *problem of ignorance about nonmoral facts*. This problem arises when an agent lacks any belief at all about whether act A has or fails to have feature F, or lacks any belief about whether some act A is one she could or couldn't perform. But how should we interpret an agent's lacking any such belief? On one interpretation, the situation should be understood as one in which the agent's being "ignorant" whether A has or fails to have F (or is or is not a genuine option for her) constitutes the agent's being *epistemically indifferent* between these two, that is, she assigns equal probability to A's having F and to A's not having F (or to A's being and not being a genuine option). On this interpretation the problem of ignorance is simply a special case of the problem of uncertainty about nonmoral facts and requires no different treatment.[24]

---

[23] As we saw in Chapter 2, there may be epistemic rules that count an agent as fully believing that P in cases where he assigns a probability of (say) 0.95 or higher to P's being true. However, the problem of uncertainty still arises for the many agents who assign probabilities lower than 0.95 to the relevant propositions.

[24] Probability theorists debate how to handle complete ignorance and have noted that interpreting it as indifference over "outcomes" only makes sense if the agent is not completely ignorant, but rather has enough information "to be able to identify which is the right partition of the outcome space over which to

On another interpretation, an agent's being ignorant whether (for example) A has or fails to have F amounts to the agent's *assigning no probability* to either one, or having no degree of credence in either one. Perhaps she declines for some reason to assign any probability, or perhaps she has never thought about whether A has or doesn't have F, and so has no beliefs on the issue at all. Suppose, for example, a visitor to Australia eats dinner at a restaurant where kangaroo meat is one of the main courses. The Levitican dietary law forbids eating meat from an animal that parts the hoof but fails to chew the cud. Not being Jewish, the visitor has never thought about this dietary law, never thought about whether kangaroos part the hoof but fail to chew the cud, is not thinking about it now, and if she did think about it, would have no idea whether or not this is true. Could the visitor use the Levitican law to decide whether eating kangaroo is forbidden by the dietary law? In this case, the visitor believes that she has the ability to eat kangaroo (that is, she satisfies clause (B) of Definition 2.1 with respect to ordering kangaroo), but she doesn't believe that if she ate kangaroo, her eating kangaroo would have the relevant feature F (that is, she doesn't believe that she would be eating the flesh of an animal that parts the hoof but fails to chew the cud). Hence she fails to satisfy clause (C) of Definition 2.1, and she is unable to use the Levitican law, even as a core guide, to derive a prescription with respect to eating kangaroo. Like the person who assigns equal probability to A's having F and A's not having F, her situation turns out to be similar to that of a person afflicted with the problem of uncertainty about nonmoral facts—someone who is uncertain whether kangaroos part the hoof but fail to chew the cud. Parallel remarks could be made about someone who lacks any belief about whether some act A is one she could or couldn't perform.

Given the fact that the problem of ignorance about nonmoral facts can be seen as one in which the agent is either subject to the problem of uncertainty about nonmoral facts, or one in which the situation of the agent seems relevantly similar to the situation of someone subject to the problem of uncertainty about nonmoral facts, I shall assume that any satisfactory response to the problem of uncertainty about nonmoral facts will also be a satisfactory response to the problem of ignorance about nonmoral facts. Hence in most of the subsequent discussion, the problem of ignorance will not be addressed separately from the problem of uncertainty about nonmoral facts.

3.2.5 *The problem of computational constraints*

A fifth problem arises when an agent possesses enough lower level factual information to calculate which act is prescribed by her principle, but she is unable (either in general, or in this case, or within the time available) to take the necessary cognitive steps to make the calculation and so identify this act. This is the *problem of computational constraints*. It should be seen as a special case of the problem of uncertainty about nonmoral facts,

exercise indifference." For discussion of these issues, and defense of the view that there are "gaps" in both objective and subjective probability assignments, see Hajek (2003), especially sections 2.3 and 7.1.1. See also Norton (2008).

because an agent caught in such a situation is uncertain which act has the relevant right-making property. Her uncertainty simply arises in a special way—from her inability to make requisite computations. For example, suppose the reaction process in a nuclear power plant starts to spiral out of control. To avert disaster, the chief engineer must decide within 30 seconds whether to close down the reactor or to add extra coolant, and if the latter, how much coolant to add. Let us imagine that the engineer wants to make this decision by reference to act utilitarianism, and that she actually has all the necessary information about the numerous possible consequences, and the corresponding values, of each option. However, she cannot calculate, in the available 30 seconds before melt-down starts, which option's total consequences would have the highest overall value.[25] Or suppose a drone operator, operating from a military base in Nevada, wants to advise army helicopters whether or not to attack a gathering crowd in a village in Afghanistan where an American convoy is forming. The operator wants to advise the helicopter squadron to attack only if he believes the crowd contains militants and does not contain innocent children. But the amount of information he receives from dozens of instant-message and radio exchanges overwhelms the drone operator's ability to process it all to arrive at a firm conclusion about the nature of the crowd.[26]

These cases are ones in which the agent has the information (by "information" I shall mean simply "beliefs," with no implication that the beliefs are true or justified) and the intellectual capacity (perhaps with the help of available supporting resources such as computers) to make the necessary calculations, but lacks the necessary time to carry them out. But it is clear that there could be some possible (and perhaps otherwise very attractive) moral principles that ascribe moral status to an action as a function of mathematically complex combinations of characteristics that might exceed the computational ability of any human being to calculate—including human beings using powerful resources such as computers to extend their own computational abilities.[27] And of course individuals with significant cognitive limitations may be unable to perform calculations that normal decision makers would find relatively easy. Consider a kindergarten child who has not yet learned basic arithmetic and who wants to distribute a limited number of Valentine's Day candies to her classmates in a way that would maximize their pleasure. Without the help of the arithmetic she doesn't yet know, she is not in a position to calculate her best option. An adult suffering from serious cognitive impairment would encounter parallel problems in calculating some arithmetical quantities that applying a given moral principle would require him to ascertain.

---

[25] See Pollack (1982), p. 32. Pollack reports experts hold that "At the time of the accident at Three Mile Island, in March 1979, the control room displays contained all the information necessary to determine the status of the plant.... Yet the operators could not sort it out fast enough and made a crucial error...that exacerbated the accident."

[26] See Shanker and Richtel (2011).

[27] For an intriguing report on how airplane pilots may be able to extend their computation capacities with the aid of an Automated Emergency Lander, see McAlpine (2015).

Agents afflicted with the problem of information processing shortcomings are unable to use their moral principle as either a core or extended decision-guide. Here again, we can treat these cases as special instances of the problem of uncertainty about nonmoral facts, since what these agents suffer from is uncertainty that happens to arise from fundamental or temporary limitations on their computational capacities.[28]

3.2.6 The problem of moral error

An agent, in appealing to a moral principle to guide her decision, may invoke a principle that is incorrect. This is the *problem of moral error*. Someone may believe that it is morally permissible to kill animals to satisfy moderately important human wants and needs. She acts on this principle throughout her life, eating meat and using products such as leather that require the death of animals. But let us suppose this individual is mistaken: it is actually morally prohibited to kill animals except for much more weighty reasons than those that arise in her life. Or, in another kind of case in which two moral considerations conflict, an agent may incorrectly weigh them against each other. For example, an overly rigorous agent may believe that it is more important to keep a promise than to render aid, and so decide not to assist a badly injured accident victim in order to keep an appointment with a student. This agent, too, is subject to the problem of moral error: although he correctly identifies relevant moral considerations, he misestimates their relative importance.

As I argued in Chapter 2, our definitions of "usability" imply that the situation of a person's being trapped in the problem of *moral* error does not imply that she is unable to use the correct moral principle, either as a core or extended decision-guide. Despite her moral error it may still be true that if she wanted to use this moral principle, she would do so. Nothing about her situation prevents her from satisfying Definitions 2.1 and 2.4 with respect to any moral principle. Her problem is that she would not want to use the correct moral principle, because she believes another principle is correct. Her cognitive limitation—her incorrect view about what moral norm should guide her—means that she will make morally incorrect choices in many cases, but the limitation itself doesn't stand in the way of her ability to use the correct moral principle to guide her choices. Her ability to use the correct moral principle depends on her beliefs about non-normative matters, not on her beliefs about normative matters.

3.2.7 The problems of moral uncertainty and ignorance

Other failures of moral information may encumber an agent trying to make a moral decision. He may be uncertain which moral principle is correct or may lack any credence at all about which moral principle is correct. These are the *problems of moral uncertainty*

---

[28] Of course many computationally constrained agents might not be aware of their inability to *accurately* compute what is needed and would proceed with a defective "computation" that would deliver (unless they are unusually lucky) the wrong prescription. These computationally constrained agents are simply special examples of agents afflicted with the problem of nonmoral error. They can use their principle in the core but not the extended sense.

and ignorance. An agent, for example, might correctly believe that utilitarianism prescribes his lying to the Gestapo to save the life of a Jewish refugee hiding in his attic, and might also correctly believe that Kantianism prescribes his telling the truth about the refugee when asked. But he may be uncertain which of these moral theories is correct. Or an agent may never have thought about which moral theory might be correct. Such agents confront either the problem of moral uncertainty or the problem of moral ignorance. In either case, it is unclear how the agent can use *morality* to make a decision. Nonetheless, according to Definitions 2.1 and 2.4, both utilitarianism and Kantianism may be usable in both the core and the extended sense by him: he could take either theory, derive an accurate prescription from it for his choice, and carry out that prescription. Still, his uncertainty about what moral norm should guide him in these instances, or his lack of belief in the correctness of any moral principle, may render him unable to make a choice that he regards as morally appropriate.[29]

We saw in discussing the problem of nonmoral ignorance that it can unproblematically be considered under the rubric of the problem of nonmoral uncertainty. On similar grounds I shall also lump the problems of moral uncertainty and ignorance together under the title the *problem of moral uncertainty*.

3.2.8 The problems of meta-moral uncertainty and error

A higher level problem arising from agents' cognitive limitations is the problem *of meta-moral uncertainty*: an agent might believe of the correct moral principle that it is correct, but be uncertain how to justify her belief in its correctness, or uncertain whether this belief is justified. She contrasts with an agent subject to the problem of moral uncertainty who is uncertain which moral principle is correct. Thus an agent subject to meta-moral uncertainty might have heard of the Golden Rule and find this rule so compelling that she adopts it as a true moral principle. However, not being philosophically or theologically sophisticated, she is quite uncertain what the *justification* is for this principle. Similarly, an agent might come to believe that act utilitarianism is correct without being able to provide a justification for this view. Alternatively, an agent might be certain that the correct moral principle is the one promulgated by God. However, she is uncertain which morality God has promulgated, so she is uncertain what moral principle is justified. She too suffers from meta-moral uncertainty. Similarly, an agent might suffer from meta-moral ignorance: never having thought about the matter, she has no credences about which moral principles are justified.

By the same token an agent might suffer from the related *problem of meta-moral error*: she believes that such-and-such is a valid justification for her moral view, but she is wrong about this. For example, she might believe that the correct moral principles are ones that could not reasonably be rejected by people who are moved to find principles

---

[29] For discussions of how an agent might best make decisions in light of moral error or uncertainty, see Guerrero (2007); Lockhart (2000); MacAskill (2016); J. Ross (2006); Sepielli (2009) and (2013); and E. Williams (2013).

for the general regulation of behavior that others, similarly motivated, could not reasonably reject.[30] She further believes that Ethical Egoism is the principle that would be so chosen—but she is mistaken in one or the other of these beliefs. All the agents just described suffer discriminable kinds of cognitive impediments to their identifying and using the correct moral theory in their decision-making. It might be demanded as a condition of any moral principle's being true that the individuals governed by it are able to ascertain that and why it is correct.[31] Here again, however, this kind of meta-moral cognitive limitation does not block any agent from using the correct moral principle in either the core or the extended sense as I have defined "usability." Of course, when we ask ourselves whether an agent suffering from the problem of meta-moral uncertainty or error is equipped to be a *perfect* moral decision maker, it is clear that she falls short in an important way, since she cannot make a moral choice that she can genuinely defend.[32]

We saw in Chapter 2 that some moral principles are flawed, even as theoretical accounts of right and wrong, and that the flaws inherent in these principles often prevent them from being used as decision-guides. But setting aside such theoretically flawed principles, we have now seen that there are still at least eight kinds of cognitive handicaps that can, and do, in some way obstruct human beings' attempts to use moral principles successfully to guide their moral decisions: the problems of (1) unintelligibility, (2) error regarding nonmoral facts, (3) uncertainty about nonmoral facts, (4) ignorance of nonmoral facts, (5) computational constraints, (6) moral error, (7) moral uncertainty and ignorance, and (8) meta-moral uncertainty and error.

These impediments to accurate decision-making can afflict all kinds of moral theories, including both consequentialist and deontological theories. In the interest of pursuing a feasible project, this book primarily focuses on the problems caused by deficiencies in *nonmoral* information. Hence I shall now set aside, without trying to address them directly, the problems of moral error, uncertainty, and ignorance, and also the problems of meta-moral uncertainty and error (although some of these will re-emerge indirectly at later stages). I have argued that the problem of unintelligibility, the problem of ignorance about nonmoral facts, and the problem of computational constraints, can all be seen (or handled) as special cases of the problem of uncertainty about nonmoral facts. This leaves two core problems to be addressed in this book: the problem of error regarding nonmoral facts (henceforward, the problem of error) and the problem of uncertainty about nonmoral facts (henceforward, the problem of uncertainty). The problem of error impedes the extended (but not the core) usability of any moral principle subject to it, while the problem of uncertainty impedes both the core and extended usability of any affected principle. These two problems show that

---

[30] Scanlon (1998), p. 4.

[31] For a discussion of this demand (which he describes as "uncontroversial among metaethicists") as applied to meta-ethical realists, see Enoch (2010).

[32] See discussion in Chapter 2, section 2.4.2, of the notion of an agent's having the ability to "do the right thing."

principles that might appear quite attractive as theoretical accounts of right and wrong may fail in many cases to be usable for actual decision-making under the actual conditions that cognitively limited human agents face. Such principles fall short of the ideal that moral principles be universally usable. How should we react to such failures?

3.3 Responses to Failures of Usability

The responses of moral theorists who have explicitly considered the epistemic limitations impairing the usability of moral principles have tended to cluster in three different categories. I shall describe each kind of response briefly, interpreting each in its most theoretically interesting form as a proposal about what the *content* of morality must be. To fix ideas I shall introduce and regard these kinds of responses as "ideal types," pure versions of the kind of response in question.[33] Previous theorists have not clearly distinguished these kinds of responses from each other, or clearly adopted one type of response versus another. We should not expect, then, to find clear-cut examples of theorists who have adopted one or the other of the responses in its purest form. However, it will be illuminating to develop the concept of an ideal type of each of the kinds of response. As the argument progresses, we can explore ways in which some theorists have shown their allegiance to one or the other kind of response, but developed it in ways that diverge from the ideal type. We will also see how advocates of one or the other type of response might have developed it in order to meet certain objections, even though no actual advocate has envisioned such a version.

The first kind of response, which I shall call the *Pragmatic Response*, has been adopted by a wide variety of moral theorists.[34] According to these thinkers, the theoretical function of morality cannot be isolated from its practical or regulative function, in the sense that one crucial test of a moral principle's theoretical correctness just *is* its practical usability by the limited human beings who will actually employ it. On this view an ethical theory is a theory to be used in guiding our choices and actions. It must,

---

[33] I am grateful to one of the anonymous readers for the Press for suggesting this way of conceiving of these responses.

[34] A representative but hardly complete list of exemplars of the Pragmatic Response would include Bennett (1995), Chapter 3, section 16; Berkeley (1929); Brandt (1979), section XIV.2; Ewing (1947), Chapter IV; Flanagan (1991); Gert (2004), p. 61; Gibbard (1990), p. 43; Griffin (1996), pp. 99–106; Gruzalski (1981); Howard-Snyder (1997); Hudson (1989); Jackson (1991); Lang (2004); Lenman (2000); Mackie (1977), p. 133; Mason (2003); Murphy (2008); Oddie and Menzies (1992); Pollock (2006), p. 190; Prichard (1968); Quinton (1973), pp. 47–54; Rawls (1971), p. 132; Rawls (1980), p. 561; Ross (1939); Scanlon (2008), pp. 47–8; Shaw (2007), pp. 465–6; Singer (1979), p. 2; and Wiland (2005). Although it is unclear in some cases, several of these theorists probably do not advocate a form of Pragmatic theory that requires universal usability of a moral theory. Although Zimmerman's Prospective view (as developed in (2006), (2008), and (2014) appears to be a type of Pragmatic theory, he describes the view as not being an attempt to render the correct moral theory usable, so his view does not qualify as Pragmatic.

For convenience of labeling I will refer to this type of theorist as a "Pragmatic theorist" or sometimes as a "Pragmatist." Note, however, that there is no intended connection between the views of these theorists and the views of the classic Pragmatists, Charles Sanders Peirce, William James, and John Dewey, whose chief "Pragmatic" focus was on epistemic issues rather than moral ones.

then, be capable of guiding us, imperfect as we are. Thus James Griffin says, "Morality is confined to the sphere of human capability. We are used to the fact that our physical and psychological capacities are limited, but so is our understanding. Moral norms are shaped for agents with all those limitations."[35]

The spirit behind the Pragmatic Response view has been expressed very well, for a slightly different human capacity, in Samuel Scheffler's account of the manner in which morality should handle human beings' strong personal motivations, which may conflict with the demands of an overly stringent moral system. According to Scheffler:

> although moral considerations do not always coincide with considerations of the individual agent's interests, moral norms do serve to regulate the conduct of human beings, and *their content is constrained by their regulative role*: they must be capable of being integrated in a coherent and attractive way into an individual human life.... It is...a practicable social goal—to achieve a measure of fit between what morality demands and what people's motivational resources can supply.... On this way of thinking, it is a crucial feature of morality that it is motivationally accessible to normal human agents...under reasonably favorable circumstances.[36]

We are concerned here with the *cognitive* frailties of human decision makers, rather than their *motivational* frailties, but those who advocate the Pragmatic Response in this arena hold a view parallel to Scheffler's. In David Lyons' description, these thinkers hold that moral principles must be designed to accommodate "the mistakes we make, the errors to which we are prone...our blockheadedness, ignorance, confusion, and stupidity."[37] Many Pragmatic Response theorists, on noting that the practical use of act utilitarianism is hindered for most decisions by our lack of information about the future, have claimed that this fact provides sufficient reason to reject act utilitarianism as a theoretical account of what makes acts right and wrong. For example, Frank Jackson, noting that agents often lack the information to apply objective act utilitarianism, says that "we are dealing with an *ethical* theory when we deal with consequentialism, a theory about *action*, about what to *do*...the fact that a course of action would have the best results is not in itself a guide to action, for a guide to action must in some appropriate sense be present to the agent's mind."[38] Finding that objective consequentialism fails to provide such a guide to action, Jackson (along with many others) rejects the theory for this reason, and instead adopts "decision-theoretic consequentialism," which recommends maximizing expected moral utility.[39] Other Pragmatic theorists have advocated replacing act utilitarianism with a different model altogether: a more readily

---

[35] Griffin (1996), p. 99.   [36] Scheffler (1992), pp. 4 and 125. Emphasis added.
[37] Lyons (1965), p. 159.   [38] Jackson (1991), pp. 466–7.
[39] Jackson (1991), *passim*. Jackson takes our obligations to depend on the actual *moral* facts, even if they do not depend on the actual *nonmoral* facts, but rather on our estimates about the likelihood of these facts. Other examples include Hudson (1989), although Hudson's discussion sometimes suggests he is advocating a Hybrid version of utilitarianism rather than a Pragmatic version; Mason (2003); and Oddie and Menzies (1992). In (1997) Howard-Snyder advocates a Pragmatic version of act utilitarianism, although her concern is focused more on the fact that objective act utilitarianism requires agents to perform acts they are unable, in the epistemic sense, to perform.

usable set of deontological rules. Thus we find Alan Donagan and P. T. Geach saying that we must accept an absolute prohibition on lying, since if we try to discriminate beneficial lies from harmful ones, we will often err.[40] Psychologist Gird Gigerenzer rejects maximizing forms of consequentialism, asking "How can maximization serve as a norm for rightness if we can neither determine, nor, after the fact, recognize the best action?"[41]

Some theorists appear to advocate rule utilitarianism as a Pragmatic Response.[42] Another example of the Pragmatic Response is provided by John Rawls, who argues that any acceptable principle of justice must be simple enough for everyone to understand, and such that ascertaining which institutions satisfy the principle does not depend on information that is difficult to obtain.[43] To use a contentious slogan, we might say that the Pragmatic Response attempts to narrow the gap between human decision-making capacities and the requirements of moral theory by *lowering* the theory to the level where fallible human beings can employ it.[44]

The second kind of response, which I shall call the *Austere Response*, claims that a moral principle's practical usability, or lack thereof, is no test of its adequacy or inadequacy as a theoretical account of right and wrong. Advocates of the Austere Response hold that a moral principle provides an explanatory theory: it tells us which acts are right and wrong, and tells us why they are right or wrong—what features make these acts have the status they do.[45] On this view it is a grave error to think that our

---

[40] See Geach (1977) and Donagan (1977), p. 39. It is notorious that Kant (1949) defended such absolute prohibitions, apparently partly on the same ground.

[41] Gigerenzer (2008b), p. 44.

[42] See Berkeley (1929), sections 4–13; Brandt (1963) and (1979); Griffin (1996); Hodgson (1967), Chapter III (although Hodgson argues in Chapter II and on pp. 63–5 that his version of rule utilitarianism is superior to act utilitarianism even under the assumption that agents make no mistaken judgments about non-normative facts); and Haslett (1984). On some interpretations, Mill (1957) belongs in the rule utilitarian camp. In (1972) Sartorius comes close to the epistemic limitations-driven rule utilitarian view. Needless to say, these theorists advocate differing versions of rule utilitarianism.

[43] Rawls (1971), p. 132, and (1980), p. 561.

[44] In (1968) on p. 25 Prichard is clear in saying that, having discovered that standard moral theories cannot be used without error, "These conclusions being all unwelcome, we naturally want to discover what *modification* of the form of a moral rule would enable us to escape them" (emphasis added). Scheffler (1992), p. 125, explicitly rejects this interpretation of his strategy. He contrasts two separate strategies for dealing with human frailties, one of which involves relaxing the requirements of morality to make them more accessible to human beings, and the other of which (his own) involves constructing morality from the outset as addressed to human beings with all their limitations. This latter strategy recognizes no "prior" moral content that must be "reduced" or "modified" when it is brought into contact with human nature. From my point of view the difference between these two approaches is likely to be minor; I classify them both as Pragmatic Responses.

There is an interesting contrast between the stance of Pragmatic theorists about morality as it applies to human beings, and the stance of theorists devising ethics for robots or other computers. The Pragmatic theorist takes human beings as a given, and asks how to design moral rules so that humans can apply them, while the person working on robot ethics may take moral rules as a given, and ask how to design robots to apply them. See Wallach and Colin (2009) and Henig (2015).

[45] For a representative articulation of this view, see Väyrynen (2006), p. 91. Väyrynen is not here asserting a full-fledged Austerity theory, which denies that the correctness of moral principles may depend on their usability.

difficulties in applying a theory make any difference at all to whether it is true, just as our difficulty in determining whether a small asteroid just hit the back side of the moon makes no difference to whether it is true that such an asteroid just hit the back side of the moon. Many Austerity theorists have consciously rejected the Usability Demand and denied that "usability" is an appropriate criterion for moral correctness. Even more Austerity theorists have endorsed moral theories on grounds that do not include any consideration of the practical usability of the theory.[46] Austerity advocates tend to view moral principles on the common-sense model of scientific laws, and point out that we do not test the truth or falsity of a scientific law by ascertaining whether it would be easy or difficult to make predictions on the basis of that law. Any difficulties we may experience in making predictions on the basis of a well-confirmed scientific law should be seen as defects in *us*, not defects in the law. Similarly, Austere Response theorists say, if we are unable to use some normatively correct moral principle to guide our choices—because we lack sufficient empirical information, or don't fully understand the principle, or are unable to perform the necessary calculations—that is a defect in us, not a defect in the theory. This kind of view is clearly expressed by Derek Parfit, who denies that a normative principle S is faulty because erroneous empirical beliefs prevent an agent from complying with S: "If this is the way in which S is self-defeating, this is no objection to S. S is self-defeating here only because of my incompetence in attempting to follow S. This is a fault, not in S, but in me."[47] In a related vein, David Lyons rejects the "general coherence" argument, that is, "the idea that a moral principle should be tested by the extent to which its general acceptance would defeat its 'point.'" He notes that "theories are not normally compared in such a way. No other kind of theory would be assessed on grounds implicit in the general coherence argument."[48] Brad Hooker agrees in rejecting such thinking: "It seems to me counterintuitive that what is morally right depends on rules designed on the assumption that we will regularly fail to comply with them. If the point of setting a rule one place rather than another is that our actions will miss their target to some degree, then a human tendency to make mistakes is shifting the line between the morally allowed and the morally forbidden."[49]

---

[46] Although it is not always clear which response various theorists adopt, a representative but incomplete list of Austerity theorists should include the following: Bergstrom (1966); Brandt (1963); Brink (1986), p. 426; Carlson (1995), pp. 20–4; Cohen (2008), pp. 323–7; Driver (2012); Graham (2010); Humberstone (1983); Lyons (1965); Moore (1993), Chapter 1, sections 16 and 17, and Chapter 5, section 89 (but see sections 91–100), and also (1965), pp. 11–12, 22, and 80–3; Resnik (1987), pp. 3–4 and 24; W. D. Ross (1930); J. J. C. Smart (1973), p. 47; Sorensen (1995); D. Sosa (1993); Spencer (1851), Chapters I and XXXII; and Thomson (1990), Chapter 9 (see especially pp. 232–3).

[47] Parfit (1984), p. 5. Parfit applies his remarks here to self-interest principles, not to patently moral principles, but also discusses the question of whether being "self-defeating" is a legitimate test for any normative theory.

[48] Lyons (1965), p. 159.

[49] Hooker (2000), pp. 76–7. Despite this statement, Hooker advocates a form of rule utilitarianism that evaluates moral codes by their expected value when adopted (pp. 32 and 72–5).

Some theorists point out that a moral norm may *inspire* us even if it is unattainable, and that striving to achieve it may uplift and improve us even if our efforts fail. To modify the norm to fit our limitations degrades this ideal, and pays a price in lowered human attainment.[50] However, since Austere Response theorists don't believe that the usability of a moral theory is relevant to its truth or explanatory power, which is what they are concerned with, they don't often attend to the epistemic problem or attempt to offer a solution for it. The capacity of a moral norm to inspire us would be at most a side interest for them, not something that should affect the norm's correctness. To the extent that Austere Response theorists address the practical use of moral principles, their slogan might be "Eliminate the gap between human decision-making capacities and the requirements of moral theory by *raising* human capacities to the level where human beings can employ the correct theory." Their advice to us might be to improve ourselves by acquiring more information relevant to moral decisions, increasing our ability to store and access this information, and employing computers or other devices to enhance our computational capacities.[51] We should not tinker with the content of the theory merely to disguise or cater to our own shortcomings. On the Austere view, the content of morality is not hostage to its usability by epistemically limited human beings.[52]

Both the Pragmatic and the Austere Responses can be seen as extreme reactions to the fact of human cognitive deficiencies. The third kind of response, which I shall call the *Hybrid Response*, rejects both extremes, and claims that the correct response involves blending the best parts of the Austere Response and the Pragmatic Response in a manner that pays allegiance to the view that the truth of a moral principle should not be affected by its practical usability, but also pays allegiance to the view that one task for moral principles is to be used for making decisions. The Hybrid Response achieves these goals by establishing a division of labor within the theory, and by

---

[50] Scheffler (1992), pp. 120–1.

[51] As Eli Shupe points out (Spring 2015 unpublished seminar note), no full-blooded Austerity theorist can *require* either that the true moral theory inspire us to higher attainments, or that it be such that improving our information or enhancing our cognitive capacities would make it possible for us to apply the theory. From the point of view of such a theorist, it is merely good luck if these improvements are possible.

[52] In an example involving decision-making broadly construed, in (1986) on p. 117 Isaac Levi takes the Austere view in defending Bayesianism as a method of evaluating options when making a decision. "No matter what principles one uses to evaluate options in a decision problem, it is to be expected that there will be some class of problems for which the theory proposed will find the task of identifying solutions computationally daunting. It does not seem to me, therefore, that objections to strict Bayesianism derived from reflections on the severe demands made upon our capacities in order to make decisions in conformity with its requirements ought to be decisive against it. We do not urge modifications of logic ... merely because the injunction to believe all logical truths or to be consistent cannot be satisfied to the letter by anyone."

For an Austere view in the theory of epistemic justification, see Conee and Feldman (2004), p. 87: "There is no basis for the premise that what is epistemically justified must be restricted to feasible doxastic alternatives ... suppose that there were occasions when forming the attitude that best fits a person's evidence was beyond normal cognitive limits. This would still be the attitude *justified* by the person's evidence. If the person had normal abilities, then he would be in the unfortunate position of being unable to do what is justified according to the standard for justification asserted by EJ. This is not a flaw in the account of justification. Some standards are met only by going beyond normal human limits."

introducing the concept of "indirectly" applying a moral theory. According to Hybrid theorists, which principle is the correct theoretical account of right and wrong is determined without any reference to the practical usability of such a principle. If the correct theoretical account proves impractical for use in making some (or all) decisions, then it is to be supplemented with appropriate second-level rules that are more readily applied in making decisions by human beings operating under limitations of information and computation. The function of these rules is to help us make decisions, so it is a test of the adequacy of the supplementary rules that they be usable as decision-guides. However, the supplementary rules do not provide an account of the features that actually make acts right and wrong. Instead they *link* the account of right and wrong with advisable decisions. The account of right and wrong, supplemented with the decision rules, constitutes the complete moral theory.[53] Perhaps the classic statement of the Hybrid Response is found in John Stuart Mill, who used it to defend utilitarianism against the objection that "there is not time, previous to action, for calculating and weighing the effects of any line of conduct on the general happiness." Mill believed that "*whatever* we adopt as the fundamental principle of morality, we require subordinate principles to apply it by."[54] This response agrees with the Austere Response in denying that the content of the account of right and wrong must accommodate human cognitive limitations, but on the other hand, it agrees with the Pragmatic Response in requiring that a *complete* moral theory have the resources to be usable for practical decision-making. The Hybrid Response seeks to make moral theory usable by accommodating our limitations through *augmenting* the theory's resources—in this case through expanding it to include normatively appropriate decision-making rules as well as principles of right and wrong. The Hybrid Response does not claim that we will always be able to apply the correct principle of right and wrong *directly* to our decisions. Rather, it introduces the idea that at least sometimes we will apply it

---

[53] It is also possible to interpret these rules as general principles of rational decision-making rather than as rules specifically designed for moral decision-making. For the time being I will interpret them in the latter way as components of a complete moral theory; we will return later to the question of whether they should be viewed more broadly.

[54] Mill (1957), pp. 30 and 32. My emphasis. It is not wholly clear that Mill has in mind by "subordinate principles" precisely what I do here. Some interpreters have seen Mill as advocating a Pragmatic Response in the form of rule utilitarianism.

It is not always easy to distinguish Austere or Pragmatic theorists from Hybrid theorists. Moreover, earlier writers didn't have the advantage of a clear distinction between rule utilitarianism and a Hybrid form of act utilitarianism. A list of theorists who arguably advocate (or describe the attractions of) the Hybrid Response would include Adams (1976); Bales (1971); Brink (1989), pp. 216–17, 256–62, and 274–6; F. Feldman (2012); Hare (1981); Jackson and H. Smith (2006); Moore (1993), pp. 162–4; Parfit (1984), pp. 24–9 and 32–43 and (2011), Chapter 7; Pettit and Brennan (1986); Pollock (2006); Railton (1984); Rawls (1980), pp. 543 and 563; Shaw (1999); Sidgwick (1907), Book I, Chapter II, and Book IV, Chapters III, IV, and V; Smart (1973); Talbott (2005) and (2010); and Väyrynen (2006). For related discussion, see Dennett (1986), and McKeever and Ridge (2006), pp. 8–11.

A parallel Hybrid strategy might be described in physics, where physicists and engineers understand Einsteinian physics to be the correct theory (as best we know), but often use Newtonian-like equations to make predictions, since predictions are easier to calculate using Newtonian equations, and sufficiently accurate in many contexts to render their use the most practical option.

indirectly, via direct application of appropriate second-level rules to our acts. Thus the Usability Demand that moral principles should be usable is weakened to the demand that they should be usable at least in this indirect sense.[55] This approach leaves open the question what a Hybrid theorist would say about a moral theory that for some reason is incapable of being supplemented by helpful second-level rules, but it suggests that such a theorist would deny that such a theory is acceptable.

Again, we should keep in mind that the three types of responses I've described are intended as "ideal types," not responses that have necessarily been advocated in their pure form by any individual theorist.

3.4 Rationales for the Usability Demand

Which of these responses to our cognitive deficiencies in applying moral principles is correct? Clearly, the answer to this question will largely depend on whether or not moral principles must be usable as practical decision-guides, what kind of usability is required, and if usability is required, *why* moral principles should be so usable. Here I will briefly describe four of the most salient reasons that have been offered to support the idea that moral principles must be usable. Although each of these reasons has some proponents, there may be no theorist who has invoked all four reasons in favor of the Demand. Clearly some rationales fit better with certain types of moral theories than with others (for example, some deontologists would have no interest in promoting a moral theory on the ground that its currency would enhance social welfare). However, our project necessitates evaluating each one, since some partisan of a given approach may have rested his or her case entirely on a single one of these reasons.

3.4.1 Usability required by the concept of morality

First, it is frequently argued that the concept of morality, or the point of morality, requires that moral principles be usable for action-guiding purposes. Sidgwick, for example, identifies the practical role of morality as its only role: "the moralist has a practical aim: we desire knowledge of right conduct in order to act on it."[56] Scanlon takes the position that "the point of judgments of right and wrong is not to make claims about what the spatiotemporal world is like. The point of such judgments is, rather, a practical one: they make claims about what we have reason to do … these judgments are ones we have reason to care about and to give great weight in deciding how to act and how to live."[57] In a similar vein Jan Narveson says, "the purpose of ethics is to guide

---

[55] Notice that motivationally oriented versions of the Pragmatic and Austere Responses are both coherent responses to the "strains of commitment" or "over-demandingness" problem that stringent moral codes may require more than human motivational capacities can supply. However, it is much less clear whether any version of the Hybrid Response would form an acceptable response to the over-demandingness problem.

[56] Sidgwick (1907), p. 5. For similar claims, see Hudson (1989), p. 22.

[57] Scanlon (1998), pp. 2 and 4.

action,"[58] Onora Nell confesses, "it is a waste of time and effort to pursue the justification of principles which are not known to be helpful in guiding moral choice,"[59] George Sher states that "morality and prudence are both action-guiding. Their central function is not merely to classify acts as right or wrong or prudent or imprudent, but rather to give us *reasons* to perform some acts and to avoid others,"[60] Peter Singer claims that "the whole point of ethical judgment is to guide practice,"[61] Terrance McConnell states that "At least one of the main points of moral theories is to provide agents with guidance,"[62] Elinor Mason says that "The most important function of a moral theory is to guide action,"[63] Jamie Dreier states that "the point of deontic verdicts, I think, is to guide us in our choices and our advice,"[64] Allan Gibbard argues that what we need is a moral standard that can be used for moral guidance in making decisions,[65] Robert Goodin states that "The point of morality is to be action-guiding,"[66] G. E. Moore holds that "the role of practical ethics is to provide guidance,"[67] J. J. C. Smart claims that "act-utilitarianism is meant to give a method of deciding what to do in those cases in which we do indeed decide what to do,"[68] and Bernard Williams notes that "especially for utilitarians, the only distinctive interest or point of the question what acts are right, relates to the situation of deciding to do them."[69]

Sometimes the idea is expressed less directly, as Prichard does when he claims that ordinary thought holds that there can be no particular duty that is not recognized as such by the person obliged to do it.[70] Other moralists, of whom R. M. Hare might provide an example, hold that it is part of the meaning of moral terms, such as "ought," that their function is to help guide choices. Hare states that when "ought" is used with its full prescriptive sense, "its function is to offer help and guidance to answering the practical question… 'What shall I do?'."[71] Clearly, to fulfill the action-guiding role Hare envisions it is necessary that the principles governing the application of these terms be usable. On all these views morality must be usable to make decisions, and it appears that any morality meeting this constraint could not suffer some of the cognitive impediments to usability I have described.[72]

This first rationale is, in a clear sense, at the heart of the debate between the Austere approach on the one hand and the Pragmatic and Hybrid approaches on the other.

---

[58] Narveson (1967), p. 112.   [59] Nell (1975), p. 2.   [60] Sher (2009), p. 139.
[61] Singer (1979), p. 2.   [62] McConnell (2010).   [63] Mason (2003), p. 327.
[64] Dreier (2011), p. 107.   [65] Gibbard (1990), p. 43.   [66] Goodin (2009), p. 3.
[67] Moore (1993), pp. 151–2.   [68] Smart (1973), p. 44.
[69] B. Williams (1973), p. 128.   [70] Prichard (1968), pp. 18–39.
[71] Hare (1965), section 4.3. See also Wallace (2011), p. 154: "on the agential interpretation I would favor, 'ought' is also constitutively suited to figure in the agent's own deliberation about [his] options." J. Ross (2012), section 5.1, identifies the fundamentally normative "ought" with the "ought of practical deliberation," where the role of this practical "ought" is to "guide our intentions, and thereby to guide our actions."
[72] For other discussions and references, see Carlson (2002) and Väyrynen (2006).
Not every theorist agrees with the claim that morality has a "point." For a trenchant rejection, see F. Feldman (1980), p. 179: "My own view, for what it is worth, is that morality doesn't have any purpose. Indeed the suggestion that morality has a purpose strikes me as being as odd as the suggestion that mathematics, or ornithology, has a purpose." See also Brandt (1979), pp. 183–4.

Someone who thinks that one of the main points or functions of morality is to provide guidance in decision-making will endorse this rationale; someone who holds that morality has a purely theoretical role will of course be likely to reject it. This is a juncture in the book's argument at which it appears that no progress can be made in determining the validity of this key rationale without appealing to background meta-ethical views about the nature and grounding of morality. As I warned in Chapter 1, I shall not attempt this. It is work that must be handed over to meta-ethicists. Instead I shall accept the first rationale as a possible starting point in addressing the epistemic problem in morality and explore what conclusions we can derive from it. Some will doubtless find this unsatisfying, but I hope they will be surprised how far we can travel even without adopting any particular meta-ethical view.

It is worth recalling that we use morality in many contexts, not just when we are deciding what to do. We invoke morality when advising other people and when evaluating the actions of agents, including ourselves in the past, who cannot be reached by our advice because their actions have already occurred or there is no way for us to communicate with them. And we often invoke morality when we simply have a theoretical interest in ascertaining what features make actions right or wrong. But all these uses—apart from the last one—require us to be able to derive a prescription from the moral code in question. We cannot advise or evaluate someone unless we can determine the moral status of at least some of her options—their permissibility, obligatoriness, or wrongness. Thus the "usability" of morality, not just to the agent but to other interested parties as well, is important. Most discussions, without explanation, give priority to usability in the decision-making context.

3.4.2 Usability required for justice

A second justification offered in favor of usability has been described most eloquently by Bernard Williams. According to Williams, there is a powerfully influential ideal according to which moral value is immune to luck.[73] On this view, "the successful moral life ... is open ... to ... all rational beings."[74] Suppose it turns out, for example, that certain moral principles cannot be used as widely by those who unluckily are dull or poorly informed as by those who luckily are highly intelligent and well-educated. Or suppose it turns out that one's worth as a moral agent depends on the chance of what decisions one is called upon to make. Such a morality would violate the ideal that the successful moral life be available to *everyone*. Williams, who traces this ideal back to Kant, claims that it has the ultimate form of justice at its heart and embodies something basic to our ideas of morality.[75] Williams himself argues that this ideal is not in fact met by morality, which is shot through with luck. On that ground he appears to abandon the ideal itself.[76] Nonetheless, he suggests that the ideal embodies something sufficiently basic to our concept of morality that forsaking the ideal may require us to ask whether

---

[73] B. Williams (1981), p. 20.   [74] B. Williams (1981), p. 20.
[75] B. Williams (1976), pp. 115–16.   [76] B. Williams (1981), p. 36, and *passim*.

we should give up the notion of morality altogether.[77] Williams is not fully transparent about what living the "successful moral life" would consist in. However, he describes the ideal of this form of justice as implying that anything that is the product of contingency is not a proper object of moral assessment. Since actions are clearly objects of moral assessment, and since some of his examples arguably involve actions that turn out to be wrong, it appears he believes that the successful moral life, if it were possible, would include the performance of right actions as well as (for example) the agent's achievement of moral worth.[78]

Although Williams rejects this form of justice as beyond our grasp, and so rejects the ideal itself, Pekka Väyrynen has embraced it as a key rationale for the Usability Demand. According to Väyrynen, "An ethical theory should make a successful moral life available to more or less any subject of its moral requirements. Such fairness seems fundamental to morality. The measure of a successful moral life is the extent to which it consists in morally right actions."[79] Thus any moral code that is unusable by normal moral agents in choosing which action to perform fails to meet the ideal of justice and should be rejected.

3.4.3 Usability required in order for morality to enhance social welfare

A third justification offered in favor of usability in moral principles holds that the function of a moral code is to enhance social welfare.[80] Warnock speaks for many when he states that "the 'general object' of morality ... is to contribute to the betterment—or non-deterioration—of the human predicament."[81] The usual idea here is that a moral code serves as a kind of informal analogue to a legal code, shaping behavior in ways that make members of society better off.[82] Although this stance is natural for utilitarians, it can be taken by non-utilitarians (such as Warnock) as well. A more restricted version of this justification is suggested by John Rawls, who requires principles of justice to serve a more specialized social role, namely to facilitate cooperative social endeavors, and to enable citizens to organize their plans for the long-term future.[83] The connection between serving these welfare-enhancing (or cooperation-attaining) functions and

---

[77]   B. Williams (1981), pp. 21 and 22.   [78]   B. Williams (1981), p. 20.   [79]   Väyrynen (2006), p. 299.

[80]   This is also the spirit behind many versions of rule utilitarianism. See, for example, Brandt (1963), p. 118, and Hooker (2000), p. 32.

[81]   Warnock (1971), p. 26. Other representative exemplars of this view include Baier (1965), especially pp. 106–9; Bentham (1949), p. 796; Berkeley (1929); Castañeda (1974); Hare (1981); Kivy (1992), p. 313; Mackie (1977), especially Chapter 5; Miller (2009); Nesbitt (1995), p. 105; and Toulmin (1950), p. 137.

[82]   Brandt (1979) states that the benefit of a moral code is primarily its influence on actions (pp. 196–7). Lessig (1999) describes law, norms, the market, and the architecture of option-presentation as multiple potential ways of shaping behavior (pp. 122–4).

[83]   Rawls (1971), sections 1, 10, 23, and 38, and (1980), pp. 553–64, especially pp. 553, 560–1, and 563. In (2004), p. 133, Jonathan Dancy describes Brad Hooker as holding, in *Ideal Code, Real World*, that "we need principles to keep society together; without principles we will not know what to expect of each other in the social sphere," and Onora O'Neill as suggesting, in (1996), "that we need principles for conflict resolution; if we have no agreed principles, there will be no common ground to work from." Mackie in (1977), Chapter 7, section 3, also points out the importance of moral principles for coordinating activities.

being usable seems to be roughly this: moral rules must be designed so that (a) they can be successfully followed, and (b) when they are successfully followed, they will increase social welfare (or attain the specified cooperative goals) through actions that avoid violent conflict, foster social cooperation, and so forth. Rules that cannot be followed cannot be guaranteed to lead to such desirable results, since consequences of the acts that result from misapplications of such rules are unpredictable and may be pernicious.

3.4.4 Usability required for the production of the best pattern of actions

Finally, a fourth justification for usability holds that a moral code should be judged by whether the actions it produces are the right ones according to that morality's own standards. Thus it might be said, with Christian Barry, that "ethics is concerned not only to evaluate but also to provide conduct-guiding structures of values and norms that shape the behavior of individual and collective agents. And like the law, ethical theories generally specify aims and objectives that their adherents ought to promote. It would seem odd indeed if these theories are exempt from being evaluated in terms of their success in promoting the aims and objectives that—by their own lights—matter."[84] One way to state this is to say that the function of morality is to produce the best possible *pattern of actions*, where what makes an action fit into the best pattern of actions is specified by the theoretical criteria provided by the morality itself. On this interpretation, if certain actions are right, then it is a good thing for them to be performed, so that truths are uttered, rights honored, debts repaid, possessions not stolen, lives saved, and so forth. If currency of a given morality in society would lead to violation of its own norms, then that is a strike against that morality. Although consequentialists may take this position, it would also be natural for deontologists. When noting a code's failure to satisfy this condition, it is common to focus on wrongful actions arising from failures of motivation: cases in which agents reject the moral code altogether, or are insufficiently motivated by it to resist the temptation to act contrary to its dictates. However, such problems can also arise from epistemic failures—agents' mistakes or uncertainty about which actions would genuinely conform to the governing moral principle. Thus the ideal pattern of actions can only be achieved if the moral principles are usable without epistemic hitch or error by the individuals subject to them. Otherwise misapplications, or failures of application, will lead to morally inferior acts.[85]

---

[84] Barry (2005), p. 223.
[85] See also Pogge (1990), pp. 649–63. Pogge endorses this rationale but does not claim that this consideration is the only one that should matter in assessing a moral theory (p. 650). See more generally Parfit's discussion of a moral theory's being "self-defeating" in (1984), Part One, and especially section 1 and pp. 36–40. Also relevant is Van Someren Greve's claim in (2014), p. 175, that a world in which agents perform more right acts is better than a world in which they perform fewer right acts.
  Careful deontologists will not say that it is generally desirable that *all* tokens of right actions be performed. Some right actions may be called for only to correct past wrongs (e.g., remedial or punitive acts are right in virtue of past injustices), and of course in the overall view of things it would be better if these acts were

3.4.5 Further considerations

It is sometimes suggested that there is a fifth justification for requiring usability, namely that it is implied by the principle that "ought" entails "can."[86] Thus in one sense Molly (from Chapter 2) is not able to obey the principle requiring her to carry out her job responsibilities. Those responsibilities require her to open the safe, and, because she doesn't know what the combination is, she would not successfully open the safe if she tried. Hence it appears that the principle stating she ought to carry out her job responsibilities violates the requirement that "ought" entails "can." However, whether or not this principle violates "'ought' entails 'can'" depends on what sense of "can" is relevant. In one clear sense Molly *can* open the safe—she can move her fingers on the dial in ways XYZ and the safe will open. She is physically able to perform this act, even though she is not epistemically able (for this contrast, see Chapter 2). The question then becomes which sense of "can" is the appropriate one for testing moral principles and their usability. Clearly any argument that the epistemic sense of "can" is the relevant one will have to be based on some further justification, and this justification is likely to be one of the four we have canvassed already. Thus the alleged fifth justification for usability turns out not to be independent, but instead to be parasitical on some more fundamental form of justification. For this reason I will not explore it further.[87]

The first two of our four rationales may be seen as "conceptual" rationales, connected with the concept of morality, while the second two rationales may be seen as "goal-oriented" rationales, connected with a goal or effect to be achieved (or avoided) by morality.

Which of the three responses—the Austerity, Pragmatic, or Hybrid Response—one finds most congenial, and which of four rationales for the Usability Demand (if any)

---

never called for and so not performed. Other right actions may be called for in response to morally neutral prior conditions (e.g., keeping a promise is called for by the neutral prior condition that the promise was made), but the deontologist need not say that the world is a better place because the promise was made and then kept, but only say that the world is a worse place if the promise is violated (see H. Smith (1997) and (2014)). The occurrence of all these actions is only desirable in light of the specific circumstances (which may not in themselves be good) that call for them.

Moreover, this standard for a deontological code would have to carefully avoid representing it as a code that advocates maximizing the number of actions deemed right by the code (for example, maximizing the number of truth-tellings, thus requiring me to tell a lie if my doing so will lead to greater numbers of truth-tellings in the future).

Note that this demand might be phrased in two different ways: (a) as the demand that promulgating the code in society would actually result in an ideal pattern of actions, and (b) as the demand that if agents wanted to follow the code, they would actually perform an ideal pattern of actions. (There are other possible variations as well.) If we were focusing upon motivational impediments to people's adherence to a code, then we might choose to phrase our demand in the first way, since a major issue would be whether or not people would want to adopt and would be sufficiently motivated by the code. However, since we are instead interested in whether people, having once adopted a code, have the information to apply it accurately in their decisions, the second phrasing of this demand is the most appropriate one.

[86] Sorensen (1995), p. 248; Carlson (2002), p. 72; and Howard-Snyder (1997). Mason, in (2003), argues for a special interpretation of this view.

[87] A more detailed version of this argument is provided by Väyrynen (2006), section IV.

one finds most compelling, may depend on one's view about the nature of morality itself. Someone who believes that at bottom morality is the product of a (possibly hypothetical) joint choice by human beings negotiating with each other to construct a viable social order may well be attracted by the Pragmatic Response and the rationale for usability citing the need for morality to enhance social welfare or cooperative endeavors. The thought would be that groups will naturally choose to adopt a code that is usable in practical decision-making contexts and which therefore will produce the best social outcomes. Someone who believes, on the other hand, that morality expresses fundamental truths about the universe, or expresses a priori truths about morality, whose validity does not depend on humanity's acknowledgment of them, is more likely to find the Austere Response compelling. However, as we shall see, it is possible to make progress in evaluating these different responses without having to take sides in these debates about the foundations of morality. Moreover, thinking about the problem of human cognitive deficiencies and how morality should respond to them is an illuminating way of testing and perhaps developing one's views about the nature of morality.

In Chapter 4 we will start by looking at the problem of error and examine the Pragmatic Response to it. To some degree, of course, it is artificial to separate our treatment of the problem of error from our treatment of the problem of uncertainty. This is especially true because there may be no clear bright line between someone who *believes* that P from someone who has a *very high subjective probability* for P. Nonetheless, drawing this distinction will allow us to avoid some of the errors that previous thinkers have fallen into by not clearly distinguishing the two problems. Failure to see the problems as distinct can result in emphasizing one problem at the expense of the other, or not noticing that a Response that works well for one of them may not work for the other. Separating discussion of the two problems will enable us to avoid these hazards.

4

Pragmatic Responses to the Problem of Error

Morality is confined to the sphere of human capability. We are used to the fact that our physical and psychological capacities are limited, but so is our understanding. Moral norms are shaped for agents with all those limitations.[1]

4.1 The Problem of Error

Let us begin by focusing on the problem of nonmoral error, which we will now call simply "the problem of error." The problem of error arises when an agent, in attempting to use a favored moral principle in deciding how to act, labors under false beliefs about the circumstances or consequences of her potential actions, and so typically makes the wrong choice. In the examples described in Chapter 3, the governor believes, falsely, that cutting state spending rather than raising taxes would maximize the general welfare, and so chooses the wrong act in his attempt to use utilitarianism in deciding what to do. Similarly the judge believes, falsely, that sentencing the offender to three years in the penitentiary would impose a punishment proportionate to the gravity of the crime, and so chooses the wrong act in attempting to use his retributive principle in deciding what to do. In the terminology we introduced, the governor's and the judge's moral principles are usable (for them) in the *core* sense, since they are able to derive prescriptions from these principles. But the principles are not usable by these agents in the *extended* sense, so the agents' attempts to use them deliver prescriptions for acts that do not in fact satisfy the principles. This is the problem pointedly raised by the problem of error.

How should we respond to the problem created for common moral principles by the fact that moral agents often labor under false beliefs about the relevant nonmoral features of their prospective acts? I shall interpret the ideal type of the Pragmatic Response as implying that acceptable moral principles must be usable as both extended and core guides for decision-making. On this conception, moral principles subject to such errors

---

[1] Griffin (1996), p. 99.

are unacceptable.[2] Principles vulnerable to the problem of error must be rejected and replaced by others that, even in the hands of fallible human beings, are error-free.[3] Advocates of this response, rejecting any division of labor within a moral theory, insist in addition that a moral system must be fundamentally unified, in the sense that a single set of principles must serve *both* as the theoretical account of rightness *and* as the action-guide. This chapter will launch our investigation of the problem of error by examining the Pragmatic Response to this problem.

Among Pragmatic Responses one might distinguish between "pure" and "concessive" variants. The pure variant denies utterly the normative significance of any principle of moral conduct that is subject to the problem of error. Thus a pure Pragmatic theorist, believing that utilitarianism is subject to the problem of error, would deny that an act's actual effect on happiness has any normative relevance whatsoever. Such a theorist might adopt a principle implying that the fact that the governor *believes* reducing state spending would maximize utility makes it obligatory for him to reduce spending. The fact that reducing spending would fail to maximize utility, and would instead send the state into a deep recession, has no moral significance at all. The concessive variant of the Pragmatic Response, on the other hand, approaches this issue by restricting what it regards as the "action-guiding" terms—such as "ought," "right," and "wrong"—to acts prescribed or prohibited by moral principles that are not subject to the problem of error. It concedes, however, that it may be acceptable to evaluate an act as "best" or "fortunate" if it would be prescribed by the error-prone moral theory from which the Pragmatic theory might be derived. Thus a concessive utilitarian might agree that an act is *best* if it would actually maximize happiness, but insist that whether or not this act is *obligatory*, *permitted*, or *wrong* depends on whether it is prescribed or prohibited by (say) an expectable consequence version of utilitarianism that is not subject to the problem of error.[4]

---

[2] We could define a type of "Quasi-Pragmatic" approach that insists only that the correct moral theory be usable in the core sense, but not necessarily usable in the extended sense. However, since actual Pragmatic theorists seem to be just as concerned about the problem of error as they are about the problem of uncertainty, I shall not further examine this approach.

Pragmatic theorists must reject the "extensionality thesis," the thesis that the only thing that matters about a moral code is its extension, i.e., the acts it identifies as right and wrong. Since two codes might have the same extensions, but differ with regard to their usability, the Pragmatic theorist would hold the two codes are importantly different. Rejecting such a view, Jamie Dreier defends the extensionality thesis in Dreier (2011), pp. 97–119.

[3] Van Someren Greve (2014) argues that the practical usefulness of a moral theory is not an evidential reason to believe it is the correct moral theory, since the theory's practical usefulness is merely a pragmatic reason, and so not the right *kind* of reason. However, this overlooks the fact that Pragmatic theorists hold that it is a *criterion* of being the correct moral theory that a theory be practically usable, so for them evidence of a theory's usefulness *is* the right kind of reason (or at least necessary evidence) to believe it is correct.

[4] Russell (1910), Part III, section 16, uses the term "most fortunate act." Hudson (1989) uses "best" or "most desirable" or "most fortunate." Russell and Hudson appear to be concessive theorists. Zimmerman seems to adopt the concessive variant of utilitarianism in (2006), p. 344, appears to reject it in (2008), pp. 29–30, and possibly to return to it in (2014), pp. 26 and 47–8. The discussions of some advocates of Pragmatic theories are vague or unclear on whether they are urging a concessive or pure form of Pragmatic theory. For example, W. D. Ross (1939) sounds for the most part like a pure Pragmatic theorist. However, when he

Most of the concessive variants of Pragmatic theory seem to me best interpreted as disguised Hybrid theories. Clearly the only relevant notion of "best" in this context is one that has all the features of the normal concept of "what the agent ought to do" (for example, the "best" act must be the best among the set of alternatives physically performable by the agent)—except for the fact that the agent may not be able accurately to identify the best act, and so may not be in a position to unerringly implement a prescription to perform it.[5] There is no discussion here about the "best" rainstorm or the "worst" earthquake: attention is focused solely on acts under appropriate human control.[6] The value reflected in what is "best" serves in an important way to organize and justify the theory that the concessive Pragmatic theorist proffers as the correct theory of what the agent ought to do. Thus it is easy to understand a concessive Pragmatic theory as deriving important normative governance from a background moral theory of what acts are "best"; the specific role for the action-guiding principles of such a Pragmatic theory is to provide decision-guides for agents *relative to* the correct theory of what acts are best. Such a theory would simply be a version of a Hybrid theory, a response that we will consider in later chapters. In light of this, I will assume that the Pragmatic theories we discuss are proposed as pure Pragmatic theories, rather than as concessive ones.

Versions of the Pragmatic Response to the problem of error, which as an ideal type insists that any acceptable moral principle must be capable of error-proof application, have attracted notable adherence from both consequentialist and non-consequentialist theorists. This chapter will examine the merits and demerits of this response. We should remember that this proposal is often attractive to its advocates as a response not just to the problem of error but also as a response to the problem of uncertainty as well. However, our concern in this chapter is with the problem of error alone.

4.2 Merits of the Pragmatic Response as a Response to the Problem of Error

Let us start with the assumption that we are looking for an *ideally* usable moral code or principle—one that is universally usable as a behavioral guide for decision-making. That is, the practical range of the principle (the set of acts for which the principle can be used without error to guide decisions) must fully match its theoretical range (the set of acts to which it ascribes moral status). In Chapter 6 we will relax this restriction and

discusses our duty to acquire information before acting, he sounds more like a concessive theorist in saying "the agent should have before his mind, as the ideal, that self-exertion which would in fact produce the right result" (p. 157).

[5] In the case of a satisficing theory, in which one is not required to perform the best act, but is permitted to perform any act above a certain threshold level of deontic or consequentialist value, this would have to be restated.

[6] See Chappell (2012) for a discussion of the differences between the judgment that an object or state of affairs is best and the judgment that an act is right.

consider the attractiveness of the Pragmatic Response if it confines itself to identifying principles that merely enhance, even if they do not fully achieve, error-free usability.

To achieve an ideally usable moral code, a Pragmatic theorist might propose either of two distinct strategies. We might call the first of these strategies the "Uniform Pragmatic Response." A Uniform Pragmatic Response says that if a moral code or principle is affected by the problem of error on even one occasion, then it must be rejected in favor of some alternative Uniform code or principle that is universally usable, that is, usable without error by every agent on each occasion for decision-making. The Uniform approach contrasts with what can be called the "Splintered Pragmatic Response." The Splintered Response, which might be developed in order to enable the Pragmatic approach to circumvent problems with the Uniform Response, says that if a moral code or principle is affected by the problem of error on one occasion, then it must be rejected as incorrect *for that agent on that occasion*. It is incorrect, both as a theoretical account of what makes acts right and wrong and also as a decision-guide for that occasion, and so must be replaced by some alternative code that is not so affected on that occasion. However, the original code or principle may be retained as correct for any occasion on which it is *not* vulnerable to the problem of error. On the Splintered view, there will be many correct moral principles covering the same field of action, but (because agents vary in their susceptibility to the problem of error) no one principle will be correct for all agents or even for the same agent on similar occasions. To see the difference between a Uniform and a Splintered Pragmatic approach, consider a Pragmatic Response to the fact that standard act utilitarianism cannot be used without error by every moral agent. A Uniform approach would reject act utilitarianism in favor of a theory that every agent could use without error—for example, a deontological code consisting of simple rules such as "Do not kill," and "Do not steal." A Splintered approach might retain act utilitarianism as the correct code for the knowledgeable elite, but propose a simpler code (such as the code containing the rules "Do not kill," and "Do not steal") for less well-informed adults and for children. Acts would be right for the elite just in case they maximized happiness, whereas acts would be right for the less well-informed just in case they conformed to the simple rules. To my knowledge all Pragmatic theorists have adopted the Uniform strategy, so I will start with a consideration of its merits and demerits.[7] We will return to Splintered Responses towards the end of the chapter.

---

[7] Notoriously Sidgwick (1907), Chapter V, section 3, discussed having a less epistemically demanding code for the common person, while act utilitarianism would be the correct code for the educated elite. However, he clearly does not view the common person's code as *defining* what acts are actually right and wrong for those persons, even though the common person may believe it does. Hence he cannot be interpreted as proposing a Splintered approach as I have defined it.

The line between Unitary Pragmatic moral theories and Splintered Pragmatic theories may not always be clear-cut. For example, consider a theory whose content is "If you are a member of the elite, maximize utility; if you are a common person, do not kill and do not steal." This theory applies to everyone (so appears Uniform), but what it requires one to do depends on what type of person one is (so appears Splintered). Clearly such a theory would itself be subject to error, since agents might mistake the social or epistemic class to which they belong.

What advantages might be gained by adopting the Pragmatic Response to the problem of error?

4.2.1 Conceptual advantages of error-free codes

When we surveyed the reasons why theorists have been concerned about the problem of error, we noted several "conceptual" reasons for concern. These concerns would seem to be satisfied by a Pragmatic Response that produces error-proof moral principles or codes.

The first of these conceptual rationales for demanding error-proof usability from a moral code was the claim that usability is part of the very concept or point of morality itself, so that a moral principle's extended usability is a necessary condition for its acceptability as a theoretical account of right and wrong. Clearly a completely error-proof moral code would satisfy this rationale, assuming it also avoided the problem of uncertainty.

The second conceptual rationale was the claim that justice would only be served by a morality that afforded each person, whether she be well- or poorly-informed, an equal chance of success in meeting the requirements of morality. Clearly, a universally usable error-proof moral code (again, assuming it avoided the problem of uncertainty as well) would do just that: however accurate or inaccurate a person's factual beliefs might be in general, nonetheless she would have the ability to apply such a morality, without error, in making each of her decisions.

4.2.2 Goal-oriented advantages: enhancement of social welfare

Other rationales for ensuring usability are goal-oriented in their focus on the impact of a morality or moral code. One of these rationales focuses on the broad consequences of a morality's currency in society. It is claimed that the function of a moral code is to enhance social welfare by fostering beneficial conduct, and further claimed that an error-proof moral code would foster more beneficial conduct than an error-prone code.[8] Let us briefly fill out this argument.

The argument that a more error-free moral code would enhance social welfare as compared to an error-prone code has typically been proposed by rule utilitarians in their criticism of act utilitarianism. These theorists claim that the point of moral codes is to enhance the general social welfare, but that individuals who attempted to apply act utilitarianism directly in their decision-making would make so many errors that they would fail to maximize human happiness, and indeed might do a great deal of damage. Notoriously people are often misled by plain mistakes of fact, as the governor is misled in estimating that cutting spending would maximize welfare. But they are also misled by mistakes induced by self-regarding bias. Such mistakes lead them to

---

[8] As Eli Shupe points out (in an unpublished seminar note), different codes may interpret "welfare" in different ways. The simplest way to compare the effects of different codes is to select a single interpretation of welfare and test each code relative to that conception. I shall assume this procedure is being used in the following discussion (and similar ones in later chapters).

misestimate the effects of their prospective actions on themselves as compared to the effects on others (perhaps the governor, a rich man, is led to believe that raising taxes would not maximize welfare partly because of his heightened sensitivity to the adverse effect this policy would have on his own family). According to this criticism, since all these mistakes would lead agents to perform acts harmful to the general welfare, act utilitarianism cannot be the correct moral code. Instead, some alternative code is correct—a code that is designed to maximize human happiness even in the hands of often fallible human beings. This code, rule utilitarians often argue, will prescribe simple, easily applied rules, often of a deontological character, such as "Killing is wrong" and "Telling lies is wrong." Of course individual acts prescribed by such rules will occasionally not match those that would be prescribed by act utilitarianism, and so fail to maximize happiness even when unerringly performed. Nonetheless, it is claimed, the overall utility produced by people's attempted adherence to a set of such rules will be far greater than what would be produced by people's attempted adherence to act utilitarianism.

4.2.3 Goal-oriented advantages: the special social role of morality

Another goal-oriented argument urges that part of the value of morality is that it can play certain important social roles. This argument claims that error-proof moral codes can play these roles better than error-prone roles. John Rawls' discussion of the rationale behind his principles of justice, and in particular the rationale for requiring them to satisfy the Publicity Condition, is perhaps the foremost modern example of this sort of argument. Two of the things that Rawls requires principles of justice to do are (1) to facilitate cooperative social endeavors, and (2) to enable citizens to organize their plans for the long-term future.[9] He appears to maintain that relatively error-proof principles are needed to promote these goals. Although Rawls himself does not spell out precisely how this is to happen, the main line of thought seems fairly easy to construct. Rawls is focusing on a well-ordered society, in which everyone is motivated to follow the principles of justice, and each person knows the others are motivated to follow these principles.[10] If we now add the assumption that each person can infer unerringly what the principles of justice require, and each believes the others can also infer unerringly what the principles require, then it appears to follow that citizens will readily be able to reach consensus about which institutions satisfy these principles. Moreover, each individual will be able to predict accurately what institutions will be adopted as just, and what the other citizens will do under those institutional arrangements insofar as their actions are governed by the principles of justice. On the basis of such predictions, citizens will be able to cooperate effectively, because inaccurate predictions about the activities of others will not impede their ability to engage in productive joint action. Thus, for example, if justice requires each to do her part in a

---

[9] Rawls (1971), sections 1, 10, 23, and 38, and (1980), especially pp. 553, 560–1, and 563.
[10] Rawls (1971), section 69.

national self-defense scheme, each *will* do her part, since all are well-motivated, all know what is required, all know this about each other, and hence no one will have reason to doubt the future participation of others. The citizens will also be able to form stable long-term plans, because they will be able to predict accurately the future social institutions and the future activities of other individuals, insofar as these are affected by the principles and institutions of justice. For example, each person will be able to form a stable life plan incorporating service in the national defense scheme, knowing that it will be maintained as a recognized just institution.

This situation compares favorably with that arising from more error-prone principles of justice, of which utilitarianism is Rawls' prime example. Because individuals can err as to what actions and institutions would maximize utility, no one can ever be sure that another will agree with him on which plan is most "just." There will be socially damaging disputes about which institutions most effectively promote utility, and pernicious doubts about whether those institutions will ever be fully agreed on and established. Without agreement, coordination is difficult or impossible. Since information and so opinions will alter over time as to which institutions would maximize utility, major social institutions will be vulnerable to constant changes reflecting the latest opinion as to what justice requires. Long-term planning will face difficult hurdles. Rawls claims, by contrast, that his notion of primary goods (publicly ascertainable items such as rights and privileges, income and wealth) renders application of his principles of justice far less open to dispute than the notion of happiness or welfare utilized in utilitarianism.[11] Adopting an error-proof code of justice seems to be an effective way of guaranteeing its capacity to play the social role that Rawls desires.

If we shift our focus to principles of natural moral duty, rather than principles of justice, much the same claim may plausibly be made.[12] It is reasonable to hold that individual morality, as well as social justice, must enable individuals to cooperate with each other and to form long-term plans. For example, it seems clear that one of the goals of the institution of promising (under which an individual may create a new obligation by making a promise) is to enable the parties involved in a promise to coordinate their activities and to form long-range plans in reliance on the promise. Here, too, it appears that these ends will best be secured if individuals do not err in their interpretation of what morality requires of them. Suppose I promise to repay a personal loan in time for the check to clear and my creditor to draw on it in order to pay her income tax. She lays her financial plans based on my fulfilling this obligation.

---

[11] Rawls (1980), pp. 563–4.

[12] Rawls (1971), p. 108 states that principles of natural duty, as well as principles of justice for institutions, are justified by the fact that they would be chosen from the original position. He believes that all these principles serve the same function, namely adjusting the claims that people make on each other and their institutions (p. 131). Certain principles of duty must be consistent with the principles of justice for institutions, since the latter are chosen first; this suggests that they must at least indirectly serve (or at least not block) the same ends as the principles of justice (section 51). Rawls explicitly claims that the duties with regard to promise-keeping are chosen to enable individuals to enter into and stabilize cooperative agreements for mutual advantage (pp. 345–7).

However, I mistakenly believe that mailing the check on April 10th will fulfill my duty. The check does not clear by April 15th and I undermine my creditor's ability to use that money to pay her income tax. Thus my error has led to my creditor's inability to successfully plan her activities in order to meet her own obligations. From examples such as this it can be argued that the role of morality in enabling social cooperation and long-term planning can best be promoted by error-proof principles.

4.2.4 Goal-oriented advantages: ideal patterns of action

One of the goal-oriented rationales for ensuring that moral principles are usable in the extended sense—in this case, for solving the problem of error—focuses on the intrinsic character of the pattern of actions performed by an agent deciding what to do by reference to a moral principle. Since, when trying to follow a principle that is subject to the problem of error, people will sometimes mistake what their duty requires, even well-motivated individuals will perform actions that, by the principle's own account, are morally sub-optimal. Thus my sending the check on April 10th fails to fulfill my promise and so is a morally sub-optimal action. By contrast, an error-proof principle—endorsed as a Pragmatic Response—could secure performance of all the morally ideal actions required by the principle, at least among morally motivated persons, and thereby help prevent the occurrence of morally objectionable actions.[13]

Note the contrast between this goal-oriented argument, which focuses on securing an ideal pattern of action, and the earlier goal-oriented arguments, which focus on the social impact of moral codes that are error-free. The "ideal pattern" argument only evaluates a moral code by reference to the actions that are prescribed by that code, whereas the social impact arguments focus both on the consequences of the actions that would be performed by adherence to an error-free code, and also on other actions and social upshots (such as ability to lay plans and coordinate actions) that may arise indirectly because an error-free code is in place.

4.3 Achieving Universal Error-Freedom by Pragmatic Responses

The grand aim of Pragmatic Responses to the problem of error is to achieve universal extended usability—that is, complete freedom from error—in a moral principle or code. Close examination reveals, perhaps not surprisingly, that none of the more standard Pragmatic Responses actually achieves complete freedom from error.

---

[13] There is a clear parallel between the concerns of theorists who worry about inferior patterns of action produced by agents attempting to follow a moral principle subject to the problem of error, and the concerns of theorists who worry about inferior patterns of action produced by agents who cannot achieve the self-sacrificing motivation necessary to adhere to a stringent and demanding moral principle. A version of the Pragmatic Response is attractive to the latter theorists as well as to the former. See Scheffler (1982) for arguments in favor of a Pragmatic Response (not his term) to the motivational problem.

One standard Pragmatic Response to the errors of application afflicting act utilitarianism is to adopt "expected consequence utilitarianism," which assesses an action as obligatory if and only if it maximizes *expected* utility (an act's expected utility is calculated by weighting each possible consequence of the act by the probability of the occurrence of that consequence; these are then summed to obtain the expected utility of the act).[14] On one version of this response, an action's expected utility derives from the *objective probabilities* of its consequences. But there is every reason to suppose that our estimates of objective probabilities (perhaps interpreted as dispositions, propensities, or long-run frequencies) are fallible. The fallibility of such estimates is implicitly recognized in our practice of consulting a meteorologist rather than relying on our own guesstimates for weather predictions. Another version of expected consequence utilitarianism derives expected utilities from the agent's *subjective probabilities* (that is, her subjective credences or estimates of the relevant probabilities) for the relevant possible outcomes. However, this version too would be subject to error. An agent may be mistaken in assessing what her own credence or degree of belief is for some outcome. Not only can an agent err in ascribing subjective probability estimates to herself, but in addition many agents would be mistaken in their estimates of subjective *expected utilities*. For example, even if an agent ascribes the correct probability estimates to herself, she might make arithmetical mistakes in calculating the overall subjective expected utilities of her prospective actions. Note the problem here does not arise because the moral theory requires an agent to *personally calculate* the expected utilities of her prospective actions. She is only required to *have* a belief about what the expected utility would be (or more precisely, a belief that the expected utility of some act A would be no less than the expected utility of any alternative action), however that belief may be arrived at. But the most common route to acquiring such beliefs is through trying to calculate these figures, and this route (like others) can lead to an erroneous belief. Hence any agent who attempted to guide her actions by expected consequence utilitarianism would occasionally, if perhaps less frequently, run into error just as surely as an agent who attempted to guide her actions by actual consequence utilitarianism. The same thing can be said about versions of utilitarianism phrased in terms of what the agent *would be justified in believing* (or what the agent has reason to believe, or what a reasonable person would believe) to be the act that maximizes expected utility. A decision maker using this form of utilitarianism must pick the action he believes he would be justified in believing to have the relevant property—but we are often mistaken as to what we would be justified in believing (or what we have reason to believe, or what the reasonable person would believe). Even when we know that our current beliefs are unjustified, we may have no good idea what alternative beliefs would be justified

---

[14]   See, for example, Jackson (1991), Mason (2003), Pettit and Brennan (1986), Smart (1973), p. 42, and possibly Broome (1991). Howard-Snyder (1997) advocates a form of subjective consequentialism but does not seem to be committed to the expected utility version of it. Good discussions of subjectivizing consequentialism are available in Driver (2012) and Lenman (2000).

instead.[15] Hence versions of utilitarianism incorporating a "justified belief" standard are fully subject to the problem of error.

Occasionally rule utilitarianism is suggested as a Pragmatic alternative to act utilitarianism, since it is easier to correctly apply simple rules such as "Breaking a promise is wrong" and "Killing is wrong" than it is to apply act utilitarianism. However, even rules such as these can lead to error: for example, as we saw before, one can be mistaken about whether or not mailing the check on April 10th will fulfill one's promise, and one can be mistaken about whether or not passing the car in front of one will lead to a collision and the death of the oncoming car's driver. Moreover, on standard interpretations of rule utilitarianism, the agent himself must do more than apply these simple rules. He must first determine *which* rules to apply. That is, he must determine which rules are such that their general acceptance would produce greater utility than general acceptance of any alternative set of rules.[16] Because this determination involves calculating complex social phenomena, it is clearly vulnerable to even more errors than the simpler project of determining, in any given choice situation, which individual act is required by act utilitarianism.[17] Actual consequence rule utilitarianism does not avoid the problem of error, and may even lead the agent into more errors than act utilitarianism. And only brief reflection is sufficient to show that expected consequence

---

[15] This problem may be especially acute for process-oriented accounts of epistemic justification, according to which a belief is only justified if it is generated by the correct sort of mental process. An individual may have no idea what belief the correct process would have produced, even if he realizes that his actual belief was produced by an incorrect process.

[16] Historically proponents of rule utilitarianism have debated whether the correctness of a set of proposed rules depends on the consequences of *compliance* with those rules, or *universal acceptance* of those rules, or *widespread acceptance* of those rules, etc. All these versions would be subject to the problem of error.

[17] Of course some advisor might calculate these matters for the agent. But this advisor would have the same problems. Again, rule utilitarianism does not require that anyone actually has to perform such calculations. But people must have the relevant beliefs in order to apply the theory, and the best route to acquiring such beliefs is typically through estimation of the consequences of various possible moral codes. The proneness to error remains even if the rules thought to be optimific are passed down from one generation to another, so that members of later generations do not need to recalculate the rules' utility. The earlier generations will inevitably have made mistakes in *their* calculations, and mistakes will persist even if each generation's experience serves to correct some of the errors of past generations, especially as it is likely that new errors will be introduced in the process of correction. All these problems arise equally if the rules are handed down to users from any human authority.

These remarks assume the standard version of rule utilitarianism, according to which it is a *normative* theory specifying that an act is obligatory just in case it has a certain complex property: the act must be such that it is required by the set of rules, general acceptance of which would maximize welfare. According to Definitions 2.1 and 2.4, to apply this principle the agent must believe of some act that it has this complex property, so he must believe of some set of rules that their general acceptance would maximize welfare. There is an alternative version of rule utilitarianism which should be conceived of as a *meta-ethical* theory (see, for example, Kagan (1992), p. 233). On this version, the normative code specifies that an act is obligatory just in case it conforms to certain rules. Which rules are correct is a matter of how their acceptance would maximize welfare, but this is a meta-ethical test, so it is not required for usability of the code that the agent believes it satisfies this test. It is only required that he believe the act satisfies the rules in question. Of course adopting this meta-ethical version of rule utilitarianism just kicks upstairs the empirical question of which rules have the benefits in question, thus substituting the issue of moral error for the issue of non-normative error. Although rule utilitarians rarely specify which version of the theory they are proposing, it is generally described as a normative theory.

rule utilitarianism has the same vulnerability to error that expected consequence act utilitarianism does.

Finally, as we can see from these examples, as well as from the initial example of the judge attempting to impose an appropriate retributive punishment, even deontological systems are subject to the problem of error, even though they are sometimes advocated as Pragmatic Responses to the problem of error for act utilitarianism. The fact that deontological rules are often easier to apply without mistake does not make them error-free. Deontological moral codes as such cannot secure universal error-free extended usability.

4.4 Achieving Universal Error-Freedom by More Radical Means: Laundry List Codes

This brief survey is sufficient to show that most of the codes standardly advocated as Pragmatic Responses do not attain error-free universal usability. However, the search for an error-free moral code is not entirely quixotic. Two more radical versions of the Pragmatic Response appear to be more promising than the more standard versions. We should note in advance that these versions of the Pragmatic Response have rarely (in one case), or never (in the other case), been advocated. Nonetheless they provide important case studies that illuminate the lengths to which a Pragmatic theorist may have to go in order to find an ideal version of the Response that may succeed where other more standard versions demonstrably fail.

The first more promising radical attempt to produce a completely error-free code is what, following Prichard, we can call an "objectivized" code—objectivized in the sense that, like most familiar moral codes, it prescribes an act in virtue of its objective features, features it has independently of the agent's beliefs about the action. Thus features such as "being a case of killing an innocent person" or "being a case of maximizing human happiness" are objective features in this sense. Such objectivized codes can be contrasted with "subjectivized" codes which prescribe an action in virtue of the agent's beliefs (or other mental states) about the action's features. We will examine subjectivized codes in section 4.5.

An error-free objectivized code can be constructed on the basis of the following phenomenon. Consider a restaurant manager who, because of her restaurant's financial difficulties, must lay off one of her employees, either Craig or Rebecca. Let us first imagine that she subscribes to a moral code instructing her, in such a situation, to lay off the least productive employee. Being ill-informed about her employees' merits, she erroneously believes that Craig is the least productive employee, and she would release him if she attempted to apply her moral code. Since in actuality Rebecca is the least productive employee, this moral code is subject to the problem of error when applied by the restaurant manager. However, the manager could without error follow the prescription of a different code that simply directed her to *release Rebecca*. As a general matter, for each action available to an agent, there is *some* accurate description of the action such that if the agent wanted to perform the action under that description, she would do so. In the case of releasing the least productive employee, the manager would not perform the act in question if she set out to do so under the description *release the least productive employee*, but would perform that act if she set out to perform it under another more accurate description, namely *release Rebecca*. This reveals that it is possible to construct, for each agent, an error-proof objectivized moral code. Such a code would contain instructions for the agent to perform a list of actions, each described in such a way that if the agent wanted to perform an action of that description on that occasion, she would perform the action in question.[18] Indeed, for each error-prone objectivized code such as act utilitarianism, one could construct a corresponding error-free objectivized code that instructs the agent to perform the very same acts as the original code, but described in such a way that the agent would be able, without error, to perform them if she derived a prescription to do so. Thus corresponding to the restaurant manager's code there would be an error-proof counterpart code that would require her to lay off Rebecca on this occasion. The *complete* code would contain instructions, not just for the restaurant manager on this occasion, but for all agents on all occasions. Such a code would be error-proof in a very strong sense, since it would be universally usable in the extended sense (if any agent governed by the code wanted to derive a prescription from it on any occasion, she would do so, and prescription so derived would conform to the code).[19]

Of course an error-proof code of this sort has little resemblance to the moral codes with which we are most familiar. To my knowledge, no Pragmatic theorist has advocated such a code. Nonetheless, it is worth examining this type of code because it may be the only way to achieve error-freedom, and so demonstrates how difficult this achievement really is. Since the choice situations that agents face are many and various, since what an agent accurately believes about the choices confronting her will vary from situation to situation and time to time, and since these beliefs will vary as well from agent to agent, it will not be possible to construct a code of this sort using just a few well-chosen act-descriptions or act-types (such as "avoiding killing an innocent

---

[18] Another way to put this point is to contrast (a) actions which the agent has the "mere" physical ability to perform with (b) actions which the agent has the "epistemic ability" to perform. Thus an agent might have the "mere physical ability" to fix his car if there is a more basic act (flipping the butterfly switch) such that if he performed that more basic act, he would fix the car. But he lacks the epistemic ability to fix his car if he doesn't know that performing this more basic act would fix it. The proposed error-free codes discussed in this section all prescribe acts that the agent has the epistemic ability to perform. See Chapter 2, section 2.3 for Definition 2.3 of "epistemic ability." Howard-Snyder (1997) briefly describes and rejects something like this kind of code as one solution to overcoming the epistemic problem for act utilitarianism. I have discovered recently that John Pollock discusses something like this proposed solution to decision-making as "universal plans," which he rejects for much the same reason that I shall. See Pollock (2006), pp. 172–4.

[19] This assumes that the universal code would include some error-proof way to index each obligation to the agent who is subject to that obligation and to the time of the performance, so that each agent can unerringly identify what act she personally is required to perform. This may be a tall order.

human being" or "maximizing human happiness"). Instead the code will often include many highly specific descriptions of the actions to be performed or avoided, descriptions that are tailored to what each agent accurately believes about his options. Such a "code" will consist for the most part of a list of individual actions to be performed or avoided, each described in terms the agent can unerringly apply. A fragment of such a code for the restaurant manager might read as follows: "At 10:30 A.M. October 21st, you ought to lay Rebecca off. At 10:35 A.M. October 21st, you ought to tell the kitchen prep cooks that Rebecca has been laid off and that they will need to wash dishes along with their other duties. At 10:40 A.M. October 21st, you ought to telephone the restaurant owner to let him know how you have handled the situation..." Because such a code is a list of individual actions to be performed, rather than the usual set of general principles, let us call any code of this ilk a "moral laundry list." Each agent will have his or her own lifetime moral laundry list and the complete code would combine these into one massive list that contains instructions for all agents for the whole of their lives.[20] Since the characteristics by which the agent can accurately identify her actions will vary significantly from situation to situation, there may be little or no similarity among the descriptions under which the various actions are prescribed. A moral laundry list, then, might be viewed as a radical type of Particularism, in which no general properties (or types) of acts are identified as being morally significant whenever they occur.[21]

---

[20] There may be situations in which even a moral laundry list would not be able to guide an agent unerringly in making decisions. An agent might, for example, have "available" some action which he could only perform if he set out to perform a different action (thus in certain children's games involving twisting the fingers together, one can only wiggle one's right index finger if one tries to wiggle one's *left* index finger instead). (I owe this example to Alvin Goldman.) Depending on your theory of human action, you might conclude that such an action is not genuinely one of the agent's options. In this case the agent's moral code need not prescribe this action. However, suppose the action is accepted as one of the agent's genuine options. Then either (a) the moral laundry list prescribes this action in terms that lead the agent to perform a different action (it prescribes the morally desirable action, wiggling his right index finger, and if he tries to do so, he will instead wiggle his left index finger), or (b) it prescribes a different action in terms that lead him to perform the desirable action (it prescribes wiggling his left index finger, and if he tries to do so, he will instead wiggle his right index finger). In either case, the code is subject to the problem of error and not usable in the extended sense. (Note that variant (b) is actually ruled out by my characterization of a moral laundry list.) This is an especially vicious form of the problem of error which no moral code could be constructed to avoid, since the action will only be performed if the agent sets out to do something different. Fortunately, these are aberrant cases in which the acts in question rarely have moral significance. Some theorists have noted morally more significant situations in which, for example, someone who sets out to maximize her own happiness will inevitably fail, given the psychology of happiness. But the moral laundry list need not include any global instruction to maximize one's own happiness; instead it would include localized instructions to perform specific actions that in fact would maximize the agent's happiness (helping others, forming personal attachments, and so forth).

[21] Of course the rationale for standard Particularism is quite different from the rationale for a laundry list code. Note that moral laundry lists lack a feature that many theorists find essential to moral codes, namely their being true in all possible worlds. Because the belief-states of any given agent will vary from world to world, the content of the correct moral laundry list for that agent will vary as well, so it will not be true in all possible worlds. Any Pragmatic theorist who advocates a moral laundry list as the solution to the problem of error must reject this standard requirement.

PRAGMATIC RESPONSES TO THE PROBLEM OF ERROR   73

Clearly there are vast multitudes of moral laundry lists that avoid the problem of error for every agent who might try to use them. This follows from the fact that each agent, on each occasion for action, typically has a great many alternative actions, each of which could be prescribed by some laundry list in a manner that the agent could unerringly use to derive a prescription. The restaurant manager could cut costs by releasing a dishwasher, or reducing the pay of all employees, or ordering cheaper meat, and so forth. But a satisfactory response to the problem of error cannot merely identify moral codes that are universally usable in the extended sense; it must identify moral codes that are *normatively attractive* as well as usable. How might a Pragmatic theorist winnow out the normatively attractive moral laundry lists from those which merit no consideration? How could such a theorist identify the *correct* moral laundry list?[22]

One strategy might be to consider only those lists satisfying additional non-normative criteria above and beyond extended usability. For example, given that the Pragmatist is moved by practical considerations, he might insist that the correct list be highly memorable, or attain some threshold degree of simplicity, or prescribe actions that a normal agent could readily be motivated to perform. These are plausible pragmatically oriented proposals, and *might* serve to narrow down the set of candidate laundry lists. Unfortunately it is highly unlikely that any moral laundry list code would actually satisfy any of these criteria. Moreover it is clear that these criteria fail to inject any specific *normative* content into the selection process. It seems equally clear that they cannot successfully narrow down the set to a unique laundry list or even to a manageably small number of lists. The Pragmatist needs some further way to identify the correct moral laundry list.

A second strategy for the Pragmatist would be to proceed as follows: first, identify *theoretically compelling* criteria of rightness and wrongness in actions, and identify which individual actions those criteria would prescribe and prohibit. Second, identify, for each of the prescribed actions, some accurate description under which the action's agent would recognize it, and which is such that if the agent wanted to perform an action of that description, he would do so. Finally, construct the correct moral laundry

---

[22] In reality the Pragmatist may not need a unique correct list. For any alternative action, there may be multiple accurate descriptions of it under which the agent could unerringly perform it if she wanted to. Thus the manager could unerringly follow one list beginning "Release Rebecca," but she could also unerringly follow a list beginning "Release the only female dishwasher." Since these two lists prescribe the very same action (under different but equally recognizable descriptions), there is no harm in maintaining both as acceptable. Any problem with multiple laundry lists would only arise if an action prescribed by one list is prohibited by another.

A troubling issue for a moral laundry list is how it should handle non-compliance by the agent(s) addressed by the list. For example, suppose the moral laundry list prescribes, for Sam, act A at t_1, act B at t_2, and act C at t_3. Sam does A but fails to do B. Given that B was not performed, it is now better for him to perform D rather than C at t_3. Does this mean that the original laundry list should have prescribed A, B, and D at their respective times? Or does it mean that the prescriptions of the laundry list will change, depending on what the agent actually does, so that the list contains the original prescriptions as of t_1, but the prescriptions for A, B, and D at t_3? Or that the prescriptions should be formulated conditionally in cases such as this? Clearly, parallel and even more complex questions can arise when two agents each have their own laundry lists, and what is best for each to do depends on what the other agent actually does.

list by prescribing the list of all these morally desirable actions, each identified by a description under which its agent would recognize it. This moral laundry list would be the error-proof counterpart of the original theoretically compelling criteria of rightness and wrongness.

Something like the availability of this strategy undoubtedly underlies the original attraction, such as it is, of constructing an error-free moral code by identifying an error-free laundry list. However, a laundry list constructed and chosen in this manner seems actually to be a covert form of a Hybrid Response to the problem of error, rather than a Pragmatic Response, because it assumes that in the background there is an independent, correct account of which actions are right or wrong and which features give them this moral status, and that the function of the laundry list is to *supplement* this by providing a decision-guide that enables the decision maker to perform precisely those actions. The laundry list itself, however, is not assumed to provide an account of what makes these actions right or wrong. Pure Pragmatic Responses, by contrast, insist that one and the same standard must serve *both* as the correct account of right and wrong, *and* as the agent's decision-guide. We can set this suggestion aside for now, then, and consider other strategies before returning to consider it under the guise of a Hybrid Response in later chapters.[23]

A third and more promising strategy might be to use some global normative feature of the list itself in order to pick out a unique list from those which are universally usable. Thus someone who thinks the function of morality is to enhance social welfare might identify the correct list as "that universally usable list which, if it were adopted, would maximally enhance social welfare," whereas someone more focused on the importance of morality's playing a certain social role might identify the correct list as "that universally usable list which, if it were adopted, would best enable people to cooperate with each other and form long-term plans." Or, inspired by contractarianism, someone might propose as the correct list "that universally usable list of prescriptions for the general regulation of behavior that no one could reasonably reject as a basis for informed, unforced general agreement."[24] This general strategy cannot be classified as a Hybrid Response, since the independent normative standard assesses features of candidate lists as a whole, rather than features of individual actions prescribed by these lists.[25] The best way to understand such theories is as providing a meta-ethical standard by which the correct normative theory is selected—where the meta-ethical standard evaluates candidate normative theories in substantive terms, that is, in terms of their

---

[23] Detailed discussion of Hybrid theories begins in Chapter 8. Note the contrast with the structure of standard rule utilitarianism. In rule utilitarianism, the *rule* is selected by reference to some feature that makes it the correct rule (its acceptance would maximize utility), and then acts are deemed to be right just in case they are prescribed by the rule. In the strategy just described, both "components" of the theory focus just on individual actions and which features make them right.

[24] See Scanlon (1998), p. 153.

[25] Footnote 17 points out that one possible way to understand such theories is as providing a meta-ethical standard by which the correct normative theory is selected—where the meta-ethical standard evaluates candidate normative theories in substantive terms, i.e., in terms of their consequences if adopted, etc.

consequences if adopted, etc. Such a theory can present the chosen list as the correct theoretical account of what makes individual actions right and wrong.

However, it is not difficult to see the weakness of this strategy as a response to the problem of error. First, a genuine moral laundry list of the sort I have described far surpasses the cognitive ability of any individual to learn the list and regulate her behavior according to it, since the list would consist of millions of prescriptions for just one agent (let alone all agents). It might be proposed that the agent doesn't need to know the content of the *entire* moral laundry list when she makes a decision which action to perform at time t_1. Instead she can proceed step by step: all she has to know at t_1 is what act is prescribed by the list for t_1 itself, and then know at time t_2 what act is prescribed by the list for t_2, and so on. But this suggestion doesn't tell us how the agent is miraculously to come up with the right prescription on each such occasion, especially as she has no general rule to guide her. And of course any agent who has mistaken beliefs about her objective circumstances C at time t_1—or mistaken beliefs about the fact that it is now time t_1—could easily be mistaken about which act is prescribed by the correct moral laundry list when she is in circumstances C at time t_1.

Second, it is clear that no individual has sufficient accurate information to ascertain accurately which list actually meets the kinds of standard just described (or other global standards that might strike us as attractive). Indeed, to accurately ascertain which list meets such standards would require typically far more factual information than would be required of an agent who more simply tried to ascertain what action act utilitarianism requires of her on some given occasion. This may be slightly less obvious for a list that is required to "enable people to cooperate with each other and form long-term plans," or a list that is required to be "such that no one could reasonably reject it as a basis for informed, unforced general agreement." But ascertaining that some candidate list is the *best* according to each of these standards is just as epistemically daunting as ascertaining that a candidate list would maximally enhance social welfare. Agents will inevitably make errors when they try to identify the best list according to these standards—errors that of course arise partly because of their erroneous beliefs about their current circumstances and options. Hence, despite its promise, this strategy cannot circumvent the human cognitive limitations that give rise to the problem of error in the first place. It doesn't help to point out that the agent herself need not have the requisite information, noting that the agent could call on the assistance of better-informed advisors to tell her which laundry list code satisfies the global criterion. But clearly, the amount of accurate information required to select the correct moral laundry list surpasses the amount of information available to any human, whether she is the agent or the agent's advisor. Appealing to advisors is no way out of this dilemma.

An advocate of this strategy might respond that this new problem of error is a problem at the meta-ethical level rather than at the normative level, so it doesn't infect the practical usability of the moral code. And indeed, Definitions 2.2 and 2.5 concerning usability do not entail that a moral principle is usable by an agent only if the agent believes it to be the correct principle. But this response reveals that this strategy for solving the problem of error at the normative level only works by *shifting* the problem to the meta-ethical level. This is not a genuine solution to the problems for moral decision-making created by our epistemic limitations. If the problem of usability at the normative theory level can only be solved by transferring it to the meta-ethical level, where it recurs with full force, we would not have genuinely escaped the epistemic problems vexing the original normative theory. Any solution to the problem of error at the normative level that depends on this sort of shift is not a strategy which a Pragmatist should want to pursue.

This situation is instructive because it is typical of a number of proposed responses to problems of usability caused by our lack of accurate beliefs. A problem that begins as a problem of lacking *nonmoral* knowledge that prevents us from applying a moral code is transformed, under the proposed response, to a problem of lacking *moral* knowledge. The new inability is the inability to identify the correct moral code. But no real progress has been made: in either case, our lack of nonmoral knowledge (whether it prevents us from identifying the morally right action, or prevents us from identifying the correct moral code) bars us from using the correct moral code to make the decision it calls for.

What if the Pragmatist watered down the global normative feature required of the correct laundry list moral code in order to make the list more readily identifiable by agents? For example, instead of requiring the correct list to be such that its adoption would *maximally enhance* social welfare, the theorist might only require the correct list to be such that its adoption would *enhance* social welfare. Or instead of requiring the correct list to be such that its adoption would *best enable* people to cooperate with each other and form long-term plans, he might only require that its adoption would *frequently enable* people to cooperate with each other and form long-term plans. Such watered-down criteria would seem to be more capable of accurate deployment by agents selecting laundry list codes than the more ambitious counterparts originally described.[26]

Of course, identifying which laundry list code would enhance social welfare, or frequently enable people to cooperate, itself faces challenging epistemic problems, since it would be necessary not only to identity a code with the desired global feature but to identify one that each agent could unerringly apply to his or her own decisions. This would require a daunting amount of accurate information about the beliefs of each agent regarding her prospective actions. Thus the epistemic problem encountered by this watered-down proposal would still be prohibitive.

However, quite apart from this epistemic problem, we can see that there is a fatal new difficulty with this version: such watered-down standards would not identify a *single* moral laundry list as the unique correct code. *Many* codes might each enhance (to some degree) social welfare, or frequently enable people to cooperate. This fact means that, on the current proposal, an agent might legitimately adopt any of these

---

[26] There would, however, be a difficult theoretical problem in specifying the baseline relative to which a code in question would enhance social welfare or frequently enable people to cooperate.

codes, and this in turn makes it indeterminate what act any agent ought to do, since one acceptable code may prescribe a given action while another acceptable code may prohibit the very same action. In itself this may not seem problematic, since we could interpret the strategy as holding that an act is permissible just in case it is required or permitted by at least one acceptable code. But this interpretation becomes problematic when we look at cases in which the cooperation of several agents is necessary in order to enhance the general welfare or achieve some other goal, in a context in which several different possible schemes of cooperation (each scheme calling for a different pattern of actions) would each be beneficial. For example, before there were any laws on the matter, there were various patterns of automobile-driving activity that would have enhanced welfare: automobile drivers could all have driven on the left, or could all have driven on the right. A contemporaneous moral code calling for either one would have been acceptable. Universal acceptance of either code would have enhanced welfare by increasing cooperation and reducing collisions. But if both moral codes were acceptable, then some agents could have legitimately adopted and acted according to the right-driving code, while others could have legitimately adopted and acted according to the left-driving code. This situation would have led to the very chaos that such codes are supposed to remedy, and would have diminished social welfare and cooperation. To secure the desired global effects, everyone needs to adopt the same code, even though both codes are equally acceptable.[27] This phenomenon shows that a strategy that fails to identify a single code to be followed by everyone does not solve the problem of error in a satisfactory manner. And this only adds to its defects in terms of epistemic demandingness.

In general, then, it appears that the hope of identifying a morally satisfactory objectivized error-proof moral code is a vain one. We can describe what such a code would be like—it would take the form of a moral laundry list—but no agent has the informational resources to accurately identify *which* such code is the correct one. Moral laundry lists merely transfer the problem of error from the nonmoral realm (identifying the correct action) to the moral realm (identifying the correct moral code). If we are to find an adequate response to the problem of error, we need to look elsewhere.

4.5 Achieving Universal Error-Freedom by More Radical Means: Subjectivized Codes

Our first radical attempt to solve the problem of error involved trying to identify an error-proof code that would characterize the action to be performed in terms of its objective features, features possessed by the action independently of what the agent

---

[27] Rule utilitarians, faced with a structurally parallel problem about how to specify the content of the ideal rules, have attempted to avoid this sort of difficulty by incorporating a description of what other agents are doing into the rule specifying any one agent's obligation. There is a long literature on whether this (or any similar) strategy can be made to work; my judgment is that it cannot. See H. Goldman (1974) and H. Smith (2010b). The most subtle and promising attempt is proposed by Regan (1980).

believes about it. Having failed to identify a satisfactory error-proof code of this sort, we now turn to the second radical suggestion. According to this suggestion, the Pragmatic Response requires "subjectivized" codes: codes that prescribe actions in virtue of the agent's internal mental attitudes towards the nonmoral features of their possible actions. (A more full-blown subjectivizing strategy would prescribe actions in virtue of the agent's beliefs about the moral status of those actions. However, that is not the kind of subjectivizing strategy we are discussing here, since we are not directly concerned with solutions to the problem of moral error.) Although it is rare for deontologists to pursue this course, a few have. H. A. Prichard is the most influential deontological proponent of this response to the problem of error, although versions of it were advocated by the later W. D. Ross. Hudson (1989) has also argued that this strategy should be adopted by deontologists. More recent act utilitarians have propounded it as well in adopting expected utility versions of utilitarianism.[28] Since act utilitarians who have advocated this kind of solution have focused on solving the problem of uncertainty rather than on solving the problem of error, this chapter will examine only those subjective codes proposed by deontologists.

One type of subjectivized code would ascribe moral status to an action in virtue of the agent's *motivations* with respect to that action.[29] Such a code might say that an action is right if the agent performing it chose the action out of a desire to act generously. Whether the act actually helped its intended beneficiary would be irrelevant to the act's moral status. As a Pragmatic Response to the problem of error, this response relies on the assumption that people cannot err in their ascriptions of motivations to themselves. According to this assumption, if I believe that my giving to United Way would arise from a desire to act generously, then I cannot be mistaken about this, and I can be assured that my act is right because it arises from the correct motive. However, most of us are aware that we are often mistaken about our own motivations: I may think I am giving to United Way out of generosity, but actually am giving in order to impress my co-workers. Contemporary psychological research supports the idea that our own motivations are often opaque to us.[30] Moreover, we can be mistaken about the

---

[28] For act utilitarians who have advocated expected utility versions of consequentialism, see note 14 in this chapter. Some theorists have advocated subjectivized versions of act utilitarianism for slightly different but related reasons. Thus Frances Howard-Snyder could be understood as proposing a subjectivized version of act utilitarianism in order to ensure that the theory issues "oughts" that the agent has the ability—the *epistemic* ability—to obey. Her argument leaves it unclear whether she would prefer a form of utilitarianism that prescribes acts based on what the agent actually believes, or based on what the agent should believe. See Howard-Snyder (1997). See Andric (2013) for a different kind of defense of subjectivism.

Note that versions of expected utility utilitarianism that employ objective probabilities, rather than subjective credences, would typically not count as subjectivizing codes as I am understanding them.

[29] Sorensen (1995), p. 257, attributes such a theory to Immanuel Kant. In my view this is a mistaken attribution: for Kant the actual springs of an action determine its moral worth, but not whether or not it is a duty. The contemporary debate about the role of motivation in determining which actions are right does not seem to be significantly driven by Pragmatic concerns. See Tadros (2011), Chapter 7, and Sverdlik (2011).

[30] See Ross and Nisbett (2011). Sorensen (1995), pp. 261–2, points out that even Kant was well aware of our inability to know our inner springs of action.

motivations with which we would perform a future action. Thus any subjectivizing solution that relies on a moral code which ascribes moral status to an action in virtue of the agent's motivation in performing it is doomed to failure as a solution to the problem of error.

More common subjectivizing theories, intended as remedies for the epistemic problem in morality, ascribe moral status to acts in virtue of the agent's *beliefs* about her action. Thus Prichard holds that the only propositions about which we can be infallibly certain are propositions about our own mental states, and hence that, in order to avoid the problem of error, our duties must be based on our beliefs about our situation and the character of the acts we might perform. For this reason he advocates a moral code that consists solely of principles of the form "Act A ought to be performed if and only if the agent believes A to have F." F itself would typically be an objective feature, such as *would involve keeping a promise*, but it is the agent's beliefs about his action's features that make it right or wrong, not the action's having feature F. Prichard claims that on a properly constructed subjectivized moral code, the agent can never make a factual mistake about whether her own action is morally required or not, for she only needs to consult the content of her beliefs about the prospective act.[31]

4.5.1 Possible conceptual advantages of subjectivized moral codes

Is a subjectivized code of this sort a satisfactory response to the problem of error—is it genuinely error-proof, and therefore universally usable as an extended decision-guide? Does it offer the advantages sought through requiring usability? As we have seen, error-proof codes are desired partly for conceptual reasons. The first conceptual

---

[31] Prichard (1968). W. D. Ross (1939), Chapter VII, followed Prichard in advocating subjectivized codes, although he adduced further reasons for this. Prichard also notes that we can never be certain of any act that we can actually perform it, and claims that one can only have a duty to do that which one can guarantee will occur. Hence the obligations he countenances are actually obligations to *try* to perform an act one believes will have a certain feature, or to *set oneself* to perform that act. For an excellent discussion of Prichard and Ross on these issues, see McConnell (1988).

Prichard (1968) distinguishes saying that "Act A has a certain property ('ought-to-be-doneness') in virtue of the agent's beliefs about A" from saying "Agent S ought to do A in virtue of S's beliefs about A" (pp. 36–8), where the former formulation ascribes a property to the act, while the latter formulation ascribes a property to the agent. He argues that the latter is the correct formulation to use. This view may be especially attractive in the context of a subjectivized theory, where many might find it problematic to say that an action is right because of the agent's beliefs about it, rather than because of its actual characteristics. However, it is not clear to me that this is a substantive distinction. In any event, as I conceive it, the Pragmatic Response in its subjectivized version is committed to precisely the view that the "oughtness" in question is a property of the act, and I have retained this formulation for consistency with Definitions 2.2 and 2.4.

Prichard and Ross concede that there is one type of "borderline" case in which a person will not be able to be certain whether he has a duty or not. This type of case is one in which whether or not the person has a duty depends on how likely the person thinks it is that a certain act would have a certain effect, but he is uncertain what degree of likelihood is necessary for the action to be morally required. (See Prichard (1968), p. 26, and W. D. Ross (1939), p. 151.) However, it is clear that this form of uncertainty is not uncertainty whether or not the act has the feature (*being believed to have likelihood N of having a certain effect*) that grounds the duty, but rather *normative* uncertainty about what feature grounds this type of duty (how large does N have to be?). Thus it is not part of the problems of nonmoral error and uncertainty as I have defined them.

reason is the claim that it is part of the meaning, or point, or function, of morality that it be capable of guiding choices. Prichard himself is moved by something like this criterion, since he rejects the idea that a person can have a duty which he does not believe himself to have, and also rejects the idea that someone does not have a duty which he believes himself to have.[32] He says, for example, in discussing the case of a would-be Inquisition torturer who (despite our best arguments to the contrary) remains convinced that torturing would save a heretic, "We think that...he would be bound to inflict the torture."[33] Prichard advocates a subjectivized moral code precisely in order to ensure that no agent will be in error as to what concrete act his or her duty requires. Insofar as subjectivized codes are error-proof, they succeed in this endeavor.

But Prichard relies on the assumption that we never make errors about the existence and content of our own beliefs,[34] and hence cannot make errors about whether or not a given action is required by our subjectivized code. This assumption may have been a commonplace at the time that Prichard wrote, but it is not so any longer. Most philosophers and psychologists now hold that a person's own beliefs are not necessarily accessible to that person (or at least accessible in the time available for making a quick decision). We can be mistaken regarding the existence or content of our beliefs, just as we can be mistaken about the objective consequences or circumstances of our actions, or about our motives. Many beliefs are tacit, remaining below the level of consciousness, even though they govern our behavior. Thus you tacitly believe the floor you are about to step out onto from the elevator is stable and will bear your weight, but typically you have no conscious awareness of this belief. Indeed, psychological research suggests that vast numbers of our mundane beliefs, perhaps for reasons of psychological economy, occur below the level of conscious awareness, and—unlike your belief about the floor—often may not be accessible even by agents who try to discover what they believe.[35] When a person's beliefs are unconscious, she may not have an accurate grasp of whether or not she holds that belief, as research on implicit attitudes shows.[36] In the more complicated cases, some beliefs are, and often remain, unconscious because we are motivated not to acknowledge them.[37] Someone raised in a racist society, but who now lives in a more progressive environment, may believe that he no longer harbors racist beliefs, but be mistaken about this. Or, alternatively, someone may have become

[32] Prichard (1968), pp. 24–5. Here Prichard seems to be advocating a full-blown subjectivizing moral theory, in which the moral status of the action depends on the agent's belief about its moral status. Sorensen (1995), p. 247, formulates a similar requirement as "Access": "If one is obliged to do x, then one can know one is obliged to do x."

[33] Prichard (1968), p. 30. This example seems to involve both nonmoral and moral mistake of fact.

[34] Prichard (1968), p. 25 ("The question whether I am thinking something likely is no more one about which I can be mistaken than is the question of whether I have a certain pain").

[35] See, for example, Evans and Frankish (2009) and Kahneman (2011).

[36] See papers listed on the Project Implicit website at <http://www.projectimplicit.net/papers.html> (accessed May 21, 2015).

[37] As Giacomo Leopardi says, people "approach life in the same way as Italian husbands do their wives: they need to believe they are faithful even though they know otherwise." This passage is quoted by Parks (2013).

convinced (through attendance at too many diversity workshops) that she *does* harbor racist beliefs, when actually she does not. A person may, without reflection, assume she has a certain belief, but under the right circumstances discover she does not have the belief at all. For example, a churchgoer brought up in a conventional religious family may assume that she believes in God, but be mistaken about this, as she discovers when challenged about this belief. Our beliefs, in other words, are not self-intimating (a belief is *self-intimating* just in case it is true that if we have that belief, we believe that we have that belief). Nor are we infallible with respect to our beliefs (we are *infallible* with respect to our beliefs just in case it is true that if we believe we have a certain belief, then we do have that belief).[38]

This means that subjectivized codes, as Prichard defines them, are not error-proof: they are not guaranteed to be usable in the extended sense. Consider the following example.

Maureen believes, in her heart of hearts, that her husband stole $100K from his company. However, she can't bring herself to acknowledge his crime, so she doesn't believe that she believes her husband stole the money. Maureen's subjectivized moral Code C_1 requires her to file a complaint with the police if she believes that her husband took the money. Since she believes her husband stole the money, she has a duty to file a complaint with the police. However, since she doesn't believe she has this belief, she has a duty of which she is unaware. Hence even though she believes her husband committed this crime, and even though she desires to follow a code requiring her to report anyone she believes to have committed a crime, she would not derive any prescription from this belief and desire because she doesn't believe she has the relevant belief. She is subject to the problem of error and her moral code is not usable by her in either the core or the extended sense.

We can expand the case to one in which Maureen, unable to ignore the evidence that the crime occurred, comes to believe that she believes her husband's workmate stole the money (although in her heart of hearts she doesn't really believe the workmate is involved). Given her unconscious belief that her husband stole the money, her moral code requires Maureen to inform the police about her husband. However, given that she can't bring herself to acknowledge her belief that her husband committed a crime, she would actually derive a prescription to inform the police about her husband's workmate. In this case Maureen's moral code is usable by her in the *core* sense (she can derive a prescription from it), but it is not usable in the *extended* sense (since she would derive a prescription to perform an act that is not required by the principle). Relative to this

---

[38] For an influential philosophical discussion of our epistemic access to our beliefs, see Williamson (2000), Chapter 4. Williamson uses the term "luminous," which he restricts to beliefs of which it is true that if we have that belief, then we are in a position to know that we have that belief. In our context the difference between "being in a position to know (or believe) something" and "actually knowing (or believing) something" may be crucial, so I have not adopted Williamson's terminology. For a seminal discussion of the different types of (possible) "privileged access" to our mental states, see Alston (1971). Although most philosophers (and almost all psychologists) would agree with my statements in the text, there has long been philosophical controversy over this point.

subjectivized code, Maureen's mistakes about her beliefs mislead her in much the same way that other agents' mistakes about the objective facts mislead them.[39]

To escape the problem that subjectivized codes as he envisions them cannot always be used as guides by decision makers, a Pragmatist such as Prichard might respond by refashioning the subjectivized code so that it grounds the prescription for an action, not in what the agent believes about the action, but rather in what the agent believes herself to believe about the action. Thus the new Code C_2 for the Maureen case would state "You ought to inform the police that S committed a crime if you believe that you believe that S committed a crime." According to this version of the subjectivized code, Maureen has no duty to inform the police on her husband and so does not violate her duty by not doing so. In the expanded version of the case she does have a duty to inform the police about her husband's workmate (because she believes that she believes him to have committed the crime) and she would derive such a duty from the code. Thus the revised code is usable by her both in the core and in the extended sense, despite her mistaken beliefs about her beliefs.

Unfortunately, the problem of the accessibility of one's own beliefs may simply reassert itself at this higher level: an agent might believe that she believes that P, but not believe that she believes that she believes P. Such an agent would be subject to Code C_2, but would not derive any prescription from it. We might be tempted to remedy this problem by raising the relevant level of belief one more step, for example revising the code still further as code C_3: "You ought to inform the police that S committed a crime if you believe that you believe that you believe that S committed a crime." But this way looms trouble. Many agents will have no such third-level beliefs. If they have no third-level beliefs, then they have no obligations under Code C_3. Adding layers to the number of beliefs involved may protect some agents from the problem of error, but at the cost of entirely eliminating this kind of duty for most agents.[40]

Yet another response would be to adopt the following version, Code C_4: "You ought to inform the police that S committed a crime if, according to the highest-level relevant belief which you believe yourself to have, S committed a crime."[41] Such a code cuts off the threat of eliminating the duty to report crime for most agents, who lack high-level beliefs, by attaching the obligation to the highest-level belief which

---

[39] Compare my remarks about Maureen's case with my remarks about unconscious beliefs in section 2.1 of Chapter 2. There I said that unconscious beliefs *could* enable an agent to use a moral principle if the existence of those beliefs would lead the agent, if she wanted to apply the principle, to derive a prescription from it. Thus Sally no longer has a conscious belief about the combination for opening the safe, but if she wanted to open the safe, she would go through the appropriate motions and open it. However, I am assuming that in Maureen's case her unconscious belief that her husband committed the crime is a belief she has repressed, so that it would *not* lead her to report her husband to the police if she wanted to follow a principle requiring her to report what she believes to be crimes. And, since the principle in question does not require her to report crimes, but requires her to report any person she *believes* to be perpetrating a crime, and she believes that she believes her husband's workmate to have stolen the money, she would derive a prescription to report him rather than to report her husband.

[40] Thanks to Ben Bronner for helping me clarify the nature of this problem.

[41] I owe this suggestion to Evan Williams and Jeffrey McMahan.

the agent believes herself to have (however high or low that level might be). According to Code C_4, Maureen ought to inform the police about her husband's workmate but not about her husband. A cognitively more sophisticated Colleen, who has no beliefs about the workmate but unconsciously believes her husband to have committed a crime, believes she doesn't have this belief, but has an additional third-level (false) belief that she believes that she believes that her husband committed a crime, would in virtue of this third-level belief have an obligation to inform the police about the husband but not about her husband's workmate. Unfortunately, although this code is usable by Maureen and Colleen, it does not ascribe any obligation at all to a third agent Aileen, who unconsciously believes, in her heart of hearts, that her husband stole the money, and also unconsciously believes that she believes her husband stole the money. Aileen has no beliefs about the workmate. Code C_4 requires Aileen to report her husband. But because her belief that she believes her husband to have stolen the money is itself unconscious and suppressed, and given the complicated nature of her set of beliefs, it is unlikely that if she wanted to follow Code C_4, she would derive any prescription at all. Thus Code C_4 is not usable in either the core or the extended sense by Aileen and so is not universally usable. Of course agents could also be mistaken about whether some belief was their highest-level belief, which would lead to more misapplications.

Other variants of this kind of subjectivized code might be explored in the hope of finding one that would deliver appropriate recommendations and also would be universally usable in the extended sense. I am dubious that this search will succeed. Errors and ignorance about our own beliefs, although perhaps less common than errors and ignorance about our objective circumstances, seem nonetheless to be fatal for the truly universal usability of subjectivized codes. A subjectivized code cannot be guaranteed to be completely error-proof.

The problem of access to the content of one's own beliefs undermines the first conceptual advantage that might be claimed for subjectivized codes, namely that they guarantee extended usability. The second conceptual advantage that could be claimed for error-proof codes is that they meet the demand of justice that the successful moral life should be available to everyone, whether the person is intelligent and well-informed, or dull and poorly informed. The thought would be that each agent, however mistaken about her circumstances, nonetheless has complete access to her thoughts about her prospective actions, and that is all that is required in order to correctly ascertain her duty under a suitably subjectivized code. And indeed, if each agent had guaranteed access to her beliefs about her prospective actions, this demand could be met by a subjectivized code (setting aside the problem of uncertainty). But, as we have seen, agents can be mistaken about or unaware of their own beliefs, just as they can be mistaken about or unaware of the circumstances in which they act. Hence subjectivized codes cannot be assured of achieving this second conceptual advantage either. Even the best-motivated agent would sometimes perform the wrong action.

4.5.2 Possible goal-oriented advantages of subjectivized moral codes

Those who hope to find error-proof codes often seek the "goal-oriented" advantages that such codes would arguably ensure, namely, the production of beneficial effects on human welfare (perhaps including the fostering of social cooperation and the formation of long-term plans), or the achievement of a desirable pattern of actions.

The first claimed goal-oriented advantage focuses on the broad social consequences of a moral code's currency in society. The first version of this argument claims that an error-proof moral code would optimally enhance those elements of social welfare affected by the human activities that can be regulated by a moral code. However, it seems clear on little reflection that subjectivized moral codes, even if they were error-proof, are not likely to secure much advantage in this regard. For the sake of argument let us assume both that agents are fully motivated to act morally and also that agents' beliefs about their own beliefs are accurate. Then individuals regulating their actions by subjectivized codes would indeed do exactly as the code requires. However, since their beliefs *about the world* would often be false, there is no guarantee that the actions they perform would enhance social welfare. Consider Ben, who believes that giving whiskey to a person suffering from hypothermia is a good way to save the person's life. If Ben tries to follow an objectivized code requiring him to save life, then Ben will give the whiskey to the hypothermia victim—and unfortunately kill the victim, since alcohol is dangerous to persons in this condition. If Ben tries to follow a subjectivized code requiring him to do what he believes will save someone's life, he will also give the victim whiskey, thereby killing him. According to the objectivized code Ben acts wrongly, while according to the subjectivized code Ben does what is right. But either way, the hypothermia victim is dead. Thus switching from an objectivized code to a subjectivized version of it does nothing to enhance social welfare. There is no reason, therefore, to adopt subjectivized codes on grounds that they will enhance social welfare more than standard error-prone codes.[42]

The second version of the hoped-for "social welfare" advantage to error-proof codes focuses on certain special social roles that a suitable moral code can play. As we have seen, Rawls requires principles of justice in a well-ordered society to facilitate cooperative social endeavors and to enable citizens to organize their plans for the long-term future.[43] One could argue that a full moral code, not just the principles of justice, should secure these same goods through moral principles requiring people to tell the truth, keep their promises, and so forth. An advocate of error-proof codes might argue

---

[42] It might be argued that social welfare will be enhanced because, although the hypothermia victim is equally dead whichever code Ben attempts to follow, at least if he attempts to follow the subjectivized code he won't feel unpleasantly guilty at performing the wrong act, as he will if he attempts to follow the objectivized code. At best this effect is likely to be small in the grand scheme of things, and one could argue that cognitive dissonance, itself a source of discomfort, might be caused by believing that acting according to one's moral code led directly to the death of such a victim—a dissonance that might outweigh the uncomfortable guilt Ben might feel after attempting to follow the objectivized code.

[43] Rawls (1971), sections 1, 10, 23, and 38, and (1980), pp. 553–64, especially pp. 553, 560–1, and 563.

that an error-free moral code would better enable people successfully to coordinate their actions than a code that is error-prone. But only brief reflection is necessary to show that subjectivizing a moral code fails to secure such coordination. Consider Maria and Juan, who agree to meet for lunch at the campus grill on the day classes start. Each subscribes to an *objectivized* code requiring them to keep their promises and each intends to do this. However, Maria believes that classes start on Tuesday, while Juan believes that classes start on Wednesday. In reality classes start on Thursday. Each will do what she or he believes to be keeping the promise, but Maria will show up at the grill on Tuesday, while Juan will show up on Wednesday, both individuals thus violating their code and failing to coordinate their actions. But their subscribing to a subjectivized version of the code, instead of the objectivized one, requiring them to do what they *believe* to be keeping their promises, would not help matters. Maria would still show up on Tuesday, while Juan would still show up on Wednesday. They would each do as their code requires, but they will still fail to coordinate their actions. Shifting to a subjectivized code does not help them coordinate their actions any more than its counterpart objective code would have done. In the case of subjectivized codes, the agents in this case are able to use their code in the extended sense. Inability to make core or extended use of the code is not their problem—their problem is caused by their false beliefs about the world. These false beliefs still stand in the way of their accomplishing their goals, even though their code is a usable one. A similar point can be made about the capacity of subjectivized codes to foster agents' abilities to plan successfully for the long-term future.

Let us look finally at the second major goal-oriented advantage of error-proof codes, namely that of securing a desirable pattern of actions through agents' use of the code. Recall that we are considering Pragmatic Responses, under which the moral code in question must serve both as the theoretical account of what makes actions right and wrong, and also as a decision-guide for the agent. Hence the only available criterion for identifying a "desirable pattern of actions" is the candidate code itself.[44] Thus the question of whether subjectivized codes secure an ideal pattern of action is the question of whether each agent who attempts to follow a candidate subjectivized code actually succeeds in performing the acts prescribed by the code. If subjectivized codes were indeed completely error-proof, the answer would be yes: such a code would be universally usable in the extended sense, which implies that each act performed by an agent attempting to apply that code would in fact conform to it. We have seen, however, that subjectivized codes fall short of universal usability in the extended sense: agents' errors about their own beliefs can lead to erroneous applications of a subjectivized code, just

---

[44] It might be proposed that the criterion for identifying a desirable pattern of actions is some independent standard that evaluates actions individually, and the question is whether the actions performed by agents following the candidate code actually satisfy that standard or not. However, this would in effect be a Hybrid Response to the problem of error, under which there are two separate standards, one serving as the account of right and wrong, and the other serving as the agent's decision-guide. This type of response will be examined in later chapters.

as agents' errors about their circumstances can lead to erroneous applications of an objectivized code. Thus we must conclude that subjectivized codes fall short of attaining the goal of securing desirable patterns of action.

Summing these arguments up, we can conclude that subjectivized codes cannot achieve full universal usability as decision-guides. Because agents are vulnerable to errors about their own motivations and beliefs, just as they are vulnerable to errors about their objective circumstances, the conceptual advantages sought for an error-proof code cannot be achieved by subjectivized codes. The vulnerability to error of subjectivized codes also implies that agents cannot be guaranteed by such codes to achieve the goal-oriented advantage of producing the pattern of actions called for by the code. And we have seen that subjectivized codes (even if we set aside their vulnerability to error) cannot achieve the welfare-related goal-oriented advantages we might hope to obtain from a Pragmatic Response to the problem of error. Since people continue to have false beliefs about their circumstances, shifting to a subjectivized code does not necessarily improve the actual consequences of their actions or their ability to coordinate activities or form long-range plans. In arguing for this latter point I have compared the goal-oriented advantages of matched pairs of codes, one of which is the subjectivized version of its partner, an objective code. To fully argue that subjectivized codes cannot secure optimal social advantages would require us to make comparisons among a wider set of codes that are not otherwise closely matched. This is not a well-defined task, and so would be a difficult one to carry out. What I hope to have shown is that merely subjectivizing a code does not guarantee that it secures social advantages that are not securable by error-prone objective codes—and of course, since subjectivized codes are not error-free, they can't in any event satisfy the Pragmatic theorist's hope for a universally usable error-free moral code.[45]

Thus subjectivized codes are not error-free and fail to achieve the full advantages that a Pragmatic theorist might hope to secure by adopting subjectivized moral codes in place of traditional objectivized codes.

4.6 The Splintered Pragmatic Response

We should examine one remaining possible version of the Pragmatic Response—the Splintered Pragmatic Response. This response initially seems more moderate than the ones we have examined so far, since it would reject the claim that a moral principle is unacceptable in general if there is even one occasion on which some agent would be subject to the problem of error with respect to it. This version would say instead that a moral principle is unacceptable as a theoretical account of right and wrong only for the specific occasions when it is not usable by the agent to guide his decision. Thus the Splintered Response Pragmatic theorist would say that utilitarianism is *not* correct as a

---

[45] There are many other grounds to reject subjectivized codes, but a discussion of these would carry us outside the bounds of our current inquiry.

theoretical account of the governor's act when he decides whether to propose cutting state spending (because his error about the nonmoral facts would lead him to draw the wrong moral conclusion), but *is* correct as a theoretical account of the moral status of his action when he decides whether to sign a bill increasing financial aid to college students (because in this case he has the facts right, and so would succeed in deriving the correct prescription from utilitarianism if he applied it). What makes his signing the bill right in the student aid case is the fact that his doing so would maximize welfare, but what would make a choice right in dealing with the budget deficit is some other feature entirely. To pursue this version of the Pragmatic Response would involve admitting a plurality of correct accounts of what makes actions right and wrong, each correct for a given agent and a given decision (or perhaps for a limited set of agents and decisions), but not necessarily correct for other agents, or for the same agent and a different decision.[46]

The Splintered version of the Pragmatic Response would be a heroic attempt to deal with the problem of error without abandoning *tout court* many traditional moral theories such as utilitarianism. However, I am not aware of anyone who has advocated it. Its disadvantages are evident: it proposes a radically splintered moral "theory," in which multiple distinct moral principles are accepted, even for the same field of action. According to this code what makes an action right in one circumstance for an agent is entirely different from what makes an action right in similar circumstances for that same agent when he has a better (or worse) grasp of his situation. The theory would also imply that what makes an action right for one agent is different from what makes an action right for another agent who is in the same situation but who has different beliefs.[47] It is difficult to see how effective moral learning could take place, since each agent would need to learn a vast array of moral principles, each tailored to the different epistemic circumstances in which she might find herself. But worst of all is the fact that in most cases, no agent would be able to ascertain which moral principle is the correct account of the moral status of her present action, or the one she should apply. By hypothesis, this Splintered version of the Pragmatic Response is proposed as a response

---

[46] Note that the Splintered Response is not a form of moral relativism as it is often understood. What action is right for the governor doesn't depend on the mores of the culture of which he is a member; nor does it depend on the culture or moral beliefs of the person evaluating his action, or on the agent's own moral beliefs. Instead it depends on what ethical code the agent *could unerringly use* in his circumstances at the time of the decision. Depending how the Splintered Response is developed, it might turn out that Governor 1 and Governor 2, each faced with exactly the same decision, but having different beliefs about the consequences of their actions, would be required to do the very same action (let's say, increase spending), but these requirements would issue from different codes, one of which is usable by Governor 1, and the second of which is usable by Governor 2.

[47] Taken to an extreme the Splintered Response might endorse a moral laundry list. However, this would only happen if each moral code has only a single occasion on which it would be applied correctly by the agent in question. It seems likely that a number of standard moral codes would be applied correctly on numerous occasions (although none would be applied correctly on every possible occasion for its use), so the "correct" set of moral codes would include at least some that are stated as (limited) general principles. Thus the Splintered Response would probably not endorse a moral laundry list consisting of a separate individual prescription for each occasion.

to the problem of error: a situation in which the agent has false beliefs about the facts relevant to a given moral principle P. But when an agent has false beliefs, she typically does not realize these beliefs to be false (or otherwise she would reject them). Thus she does not realize she is faced with the problem of error with respect to P. She is not in a position to recognize that P is not, for her, the correct account of the rightness and wrongness of her prospective actions, or to recognize that she would be making a mistake if she used P to decide what to do. Thus on this version of the Pragmatic Response, what started out as the problem of error with respect to nonmoral facts has once again been converted to a problem of error with respect to *morality*: the agent is now interpreted as mistaken about which moral principle is the correct account of right-making characteristics, and correct decision-guide, for her in her specific circumstances. Such a response fails to rescue agents from their cognitive limitations, but simply redescribes those limitations as occurring at another level. Since this is no progress, we may reject the Splintered Pragmatic Response.

4.7 Conclusion

In this chapter we have examined Pragmatic Responses to the problem of error: responses which accept the thesis that a unified moral code must serve both as the theoretical account of what makes actions right and wrong, and also as a decision-guide for agents. The ideal is to find a *universally usable* moral code that could successfully be used by all agents both in the core and in the extended sense, even though their information about their circumstances may be impoverished or mis-taken. The hope behind the Pragmatic Response is to find a type of moral code that will successfully achieve at least some of the advantages that it is claimed can be secured through an error-free moral code: the conceptual advantages of usability as a decision-guide and satisfaction of a basic form of justice that makes the successful moral life available to everyone; and the goal-oriented advantages of enhancing social welfare and cooperation, and generating the performance of an ideal pattern of actions by agents who try to follow the code. Unfortunately, we have found no Pragmatic Responses that provide effective remedies for the problem of error. Any theorist who seeks a theory that achieves one of these four advantages through universal usability must reject the ideal Pragmatic approach.

Standard proposals for Pragmatic theories (such as expected consequence utili-tarianism, rule utilitarianism, and standard deontological theories) all fail to provide universally usable moral codes, since agents' mistakes infect the remedies supplied by these theories. It is possible to describe a more radical objective Pragmatic theory, the moral laundry list. But it only succeeds at achieving universal usability by shifting the problem of error from the level of normative theory to the level of meta-ethical theory, so the advance it procures is fundamentally illusory. A second radical Pragmatic Response is the adoption of the kind of subjectivized code that Prichard, Ross, and some expected consequence utilitarians have advocated. However, such subjectivized codes are themselves vulnerable to the problem of error, since human beings have mistaken beliefs about their own beliefs, just as they have mistaken beliefs about the objective circumstances of their actions. Moreover, even if they were error-proof, subjectivized codes would fail to achieve the goal-oriented advantages that it is often hoped Pragmatic theories can attain—agents' mistakes about their objective circumstances would still lead, under a subjectivized code, to actions that fail to enhance general welfare, fail to coordinate the actions of different agents, and fail to ensure the success of long-term planning.

Taking into account all these considerations, we have reason to conclude that Pragmatic Responses cannot provide universally usable moral codes that will satisfactorily solve the problem of error. Hardy souls have hoped it would, but their hope proves to be in vain. In Chapter 6 we will consider whether Pragmatic Responses fare better if we weaken the demand that they provide universally usable codes to a demand that they merely provide codes that are *more usable* than standard moral theories. However, before undertaking that examination, in Chapter 5 we will look at another drawback to subjectivized codes that should persuade even the most committed Pragmatic theorists to abandon them as a solution to the problem of error. This drawback is the fact that no subjectivized deontological moral code can provide a rationale for the duty to seek more information. Since the discussion in Chapter 5 is, strictly speaking, a digression from the main argument of this book, readers should feel free to skip this chapter and move directly on to Chapter 6.

5

A Further Disadvantage of Subjectivized Moral Codes

One cannot always be in an investigative mode, but one fails to investigate at one's risk.[1]

In the previous chapter we examined both objectivized and subjectivized moral codes as proposed solutions to the problem of error. We saw that such codes fail to fully solve the problem of error: laundry list objective codes require just as daunting an amount of information (raised to the meta-ethical level) as the standard codes they seek to replace, and subjectivized codes are vulnerable to the fact that agents are often mistaken about their own beliefs and motives. Moreover, even completely error-free subjectivized codes cannot fully satisfy the goal-oriented aims a Pragmatic theorist hopes to achieve in requiring that an acceptable moral code must be usable. In the hunt for Pragmatic solutions, it now behooves us to inquire whether moral codes that provide less than ideal solutions to the problem of error—ones that *improve* our success rate in applying them, even though they cannot guarantee full elimination of the problem of error— would nonetheless be acceptable responses. Our question will be whether such codes are *good enough*. That examination will be undertaken in Chapter 6.

Before we turn to that task, however, it is worth showing that subjectivized codes have an additional severe disadvantage beyond their failure to serve as full and satisfactory solutions to the problem of error. This chapter will outline this disadvantage, focusing on the most common forms of subjectivized codes, which ascribe moral status to an action in virtue of the agent's beliefs about that action. Of course subjectivized codes have many further disadvantages, but it would take us far from our main quarry to describe these. As I noted at the end of Chapter 4, the material in this chapter is not part of the central argument in this book, so the reader who is short on time may proceed directly to Chapter 6 without losing the main thread.

As we've noted, consequentialist theories have borne the brunt of the criticism arising from the epistemic limitations that prevent agents from applying these theories accurately to their decisions. Deontologists have paid less attention to the epistemic

---

[1] Putoto (2012).

difficulties that decision makers may have in applying deontological codes, perhaps relying on their sense that deontic duties are less subject to epistemic problems than consequentialist obligations. However, we have seen numerous examples of cases in which an agent, because of her false beliefs, would go astray in making a decision by reference to her deontological code. Deontologists who are aware of this problem have sometimes advocated some version of a subjectivizing moral theory.[2]

I will argue, however, that subjectivized deontic codes cannot underwrite the widely endorsed duty to gather information before making a morally important decision.

5.1 The Moral Duty to Inform Oneself before Acting

Pragmatic theorists, who aim to find a moral code that avoids the problem of error, advocate the adoption of a moral code that is usable by any agent, no matter how impoverished or inaccurate his beliefs about the world.[3] Such a code accommodates the less than perfect information agents often have about their circumstances and the consequences of their actions. Even so, Pragmatic theorists never deny that we have an obligation to *improve* our information whenever we have a suitable opportunity to do so. Indeed, I take it as a datum that we all believe there often is such an obligation, and a very strong one.[4] If you are a military leader whose lieutenants recommend bombing a compound that might house enemy soldiers, you have an obligation to investigate—before bombing it—whether the compound really does house enemy soldiers, and whether it houses innocent civilians as well. If you are backing your car out of your garage, you have a duty to check your rearview mirror before proceeding. If you are a faculty member considering how to vote in an upcoming tenure case, you have an obligation—before voting—to inform yourself about the achievements of the tenure candidate.

Some philosophers have raised questions about whether a subjectivized moral code can underwrite such obligations to inform oneself before acting. Prichard himself took this to be a significant (although answerable) worry about the subjectivized code

---

[2] As we've seen, the most famous such advocates are Prichard (1968) and W. D. Ross (1939), Chapter VII. In (1989) Hudson argues that non-utilitarian theories, as well as utilitarian ones, should be subjectivized. In (1990) at p. 43, Gibbard argues that we only need a "subjective" sense of "ought" in morality. In (2004) at p. 61, B. Gert claims that "...it is foreseeable goods and evils that are most relevant to the making of moral judgments," not what the agent did not know, or what he should have known but did not. For a discussion of the need to accommodate false beliefs by a non-consequentialist virtue ethicist, see Baehr (2011), pp. 123–7. Virtue ethicists who hold that what makes an act virtuous is its issuing from a good motive can be seen as implicitly adopting a subjectivizing strategy, since the agent's motive will link up with his beliefs in order to issue in action.

[3] Much of the material in sections 5.1–5.5 originally appeared in H. Smith (2014).

[4] Thus Donagan (1977), p. 130, quoting Whewell, asserts that we have a duty to do "all that is in our power" to free our actions from the defects of ignorance and error. In a representative contemporary example, Väyrynen states, "In the moral case, we can reasonably require agents to inquire into the nature of the situation when deciding what to do" in (2006), p. 300.

he advocated, and subsequent authors have raised the same question.[5] In this chapter I examine this question. I will argue that both objective and subjectivized consequentialist codes can easily accommodate an appropriate obligation to gather information, since this duty is encompassed by the basic obligation under such codes to produce good consequences. In the case of objective deontological codes, I will examine two different strategies for accommodating the obligation to gather information. The first strategy attempts to define a special, free-standing deontic duty of this type. I will argue that this strategy is not promising, and advocate an alternative approach, namely defining a derivative obligation to gather information so as to ensure that one satisfies one's subsequent deontic duties. Although this approach appears successful in the case of objective deontological codes, I will argue that neither it nor the alternative "free-standing duty" approach is successful in the case of subjectivized deontological codes. Thus Prichard was right to worry: it appears that subjectivized deontological codes cannot underwrite an obligation to gather information before acting. Even if one holds, despite the arguments in Chapter 4, that subjectivized deontological codes do provide an effective solution to the problem of error, one should reject such codes on the ground that they cannot include a suitable obligation to investigate before acting.

5.2 Three Caveats

Several caveats before we begin. First, since we are considering the Pragmatic Response to the problem of error, in this chapter I shall focus primarily on agents who have false beliefs or no relevant beliefs, rather than agents who are subject to uncertainty. This restriction will not distort the inquiry or its outcome. If a moral theory flunks the test of appropriately handling the duty to gather information for agents having false beliefs or no relevant beliefs, then it is inadequate, even if it passes this test for agents laboring under mere uncertainty.

Second, we will be inspecting subjectivized moral codes that prescribe actions in light of the agent's beliefs—her *actual* beliefs. But some may think this sets us off on the wrong foot, holding that what a person ought to do depends on what *it would be reasonable* for the person to believe, not on what the person *actually believes*.[6] These theorists

---

[5] Prichard (1968), pp. 27–8. See also Gruzalski (1981), who mentions (and dismisses) this as a possible objection to foreseeable consequence utilitarianism (p. 169). Parfit takes a similar line in (2011), pp. 160–1. In (1995) at p. 254 Sorensen argues against the requirement that all one's obligations be knowable on the ground that such a requirement would enable one to "mute the call of duty by diminishing one's cognitive capacity." Whether or not the duty to acquire information can be justified in a subjectivized code is discussed by McConnell (1988). In the same vein, Michael Zimmerman criticizes the subjectivized view (which he characterizes somewhat differently, as saying that an act is right if the agent believes it to be right) as follows: "the [subjectivized 'ought'] implies that the failure to believe that any act is best would make it the case that one has no obligations. But it is absurd to think that, for example, simply failing to attend to one's situation...should suffice to free one from obligation" (Zimmerman (2008), p. 14).

[6] Advocates of this view are legion. They include Gruzalski (1981); Hooker (2000), section 3.1; Kagan (1989), p. 1; Scanlon (2008), pp. 47ff.; and Zimmerman (2008).

would argue that we should concentrate on reasonable-belief versions of these codes, which may elude the problems I raise for actual-belief versions.

My primary focus will be on actual-belief codes. But I shall argue later in this chapter that certain reasonable-belief versions of subjectivized codes are subject to the same problems that I shall describe for parallel actual-belief versions.

Third, although I will examine situations in which agents have false beliefs, or no relevant beliefs, about *nonmoral* facts (such as what one promised to purchase at the store), I will assume that these agents all have correct beliefs about *moral* facts (such as whether or not violating a promise is prima facie wrong). Of course agents make mistakes or are uncertain about moral facts as well as nonmoral facts. However, I argued in Chapter 2 that uncertainty or mistake about moral facts does not impede the usability of the moral code in question. And the general question of how best to choose when faced with moral uncertainty must be left for another occasion.

5.3 Epistemic Duties

It may seem as though the question of whether there is a duty to gather information is a question for epistemology: is there an *epistemic* duty to acquire more information, and if so, what is its content? If epistemology provides us with an account of this duty, then perhaps moral theory may simply defer to epistemology.

Regrettably, seeking help from epistemology is not straightforward. Until fairly recently, attention to the duty to gather evidence has been relatively neglected in epistemology. Fortunately, some contemporary epistemologists are now actively debating whether there is any duty to gather evidence, and if so, what the nature of this duty is. Among those engaged in this debate, some hold that there is such a duty, but that it is simply a special kind of moral duty to perform "epistemic" actions.[7] Others hold that there are distinctive epistemic duties, independent of any moral duties, which typically include a duty to acquire information. Epistemologists in this second camp often (but not always) consider the duty to gather information to be a duty to acquire special "intellectual goods" such as warranted true beliefs or knowledge, avoidance of false beliefs, understanding, intellectual acquaintance,[8] or more generally consider it as a duty to establish "the best kinds of cognitive contact with reality."[9] Still other epistemologists don't address the question of whether there is a moral duty to acquire information, but their other claims imply that there is no such epistemic duty: on their view, the *only* distinctive epistemic duty is fitting one's beliefs to one's current evidence.[10]

---

[7] Zagzebski (1996), p. 255 is a prime example of a theorist who views epistemic duties as a sub-category of moral duties.

[8] See Driver (2003) and Roberts and Wood (2007), Chapter 2.   [9] McKinnon (2003), p. 247.

[10] Among those who accept epistemic normativity as extending beyond fitting beliefs to current evidence, and possibly including a duty to acquire information, are Axtell (2011); Axtell and Olsen (2009); Baehr (2011); Code (1987); DeRose (2000); Foley (2010); Hall and Johnson (1998); Kornblith (1983); Monmarquet

If there is no specifically epistemic duty to seek evidence, then we can draw no help from epistemology. On the other hand, if the "epistemic" duty to seek evidence turns out to be a special kind of moral duty, then we may hope that epistemologists have offered insights into the nature of this duty which we can use in developing a detailed account of it. Finally, if the epistemic duty to seek evidence turns out to be completely independent of any moral duties, then our situation is more complicated. We will face the question of how to balance such an epistemic duty against conflicting moral duties.[11] For example, if there is an epistemic duty to gather as much evidence as possible, it will sometimes conflict with the role-based moral duty to save lives, as in the case of an emergency medical technician who gathers evidence about the name, address, age, weight, length of time submerged, and so forth of a drowned child, instead of immediately applying CPR. Some epistemologists have argued that epistemic and moral duties are incommensurable, and that such conflicts cannot be rationally resolved.[12] Others hold such conflicts can be resolved, but offer little guidance how to resolve them. More pressingly for our immediate purposes, if we accept the existence of a strictly epistemic duty to gather evidence, we cannot assume that the existence of this duty entails the existence of a parallel moral duty—or that if there is such a moral duty, the moral duty mirrors the character of the distinctively epistemic duty. We may hope that epistemologists' proposals about the nature of the epistemic duty give us useful clues about how to understand the nature of the moral duty, but we cannot assume this will turn out to be the case.

The following discussion will include an examination of proposals from epistemologists about the content of an evidence-gathering duty. Unfortunately, most epistemologists have focused on more abstract issues, such as how the epistemic and moral virtues or duties relate to each other, or how having justified beliefs connects with being responsible in forming beliefs, so we will find relatively little help in working out the character of the duty to gather evidence.

5.4 The Duty to Acquire Information before Action: Objective Moral Theories

Our normal view is that when we must make an important choice in the future, we have a duty now (or at some point prior to the choice) to obtain information that will reveal which option we ought to choose on that future occasion. The question is whether

(1993); Nickerson (2008), p. 140; Nottelmann (2007); Roberts and Wood (2007); E. Sosa (2014), section C; and M. Williams (2008). Many of these theorists are virtue epistemologists.

Among those who deny that epistemic normativity includes a duty to gather information or extends beyond fitting one's belief to the evidence are R. Feldman (2000) and (2002) and Dougherty (2012).

A more nuanced division of possible views about the relation between epistemic and moral duties is offered in Haack (2001).

[11] For discussion of recognition among epistemologists about these conflicts, see Chignell (2013). Of course one additional possible view is that we have a moral obligation to uphold our distinctively epistemic obligations. Chignell discusses this interpretation of W. K. Clifford's position. For Clifford's views, see Clifford (1999).

[12] R. Feldman (2000), section III.

subjectivized codes can accommodate such a duty. Some can—but importantly, some cannot. To see this, let's start by considering how such a duty arises within *objective* codes, codes in which the agent's obligations depend on objective facts about the world, not on what the agent believes about the world.

Consider an agent who must lay off an employee during a financial retrenchment. Claire is a human resources manager, who tomorrow (Tuesday) must lay off one of the employees from her financially stressed company, and who will have a duty to carry out this task in the best manner possible. As of today (Monday) Claire knows relatively little about the two employees, Max and Mina, who are candidates for being laid off. However, she could spend time today gathering accurate information about the employees' length of service, productivity, number of dependents, and so forth, and if she did so, she would have enough information to make a good decision tomorrow. Normally we would think that Claire has a duty to gather this information about the employees before making her decision.

But *why* does Claire have this duty, within an objective moral code, to acquire information? The answer depends on the normative content of the code in question. Consider a code that requires agents to act so as to maximize general human welfare. Suppose Max has fewer dependents than Mina. It would maximize welfare—that is, mitigate negative impact on welfare—for Claire to lay off Max tomorrow. However, suppose that as things are, Claire believes that it would maximize welfare for her to lay off Mina, since she (falsely) believes Mina has fewer dependents. Nonetheless if she investigated she would come to believe (correctly) that it would maximize welfare to lay off Max rather than Mina. Thus, assuming that Claire is disposed to follow this code, it is true that if she investigated, she would subsequently lay off Max rather than Mina. Hence Claire's gathering information in this situation *just is* her maximizing welfare, in virtue of this act's leading to her subsequent act of releasing the employee whose dependents would be least badly affected by losing the job.[13] This example shows that objective welfare-maximizing codes can readily explain the duty to acquire information about one's future acts, because acquiring information is often just a *way* of bringing about the best consequences. Of course this is not always true: sometimes investigations can mislead the investigator and so result in bad consequences over the long run, and sometimes investigations are so costly that the good consequences they would secure do not counterbalance the bad effects they occasion. But even in these cases an objective welfare-maximizing code provides a recommendation that we find appropriate for such a code, precisely because it takes these factors into account in determining whether or not the agent has a duty to investigate before acting.[14] We do

---

[13] On a coarse-grained approach to act-individuation, there is one act which can be described in two different ways, as "gathering information" or as "maximizing welfare." On a fine-grained approach to act-individuation, there are two act tokens, but the token of gathering information generates the token of maximizing welfare, and so inherits its moral status.

[14] Recall that in this chapter we are primarily considering situations in which the agent may have *erroneous* nonmoral beliefs, not situations in which the agent is *uncertain* about the relevant nonmoral facts. Thus

not think, for example, that Claire ought to spend time investigating if doing so would distract her from responding to a law suit that would send her company into bankruptcy. Sometimes, according to a welfare-maximizing code, an agent does not have a duty to investigate.

Note that this discussion assumes that consequentialist theories should be framed in terms of actualism rather than possibilism (where actualism says that our current duty depends on what it would actually lead us to do, while possibilism says that our current duty depends on what it would enable us to do). According to actualistic consequentialism, Claire ought to investigate because doing so *would lead her to* perform the subsequent welfare-maximizing act. Possibilism often seems ill-equipped to generate appropriate duties to gather information before acting. Since Claire (and many other agents faced with a decision whether or not to acquire more information) *already* is able—whether or not she investigates—to do the right thing in the future, namely lay off Max, a possibilistic version of consequentialism would not generate any objective duty for her to investigate. Moreover, as I shall argue later, it makes no difference to an agent's subjectivized duty in a key case whether one analyzes the case in actualist or possibilist terms. For these reasons I will assume consequentialism (and later, deontology) should be phrased in terms of actualism.[15]

The epistemic duties to gather evidence discussed by many epistemologists fit this general consequentialist framework, although the "consequences" of interest are specifically epistemic goods, rather than the more general good of human welfare. Thus we see the following types of proposals discussed (if not necessarily advocated):

P_{E1}. One has a prima facie duty to act in ways that maximize the number of true beliefs and minimize the number of false beliefs.[16]

P_{E2}. One has a prima facie duty to act in ways that lead to knowledge.[17]

I am not addressing the question of how to define the obligation to acquire information when the agent is uncertain about the consequences of her action. However, there is a developed literature on this question. In general, decision theorists argue or assume that gathering information is just like any other act in the sense that one should gather information if and only if it would maximize utility or expected utility (as it may not if the information is costly). For an example, see Jackson (1991), p. 465, and Parfit (2011), pp. 160–1. For a statement of the proof that this is the best decision rule regarding the gathering of more evidence, see Horwich (1982), pp. 125–6.

[15] There is an extensive discussion of actualism vs. possibilism in the literature. For my earlier discussions of these views, see H. Goldman (1976) and (1978). Another influential account is offered by Jackson and Pargetter (1986).

Ben Bronner points out (unpublished seminar note) that the possibilist might try rescuing her position by restating it as "our current duty depends on what it would render us epistemically able to do." This would require a problematic revision of the common underlying assumption that "ought" implies "can" to restrict the ability in question to epistemic ability, and in any case would not address the problem arising for the key case even for possibilists.

[16] See R. Feldman (2002), p. 372; Kornblith (1983), p. 34; and Driver (2000), who states that "A character trait is an intellectual virtue iff it systematically (reliably) produces true belief," p. 126.

[17] R. Feldman (2002), p. 379.

P_{E3}.   One has a prima facie duty to act in ways that lead to justified cognitive attitudes.[18]

P_{E4}.   One has a prima facie duty to act in ways that will lead to accurate and comprehensive beliefs.[19]

Other epistemically desirable consequences might be mentioned as well, such as maximizing understanding.[20] It is clear that if one takes this consequentialist view about the nature of epistemic duties, then a duty to gather information can be considered simply as a special case of fulfilling one of these duties, since gathering additional information will (typically) be a *way* of acting so as to maximize true beliefs and minimize false beliefs, or a way of producing knowledge, or a way of producing justified cognitive attitudes, and so forth. (And in cases where it would not have the desired results, there would be no duty to acquire the information.) Thus, if a *moral* code includes duties modeled after P_{E1}–P_{E4}, the moral code has a ready-made consequentialist technique for explaining the existence of a duty to gather information. For objective consequentialist moral codes, then, it is easy to explain the nature of the duty to acquire additional evidence.

However, the situation is less clear-cut when the objective code incorporates non-welfare-maximizing elements, such as duties to keep promises, to compensate others for past wrongs, and to act justly. Let us call these "deontic duties" (and codes containing them "deontological codes"). Clearly we think that one can have a duty to gather information now in light of one's subsequent deontic duties. Just as one has a duty to investigate in order to ensure that one subsequently acts to maximize welfare, so too, if one has backed one's truck into another person's car, one has a duty to investigate whether one has caused any damage, so that one can fulfill any duty to compensate the car's owner. But although we can understand gathering information as a way of maximizing welfare, and hence as merely a special case of one's duty to maximize welfare, the same approach is not possible in the context of gathering information in order to ensure one fulfills the deontic duties I described. Gathering such information is *not* a way of keeping a promise, or compensating others, or of acting justly.[21] If there

---

[18] R. Feldman (2002), p. 379. See also Baehr (2011), p. 82.   [19] Foley (2010), p. 136.

[20] Roberts and Wood (2007), p. 33. Selim Berker critiques certain "consequentialist" approaches to epistemic duties, most persuasively in Berker (2013).

[21] On a coarse-grained approach to act-individuation, in this case there is no one act which can be described in two different ways, as "gathering information" and as "keeping a promise." Instead, the act of gathering information occurs first, followed by the act of keeping the promise. On a fine-grained approach to act-individuation, there are two act tokens, but they occur on two different act-trees that occur at different points in time. The act-token of gathering information does not generate the token of keeping a promise.

Indeed, in calling these duties "deontic duties," in this context I primarily mean to indicate that these duties are ones about which it is not plausible to say that gathering information that leads to one's fulfilling such a duty *itself counts* as a special case of fulfilling that "deontic" duty. There are, of course, other duties traditionally recognized as "deontic," such as the duty not to injure others or the duty to care for one's elderly parents. However, these duties could arguably be thought of as essentially consequentialist in

is a duty to gather information in connection with these duties, a different account of it must be given.

Suppose Claire's moral code doesn't require her to maximize welfare in selecting which employee to lay off, but instead requires her to act justly in making this decision. In particular it stipulates that justice requires someone in Claire's position to first lay off those employees who are least productive. Mina is the least productive employee, so Claire will act justly only if she releases Mina. However, Claire falsely believes Max to be the least productive employee, so if she doesn't gather any additional information, she will lay off Max. On the other hand, if she were to gather more information, she would come to believe that Mina is the least productive employee, and act justly by laying her off instead of Max.

Under this code, should Claire gather information before deciding whom to lay off? The question becomes one of whether such a code contains a special rule requiring agents to gather information before they make such a decision. Of course, one possibility is that the code contains no such rule. In that case, Claire and others like her have no duty to acquire information. Since such a code would clearly be highly deficient, an adequate code of this sort must incorporate a special rule requiring information to be gathered before taking action that may be just or unjust. What would be the *content* of such a rule? Some theorists, grappling with this issue, have tried to formulate such a duty as a free-standing deontic duty to gather information: free-standing in the sense that it is not defined or justified in terms of the consequences of gathering information for the agent's subsequent choice. Thus (if we convert Prichard's remarks about a subjectivized code into remarks about an objective code) Prichard suggests that

P_{M1}.   One has a prima facie duty to consider the circumstances as fully as one can.[22]

character—the first is a duty not to produce a certain kind of consequence, namely harm to another person (or harm that the person could reasonably reject), while the second is a duty to ensure one's elderly parents have sufficient shelter, food, affection, medical care, etc. Hence the duty to acquire information in order to ensure one fulfills the duty not to injure others, or the duty to care for one's elderly parents, could potentially be analyzed in the same way that we analyzed the duty to acquire information in order to ensure one fulfills the duty to maximize general human welfare. On such an analysis, one has the duty to acquire this information because acquiring the information is a *way* of not harming another person, or a way of caring for one's parents. Admittedly, this analysis is something of a stretch. However, to ensure that we are discussing the duty to acquire information in connection with fulfilling pure deontic duties that can't be conceptualized as types of consequentialist duties, I am restricting my attention to the examples in the text. Almost all deontological theories recognize such duties, so some way of dealing with the acquisition of information relevant to them must be found. If the duty not to harm and the duty to care for one's elderly parents are at core non-consequentialist, then they would fall under the same analysis as the more clear-cut deontic duties to keep promises, etc.

[22] Prichard (1968), p. 27. Making a similar suggestion, Gigerenzer and Goldstein (1999) describe the following "commandment" as characteristic of rational judgment: "Thou shalt find all the information available" (p. 83). In the same vein Chignell (2013) discusses the epistemic norm to "gather as much evidence as possible."

If we convert Ross's remarks on this question to a suggestion about an objective code, we may interpret him as advising that

P_{M2}. One has a prima facie duty to investigate the circumstances relevant to an upcoming duty until either (a) one must act because time has run out, or (b) one has reached the point where no further consideration would enable one to judge better of the circumstances relevant to the duty.[23]

More recently Gideon Rosen has asserted that "We are under an array of standing obligations to inform ourselves about matters relevant to the moral permissibility of our conduct: to look around, to reflect, to seek advice, and so on." He notes that "The content of this obligation varies massively from case to case," and gives as an example "I am under an obligation to look out for other people when I'm out walking."[24] We could construe this advice as follows:

P_{M3}. One has a great variety of prima facie obligations to inform oneself about matters relevant to the moral permissibility of one's future conduct, such as an obligation to look out for other people when one is out walking.

Let us review these proposals, construing them as descriptions of duties that can be defined or justified without reference to their impact on the agent's subsequent actions or states. One virtue of these proposed duties is that an agent who lacks significant information about his upcoming act would nonetheless (in principle) be able to follow a free-standing rule to decide whether or not to gather more information about his prospective act. But a review of the proposed rules suggests they are uniformly ill-conceived. They are ill-conceived precisely because they interpret the duty to gather information as free-standing. Considering the circumstances as fully as one can, as Prichard suggests, may lead one to spend unnecessary time and effort on this endeavor, since one may already have enough information to incline one to perform what is one's subsequent duty, or one may obtain such information with very little effort, or further investigations won't improve one's information, or will even degrade it. Investigating until time has run out, as Ross suggests, has the same defects. Ross's suggestion that one should gather information to the point where no further consideration would enable one to judge better of the circumstances relevant to the duty is more promising. But it too may be misguided. There is an ambiguity in what Ross means by "judge better of the circumstances." If he means "gather information until one has achieved a true opinion about the matter," then this may be an impossible task, because there may be no available information that would lead to a true opinion.[25] If he means "gather information until no further consideration would render one better *justified* in one's

---

[23] W. Ross (1939), p. 57.   [24] Rosen (2002), p. 63.
[25] Ben Bronner suggests (in an unpublished seminar note) that the prima facie duty to "gather information until one has achieved a true opinion about the matter" should be qualified by adding the phrase "if possible." But if achieving a true opinion is not possible, it then becomes unclear what the agent is supposed to do—perhaps nothing, which seems contrary to the spirit of Ross's proposal.

opinion," then it is not clear why one should expend the effort to achieve maximum justification, when (even if there are no conflicting prima facie duties) less effort might lead one to the same belief about the matter, or when less effort might render one less well-justified but with a more accurate opinion (since one can be well-justified in believing a falsehood). Nothing inherent in Ross's description of this duty provides any guidance about what to do in cases where one should not aim at maximum justification. And Rosen's suggestion that a proper deontic code would include a raft of substantive rules to carry out certain kinds of investigations in different types of circumstances doesn't provide us what we need unless the *content* of those rules can be specified, a difficult challenge that Rosen doesn't undertake. Thus having a duty to "look out for people when one is out walking" may be reasonable when one is walking on a crowded street, but not reasonable when walking on a mountain trail little trafficked by other hikers.[26]

Some theorists have suggested that there are many specific evidence-gathering duties that are attached to roles or jobs people occupy.[27] Thus a surgeon has a duty to double-check which arm of his patient is diseased before performing an amputation and a cashier has a duty to check a customer's signature before accepting her credit card. Such investigatory duties are often spelled out in institutional rules adopted to ensure that people occupying certain positions will secure the information they (or others) need in order to carry out their other duties effectively. But not all decisions whether to gather evidence are made by people insofar as they occupy one of these role-based positions, and we need to define the more general deontic duty to acquire information that applies in these broader circumstances. Rosen seems to be attempting this task, but his suggestions fall short.

Lacking adequate suggestions from moral philosophers for free-standing deontic duties to gather information, we might turn to epistemologists for guidance. Indeed,

---

I am assuming that on this objective version of Ross's moral theory, the duty to gather information would be a prima facie duty. If not, the stricture to gather information to the point where no further consideration would enable one to judge better of the circumstances suffers another fatal defect, namely that carrying out such an investigation may involve neglecting some other and more important duty in order to acquire information relevant to an upcoming trivial duty. On the other hand, if the duty to gather information is merely a prima facie duty, it is difficult to see how the *strength* of such a duty could be settled without reference to the consequences (at least for one's subsequent duties) of following or not following it, and this would necessitate importing considerations about the impact of following the duty on one's future actions, making it no longer a free-standing deontic duty.

[26] No doubt a theorist attempting to define the free-standing duty to acquire information could try to formulate a suite of such rules, each rule designed to be used in a different situation. But then the question would arise why *these* rules rather than others? It appears that answering this question would either involve moving to a type of rule consequentialism (these rules would tend to produce the best consequences), or a type of rule-deontology in which the rules are adopted because they do the best job of leading adherents to carry out their subsequent duties. The former rationale abandons deontology for a form of consequentialism, while the latter imports a version of the derivative deontological rationale for gathering information that I advocate later in the chapter.

[27] This was suggested to me by members of an audience at Fordham University and by an anonymous referee for *Ethics*. Foley (2010) discusses it on p. 138.

a number of epistemologists have discussed the duty to gather evidence as such a free-standing, non-consequentialist duty. Suggestions gleaned from this literature would include the following proposals:

P_{E5}. For any proposition P, time t, and person S, if P is less than certain for S at t, then S has a prima facie duty at t to gather additional evidence concerning P.[28]

P_{E6}. If S is unjustified in believing P, then S has a prima facie duty to gather additional evidence regarding P.[29]

P_{E7}. S has a prima facie duty to gather additional evidence regarding P if (a) P is important, or (b) there is a strong likelihood of S's gaining additional evidence, or (c) the evidence that S would gain would conflict with S's current evidence.[30]

P_{E8}. One has prima facie duties to be inquisitive, attentive, careful and thorough in inquiry, open-minded, and fair-minded.[31]

P_{E9}. One has a prima facie duty to use one's cognitive faculties carefully and in appropriate ways, where the standards of "appropriateness" are implicit in community practices.[32]

Examination of these proposals, however, shows that they suffer the same weaknesses as the proposals from moral philosophy. For example, P_{E8} and P_{E9} sound plausible, but give no precise guidance regarding when, or on what kinds of occasions, and how energetically one should seek additional evidence.[33] P_{E5} and P_{E6} have the same problems as Prichard's and Ross's suggestions: they claim there is a prima facie duty to

---

[28] R. Feldman (2002), p. 370. Feldman suggests this as one interpretation of what Clifford had in mind in "The Ethics of Belief."

[29] R. Feldman (2002), p. 371. There is an interesting relationship between this principle and the kinds of principles proposed by epistemologists who advocate what is often called "pragmatic encroachment" views about knowledge. For example, Hawthorne and Stanley (2008) defend the "Action-Knowledge Principle," according to which one should treat the proposition that p as a reason for acting only if one knows that p (p. 577). They further argue that whether or not a given doxastic state counts as knowledge depends partly on the stakes at issue. Thus someone for whom not much is at stake can be said to know, on the basis of fairly casual evidence, that the bank will be open on Saturday, whereas someone to whom it makes a major financial difference would not be said to know the bank will be open on Saturday, even though she may have exactly the same evidence as the first person (pp. 571 and 576). An anonymous referee for *Ethics* suggests that from Hawthorne and Stanley's principle one might infer a further principle, namely that "If one is going to use p as a reason for acting, one must investigate until or unless one knows that p." Taken by itself as a principle to be used in the context of an objective deontological moral theory, this principle suffers the same defect as P_{E5} and P_{E6}—it ascribes invariant value to acquiring knowledge about p, whether or not knowledge is obtainable, however much or little difference knowledge of p might make to S's future action, and however important that future action is. However, it seems reasonable to speculate that a pragmatic encroachment theorist would stipulate that how much investigation is required (in order for the agent to count as having achieved knowledge about p) would vary depending on the moral seriousness of the agent's future action. On this pragmatic interpretation, the proposed principle begins to look very much like the one I will advocate, Principle P_{OD}.

[30] R. Feldman (2002), p. 371.

[31] This is adapted from a list of intellectual virtues in Baehr (2011), p. 89.

[32] McKinnon (2003), pp. 249–50.

[33] A number of virtue ethicists address this problem by stating that the details of any duty to seek more evidence must be discerned through the use of "practical wisdom." (See, for example, Roberts and Wood (2007), p. 78, and more generally Chapter 12.) Unfortunately this provides us with little substantive guidance.

gather additional evidence whether or not doing so will lead to the agent's being in a better epistemic state, or how important it is to be in that state. P_{E7} attempts to address this kind of problem by restricting the duty to gather evidence to occasions when the proposition in question is important, or there is likelihood of gaining such evidence, or if the evidence would be epistemically valuable relative to the agent's current epistemic state. But again, too much is left up in the air for this "duty" to be apt. How important must the proposition be? How likely must it be that new evidence will be gained? How epistemically valuable must the likely new evidence be?

Scrutiny of all these proposed free-standing duties to seek information reveals that either they provide poor advice, or provide insufficiently detailed advice. On reflection it seems clear that what a deontologist should want is a duty to gather information designed so that the agent who fulfills this duty will then be able to fulfill her subsequent substantive obligations. The proposed duties we have examined fall short of this goal. They fail to clarify that this is the goal of the duties they describe, and it seems clear that the duties they describe do not take into account enough factors to ensure that satisfying the duty in question would be effective in achieving the goal.

The most natural way to frame the duty to acquire information in a manner that takes this aim into account is for the code to incorporate a duty to gather information just in case doing so would lead the agent subsequently to satisfy any deontic duty incumbent on him at that later time to keep his promise, compensate others, or act justly. Let us call this non-free-standing duty a "derivative" duty to gather information, since the fact that it is a duty derives from the subsequent duties it would lead the agent to satisfy. This duty will of course be a prima facie duty, since it may conflict with, and sometimes be overridden by, other more stringent duties incumbent on the agent.

If Claire's code included such a derivative duty, Claire would have a prima facie duty to gather information about her employees on Monday so that she would act justly in choosing on Tuesday which employee to lay off. It appears that a code containing a derivative duty of the sort described can provide an acceptable account of duties to gather information, precisely because it suitably grounds the duty to acquire information on the effects of the agent's fulfilling this duty on her carrying out her subsequent deontic duties.

However, such a derivative duty must be somewhat more nuanced than this. Although we have focused on cases in which the agent has the option of gathering information at time t_1 to inform her decision at later time t_2, real life is more complex than this. Sometimes, for example, the information gathered at t_1 will be useful to more than one decision to be taken later on. Thus a prosecutor might gather information at t_1 in order to inform his decision at t_2 about whether to bring charges against an alleged law-breaker, but also to inform his subsequent decision at t_3 about what penalty to recommend if the defendant is found guilty. Moreover, these subsequent duties may have different degrees of stringency that may sometimes need to be weighed against each other. To accommodate these facts, let us introduce the notion of the "deontic weight" of different deontic duties. The deontic weight of an act expresses the weight, or stringency, of the duty to perform (or not to perform) an act of that type (or, in other terminology, the force of the moral reason to perform or not to perform that action).[34] Thus the deontic weight of saving a person's life is greater than the deontic weight of keeping a minor promise. In determining what one ought all-things-considered to do, one considers the deontic weight of the various (sometimes conflicting) duties involved. If one has to choose between saving a life versus keeping a minor promise, one ought all-things-considered to save the life, since the deontic weight of this act is greater than the deontic weight of keeping the promise. This concept would need further refinement to support certain kinds of constraints that are often built into deontic theories, such as the constraint that it would be all-things-considered wrong for me now to violate my duty not to kill a person even if killing the person ensures that you (or I myself) kill fewer people in the future. Since issues raised by these kinds of constraints are not implicated by the questions of this chapter, I shall not attempt to refine the concept of deontic weight in order to reflect them.[35]

Using the notion of deontic weight, we are in a position to accept the following:

P_{OD}.   An agent has an objective derivative prima facie duty to acquire information if and only if doing so would lead the agent subsequently to produce the maximum possible amount of deontic weight (typically through his carrying out the various deontic duties that would later be incumbent on him).[36]

---

[34] Prohibitions and permissions, as well as obligations, have deontic weights.
I shall use the concept of deontic weight as it plays a role in comparing the relative weights of different moral obligations (or permissions or prohibitions). However, we should note that the importance, or deontic weight, assigned by a code to a given principle may also play a role in determining whether complying with that principle takes precedence over fulfilling some conflicting nonmoral requirement, e.g., a requirement of prudence. I shall assume that if one moral principle has greater deontic weight than a second moral principle, it also has greater weight than the second principle when compared to a nonmoral requirement, such as a norm of prudence. For moral theories in which there is only one principle (such as act utilitarianism), the deontic weight of the principle is primarily of use in balancing it against nonmoral considerations, and in comparing the importance of complying with the moral principle as compared with the importance of complying with a moral principle from a different moral theory.

[35] The notion of this sort of "deontic weight" has been recognized, implicitly or explicitly, by a number of authors, and has often been in the background of discussions about actualism vs. possibilism, and about the possibility of representing deontological theories as consequentialist theories with distinctive values. See H. Goldman (1976); Nozick (1974), unnumbered footnote on p. 29; Jackson and Smith (2006); Huemer (2010); Kagan (1988); Dreier (1993); Broome (1991), Chapter 1; Lockhart (2000), pp. 80–97; and J. Ross (2006), pp. 754–5. Taking a slightly different approach, Portmore (2011) defines an act's "deontic moral value" as "a measure of how much [objective] moral reason there is to perform it" on p. 19, n. 36. Some theorists doubt that a concept of quantified deontic weight can be devised that appropriately reflects apparent breakdowns of transitivity (see Temkin 2012) or reflects special deontological features, such as absolute precedence of some duties over any number of violations of lesser duties, agent-centered options, supererogatory acts, or the self-other asymmetry (terminology from Portmore, p. 8). I believe the jury is still out on this question. One of the lessons of this chapter is that a deontologist who rejects the notion of "deontic weight" will be very hard-pressed to define a suitable duty to acquire information before acting. I am grateful to Nick Beckstead for reminding me of the importance of the approach using "deontic weight."

[36] Suppose an agent has two alternatives at t_1, investigatory acts A and B. Performing A would lead to his subsequently performing a just act, while performing B would lead to his subsequently keeping his promise. We might conceive of the agent as having *two* prima facie derivative duties to investigate at t_1—a prima

This derivative duty is still merely prima facie, since it might conflict with, and even be outweighed by, a stronger duty to carry out some other deontic obligation at the very time the agent would investigate. For example, the only way to gather information may involve torturing an innocent person, and so violate the more important duty not to torture. According to P_{OD}, Claire has a derivative duty to seek information on Monday before she releases one of the employees on Tuesday, since her seeking this information would lead to her successfully carrying out her later duty to act justly when she makes the lay-off decision.

Our tentative conclusion should be that objective moral codes including duties to maximize welfare, keep promises, compensate others for past wrongs, and act justly, can include normatively appropriate duties to gather information. In the case of the duty to maximize welfare, the duty to gather information that will lead to one's maximizing

facie derivative duty to do A, and a prima facie derivative duty to do B. However, for simplicity of exposition, I am conceiving of the structure of the derivative duty so that the agent has *only one* prima facie derivative duty at t_1, namely the "cumulative" prima facie duty to do whichever of A or B would produce the *maximum* deontic weight at the later time.

This definition of the derivative objective duty to seek information is an actualistic one. One could propose a possibilist version as well: such a duty would require the agent to seek information if doing so would *enable* her to carry out her subsequent duties. However, just as we saw before in Claire's case, she is able to carry out her subsequent duty to act justly by laying off the least productive employee *whether or not she investigates*. Thus the possibilist version would impose no duty to investigate on her. Since this is counterintuitive, I shall maintain the actualist version.

A referee for H. Smith (2014) questioned the truth of P_{OD} in light of the following case: Jim, a demolition engineer, has an obligation to see whether anyone is in the Fairlake Apartment Building, because he is going to demolish the building. In investigating the interior of the building, he sees his partner having an affair. This leads Jim to commit suicide, leaving his younger orphaned sister to fend for herself, violating both a promise he made to his parents to watch out for her, and a familial duty he had to care for her. In fact, at the time Jim would have demolished the building, everyone would already have vacated. The referee contended that it is plausible that (a) Jim had a prima facie duty to investigate the interior of the building, and (b) Jim had an all-things-considered obligation to investigate the building, and (c) investigating did not maximize deontic weight. He concluded that duty P_{OD} I describe in the text isn't correct. However, although I agree with all of (a), (b), and (c), I don't agree the case shows P_{OD} to be mistaken. The case is a complex one, with a number of factors influencing how we assess Jim's action. For one thing, our intuition that Jim has a duty to investigate may heavily reflect our sense that Jim would be blameworthy for not investigating, given that he couldn't possibly foresee the actual consequences of his investigating. It's often hard to separate one's intuitions about what is objectively obligatory from what is blameworthy. (Recent research has shown that information about blameless transgressions distorts people's description of the agent's conduct. When an agent has blamelessly broken a rule, half the subjects deny a rule was even broken. See Turri and Blouw (2015).) Second, the case raises the possibility that the derivative duty to investigate should exclude subsequent duty-fulfillments that arise through what are sometimes called "deviant causal chains." (It is only by a deviant causal chain, not the normal causal chain we expect to link action to consequences, that Jim's investigation leads to his subsequent violations of his promises.) This is an interesting possibility that I will not try to explore here. Third, I think that Jim's duty to investigate arises from an independent source, namely his role-based obligations as a professional demolitions contractor. The duty I characterize in the text is only meant to be a *derivative* prima facie duty that arises from the way in which the agent's investigating would or would not affect his fulfillment of his subsequent duties. Such duties can conflict with other kinds of duties and sometimes be outweighed by them. Thus in this case Jim's prima facie derivative duty not to investigate may be outweighed by his role-based duty to investigate. Finally, the case may provide evidence that the deontic duty to investigate should be time-centered.

The case also reveals the built-in weakness of role-based institutional obligations: they must be framed to deal with what is most likely, and so sometimes cannot correctly handle actual cases.

welfare is just a special case of the duty to maximize welfare. In the case of the deontic duties, the duty to gather information relevant to these duties is a specially defined *derivative* prima facie duty that requires one to gather information when doing so ensures that one will maximize the weight of one's subsequent deontic duties.

5.5 The Duty to Acquire Information: Subjectivized Moral Theories

I have charted out ways in which both objective consequentialist and deontological theories can successfully define a duty to acquire information before making a subsequent morally significant choice. But our main focus of interest is *subjectivized* moral codes, not *objective* ones. Given our conclusions about the ways in which objective codes can incorporate satisfactory duties to gather information, what can be said about subjectivized codes?

5.5.1 *The duty to gather information in subjectivized welfare-maximizing codes*

Let's look first at the kind of subjectivized code that characterizes an agent's duties relevant to welfare-maximization. It appears such a subjectivized consequentialist code can readily explain why we have a duty to do what we *believe* would be gathering information. According to such a code, our general duty is to do what *we believe* would maximize welfare.[37] Suppose Claire realizes that she has no relevant beliefs about whether laying off Mina or Max would maximize welfare—she doesn't have beliefs about their dependents, their alternative job prospects, and so on. She believes, therefore, that if she makes the lay-off decision with no more than her current information she may fail to maximize welfare. She also believes that if she spends the afternoon acquiring relevant information, she will obtain it, and will come to have true beliefs about which employee would be least badly affected by being laid off, and that she will then choose to do what she believes to be maximizing welfare when she makes the eventual decision. Thinking this about herself, she will believe that gathering information will itself maximize welfare. Assuming she believes she has a duty to do what she believes will maximize welfare, she will conclude that she has a duty to do what she believes is gathering this information. In cases such as this, because doing what the agent believes is gathering information is a *way* of doing what the agent believes to be maximizing welfare, it follows that she has a duty to do it on a subjectivized welfare-maximizing code. Of course sometimes the agent will believe that gathering information would *not* lead to maximizing welfare (for example, when she believes that gathering information is too costly or would be fruitless), and then she will have no duty on this

---

[37] Recall that we are not considering cases in which the agent may be (and may remain) uncertain what the consequences of her actions would be, and so, arguably, has a duty to do what she believes would maximize the chance of maximizing welfare, or would maximize subjective expected welfare.

code to gather information. But, as we saw before, this is as it should be: even on an objective code, the consequentialist duty to gather information is not absolute, but depends on what would be achieved by doing so. A subjectivized welfare-maximizing code reflects this in saying that the duty to do what one believes is gathering information is not absolute, but depends on what the agent believes would be achieved by doing so.

5.5.2 *The duty to gather information in subjectivized codes that include deontic duties: free-standing duties*

Since it appears there is no problem incorporating a plausible duty to gather information into a subjectivized welfare-maximizing code, let us turn our attention to the question of whether subjectivized codes involving what I'm calling "deontic duties," such as the duties to keep promises, compensate others, and act justly, can incorporate a suitable duty to gather information. I will examine two different ways in which this might be done, and argue that neither of them deliver the kind of duty to gather information that we believe is appropriate.

The first approach to defining such a subjectivized duty to gather information (suggested by the parallel approach to the objective duty) would be to characterize this duty as a free-standing duty, *not* defined by reference to the effect that the agent believes satisfying this duty would have on her fulfillment of her subsequent deontic duties. But reasoning similar to our previous deliberations about objective free-standing duties to gather information suggests it is unlikely that the strategy of invoking such a free-standing duty will generate a normatively acceptable subjectivized duty. Just as any acceptable *objective* duty to gather information must take into account the consequences of gathering information on the agent's subsequent actions, so any acceptable *subjectivized* duty to gather information must take into account the consequences the agent *believes* the act would have on her later actions. The kinds of free-standing duties to gather information suggested by Prichard, Ross, Rosen, and various epistemologists, when translated into subjectivized terms, fail this test. For example, a subjectivized duty to do what you believe is considering the circumstances as fully as you can is not a satisfactory account of this duty. Why should you do what you believe is considering the circumstances as fully as you can, when you believe that doing so will commit you to spending far more effort in gathering information than is necessary in order to arrive at the truth? Similarly, a subjectivized duty to do what you believe is investigating until you believe your time has run out is not an appropriate duty. How could such a duty be justified in a case in which you believe that fulfilling it would bring you no closer to the truth, or would lead you astray? Similarly there is little to be said for a subjectivized duty to do what you believe is investigating until you have reached the point where you believe that no further consideration would enable you to judge better of the circumstances. Why should you do this, if you believe that doing what you believe to be investigating until you have reached the point of being maximally justified would not change your opinion from the opinion you would have achieved at an earlier stage?

Or why should you do this, if you believe that no matter how much you investigate, you will never reach the truth of the matter? Finally, we have no substantive proposal for what the content should be of a Rosen-type array of standing specific subjectivized investigatory duties, such as the duty to do what one believes is looking out for people when one is out walking. Similar criticisms can be made of subjectivized analogs to the epistemologists' proposals P_{E5}–P_{E9}. Thus trying to define a subjectivized duty to gather information as a free-standing duty appears to be the same blind alley that it was in trying to define an objective duty to gather information.

5.5.3 The duty to gather information in subjectivized codes that include deontic duties: derivative duties

Since the first "free-standing" duty approach to defining the subjectivized duty to gather information relevant to deontic duties appears wrong-headed, let us turn to a second approach. Modeled after the second approach to defining the objective duty to gather information relevant to deontic duties, this approach defines the subjectivized duty to gather information as a *derivative* duty. As we saw before, this derivative duty must reflect the fact that the agent may believe that her informing herself now may have an impact on her carrying out multiple deontic duties at later times, and that these duties may have different degrees of stringency. In light of this, we can propose the following:

> P_{SD}.   An agent has a derivative prima facie subjectivized duty to do what he believes is acquiring information if and only if he believes that doing what he believes is gathering information would lead him subsequently to produce the maximum amount of deontic weight (typically through his doing what he then believes to be carrying out the various deontic duties that would then be incumbent on him).

Just as in the case of objective duty, this appears to be a natural way to define the derivative subjectivized deontic duty to gather information.[38] It, too, is merely a prima facie duty, since even when the agent believes that gathering information itself would lead him to subsequently produce the maximize amount of deontic weight, he may also realize that the process of gathering information may simultaneously violate some more important deontic duty (such as the duty not to engage in what he believes is torture).

---

[38] Guerrero (2007) considers at some length what duties an agent has to inform herself before performing a morally significant act. He adopts what he calls "modest moral epistemic contextualism," stated as follows: "How much one is morally required to do from an epistemic point of view with regard to investigating some proposition p varies depending on the moral context—on what actions one's belief in p (or absence of belief in p) will license or be used to justify, morally in some particular context" (p. 70). This appears to be a statement of something very much like my P_{SD}, except that one can interpret it as phrased in terms of what the agent would reasonably believe after he investigates rather than in terms of what the agent would believe *simpliciter*. Guerrero means his principle to be a *moral* requirement to engage in certain epistemic activities.

To see how this approach would work, suppose that Claire, the human resources manager tasked with laying off an employee, is governed by the following subjectivized Code C, which includes a prima facie deontic duty to do what the agent believes to be laying off employees justly and a derivative prima facie duty to do what the agent believes to be gathering information before acting.[39] Justice will be best served by doing what the agent believes to be laying off the least productive employee, but in a case of employees who are all tied for minimum productivity, or a case in which the manager does not know which employee is least productive, the second-best solution called for is to lay off the person the agent believes to be the most recently *hired* employee.

Code C:

(1)   When an agent believes she has been tasked to lay off employees in light of a financial retrenchment, the agent ought prima facie either to

(a)   do what she believes to be laying off an employee if she believes that person to be the least productive employee, or

(b)   do what she believes to be laying off the most recently hired employee if she does not believe of any employee that he or she is the least productive employee.

(2)   When an agent believes she has the opportunity to gather information relevant to a subsequent duty, then the agent ought prima facie to do what she believes to be gathering relevant information before fulfilling her subsequent duties if and only if she believes that doing so would subsequently lead her to produce the maximum amount of deontic weight.[40]

Code C contains an apparently plausible subjectivized derived prima facie duty to do what the agent believes to be gathering information relevant to her subsequent deontic duties. But does such a code impose *actual* appropriate duties to acquire information? Would agents governed by Code C ever be obligated—even prima facie—to gather information? To see the answer to this, we need to assign deontic weights to Claire's carrying out, or violating, her various substantive deontic duties. Let's assume that the duty she would have to select the most recently hired employee for lay-off if she doesn't believe of any employee that he or she is least productive constitutes a lesser form of justice than her duty to lay off an employee whom she believes to be least productive—it provides a second-best solution.[41] Thus fulfilling this duty has less deontic weight than

---

[39] For simplicity in presenting this case, I am assuming that Code C contains no duty to maximize welfare.

[40] For brevity I have not stated the obvious clauses governing when seeking information would be wrong or merely be permissible. To avoid an overly cumbersome formulation of this code, I have left out some of the "what she believes to be" clauses.

[41] This assumption may or may not be plausible. But to establish the points to be made in connection with this case, we need an example in which the duty that would arise if the agent failed to investigate is a less weighty duty, and I shall assume it is true in this case.

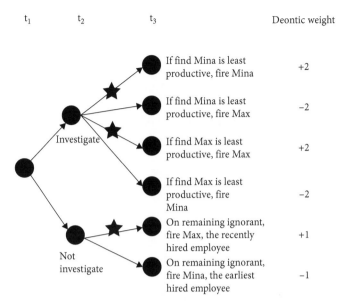

Figure 5.1

fulfilling the duty to lay off the least productive employee. After we plug in plausible numbers for the deontic weights of her acts, Figure 5.1 represents Claire's options.[42]

In this case, Claire currently doesn't have any beliefs about *which* employee is least productive, although she (correctly) believes that one of them is more productive than the other. Let us assume she believes that Max is the most recently hired employee. Claire truly believes that if she does what she believes is gathering information she will come to accurately believe of one of the employees that he or she is least productive, whereas if she does what she believes to be omitting to gather information, she will continue not to believe of any employee that he or she is least productive. If she gathers information, she will have a subsequent duty (by clause 1(a) of Code C) to do what she believes to be laying off the least productive employee, whereas if she omits to gather information, she will have a subsequent duty (by clause 1(b)) to lay off Max, whom she believes to be the most recently hired employee. (The stars in Figure 5.1 represent which choice Claire would actually make, depending on what information she has at t_2 after she either investigates or fails to investigate.) Claire truly believes that she will carry out whichever of these subsequent duties is incumbent upon her.

From this diagram we can see that Code C tells Claire to do what she believes to be gathering information, since she believes that her doing so will create a duty either to

---

[42] To avoid over-counting in calculating whether or not Claire has a derivative duty to investigate, I have assigned investigating (and not investigating) no deontic weights of their own in this figure. Once it is established whether or not there is a prima facie derivative duty to investigate, that action would have to be assigned a deontic weight (arising from this derivative duty) in order to weigh this against other potentially conflicting duties.

lay Mina off or to lay Max off (depending on what she discovers about their productivity), either of which has a weight of +2 when she carries it out. By contrast, she believes that doing what she believes to be not gathering information will create a weaker duty to lay off Max (whom she believes to be the most recently hired employee) merely having weight of +1 when she carries it out. (Note that if she fails to investigate, she then has no duty to do what she believes to be laying off the least productive employee.) She can maximize deontic weight by doing what she believes to be gathering information, and according to clause 2 of Code C this is what she should do. This is indeed the duty we want to ascribe to Claire in this situation; she should do what she believes to be gathering information. Thus this approach to the subjectivized duty to gather information seems to ascribe the duty to gather information in a normatively appropriate way in Claire's case.

5.5.4 A problem for this approach, and the solution

But further reflection reveals a problem for this approach. Claire's Code C is a subjectivized code. This means that her actions at t_2 of investigating (or not investigating) *create* her later duties at t_3, since what duty she has at t_3 depends on what she believes at t_3, and what she believes at t_3 in turn depends on whether or not she has investigated at t_2. Her doing-what-she-believes-to-be-investigating at t_2 creates a duty at t_3 to do-what-she-believes-to-be-laying-off-the-least-productive-employee, while her doing-what-she-believes-to-be-not-investigating at t_2 creates a later duty at t_3 to do what-she-believes-to-be-laying-off-the-most-recently-hired-employee. Code C implies that she ought to do-what-she-believes-to-be-investigating at t_2 because that will create a more weighty duty (worth +2 rather than a mere +1) which she will then fulfill at t_3. But is it really true that one should act so as to create a weightier duty for oneself which one would then carry out, as opposed to creating a less weighty duty for oneself which one would then carry out? This assumption lies behind our "derivative duty" approach to the duty to gather information, but I believe it is mistaken.

We can get some grip on this question by considering promises, which are one prominent way, even under an objective moral theory, that a person can create duties for herself. *If there is no independent moral reason to make any promise,* should one make a weightier promise as opposed to making a less weighty promise? Suppose Devon receives two email messages: one from Kate, who asks Devon to take care of Kate's cat next week while she is on vacation, and one from Fred, who asks Devon to take care of his goldfish next week while he is on vacation. Both friends say that if Devon can't do it, they can find another equally competent caretaker. On the other hand, if he promises, then the pet will only be fed if Devon himself does it. Should Devon make a promise to take care of Kate's cat, rather than make a promise to take care of Fred's goldfish, because the duty he would create to take care of the cat would be a *weightier duty* (weightier because it would be worse if he fails to carry out the promise) than the duty he would create to take care of the goldfish? This doesn't seem right: given that someone else would ensure that each creature would be cared for if Devon doesn't make the promise, there is no more reason for him to promise to take care of the cat than to promise to take care of the fish just because it would be more important to carry out the first duty (if it came into existence) than to carry out the second duty (if it came into existence).

In earlier work I argued that it is counterintuitive to judge that someone like Devon ought to promise to take care of the cat rather than the goldfish because it would give rise to a weightier duty, and that it is even more counterintuitive, in certain kinds of cases, to be forced to conclude, on the basis of the positive weight that keeping a promise would add, that an agent has a duty to make a promise that would convert an otherwise wrongful act into an obligatory one. I then presented an extended argument that the best way to avoid these counterintuitive implications is to hold that, while breaking a promise has negative weight, keeping a promise has *no positive weight*—no value above and beyond what the promised act would have had if it had not been promised.[43] On this view there is reason to avoid breaking a promise and also a reason to avoid breaking a weightier promise rather than breaking a conflicting lesser promise. However, there is no obligation to *make* a weightier promise as opposed to a weaker promise, assuming one would keep whichever promise one made. Of course, there might be other, non-deontic reasons to make and then keep a weightier promise, but the fact that one promise is weightier than another does not *in itself* provide reason to make it. And, since breaking a promise has negative weight, this negative weight may imply that one ought not to make that promise in the first place. Thus suppose that if Devon promised to take care of the cat, he would then fail to do so, whereas if he promised to take care of the goldfish, he would carry out this duty. Since we ascribe negative weight to Devon's violation of his duty to care for the cat (even if we don't ascribe positive weight to his keeping his promise), in this case we can see that Devon ought to promise to take care of the goldfish, and then ought to do so, even though his possible duty to take care of the cat would be a weightier duty than his possible duty to take care of the goldfish.[44]

---

[43] H. Smith (1997). To aid understanding I will represent the fact that an act of fulfilling a created duty receives "no positive weight" by assigning it a weight of 0. This number, along with other weight numbers ascribed to acts, could be interpreted as measures on an interval scale, in which case the 0 is arbitrary. The point is not that we ascribe any particular numerical weight, such as 0, to the act that fulfills a created duty, but rather that our ascribed weight to this act is the same weight the act would receive if it were a morally neutral act.

Tom Hurka has pointed out to me that A. C. Ewing also claimed that promises should be treated asymmetrically, with the agent receiving no positive credit for keeping a promise, but negative credit for violating one. See Ewing (1939), pp. 9–10. In the same vein Kagan (2005), pp. 16–17, explores whether a person's getting what she deserves is a positive good or just the absence of a bad. See also Anderson (1996), p. 542, who says of agents acting under a deontological theory, "...they do not take as their reason for action...[the] thought that it is good to promote states of affairs in which commitments are fulfilled. This thought would, incoherently, encourage them to make commitments willy-nilly, just so that more commitment fulfillments can exist in the world."

[44] In a critical article Conee (2000) rejects this asymmetrical view about the values of keeping and breaking promises. But he does this at the price of denying that *either* keeping or breaking promises has any intrinsic deontic weight; on his view, the values that promise-keeping and promise-breaking might have

The problems encountered by ascribing positive weight to keeping a promise arise because in making the promise *one creates a new duty*. If we hold that one has a duty to create a new duty in order to garner positive weight from subsequently fulfilling the newly created duty, we run into the kind of difficulties described in Devon's case. There are other kinds of cases as well in which a person's action may create a duty, which the person would then fulfill, but we don't conclude the person ought to create the duty just so that he would act rightly in fulfilling it. Thus if a man impregnates a woman, he creates a duty to provide child care and support. Even if he would carry out this duty, we don't conclude from this that he has a prima facie duty to impregnate the woman and create the subsequent duty for himself. Similarly a driver might back her truck into a car, thus creating a duty to compensate the car's owner. Even if she would carry out this subsequent duty, we don't conclude from this that she has a prima facie duty to back her truck into the car and create the subsequent duty for herself. The lesson from these cases is that there is no positive weight to satisfying a created duty, but only negative weight to violating such a duty.[45] While it is tempting to suppose that one has a deontic duty to create duties and then fulfill them in order to maximize deontic weight, in fact this temptation must be resisted if we are to avoid counterintuitive implications in cases involving agents such as Devon (and other promise-makers), the father, and the driver.

Just as making a promise, impregnating a woman, or backing one's truck into a car create new duties, so, within a subjectivized deontological code, acquiring morally relevant information creates a new duty. For example, let's suppose that if Claire investigates, she will come to believe of Mina that she is the least productive employee, and so will come to have a prima facie duty to do what she believes to be laying Mina off. On the other hand, if she doesn't investigate, she will not believe of any employee that he or she is least productive, and so will come to have a prima facie duty to do what she believes to be selecting the most recently hired employee for lay-off.[46] Thus, according to a subjectivized deontic moral code, gathering information (or failing to do so) can create subsequent duties for the agent because gathering information produces belief-states that provide the grounding for the new duties. To avoid problems, these created duties must be handled in the same way that the duties created by making a promise are: fulfilling such prima facie duties must be accorded no positive weight, even though violating these duties is accorded negative weight.

---

only arise from their being the exercise of a virtue or vice. If one holds that keeping or breaking promises have intrinsic deontic moral significance, then Conee's proposal will not be acceptable.

[45] In H. Smith (1997) I argued only that the fulfillment of created duties must not be accorded any positive value. I now believe this conclusion should be extended to *all* duties, not just created duties. However, I will defer arguing for this extended position to a later occasion.

[46] In this particular case of not investigating, it may be more accurate to say that not investigating maintains, rather than produces, the lack of a belief about any employee that he or she is least productive. However, since Claire has an alternative (investigating) that would have eliminated this epistemic state, not investigating should be understood as playing an active role.

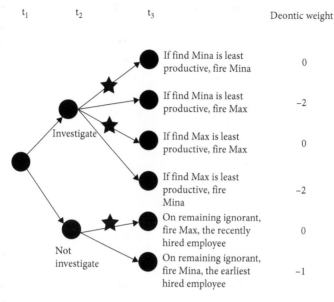

t₁   t₂   t₃   Deontic weight

Figure 5.2

When we accept this, Claire's choices should then be represented as having the revised deontic weights shown in Figure 5.2.

Figure 5.2 incorporates the new assumption that no fulfillment of a duty receives any positive weight. The stars in Figure 5.2 indicate that if Claire investigates, she will rightly lay off whichever employee she discovers to be the least productive, for a weight of 0, while if she doesn't investigate, she will then lay off Max, whom she believes to be most recently hired, also for a weight of 0. Thus Claire's doing what she believes is gathering information and her doing what she believes to be not gathering information would lead to acts having the same weight (0), and, according to Code C, it is not morally obligatory for her to gather information, since she foresees all this and (correctly) believes that gathering information would not maximize deontic weight. She would achieve the same deontic weight whether she investigates or not. This flies in the face of our assumptions about what it is morally incumbent on Claire to do, even according to a subjectivized code. We have been compelled by cases like Devon's to adopt a new way of assigning deontic weights to the fulfillment of duties, but this has resulted in the completely counterintuitive conclusion that Claire has no subjectivized duty to investigate. This is hardly the result that subjectivizing deontologists hoped for.[47]

---

[47] For fans of possibilism, it's worth pointing out that possibilism has the same result. Since Claire will do her duty at t_3 whether she investigates or not, possibilism also implies that it makes no difference to her derivative duty at t_2 whether she investigates or not. The two actions are each morally permissible, since each would lead to a subsequent action having a value of 0.

On this new way of calculating the relevant deontic weights, we do obtain a different prescription if we assume that Claire would *fail* to carry out some of her subsequent obligations. Thus suppose Claire (who continues to believe Max is the most recently hired employee) dislikes Mina. If she investigates she will lay off whichever employee she comes to believe to be least productive. However, if she doesn't investigate she will bend the rules a bit by laying off Mina rather than doing what she believes to be laying off the most recently hired employee, namely Max. In this case investigating would have a deontic weight of 0, but not investigating, which would lead her to violate her duty, would have a deontic weight of –1. Since she foresees all of this, she would have an obligation to investigate. However, this kind of effect only occurs when the agent would fail to carry out her subsequent duty.[48] In cases having the structure of Claire's case, if the agent *would* carry out her subsequent duties, she has no duty to investigate. It is hardly a satisfactory account of the duty to investigate if it obtains only when one would *not* carry out one's subsequent duty if one failed to investigate.

To complete this picture it is important to point out that some cases will include an *independent reason* to investigate—independent of the deontic weight the agent believes that investigating would subsequently produce. In this sort of case things may turn out differently than they do when the only source of a duty to investigate is the derivative duty. For example, Claire might have signed a contract requiring her, as the company's human resource manager, to investigate employee productivity records before conducting lay-offs during financial exigencies. In such a case Claire would then have a credible "backwards-looking" duty to gather information, based on her contractual promise.[49] But in the original case there is no such independent duty to investigate: in that case, whether or not Claire has an information-gathering duty depends *solely* on whether doing so would produce the maximum amount of subjectively expected deontic weight.

---

[48] McConnell (1988) on p. 17 also points out this phenomenon.

[49] To spell out the example, suppose her contract requires Claire to investigate employee productivity records before releasing any employee in a financial exigency. Remembering that she signed the contract, she believes she has such a duty. Since she created this duty for herself by signing the contract and coming to believe it is in force, the deontic weight of fulfilling her duty to do what she believes is fulfilling her contract is 0, while we might stipulate that the deontic weight of doing what she believes is violating it is –3. Thus the deontic weight of each sequence of acts following her doing what she believes to be not investigating (and so doing what she believes to be breaking her contract), would gain an additional disvalue of –3, while her act of doing what she believes to be investigating (and so doing what she believes to be honoring her contract) would gain an "additional" deontic weight of 0. Thus investigating would turn out to maximize deontic weight (it would produce a total deontic weight of 0, whereas her doing what she believes to be not investigating would produce a total deontic weight of –4). Hence, because of the existence of this independent reason, Claire would have a duty to do what she believes to be investigating.

Similarly, there could be independent reasons for Devon to make a promise to take care of Kate's cat. For example, Devon may believe (correctly) he owes a favor to Kate, since she took care of his pet the last time he went on vacation. He believes he owes no similar favor to the owner of the goldfish. Devon's caring for the cat would constitute repaying Kate's favor, while his caring for the goldfish but not the cat would constitute his failing to repay the favor. Thus there is an independent negative value to his promising to care for the goldfish, even if he carries out this promise, since doing so constitutes failing to repay a favor to Kate.

It may be tempting to suspect that Claire's case is somehow unique, and that to prove that subjectivized deontological codes cannot show agents have suitable duties to investigate before they act, we need to canvass a great many such cases. However, there is no need to canvass more such cases. One can demonstrate fairly readily that Claire's case is not unique: if fulfilling a duty has no positive deontic weight, then in any case in which the *only* moral reason to do what the agent believes is investigating, or to do what the agent believes is not investigating, is the derivative reason attached to the action's leading the agent to fulfill or violate subsequent duties, there will never be a duty to do what the agent believes to be investigating if the agent believes that both investigating and not investigating would lead to her fulfilling a subsequent duty.

Here is the informal proof: suppose the agent has two options, doing what she believes to be investigating (act A) and doing what she believes to be not investigating (act B).[50] She believes that if she does A, she will then believe she has three (or more) sets of options, X, Y, and Z. X is deontically better than either Y or Z, so X is obligatory. According to our assumption that fulfilling a duty has no positive value, the deontic weight of X is 0.

Assume next that the agent believes that if she does B (not investigating), she will then believe she will have three (or more) sets of options, K, L, and M. K is deontically better than either L or M, so K is obligatory. According to our assumption that fulfilling a duty has no positive value, the deontic weight of K is 0.

Assume that the agent believes that if she does A she will carry out what she then has a duty to do, that is, she will do X. Assume also that the agent believes that if she does B she will carry out what she then has a duty to do, that is, she will do K. Since both X and K have a deontic weight of 0, the agent has no derivative duty to do A or to do B, since neither leads to greater deontic weight. (This proof can be extended to cases in which some of the best actions subsequent to A, e.g., X and Y, have the same deontic weight, if we assume, plausibly, that merely permissible actions also have no positive deontic weight.) Thus in any case having a similar structure to Claire's case, and in which the agent will fulfill any duties she believes herself to have, the agent will have no duty to seek additional information before acting.

5.5.5 Extension of Principle P_{SD} to cases of uncertainty

In section 5.1, I noted that, for simplicity, I would focus primarily on cases involving agents who have false beliefs or no beliefs rather than uncertain beliefs about the circumstances and consequences of their actions. Claire's case closely fits this description; while

---

[50] Of course Claire's options might be more complex. For example, she might have different *ways* of investigating: she could read the company's personnel records, she could consult her assistant manager, or she could observe Max and Mina for an hour to see which one seems least productive. These acts might have their own prima facie values (thus observing Max and Mina might humiliate them), and these would have to be taken into account in deciding what Claire's best overall course of action is. The proof assumes that we are focused only on the derivative values arising from Claire's epistemic state after she investigates or fails to investigate.

some of her beliefs are true, others are false or simply lacking altogether. However, most agents are not in this situation: they have beliefs with varying degrees of certainty and uncertainty. Thus Claire, instead of being certain at t_1 that Max is the most recently hired employee, might think there is a 0.9 chance that Max is the most recently hired employee, or might think there is only a 0.8 chance that she will fire the person she identifies as the least productive employee. Principle P_{SD}, together with the prohibition against assigning positive deontic weight to fulfilling an obligation, must be extended to cover such cases as well. But doing so involves resolving dauntingly complex theoretical issues. For example, how would one restate Code C to apply to cases in which the agent is uncertain about the relevant facts? This seems clear enough for clause 2: a plausible restatement would be "An agent subjectively ought prima facie to gather information before fulfilling her subsequent duties if and only if she believes that doing so would maximize her subjective expectation of deontic weight through her subsequent actions." But what about clause 1? Recall that clause 1 is stated as follows:

(1)   When an agent believes she has been tasked to lay off employees in light of a financial retrenchment, the agent ought prima facie either to

(a)   do what she believes to be laying off an employee if she believes that person to be the least productive employee, or
(b)   do what she believes to be laying off the most recently hired employee if she does not believe of any employee that he or she is the least productive employee.

It makes no sense to import the concept of "subjective expected value" into clause 1, because the fulfillment (or violation) of clause 1 is what itself *bears* value. It doesn't ascribe a duty to the agent in virtue of something else her action has some probability of producing. Nonetheless Claire could well be uncertain whether laying off Mina would be laying off the least productive employee. This suggests we need a new code incorporating multiple clauses in place of clause 1. Each clause would define a distinct duty, such as a duty to "lay off a person who you think has a 0.9 chance of being the least productive employee," a duty to "lay off a person who you think has a 0.8 chance being the least productive employee," and a duty to "lay off a person who you think has a 0.7 chance being the least productive employee."

Then there will be the question what the deontic weight is of fulfilling these various duties. Perhaps, if laying off a person you think has a 1.0 chance of being the least productive employee has a deontic weight of 2 (as I originally assumed), then laying off a person you think has a 0.9 chance of being the least productive employee has a lesser deontic weight of 1.8 (2×0.9). But what is the deontic weight of laying off a person you think has merely a 0.4 chance of being the least productive employee? Should this be a small positive value or a negative value? Should this depend on how many options you believe you have and how you've partitioned the probabilities among them? Moreover, if laying off a person you think has a 1.0 chance of being the least productive employee has a value of 0 rather than 2 (as I have argued), then what is the deontic weight of laying off a person you think has a 0.9 chance of being the least productive employee? Should this value also be 0, or should it be less than 0, or more than 0?

Another issue is how to handle an agent's not having any belief about some matter. If Claire doesn't investigate, should she be understood as thinking there is a 0.5 chance that Mina is the least productive employee and a 0.5 chance that Max is the least productive employee? This may be appropriate in cases where the list of prospective employees is believed by Claire to have a definite number of candidates, so that she can partition her credences equally among them. But what if she doesn't have any idea how many individuals are candidates for lay-off? Some decision theorists have argued persuasively that in certain cases of this type there is no way for the agent to partition her credences so that she assigns equal probabilities to each one.[51] All this makes exploration of how to extend Principle P_{SD} to probabilistic cases highly complex because of the theoretical issues that need to be addressed. In light of these complexities, I shall have to leave the extension of Principle P_{SD} to cases involving uncertain beliefs for another occasion. Nonetheless it is clear that P_{SD}, together with the assumption that fulfilling an obligation has a deontic weight of 0, generates an unacceptable answer to the question of whether Claire ought to investigate in the case in which she assigns a probability of 1.0 to the various possible upshots of her investigating and not investigating. Principle P_{SD} goes wrong in at least this central case, and its doing so raises doubts that it will go any better in cases involving uncertainty.

5.5.6 Reasonable belief versions of the subjectivized duty to investigate

At this point one can ask what would be said about Claire's obligation by a theorist who believes "subjectivized" obligations are determined by what it would be *reasonable* for the agent to believe, not by what the agent *actually* believes. Would switching to the "reasonable belief" account rescue the subjectivized deontic duty to investigate? To answer this, let's restate Code C as follows in a "reasonable belief" version:

Code C_1:

(1)   When an agent reasonably believes she has been tasked to lay off employees in light of a financial retrenchment, the agent prima facie ought either to

(a)   do what she reasonably believes to be laying off an employee if she reasonably believes that person to be the least productive employee, or

(b)   do what she reasonably believes to be laying off the most recently hired employee if she does not reasonably believe of any employee that he or she is the least productive employee.

---

[51] See Hajek (2003), especially sections 2.3 and 7.1.1.

(2)   When an agent reasonably believes she has the opportunity to gather information relevant to a subsequent duty, then the agent ought prima facie to do what she reasonably believes to be gathering relevant information before fulfilling her subsequent duties if and only if she reasonably believes that doing so would subsequently lead her to produce the maximum amount of deontic weight.

The phrase "what it would be reasonable for the agent to believe" has been interpreted in a number of different ways. What Code C_1 requires Claire to do depends on how we interpret it. According to one of the most prominent interpretations, this phrase refers to *what the agent would be justified in believing given the evidence actually accessible to her.* On this interpretation, Claire's beliefs at t_3 count as reasonable if she investigates and comes to have evidence that would justify her in believing at t_3 that Mina is the least productive employee. So do her beliefs at t_3 if she fails to investigate and so has evidence that would justify her in believing that Max is the most recently hired employee, but doesn't have evidence that would justify her in believing of any employee that he or she is least productive. Again we can assume that Claire will carry out her duty as she perceives it at t_3. Then, on this interpretation of "reasonable beliefs," Code C_1, together with the view that fulfilling created duties itself has no positive value, would counterintuitively imply—like the actual belief view—that Claire has no obligation to do what she believes to be investigating, since investigating would not maximize deontic weight.

According to the other leading interpretation of "what it would be reasonable for the agent to believe," the phrase means *what the agent would believe if she had investigated as thoroughly as she ought to have done.* In the context of a subjectivized theory, the "ought" in "investigating as thoroughly as the agent ought to have done" must be reinterpreted in terms of the investigation it would have been reasonable for her to carry out if she had investigated the issue of whether or not to investigate as thoroughly as she ought to have done. It's clear that a troublesome circularity emerges in trying to use this interpretation in the context of Code C_1. Code C_1 purports to provide the account of whether or not the agent ought to investigate—but given this interpretation of "reasonable belief," Code C_1 can't complete the account until it is clear whether or not the agent ought to investigate! Ignoring the lessons of the rest of this chapter, we might simply push this issue aside and mandate that Claire's beliefs only count as reasonable if they would have arisen if she had investigated. On this finding, her beliefs after she investigates would count as reasonable. But at least one of Claire's actual "beliefs" *after she fails to investigate*—namely her suspension of belief about which employee is least productive—doesn't qualify as "reasonable." Instead it would be reasonable for her, having failed to investigate, to nonetheless believe that Mina is the least productive employee, since this is what she would believe if she had investigated as thoroughly as she ought to have done. But, since Claire didn't investigate, doesn't have this belief, and has no way to know at t_3 (when she must decide whom to lay off) what the content of this belief would be, a theory of subjectivized obligations couched in these terms cannot give Claire any advice that she can follow, despite its aim to do so. For this reason, in addition to the problem of circularity, a theory of subjectivized obligation resting on this interpretation of "reasonable belief" must be rejected as incapable of providing guidance to decision makers. Although other interpretations of "reasonable belief" could be reviewed, there is reason to fear that all would fall prey to one or the other of the problems described for these two leading interpretations.[52]

5.5.7 Summary for subjectivized deontic theories

In ascertaining whether or not we have a derivative deontic subjectivized duty to gather information, the most attractive approach we have canvassed is the view that such a derivative duty depends on the deontic weight the agent believes that carrying out (or violating) his subsequent duties would have if he investigated. But we also noted that in the context of a subjectivized code such as Claire's, gathering information *creates* subsequent duties about how to act in light of the agent's ensuing beliefs. As reflection on the case of promises has revealed, we must interpret the derivative duty concerning investigating so that it ascribes no positive weight to fulfilling a created obligation, although it ascribes negative weight to violating such an obligation. Once we ascribe zero deontic weight to fulfilling such created duties, it emerges that we have no duty to create subsequent duties even though our then carrying them out would fulfill a stronger duty than the one we would fulfill if we didn't create the duty in question. Code C's clause 2, therefore, does not generally underwrite a subjectivized duty to gather information, even in cases where the duties one would fulfill on gathering information are stronger than the duties one would fulfill on omitting to gather information.

This approach to interpreting duties to gather information as derived duties to maximize the deontic weight of the subsequent course of action appears to be the correct approach, since it captures the essential point of acquiring information before one makes a morally important choice. However, in the context of a subjectivized moral code—because of its special feature that gathering information creates beliefs, and so creates the agent's subsequent duty to act in light of those beliefs—this approach does not provide any rationale for appropriate actual duties to gather information, even in cases where this should seem straightforward. Lacking a better approach to explaining this duty, it appears that subjectivized deontological moral codes cannot require a moral agent to gather information before making a morally consequential choice.

5.5.8 Implications for objective deontological codes

It might reasonably be feared that barring the ascription of positive weight to the fulfillment of duties is too powerful a strategy and consequently undermines the case for there being a duty to gather information in the context of *objective* deontological

---

[52] Treatments of this issue have also been published in H. Smith (2010a) and (2011).

moral theories. Fortunately no such problem arises. In discussing objective duties we said that an agent has a derivative duty to gather information if and only if doing so would maximize the deontic weight of the course of action he would follow if he gathered the information, as compared with the deontic weight of the course of action that would follow his omitting to gather information. The first thing to note is that in the case of an objective deontological code, the agent's subsequent duty (for example, Claire's duty to lay off the least productive employee) is not obviously a *created* duty. Claire's investigating which employee is least productive does not create her duty to lay off Mina; she has this duty on Tuesday whether or not she has investigated.

I have here only claimed that it is created duties whose fulfillment should be accorded no positive weight. Thus the bar on ascribing positive weight doesn't apply in the case of fulfilling objective duties. However, it is worth exploring what the upshot would be if we did import this bar to the case of non-created duties. If we import the caveat that fulfilling any obligation has no positive weight, we can understand Claire's case as follows, taken as a case in which she has an objective duty of justice to lay off the least productive employee (regardless of what she happens to believe about the case). Code C, restated as an objective code, then appears as Code C_2:

Code C_2:

(1)   When an agent has been tasked to lay off employees in light of a financial retrenchment, the agent prima facie ought either to

  (a)   lay off an employee if that person is the least productive employee, or
  (b)   lay off the most recently hired employee among those who are tied for least productive if there is no unique least productive employee.

(2)   When an agent has the opportunity to gather information relevant to a subsequent duty, then the agent ought prima facie to gather relevant information before fulfilling her subsequent duties if and only if doing so would subsequently lead her to produce the maximum amount of deontic weight.

Note that the "lesser" duty to lay off the most recently hired employee only kicks in—that is, an agent only counts as fulfilling or violating this duty—in cases in which the agent has no "higher" duty to lay off the least productive employee because clause 1(a) is not satisfied. Assume Mina is the least productive employee, but Max is the most recently hired employee. Claire's objective options are represented in Figure 5.3.

Assume that if Claire investigates, she will discover that Mina has been least productive, and so will lay her off, for a deontic weight of 0. Assume also that if she fails to investigate, she will continue to be uncertain which employee is least productive, and in fact she will lay off Max, who, although most recently hired, is not the least productive employee (a violation of duty worth −2). These facts are represented by the stars in the diagram. Under these circumstances, she has an objective duty to investigate, since doing so will maximize the weight of her subsequent course of action.

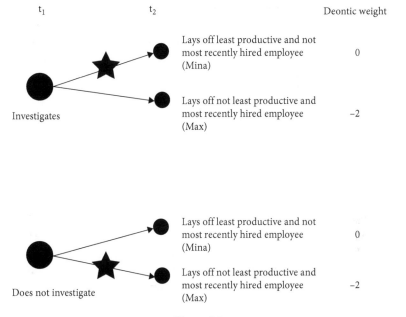

Figure 5.3

Consider a different version of this case in which there are three candidates for lay-off: Max and Mina, who tie for being least productive, and Rachel, who is most productive. Again, as Claire believes, Max is the most recently hired employee. Claire's objective choices are represented in Figure 5.4.

In this version of the case, since there are two employees tied for being least productive, Claire has an objective duty to lay off Max, the most recently hired of these employees. As the stars in the diagram indicate, if she investigates she will discover the tie for productivity, and following clause 1(b) of Code C_2, will lay off Max. Since this fulfills her duty, it receives no positive weight. On the other hand, if Claire fails to investigate, then given that she doesn't know the comparative productivity of all the employees, she will still lay off Max, whom she already believes to be most recently hired. Since this in fact is the objectively right act, it still receives no positive weight. Thus Claire has no derivative obligation to investigate, since luckily she will carry out her subsequent duty whether she investigates or not. We may find this startling, but it is a feature of objectivized codes in general when an agent would be lucky in her choice—it doesn't arise specifically for such codes' derivative duties to gather information. Thus it is the correct prescription for an objective code. Hence we retain the intuitively correct objective prescriptions regarding investigation, unlike the situation with subjectivized duties.

Why is there this difference between objectivized and subjectivized deontic duties? The difference arises precisely because (in the first scenario) Claire objectively ought to lay off the least productive employee, regardless of whether she has investigated or not,

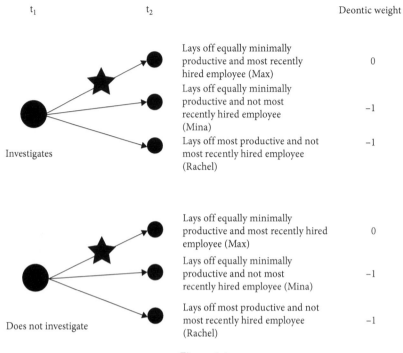

t₁   t₂   Deontic weight

Figure 5.4

and regardless of what she believes. In contrast to this, her subjectivized duty depends on what she believes, which in turn depends on whether or not she has investigated. On the subjectivized code, if she hasn't investigated and doesn't believe of any employee that he or she is least productive, then she has no duty to lay off the least productive employee. Duties under the objectivized code are not dependent on beliefs in this fashion.

We can conclude that even when we import the assumption that fulfilling even a non-created duty receives no positive weight (an assumption for which I have not argued), our recommended approach to determining an objectivized deontic duty to investigate still provides the answer we want: if the agent would suitably follow up her successful investigation, then generally speaking she has a duty to investigate. As we saw before, it will not turn out that she has a duty to investigate if the cost of doing so is too large, or the investigation would not lead to her carrying out her subsequent duty, or if she would luckily lay off the correct employee even if she failed to investigate. These are appropriate outcomes for an objective code.

5.5.9 Upshot: subjectivized deontic moral codes cannot appropriately underwrite the duty to gather information prior to acting

Because decision makers frequently lack the information necessary to use standard objective moral theories for guidance in making moral decisions, some Pragmatic theorists have proposed that we cast these theories aside in favor of subjectivized theories that ascribe moral status to actions as a function of what the agent *believes* about her prospective actions' circumstances and consequences, rather than as a function of the actions' actual circumstances and consequences. Some of these theorists, including Prichard, who famously advocates this "subjective turn" in normative theory, have asked whether such subjectivized theories can properly underwrite a duty to gather information before one makes a morally momentous choice.[53]

We have seen that subjectivized *welfare-maximizing* codes can incorporate a normatively appropriate duty regarding information-gathering.[54] But the story is different with subjectivized codes that include "deontic" duties to do what one believes to be keeping promises, compensating others for wrongs one has done them, and acting justly. We considered two ways to incorporate an information-gathering duty into a subjectivized deontological moral code: (1) as a free-standing duty characterized without reference to what the agent believes about how carrying out that duty would affect whether or not she carried out her subsequent deontic duties; and (2) as a duty to do what the agent believes is gathering information if and only if she believes that doing so would maximize the deontic weight of her subsequent actions. I have argued that the second of these two approaches is the correct one, but that it fails to deliver what subjectivized deontological theories need: a normatively plausible duty to do what an agent believes is gathering information. If subjectivized deontological moral codes are to provide a satisfactory account of a duty to gather information, the task remains to be accomplished. Absent such an account, it appears that such subjectivized codes fail to define adequately, or actually impose on us, an important type of duty that

---

[53] The full statement of this concern in Prichard (1968) is as follows (he is considering a case in which a man has fainted and the question is whether Prichard should shout in order to revive the man): "Nevertheless the idea that, where we have not done so, we ought to consider the circumstances fully, is itself not free from difficulty. This becomes obvious as soon as we ask; '*Why*, for instance, when it first strikes me that shouting might cure the man, am I bound to consider fully whether it would?' For the answer which we are first inclined to give is: 'Because, if I were to consider the matter fully, I might come to think shouting in a certain degree likely to cure him, and, if I did, I should then be bound to shout.' And yet this answer cannot be right. For plainly the duty of doing one action cannot possibly depend on the possibility of the duty of doing another the duty of doing which cannot arise unless the former action has actually been done. Moreover, if the answer were right, I could always escape a duty to shout merely by abstaining from considering the circumstances, and yet no one thinks this possible. The truth is that our having a duty to consider the circumstances cannot be based on the possibility of our having a future duty of another kind if we were to consider them. Rather, to vindicate such a duty, we must represent the two so-called duties as respectively an element and a possible element in a *single* duty, viz. to consider the circumstances, and then *if*, but only if, as a result, we reach a certain opinion, to do a certain future action" (p. 27). This is a very compressed statement of the problem as Prichard sees it and is not easy to interpret. I suspect Prichard had in mind at least some of the issues I have pointed out in this chapter, although he does not fully grasp the problem about the value of created duties. However, his proposed solution amounts to proposing yet another (more complicated) free-standing subjectivized duty and is subject to the problems I found with the simpler free-standing duties considered in the text.

[54] The view that fulfillment of duties has no positive value does not distort either objective or subjectivized *consequentialist* theories, since on these theories the rightness or wrongness of investigating depends, not on the deontic weight of the agent's subsequent fulfillment or violation of duties, but rather on the value of the events and states of affairs (such as effects on human welfare) to which her investigating would lead. For brevity I will have to defer the argument for this claim to another occasion.

we all believe we have.[55] Theories failing to contain or prescribe such duties are crucially defective. Prichard may have been right to fear this could be a fatal flaw in a subjectivized deontological theory.[56]

5.6   Conclusion

In Chapter 4 we saw that theorists wishing to promote the Pragmatic Response to the problem of error could advocate an objective moral code—the moral laundry list— that would indeed be error-free in the hands of each agent who tried to use it. However, this solution was rejected because it simply elevates the problem of error from the level of choosing what act to perform to the level of identifying which code is correct. We then reviewed pure subjectivized codes, of the kind that Prichard and Ross advocated, and saw that they, too, fail as responses to the problem of error. Because people may have erroneous beliefs about their own beliefs, just as they may have erroneous beliefs about the objective circumstances in which they act, a subjectivized code cannot provide universal usability as an extended guide to decision-making. Moreover, even if they were error-proof, such codes would fail to achieve the goal-oriented advantages that have been hoped for by many Pragmatic theorists—the codes would not secure better social welfare or foster more successful coordination and long-run planning. Agents' mistakes about their circumstances would often prevent subjectivized codes from achieving these goals in precisely the same circumstances that they prevent the counterpart objective codes from achieving them.

In the present chapter we have seen that one important variety of subjectivized codes has a special disadvantage of its own: subjectivized deontological codes cannot account for a duty to acquire information in circumstances where we think there is such a duty. We should note that this disadvantage is not restricted to *pure* deontological codes. The most plausible, and certainly most popular, moral codes are mixed consequentialist and deontological codes, ones requiring attention both to the consequences of one's action for human welfare and to issues of whether or not one would keep a promise, compensate others for past wrongs, and act justly. Presumably it follows that the most plausible subjectivized codes will also be mixed deontological and consequentialist in nature. But these mixed codes will also be unable to account adequately for a duty to acquire information when at least one of the subsequent duties is deontological in nature. Hence the problem afflicts virtually all of the most plausible subjectivized codes.

---

[55] There is a lesson here for any epistemologist interested in defining a "deontic" subjectivized duty to acquire additional evidence.

[56] Note that other actions, beyond investigating, may be important for "preparing" for a deontic duty that may arise later. An example would be a government's preparing to rescue citizens injured by a predictable natural disaster. We normally believe governments have a derivative obligation to perform these preparatory acts. Insofar as this duty is linked to the later performance of a deontic duty it will be vulnerable to the same problem within a subjectivized code that afflicts the derivative duty to acquire information.

All things considered, we have found conclusive reason to reject subjectivized codes as an acceptable response to the problem of error.

In this and the previous chapter we have tried to find *ideal* Pragmatic Responses to the problem of error: codes that would entirely eliminate agents' errors in using the codes to make decisions. Having failed to find any satisfactory codes of this sort, we must turn next to consideration of codes that fall short of universal usability, but at least achieve greater usability than that achieved by standard moral codes.[57]

[57] Support for work in sections 5.1–5.5 was generously provided by a Research Fellowship from the School of Philosophy at Australian National University during 2011. I am also grateful for comments from the anonymous *Ethics* referees on the published version of these sections material, as well as for discussion by groups at the University of Toronto, Fordham University, the City University of New York Graduate Center Philosophy colloquium, the graduate student Faculty Talk series at Rutgers University, the University of North Carolina at Chapel Hill Colloquium, and especially for insightful comments provided by Nick Beckstead, Philip Swenson, and by participants in my Spring 2015 graduate seminar. Julia Annas, Peter Klein, Ernest Sosa, and Kurt Sylvan were very helpful in discussing epistemological sources in which a duty to gather evidence is considered.

6

Non-Ideal Pragmatic Responses to the Problem of Error

It's enough to be workably suboptimal.[1]

In Chapter 4 we examined attempts to find completely error-proof moral codes—codes that are universally usable in the extended sense as decision-guides. An error-proof code would enable agents to determine what concrete duties the code assigns them without running any risk of mistake. As we saw, one strategy for identifying such codes is to adopt subjectivized codes, codes that make an action's rightness or wrongness depend on the agent's beliefs about its nonmoral properties. However, since agents are sometimes mistaken about their own beliefs, subjectivized codes cannot achieve full error-freedom. Moreover, as we saw in Chapter 5, such codes have the independent severe disadvantage of being unable to support an appropriate duty to seek information. Chapter 4 did identify at least one kind of code that could achieve complete error-freedom: the moral laundry list. The laundry list consists of a vast list of objectivized prescriptions for individual acts. Each prescription is tailored to the agent's epistemic state so that he or she would be able unerringly to identify and choose to perform the action prescribed by the list. But even though this code attains complete error-freedom, it fails to achieve most of the important desiderata that have led theorists to search for an error-proof code. Most crucially, the moral laundry list is useless as a strategy for fully circumventing the epistemic limitations that led us to seek an error-free code, since no agent (or her human advisors) is in an epistemic position to identify *which* laundry list prescribes the morally correct actions. In the laundry list solution, the errors that create the problem of error at the level of the normative code simply reappear as error or ignorance at the meta-ethical level, preventing identification of the *correct* moral laundry list, and so in an important sense preventing its application as well.

Thus the sole completely successful error-free code, the moral laundry list, is not an attractive Pragmatic solution to the problem of error. And indeed, many advocates of a Pragmatic Response (perhaps because they did not realize that a fully error-free code is possible) have contented themselves with advocating codes that may fall short of

[1] Brooks (2012).

achieving *complete* error-freedom but at least achieve *a greater degree* of error-freedom, and thus a higher degree of extended usability, than rival moral codes. Thus some theorists have implicitly defended deontological codes on grounds that these codes, while not universally usable, are at least less prone to error, and hence more widely usable, than consequentialist codes such as act utilitarianism. Similarly some expected-consequence utilitarians have implicitly defended their version of act utilitarianism on grounds that it is less prone to error than actual-consequence utilitarianism.[2] In this chapter we will explore more carefully how to define such non-ideal versions of the Pragmatic Response to the problem of error.[3] Devising the kind of concepts the Pragmatic theorist needs for her project will take some ingenuity, but is important for assessing the success of the project. Our aim will be to provide the most sympathetic possible reconstruction of the non-ideal Pragmatic solution to the problem of error. In Chapter 7 we will then examine whether the non-ideal Pragmatic Response, so understood, actually achieves the advantages the Pragmatic theorist hopes for. A warning: the ride is considerably rougher in this chapter, so readers should be prepared to fasten their seatbelts.

6.1 Defining "Greater Usability"

The search for a reduced error-prone Pragmatic Response might be thought of as motivated by the following standard for assessing moral codes:

Standard 6.1.   If moral Code X has higher extended usability than moral Code Y, then, other things being equal, X is better than Y.[4]

Standard 6.1 asserts that higher extended usability[5] always has (as Particularists would say) "positive valence": a code's higher usability as compared to another code is always

---

[2] Most such utilitarians, however, have focused more explicitly on the value of expected-consequence versions of the theory for handling cases in which the agent is balked by the problem of uncertainty rather than by the problem of error.

[3] Whether or not a satisfactory non-ideal Pragmatic solution could involve a code containing at least some subjectivized principles is not a question I shall address, although the argument in Chapter 5 should reveal the problematic character of such principles.

[4] Such a standard for assessing moral theories or codes is explicitly advocated as appropriate for the Pragmatic approach (not his term) by Väyrynen (2006), who introduces the *Guidance Constraint*: "Other things being at least roughly equal, ethical theories are better to the extent that they provide adequate moral guidance" on p. 292.

Note that Standard 6.1 and its successors in this chapter imply that the correct code is not necessarily correct in all possible worlds. How usable a given code is depends on the contingent cognitive capacities of the creatures subject to the code. Thus some Code C might be the correct code in possible world W_1 (where the creatures subject to morality have the capacity to use it without error on most occasions), whereas it would not be the correct code in possible world W_2 (where the creatures subject to morality in W_2 would err in using Code C on many occasions). For theorists who hold that fundamental moral principles are true in all possible worlds, or true in all reasonably close-by possible worlds, this implication would be fatal for Standard 6.1 in particular and the Pragmatic Response more generally.

[5] In this chapter "usability" will always mean "extended" usability unless explicitly noted otherwise.

relevant to its overall acceptability, and it always contributes positively towards the first code's being more acceptable than the second. If two codes are equally acceptable on other grounds, but the first more usable than the second, the first code is always superior to the second. The clause stipulating that other things must be equal makes room for Pragmatic theorists who maintain that further factors, such as the capacity of a code to motivate users, or to be easily teachable, are also relevant to which code is better overall. Standard 6.1 accurately reflects the fact that there is nothing inherently limited in the demand for usability. Any limitations that are accepted must be conceded because of pressure from conflicting considerations, or failure to achieve full usability.

Why would a more usable code be superior to a less usable code? The answer, presumably, refers to the various claimed advantages of usability that we have canvassed already. The thought must be that a more usable code would have more of the relevant advantages (or have them to a greater degree) than a less usable code: it would come closer to satisfying the demand that a moral code be usable for making decisions; or would enhance justice by enabling a greater number of people to lead successful moral lives; or would produce greater social welfare or more effectively play the crucial social role required of morality; or would produce a better pattern of actions.[6] Recall that not every theorist invokes all of these advantages, so different theorists will vary in their views about which advantages are relevant to evaluating which codes are best.

Having determined that the sole universally usable moral code (the moral laundry list) fails to secure these advantages, we now need to investigate whether the Pragmatic theorist who lowers his sights by seeking only relatively high usability can find moral codes that thereby secure these advantages to a greater degree than codes more heavily afflicted with the problem of error.

Before turning directly to this question, we must first clarify what "more usable" should mean when two codes are being compared. As we noted in Chapter 3, section 3.1, different moral principles often have very different theoretical domains (the actual and possible acts to which the principle ascribes moral status).[7] Since an error-proof principle's extended practical domain (the acts for which it can be used without error for guiding decisions) typically matches its theoretical domain, the fact that two error-proof principles may have different theoretical domains means that even two universally usable principles might have extended practical domains of very different sizes. For this reason it would often be misleading to compare the usability of two rival principles by calculating the number of occasions on which an agent could, without error, use one principle as compared with the other. If the first principle has a much smaller theoretical domain than the other, even if it is completely error-free there may

---

[6] Of these goal-oriented advantages, Väyrynen (2006) in section III explicitly appeals to the idea of enhancing justice.

[7] The discussion of principles in this chapter will often concern principles that issue prima facie or pro tanto prescriptions, rather than principles issuing all-things-considered prescriptions. However, since this will not affect the discussion, for brevity I will not explicitly qualify the principles under discussion as prima facie principles.

still be fewer occasions on which an agent could use it without error than she could use the more error-prone principle having a broader domain. Thus even if the small-domain principle "It is wrong to lie to one's spouse" were error-free, it might generate a smaller number of compliant acts than the larger-domain principle "It is wrong to lie" even if the latter were more error-prone. The most natural way to circumvent this problem is to compare two rival principles in terms of their *ratios* of usability—that is, to calculate for each principle the ratio between the principle's extended practical domain and its theoretical domain (in other words, the ratio between the number of occasions on which agents could use the principle without error and the number of acts to which the principle ascribes moral status).[8] We can call this the principle's "P/T ratio" (for Practical domain/Theoretical domain). Thus if Principle P could be used without error on 100 occasions, but it ascribes rightness to 400 possible acts, then its P/T ratio of usability would be 1 to 4 (or expressed as a percentage, 25 percent). If some rival Principle P* has a P/T usability ratio of 1 to 5, then P would count as more usable than P*, even though P's theoretical domain might be much smaller than the theoretical domain of P*.[9] Later in this chapter I will utilize this technique for comparing the usability of two principles. However, using it at this point would make exposition of certain interim points unduly cumbersome. So I will not use the concept of a P/T ratio in characterizing a principle's usability until later, but will instead assume that a principle's usability is the total number of occasions on which agents could use the principle without error. Examples will be constructed so that this simplification does not distort our conclusions.

Whether we define a principle's usability in terms of the *principle's* P/T ratio or in terms of the number of occasions on which it could be used without error, we still need to address the problem of different theoretical and practical domains at the level of the moral *code*. The problem arises because some standard codes have much smaller theoretical domains than others, since the smaller-domain codes contain principles prescribing only a limited set of types of act. Thus act utilitarianism has a much larger

[8] Thanks to John Carroll for persuading me that we need to use the P/T ratio rather than the raw number of usable occasions to measure usability.

[9] As Ben Bronner points out (in an unpublished seminar note), the attempt to compare two principles' "usability" may immediately encounter mathematical problems. I have defined the theoretical domain of a principle as all the actual and possible acts to which the principle ascribes moral status. It is arguable that this domain is infinitely large. Similarly, it is arguable that the practical domain of the principle is infinitely large. If both these domains are infinitely large, then neither principle qualifies as more usable than the other if we simply compare the number of times each principle could be used without error. And if we construct a P/T ratio for each principle, these ratios will both be undefined, so neither principle qualifies as more usable than the other. Even if the practical domain (but not the theoretical domain) of each principle is smaller than infinity, the P/T ratio of each principle is undefined (more precisely: the limit of 1/x as x approaches infinity is 0). Again, neither principle qualifies as more usable than the other. This is a problem that the Pragmatic theorist must solve, presumably by defining the theoretical and practical domains of principles in such a way that they are not infinitely large. In what follows I shall assume this can be done. Since any moral theory selected on grounds that it is widely usable will not be true in all possible worlds (given that agents' psychological capacities and information vary from world to world), the non-ideal Pragmatic theorist must in any event forswear the aim of identifying a moral theory true in every possible world.

theoretical domain than the Ten Commandments, since act utilitarianism generates a prescription for every possible act, whereas the Ten Commandments code only generates prescriptions for a restricted set of acts (honoring one's father and mother, not killing, not committing adultery, and so on). To avoid distortions in comparing codes we could use the same technique we used to handle comparisons among principles that have theoretical domains of different sizes: we could compare two codes in terms of the P/T ratios between their practical domains and their theoretical domains. However, here again it will simplify exposition to temporarily define the usability of a code in terms of the number of occasions on which it can be used without error. This gives us Definition 6.1.

> **Definition 6.1.   Comparative extended usability for codes:** Code X is more usable (in the extended sense) than Code Y if and only if there are *more occasions* on which agents can use Code X without error to select their potential actions than there are such occasions for Code Y.[10]

However, this does not address all the issues that must be taken into account in determining a code's usability, since we have only defined the extended usability of a principle in terms of the agent's ability to derive a correct prescription from the principle when it assigns moral status to an act. This leaves untouched the reverse issue: an agent's disposition to derive unwarranted prescriptions from that principle in cases where it does not apply. Thus, when considering possible actions of committing adultery, an agent might unerringly hold adulterous acts to be wrong which are indeed forbidden by the Ten Commandment prohibition against adultery. But the agent might also, mistakenly, identify an act that is *not* adulterous as one prohibited by this rule. Consider a case in which a husband has been away for a prolonged period, and returns to his native city much changed. His wife does not recognize him, but feels sexually attracted, and considers having intercourse with the "stranger."

---

[10]   Recall that the codes we are discussing may still be vulnerable to the problem of uncertainty, even if they are not vulnerable to the problem of error. Thus the actual "extended usability pattern" for a given code might break down as follows: 30 percent error-free usability, 20 percent error-stricken non-usability, and 50 percent non-usability because of agents' uncertainty.

Notice that Definition 6.1 implicitly addresses the issue of how codes should be compared when which code people subscribe to affects the decisions they make, and the decisions they make in turn affect how long their lives will be, how many and which children they will have, and in general how many opportunities to make moral decisions will confront human agents throughout history. Applying Standard 6.1 in conjunction with Definition 6.1 implies that a Code C is more usable than a Code C* if the general use of Code C would lengthen people's lives and increase the population over time, as compared to the general use of Code C* which would not increase the population, even though within any given individual's life she would apply Code C* with a higher success rate than the success rate of individuals applying Code C. (For an extreme example, consider Code C as act utilitarianism and Code C* as consisting of one rule, "It is obligatory to commit suicide as soon as possible." Assume that there would be a moderately high percentage of errors in applying Code C, but that everyone would be able without error to apply Code C*. Even so, according to Definition 6.1, Code C is more usable than Code C*, since the number of occasions on which it would be accurately used is higher.) If, on the other hand, we use the P/T ratios of the two codes, Code C* will be more usable than Code C. Which of these is the right approach to the effect of population issues is an important question the Pragmatic theorist would need to address.

She incorrectly believes that if she did so, she would be committing adultery and violating the Commandment prohibiting adultery. On Definition 2.4 of ability to use a moral principle this kind of incident does not show that the rule against adultery is not usable in the extended sense by the wife, since she does not mistake an adulterous act for one which is not adulterous. Instead, she over-extends the rule, deriving a prescription from the rule for an act to which it actually assigns no moral status. We could of course change Definition 2.4 so that it implies the rule is not usable in the extended sense by the wife or other agents who would make similar errors. However, this seems inappropriate. From the perspective of the rule prohibiting adultery, the wife's over-extension of the rule is not a problem: the rule itself does not assign any moral status to her act. But it seems to be a problem from the perspective of the code of which that rule is a part, since she judges an act to be wrong even though it is not prohibited by this or any other rule of the code.

To address this kind of situation we should interpret the concept of a moral code so that a code always has an "exhaustive theoretical domain"—that is, it ascribes moral status to every actual and humanly possible action. This will involve augmenting many traditional codes that explicitly address only a small number of types of actions. Without seriously distorting their original intent, we can reinterpret these codes so that they explicitly ascribe moral status to *all* actions. This can be done by adding a closure principle according to which all acts "unaddressed" by the provisions of the original code are deemed to be morally optional or permissible. As an example, consider again the Ten Commandments. Although the Ten Commandments do not explicitly prescribe or proscribe acts of honoring one's elder sister or brother, we can augment the Commandments so that they accord moral permissibility to acts of honoring one's elder siblings (and also to omitting to honor them), and indeed accord permissibility to every act not explicitly addressed in one of the original Commandments. According to this augmented version of the Ten Commandments, having intercourse with one's spouse is permitted. Thus the wife who derives a proscription against having intercourse with the "stranger" counts as able to use the rule prohibiting adultery, but she also counts as *unable* to use the Ten Commandments augmentation rule that deems all acts not permitted or proscribed by the other rules as permissible. This is the result we want, since the wife is someone who surely qualifies as subject to the problem of error when she tries to use the Ten Commandments as a whole code. Moreover, when we use this way to regiment moral codes, comparisons between codes using Definition 6.1 do not introduce distortions since all codes have the same theoretical domain (setting aside population-change issues).

Employing Standard 6.1 for assessing codes in virtue of their degree of extended usability, and Definition 6.1 for measuring the comparative usability of codes, we are better placed to turn to the question of whether comparatively more usable—although not perfectly usable—codes provide satisfactory Pragmatic Responses to the problem of error. A satisfactory response would adequately secure the relevant conceptual and goal-oriented advantages of solving this problem. However, before assessing whether more (but not perfectly) usable codes do provide a satisfactory response, we need to look more closely at the concept of "usability" and the circumstances under which a moral code's being usable appears to be genuinely valuable.

6.2   A Closer Look at "Usability"

Pragmatic theorists have wanted to find less error-prone codes that would be more usable, in the extended sense, to guide actual choice. However, our current project of comparing the advantages of two codes which have merely imperfect usability highlights our need to take a closer look at usability.

6.2.1   Comparing the value of usability in more and less important principles

Consider two incompletely usable codes that have precisely the same degree of error-proneness: suppose both Code C and Code D are usable in the extended sense on exactly 65 percent of the occasions for their use. Suppose, however, that Code C is usable without error primarily on what it deems to be the most important occasions for moral decision ("Should I take this opportunity to embezzle several million dollars from my employer?"), whereas Code D is usable without error primarily on occasions for what it deems to be more trivial moral decisions ("Should I phone in sick so I can attend the baseball game?"). Code D is rarely usable for important moral decisions. It is hardly clear that Codes C and D are, other things being equal, equally attractive because their degrees of error-proneness are identical.

One might begin to respond to this kind of case by noting that Definition 6.1 concerns what we can call "bare usability," where bare usability is simply the number of occasions on which a code can be used without error to derive a prescription. The case of Codes C and D suggests that the usability of a moral code should be judged, not simply by its bare usability, but rather by some measure that takes into account the importance of the principles which are usable, as assessed by the code itself. Let us call this "code-weighted usability." Thus Code C is better in terms of code-weighted usability than Code D, despite the fact that the two codes' bare usability is identical, because Code C can be used for a greater percentage of what it deems to be *important* moral decisions than can Code D.

It appears that bare usability should be discarded as a measure of a code's usability, and instead we should consider its code-weighted usability, contrary to Standard 6.1. Suppose, for example, that there are 100,000 occasions on which Codes E and F might be used. Code E is usable without error on only 40,000 of those occasions, while Code F is usable without error on 70,000 occasions. However, Code E is usable on many occasions deemed by the code to be highly important, while Code F is only usable on occasions it deems to be of modest importance. In Chapter 5 we introduced the concept of "deontic weight," according to which an act's deontic weight expresses the weight, or stringency, of the duty to perform (or not to perform) an act of that type, or the force of the moral reason to perform or not to perform that action. When a code assigns a given principle great "importance," it is assigning the principle high deontic weight. For the present discussion it is useful to introduce numerical scores to express these assignments of deontic weight. These scores need to be rich enough in mathematical terms to support the operations of addition, subtraction, and multiplication. Such scores provide the foundation for being able to judge, for example, that according to the code, one should perform an act that complies with two moderately important principles even at the cost of violating a highly important principle. More problematically, if we need to compare codes with each other, the deontic weight scores need to support comparisons between the deontic weight of a principle (as assigned by one code) and the deontic weight of another principle (as assigned by a second code). To my knowledge, no one has yet proposed a theoretically acceptable technique for doing this.[11] However, it is crucial for a number of normative questions that this problem be solved. Hence I will optimistically assume that the problem will be solved, and in the meantime will simply proceed as though such cross-code comparisons of deontic weight are meaningful.

Given this background, let's assign a deontic weight of 1 to each occasion on which Code E or F can be used at all; a deontic weight of 2 to each modestly important occasion on which Code E or F can be used; and a weight of 10 to each highly important occasion on which one of these codes can be used. We can then compute the total score earned by each code in light of its pattern of usability as in Table 6.1.

If we measure the usability of Codes E and F by their bare usability scores (40,000 and 70,000 respectively), then Code E is inferior to Code F. But if we measure their usability by code-weighted usability (160,000 and 140,000 respectively), then Code E is superior to Code F, even though Code E is usable on fewer occasions, because a quarter of the occasions on which Code E can be used are highly important ones, whereas none of the occasions on which Code F can be used are important.

Table 6.1

Code	Number of total occasions for use	Number of usable occasions	Number of highly important uses	Number of modestly important uses	Bare usability	Code-weighted usability
Code E	100 K	40 K	10 K	30 K	40 K	160 K
Code F	100 K	70 K	0	70 K	70 K	140 K

[11] For seminal work on the issue, see Lockhart (2000); J. Ross (2006); and Sepielli (2009) and (2013). Gustafsson and Torpman (2014) review the state of the literature on this issue, claim the cross-theoretical comparison problem may be insurmountable, and argue in favor of following the theory deemed to be most likely to be correct.

Assessing a code's usability in terms of its code-weighted usability instead of its bare usability seems like a much more plausible assessment. On such a scheme *usability* is still captured—every occasion on which a code is usable plays a role in determining its overall score—but different deontic weights are assigned to these different occasions, depending how important the decisions are. Of course, even on this scheme it is always possible that a vast number of modestly important usable occasions for one code might well outweigh a smaller number of highly important usable occasions for a rival code. But this effect is precisely what we expect in any scheme that weighs important decisions against less important decisions: it can arise any time we balance a great many items having smaller weight against a much smaller number of items having larger weight.[12]

Thus Standard 6.1 is incorrect in positing bare usability as contributing to the superiority of a moral principle. If usability affects the superiority of principles, it must be the more nuanced property of *code-weighted usability*.

In order to propose a scheme for taking code-weighted rather than bare usability into account, we first need a new definition:

Definition 6.2.   Code-weighted extended usability of a moral code: The code-weighted extended usability of a code equals the sum of the occasions on which it is usable in the extended sense, each weighted by the deontic importance of those occasions as determined by the code in question.

The advocate of "usability" as a test for moral codes must reject Definition 6.1 and Standard 6.1 and replace them with Definition 6.2 and a new Standard 6.2:

Standard 6.2.   If the code-weighted extended usability of moral Code X is greater than the code-weighted extended usability of moral Code Y, then, other things being equal, X is better than Y.

Standard 6.2 agrees with Standard 6.1 in according positive valence to greater usability: a code's greater code-weighted usability as compared to another code is always relevant to its overall acceptability, and it always contributes towards the first code's being more acceptable than the second. But on Standard 6.2 the code's code-weighted usability, not its bare usability, makes the difference. Like Standard 6.1, Standard 6.2

---

[12] Some deontological codes may try to introduce special devices to prevent the possibility of multiple acts of compliance with a lower-weight principle outweighing a single act of non-compliance with a higher-ranked principle. One device sometimes invoked involves arranging a code's principles in a lexical weighting order, so that conflicts between the lower and the higher lexically weighted principles are always resolved in favor of the higher weighted principles no matter how many violations of the lower weighted principles may occur. Alternatively, principles can be arranged in groups such that principles within a single group can be weighed against each other, many violations of one principle within the group potentially outweighing a single violation of another principle in the same group, but conflicts between a principle from a higher group with a principle from a lower group are always resolved in favor of the principle from the higher-ranked group. For pessimistic discussions of possible techniques for doing this in the context of risky choices, see Jackson and Smith (2006) and Huemer (2010).

implicitly claims that a more usable code is better according to the four advantages
that the Pragmatic theorist seeks to secure.[13]

6.2.2 Comparing the value of usability in principles having better or worse content

Consideration of Standard 6.2 raises another issue. Suppose Code G is highly but not
perfectly usable. Code G includes only two duties. Its most important duty is paying
what one owes in taxes and its least (and modestly) important duty is not cutting into
movie queues. Since accurately calculating one's taxes is difficult but avoiding inad-
vertent queue-cutting is easy, suppose further that the usability rates of these two
duties are as shown in Table 6.2.

Now let us define a new Code G* by transposing the *ranking, and so the importance,*
of these two duties as Code G* weights them. Let's assume that the usability rates for
each duty would remain the same, as shown in Table 6.3.[14]

Code G* has higher code-weighted usability than Code G, since Code G* ascribes
greater weight than Code G does to the most usable principle (not cutting into movie

Table 6.2

Code	Paying taxes (highly important)	Not cutting queues (modestly important)
Code G	30% usability	90% usability

Table 6.3

Code	Not cutting queues (highly important)	Paying taxes (modestly important)
Code G*	90% usability	30% usability

[13] As Ben Bronner points out (in an unpublished seminar note), both Standard 6.1 and Standard 6.2
open up an unfortunate possibility. Suppose some Code C has the highest code-weighted usability of any
imperfect code we can identify. Code C then looks like a good candidate for adoption by a Pragmatic theorist. However, we can readily describe a new Code C* that is guaranteed to have higher code-weighted
usability than Code C: Code C* has exactly the same principles as those in Code C, but assigns them
greater weight. Code C* then has higher code-weighted usability than Code C. And we need not stop with
Code C*, since we can use the same strategy to describe a Code C# which has all the same principles but
assigns them even higher weight than the weight assigned by Code C*. Code C# then has higher code-weighted
usability than either Code C or C*. To cut off this sort of infinite regress, it appears the best technique for
the Pragmatic theorist is to impose a cap on the total weight that can be assigned by a code to all of its
principles taken together. I shall assume this can be done without trying to specify what this cap is.

[14] Although it seems plausible that the extended usability rate of a principle would remain the same
whatever its ranking within a code, this may not be true. For example, if the principle is ranked very highly
by a code, then people may try harder to obtain the information necessary to apply that principle, so that
it would be more highly usable under those circumstances. This is something a non-ideal Pragmatic theorist would have to take into account. However, the size of this kind of effect is not easily predictable, so to
facilitate comparing codes, I will assume throughout that a principle's usability does not vary as a function
of how much importance the code places upon it.

queues). Clearly it would be perverse to rate Code G* as superior to Code G, even though it has higher code-weighted usability. From a perspective outside Codes G and G*, it matters less how frequently people are able to successfully avoid cutting into queues than it matters how often they are able to accurately pay their taxes. Of course, Standard 6.2 doesn't necessarily rate G* as better than G, because it includes an "other things being equal" clause. But this case alerts us to the fact that the Pragmatic theorist should not want to focus on code-weighted usability alone, since doing so doesn't take into account everything about usability relevant to a code's superiority.

This concern is enhanced by considering another pair of codes, Codes H and I. Code H includes a *corrupt* principle—one that prescribes actions that are *thoroughly wrong* from a perspective outside Code H itself. Code H includes Principle P1, "It is permissible to lie only when doing so will violate important rights." Code I is otherwise identical to Code H, but instead of P1 it includes a slightly less corrupt Principle P2: "It is permissible to lie to anyone except members of one's family." Codes H and I assign each of these principles the same importance, and let's assume the perspective outside these codes assigns them (as the rules regarding the permissibility of lying) the same importance as well. Let's further suppose that Code H and Code I have identical patterns of code-weighted usability as regards their other principles, but that Code H's Principle P1 is more frequently usable than Code I's Principle P2. It follows that Code H has higher code-weighted usability than Code I. We are not, however, prepared to say that Code H is the better code because people governed by it would more often be successful in deriving correct prescriptions from its corrupt principle. This would be hard to swallow: surely no value at all is achieved for Code H by the high usability of its corrupt Principle P1. Again, the "other things being equal" clause in Standard 6.2 shields it from implying that Code H is all-things-considered better than Code I. But this case, too, alerts us to the fact that the Pragmatic theorist should want to take into account more factors than code-weighted usability in evaluating codes. The standard for "betterness" should explicitly include a factor reflecting the appropriateness of content of the code, as well as a factor measuring its code-weighted usability.

These arguments about the relative superiority of Codes G to G* and Codes H to I assume that there is some authoritative perspective from outside any of these codes that can be used to evaluate the acceptability of their principles' *content* as well as the acceptability of the *weight* the code assigns to its principles. Pragmatic theorists should have no objection with this assumption. They don't maintain that high usability is a *sufficient* condition for a moral code's acceptability. Rather they hold that a code's high usability is a *necessary* condition for its acceptability, but also readily grant that the correct code must meet other kinds of criteria as well, criteria including the normative acceptability of its content and presumably the acceptability of the importance it assigns its principles.[15]

---

[15] It should be said, however, that few normative ethicists have paid explicit attention to the importance of proper weights. Rosen (2004) at pp. 305–6 comes close by pointing out that an agent can be ignorant of the relative force of moral, as compared to prudential, reasons to act.

Thus imagine a Pragmatic theorist who is offered a magic wand by which any moral code could be made universally usable. The theorist would be able to review the content and weight assignments of all the possible codes and select, in virtue of its content and weight assignments, the code she would choose to make universally usable. For the Pragmatic theorist, this code would qualify as the deontically perfect code. Alas, there is no such magic wand, so the Pragmatic theorist is willing to relinquish some ideal content and weight in order to attain greater usability. However, she does not give up the importance of good content and appropriate weight as factors to be taken into account.

In light of these considerations, I will introduce the notion of a "deontically perfect code," or a "perfect code" for short—a code that has all the deontically correct features, whether or not it is widely usable. As we've seen, such a perfect code has two features of special interest to us. One feature is the *content* of its principles. Thus the perfect code might include a principle stating that telling a lie is wrong unless doing so is necessary in order to protect important rights. Another less perfect code might include a principle stating that telling a lie is wrong unless doing so is necessary to maximize welfare. The content of the second principle diverges from the ideal and so renders its code less than perfect. The second important feature of the perfect code is the weight or importance that it assigns its various principles. Thus the perfect code assigns greater importance to its prescription to pay taxes than it assigns to its proscription not to cut into movie queues.

The perfect code can serve as the standard by which we judge what I will now call the *deontic merit* of a code. The deontic merit of a code depends on two factors: its *content merit* and its *weight merit*. The *content merit* of the code rises or falls as the content of its principles resembles or diverges from the content of the perfect code's principles. The *weight merit* of a code rises or falls as the weight it ascribes to its principles resembles or diverges from the weight ascribed to them by the perfect code. If some Code C has exactly the same content as the perfect code, and assigns its principles exactly the same weights as those assigned to them by the perfect code, then we can say that Code C has the maximum amount of deontic merit. If a code's content or its weight assignments diverge from those of the perfect code, then its deontic merit is diminished. Once we've introduced the concept of deontic merit, we can further introduce what I will call a code's "usability value," which will depend on two different factors: its deontic merit, and how usable its principles are. Thus the inclusion in Code H of a principle permitting lying only when doing so will violate important rights decreases (or fails to increase) the usability value of Code H, even though it is highly usable. The aim of the non-ideal Pragmatist is to find the code with the maximum usability value.

Of course other factors, such as a code's capacity to motivate agents to comply with it, may also be relevant to its overall normative acceptability. For this reason I am using the term "usability value" rather than "overall value." Since we are not directly concerned with these other factors, I will leave room for them to be covered by the "other things being equal" clause in standards for judging codes, but will not attempt to determine how they relate to either the deontic merit or usability value of a code.

To understand what I mean by the merit of a code's "content," we should note that two principles might have different semantic content but, because they employ different but co-referring terms, prescribe exactly the same acts. Thus one principle prescribes donating one-tenth of one's income to charity, while another prescribes tithing for charity. These two principles prescribe exactly the same acts. Or a principle prescribes obeying God, while another principle prescribes obeying the unique all-good, all-knowing, and all-powerful being. Like the tithing principles, these two principles also prescribe exactly the same acts. Since what is deontically important about these principles is the acts they prescribe, not the concepts or terms under which they do so, I shall interpret the "content" of a code to refer to the set of acts the code prescribes (in the relevant possible worlds).[16] Thus I shall say that the two tithing principles have the same content and thus have the same content merit. The same thing holds for the two principles about obeying a supreme deity.

Using the notion of deontic merit, according to which the deontic merit of a code depends on its content merit and its weight merit, we can judge that Code G, which gives more importance to paying taxes than to avoiding cutting into queues, has greater deontic merit than Code G*, which illegitimately reverses the importance of these two duties. Notice that a choice must be made here. One option would be to define a code's deontic merit so that it is a function of two factors: (a) how much divergence there is between the content of the code's principles and the content of the perfect code's principles, and (b) what importance the perfect code assigns to the code's principles. Factor (b), although tempting, would not serve our purposes. If this were how deontic merit were defined, then Code G and Code G* (which contain only the principles requiring one to pay taxes and not cut into movie queues) would have the same deontic merit, since each of the two principles is included in both codes, each of these principles (let us assume) is included in the perfect code, and each principle, whichever code it appears in, is accorded the same level of importance by the perfect code. However, we want a concept of deontic merit that *differentiates* Code G and Code G*, telling us that Code G has greater deontic merit than Code G*. This implies that a code's deontic merit, in our sense, is not simply determined by the importance the perfect code accords its principles. Rather our concept of deontic merit must take into account both how much the content of a code's principles diverges from the content of the perfect code, and also how much the weights *assigned to the principles by the code* diverge from the weights assigned to those principles by the perfect code. Codes G and G* differ only with respect to the latter factor, since the two codes share the same principles but assign different weights to them. But this implies, as we want, that these codes have different deontic merit.

---

[16] Nonetheless the semantic character of a code can be important in other ways, a point to be examined in section 7.1 of Chapter 7.

This notion of deontic merit can now be used to compare other codes we have discussed. For example, recall that Code H includes Principle P1, "It is permissible to lie only when doing so will violate important rights," while Code I, which is otherwise identical to Code H, instead of P1 includes a slightly more acceptable Principle P2, "It is permissible to lie to anyone except members of one's family." Codes H and I assign the same weights to these principles, but the content of Principle P1 diverges far more from the content of the perfect principle concerning lying than does the content of Principle P2 (that is, the overlap between the acts deemed permissible by the perfect code with those deemed permissible by P2 is greater than the overlap between the acts deemed permissible by the perfect code and P1). Hence Code I has greater deontic merit, in view of its higher content merit, than does Code H.

Having introduced the concept of deontic merit of a moral code, we can note that the deontic merit of a code arises from the deontic merit of its component principles. The deontic merit of a principle, like that of a code, depends on both its content and its importance, and in particular how much these diverge from the ideal. However, a moral principle taken in isolation has no importance; rather it is assigned that importance by a code of which it is a part. Since the importance of the principle depends on the code which includes it, a principle may have one deontic merit as part of one code, and a different deontic merit as part of a different code. Thus the principle forbidding cutting into movie queues has greater deontic merit as part of Code G (which properly assigns it low importance) than it does as part of Code G* (which assigns it unsuitably high importance). The deontic merit of a principle depends on both its content and its code-assigned importance, each as assessed in comparison to the content of the relevant perfect principle and the importance assigned by the perfect code to that principle.

6.2.3 Further refinement of the notion of deontic value

We have sketched concepts of the deontic merit of a code and of a principle, but these concepts need more refinement. To fully spell out this notion, we need to look more deeply into the normative appropriateness of the content of a principle or code. Let us start with the content of principles. We've described some principles as "corrupt"— ones that prescribe or permit actions that are assessed as thoroughly wrong by the perfect code. For example, Code H includes the principle "It is permissible to lie only when doing so will violate important rights." This principle certainly seems corrupt.

However, we should recognize that some principles diverge in content from the content of principles in the perfect code, and yet do not seem corrupt. Suppose a Principle P3 stating that "It is obligatory to keep a promise unless it has been elicited by deceit" is fully endorsed by the perfect code. Now consider Principle P4, which is similar but not identical in content to Principle P3. Principle P4 states that "It is obligatory to keep every promise"—requiring promising-keeping whether or not the promise has been elicited by deceit. Suppose Code J includes all and only those principles fully endorsed by the perfect code, except that it includes Principle P4 instead of Principle P3. Code J accords P4 the same importance given to P3 by the perfect code. Although P4 is not identical to P3, nonetheless its content is similar enough to P3 that it seems to have positive deontic merit, although less merit than Principle P3 itself would have. A code containing Principle P4 would be better than a code containing no obligation to keep promises at all, or an obligation to keep promises only to one's friends and family. For a Pragmatic theorist, it would make Code J better if P4 were highly usable than if it had only low usability. Thus the notion of deontic merit must be able to assign some positive merit to principles such as P4 which are not so thoroughly wrong as to be corrupt and yet deviate from the exact content of principles endorsed by the perfect code. By extension, Code J, which contains Principle P4, must be accorded some positive deontic merit in virtue of its inclusion of P4, although it has less deontic merit than would an otherwise identical Code K that included the fully endorsed P3 rather than P4.

6.2.4 Combining the content merit and weight merit of codes and principles

We now have two questions. How do the two components of a principle's deontic merit—its content merit and its weight merit—combine with each other to constitute the overall deontic merit of the principle? And how do we determine a code's usability value once we have determined the deontic merits of its component principles? It turns out that answering these questions is far from simple.

To assess what can be accomplished by the Pragmatic approach to the problem of error, and to see what challenges this approach faces, it would be helpful to be able to express the Pragmatic approach in a formula that shows precisely how a code's usability value depends on such factors as its content merit, its weight merit, and its usability. Of course such a formula may exceed the degree of precision that is genuinely possible in this field. However, the search for a formula of this sort will clarify what the Pragmatic approach really amounts to, and what its strengths and weaknesses are. Once we have found a formula and gleaned these insights from it, we can note that it may represent the Pragmatic approach in a more precise form than the Pragmatic theorist herself would claim is possible.

Let's start with our first question: how do the two components of a principle's deontic merit—its content merit and its weight merit—combine with each other to generate the deontic merit of the principle?[17] Recall that the principle's deontic merit arises from how much its content approaches or diverges from the ideal content, while its weight merit arises from how much the weight assigned to the principle by its code approaches or diverges from the weight assigned to the principle by the perfect code. The Pragmatic theorist presumably wants the method of combination to meet the following two criteria:

Criterion 6.1:   If Principles P and Q have the same content merit, and P's weight merit is greater than that of Q, then P has higher deontic merit.

---

[17] I am grateful to Thomas Hurka for pointing out to me some of the mathematical traps threatening some otherwise plausible formulas of this type, and especially grateful to John Carroll for his great generosity in helping sort out which formulas work and which ones do not.

Criterion 6.2:   If Principles P and Q have the same weight merit, and P's content merit is greater than that of Q, then P has higher deontic merit.

The most natural way of combining the two types of merit that meets these criteria is simply to multiply the two merit values of a principle (within a given code).[18] In effect this *weights* the content value of the principle by its weight value (or vice versa). On its face this certainly appears plausible, since a principle with deviant content is less problematic in a code if it has low importance. To see how this works, let's introduce numerical scores to represent content merit and weight merit.

There are several hurdles to doing this. In the case of content merit, the problems are not difficult to overcome. Recall that a principle's content merit is a measure of how much its content approaches or deviates from the content of the corresponding perfect principle which addresses the same realm of action. Let us proceed, then, by arbitrarily assigning a content value of 50 to any perfect principle, where a perfect principle is one contained in the perfect code. As an example, putatively perfect Principle P3 "It is obligatory to keep a promise unless it has been elicited by deceit" has a content value of 50. Insofar as the content of a principle deviates from the perfect content, it will have a value that is less than that of the perfect principle. Thus the imperfect principle P4 "It is obligatory to keep every promise" might have a content value of only 40. At this point it is tempting to represent the content merit of the principle as the absolute value of its *deviation* from the perfect content. In case of P4, its content merit would then be 10. But if we use this method of representing content merit, unfortunately the score representing the content merit of a principle will *rise* as its deviation from the perfect content rises. Thus consider Principle P5, "The only promises it is obligatory to keep are promises to one's friends and family," whose content has a lesser value of 20 and so deviates by 30 from the ideal 50. On the proposed scoring method Principle P5 would receive a content merit score of 30, higher than the content merit score of P4, whose content value only deviates by 10 from perfection. If we assume that P4 and P5 have the same weights within their respective codes, then P5 should have *worse* deontic merit than P4, because its content diverges further from the perfect content. Since adopting the proposed scoring method would assign principle P5 higher deontic merit than P4, it must be rejected.[19]

To avoid this problem, we need to represent the content merit of a principle in such a way that the content merit score rises as the principle's content more and more closely resembles that of the corresponding perfect principle. The obvious way to do this is to express the principle's content merit by its content *value*, which rises as its content

---

[18] For the seminal discussion of different ways in which normative factors can interact with one another in determining overall value, see Kagan (1988).

[19] We might try to avoid this by representing deviation scores as negative numbers rather than absolute numbers. However, if we do this for both content and weight deviation scores, it will turn out that no deontically imperfect principle can ever have higher usability value than a deontically perfect principle (however low its usability), since the imperfect principle's deontic value will be negative, and multiplying a positive usability score by a negative deontic score will yield a negative value. Given the Pragmatic theorist's project, she would reject this.

more closely approaches perfection. Thus Principle P4 receives a content merit score of 40, while Principle P5 receives a content merit score of only 20. Assigning content merit scores in this fashion measures, albeit indirectly, how closely a principle's content approaches perfection. To avoid problems dealing with negative values, and to normalize the values of all principles, we should also regiment the underlying content values of principles so that the highest content value any principle may receive is 50, while the lowest value it may receive is 0. The highest and lowest possible content merit scores are 50 and 0. Assigning a principle a content value, and so a content merit, of 0 expresses the fact that the principle's content is sufficiently corrupt that no matter how widely it is usable, its usability does not contribute positively to its deontic value.[20] Of course, corrupt principles may, from another perspective, vary in how corrupt they are. For example, a principle prescribing murder at every opportunity is more corrupt than a principle prescribing lying at every opportunity. But for purposes of calculating a principle's usability value we do not need to make such discriminations: high usability in either such principle fails to add to the principle's usability value.[21]

The case of assigning numerical scores to weight merit is more complicated for two reasons. One is that the perfect code will typically contain multiple principles to which it may assign different weights. This contrasts with our assumption that all principles with perfect content have the same value of 50. As an example of different assigned weights, the perfect code might assign a weight of 40 to the perfect Principle P6, "It is obligatory to pay what one owes in taxes," while assigning a weight of merely10 to the perfect Principle P7 "It is obligatory not to cut into movie queues." Of course imperfect codes will assign various weights to their component principles as well, and these assigned weights may or may not match the weights assigned to these principles by the perfect code. Moreover, in the case of content value, the content value (and so the content merit) of a principle can never exceed the content value of its counterpart perfect principle. No principle can have *better* content than a perfect principle. But a code can either *under-weight* or *over-weight* the importance of a principle as compared to the weight it is assigned by the perfect code. Thus Code G* under-weights P6, the obligation to pay taxes (assigning it a weight of 10), but over-weights P7, the obligation not to cut into movie queues (assigning it a weight of 40).

To accommodate these features of weight merit so that weight merit scores satisfy Criteria 6.1 and 6.2, we can adopt the following strategy. First we can normalize all weight assignments to a principle so that the range of possible weights is 0 to 50.[22] We can then calculate the absolute amount by which a weight assigned to a principle by its code

---

[20] Presumably a principle has a content value of 0 when its prescriptions have no overlap at all with the prescriptions of its corresponding perfect principle.

[21] Thanks to John Carroll for proposing this method for dealing with corrupt principles.

[22] Recall that we suggested that a cap must be placed on the total weight that can be assigned by a code to all of its principles taken together; this will further constrain what weights can be assigned to individual principles within a single code. However, the capping constraint may lose importance at this point in the development of the Pragmatic position, since a principle's weight merit doesn't automatically increase as its weight increases.

Table 6.4

Principle	Perfect weight	Code-assigned weight	Absolute deviation	Weight merit (50 – absolute deviation)
P6 in G	40	40	0	50
P7 in G	10	10	0	50
P6 in G*	40	10	30	20
P7 in G*	10	40	30	20
P8	30	0	30	20
P9	0	20	20	30
P1	20	20	0	50

deviates from that assigned to it by the perfect code. That deviation is then subtracted from 50 (no matter what that principle's perfect weight happens to be). The resulting number is the score for weight merit for that principle.[23] Thus the weight merit scores of the two principles in Code G and Code G*, along with the weight merit scores of additional sample principles P8, P9, and P1, would be as shown in Table 6.4.

Using this technique ensures that the scores for weight merit rise as the weight assigned to the principle by its code approaches the weight assigned to it by the perfect code. Thus Principle P6 is assigned the perfect weight by Code G, but it is under-weighted by Code G*, and so receives a lower weight merit (20) in Code G* than it does in Code G (50).[24] Recall that P1 is the previously described corrupt principle "It is permissible to lie only when doing so will violate important rights." Assume that the code of Principle P1, like the perfect code, ascribes it a weight of 20, so its weight merit is 50—just as high as the weight merit of Principle P6 in Code G. This may seem surprising, but on reflection it seems right, even though Principle P1 is corrupt: the code

[23] Technically we can think of the formula for calculating content merit as identical to the formula for calculating weight merit (i.e., content merit = 50 minus the absolute value of the principle's content; while weight merit = 50 minus the absolute value of the principle's weight). I simply picked the value 50 from which the absolute weight divergence values are subtracted so that it is identical to the content value of a perfect principle.

[24] It is tempting to think that we should subtract the absolute deviation in a principle's weight from its own ideal weight. However, this would be a mistake. Consider the two principles shown in Table 6.5.

Table 6.5

Principle	Perfect weight	Code-assigned weight	Absolute deviation	Perfect weight – absolute deviation	Weight merit (50 – absolute deviation)
P10	40	30	10	30	40
P11	10	7	3	7	43

If we subtract the deviation from the principle's perfect weight, Principle P10 would receive a higher "merit weight" (30) than Principle P11 (7). But this would be a mistake: since P10's weight deviation is greater than P11's weight deviation, its weight merit should be lower. We achieve this result by subtracting the weight deviation from 50, thus counteracting the distortion produced by the fact that P10's perfect weight is greater than P11's perfect weight.

containing P1 does well to assign P1 a weight of 20, the same as the weight assigned by the perfect code to the corresponding correct principle for P1's field of action.

Partly to maintain parity between content merit scores and weight merit scores, this scoring scheme always subtracts the deviation of a principle's weight from 50. According to the scheme, a principle's content merit and its weight merit play equal roles in determining its deontic merit. Some theorists might reject equality between content and weight merit, believing, for example, a principle's content merit should make more of a difference to its deontic merit than its weight merit does. They could capture their view by multiplying the principle's content merit score by some suitable positive constant greater than 1.

Notice several features of this method of assigning content and weight merit. First, if any two principles have content fully endorsed by the perfect code, they will be accorded the same content merit, even though they may differ in content and in importance. Their content merit simply measures how closely their content mirrors that of their corresponding perfect principles. Thus if "It is obligatory never to kill an innocent person" and "It is obligatory to pay one's taxes" are both fully endorsed by the perfect code, they will have the same content merit, even though the first principle should have greater weight than the second principle. Content merit is not intended to reflect the importance of a principle.

Second, the recommended method for measuring weight merit does not imply that two principles will have different weight merit if they are assigned different weights by the perfect code. For example, suppose we are comparing the weight merit of a Principle P12 (which is accorded a weight of 12 by its own code, but a weight of 8 by the perfect code) and the weight merit of a Principle P13 (which is accorded a weight of 1 by its code, but a weight of 5 by the perfect code). The deviation in both cases is 4, so they each are assigned a weight merit of 46 by the proposed method. The fact that P12 is deemed more important than P13 by the perfect code does not imply that P12's deviation is worse than P13's deviation. Although theorists might argue that the deviation between 12 and 8 is more important than the deviation between 1 and 5, I shall assume this is not the case. This example, as well as the cases of P6 and P7 in Table 6.4, also show that deviation upward has the same impact as deviation downward: it doesn't matter to a principle's weight merit whether its code over-weights or under-weights it relative to its ideal weight.

At the beginning of this section I said that the most appropriate way to combine a principle's content merit and its weight merit is simply to multiply these two factors to yield its deontic merit. Table 6.6 shows comparisons of deontic merit among some sample principles.

In this table I am assuming that, while P6 and P7 each have perfect content (so they have a content merit score of 50 in both Code G and Code G*), these principles are weighted correctly in Code G but mis-weighted in Code G*. Accordingly their deontic merit scores in Code G* are lower than their scores in Code G, as we recognized would be appropriate in our previous discussion of these principles. Principle P1 (the corrupt

Table 6.6

Principle	Content merit (50 – absolute deviation	Weight merit (50 – absolute deviation)	Deontic merit of principle
P6 in G	50	50	2,500
P7 in G	50	50	2,500
P6 in G*	50	20	1,000
P7 in G*	50	20	1,000
P1	0	50	0
P14	6	10	60
P15	10	6	60
P16	3	10	30

principle) receives a weight merit of 50, because its code assigns it the same weight as the perfect code assigns it. Because it is corrupt, it receives a content merit score of 0. Since one of its scores is 0, it has no overall deontic merit, as seems appropriate. The deontic merit scores of principles P14 and P15 reveal, unsurprisingly, that reversing the merit scores in the content and weight columns yields the same deontic merit. These assignments of deontic merit all seem plausible, and they illustrate how the proposed methods satisfy Criteria 6.1 and 6.2: if two principles have the same content merit, but one has a higher weight merit, then the latter's overall deontic merit will be higher, while if two principles have the same weight merit, but one has a higher content merit, then the latter's overall deontic merit will also be higher. Principles P6 in G and P6 in G* have the same content merit, but P6 in G* has less weight merit, so its deontic merit is less. Principles P14 and P16 have the same weight merit, but P14 has greater content merit, so its deontic merit is greater.

6.2.5 Tying up a loose end: assigning weights to imperfect principles

In assigning weights to principles with imperfect content (such as principles P1 and P14–P16) I have simply assumed that such weights are available. However, determining a principle's weight disvalue is far from straightforward in cases in which the principle's content diverges from that of a perfect principle. Such an imperfect principle would not be part of the perfect code, so how can we determine what weight the perfect code would ascribe to it?

Let's look at the case of merely imperfect (but not corrupt) principles first. Recall that the imperfect Principle P4 says, "It is obligatory to keep every promise," whereas we assumed that the perfect content is that of Principle P3, which says, "It is obligatory to keep a promise unless it has been elicited by deceit." To calculate the deontic merit of Principle P4 we have to know how much weight would be assigned to P4 by the perfect code. However, the perfect code assigns *no* weight to P4, since P4 is not included in the perfect code. Fortunately it appears there is at least a rough and ready way for the Pragmatic theorist to surmount this problem. To ascribe a principle such as P4 a content merit from the perfect code perspective, we need to identify some principle, fully endorsed by the perfect code, to which we can appropriately compare P4 as its counterpart.[25] For example, P4 is most similar to the perfect P3, so we can compare P4 to P3. Of course there are other perfect principles to which we could also compare P4 in terms of content—for example, we might compare P4 to a perfect Principle P17, which says, "It is obligatory to offer your seat on public transportation to elderly persons." But P4 bears no similarity to P17—there is little overlap in the actions they prescribe—so this comparison seems irrelevant. We need to identify the appropriate principle, fully endorsed by the perfect code, to which we should compare P4. This principle will presumably apply to the same field of action as P4, namely keeping promises. Once we have identified this counterpart principle, we can estimate how closely the content of the imperfect P4 resembles the content of its perfect counterpart (this provides us with the measure of content merit deserved by the imperfect principle).[26] By extension we can then ascribe to the imperfect P4 the *weight* ascribed by the perfect code to its perfect counterpart principle. In this case, as we have seen, it seems appropriate to compare Principle P4 to Principle P3. The weight merit of P4 would be calculated by finding the deviation between its ideal weight and the weight assigned to it by its code. Thus if the perfect code assigns a weight of 40 to Principle P3, it would also, by stipulation, assign the same weight to the imperfect P4. If P4's own code also assigns a weight of 40 to P4, then P4's weight merit is 50 (50 minus 0 deviation). If the code assigns a weight different from 40 to P4, then its weight merit will be lower. Of course the *content* of P4 diverges from the content of Principle P3, so P4 will have a content merit lower than 50.[27]

The task of assigning weight merit to a corrupt principle, such as Principle P1, can proceed along the same lines. P1 says, "It is permissible to lie only when doing so will violate important rights." To establish that P1 is corrupt we need to identify the perfect principle to which it should be compared. This will be a perfect principle covering the same field of action (lying) as does P1. Perhaps the perfect counterpart of the corrupt

---

[25] This implicitly assumes that each principle within a candidate code has a unique counterpart principle with perfect content to which it should be compared. It seems possible, however, that a principle might equally resemble several perfect principles. Should one of these be picked out as the unique counterpart principle? Or should the principle gain content-value from comparing it to several counterparts? It is also possible that the perfect code includes only one principle for a given field of action (such as keeping promises), whereas an imperfect code divides up the field of action, including several principles for obligations relating to that field (or vice versa). There are inevitable complexities here that we need not address in order to pursue the main argument, leaving it to the Pragmatic theorist to work them out.

[26] As Nate Flores points out (in an unpublished seminar note), we should be able to do this numerically by comparing how much overlap there is in the prescriptions of the perfect principle and the prescriptions of the various candidate imperfect principles.

[27] In discussion at North Carolina State University, Robert Mabrito asked how this could work in a case where the candidate code includes such a bizarre principle (for example, "It is forbidden to eat beans while wearing polyester") that it would be impossible to find a perfect counterpart to which it could be compared. However, since the perfect code is exhaustive, its general permission clause would implicitly include a permission to eat beans while wearing polyester (and a permission to not eat beans while wearing polyester). This is the "counterpart" to which the bizarre principle would have to be compared.

P1 is something like P18, "It is obligatory not to tell a lie unless doing so is necessary in order to protect important rights." Presumably there is little or no overlap between the acts prescribed by P1 and those prescribed by P18, so we evaluate P1 as corrupt.[28] Once the perfect counterpart to P1 has been identified, we can stipulate that the perfect code ascribes the same weight to P1 that it ascribes to P1's perfect counterpart. Thus if the perfect code ascribes a weight of 45 to the perfect principle P18, then the perfect code also assigns P1 a weight of 45. If its code assigns it the very same weight, then P1's weight does not diverge from that of its corresponding perfect principle, and the upshot of this procedure is that P1's weight merit is 50 (50 minus 0 deviation). If its code-assigned weight diverges from that of the perfect corresponding principle then its weight merit will be lower. Of course, since P1 is corrupt, its content merit is 0. The difference between imperfect principles whose content is merely imperfect and those whose content is corrupt is the difference between how far the prescriptions of the imperfect principle diverge from those of the corresponding perfect principle.[29]

6.2.6 Tying up further loose ends: potentially controversial implications of our proposals

It's worthwhile noting two potentially controversial implications of the proposals described in section 6.2.4. To see the first implication, consider two codes L and M which both include a principle P whose content is fully endorsed by the perfect code. The perfect code assigns P a weight of 10, but Code L assigns it a lower weight of 5 and Code M assigns it a greater weight of 15. On the proposals I've just described, Principle P would have the same weight merit of 45 (50 minus 5) in Codes L and M. However, it could be argued that Code L does worse than Code M because it *under-weights* Principle P relative to the weight assigned to it by the perfect code, whereas Code M *over-weights* it. Someone persuaded that the distortion of under-weighting is worse than the distortion of over-weighting (or the reverse) might be able to accommodate this view by multiplying the variance of under-weighting but not the variance of over-weighting (or the reverse) by some constant. Implementation of this procedure would yield the result that the weight merit of P in Code L is less than the weight merit of P in Code C^*. I shall not adopt this course, but instead view under-weighting and over-weighting as equivalent distortions.[30]

To see the second controversial implication, note that it might be argued that it is more crucial for a code to assign the correct weight to principles that are deemed by the perfect code to be most important than for the code to assign the correct weight to

[28] In the case of principles prescribing acts as obligatory, a corrupt principle may prescribe *too many* acts—ones not prescribed by its perfect counterpart. We might need to fill out our understanding of corruption by adding the stipulation that these acts are forbidden by other principles in the perfect code.

[29] If it is not possible to identify a corrupt principle by measuring the extent to which its prescriptions diverge from those of its counterpart perfect principle, then it will be up to the Pragmatic theorist to decide exactly which principles qualify as corrupt, in the sense that no matter how widely usable the principle is, its usability contributes nothing positive to its deontic value.

[30] For an illuminating discussion of asymmetries in value assignments in other contexts, see Hurka (2010).

principles that are deemed less important by the perfect code. On this view, a weight match for a principle assigned an importance of 40 by the perfect code should have more weight merit than a match for a principle assigned an importance of only 10 by the perfect code. However, mismatches in assigned weights, even for less important principles, will reverberate through the whole system, since principles within a code are weighed against each other in cases of conflict. In view of this I feel that, when calculating the weight merit of a principle, it is more reasonable to give all weight matches (and mismatches) the same merit, whether they occur in highly important principles or less important ones.[31] However, the importance of the mis-weighted principle is a crucial factor that we should not lose track of, as we shall see in the next section.

6.2.7 Introducing usability weight

I've now argued that the appropriate way to combine a principle's content merit and its weight merit is simply to multiply the two factors to yield its deontic merit. We now can turn to our second question: how should the deontic merit of a code or a principle combine with its usability to determine its overall usability value?

Before determining how to calculate a principle's usability value, we have to recognize that one element is still missing. Earlier in section 6.1 we noted that, in comparing the usability of two codes, we need to take into account not just how often the code could be used, but also how important the usable principles of each code are. If Code C is usable partly because agents can use its important principle prohibiting embezzlement (even though they can't use less important principles), whereas Code D is usable partly because agents can use its modestly important principle prohibiting employees' phoning in sick in order to attend a baseball game (even though they can't use any more important principles), then Code C is surely the more attractive code. In that discussion we characterized the relative "importance" of these two principles in terms of the importance each principle is assigned by its own code. But now that we have introduced the concept of the perfect code, we can see that what drives our judgment that Code C is more attractive than Code D is that it's genuinely more important— from a perspective outside these codes—that agents be able to apply a rule barring embezzlement than that they be able to apply a rule barring false sick day claims. Thus it's the importance assigned to these principles by the perfect code, not the importance assigned to them by their own codes, that is crucial here. Our concept of the deontic merit of a principle does not capture this feature of it, since the principle's weight merit only registers how much deviation there is between the weight assigned to the principle by its code and the weight assigned to it by the perfect code. Two principles might have very different weights but nonetheless have the same weight merit, since their code-assigned weight deviates by the same amount from their ideal weight. Since it makes a difference to the attractiveness of a code whether it is important or trivial

---

[31] My thanks to Thomas Hurka for raising questions about this kind of issue.

Table 6.7

Principle	Deontic merit of principle	Perfect weight	Usability weight
P6 in G	2,500	40	100,000
P7 in G	2,500	10	25,000
P6 in G*	1,000	40	40,000
P7 in G*	1,000	10	10,000

principles—as judged by the perfect code—that are usable, we need to incorporate a factor in the principle's usability value that reflects this.

The most natural way to do this is to multiply the principle's deontic merit by the weight assigned to that principle by the perfect code (a weight that will vary between 0 and 50). Let us call this the "usability weight" of the principle, as set out in Definition 6.3.

Definition 6.3.   Usability weight of a principle: The usability weight of a principle is the deontic merit of the principle multiplied by the weight assigned to that principle by the perfect code.

As an example, the usability weights of Principles P6 ("It is obligatory to pay what one owes in taxes") and P7 ("It is obligatory not to cut into movie queues") are shown in Table 6.7.

Having introduced usability weight, we can now turn to the question of how usability weight and usability itself combine to generate a principle's usability value—the overall value that takes into account the principle's deontic merit, its usability weight, and its extended usability.

6.2.8 Combining usability weight and usability into usability value

There are various methods by which usability and usability weight (which incorporates deontic merit and perfect weight) might be combined to determine a principle's usability value. We should start, then, by asking what criteria a Pragmatic theorist would want such a method to satisfy. The following seem to be the obvious candidates. They express two claims that are crucial for a Pragmatic theorist who wishes to argue for a non-ideal solution to the problem of error. The first claim is that both usability weight and usability make a difference to the usability value of a principle, with higher scores in either resulting in a higher usability value. The following Criteria 6.3 and 6.4 reflect this claim. The second claim is that greater usability can compensate for smaller usability weight. Criterion 6.5 highlights this claim. Criteria 6.4 and 6.5 are especially important for the Pragmatic theorist, because these claims are what enables the Pragmatic theorist to argue that a principle which is less ideal in terms of usability weight—perhaps because it has less deontic merit—but is more usable is superior to a principle that has greater usability weight but less usability. This is the basis for the Pragmatic theorist's argument that, for example, a set of simple deontological rules is superior to act utilitarianism, because the former is more usable than the latter, even though it may be less perfect in terms of its content, and therefore has less usability weight.[32]

Criterion 6.3: If Principles P and Q have the same extended usability, and P has higher usability weight than Q, then P has higher usability value than Q.

Criterion 6.4: If Principles P and Q have the same usability weight, and P is more usable in the extended sense than Q, then P has higher usability value than Q.

Criterion 6.5: If Principle P has higher usability weight than Principle Q, there is some possible level at which Q's extended usability could exceed P's extended usability such that Q would have greater usability value than P.

Once we have the final component of usability weight, arrived at by weighting a principle's deontic merit by its perfect weight, it becomes natural to calculate a principle's usability value according to Formula 6.1. This formula multiplies the usability weight of the principle by its usability, so that a principle with low usability weight but high usability can have higher usability value than a principle with high usability weight but low usability.

Formula 6.1: The extended usability value of principle P = P's usability weight × P's extended usability (or $UV_P = UW_P \times EU_P$).

Note that in this formula we revert to using what I previously called the principle's *bare (extended) usability*, or roughly the number of times it can successfully be used without error. However, by multiplying the principle's bare usability by its usability weight, we are in fact taking into account all the factors that I earlier argued were necessary: the value of a principle's usability is affected both by how closely the content and the code-assigned weight of the principle approach the relevant perfect content and weight, and also by how important the principle is (now explained as its importance as assessed by the perfect code). Applying this formula to Principles P6 and P7 in Codes G and G*, and supplying usability scores, we obtain the results shown in Table 6.8.

Table 6.8

Principle	Usability weight	Extended usability	Extended usability value
P6 in G	100,000	300	30,000,000
P7 in G	25,000	900	22,500,000
P6 in G*	40,000	300	12,000,000
P7 in G*	10,000	900	9,000,000

---

[32] Criteria 6.3 and 6.4 might be interpreted as entailing Criterion 6.5. However, it is helpful to have Criterion 6.5 as well as 6.3 and 6.4 to make explicit a bar against any system which places a cap on the total amount of usability that can count towards a code's usability value.

Table 6.8 partly illustrates the fact that our formula for calculating a principle's extended usability value satisfies Criteria 6.3 and 6.4.[33] Criterion 6.3 is illustrated by P6 and P7 in Code G, which respectively have higher usability weight than P6 and P7 in Code G*, and so correspondingly have higher usability value, even though they are equally usable in both codes. Adding another principle PN in G* which has a usability weight of 10,000 and an extended usability of 1,000 would illustrate Criterion 6.3, since it has the same usability weight as P7 in G*, but more usability, and therefore has higher usability weight (10,000,000). Moreover, it appears that the formula satisfies Criterion 6.5. P6 in Code G* has lower usability value than P6 in Code G, because it has lower usability weight. But if for some reason the usability of P6 were much higher in Code G* than in Code G—if, say, it had a usability score of 1,000, then it would have a higher usability value (40,000,000) in Code G* than in Code G. This gives the Pragmatic theorist the hope that for each deontically perfect principle (such as P6 and P7 in Code G) with low usability, it will be possible to identify a replacement principle whose lower usability weight is compensated for by its higher usability, so that the replacement principle accrues a higher usability value. This is the kind of principle the Pragmatic theorist wishes to recommend as superior to many standard moral codes. Because these standard codes are not framed to enhance their usability, they wind up leading epistemically challenged decision makers astray when they try to use these codes in deciding what to do. The Pragmatic theorist wants to find moral codes that do a better job.

However, at this point we need to think more carefully about what is meant by "extended usability" in Formula 6.1. I've temporarily been describing a principle's usability as the number of occasions on which it would be possible for the agent (given her information) to use the principle without error in deriving a prescription from the principle. Of course this doesn't translate into the number of occasions on which the agent *actually uses* the principle: she might not be interested in applying it and so never attempt to derive a prescription, although she would derive the correct one on these occasions if she did try. However, we should now notice a disadvantage of our interpreting a principle's usability in this manner. Consider Principle P19, which states that "It is permissible to break a promise if it has been elicited by fraud," and Principle P20, which states that "It is permissible to break a promise if it has been elicited by coercion." Assume that P19 and P20 have the same usability weight (perhaps even that their deontic merit, weight merit, and ideal weight are the same). Suppose the Pragmatic theorist is trying to decide whether to incorporate P19 or P20 into her favored code. In order to do so, she needs to determine whether P19 or P20 has the highest usability value. To do that, she needs to multiply the usability weight of each principle by its usability. Let us suppose the number of promises elicited by coercion

---

[33] Note that our selection of 50 as the highest content and weight values, although arbitrary, does not affect the adequacy of Formula 6.1. We could have picked any other positive integer in place of 50 and the rank-ordering of principles by usability value would have remained the same.

Table 6.9

Principle	Theoretical domain	Percentage errors	Practical domain
P19	1,000	22%	780
P20	800	5%	760

greatly outnumbers the number of promises that are elicited by fraud. Then the number of occasions on which Principle P19 actually issues a prescription (that is, occasions on which the agent may break a promise elicited by fraud) is significantly smaller than the number of occasions (that is, occasions on which the agent may break a promise elicited by coercion) on which Principle P20 does so. This means that the usability of P19, as we are now interpreting it, may be smaller than the usability of P20—even though (let's assume) on a percentage basis agents would make more mistakes in applying P20 than they would in applying P19. This distortion could easily result in P20 having higher usability value than P19. This seems like the wrong judgment, since agents would make a greater percentage of errors in applying P20 than in applying P19. We can see this in Table 6.9, which supplies usability figures for P19 and P20.

Although this effect might be taken care of at the code level, because every code will apply to all possible human acts, it will make the job of the Pragmatic theorist in selecting the best principles much easier if we can remove this distortion at the level of the principles.

Fortunately we already have the tool in hand to remove this distortion, namely to revert to an earlier suggestion in section 6.1. According to that suggestion, we should interpret a principle's usability, not as the number of occasions on which it would be used without error, but rather as the ratio between the principle's extended practical domain (all the occasions on which an agent is able to use it without error) to its theoretical domain (all the occasions on which the principle issues prescriptions).[34] As before, we will call this the "P/T ratio" of the principle. We can then revise our definition of "usability" as follows:

Definition 6.4.   Comparative extended usability of a principle: Principle P is more usable (in the extended sense) than Principle Q if and only if the P/T ratio of Principle P is greater than the P/T ratio of Principle Q.

---

[34] Expressing this accurately may be slightly more complicated than this phrasing suggests. As John Carroll proposes, it would clarify matters if we thought of every principle as having the following form: It is obligatory for S to do A if conditions C obtain. Then for a principle to prescribe an action to a particular agent on a particular occasion, the conditions C must obtain. For an agent to be usable by an agent on a given occasion, it must be the case that the principle prescribes an action on that occasion (i.e., the act is possible, and conditions C obtain), and also be true that if the agent wanted to derive a prescription from the principle on that occasion, he would derive the correct prescription. So if Principle P19 states that "It is permissible to break a promise if it has been elicited by fraud," it only prescribes an action to an agent on an occasion on which the agent has made a promise, there is opportunity for the agent to act in a way that fulfills the promise, and the agent's making the promise was elicited by fraud.

Table 6.10

Principle	Usability weight	Extended usability (P/T ratio)	Extended usability value
P6 in G	100,000	0.6	60,000
P7 in G	25,000	0.9	22,500
P6 in G*	40,000	0.6	24,000
P7 in G*	10,000	0.9	9,000

So, for example, suppose as above that the theoretical domain of P19 is 1,000, and its extended practical domain is 780, while the theoretical domain of P20 is 800, and its practical domain is 760. Then the P/T ratio for P19 is 780/1,000 or 0.78, while the P/T ratio for P20 is 760/800 or 0.95. Although P20 can be successfully used on fewer occasions, its P/T ratio is superior to that of P19, so it should rank higher in terms of usability. When deciding which principle has the highest usability value, we should measure each principle's usability as defined by Definition 6.4 in terms of its P/T ratio. Thus our evaluations of P6 and P7 in Table 6.8 would be restated as in Table 6.10, in which I assume that P6 can be used 300 times, while its theoretical domain is 500, for a P/T ratio of 0.6, and that P7 can be used 900 times while its theoretical domain is 1,000 for a P/T ratio of 0.9.

Calculating usability in this way preserves compliance of Formula 6.1 with Criteria 6.3, 6.4, and 6.5. We seem to have found a way for the Pragmatic theorist to attain her goal: to conceptualize the relations among a principle's crucial features (its content merit, its weight merit, its importance as assessed by the perfect code, and its extended usability) in a manner that enables her to calculate the usability values of principles. According to this conception, the extended usability value of a deontically imperfect principle can exceed the extended usability value of a deontically more perfect principle by virtue of having higher usability.

6.2.9 The extended usability value of a code

Having found an appropriate formula for calculating the usability value of a *principle*, all that remains to establish is the usability value of a *code*. At this point it seems clear that the usability value of a code is a function of the usability values of its various principles. We need to construct this function to avoid certain distortions: those that might arise simply because one code has more principles than another, and those that might arise because the prescriptions of several principles of a code might overlap, so that these principles all generate prescriptions regarding a single act. This can be done by construing the extended usability value of a code as equal to the *average* extended usability value of the code's principles, as is set out in Definition 6.5.[35]

---

[35] In discussion at North Carolina State University, Michael Pendlebury raised the question of whether simply adding the usability values of a code's principles would unfairly distort the results in favor of codes that have more principles, as compared to codes that have fewer principles. John Carroll

Table 6.11

Principle	Extended usability value of principle	Extended usability value of code
P6 in G	60,000	41,250
P7 in G	22,500	
P6 in G*	24,000	16,500
P7 in G*	9,000	

Definition 6.5.   Extended usability value of a code: The extended usability value of a code equals the average extended usability value of the code's principles.[36]

The resulting usability values of Codes G and G* (insofar as these values arise from Principles P6 and P7 alone) are shown in Table 6.11.

As we anticipated, the usability value of Code G is higher than that of Code G*, since Code G* mis-weights its principles. Of course the scores in Table 6.11 for the usability values of these codes aren't their complete scores. Any adequate code would include principles covering conduct not addressed in Principle P6 and P7. And even if Code G and G* contain no more normative substance than that incorporated into Principles P6 and P7, each must also include principles stating that violating P6 or P7 is wrong, as well as a closure principle stating that all acts which are neither obligatory nor wrong are permissible. Here we need not try to calculate these codes' total deontic values.

In light of our findings, we can reject Standard 6.2 in favor of a new Standard 6.3, which utilizes the definition of extended usability value in Definition 6.5:

Standard 6.3.   If the extended usability value of moral Code X is higher than the extended usability value of moral Code Y, then, other things being equal, X is better than Y.

is responsible for the suggestion that one could remedy this problem by focusing on the average usability value of the code's principles rather than their total values. This technique also addresses the issue of overlapping prescriptions.

[36] Eli Shupe (in an unpublished seminar paper) points out that the Pragmatic theorist would want the measure for deontic merit of a code to reflect not merely its content merit and its weight merit, as I have defined them, but also to reflect certain holistic features of the weights it assigns to its principles as compared to the weights assigned to them by the perfect code. For example, a better code would preserve the rank order of the principles as assigned by the perfect code. Thus suppose the perfect code assigns the principle prohibiting murder a weight of 40, and the principle prohibiting torture a weight of 35. One imperfect code assigns the principle prohibiting murder a weight of 47 and the principle prohibiting torture a weight of 35, while a second imperfect code assigns the principle prohibiting murder a weight of 40 and the principle prohibiting torture a weight of 42. These two codes have identical weight merit as I have defined it (since the weights assigned to these two principles deviate from the perfect weights by the same total amounts), but the second code seems worse, since it assigns torture a greater weight than it assigns murder and so reverses their rank order. A superior measure of a code's weight merit would not only take into account the amount of deviation in the weights from those assigned by the perfect code, but would also take into account holistic features such as degree to which rank-ordering of weighted principles is preserved by the imperfect codes. I have not tried to develop such a measure here. Incorporating such a measure should make no difference to points in this and the subsequent chapter.

This standard, like its predecessors, is phrased in terms of "other things being equal," since some Pragmatic theorists may want to claim that additional features of moral codes (such as their capacity to motivate agents to comply with them) are relevant to their overall superiority. Since the definition of the extended usability value of a code appropriately reflects the contributions of the various factors that determine extended usability value, I will interpret the "other things being equal" clause to refer to factors (such as agents' capacity to be motivated to follow the code) *beyond* the components of a code's extended usability value. Once again, what this standard implicitly asserts is that a code with higher usability value is better than one with lower usability value in regard to satisfying at least some of the four postulated advantages for usability.

This standard applies to the comparison between two codes. It does not say that if the usability value of moral Code X were higher than it actually is, then Code X itself would be better. This might be true. But since we are regarding the usability value of a code as a given, the job of Standard 6.3 is to tell us what makes one code superior to another.

I think it is fair to say that no non-ideal Pragmatic theorist has actually done the hard work of trying to sort out what factors should be taken into account in determining what I am calling the "extended usability value" of a code, or to balance these factors against each other, or to balance the usability weights of candidate codes against their usability scores, or to utilize the outcome of such a process to figure out which among all the rival non-ideal solutions is actually best. But Definition 6.5 and Standard 6.3 together provide the tools by which this can in principle be done. In Chapter 7 we will examine the question of whether Standard 6.3 is correct: that one code's greater usability value as compared to another code's usability value genuinely guarantees that the first code is superior (other things being equal) to the second code, in terms of better securing one or more of the four conceptual and goal-oriented advantages that the Pragmatic theorist hopes her solution to the problem of error will achieve: increase in usability for decision-making, enhancement of a basic form of justice, increased social welfare and cooperation, and performance of a better pattern of actions.

7

Assessing Non-Ideal Pragmatic Responses to the Problem of Error

Even a bad decision, I was told, is better than no decision at all.[1]

In Chapters 4 and 5 we looked at attempts to find completely error-proof codes—codes that are universally usable without error as decision-guides. The codes we examined either fell short of being universally usable, or else suffered from other flaws that rendered such codes extremely unattractive as solutions to the problem of error. With this background, we turned our attention in Chapter 6 to an alternative Pragmatic solution to the problem of error: identification of a code that would not be usable by every agent on every occasion, but would nonetheless be more highly usable than many standard codes, and for this reason be superior to these standard codes. Chapter 6 was dedicated to trying to spell out, in a way that is sympathetic to the Pragmatic theorist's project, how to understand and estimate the value of a "non-ideal" code, that is, a code that achieves significant, although imperfect, usability. We found a formula that the Pragmatic theorist can use for measuring what we called the "extended usability value" of a principle, and a method for using the usability values of principles to measure the overall usability value of the code that contains them. These methods reveal how (as the Pragmatic theorist hopes) a code might be deontically less perfect but more usable, and hence may have a higher extended usability value, than deontically more perfect but less usable rival codes.

This conceptualization involves measuring the "usability value" of a principle according to the following formula:

Formula 6.1: The extended usability value of principle P = P's usability weight × P's extended usability (or $UV_p = UW_p \times EU_p$).

The extended usability value of a complete code is then calculated by calculating the average extended usability value of the code's component principles. We concluded that the appropriate standard for assessing whether one code is superior to another in part because of its usability value is the following:

---

[1] Kudo (2015).

Standard 6.3.   If the extended usability value of moral Code X is higher than the extended usability value of moral Code Y, then, other things being equal, X is better than Y.

Standard 6.3 seems the best expression of the Pragmatic theorist's view that greater usability makes a moral code better, and can outweigh superior deontic merit in a less usable code. This chapter will now examine whether Standard 6.3 is correct: that a code's greater usability value as compared to a rival code genuinely guarantees, other things being equal, one or more of the four conceptual and goal-oriented advantages that the Pragmatic theorist hopes his solution to the problem of error will secure: greater usability for decision-making, enhancement of a basic form of justice, increased social welfare, and performance of a better pattern of actions.

7.1 Problems for the Non-Ideal Pragmatic Approach

Before turning directly to look at the impact of usability value on the four advantages, we can now see that the Pragmatic approach is seriously defective on more general grounds. The first ground is revealed by considering the array of principles in Table 7.1, in which it is assumed that the principles all have the same ideal weight.

Principle 21 has perfect deontic merit (a score of 2,500), but its usability ratio is only 0.1, so its usability value is 10,000. The principles arrayed below P21 have the same usability value (10,000) but they must achieve this value by greater bare usability than P21, since the deontic merit (and therefore usability weight) of each is smaller. Thus Principle P22 also achieves a usability value of 10,000, but because its deontic merit is only 50 percent of P21's deontic merit, it has to be twice as usable as P21. Principle P23, which has only 25 percent the deontic merit as P21, must be exactly four times as usable as P21 to achieve the same usability value. And of course each of these principles would have to be at least slightly more usable than what is shown here in order to achieve a usability value superior to that of P21.

What this shows is that exceeding the usability value of a deontically perfect principle by finding a more usable, if less deontically perfect, principle does not necessarily come cheaply. The deontically less perfect principle will typically need to be substantially more usable than the deontically perfect principle.[2] The non-ideal Pragmatic solution to the problem of error is not an easy one to achieve.

---

[2] Of course there are some exceptions to this. Consider two principles P and P* that are identical except that the statement of P leads to fewer mistakes in application than the statement of P* (perhaps P is phrased in terms of more easily understood frequencies while P* is phrased in terms of less easily understood probabilities). Then the deontic merit of P and P* is identical, but P is more usable than P*. This is the kind of phenomenon to which Pragmatic theorists (as well as legislators in formulating statutes) should pay attention.

Note that how much more usable a principle with lower deontic merit would have to be depends on what the relative weightings of deontic merit and usability weight are in setting the usability value of the principles.

Table 7.1

Principle	Content merit (50 – absolute deviation)	Weight merit (50 – absolute deviation)	Deontic merit	Perfect weight	Usability weight	Usability (P/T ratio)	Usability value of principle	Usability increase over P21 needed to match P21's usability value
P21	50	50	2,500	40	100,000	0.1	10,000	0 ×
P22	50	25	1,250	40	50,000	0.2	10,000	2 ×
P23	25	25	625	40	25,000	0.4	10,000	4 ×

But there is another and more troubling way in which the non-ideal Pragmatic solution does not come cheaply. To *identify* the best moral code (even one with incomplete usability), the Pragmatic theorist must have extensive moral knowledge[3] about the deontic merits of the candidate codes, and must know (at least roughly) how usable the various candidate imperfect codes are. This requires him to calculate the P/T ratios of the principles that are included in each code. Recall that the P/T ratio of a principle is the ratio between the principle's extended practical domain (all the occasions on which an agent is able to use it without error) and its theoretical domain (all the occasions on which the principle issues prescriptions). He needs this ratio for each principle so that he can identify the usability value of each principle and of the code containing it, and so ascertain which code has the highest usability value. Even if we assume that the theorist can appeal to moral knowledge alone in order to ascertain the content and weight merits, as well as the usability weights, of the rival principles, his calculation of the P/T ratios requires a massive amount of *nonmoral* knowledge about the world and about the kinds of ignorance and mistakes under which agents tend to labor. This is true for both consequentialist and deontological codes.

Of course the Pragmatic theorist may have enough relevant knowledge about certain regularities in the ways human decision makers fall into error that he can rule out certain kinds of candidate codes as non-contenders. He may know, for example, that human decision makers make more errors of judgment when they calculate using decimals rather than fractions, and he may know that decision makers are more likely to make erroneous judgments when statements are phrased using socially denigrated racial or ethnic labels.[4] This kind of knowledge would enable the Pragmatic theorist to reduce the number of contending codes. For example, suppose the theorist is considering two codes. Code C_1 recommends donating 1/100 of one's income to charity, while the otherwise similar C_2 recommends donating 0.01 of one's income to charity. Knowing that people make fewer arithmetical errors using fractions, the theorist can knock C_2 out of contention. But it hardly follows that C_1 is the *best* code. How would its usability value compare to C_3, which recommends donating 1/95 of one's income to charity? Clearly C_1 is mathematically simpler to use, but even fraught with errors C_3 might secure more actions closer to the deontically perfect actions, which involve (let us say) donating 1/92 of one's income to charity. Or it might not—who knows? To select the best among the codes remaining after the obviously epistemically problematic codes have been rejected would appear to require an amount of nonmoral knowledge significantly greater than the amount required to identify the deontically perfect moral laundry list. To assemble the correct moral laundry list the theorist must know, for each possible occasion for action, (a) what action is prescribed by the deontically perfect code, and (b) what beliefs the agent in that situation would have about that prospective action, so that a prescription can be framed which would lead the agent to perform

---

[3] By "knowledge" and "know" I mean "have a true belief about."
[4] I owe this point to Nate Flores and Eli Shupe (in unpublished seminar notes).

the right action if he wanted to. By contrast, to identify the non-ideal moral code with the highest usability value the theorist must calculate the usability values for *each* of the many rival imperfect codes (the ones that remain after he has knocked out the codes that would obviously fall prey to general human proclivities towards certain types of error). This requires calculating, for each principle in each non-ideal code under consideration, how many occasions there are on which the principle prescribes actions to agents, and how frequently agents who are prescribed actions by such a principle would fail to apply it successfully. This is a truly daunting amount of nonmoral information for the theorist to obtain, and because it requires information about a multitude of codes rather than just one, it seems to be an even greater obstacle than the information required to identify the moral laundry list.

Of course, once the theorist acquires this information, and also calculates the usability weights of the codes under consideration, he can identify the code with the highest usability value. At this point the theorist's knowledge could in principle be promulgated widely in society and down through the generations so that individual agents are not required to calculate it themselves, or to have more nonmoral information than they normally possess in order to apply the recommended code to their decisions. However, even this claim may be questionable. Individual agents' cognitive powers and nonmoral information are likely to change over the generations, so that the P/T ratio, and hence usability value, of any given code will change over time. This suggests that it will be necessary to inculcate different codes from one generation to the next. Either this means the original theorist must take into account these kinds of changes, or that a new theorist will be needed for each generation in which they occur.[5] But even if we concern ourselves only with the epistemic hurdle the original theorist must surmount for her own generation, it seems far beyond the capacity of any human being. In effect the Pragmatic solution, even when it recommends non-ideal codes as the best solution to the problem of error, removes the epistemic burden from the individual decision maker only to bury the theorist under an even greater burden, when the theorist is no more capable of shouldering his burden than the original decision maker was.

A Pragmatic theorist might respond by arguing that his task is not to successfully identify the correct moral code, but only to propose the one that, to the best of his information, is most likely to be the correct code. But if this is a satisfactory answer for the theorist hampered by false or uncertain beliefs, it should also be a satisfactory answer for the individual decision maker hampered by false or uncertain beliefs. On this view, the decision maker too could say that his task is not to successfully identify the action he ought to perform, but rather to identify the action that, to the best of his information, is most likely to be the action he ought to perform. But the Pragmatic

---

[5] This raises another difficult problem for the non-ideal Pragmatic theorist. Suppose each generation has better information than the previous generation. Then Code C might be best for Generation 1, Code C* might be best for Generation 100, and Code C# might be best for the "average" generation. Should Generation 100 be guided by Code C, C#, or C*? A parallel question can be posed for differentially informed individuals within the same generation.

theorist is committed to rejecting this view, since to accept it would be to abandon the Pragmatic approach (which insists that the account of right-making characteristics is identical with the correct decision-guide) in favor of the Hybrid approach (which countenances a separation between the correct account of right-making character- istics and the correct decision-guide). Why should a moral theory be acceptable even though the theorist's endorsement of it is based on a belief that it is most likely (although not certain) to be correct, but a moral theory must be rejected as unaccept- able because an agent who derives a prescription from it as most likely to be right would sometimes be mistaken? It seems incoherent for the Pragmatic theorist to accept nonmoral error at the theoretical level as innocuous, but reject nonmoral error at the practical level as fatal. We should conclude that for the Pragmatic theorist there is no escape from the epistemic burden by taking this route.

To evade this problem the Pragmatic theorist might argue that no single theorist (or even group of theorists) needs to shoulder this burden. Rather the theorist may claim, following Mill, that we can rely on the collective experience of mankind to gradually reveal the necessary facts to humanity.[6] But there is a crucial difference between Mill and the Pragmatic theorist on this issue. Mill holds that the *content* of the correct moral code (that is, the utilitarian principle) can readily be known. What the experience of mankind reveals to us is which individual acts or types of acts tend to *accord with* that code. But the non-ideal Pragmatic theorist holds that what types of actions are right or wrong is determined by the code with the highest usability value, and hence that we cannot even know the content of the correct code until we have sufficient nonmoral information to identify that code. Until this stage of complete nonmoral knowledge is reached, decision makers cannot even know what kinds of actions they should be aiming at. Thus for the Pragmatic theorist, although not for Mill, knowledge of the correct moral code depends on acquiring full nonmoral knowledge of the sort described above.

The Pragmatic theorist might respond to this by pulling in his horns and saying that he needn't identify the moral code with the *highest* usability value; all he needs to find is one that reaches a certain threshold acceptable level of usability value which (he assumes) the deontically perfect code fails to reach. Of course, if the Pragmatic theorist adopts this "satisficing" approach, he will have to identify what the crucial threshold level is, doubtless a controversial matter. Since the Pragmatist only needs to find one code that reaches or exceeds the threshold level, the amount of information required is less than if he has to evaluate many codes in the search for the very best one. But even if this information is more easily available than the information required to identify the best less-than-perfect code, the satisficing option is not an attractive one. Identifying a single code that has a usability value above that threshold level would itself require a daunting amount of information about that code, and of course the search for a satis- factory code may involve examining a number of candidate codes. Moreover, adopting

---

[6] Mill (1957), Chapter II.

the satisficing approach brings with it all the issues people have found with satisficing, including the fact that the satisficing Pragmatic theorist would allegedly be fully rational, having found a "satisfactory" code, to reject other codes, even if he is certain that their usability values are higher. In addition, since multiple codes might reach the satisficing threshold, there is also the problem that different theorists might select different codes. Thus some agents might follow the code endorsed by one theorist, while other agents might follow different codes endorsed by other theorists. This would inevitably lead to failures to appropriately coordinate their activities among even well-motivated and well-informed agents. Finally, we can again ask why it is legitimate for the theorist (who lacks sufficient information to identify the best theory) to use a satisficing approach to identify an acceptable moral theory, when the same theorist denies that it is legitimate for an agent (who lacks sufficient information to identify the best action according to the correct theory) to use a satisficing approach to identify an acceptable action. What is sauce for the goose ought to be acceptable sauce for the gander. All things considered, the non-ideal Pragmatic theorist should not be tempted by a satisficing approach to determining the correct moral theory.

The discussion of the last few paragraphs actually overlooks something crucial. We are discussing *non-ideal* Pragmatic Responses to the problem of error—responses that don't require universal usability of the correct code, but accept something less than full usability, recognizing that full usability may be epistemically beyond our reach.[7] However, the Pragmatic theorist still tries to maximize usability value within the sphere of attainability. Given Definition 6.5 for calculating the extended usability value of a code (according to which the extended usability value of a code equals the average extended usability value of the code's principles), it should be clear that the moral laundry list is in fact the code that maximizes extended usability value. Since its prescriptions exactly coincide with those of the deontically ideal code, and since it is perfectly usable, no other code can surpass its usability value. But we have already dismissed the moral laundry list as epistemically unattainable: thus in trying to spell out the non-ideal Pragmatist's strategy we find ourselves thrust back again into the clutches of the same epistemically unavailable solution. To avoid this conclusion, the non-ideal Pragmatist would have to establish some further constraint that would eliminate the moral laundry list from contention, and it is not clear what such a constraint could be. In Chapter 13 I will discuss possible constraints of this sort, but they seem unlikely to assist the Pragmatic theorist's project. Lacking any such constraint, it appears that the non-ideal Pragmatist position is actually unstable. The logic of the position pushes it ineluctably towards the ideal Pragmatist position and the moral laundry list, solutions we have already rejected.

---

[7] A Pragmatic theorist may seek a code offering less than perfect usability for another reason: such a code might better advance other goals he has for moral codes, such as their capacity to motivate those governed by them. However, before settling whether a given non-ideal code would be acceptable for this reason, he must first determine how effectively it would achieve the distinctive goals of usability as such. The considerations in this section show how epistemically difficult it would be to determine this.

The non-ideal Pragmatic theorist sets out to avoid the epistemic problem for morality by seeking a moral code that is imperfectly usable but nonetheless more usable by normal epistemically challenged agents than the standard moral codes. He hopes to find codes that will better achieve one or more of the four advantages he seeks for the correct moral code. However—even if we find that the correct code does indeed achieve these four advantages—once again the strategy for selecting the correct code just transfers the epistemic problem from the agent trying to use a code to the theorist trying to identify the best code. This epistemic challenge at the level of the theoretician is sufficiently daunting to raise grave doubts about the attractiveness of the non-ideal Pragmatic solution to the problem of error. Moreover, it appears that the non-ideal Pragmatic solution cannot be prevented from morphing into the ideal Pragmatic solution, a solution we have already seen to be fraught with lethal problems.

7.2 Conceptual Advantages of Codes with Higher Usability Values

Standard 6.3 states that if the extended usability value of moral Code X is higher than the extended usability value of moral Code Y, then, other things being equal, X is better than Y. Let us turn to the question of whether a code that prevails according to Standard 6.3 will, other things being equal, necessarily better attain the conceptual advantages the Pragmatic theorist hopes to attain than these advantages can be attained by its rivals having lower usability. It is worthwhile seeing that the picture here isn't as rosy as the Pragmatic theorist hopes, even while we acknowledge the epistemic challenges of identifying the code with the highest usability value.[8]

7.2.1 The conceptual advantage of usability per se

The first conceptual advantage that theorists have hoped for codes with high usability value derives from the claim that the concept of morality, or at least one of the chief functions of morality, requires that a moral code be usable, in some robust sense, to guide actual choices. For the Pragmatic theorist the "robust sense" in question requires usability in the extended sense, and we have incorporated that into our metric for usability value.

Our suggested method (encapsulated in Definition 6.5, according to which the extended usability value of a code equals the average extended usability value of the code's principles) for measuring the usability value of codes does seem to secure the Pragmatic theorist what she needs in order to argue that deontically imperfect codes can be superior to deontically perfect ones that have lower usability.

---

[8] In sections 7.2.1–7.3.3 I am temporarily waiving my claim that the code with the highest extended usability value is the moral laundry list, and focusing instead on codes whose usability value falls short of perfection.

In assessing this claim, we must remember that a code's usability value is equal to the average extended usability value of its component principles. In turn the usability value of a component principle is a function of two things: its usability weight (itself a function of the principle's deontic merit and the weight assigned to it by the perfect code) and its extended usability. Although the Pragmatic theorist tends to focus on codes that have greater usability value because they are more usable, there are also codes that have greater usability value, even though they have lower *usability*, because they have higher deontic merit. In Table 7.1, for example, Principle P23 has a usability value of 10,000. Table 7.2 shows the addition of a new Principle P24 with slightly lower usability than that of P23, but somewhat higher deontic merit and the same ideal weight, so that it would have a higher usability value than P23, even though P23 is more usable. Then a Code C that contains P24 would have higher usability value than a Code C* that is otherwise identical but contains P23, the more usable principle.

This reinforces our finding that usability value does not simply track usability. Thus the Pragmatic theorist cannot say that a code with higher *usability value* necessarily has higher *bare usability*. It may instead have less bare usability, and so be usable as a decision-guide by fewer agents or on fewer occasions.

However, this does not seem to undermine the true spirit of the Pragmatic approach, since the higher deontic merit of P24 (as compared to P23) would mean that the usability of P24 is *worth* more than the usability of P23. Since P24 has higher deontic merit than P23, an agent's acting in accord with P24 is worth more than an agent's acting in accord with P23, a fact that is duly reflected in the higher usability value of P24. We have assumed this means that an agent's being able to derive the correct prescription from P24 is more valuable than an agent's being able to derive the correct prescription from P23. Thus Standard 6.3, which incorporates our method for calculating usability value, appears to provide what the Pragmatic theorist *should* want (even though she may not have fully realized it) in terms of the connection between a code's usability value and its value for guiding decisions. She should give up the hunt for greater bare usability in favor of a hunt for greater usability value, and in adopting Standard 6.3 she does so. Even though this is the best approach for the Pragmatic theorist, it may still come as hard news to her. She can argue that a code with higher usability value achieves something important in the realm of usability that is not achieved by a code with lower usability value. But she cannot claim that, other things being equal, the best code is necessarily more usable in the bare sense than its rivals.

Table 7.2

Principle	Content merit (50 – absolute deviation)	Weight merit (50 – absolute deviation)	Deontic merit	Perfect weight	Usability weight	Usability (P/T ratio)	Usability value of principle
P23	25	25	625	40	25,000	0.4	10,000
P24	25	26	650	40	26,000	0.3999	10,397.4

7.2.2 The conceptual advantage of securing justice

In section 7.2.1 we examined the first sought-after conceptual advantage of more usable moral codes: their usefulness for guiding decisions. We learned that the most usable codes may not have the highest usability value. Still, usability value, rather than mere usability, seems to be the conceptual advantage that we should seek, as Standard 6.3 proposes. The second sought-after conceptual advantage for more usable moral codes derives from the claim that a basic form of justice requires that moral codes be such that everyone—intelligent, slow-witted, well-informed, or poorly-informed—be able to live the moral life successfully. When "being able to live the moral life successfully" is interpreted as "being able to conform to morality," and this in turn is understood to require "being able to identify accurately what is required to conform to morality," then the considerations adduced in Chapter 6 suggest that whether or not a code satisfies this goal better than a rival code depends on something more complex than the mere number of occasions on which agents would be able to correctly identify what the codes prescribe. Relative satisfaction of the goal of justice should depend not just on the number of times correct prescriptions would be derived, but also on the *nature* of the prescriptions. For example, if the use of a Code C would produce fewer correct prescriptions, but ones involving decisions deemed by both Code C and the deontically perfect code to be highly significant moral decisions, whereas the use of Code C* would produce a greater number of correct decisions, but ones deemed by Code C* and the perfect code to be trivial decisions, then this basic form of justice may be better served by Code C, despite its lesser degree of bare usability. Furthermore, the content of the code also matters: a person is hardly able to live the successful moral life merely because she can accurately identify the duties imposed by a corrupt moral code. Our concept of usability value takes these aspects of a code into account in making usability value depend partly on usability weight. So thus far Standard 6.3 seems to be on the right track: the form of justice in question seems to be better promoted by a code possessing higher usability value as we have defined it. Recognition of this leads us to abandon the view that higher bare usability per se leads to more opportunities to lead the morally successful life.[9]

However, the appearance that higher usability value necessarily secures greater justice (other things being equal) is misleading. Consider the question of *how wrong* the acts are that would be performed by agents who would be *unable* to comply successfully with the code in question. Consider a Code C, which has higher usability value than Code C*. From what we have said so far, the agents who would to be able to comply completely with C would be able to achieve, as a group, more successful moral lives than the smaller number of agents who would be able to comply completely with C*.

---

[9] This characterization of the "successful moral life" shows that it is not content-neutral: living such a life requires conformity to a deontically worthwhile moral code, not just to the code under consideration. However, the problem raised in the next paragraph would apply with equal force to a characterization of the successful moral life that is content-neutral, simply requiring conformity with whatever code is under consideration.

But what about the agents who would be unable to comply with C, or with C*, on some occasions? If the agents who would be unable to comply with C would perform acts that are much worse (according to C and the perfect code) than the acts that would be performed by the agents who are unable to comply with C* (according to C* and the perfect code), then it could easily be the case that the overall level of possible successful moral living is worse under C than it is under C*. The degree to which an agent has the ability to live a successful moral life must surely depend, not only on what number and kinds of *right* acts the agent would be able to perform, but also on the number and kinds of *wrong* acts he would perform if he were unable to ascertain which acts are right. Thus contrary to first appearances, the fact that C has higher usability value than C* does not entail, other things being equal, that C would foster a higher level of the ability to lead a successful moral life than would C*. We will return to a consideration of this point in section 7.3.3 when we take up the question of whether a code like C can necessarily secure a better pattern of action than a code like C*.

The Pragmatic theorist, then, should accept that usability value, rather than bare usability, is what, if anything, is relevant to justice. However, because patterns of unjust actions may vary under different codes, he cannot argue that a moral code with higher usability value has the conceptual advantage, even where all else is equal, of securing greater basic justice than a code with lower usability value.

7.3 Goal-Oriented Rationales for Usability

Some Pragmatic theorists defend their view that usability is a key feature of moral codes by invoking, not only the conceptual rationales for usability we have just examined, but also by invoking more goal-oriented advantages that more usable codes are claimed to have. Using the tools we have developed, let's turn to an examination of this claim.

7.3.1 Enhancing social welfare

The first goal-oriented advantage claimed for more usable codes is that such codes will better enhance social welfare. Our question now is whether higher usability value in one code means that, other things being equal, it makes a greater positive contribution towards enhancing social welfare than the contribution made by a second code with lower usability value.

In discussing this issue we should acknowledge that a moral code is an abstract object, and of course by itself cannot affect welfare one way or another. Codes only affect welfare insofar as they are adopted and used. As rule utilitarians have found, there are many ways in which the concept of a code's being adopted and used can be interpreted. For example, we might ask what pattern of behavior is relevant (mere attempts to comply with the code? Successful attempts to comply with the code?), what populations are relevant (everyone presently alive? Everyone throughout history? Everyone in our society?), and what percentage of the population is assumed to participate (everyone? Ninety percent of the population? A majority?). Clearly the effects would be different under different hypotheses, and a code that surpassed rival codes under one hypothesis might do worse under a different hypothesis. Pragmatic theorists interested in arguing for usable codes because of their beneficial effects on social welfare would need to identify which hypothetical scenario is the appropriate one to use in testing the candidate codes. Fortunately we do not need to undertake that task to accomplish our purposes. For our project it suffices to stipulate that the rival codes are all tested under the same hypothesis, whatever the appropriate hypothesis is. I shall assume this in the following sections, and for brevity simply refer to outcomes such as changes in social welfare as "the effects of the code."

Different moral codes can, of course, have different effects on social welfare. Assessing the potential impact of a given code depends partly on what we assume about the relevant agents. Since we are examining non-ideal Pragmatic solutions to the problem of error, we are considering moral codes that fall short of universal usability because of agents' inaccurate nonmoral beliefs. But should we assume that there are sometimes additional factors preventing agents' successful use of the code in question—factors such as weakness of will, or low regard for morality? Since we are focusing on the problem of nonmoral error, it seems most appropriate to set such factors aside, and to evaluate the social impact of any code by making the assumption that all the relevant agents would be adequately motivated on every occasion to conform to that code, and would only fail because of epistemic limitations—errors about nonmoral facts that would mislead them as to what the code requires.[10]

We may begin by asking whether, other things being equal, a code's greater usability value as compared to that of a rival code always enables the first code to produce greater social welfare than the second. Of course, it's impossible to fully answer this question without knowing what the content of the *deontically perfect* code is, since its content affects the deontic merit, and so the usability value, of all the imperfect codes. While Mill pointed out that "Any ethical standard whatever will work ill if we suppose universal idiocy to be conjoined with it,"[11] the Pragmatic theorist should point out the reverse: universal perfect information can also work ill if it is conjoined with perverse ethical standards. Less dramatically, it might turn out that some principles of the perfect code require actions that reduce social welfare overall. For example, many theorists hold that the perfect code prohibits the direct killing of a terminally ill patient in irremediable pain, even though the code permits allowing such a patient to die. Arguably, following such a code results in more suffering than if direct killing in these circumstances were permitted. Imperfect principles whose content approaches that of perfect principles of this type are also likely to decrease social welfare, even if they are highly

---

[10] As Ben Bronner points out (in an unpublished seminar note), the effects of epistemic limitations may be entwined with the effects of motivational limitations in such a way that we cannot realistically disentangle them. For example, if it is too difficult for people to ascertain what a moral code requires of them, their motivation to follow it may decline. Given the complexities of trying to take such entanglements into account, I shall not attempt to do so here.

[11] Mill (1957), Chapter II.

usable and so have high usability value. The Pragmatic theorist's claim that usability increases social welfare is most plausible if the perfect principles are such that, when successfully followed, they tend to increase social welfare—and it may not be the case that all perfect principles have this attribute.

However, even if we assume all perfect principles would tend to increase social welfare if they were successfully followed, it does not follow that a code with higher usability value will necessarily (other things being equal) have greater social utility than a code with lower usability value. Lower social utility may arise because compliance with different principles can have different effects on social welfare, even if compliance with each of these principles is generally beneficial. Consider two codes that have identical principles, except that one includes Principle P ("It is obligatory to offer your seat on public transportation to people on crutches") and the other instead includes Principle P* ("It is obligatory to open the door for people on crutches"). Assume that P and P* have the same deontic merit and usability weight—they deviate by exactly the same small amount from the content of their respective counterparts in the perfect code, their code-assigned weights deviate by exactly the same small amount from the weights assigned to their counterparts by the perfect code, and the perfect code assigns them the same weight. Assume further that Principles P and P* have exactly the same sized theoretical domains, but that Principle P* has a slightly higher usability score than Principle P. Then the usability value of P* is larger than the usability value of P. But we can also assume that giving up one's seat on public transportation for people on crutches (as P requires) is generally more beneficial to the person on crutches than is opening the door for people on crutches (as P* requires). The greater benefit from people's complying with Principle P (even though slightly fewer do so) outweighs the smaller benefit from people complying with Principle P* (even though slightly more of them do so). Principle P*, the principle with the higher usability value, does not have greater social utility than Principle P, the principle with the lower usability value. The same thing will be true of the codes of which they are members. We cannot say that a code with higher usability value will, other things being equal, have greater social utility than a code with lower usability value, even though the codes in general promote social welfare.

Another type of consideration shows just as clearly that it is not always the case that higher usability-value codes comparatively enhance social welfare. Consider two codes, identical in all respects except that Code N requires (with weight 30) individuals to contribute 0.017 percent of their income to charity, while Code O requires (also with weight 30) individuals to contribute the same percentage of their income to charity that their nation provides in foreign aid as a percentage of its Gross National Product. Suppose the United States provides 0.017 percent of its Gross National Product in foreign aid. In this situation Codes N and O require exactly the same acts from US citizens. Since we have defined content merit in terms of the acts required by a code, the two codes in question have the same content and weight merit, and thus the same deontic merit (restricting our attention to the acts of US citizens and this world).

We may even assume that these two codes have perfect deontic merit and that the perfect code assigns these two principles the same weight. However, since many Americans significantly mis-estimate how much their country provides in foreign aid, many fewer errors would be made by US citizens using Code N than would be made by citizens using Code O. Thus Code N has greater usability value than Code O, because it has the same usability weight and is more usable. The Pragmatic theorist may expect, then, that greater social welfare would be produced by the more highly usable Code N. However, in this instance the opposite is the case. The Americans who mis-estimate what percentage of the Gross National Product is spent on foreign aid typically *over-estimate* this amount. Thus Americans using Code O would (mistakenly) give *more* to charity, thus arguably enhancing social welfare more than the people making fewer errors using Code N.

This example shows that usability value, even in the context of normatively meritorious codes and principles, does not affect social welfare in any simple way. It all depends on the types of errors to which each code is vulnerable: some errors *enhance* social welfare (as in this case), while others *decrease* social welfare. The charity example shows we cannot infer that greater usability value always tends to contribute positively towards the enhancement of social welfare (even when it is outweighed by some countervailing factor). Thus the Pragmatist cannot reject this counterexample by appealing to the "other things being equal" clause in Standard 6.3.

This example highlights the fact, not much examined by moral philosophers, that one way of *expressing* a moral principle may have very different effects, in terms of applicability, than another way of expressing the same principle. Since a person's ability to apply a principle depends on the exact way she represents its content to herself, theorists concerned about the usability of moral principles must pay heed to the way a principle is expressed, not just to the moral proposition it expresses, or to the set of acts the code prescribes.[12]

Our conclusion should be that there is no reason to think that relatively higher usability value inevitably improves the social impact of a moral code, or even improves it if all other factors are held equal. Of course this varies: sometimes a code with higher usability value will indeed have a better effect on social welfare than a similar but less usable code. But there is no guarantee that this will be so.

7.3.2 The special social role for morality in enhancing consensus and cooperation

One variant of the claim that more usable codes will better promote social welfare is the narrower claim that a code with higher usability value will be able to better play the

---

[12] An important real-life example of this is described in a *New York Times* article, which details the mistakes elderly people make in determining when to take their various medications. According to the article, almost 80 percent of participants aged 55 to 74 did not understand that they could take two drugs together even though one label read "every 12 hours" while the other label read "twice daily" (Span, 2015). Which instruction was given to the patients made a difference to how they understood what they were to do.

special social role often required of moral systems—the role of fostering the social consensus that makes long-term planning and cooperation possible. The implicit argument for higher usability value in this context seems clear: if, for example, the members of a society easily reach agreement about what kinds of institutions would be just, and this judgment is not overthrown, then stable institutions will be formed which enable individuals to plan their lives over the long term and cooperate with each other within the framework set by the institutions. Thus if the citizens agree once and for all that justice requires the military conscription of women as well as men, then youths of both sexes will be able to form educational and career plans in light of their likelihood of being drafted. But if shifting opinions about the impact of this policy lead to recurrent revisions of this judgment, then fewer people will be able to predict accurately whether they or their partners are likely to be called up for service over the next five or ten years, effective planning will be difficult, and lives will be disordered.

Despite the plausibility of this argument, here again we can see that whether or not a moral code would produce a high degree of consensus depends on a wide variety of factors. While higher usability value may sometimes tend to promote consensus through higher usability, conversely it may sometimes work to undermine consensus. Neither bare usability nor usability value have any intrinsic propensity to increase the possibility of achieving consensus. Our earlier discussion of completely subjectivized codes makes this point clear. A subjectivized code may reduce (although not entirely eliminate) agents' errors about what their code requires of them, but it leaves intact agents' disagreements about the underlying facts about the world—facts which can be the real basis for lack of consensus and cooperation. The two agents in the Chapter 4 case trying to meet for lunch are each able to identify accurately what their subjectivized code requires of them (that is, doing what they believe to be fulfilling their promises), but they still fail to meet, since one agent believes they are to meet on Tuesday while the other believes they are to meet on Wednesday. This kind of case shows that a highly usable subjectivized code may produce no more successful cooperative endeavors than its counterpart objectivized but more error-prone code. This in itself demonstrates that we should not adopt a code with higher usability value (because of its high usability) on the ground that its usability will necessarily improve a code's ability to play the special social role of inducing consensus and cooperation (even if other factors are equal, such as the agents' motivational commitment to the respective codes).

What about a code that achieves high usability and so high usability value, not by incorporating subjectivized duties, but rather by tailoring the content of objectivized duties to the cognitive capacities of the great mass of agents applying it? Perhaps higher usability, and so higher usability value, doesn't necessarily help subjectivized codes, but does help objectivized codes. Unfortunately, even in this restricted category of codes we cannot assume that a code with higher usability value will produce more consensus than a code with less usability value. There are several factors that explain this. For one thing, errors in application do not necessarily undermine consensus. If a particular error of application is widely, or even universally, shared among all decision makers, then consensus may still be reached—even though it is a consensus based on a common mistake. Thus, if at a certain stage of medical knowledge, everyone falsely believes that human fetuses are not alive before "quickening," there may be consensus that before quickening abortion is morally permissible. Conversely, improved accuracy of knowledge about fetal development may well lead to less agreement on whether early abortion is permissible, because although people agree that the fetus prior to quickening is alive, they may still not have enough information to agree at what stage the fetus achieves the features (such as consciousness) felt to be necessary and sufficient for personhood.

A second factor may be the need for a threshold level of agreement in order to produce effective social consensus. Suppose 35 percent of the population can apply a Code R without error to the question of military conscription for women, but only 20 percent can apply Code S to the same question without error. Assume that Codes R and S are otherwise similar, so Code R has a higher usability value because of the higher usability of its principle concerning military conscription. But suppose in this society political procedures require a 51 percent consensus in order to adopt a policy on the question of conscripting women into the military. Neither code reaches this threshold level of agreement. Thus the fewer errors generated by use of Code R do not enable it to produce the kind of social consensus that enables young adults to plan around their prospects for military service.

A third factor is the nature of the errors engendered by the rival codes. For example, some errors are less tractable than others. Although the more usable Code R generates fewer errors, these errors may be based on more deeply-ingrained (and therefore much more difficult to correct) nonmoral beliefs than the greater number of errors induced by Code S, which are based on more superficial and hence more easily dislodged nonmoral beliefs. Thus adopting Code S, which has lower usability value, might enable society to reduce its disagreements and ultimately reach effective consensus, whereas adopting Code R, which has higher usability value, might generate fewer errors, but ones so intractable that they would permanently block any such consensus-building process.[13]

In response to this some Pragmatic theorists might argue codes should be directly assessed in terms of their tendency to foster socially important levels of consensus. If so, perhaps neither Code R nor Code S would receive favorable assessment, on grounds that neither secures the required level of consensus. Or perhaps Code R (but not Code S) might be rejected on grounds that the errors it generates are intractable. But what the need for this stratagem reflects is the fact that higher usability value cannot itself necessarily secure greater social consensus, and does not even contribute positively towards greater social consensus in all cases. If enhancing social consensus is a feature by which a code should be judged, it must be handled separately from usability value, since usability value may sometimes operate to diminish social consensus.

---

[13] This kind of case illustrates the importance of determining whether the relevant error rate of a code is the error rate at a given time or the error rate over a long span of time. If the error rate over the longer span of time is taken as dispositive, then Code S may have a higher usability rate than Code R.

The discussions in this and the previous section show that a higher usability value has no uniform connection with a code's tendency to improve social welfare or its capacity to foster social cooperation, even if we hold other plausible factors such as agents' moral motivations equal. A high error rate may be part of the constellation of factors that reduce a code's social benefits, or it may have no impact on these outcomes, or it may enhance the code's social benefits. It will sometimes be true of some traditional-style codes which are fairly similar in content but have different rates of usability that the code with higher usability value may achieve greater social benefits because it is more usable. But the foregoing discussion shows that we cannot assume that a code's higher usability value, even other things being held equal, will always make a positive contribution to social welfare or consensus, much less that such a code would actually produce a more salutary effect on these social benefits than a rival code with lower usability value. Theorists who hold that a code is superior insofar as it would increase social welfare or consensus must evaluate codes directly on their success in meeting these desiderata, rather than relying on the codes' usability values as proxies for this judgment.

7.3.3 Fostering ideal patterns of action

The second claimed distinct goal-oriented advantage for a code's high usability value is that of leading to a better pattern of actions among agents attempting to apply the code in their decisions. Originally we interpreted the concept of a "better pattern of actions" to mean a pattern of actions which is better insofar as the actions accord more closely with the code in question. However, our introduction in Chapter 6 of the deontically perfect code opens up several alternative possibilities for defining a better pattern of action, some of which provide a role for the perfect code as well as a role for the code in question. Let us examine four obvious such interpretations, and ask, relative to each one, whether the fact that one code has higher usability value than another code shows that, other things being equal, the first code would result in a better pattern of actions than the second code.

On the interpretation that interprets a better pattern of actions as simply a pattern that accords more closely with the requirements of the code under review, the answer is clearly "no." Consider two codes, Code C and Code C*, each of which has only one principle. Code C may have higher usability value than Code C*, not because it is more usable than Code C*, but rather because its principle has higher usability weight than the principle of Code C*. For example, the deontic merit of the principle in Code C might be sufficiently high to outweigh the higher usability of the principle in C*, resulting in a higher usability value for Code C. Thus C, despite having higher usability value, would result in fewer actions conforming to its prescriptions than would C*—a worse pattern of actions on this interpretation of "better pattern of actions."

This suggests a second interpretation, according to which what counts as a better pattern of actions incorporates not just the number of actions conforming to the code, but also a measure of how important those actions are from the perspective of the code itself—their code-weighted importance. But in this case again, the fact that Code C has higher usability value than Code C* does not imply that, other things being equal, the pattern of actions resulting from adoption of C would be better than the pattern of actions resulting from adoption of C*. Remember that the usability value of a code reflects not only the code-weighted importance of its principles, but also how far their code-weighted importance diverges from the importance assigned to those principles by the deontically perfect code. Code C* might have lower usability value than Code C because, although it assigns very high value to its most usable principles, the value it assigns them is far higher than the value assigned to them by the perfect code. Then, on this interpretation, adoption of Code C* could result in a "better" pattern of actions than adoption of Code C, because Code C* results in more actions deemed to be highly important by C* itself—but deemed to be of little importance by the perfect code. On this interpretation, too, the code with the higher usability value (in this case Code C) will not necessarily, other things being equal, result in the better pattern of actions.

The third interpretation attempts to correct for this distortion by setting aside the prescriptions of the imperfect code under review in order to focus exclusively on the prescriptions of the deontically perfect code. This interpretation defines one pattern of actions as better than another if the first pattern includes more actions prescribed by the perfect code (weighted by their importance as assigned by the perfect code) than the second pattern. The idea behind this interpretation is that even if, as the Pragmatic theorist argues, we should judge moral *codes* by how usable they are, there is no similar argument showing that one *action* is morally better than another if it is "more usable" than the second action (whatever that might mean). Usability (or usability value) may be important for codes, but perhaps the moral value of an action is simply a function of its conformity with the perfect code.

To carry out this idea, the assessment of a pattern of actions resulting from a code must determine how many times the agents trying to follow that code would succeed in doing what the perfect code recommends (weighted by the importance of the perfect principles that prescribe these actions). But further reflection shows that if one code has higher usability value than another code, it doesn't follow that the pattern of successful actions resulting from adoption of the first code would, other things being equal, be better (according to the third interpretation) than the successful acts resulting from adoption of the second code. Of course, from the usability weight and usability scores of a principle we cannot know exactly how many of the acts that would be performed by agents trying to apply it would actually accord with the perfect principle. Still, a principle's having higher deontic merit indicates that its content and weighting of principles is closer to the content and weight of the perfect code, and it's not unreasonable to think the principle's deontic merit is a reasonable proxy for the degree to which actions conforming to that principle also conform to the corresponding perfect principle. But even if this is so, it doesn't follow that a principle with higher usability value will result in a better pattern of actions (on the current interpretation) than a principle with lower usability value. Examination of Table 7.3 shows how this can happen.

Table 7.3

Principle	Content merit (50 – absolute deviation)	Weight merit (50 – absolute deviation)	Deontic merit	Perfect weight	Usability weight	Usability (P/T ratio)	Usability value of principle
P23	25	25	625	40	25,000	0.4	10,000
P25	24	24	576	30	17,280	0.5	8,640

In Table 7.3 our old friend Principle P23 is compared to a new Principle P25 that has lower deontic merit than P23. The weight accorded P25 (30) by the ideal principle is also less than that accorded to P23 (40). However, P25 has higher usability (P/T ratio). The upshot is that P23 has higher usability *value*, even though it is less usable than P25. Suppose the theoretical domains of P23 and P25 each include 1,000 actions, so that the usability ratios in Table 7.3 indicate that P23 is usable on 400 occasions, while P25 is usable on 500 occasions. The total deontic merit of the actions complying with P23 is 250,000 (400 × 625), while the total deontic merit of the actions complying with P25 is 288,000 (500 × 576). Thus, on this interpretation, the pattern of actions resulting from P25 is "better" than the pattern of actions resulting from P23, even though P23 has higher usability value.

If P23 and P25 were embedded in two codes with otherwise identical content, the code containing P23 would have higher usability value, but would give rise to a pattern of actions diverging more from those prescribed by the perfect code. The code containing P25, despite having lower usability value, would result in a pattern of actions conforming more closely to those prescribed by the perfect code—a better pattern of actions on this interpretation of "better pattern of actions."

This suggests a final, fourth interpretation of "better pattern of actions." The problems we have found with the preceding interpretations emerge from the fact that the factors that generate a code's higher usability value are not identical to the factors that determine whether one pattern of actions is better than another. Given this divergence, inevitably the pattern of actions produced by adoption of a code may not completely mirror its usability value. What we need, it appears, is an interpretation of "better pattern of actions" that takes into account *all* the factors that go into a code's usability value. One way to do this would be to interpret the concept of a "better pattern of actions" in terms of what we can call the *usability value* of the actions that would comply with the code. So far we've only defined the "usability value" of principles and codes, where a principle's usability value is the usability weight of the principle multiplied by its extended usability (Formula 6.1), and the extended usability value of a code is the average extended usability value of the code's principles (Definition 6.5). But clearly we can extend this idea to define a parallel notion of the usability value of an action relative to a code.

On this extension, an action's usability value is simply the usability value of the principle in the code that prescribes it. Often an action will be prescribed by more than one principle, as in the case of an action that both fulfills a promise and benefits a family member. In such cases it seems plausible to simply sum the usability values of all the principles that prescribe the act in question.

> **Definition 7.1.   Usability value of an action relative to Code C:** The usability value of act A, relative to Code C, is the usability value of the principle in Code C that prescribes A (or, if A is prescribed by more than one principle in C, the combined usability values of those principles).

For example, if Principle P6 ("It is obligatory to pay what one owes in taxes") has a usability value of 30,000 in Code G, then an agent's act of paying what she owes in taxes (assuming it is prescribed by no other principles in Code G) has a usability value of 30,000 relative to Code G. Using this concept we can understand a "better pattern of actions" as a pattern in which the actions in the pattern, taken together, have higher total usability value (relative to one code) than the actions comprising a second pattern of actions (relative to another code).

> **Definition 7.2.   Relatively better pattern of action:** One pattern of actions is better, relative to Code C, than another pattern of actions is, relative to Code C*, if and only if the actions comprising the first pattern have a higher total usability value relative to Code C than the total usability value relative to Code C* of the actions comprising the second pattern.

Thus this notion of a better pattern of actions is framed relative to both the codes in question and to what is required by the perfect code, and is explicitly sensitive to the codes' usability.

Clearly, since a non-ideal code is not fully error-free, agents who attempt to follow the code will sometimes fail. Their ensuing pattern of action is thus likely to fall short of the perfect pattern of actions. Nonetheless, to the degree that the code has a high usability value we might expect that the pattern of actions performed by agents attempting to follow it would be better, other things being equal, than the pattern performed by agents attempting to follow a code with a lower usability value.

However, a concern already raised in this chapter (in section 7.2.2) shows that we cannot sustain this conclusion. To see this, let's give the Pragmatic theorist her best shot by assuming that each agent who is able to derive a correct prescription from the code under consideration does so, and moreover follows through with performance of the prescribed action. For simplicity assume that those agents who (through nonmoral error) cannot derive a correct prescription fail to comply with the code. Even under these assumptions, two codes with precisely the same usability value will not necessarily produce patterns of action that are equally good. This is revealed when we ask what actions the agents would perform who, through errors about nonmoral facts, would *not* succeed in deriving a correct prescription and following the codes in question.[14] Clearly some agents, trying but failing to follow a given moral principle, would commit only minor wrongs—their failures would be moral misdemeanors, but not moral disasters. But other agents, trying but failing to follow the very same principle, would perform much more seriously wrong acts. Thus one hunter, seeking to comply with the principle "It is wrong to shoot a human being," may shoot at a movement in the trees, erroneously thinking it is a deer, but hit another hunter in the arm. Another hunter, aiming to comply with the same principle, may shoot at a movement in the trees thinking it is a deer, but hit another hunter in the heart. The failure of the first hunter is moderately bad, while the failure of the second hunter is catastrophic.

Extending this point to code comparisons allows us to see that two codes with different contents but the same usability value may give rise to patterns of action that are not equally good. Consider two codes that are identical in every respect except that Code S includes Principle P26, "It is obligatory to always tell the truth," while Code T includes Principle P4, "It is obligatory to keep every promise." Assume that these two principles have the same usability values. But as a general rule, individuals who unwittingly violate P26 tell only minor lies, whereas individuals who unwittingly violate P4 frequently break highly important promises. Despite the fact that Code T has the same usability value as Code S, T would result in a worse pattern of actions than S. We can see from these examples that Definition 7.2 (based on Definition 6.5 of the usability value of the code) is inadequate. In assessing a pattern of actions, it takes into account only actions insofar as they comply with the code in question. It does not take into account the actions that violate the code. But clearly the value of a pattern of actions must take into account the value of *violations* as well as the value of compliant acts. The example shows that two codes might have patterns of success with precisely the same value, but patterns of failure with very different values. Although the percentage of failures is a function of the percentage of successes, the *nature* of the failures is not a function of the percentage of successes. In consequence, merely knowing that one code has higher usability value than another does not allow us to compare the overall values of the patterns of actions that would be produced by currency of the codes, since this depends on the failures as well as the successes. In light of this, we must conclude that greater usability value in a code does not guarantee a better pattern of actions, and does not necessarily contribute positively, other things being equal, to the production of a better pattern of actions.[15]

One response to this discovery might be to say that Definition 6.5 of the usability value of the code needs to be restated to take into account not only the number and importance of the successes, but also the number and seriousness of the failures that people would encounter in applying the code. Although such a change would extend

---

[14] For further discussion of this point in the context of rule utilitarianism, see H. Smith (2010b).
[15] Note the importance of our earlier caveat that Standard 6.3 only applies to one code's having higher usability value than another code, not to the question of whether a code would be better if its own usability value were higher. Doubtless Code S would produce a better pattern of actions if *it* could be used successfully more often. But that is not the question we are asking.

well beyond the core mandate of the Pragmatic theorist, whose focus is on the number of times a code can successfully be applied by agents trying to use it, the change could be seen as a friendly amendment for any non-ideal Pragmatic theorist trying to find a code that would produce the best possible pattern of actions.[16] No doubt such a new account of usability value could be developed, a task that would require a measure for how seriously wrong various failures to successfully apply the code would be. (Note that this measure would also be helpful in allowing the non-ideal Pragmatic theorist to address the very similar problem I raised in section 7.2.2 for his ability to argue that a non-ideal moral code would secure greater justice than a less usable code. In effect the definition of "usability value" would have been altered to guarantee this result.) Unfortunately our theory as developed so far does not provide the tools for developing such an account. Although we have introduced a way to measure how far the content of a given principle diverges from the content of its perfect counterpart, this method only requires assessing how much overlap there is between the set of actions required by the principle and the set required by its perfect counterpart. Clearly this particular measure cannot be utilized in assessing how seriously wrong an individual wrong action is. I will have to leave the development of such a measure to future Pragmatic theorists who wish to propose non-ideal versions of their approach as the best solution to the problem of error. However, we should note that requiring the evaluation of a code's usability value to include the various disvalues of all the wrong acts that agents would perform would dramatically exacerbate the epistemic burden faced by the theorist trying to identify the best non-ideal code. Although development of a more sophisticated account of usability value might strengthen the non-ideal Pragmatic theorist's argument that a non-ideal code with higher usability value secures a better pattern of actions than a code with less usability value, it would still leave him in the untenable position of promoting a code which no agent or theorist is in an epistemic position to identify.

In the course of examining four different interpretations of the standard for a better pattern of actions, we have found that the theorist who wishes to evaluate codes in part by the quality of the pattern of actions their currency would produce cannot count on high usability value to secure a high quality of actions, or even to invariably contribute positively towards it, other things being equal. Instead, if what this theorist cares about fundamentally is patterns of actions, she must invoke a separate standard for her evaluation of moral codes that directly appraises the value of the total pattern of actions—both successes and failures—that would be produced by currency of the code.

7.4 Non-Ideal Splintered Pragmatic Responses

When assessing the ideal Pragmatic Response to the problem of error we discussed the Splintered Pragmatic Response. According to the response, if a moral code or principle is affected by the problem of error on one occasion, then it must be rejected as incorrect

---

[16] As a reader for the Press suggests.

for that agent on that occasion. Being incorrect, both as a theoretical account of what makes acts right and wrong and also as a decision-guide for that occasion, it must be replaced by some alternative code that is not so affected on that occasion. However, the original code or principle may be retained as correct for any occasion on which it is *not* vulnerable to the problem of error. On the ideal Splintered view, there are many correct moral principles, but (because agents vary in their susceptibility to the problem of error) no one principle will be correct for all agents or even for the same agent on similar occasions.

It is possible to imagine a parallel *non-ideal* Splintered Pragmatic Response to the problem of error. It would maintain that there are many moral codes, each devised for some set of agents and occasions for decision, and each such that it has high (albeit not necessarily perfect) usability value for that set of agents and decisions. It is not easy to see exactly how this would be worked out. If some Code C has somewhat low usability value for Set S of agents and decisions, should the non-ideal Pragmatic theorist search for some alternative Code C* that would have higher (if not perfect) usability value for Set S, or should he define some new Set S* (perhaps a subset of S itself) such that Code C has higher usability value for the members of Set S* than it does for the members of the original Set S? However, we need not try to settle such questions. It seems clear that the non-ideal Splintered Pragmatic Response would inherit all the problems and shortcomings we have now found in the non-ideal Uniform Pragmatic Response. We can reject the Splintered version of the non-ideal Pragmatic Response as well as the Uniform version.

7.5 Conclusion

In Chapter 4 I argued that there is only one Pragmatic Response to the problem of error—the moral laundry list—that arguably achieves universal extended usability as a decision-guide. Unfortunately this solution only secures universal usability at the cost of shifting the problem of error from the normative level to the meta-ethical level. Another proposed Pragmatic Response, Prichard's subjectivized code, not only fails to achieve universal usability, but also fails to achieve the hoped-for advantages of solutions to the problem of error, and cannot underwrite any deontological duty to inform oneself before acting.

Finding that no satisfactory Pragmatic Response to the problem of error achieves universal extended usability, a realistic advocate of Pragmatic solutions might urge that we should weaken our demand for a universally usable moral code. Instead, this Pragmatist may urge, we should seek to find, among the imperfectly usable moral codes, the one that is best because it boasts the highest attainable usability. This proposal, examined in this and the previous chapters, is captured in Standard 6.1. However, after looking more deeply into the nature of usability and what makes it plausibly valuable in a moral code, we concluded that the realistic Pragmatic theorist should reject Standard 6.1 and instead adopt Standard 6.3, which states that if the extended *usability value* of moral Code X is higher than the extended usability value of moral Code Y, then, other things being equal, X is better than Y. The usability value of a code incorporates measures of the code's usability ratio, but also incorporates measures of the deontic merits of its principles together with a measure of the importance assigned to its principles by the deontically perfect code. A code with higher usability value is indeed more usable in ways that matter, while a code that merely has higher bare usability is not necessarily so.

We then turned to the question of whether Standard 6.3 is correct—whether a code with higher usability value inevitably does better, other things being equal, in terms of the postulated advantages for usability than a code with lower usability value. If so, then the Pragmatic theorist would be correct in holding that a deontically imperfect code with higher usability value could be superior to a deontically perfect but less usable code in terms of one or more of the four claimed advantages for more usable codes: being usable as a decision-guide, increasing the basic form of justice that makes the successful moral life available to everyone, enhancing social welfare and social consensus, and producing a deontically valuable pattern of actions. The Pragmatic theorist's favored code—the one with higher usability value—could then be defended on the ground that its greater usability value makes it superior to more traditional codes crippled by their greater vulnerability to the problem of error.

This chapter has argued that this strategy falls far short of its goal. First, we saw that greater usability value does not come cheaply: a principle having only half the deontic merit of a deontically perfect principle must typically have significantly more usability than the perfect principle, and such principles may be hard to come by. But even worse, we saw that comparing non-ideal codes for their usability value is an even more daunting task, in terms of the amount of nonmoral information required, than the task of identifying a code with perfect usability. The lack of information that ordinary agents experience when trying to apply the standard moral codes is simply transmuted into an even more challenging epistemic problem for the theorist trying to identify the best non-ideal code, since this theorist must correctly predict general patterns of ignorance and mistake in assessing the comparative values of multiple candidate codes. Even if the non-ideal Pragmatic approach in principle could secure the four hoped-for advantages, there is no realistic expectation of identifying a code that could provide this solution. Moreover, we saw that the logic of the standard for measuring usability value actually drives the non-ideal Pragmatic theorist back into the arms of the perfectly usable (but undiscoverable) moral laundry list, since it is identifiable as having the highest usability value of any possible candidate code.

Finally, it turns out on inspection that there is no sure-fire connection between a code's usability value and its superiority as regards the four rationales for valuing extended usability in a moral code. In the case of the first rationale, increasing a code's usability as a decision-guide, we saw that what the non-ideal Pragmatic theorist should really want is not a code with high bare usability, but rather a code with high extended usability value (which can arise from either high deontic merit or high usability).

Of course by definition a Code C with higher usability value does achieve more of this advantage than a Code C* with lower usability value. Although usability value is what the non-ideal Pragmatic theorist should seek, she may find it somewhat discomforting to give up the goal of bare usability and recognize that a code with lower bare usability might be preferable to a code with higher bare usability.

In the case of the special form of justice, we found that, on the present interpretation of usability value, a code's greater usability value does not necessarily, other things being equal, contribute positively towards an enhancement of this form of justice, since the injustice created by the errors that would be made in attempting to apply the code might outweigh the justice engendered by the potential successful attempts to apply it. The connections between a code's usability value and its tendency to promote social welfare and social consensus are similarly (although for different reasons) not what the Pragmatic theorist hopes for. And last, there is no automatic tendency, other things being equal and on the present interpretation of usability value, for a higher usability-value code to produce better patterns of action than those produced by a lower usability-value code. Greater usability value does not invariably, other things being equal, contribute positively towards the production of these three advantages, much less ensure that they will actually be achieved. Thus theorists who view three of the four advantages as reasons to insist that a moral theory must be highly usable, or must have higher usability value, make a mistake. Aside from usability value itself, the other three goals might be promoted by higher usability value, but they might also be impeded by it. If the theorist insists that a moral code must promote the special form of justice, or the social outcomes we've described, or a better pattern of actions, it may be that the best way to achieve this is to impose independent standards for evaluating moral codes on these grounds, not by insisting that higher usability value, other things being equal, will promote these goals.

Chapters 4, 5, 6, and 7 have left us with five major conclusions. First, although we have seen that the moral laundry list would qualify as an ideal error-proof moral code, we have also realized that the epistemic challenge of identifying which laundry list is the correct one is insurmountable. Worse, the epistemic challenge of identifying the best *non-ideal* moral code is, if anything, even harder to surmount. Second, we have seen that bare usability does not capture what the Pragmatic theorist needs in usability of a moral code, and that instead he should focus on a code's usability value. Third, we have seen that the logic of the non-ideal Pragmatic position actually drives it back to the ideal Pragmatic position, which has fatal epistemic costs. Fourth, we have seen that selecting a code for its high usability value does indeed guarantee high usability value in that code, the type of usability that a Pragmatic theorist should be seeking. However, high usability value fails to systematically promote, other things being equal, the achievement of the special form of justice and the goal-oriented advantages often claimed for highly usable moral codes. Even holding all else equal, sometimes higher usability value works to promote these advantages, but sometimes it doesn't.

Finally, and perhaps most importantly, we have seen that even if non-ideal Pragmatic solutions were epistemically attainable, they would typically come at the price of accepting a decrease in the deontic merit of the best code, since deontic merit must often be compromised in order to attain increased usability. To develop a satisfactory concept of usability value, the Pragmatic theorist must recognize that moral codes should be evaluated by their deontic value as well as by their usability. Because the Pragmatic theorist values usability, to find a code with the highest usability value he must typically accept a code with reduced deontic value. This is true even for the Pragmatic theorist who cares about the usability of moral codes but cares nothing for the other three advantages of achieving justice, enhancing social welfare, or attaining the best possible pattern of actions. This is the crucial point at which the Pragmatic theorist disagrees with the Austere theorist. The Austere theorist has no concern for usability, and so seeks to identify the code with perfect deontic value. The Pragmatic theorist cares about usability, and so accepts a trade-off of deontic value for greater usability. To determine which approach to this key issue is correct would require us to delve into meta-ethical theories about the foundation of morality, an inquiry that is beyond the scope of this book. Even so we can highlight the fact that such a trade-off is unavoidable for the Pragmatic approach, and that the deontic price of a highly usable moral code may be higher than most of us want to accept. And we can reiterate our finding that the epistemic challenge for a Pragmatic theorist who hopes to find the moral code—even a non-ideal code—displaying the best combination of deontic value and usability seems insurmountable.

Although I have argued for these conclusions on the basis of accepting Formula 6.1 (according to which the extended usability value of principle P = P's usability weight × P's extended usability) as the best account of the Pragmatic theorist's fundamental conception of what makes one principle "more usable" than another, I believe this exact formula itself is not necessarily essential in drawing these conclusions. Perhaps some other, better, formula will be found, or the point could be made with a less precise expression of the relation between a principle's usability and its deontic merit. But it appears that whatever the nature of that formula, so long as it captures an essential element of Pragmatic thought, the same conclusions will follow from it as have followed from the formula actually used in Chapters 6 and 7.

Given these conclusions, we should conclude that the search for Pragmatic solutions to the problem of error is best abandoned as quixotic. We now know that Pragmatic solutions should focus on finding a moral code with the highest extended usability value. But the epistemic burden of finding such a code is too high, and the code itself would reliably only achieve the first of the goals (reinterpreted as usability value) for which it has often been sought. It is time to turn our attention to other proposed solutions.

8

Hybrid and Austere Responses to the Problem of Error

> The information's unavailable
> to the mortal man.[1]

In Chapters 4, 5, 6, and 7 we explored ideal and non-ideal Pragmatic Responses to the problem of error: responses that attempt to achieve extended usability for a moral code by rejecting error-ridden moral codes in favor of ones that are error-free or at least more error-free than traditional codes. Finding severe problems and inadequacies in such responses, our conclusion was that we need to look elsewhere for a solution to the problem of error.

The preeminent two other general approaches to the problem of error are the Hybrid Response and the Austere Response. The Hybrid approach attempts to solve the problem of error by introducing two-tier moral systems in which there is a division of labor: the top tier provides the theoretical account of right and wrong, while the second tier provides more usable decision-guides that can be utilized by epistemically limited agents in making their decisions. The Austere approach maintains that all we should require from a moral system is a theoretically satisfactory account of right and wrong. If human decision makers have difficulty in applying such a system to their decisions, that is not a flaw in the system, but rather a weakness in the decision makers that they should try to overcome. In this chapter we will examine each of these approaches to the problem of error, once again deferring consideration of the problem of uncertainty to a later chapter. It will facilitate developing our argument to begin by considering the Hybrid approach.

8.1 Hybrid Approaches

Let us start with the Hybrid approach to the problem of error, which attempts to solve the problem by advocating what is sometimes called a *two-tier* moral system.[2] In this

---

[1] Paul Simon, "Slip Slidin' Away." <http://www.paulsimon.com/song/slip-slidin-away/>. Copyright © 1977 Paul Simon. Used by permission of the Publisher: Paul Simon Music.
[2] Portions of the material in this chapter originally appeared in H. Smith (1989).

system, the top tier consists in a set of principles, or a code, that provides the correct theoretical account of what makes actions right and wrong. Let us label such a moral code "C." The lower tier consists of a set of decision-guides: rules that are to be used for actual decision-making. Let us label the set of lower-tier rules "C*."[3] The top-tier rules—encoded in C—are typically subject to the problem of error: since people are sometimes mistaken about the nonmoral nature and circumstances of their prospective acts, they would at least occasionally err as to which acts are required by C.[4] In attempting to follow C they would sometimes perform acts that it forbids. In an ideal Hybrid approach, the lower-tier rules—encoded in C*—are so constructed that agents who attempt to apply these rules would actually do what the top-tier code C prescribes. We can say that the lower-tier rules are designed to secure *indirect* extended usability for Code C. Agents are typically instructed to attempt to apply C* rather than C itself, because their attempts to apply C would sometimes (unbeknownst to them as they make any particular decision) lead them astray. Hybrid solutions of this sort differ markedly from the Pragmatic approaches examined in the last several chapters, since they abandon the requirement that a *single* moral code serve *both* as the theoretical account of right and wrong *and* as the decision-guide. Instead they countenance a division of moral labor: one code serves the first function, while a second code, with different semantic content, serves the second function.[5] In the ideal case the two codes are *pragmatically co-extensional* in the special sense that the acts the agent would perform if she attempted to follow C* are the acts actually prescribed by C.[6]

Two-tier Hybrid solutions of this sort are most familiar in the philosophical literature when the top tier is consequentialist and the lower tier is deontological. Sidgwick's view that common-sense morality ought to be used by most people in decision-making,

---

[3] In earlier chapters I have often introduced Codes C and C* as rivals to each other. From Chapter 8 on, the referents of these labels will be restricted in the way indicated in the text.

[4] Of course there might be highly implausible moral codes, such as "It is permissible to do whatever you feel like," that might be directly usable in the extended sense by each agent without any need for supplementation by extra decision-guides. But we can restrict ourselves to moral codes that are normatively plausible enough to be subject to the problem of error.

[5] It is possible, as Sidgwick imagines, that the second-tier rules are only needed by certain populations of ill-informed agents in making their decisions, while the first-tier rules can serve both functions for a putative population of perfectly informed agents. See Sidgwick (1907), Book IV, Chapter 5.

[6] The rules need not have the same extension in *every* possible world, but only in the actual world (or perhaps in worlds sufficiently close to it).
As Eli Shupe points out (in an unpublished seminar note), there is a tricky issue here raised by the fact that the second-tier rules may themselves be subject to the problem of error. Thus if the top-tier rule is "Act so as to maximize utility," a second-tier decision-guiding rule might be "Donate one-tenth of your annual income to charity." But an agent might regularly miscalculate the amount she should give according to the second-tier rule, and wind up failing to maximize utility because she donates only one-twentieth of her income to charity instead of the required one-tenth. On the other hand, if the second-tier rule were "Donate one-fifth of your annual income to charity," the agent would also regularly miscalculate, but would wind up maximizing utility because she would donate the required one-tenth of her income to charity. Given the possibility of this sort of mishap, should the second-tier rule be "Donate one-tenth" or "Donate one-fifth"? Settling this issue is complex, so I shall side-step it by assuming that it is a requirement of the second-tier rules that they are not themselves subject to the problem of error. Future Hybrid theorists will need to settle this question.

even though utilitarianism is the correct account of right and wrong, may be interpreted as an example of this kind of proposal.[7] Other influential consequentialist examples are provided by J. J. C. Smart's version of utilitarianism and by R. M. Hare's "two levels" of moral thinking, one of which is utilized by the "archangel," who is hindered by none of the usual human frailties, and the other of which is utilized by the "prole," who is afflicted with all the usual human frailties, including mistaken beliefs.[8] However, any combination of deontological and consequentialist tiers is possible. For example, someone who believed the top tier should be deontological in character might recognize that the correct principles are both subtle and complex, and would be misapplied by many people, owing to their mistaken beliefs about the world. Such a theorist could advocate for the lower tier a set of principles less subject to erroneous application: these could either be simpler deontological principles or even simple consequentialist ones referring to a restricted list of easily ascertained effects of actions. Thus a deontologist might believe that in certain extreme circumstances, the use of torture by military officials is justified; but he might also believe that the likelihood of such officials' incorrectly believing themselves to be in these circumstances is so great, and the results so damaging, that it would be better if they settled the issue of torture by reference to the simple lower-tier rule "Never use torture."[9]

8.1.1 Ideal Hybrid approaches

Like Pragmatic approaches to the problem of error, Hybrid approaches come in both ideal and non-ideal versions. For purposes of assessing the adequacy of the two-tier Hybrid approach, let us begin by considering an *ideal* C*—that is, one such that attempts to apply it would *always* lead the decision maker to derive a prescription for the act that C prescribes. Proponents of this approach tend to write as though there are something like laws of nature connecting the morally significant act-types identified by C and those identified by C*. Such a law of nature might state that, for example, every act of telling a lie (forbidden by C*) is also an act of failing to maximize utility (wrong according to C). The act-types included in C* must be ones which agents are always in a position to ascertain they can perform. But it seems unlikely that, for any C of genuine normative interest, there exist simple correlations between the occurrence of general C-identified act-types and any act-types that could serve in a corresponding C* code. Lying, for example, does not always involve failing to maximize utility, and even if it did, agents are not always infallible in their beliefs about whether a prospective act would be a case of lying. Parallel remarks are true of every act-type that might be

[7] Sidgwick (1907), Book IV, Chapter 5.   [8] Smart (1973), pp. 49–53, and Hare (1981).

[9] The two-tier approach is sometimes recommended for prudential as well as moral decision-making. Parker (2008) pursues something like this approach and provides entertaining examples of second-tier rules of thumb such as "Between two barbers in a shop, choose the one with the worse haircut; barbers cut each other's hair," and "When handling pythons, anacondas, boas, and other large constrictors, it's wise to have one person for every four or five feet of snake" (pp. 13 and 65). Parker defines a rule of thumb as "A homemade recipe for making a guess. It's an easy-to-remember guide that falls somewhere between a mathematical formula and a shot in the dark" (p. vii).

mentioned as a candidate for inclusion in a C* code. There seems no prospect of finding any laws of nature that can connect the prescriptions of a plausible C with the prescriptions of a suitable ideal C*.

But this does not mean that decision-guides capable of serving in the position of C* do not exist. Given our discussion in Chapter 4, we already know what one ideal C* would be: it would be a moral laundry list, now considered not as a free-standing and usable account of right and wrong but rather as a decision-guide supplementing some moral code C, where C is the code serving as the theoretical account of right and wrong. No other rule or set of rules seems likely to have the requisite character of being at once usable by every agent and also such that each agent's using it would lead her to perform the act required by the governing C.

For example, suppose C instructs the agent, as a jury member, to vote for an award to the plaintiff that would exactly compensate him for his injury. The juror believes that her prospective act of awarding the plaintiff half a million dollars would exactly compensate him for his injuries. Her belief is incorrect, since it would require a full million dollars to compensate him. If the juror tried to follow C she would violate it. But she does know how to perform an act of the type *vote for an award of one million dollars to the injured plaintiff*. Let's suppose that the juror's vote will carry the day, so that this act would exactly compensate him for his injury. Then a C* instruction to vote for an award of one million dollars, if the juror followed it, would result in her fulfilling the prescription of C itself—even though the juror herself would not believe this. Of course, which act-type correlates with the C-prescribed type, and is also such that the agent knows how to perform it, will vary from case to case, depending on the circumstances and the agent's beliefs. Thus we cannot use this phenomenon to identify any simple general rule to supplement C. But we can use it to create a moral laundry list to serve as a decision-guide C* that would enable agents to carry out the prescriptions of C. In Chapter 4 the moral laundry list was examined as an error-free theoretical account of right and wrong that could serve as a Pragmatic solution to the problem of error. Here we find it could serve as an ideal lower-tier code that supplements the correct theoretical account C and guides error-prone agents aright when they would be misled if they tried to follow C itself. Such a C* will take the form, as we saw in Chapter 4, of an extended list of prescriptions to perform individual actions. Each individual action would be prescribed in terms of an act-type having the feature that if the agent tried to perform an action of that type, he would successfully perform that act, and it would be the act actually required by the upper-tier C in those circumstances. Such a list might contain prescriptions for our juror that would read (in part) as follows: "At 10 a.m., you ought to vote for an award of one million dollars. At 11:00 a.m., you ought to decline to speak to the press about jury deliberations. At 1:00 p.m., you ought to return to work. At 5:00 p.m., you ought to drive no more than 35 mph on your way home..." and so forth. Presented with such a list, the agent could follow it and so do everything required of him by C—even though he might not believe each of these acts to fulfill moral Code C. Code C* itself would consist of a super-list, compiled from the individualized lists for each moral agent. An agent armed with a suitably designed list of this sort, and properly motivated, would perform each of the acts prescribed by C.

So appropriate ideal lower-tier codes C*, of a peculiar kind, do exist. But their mere existence does not show they provide a viable solution to the problem of error. We have already seen the major obstacle to success. Although for each C an appropriate laundry list C* exists, there is no reason to believe that anyone knows, or could find out, what the content of any appropriate C* is. Certainly the decision maker herself cannot determine what the content of the appropriate C* is, for the decision maker could only determine this if she knew what C requires in each particular case—something that by hypothesis she does not know. For example, since the juror believes that a mere half million dollar award would exactly compensate the plaintiff, she would reject the correct C* requiring her to vote for a larger award. No one who needs a C* code to avoid the problem of error can construct or identify the code herself at the time of action. Of course, in any case where the decision maker would err, there might be some *other* individual who knows which act is to be done, and who might even know under what description of it the decision maker would be led to perform the correct act. In rare cases the decision maker herself might know in advance what it will be right for her to do later, know that she would hold a different and incorrect belief at the time for action, and so give herself an appropriate C* rule to follow when the time for action comes. But there is no reason to believe that, for *every* decision the decision maker must make, there is someone who would know this. Nor is there reason to suppose that a person possessing this knowledge is always in a position to credibly instruct the decision maker what to do. There is even less reason to think that there is any one human being, or group of human beings, who has this kind of knowledge about every act and every decision maker subject to the problem of error, and who has instructional access to all these decision makers. Even Sidgwick's envisioned "elite" do not possess this kind of knowledge. But this is what would be required for this ideal Hybrid solution to work. Moreover, the kind of rule that this C* requires—an extended list of individual acts—is not simple enough to be learnable in advance by any person of normal intelligence. Hence the moral elite (assuming, implausibly, that they had the requisite knowledge) could not teach agents Code C* in advance, but instead would have to operate literally as guardian angels, hovering constantly about and advising the decision makers from moment to moment what they should do. Thus it is not only true that agents lack the necessary information to utilize this kind of ideal Hybrid approach; even advisors hoping to implement the approach by teaching the ideal C* to decision makers, or advising them what to do from moment to moment, would have to surmount overwhelming practical difficulties.

How critical is this problem? The rules of C* are designed to serve a *practical* function only: to enable decision makers to act as C commands. The difficulty we have just seen shows that they cannot do this. What we wanted was a practical solution to a practical problem. An analogy here might be our needing a solution to a practical problem such as taking expired license plates off our car. To get the plates off we need a Phillips screwdriver. It is no solution to the problem to be told that a Phillips screwdriver exists somewhere in the house: to get the plates off, we need the right screwdriver actually in hand. If we cannot find it, we cannot solve our original problem. Similarly, if one's practical problem as an agent suffering from mistaken factual beliefs is to do what C prescribes, or one's practical problem as an advisor is to bring it about that agents with mistaken factual beliefs do what C prescribes, it is no help to be told that a certain C* exists which is such that if decision-making agents attempted to follow it, they would do what C demands.[10] For an agent to do what C demands, she must have the correct C* actually in hand. And for an advisor to get agents to do what C demands, he needs the right C* actually in hand. Since neither agents nor advisors can identify this C*, it does not solve the problem of error.

8.1.2 Non-ideal Hybrid approaches

The ideal Hybrid approach to the problem of error attempts to find a two-tier code in which the decision-guiding tier secures universal indirect usability for an upper tier that provides the theoretical account of right and wrong. Although we can describe a two-tier code that in principle has this feature, in fact it doesn't provide a practical solution to the problem of error, because identifying the code requires more information than any agent, advisor, or theorist possesses.

A non-ideal Hybrid approach retains the central concept of a two-tier code embodying a division of labor, but gives up the idea that such a code could secure universal indirect usability for C, the theoretical account of right and wrong. Instead the non-ideal approach lowers its sights, and seeks a decision-guide C* that would merely secure high, if not perfect, indirect usability for C.[11] By contrast with the non-ideal Pragmatic approach, the non-ideal Hybrid approach does not need to manipulate its account of right-making characteristics in order to achieve greater usability. It can retain a deontically pure C, and attempt to supplement this with a C* that caters to agents' epistemic limitations while retaining the appropriate connection with the deontically unalloyed C.

Profiting from our work in Chapter 6, the non-ideal Hybrid theorist should realize that finding a lower-level tier that secures high *bare* usability for C is not in fact what

---

[10] Of course there is also the problem of how to *motivate* agents to follow C*. If they believe C is the correct account of what makes actions right, and fail to see the connection between C and C*, they are unlikely to try to follow C*. This suggests, as Sidgwick recognized, that the agents in question must be left in the dark about the true account of right and wrong. Of course an agent might believe that following C* is very likely to lead him to conform to C. But if the agent thinks of C* in this latter way, C* does not really operate as a normative decision-guide, but instead as a bit of epistemic evidence about what is likely to be the best choice (as Van Someren Greve (2014), p. 176, seems to point out). This issue will be addressed when we consider the problem of uncertainty.

[11] At this point the non-ideal Hybrid solution to the problem of error begins to shade over into the Hybrid solution to the problem of uncertainty, which we will begin to examine in Chapter 9. However, I shall continue to construe the current target as a proposed solution to the problem of error.

she wants, since the value of usability depends on how important the (indirectly) usable principles are. For example, high indirect usability of a principle to which code C gives little weight is less valuable than high indirect usability of a principle to which that C gives great weight. Since the Hybrid theorist posits a top-tier Code C that is identical to the deontically perfect code, the weight given to a principle by the top-tier code is identical with the weight given to it by the perfect code. Thus the Hybrid theorist should be concerned, not to secure high bare usability, but rather to secure high code-weighted usability. For example, consider a theoretical account C which assigns substantial weight to Principle P6, which states it is obligatory to pay one's taxes, and assigns less weight to Principle P7, which states it is obligatory not to cut into movie queues. Suppose that acceptance of lower-tier Code C* would lead to many acts complying with P6, but only a few acts complying with P7, while acceptance of a different lower-tier Code C# (identical to C* except for the decision-guides relevant to P6 or P7) would lead to only a few acts complying with P6 but many acts complying with P7. Clearly C* is the better decision-making code to supplement C, since C rightly regards conformity to P6 as more important than conformity to P7. In light of this the non-ideal Hybrid theorist should subscribe to the following standard for evaluating lower-tier codes relative to C:

> **Standard 8.1.**   Decision-guiding Code C* is a better decision-guiding second-tier code for theoretical account C than decision-guiding Code C# if and only if C* has higher Code C-weighted usability than does C#.

Searching for a supplementary decision-guide that has greater C-weighted usability in relation to its top-tier Code C certainly appears to be more realistic than searching for one that has *perfect* C-weighted usability. However, the central lesson of Chapter 7 carries over from non-ideal Pragmatic Responses to non-ideal Hybrid Responses. The advocate of a non-ideal Hybrid Response must still compare the C-weighted usability of the various candidate decision-guiding codes. Comparing the C-weighted usability of candidate codes would require an enormous amount of nonmoral information on the part of the theorist: among other things she must know not only which particular acts are prescribed by C, but also, for every candidate Code C*, she must know which acts agents would perform if they tried to apply C* in their decisions, and how frequently these acts would be identical to the acts actually prescribed by C itself. Acquiring this information is even more daunting than an agent's acquiring the information necessary to correctly apply her C, since it requires knowledge about *all* agents, not just about a single agent, and requires knowledge about agents' potential patterns of action in trying to apply both C *and* in applying all the candidate C*s. Thus even if the correct supplementary decision-guiding code could take a more general form than the moral laundry list (since it does not need to lead agents to perform the C-correct act on every single occasion), identifying the content of this code still surpasses the epistemic capabilities of any agent or advisor, and is a more difficult epistemic problem than the original problem of error it is supposed to remedy.

This problem might be moderated by recognizing that there might be arenas of decision-making about which experts already know that people often make mistakes when asked to apply a principle from Code C, but that they rarely make mistakes if asked to apply some suitably related decision-guiding principle from Code C*. For example, cognitive scientists advise us that people make many more mistakes applying principles phrased in terms of probabilities than they do when they apply principles phrased in terms of frequencies.[12] The epistemic problem for the Hybrid theorist might also be mitigated by recognizing that different groups of agents, differentially characterized by their areas of special obligation or their epistemic capabilities, might be given different decision-guiding principles from C*. It might be claimed that there is a single correct C* but that the epistemic work of identifying the components of this code can be divided up. Thus one expert could know what decision-guiding principles of C* are appropriate for experienced surgeons (relative to C), and could feasibly promulgate such rules. Another expert might know what decision-guiding principles of C* are appropriate for inexperienced surgeons, yet another expert might know what principles are appropriate for anesthesiologists, another might know what principles are appropriate for obstetricians, and so forth. Such limited-scope experts would not face such a daunting epistemic challenge as a single expert who has to know *all* of the appropriate principles in C*. Identifying types of decisions and categories of agents for which effective rules are known or knowable would certainly help the non-ideal Hybrid theorist construct the rules of Code C*. However, even if we could call on epistemic expertise in this fashion, there are many agents who must make decisions in situations that would not easily fit into the obvious decisional or agential categories such as "decisions requiring probability estimates" or "experienced surgeons." Many agents must make decisions in arenas outside the ones for which effective decision-making rules are known. Examples might include the woman who mistakenly remembers that she promised her elderly mother she would buy bread at the supermarket, but actually promised to buy milk, or the juror who mistakenly believes that half a million dollars would fully compensate the injured plaintiff. It's unlikely that any advisor would have enough information to construct a set of decision-guides for all agents who find themselves in situations that fall outside obvious decisional- and job-related categories. But this multitude of non-classifiable agents, just like the experienced surgeon, need decision-guiding principles from C* as well, and the appeal to experts over more limited epistemic realms does not work for them. We must conclude that full non-ideal Hybrid solutions, like ideal Hybrid solutions, are therefore out of epistemic reach.

The situation is actually worse than this. Brief thought shows that the moral laundry list, now construed as a decision-guide, is evaluated by Standard 8.1 as the best decision-guide in a Hybrid code. Since all its prescriptions are usable, and they correspond exactly with what C itself recommends, it has the highest code-weighted usability. Once again the non-ideal theorist is driven back into the arms of the ideal theorist. And we know that the ideal theorist faces an insurmountable epistemic problem in trying to identify which Code C* is best.

Hybrid approaches to the problem of error have attracted more than their share of criticism. How is an agent, for example, supposed to view the relation between C (the account of right and wrong) and C* (the supplementary decision-guide)? On some "Esoteric Morality" versions of this solution, an enlightened elite understand that C is the correct account of right and wrong and follow it accurately in making their own decisions, but foster (or allow) the belief among less well-informed populations that C* is itself the correct account of right and wrong. On other "Self-Effacing Morality" proposals, even the enlightened elite see that it would be best if *they* no longer believed C to be the correct account of right and wrong, so they manipulate themselves, replacing their belief in C with a false belief in C* as the correct account of right and wrong. On a variant on this story, the first enlightened generation teaches their children that C* is the correct account of right and wrong and the code by which they are to make decisions, so that over time no one remains who believes in C.[13] On other accounts, agents are fully aware of the two-tiered structure of their moral code, and know that C is the correct account of right and wrong and that C* is merely the code which is to guide their decisions.[14] On this variant, each agent who wants to comply with C, and who believes that some act A would comply with C, nonetheless aims to adhere to the recommendation of C*, which may be to perform act B rather than act A.[15] Each of these versions has its problems, although many of the standard criticisms seem much less cogent when lodged against ideal rather than non-ideal Hybrid solutions. However, all these versions can be dismissed because they face an insurmountable epistemic problem at the meta-ethical level: no one (or set of persons) is in an epistemic position to identify which decision-making C*s would best supplement any given error-ridden C as a theory of right and wrong. We will return to consideration of Hybrid approaches when we consider approaches to the problem of uncertainty, where they are more promising. But neither ideal nor non-ideal Hybrid solutions can help with the problem of error.

In light of our conclusion that neither the ideal nor the non-ideal Hybrid approach can solve the problem of error, we need not inquire further whether either of these approaches would fulfill the requirement that the codes it endorses would better enable agents to make decisions, promote the special form of justice that requires the successful moral life be available for everyone, enhance social welfare, or foster ideal patterns of action. The reasoning here would be similar to that used to explore these questions in the case of Pragmatic approaches. But whatever the outcome of this reasoning, it could not overcome the epistemic objection to Hybrid approaches to the problem of error.

---

[13] See Sidgwick (1907), Chapter 5; Parfit (1984), section 17; B. Williams (1973), pp. 138–9; and Lazari-Radek and Singer (2014), Chapter 10.

[14] It appears that the view Hare (1981) espouses falls into this category. See also Varner (2012).

[15] Recall that we are discussing the problem of error, so the agents in question are not *uncertain* whether (say) A is prescribed by C; instead they believe this—and nonetheless ought to turn to C* for advice.

8.2 Austere Approaches

Advocates of the Austere approach hold that morality does not need to make any concession to the fact that human beings often suffer from false beliefs about the world in which they make their decisions. On the Austere theorist's view, a moral code's practical usability, or lack thereof, is no sign of its adequacy or inadequacy as a theoretical account of right and wrong. In particular, the fact that individuals attempting to do what the code recommends sometimes perform wrong acts because they are led astray by false beliefs about the world is not seen as any indictment of the code, but rather as an unsurprising symptom of human beings' lack of omniscience. Insofar as we care about applying moral codes to our decisions, the remedy is to improve our knowledge, not to abandon the code in favor of some less demanding one.[16] Thus, in the terminology introduced in Chapter 6, the Austere approach maintains that the overall acceptability of a moral code depends solely on its deontic merit, not on its usability or even its usability value. It's a chief virtue of the Austere approach that it refuses to countenance any moral theory that distorts or dumbs down the theoretically correct account of what makes acts right or wrong.

The Austere stance may seem most natural for those who hold that moral codes have their foundation in some independent reality, such as natural or metaphysical facts— perhaps facts about rationality or human evolution, or about a deity's commands, or facts about non-natural moral properties. But those who hold these views are not necessarily committed to an Austere Response to the problem of error. For example, someone who holds that moral principles are the outcome of evolution might hold that evolution would eventually equip us with a code that would enable us, as epistemically limited creatures, to effectively make the kinds of decisions necessitated by our environment. Someone who holds that moral principles are grounded in rationality might similarly argue that genuinely rational principles would take into account common cognitive deficiencies in decision makers. Or someone who holds that moral principles are commands of a deity might maintain that an all-wise deity would shape these commands so that human beings, in trying to follow them, would always have enough information to follow them successfully. Such theorists would reject the idea that usability is irrelevant to the truth of moral principles.

By parallel reasoning, rejection of the Austere Response to the problem of error might seem most natural for those constructivists who hold that moral principles are the products of actual or hypothetical human choices, rather than rooted in some independent reality. For example, someone who believes that the correct moral principles are those that would be chosen by agents in a hypothetical "original position" might well conclude that such a choice would be strongly governed by practical considerations, and that the hypothetical choosers would select principles that could typically be used

---

[16] For a sample discussion of how we might improve our inferential practices, see Nisbett et al. (1982). For a list of theorists who seem to advocate the Austere solution, see Chapter 3, note 46.

even by cognitively imperfect human decision makers. Such a theorist might reject the Austere approach and defend principles that represent a compromise between "pure" deontic considerations and "practical" accommodations to human decision makers' foibles. However, constructivists are not necessarily committed to pursuing a non-Austere solution to the problem of error. They might readily maintain that other machinery can be built into the normative theory, such as a theory of excusing conditions, to provide the necessary accommodation to human epistemic shortcomings without weakening the theory's commitment to a deontically pure account of what makes acts right or wrong.

Of course, virtually all moral theorists would agree that moral principles are principles governing *human* beings, and hence must be appropriate for them.[17] For this reason virtually all theorists agree, for example, that no correct moral principle can prescribe types of actions as obligatory that are beyond the physical capabilities of any human being (such as flying without mechanical assistance), or can demand an individual agent perform an action that is beyond his personal physical capability (such as a quadriplegic's swimming into a lake to save a drowning child). If angels have different physical capabilities than human beings, then what they are morally required to do may be different from what human beings would be required to do in precisely the same environment.[18] There is broad agreement that "S ought to do A" entails "S can do A" at least in some suitable sense of physical ability to do A.[19]

8.2.1 Must a moral code be usable?

Our present question is whether moral codes should bend even further to accommodate human limitations, so that they are "usable" in some stronger sense than one that merely accommodates physical limitations. Both the Pragmatic and Hybrid approaches to the problem of error can be seen as driven by the view that moral codes must be usable by human beings thwarted by epistemic as well as physical limitations. The question for us in this section is whether the Austere Response to the problem of error should be rejected because it insists that human epistemic limitations provide

---

[17] Some theorists, such as Kant, would state that moral principles are principles for an expanded set of beings—perhaps all rational beings, or human beings plus angels and intelligent aliens. But they would agree that human beings are among those to whom the principles under discussion apply.

[18] Note, however, that this does not imply that the basic moral requirements on angels and on human beings must be fundamentally different: just that the types of concrete actions they are required to take in order to fulfill those basic requirements may be different. For example, if both angels and human beings are required not to cause gratuitous pain, then for the angels this might mean not smiting an innocent person with a thunderbolt, whereas human beings, having no such possibility, have no duty to refrain from smiting with thunderbolts.

For a more complex account of what angels might be required to do, acknowledging that the obligations of idealized agents might differ from those of human beings for other reasons, see H. Goldman (1976) and (1978).

[19] There is active contemporary discussion about this requirement and how best to interpret it. See, for example, Gardner (2004) for a contrary point of view and a refutation of Kant's apparent argument that there can be no duty to succeed, but only a duty to try.

no reason to revise or supplement moral codes to make them usable, or indirectly usable, in the extended sense. If the Austere Response is wrong in saying that we should accept moral theories that permit error, then it appears moral theory is in serious trouble, since we have now rejected as inadequate the Pragmatic and Hybrid proposals for solving the problem of error, and no other prospective solutions seem to be on offer. In exploring why it might be demanded that moral codes be usable despite agents' imperfect knowledge about the world, we described four different types of rationales for this demand. Let us reconsider these as they apply to the Austere approach.

The first rationale states that a moral code must be usable for making decisions because one of the functions or purposes—perhaps the primary or even sole function—of a moral code is to guide an agent as he or she chooses which actions to perform. Clearly, the natural line of thought for the Austere theorist is to reject the view that the function of morality is to guide conduct in this sense. Such a theorist might compare moral theories to scientific theories, and say that just as the role of a scientific theory is to articulate the scientific laws that govern events and states of affairs, so the role of a normative theory is to articulate the normative principles setting out how the normative properties of acts are grounded in their nonmoral features. Once such normative principles are available, it may be possible for us to use them in appraising and evaluating actions and in guiding our choices of how to act. But the validity of the normative principles governing actions does not depend on anyone's ability to make such appraisals or to conform her action to these standards—just as the truth of a scientific theory does not depend on any scientist's ability to demonstrate how a particular event is explained by it, or on any engineer's ability to use the theory in constructing a bridge or rocket ship. Similarly, a person's epistemic limitations may make it difficult for her to discern which action is right according to the correct moral standards. Of course she might be able to improve her knowledge, for example by checking the Internet for more information, or by finding an algorithm that would enable her to rapidly calculate some outcome. But no one should argue that the truth or falsity of her moral standard depends on the availability of the Internet or the algorithm. Nor should we argue that the correct moral standards must include built-in concessions to human frailties in order to serve a false goal of usability. Rather, the Austere theorist says, the standards for right action must capture what would be genuinely ideal in human action. If the standards for right action set out some criterion that falls short of this ideal, then they are not worthy of our aspirations.

This stance of the Austere theorist is a coherent one and has undeniable attractiveness. Deciding whether or not a moral code must serve both a theoretical and a practical function, or need only serve a theoretical function, would (as I have noted before) require a deeper examination of fundamental issues in meta-ethics than this book will attempt. But we cannot lightly dismiss the Austere claim that a moral code's service as a theoretical account of right and wrong is the single preeminent role that governs its content.

However, someone who disagrees with the Austere theorist, and holds that the correct moral code must be able to serve both a practical as well as a theoretical role, can nonetheless find some attractions in the Austere solution. For a moral code to serve in a practical role it must be capable of guiding decisions. But there are two interpretations of what is required for a moral code to guide decisions. So far we have followed the Pragmatic theorist in assuming that "guiding decisions" must be interpreted as "enabling agents to use the code in the *extended* sense of usability"—that is, as enabling agents to avoid the problem of error. But it can be argued that the search for universal extended usability is not only doomed to fail, but it is seeking a greater prize than we really need. On this view, a practical moral theory does not require extended usability; the need to guide decisions is satisfied so long as the theory offers *core* usability. A principle can serve to guide decisions in the core sense if it is such that, when an agent is faced with a choice, the agent can use the principle to select an action she knows how to perform out of a desire to conform to the principle and a belief that the action does conform. An agent can use a principle in the core sense whether or not the action she would select would *actually* conform to the principle. A principle capable of being used in this way would place the agent who accepts the principle in a position to make choices informed by her moral values. Such an agent is not morally rudderless, but has access to a principled way to determine what conduct to engage in. The fact that agents sometimes, or even often, have false beliefs about features of the world does not in itself prevent these agents from making core use of a moral code. If the shopper believes that she promised her mother to buy bread, she can derive a prescription from a code requiring her to keep promises. If her belief is false, then the prescription she derives will be mistaken. But this does not undercut the fact that she is able to make core use of this code in guiding her action.[20] If she later becomes aware of her mistake, she will presumably regret that she didn't know better. But at the time of the decision, if she wishes to act in accord with that principle, it is possible for her to shape her *choice*, if not her resulting action, in accord with the value she holds to be most important. On this view, what makes the usability of moral principles important is not that a usable principle guarantees that suitably motivated agents will perform the actions it prescribes. As we have seen, no attractive moral theory can feasibly guarantee that. Rather the usability of a principle is important because it ensures that motivated agents can achieve a certain form of autonomy in making their choices. An agent who cannot find any way to translate his moral values into his *choice* of what to do is an agent who cannot find a way to govern his decision by the considerations he deems most relevant.

---

[20] In the case of the problem of error, there are various possible outcomes that might arise from the agent's selecting an action despite erroneous nonmoral information. The situation could be one in which the person believes that he ought to do A, when in fact A is not required (perhaps A is wrong, or possibly A is simply permissible rather than obligatory). Or the situation could be one in which the person believes no duty is incumbent upon him, but actually B is obligatory—and he fails to do B. Or he could actually do B, but act in ignorance of the fact that he is thereby doing his duty. Thus an agent laboring under the problem of error might (luckily) satisfy his duty, or perform a morally neutral act when no duty is incumbent upon him, or he might (unluckily) violate his duty. Although our focus will usually be on the most dramatic cases in which the agent's erroneous beliefs about the world lead him to violate his duty, we should remember this will not always be the outcome.

His decision does not express his moral values, and so in an important way undermines his autonomy.[21] But if his moral principle is usable in the core sense, it secures this type of autonomy, even if the agent has mistaken beliefs about the world and so does not succeed in performing an action that accords with his principle.[22] The importance of core usability, then, can be understood as preserving this type of autonomy. A principle secures an agent's autonomy (with respect to it) if the principle is usable in the core sense, since adopting such a principle enables the agent to translate her moral values into her choice of what to do.

Thus it is possible to agree that it is part of the function of moral principles to guide decisions, but note that this function is sufficiently carried out by a moral code that is usable in the *core* sense, even if (because of the problem of error) it is not always usable in the *extended* sense. Someone who takes this tack can accept the Austere theorist's account of which moral principles are correct, while maintaining that these principles are untarnished by the problem of error in the sense that errors about the world do not render them unusable in the core sense, and so do not undermine agents' autonomy. Of course the Austere theorist herself would have no interest in this feature of her solution. But others, otherwise attracted to the Austere approach but still wanting to preserve some important measure of usability, can be satisfied that principles that satisfy the Austere approach nonetheless can be defended against the charge of "lack of usability."

Looking ahead, however, we can see that insofar as a moral code is subject to the problem of *uncertainty*, it is not always usable even in this core sense. The agent whose code requires her to keep her promise to her elderly mother can use her code in the core sense so long as she believes, even if falsely, that buying bread will keep her promise. However, if she is *uncertain* which act would keep her promise, then she

---

[21] For my earlier discussions of this idea, see H. Smith (1988), section V, and H. Smith (2010a), section II.A. Väyrynen (2006) pursues this suggestion. For related accounts of autonomy, see Christman (2015), who states that on certain approaches "autonomy requires the ability to act effectively on one's own values," and Buss (2014), who states that "Autonomous agents are self-governing agents." McLeod (2005), p. 109, holds that "According to the dominant view in contemporary moral theory, to be autonomous is to exercise a psychological ability to govern oneself." Although McLeod's description of this view is ambiguous between a "core usability" interpretation and an "extended usability" interpretation, one can see the type of autonomy I describe in the text as a version of this dominant view. On the other hand, Sher (2014) seems to argue in favor of a view requiring usability in the extended sense, when he takes our fundamental interest to be "living our lives effectively," where that involves accurately discerning what we have reason to aim at, seeing what we need to do to get it, and succeeding at doing what needs to be done (p. 114).

[22] The type of autonomy available to such agents, as I have characterized it, does not require that their beliefs about which values are most important be *correct*. For example, suppose Kantianism is the true moral system. On my conception an agent qualifies as autonomous even if she mistakenly believes that utilitarianism is the correct moral system and is able in the core sense to use utilitarianism to derive prescriptions for what actions to perform. Some moral theorists may hold that an agent is only autonomous if she has identified and is able to derive prescriptions from the correct moral system (see, for example, Van Someren Greve (2014), 172–3, and for different reasons, Wolf (1990), Chapter 4). My remarks in the text assume that the agent's primary aim is to make a decision guided by morality rather than some other type of value. If she places more importance on, say, prudence, then her inability to derive a prescription from her moral code may be seen as having less effect on her autonomy.

cannot connect her choice with her guiding moral code. Thus Austere solutions only secure core usability in cases of error, but not in cases of uncertainty. Harking back to the discussions in Chapter 3, we should recall, also, that a moral principle or code might be unintelligible to a given agent, for example because the agent is unable to grasp some of its crucial concepts or to comprehend the overall structure of the principle. An unintelligible principle is unusable by that agent, even in the core sense. I argued in Chapter 3 that unintelligibility, as a block to usability, should be handled in the same way that nonmoral uncertainty should be handled. So the possibility of its being unintelligible may prevent the code identified as correct by the Austere approach from being usable in the core sense.

We should now note that the Pragmatic and Hybrid solutions to the problem of error can also claim to secure a similarly limited type of core usability. If such solutions could be identified, they, too, would typically also consist of moral codes that, whether or not they provide universal extended usability, nonetheless would provide core usability (or indirect core usability in the case of Hybrid solution codes) for situations in which the agent has false beliefs about the world. For example, an agent who subscribes to a subjective code requiring her to do what she believes to be keeping her promise, and who believes that buying bread will keep her promise, can make core use of her code. (Of course, if she is uncertain what she promised, or the code is unintelligible to her, she cannot even make core use of this code.) However, since the professed aim of Pragmatic theorists is to secure *both* core and extended usability, the fact that their preferred theory would secure core usability alone is probably of little solace to advocates of this approach. The Hybrid theorist may be more flexible about this aim. In any event, we have seen that Pragmatic and Hybrid solutions cannot be identified without assuming the theorist can overcome the epistemic limitations that impede agents themselves, so there is decisive reason from the point of view of solving the problem of error to adopt an Austere solution rather than a Pragmatic or Hybrid solution. Moreover, the Austere solution achieves core usability (setting aside cases where the agent is plagued by uncertainty or unintelligibility) without having to give up some of the deontic merit that must often be traded off for greater extended usability by non-ideal Pragmatic solutions.[23] Thus the Austere solution to the problem of error is preferable to the Pragmatic and Hybrid solutions, even though all three of them could in principle secure significant core usability and so preserve agents' autonomy.

8.2.2 Must a code make the successful moral life available to everyone?

The second rationale for usability states that an unusable moral code would violate the special form of justice requiring that the successful moral life be available to everyone,

---

[23] There is an interesting question here about the comparative importance of extended versus core usability. It is possible that some Code D has greater extended usability but less core usability than another Code D* which has less extended usability but more core usability (Code D has more occasions on which agents have the relevant true beliefs, but also more occasions on which agents are handicapped by uncertainty). Which profile is better? I don't think we yet know how to answer this, considering "usability" purely as a conceptual rationale.

whether they are dull, poorly informed, or highly intelligent and well-educated. On this view, a moral code subject to the problem of error unfairly condemns poorly informed agents to an "unsuccessful" moral life.

So far we have accepted the assertion that a special form of justice is violated by these circumstances. But the proponent of the Austere approach to the problem of error may wish to challenge this claim. To spell out this challenge, it is useful to distinguish two different conceptions of a "successful moral life" and the hindrances that cognitive incapacities might pose to the attainment of such a life.[24]

What I shall call the "strong" conception of a successful moral life is the conception of a life in which the agent never does wrong and is never blameworthy for any of her actions. Of course we know from hard (and often personal) experience that not everyone is adequately motivated to choose the right act on every occasion: malicious intentions, insufficient concern for morality, and weakness of will can often impede people's achievement of the strong successful moral life. But we can retain the ideal that each person should have the *opportunity* to achieve this life, in the sense that if a person has good motivations, then nothing—including mistakes of fact—would prevent her from fulfilling her desire to do what is right. This seems to be an attractive thought. In particular we may be moved by a concern that relative lack of intelligence (which derives largely from genetic and social factors over which the agent has no control) or education (which is largely a function of the agent's socio-economic class, over which she has no control during her crucial formative period) should not stand in the way of anyone's living a successful moral life. We feel that socio-economic factors should not make a difference to one's ability to lead the *moral* life, even if they may make a difference to one's ability to achieve happiness or material success. Even if what one agent can accomplish through right action is more than what another agent can accomplish—a wealthy entrepreneur such as Bill Gates can contribute billions to charity, while a poor widow can only give her mite—still Gates and the widow should have the same opportunity to do what is morally right for their own circumstances.

But realism intrudes on this picture. Even two agents who are well and similarly situated in terms of their wealth, education, and intelligence may nonetheless have different beliefs (even reasonably different beliefs) about their factual circumstances, leading one agent to draw erroneous conclusions about which of his actions would be right, and the other to draw correct conclusions about the moral status of the available options. Billionaire Bill Gates, believing that Research Team A will discover a vaccine for HIV, concludes that his family foundation's investing the available millions in Team A is the right action. His wife and foundation co-director Melinda Gates, believing that Research Team B rather than Team A will discover a vaccine for HIV, concludes that investing the available funds in Team B is the right action. As it happens,

---

[24] As Douglas Blair has pointed out in a private communication, one can also distinguish a third type of "morally successful life" in which the agent is successful in discerning the fundamental moral truths, whether or not she can ascertain what actions they require of her. Since we are not directly concerned with the problem of moral error and uncertainty, I will not attempt to discuss this proposal.

Melinda is correct, but Bill wins the argument and directs the foundation to invest the funds in the wrong research team. By this action Bill fails (in this instance) to lead the "successful moral life" even though he tries in good faith to do the morally optimal action. Is there any unfairness in this? Should we adjust the content of the applicable moral code to "rescue" Bill and make it possible for him to lead a morally successful life even though he invests the funds in a research team that is destined to labor in vain? To the Austere theorist, this seems silly. Bill's failure is not a reflection of some inherent unfairness in the moral code; it is simply a reflection of the fact that human beings—even rich, powerful, and highly intelligent human beings—are not and can never be omniscient.[25]

Of course if an agent were *punished* or *blamed* for failing to do what is right because he lacks knowledge, we would all feel that this was unfair (at least if we assume he could not have discovered what was right even if he had tried). It is wrong to visit unpleasant consequences or criticism on someone for doing something which he did not know to be wrong (or could not have known to be wrong). But the moral code evaluating a mistaken action as wrong need not have this upshot. Most moral codes recognize that ignorance of one's duty, arising from a non-culpable mistake of fact, is an excuse for failing to carry out that duty. People are neither punished nor thought to be morally blameworthy for wrongful actions that arise from such mistakes. Hence there is no need to change the character of the duties constraining human beings in order to protect them from this form of injustice. The apparatus of excusing conditions, which includes excusing impermissible acts resulting from ignorance about the world, is a fully effective way of precluding such injustice. We do not need the strong conception of a successful moral life, which insists that morally successful agents neither do wrong nor are ever blameworthy, to avoid this kind of injustice. Agents can avoid blame-worthiness even though they sometimes do wrong.

Reflection on these facts leads naturally to recognition of the attractions of the second interpretation of the successful moral life: the "modest" conception. According to the modest conception, the successful moral life is one in which, although the agent may sometimes act wrongly in striving to do right, nonetheless she is never blameworthy for any of her actions. When her actions fall short of what morality requires, there is always some factor that excuses her for any infraction: she is mentally incompetent, immature, insane, under the involuntary influence of hypnotism or drugs, non-culpably ignorant of the nature or consequences of her acts, and so forth. In short, although she does not always succeed in doing what morality requires, nonetheless she is never blameworthy for what she does. This conception of the modest successful

---

[25] Of course Bill Gates famously did not complete his bachelor's degree at Harvard, but it seems dubious that anyone will urge this "lack of education" as an excuse for Bill's mistake. Someone might also say that Bill and Melinda both err by putting all their philanthropic eggs in one basket—they should divide the funds between Team A and Team B. For purposes of this example, we should understand that neither team can get its work successfully off the ground unless it is supported by the full available amount.

moral life is the most viable one, given the realities of the human condition.[26] But this more modest ideal form of life can in fact be available to agents under moral codes endorsed by the Austere approach. It is true of such agents that they sometimes fail to carry out their duty because their erroneous beliefs about the world mislead them into choosing the wrong act. But under an Austere code that incorporates a provision excusing an agent when she makes a non-culpable error of fact, such an agent will succeed in avoiding blameworthiness so long as she tries to do her duty and only falls short because she non-culpably mistakes the pertinent facts.[27] Such an agent has it within her power to lead a successful moral life according to the modest conception of such a life, even though she may be unintelligent, ill-educated, and poorly informed. According to this conception the appropriate ideal is that each of us has the opportunity to lead this modest morally successful life. This ideal is indeed available under any moral code that admits suitable excusing conditions, including factual error, which preclude blameworthiness.[28]

I believe that the concept of the modest successful moral life and the ideal associated with it are tenable conceptions, and are appropriately more realistic than the strong conception of the successful moral life, despite the initial attractions of the latter. Hence it appears that while we may accept the ideal that the successful moral life should be available to everyone, we must give it a suitable interpretation. The modest conception of such a life can be satisfied by Austere solutions, as least as regards the problem of error, so long as these solutions are codes that include appropriate excusing conditions.[29] Of course some agents, in attempting to apply a code endorsed

---

[26] Bernard Williams, in introducing the ideal of the morally successful life, is not very clear on what it would consist in. However, his comments suggest he may have had in mind something similar to what I am calling the "modest conception." See B. Williams (1976), pp. 115–16. By contrast Väyrynen (2006) clearly espouses a concept of the morally successful life that includes performance of the morally required actions (p. 299) and so is closer to the strong conception.

In an unpublished seminar note, Nate Flores points out that we could define a fourth concept of the successful moral life according to which the agent has opportunities, not only to avoid blameworthiness, but also to achieve creditworthiness for performing right actions. But since one is creditworthy whenever one performs a right action (with acceptable motives), it appears this third conception would actually be co-extensive with the strong conception.

[27] Here I have phrased the relevant excusing condition as one requiring any mistake of fact to itself be non-culpable: the agent must not have acted out of culpable ignorance. As I argued in Chapter 5, all acceptable moral codes must require agents to make reasonable efforts to acquire the information relevant to their future morally significant choices. An agent who fails to make such efforts and does so without excuse or justification is culpable for this failure. Theorists are divided on the question of whether the agent's subsequent act, done in culpable ignorance, is also, by virtue of the fact that the act is done in culpable ignorance, itself blameworthy. For my work on this issue, see H. Smith (1983) and (2016), in which I argue that wrongful acts done from culpable ignorance should not be judged by this fact alone to be blameworthy. However, in the present book I wish to leave this question open, so will vary in my description of when ignorance excuses.

[28] It will be necessary to discuss in subsequent chapters how the problem of uncertainty affects availability of this ideal. In this chapter we are focused only on the problem of error.

[29] Some agents are hampered in their pursuit of the successful moral life by the inability to imagine the alternatives that would provide the best solution to their dilemmas. Consider an example provided by Peter Geach in which St. Athanasius once encountered Roman persecutors who, not recognizing him, demanded

by the Austere approach, will perform the wrong action because the agent has false beliefs about the world. And the wrongness of these actions may vary from case to case. However, so long as the agent is excused for his ignorance, he will not be blameworthy for the act. And even though the degree of wrongness of the acts which the agent performs in non-culpable ignorance may vary, this will not affect the degree of blameworthiness which the agent accrues, or the degree to which the code enables agents to live a modest successful moral life.

This discussion has focused on whether the Austere Response can be criticized for unfairness because it condemns agents who are subject to the problem of error to an unsuccessful moral life. I have answered that it does not, because the most plausible conception of the successful moral life is the modest conception, in which a properly motivated agent can always avoid blameworthiness for her acts, even though she sometimes, through mistaken beliefs, performs an act that is wrong. Such a conception is consistent with the Austere approach. On this view the Austere Response cannot be criticized for the injustice implied in the "unsuccessful moral life" objection—namely, the criticism that the Austere Response unjustly condemns agents to unfair punishment or disapprobation because they fail, through mistakes about the world, to perform the morally right act. So long as the Austere moral code in question has a suitable account of excusing conditions under which agents are not to blame for morally wrong acts done in ignorance (or in non-culpable ignorance), no agent will be unjustly blamed for choices made from non-culpable mistakes about the world.

It is worthwhile pausing to ask whether Pragmatic and Hybrid solutions could secure the opportunity to live the *modest* successful moral life just as effectively as the Austere solution. In the case of the Austere solution, access to this life is secured (setting aside cases in which the agent suffers not from error but from uncertainty

to know "Where is the traitor Athanasius?" "Not far away," the saint replied, and went on his way unmolested. Geach holds that lying is always wrong, but praises Athanasius's non-lying deception as follows: "Such is the snakish cunning of the Saints, commended in the Gospel" (Geach 1977, p. 115). Clearly not every agent would be able to think of a stratagem, such as that adopted by Athanasius, that would enable him both to avoid violating an absolute moral stricture against lying and also to save his life in these circumstances. Some less clever agents in the same position might not be able to concoct a way of avoiding further persecution except by lying, in which case they would violate their duty as Geach understands it. Other agents might attempt to evade detection while also avoiding lying, but fail and wind up apprehended and martyred by the persecutors. Cleverness gains Athanasius the avoidance of wrong-doing, the avoidance of blameworthiness, and the continuation of his life and activities without molestation by hostile authorities. (It is noteworthy that political leaders deliberately hire quick-witted spokespersons who can figure out ways to avoid the pitfalls of either lying or revealing more of the truth than the leader wants revealed.) It can indeed seem unfair that a slower-witted agent, placed in this position, might through his slow-wittedness suffer a less favorable fate. However, it is not plausible to assume that the "successful moral life" includes not only avoidance of blameworthiness, but also the achievement of a high level of personal welfare. The slower-witted agent who cannot think of the clever response of an Athanasius chooses his inadequate response in the false belief that it is the best answer he can make to the Roman persecutors. He, too, is subject to the problem of error, and is not blameworthy for his mistake, so he achieves the modest successful moral life, even though he fails to perform the right act and unfortunately suffers for it at the hands of unjust authorities.

about the world) by recognizing that moral systems must include both an account of right and wrong and also an account of excusing conditions that includes an excuse for actions done from (non-culpable) error. The answer for a Pragmatic solution is more complex. An ideal Pragmatic solution code (if it could be identified) would be universally usable in the extended sense, so agents attempting to follow it would never perform a wrong act from nonmoral error (culpable or not). Such a system would have no need for a component excusing actions done in error. Although some agents, such as those with malign intentions, would perform wrong acts and do so in a manner that renders them blameworthy, no one would perform a wrongful act from nonmoral error. Competent agents with the correct intentions would thus be enabled to lead a successful moral life in the strong sense, and therefore in the modest sense as well. But as we have seen, the identification of a satisfactory ideal Pragmatic solution can only be accomplished by shifting the burden carried by epistemically limited decision makers to the level of the meta-ethical theorist.

Under a non-ideal Pragmatic solution code, agents would sometimes perform impermissible acts because they would act out of erroneous beliefs about the world. Such a code, like an Austere solution code, would need a component excusing agents who act in (non-culpable) error. This component would shield erring agents from blameworthiness. In discussing usability value in Chapter 7, we saw that the "best" non-ideal Pragmatic code—the one with greatest extended usability value—does not necessarily do the best job of enabling agents to live the strong successful moral life, since the code with the highest (but less than perfect) usability value may nonetheless have lower usability than codes with lower usability value. Because of this phenomenon, high usability value does not in every case contribute positively to enabling agents to agents' living the strong successful moral life. Despite this, a Pragmatic solution including a suitable excusing condition could, like an Austere solution, offer the opportunity to live the *modest* successful moral life to all suitably motivated and competent agents (again, setting aside cases in which the agent suffers not from error but from uncertainty about the world). However, we also saw that epistemic limitations prevent non-ideal Pragmatic theorists, like ideal Pragmatic theorists, from identifying which code is best, so the fact that non-ideal Pragmatic solutions could in principle guarantee well-motivated agents a modestly successful moral life still leaves Austere solutions in a superior position.

Parallel remarks would hold for ideal and non-ideal Hybrid solution codes. As we have seen in this chapter, these approaches to solving the problem of error are subject to epistemic difficulties no less serious than those facing the ideal and non-ideal Pragmatic approaches. Their capacity to provide a modestly successful moral life cannot overcome this drawback to render them superior to the Austere approach.

It appears from the discussions in this and the previous section that the Austere solution to the problem of error can be shown to satisfy the (suitably reinterpreted) conceptual rationales for a solution to this problem. The Austere solution provides agents caught by the problem of error (although not those caught in the problem of uncertainty) with a moral code that is usable in the core sense, if not in the extended sense (although this fact is of no interest to Austere theorists themselves). A code that is usable in the core sense enables an agent accepting that code to guide her choices by the values to which she is committed, and so to achieve an important type of autonomy. Austere solutions incorporating appropriate excusing conditions also offer all well-motivated agents the opportunity to lead a modestly successful moral life, the most defensible concept of a "successful moral life." Thus Austere solutions are not unjust, either in the sense of preventing agents from leading the successful moral life, or in the sense of necessarily exposing them to blame and punishment when they act from (non-culpable) mistakes about the world. My conclusion is that the problem of error does not prevent the Austere approach from satisfying the conceptual rationales for usability.

8.2.3 The argument for enhancing social welfare

The last two sections have explored whether the Austere Response to the problem of error can satisfy the conceptual rationales for requiring that a moral code be immune to the problem of error: the rationale that a central purpose of morality is to enable agents to use it in guiding their decisions, and the rationale that morality must satisfy a basic form of justice by enabling all agents to life a successful moral life. We have now found that the Austere Response does satisfy plausible scaled-back versions of these rationales. But what about the goal-oriented rationales—the rationales that usability is needed to enable morality to enhance social welfare and to produce the best possible pattern of actions?

In this section we will examine the Austere solution's capacity to enhance social welfare. We have seen that a moral code's influence on social welfare can indeed be affected by its extended usability. However, while greater extended usability sometimes increases the code's positive effect on social welfare, it can also result in the code's having a negative effect (for example, this occurs when a deontically imperfect code's provisions require actions that are detrimental to welfare, or when the wrongful actions of those who cannot successfully use a highly usable code would be more injurious than the wrongful actions of those who cannot successfully use a less usable code). Similar remarks hold for core usability. Of course higher core usability may, perhaps in small ways, increase a code's positive impact on social welfare. For one thing, in cases involving the problem of error agents would have core guidance for each of the decisions they must make, so they would not be frustrated at being unable to find a way to translate their moral code into a decision. Second, if agents understood their code to be endorsed by the Austere approach, they might feel some gratification that they are making their decisions in accord with moral principles that have the highest deontic merit, not with principles that have been debased in order to accommodate human shortcomings. Third, their moral system could include an appropriate derived duty to seek information when they must make a morally significant decision in the future.[30] Understanding that factual errors can lead them to perform the wrong acts, these agents would seek to minimize this by enhancing their information regarding future acts. Such information-seeking would normally reduce the overall incidence of violations of the code. Insofar as adherence to the code's non-derivative requirements would enhance social welfare, reducing the number of violations will help.

Despite these potentially welfare-promoting features, it is also true that an Austere code might decrease social welfare—for example, it would do so if those who can derive prescriptions from the code would nonetheless systematically perform actions that fail to promote social welfare, either because such actions are required by the code (as in the case of not killing a terminally ill patient in irremediable pain), or because prescriptions mistakenly derived from the code would lead to such acts. Thus the Austere theorist is not in a position to argue that, other things being equal, the moral code he endorses would necessarily have a favorable effect on social welfare. But in this regard the Austere theorist is no worse off than Pragmatic or Hybrid theorists, who cannot make this claim either.

A variant on the idea that an acceptable moral code must enhance social welfare is the view that a moral code should foster social cooperation and consensus. As we have seen, neither the Pragmatic nor the Hybrid solution theorists can claim that the best codes on their view necessarily have these effects. Because the Austere solution does not enable agents to rise above actual mistakes of fact that may lead to lack of cooperation or consensus, it too fails to fully meet this desideratum.

8.2.4 The argument from ideal patterns of action

One of the arguments for requiring usability of moral codes is the argument that an important function of a moral code is to produce the best possible *pattern of actions*. The Austere theorist, in determining which code is the correct theoretical account of right and wrong, only takes into account the deontic virtues of candidate codes, not their pragmatic virtues. So in the context of an Austere approach, the code endorsed by the Austere approach is identical to the perfect code. Thus conformity with the code in question is the same as conformity with the perfect code. Given this, the "best pattern of actions" should be interpreted as those actions that conform to the code in question. Clearly a code endorsed as an Austere solution to the problem of error cannot be guaranteed to produce the best possible pattern of actions on this interpretation. Agents' errors would (except by unlikely accident) lead them to violate the code's own requirements on at least some occasions, falling short of perfect compliance.

As we have seen, ideal Pragmatic and Hybrid solutions to the problem of error are epistemically unavailable. Non-ideal Pragmatic and Hybrid solutions are also

---

[30] Here I am assuming that the Austere code in question is an objective code. However, subjective codes could also count as Austere codes if a suitable deontic justification for them were found. As I argued in Chapter 5, subjective codes have difficulty in incorporating effective derivative duties to acquire information.

unavailable epistemically, and I have argued that there can be no guarantee, even holding other things equal, that either the best imperfect non-ideal Pragmatic solution code or the best imperfect non-ideal Hybrid solution code would produce the best pattern of actions.[31] Nonetheless it may be possible to judge that the code advocated by the Austere theorist would produce a worse pattern of actions than a certain kind of more usable code that might be advocated by a Pragmatic or Hybrid theorist. Consider the following case.

We earlier claimed (for the sake of argument) that the deontically perfect code contains Principle P6, "It is obligatory to pay what one owes in taxes." This principle would be included in an Austere code. But people make mistakes in attempting to follow this principle. According to a study conducted by the Internal Revenue Service of the US Department of the Treasury, the average underpayment in wage and salary tax for the US income tax in 2001 was 1 percent of the amount that should have been paid.[32] Employees are generally aware that wages and salaries are automatically reported by employers to the Internal Revenue Service, so they have little incentive to try to misreport their wages and salaries. Indeed, the percentage of underpayment for categories of income that are not automatically reported by the payer (such as self-employment business income) is sharply higher, providing empirical support for the claim that for the most part individuals calculating the tax due on their wages and salaries aim to report and pay the correct amount, since they believe that under-payment will easily be caught by the IRS. Thus most of the 1 percent underpayment is likely to arise from errors made in calculating the amount due. We can reasonably conclude that US taxpayers, aiming to obey Principle P6 by paying the taxes they owe on their wages and salaries, make errors in applying this principle, underpaying by 1 percent of what is owed.

In light of these facts, a non-ideal Pragmatic theorist, seeking to formulate a moral code that would produce a better pattern of actions (as judged by what the perfect Code C requires) than the perfect code, might propose a Code C# that would be identical to the perfect code except that it would include, instead of the perfect Principle P6, an imperfect Principle P6*, "It is obligatory to pay what one calculates that one owes in taxes, plus 1 percent." The Pragmatic theorist could argue that adoption of his proposed Code C# would produce a better pattern of actions than adoption of perfect Code C, since people trying to follow the perfect code and Principle P6 would some-times violate P6, whereas people who adopted Code C# and P6* would more often actually pay what they owe in taxes and so perform the correct action according to the

---

[31] The best *ideal* Pragmatic solution code and the best *ideal* Hybrid decision-guiding code would be the moral laundry list, which would guarantee performance of exactly those acts required by the moral code in question. However, as I've argued, there is no way to identify what the content of those laundry lists would be.

[32] Slemrod (2007). This figure includes only underpayment, not failures to pay.

perfect code (even though errors would sometimes lead them to violate imperfect P6*).[33] Using this technique of identifying narrow fields of action in which it is known what kind of errors are made in attempts to apply certain kinds of moral principles, the Pragmatic theorist might construct a moral code that would improve on the pattern of action that would be produced by the perfect code itself.[34] The non-ideal Hybrid theorist might adopt a parallel strategy, proposing that Principle P6 be recognized as part of the correct account of what makes actions right and wrong, but that it be supplemented by Principle P6* in the guise of a decision-guide to be used whenever agents decide how much income tax to pay on their wage or salary.[35]

But this strategy of the non-ideal Pragmatic and Hybrid theorist is an unstable one. As soon as information about errors becomes available in some new field, then the code that has been provisionally adopted by the Pragmatic and Hybrid theorist (to respond, say, to known systematic errors in tax calculation) would have to be discarded in favor of a code revised in light of this new information. Moreover, these theorists aim to identify the best code overall, not just a code that would produce a better pattern of actions than the perfect code in certain limited arenas. However, we've seen that this aim is blocked by the amount of nonmoral information that would be needed to identify such a code. Although the non-ideal Pragmatic and Hybrid theorist may be able to identify codes that would produce better patterns of action than the Austere code, they are prevented by their own epistemic limitations from identifying the *best possible* code.

Our conclusions about the patterns of actions securable through the Austere approach may be the following. There seems to be no in-principle way to tell whether the correct Austere code would produce a better or worse pattern of actions (interpreted as conformity to that code) than the best less-than-perfect Pragmatic or Hybrid solution codes (interpreted as conformity to the Pragmatic or Hybrid code in question, and setting aside the fact that the best such code is actually the moral laundry list). It is true that it may be possible for the Pragmatic or Hybrid theorist to take advantage of known patterns of error in particular fields of action (such as income tax estimation) to formulate a Pragmatic or Hybrid code that would produce a better pattern of action

---

[33] Of course, this is setting aside the fact that no single taxpayer may actually underpay by exactly 1 percent, even though the average underpayment is 1 percent. This is not a perfect example, since the argument assumes that every taxpayer underpays. If, say, only 1 percent underpay, then implementing this system would result in the "underpayers" paying the correct amount, while the "correct payers" would pay too much.

[34] In unpublished seminar notes, both Nate Flores and Eli Shupe argued for consideration of this strategy on the part of the Pragmatic theorist.

[35] In section 8.1.2 we raised the question of how the agent is to view such a decision-guide. It seems quite possible that the agent would view the guide as a piece of evidence that she has underestimated how much income tax she owes, and that she should raise her estimate by 1 percent. If this is her perspective, it appears that P6* really functions for her as epistemic evidence about how much tax is owed rather than as a decision-guide per se.

(now judged by compliance with the perfect code) than the pattern of action that would be produced by the perfect Austere code itself. However, given that neither the Pragmatic theorist nor the Hybrid theorist can identify the content of the code they seek, their views still labor under an insurmountable epistemic burden. It does little good to claim that the best Pragmatic code would produce a better pattern of actions than the Austere code if it is impossible to identify what the content of that Pragmatic code is.

8.3 Conclusion

This concludes our discussion of the problem of error. On the one hand, it appears that neither Pragmatic nor Hybrid solutions—whether in their ideal or non-ideal embodiments—provide acceptable remedies for this problem. On the other hand, the Austere solution has distinct attractions. It is true that codes endorsed by the Austere approach cannot be shown to meet the "goal-oriented" desiderata of maximizing social welfare, or facilitating social cooperation and long-range planning, or guaranteeing the occurrence of the ideal pattern of actions. But Austere-endorsed codes do satisfy the conceptual desiderata for "usable" moral theories in the core sense of "usability." They provide agents (even in cases in which they have false beliefs about the world) with a way to make decisions that accord with their values, and so a way to achieve an important form of autonomy. They also provide agents hampered by nonmoral false beliefs with the opportunity to live a successful moral life, according to the modest conception of this life. Furthermore, they do not accede to a decrease in deontic merit in order to achieve greater usability. And unlike Pragmatic and Hybrid approaches, the Austere approach does not confront any devastating epistemic problem at the meta-ethical level. The Austere solution then appears to be the best response to the problem of error, even though it cannot guarantee that agents will successfully perform the actions required by their code. The virtues of the Austere approach suggest that the problem of error is, in some respects, less serious than we may originally have thought. Our deliberations in the last few chapters show that the only acceptable remedy for error is a strong derivative duty for agents to gather information before acting in order to prevent or remove any errors into which they may fall. Of course, gathering information is not always worth the cost, and even when it is worthwhile it may not correct our errors. But it is the only hope we have.

In Chapter 9 we turn to a consideration of the problems of nonmoral ignorance and uncertainty, which may require a different kind of solution.

9

The Problems of Ignorance and Uncertainty

Uncertainty is an inevitable part of life and only the foolish imagine they can eliminate it.[1]

In the past few chapters we have examined possible solutions to the problem of error—the problem raised for a moral code by the fact that all-too-human decision makers often have erroneous beliefs about the world, and so (unless they are lucky) would derive mistaken prescriptions from the code if they tried to use it for guidance. Thus the jury member falsely believes that a half a million dollar award to the plaintiff would fully compensate him for injuries, and so incorrectly concludes that justice requires him to vote for this award (rather than the correct award of a full million dollars); the state governor falsely believes that cutting spending would maximize the general welfare, and so mistakenly concludes that this act (rather than raising taxes) is called for by utilitarianism; and the woman who has promised her mother to buy milk at the super-market falsely remembers she promised to buy bread, and so erroneously judges that she can carry out her duty by buying bread. In canvassing possible responses to this problem, we concluded that the Pragmatic and Hybrid Responses, in either their ideal or non-ideal forms, could not provide workable solutions to error, most prominently because they simply substitute an insurmountable epistemic problem at the theoretician's level for the original insurmountable epistemic problem at the agent's level.

However, we also concluded that the Austere Response could be accepted as a satisfactory solution to the problem of error. It is true that a moral code endorsed by the Austere Response does not normally enable agents hampered by false beliefs to perform the action the moral code actually requires of them. However, an Austere code does assure agents of an important form of autonomy: they can use the code, in the core sense, to derive a prescription for what to do, and so they are not left without moral guidance in making their decisions. Moreover, an Austere code with a suitable

---

[1] Leonhardt (2006), p. C1. Leonhardt attributes this to Robert Rubin as one of the two "big ideas" he brought to Washington in 1982. The actual quotation is slightly different: "Uncertainty was an inevitable part of life and only the foolish imagined they could eliminate it."

account of responsibility provides agents with the opportunity to live a successful moral life, when this is interpreted to mean a life without blame. In addition, the Austere approach does not countenance any dilution in the deontic merit of a moral code in a quixotic search for greater extended usability. Finally, it confronts no special epistemic problem at the theoretical level. Our conclusion is that the Austere approach is the best response to the problem of nonmoral error.

In this chapter we turn to two further epistemic barriers for agents trying to guide their actions by consulting their moral codes: the problem of nonmoral ignorance and the problem of nonmoral uncertainty. (Henceforward I will usually drop the qualifier "nonmoral"—all our focus will be on nonmoral epistemic difficulties.) Let us look at these in turn.

9.1 Defining the Problem of Ignorance and the Problem of Uncertainty

Before examining solutions to the problems of ignorance and uncertainty, we need a more careful statement of what these problems are.

9.1.1 The problem of ignorance

Until now I have often used the term "ignorance" somewhat loosely to refer both to false beliefs and to lack of beliefs about some fact. But we now need to introduce a more precise definition of "ignorance" in order to obtain a clear understanding of the problem of ignorance.

Suppose an agent is trying to apply some moral code to her decision, and believes that the code prescribes as permissible actions having one or more of nonmoral properties F, G, or H. In Chapter 3, section 3.2.4, I roughly characterized the problem of ignorance as the problem of an agent's being ignorant whether a given act A has or fails to have one of properties F, G, or H, or lacks any belief whether A is an act she can or cannot perform. But the problem should be characterized for a broader context. An agent might know, for example, that she must choose among options A, B, and C, might be ignorant whether or not act C has a nonmoral property that makes it permissible or not, but nonetheless believe that acts A and B both have nonmoral property F that makes them permissible. Such an agent is ignorant about act C, but not ignorant about the situation as a whole, since she has information indicating that it would be permissible to perform either act A or B. Her ignorance does not impede her ability to make a decision. Our concern in defining the problem of ignorance should be with agents afflicted with a broader form of ignorance in which the agent lacks enough information to guide *any* choice in her situation. The agent just described is not handicapped in this manner. We must also relativize the notion of ignorance to particular moral codes, since an agent might be ignorant about the nonmoral properties relevant to Code C but not ignorant about the properties relevant to a different Code D. To spell this out we can say the following:

Definition 9.1:   An agent is impeded by the problem of ignorance relative to moral code C and her possible actions at t_1 if and only if:

(1)   in any suitable set of exhaustive options for an agent, at least one of the options has at least one of nonmoral properties F, G, or H,[2] and

(2)   Code C prescribes as permissible or obligatory all and only actions having at least one of F, G, or H, in virtue of their having F, G, or H, and

(3)   either

(a)   S has options available for performance at t_1, but lacks the belief she has such options (and does not believe there are no such options), or

(b)   S believes there are actions that may be epistemically available to her as options for performance at t_1, and for each act A that the agent believes may be epistemically available to her for performance at t_1, she lacks any belief that act A would have F, G, or H.[3]

Unlike some of my previous uses of "prescribes," this definition requires that the code prescribe actions *positively*, that is, prescribe them as either permissible or obligatory. Clauses 1 and 2 jointly require the moral code to satisfy the formal requirement that it identify, in each suitable set of exhaustive options for an agent, at least one act that is permissible or obligatory. Clause 3(a) implies that an agent is impeded by the problem of ignorance if she has options at t_1 but is unaware of this. Such cases are presumably rare. Note that clause 3(a) rules out a case in which an agent affirmatively believes that she does not have any options at t_1; such an agent is impeded by the problem of error, not ignorance. Let us say that the nonmoral properties in virtue of which the code prescribes an act as permissible or obligatory are "right-making" properties. Thus clause 3(b) requires the agent to lack beliefs about the right-making properties of her possible actions, although it does not require her to lack beliefs about their wrong-making properties. This feature is appropriate because there are cases in which an agent might believe that one or more of her options has a wrong-making property without believing of any option that it has any of properties F, G, or H (which in fact are right-making according to C).[4] Such an agent has enough information about her situation to

---

[2] I have qualified this set of options as "suitable" to flag the fact that more is needed in order to ensure that the set qualifies as a genuine set of alternatives. How to do this is controversial (see Bergstrom (1966) for seminal work on this problem) and I shall not attempt it here.

[3] Since an agent's beliefs can change over time, a more complete definition would also specify the time at which the agent has (or lacks) the relevant belief. However, doing so is unnecessary for the present discussion. Assume the time in question is the last time at which the agent must make a decision with respect to her possible options at t_1.

An insightful account of "ignorance" (as it plays a role in assessing blameworthiness) is offered by Rene van Woudenberg (2009), section 1. However, van Woudenberg seems to focus, as did I in Chapter 3, on ignorance about individual acts, not on ignorance about a decision situation.

[4] I use this locution, somewhat awkwardly, to indicate that the agent herself need not believe that these properties are right-making according to C. We need the definition to determine whether the agent is impeded by the problem of ignorance with respect to C in the sense that her uncertainty about the relevant nonmoral properties would leave her unable to apply it if she were to try to do so. In reality she herself may

rule out some acts as impermissible, but she does not have enough to identify what she positively may do. Note that clause 3(b) does not require that Code C actually prescribe any actions for the agent, since we want it to apply to the rare case in which the agent has no options at all, but nonetheless believes that she may have options among which she must make a choice (perhaps, unbeknownst to her, she has been paralyzed by a stroke). Even in this situation, if the agent cannot identify any supposed options that have F, G, or H, she is confronted with the problem of ignorance. Of course the definition does not, and should not, stipulate in clause 3(b) that the agent lacks *true* belief that any action has F, G, or H. She would count as lacking true belief if she either has a false belief or lacks any belief on the question. But if she has a *false* belief that some act has F, G, or H, she is enmeshed in the problem of error with respect to C, not the problem of ignorance. Ignorance requires *lack* of any relevant belief. Clause 3(b) also stipulates that the agent believes of some act that it *may be* epistemically available to her—she need not believe it actually is available to her.[5] Thus if she believes act B might be an option for her, but does not believe of B that it has F, G, or H (and she doesn't believe this of any other act she believes may be an option), then she qualifies as being subject to the problem of ignorance, whether or not B is not actually one of her options. Finally, if she believes about some act-type that any action of this type would have F, G, or H, but also falsely believes that such an act is not an option for her, and in addition lacks any belief that the acts she thinks may be options for her have, or might have, properties F, G, or H, then according to clause 1(b) she is impeded by the problem of ignorance.

For a simple example, suppose Celia yesterday promised her husband, who is concerned about the dangers of icy road conditions, that she would take a certain route to work during her commute today in order to avoid the ice. Code C requires agents to keep their promises. As Celia drives away from the house she remembers that she made the promise but can't remember whether she promised to take Route 1, Route 27, or Route 533. She believes that taking one of these routes would have property F—keeping her promise—but she doesn't believe of any of these acts that it is the one that would have F. Her successfully doing what Code C requires is impeded by the problem of ignorance. We can also describe this situation as one in which she is ignorant *how* to keep her promise (by taking Route 1, taking Route 27, or taking Route 533). Definition 9.1 covers situations in which an agent knows of some act (for example, *driving on the route I promised my husband I would take*) that it has a relevant property F (keeping her promise) but doesn't know *how* to perform an act of that type. Ignorance about how to perform an act needs no separate treatment under Definition 9.1.

---

never have heard of C, or have any interest in applying it to her decision, so she may not believe that F, G, and H are right-making.

[5] Clearly this sense of "may" is stronger than mere logical or metaphysical possibility. We need not try to specify it further here.

The commuter case illustrates how difficult it is to draw a clean distinction between ignorance and uncertainty.[6] For example, under Definition 9.1 the commuter would count as ignorant with respect to Code C because she "lacks any belief that act A would have F, G, or H," even if she held modest credences (degrees of belief) about each of her options that it would fulfill her promise. Thus she might think there is a 60 percent chance taking Route 1 would keep her promise, a 15 percent chance that taking Route 27 would keep her promise, and a 25 percent chance that taking Route 533 would keep her promise. None of these credences is strong enough to count as *believing* the proposition in question. (Of course, if Celia gives full credence to one option's being the one that would keep her promise, then this counts as her believing the proposition in question. Either this belief is false and she is facing the problem of error, or this belief is true and she is not facing any epistemic problem at all.) So long as none of these credences rises to the level at which it counts as full-on belief, she would qualify under Definition 9.1 as ignorant if she has the described credences, although it would be more natural to describe her situation as one of uncertainty.

Indeed, as I argued in Chapter 3, there is reason to treat the problem of ignorance as a special case of the problem of uncertainty. For example, if Celia assigns the different levels of credence just described to each of her various options' keeping her promise, then her situation counts as one of uncertainty, even if one of the credences she assigns is very high, so long as it falls short of full credence. If Celia is epistemically *indifferent* about which of her options would keep her promise, where this is understood as her assigning equal credence (in this case, a 1/3 chance) to each option's being the one that would keep her promise, her situation is still best understood as one of uncertainty. If she assigns no credence at all to any option's being the correct one, or regards the relevant probabilities as being indeterminate, then as a decision maker she is nonetheless in the same position as an agent who assigns some less-than-full credence to each of her option's being the correct one: she cannot derive any prescription from the code that prescribes keeping her promise. We need a response to the problem of uncertainty that will address all of these situations, even though they would be classified by Definition 9.1 as instances of ignorance.

Given the fact that the problem of ignorance seems best interpreted as a special case of the problem of uncertainty, I will subsume it (with one exception, to be explained) under uncertainty, and focus the discussion in the rest of this chapter on the problem of uncertainty construed so that it includes the problem of ignorance. Thus I am treating error, ignorance, and uncertainty (and the problems associated with them), not as psychological natural kinds, but rather as categories unified by the kind of remedy best suited to them. Similarly, one might treat certain kinds of computer problems as all being of the same kind, not on the ground that they are all caused by the same underlying software malfunction, but rather on the ground that

---

[6] Recall that in this book I am using "uncertainty" to describe cases that decision theorists standardly describe as involving "risk."

they are all best treated by the same kind of remedy, such as powering down the computer and then powering it up again.

9.1.2 The problem of uncertainty

Given our discussion of the problem of ignorance, we can now define the problem of uncertainty as follows, incorporating the problem of ignorance under it. We need a quite broad definition that will cover all the different kinds of cases in which an agent is less than certain whether any of her options have the properties that are relevant under the code in question.

> **Definition 9.2:**   An agent is impeded by the problem of uncertainty relative to moral code C and her possible actions at t_1 if and only if:
>
> (1)   in any suitable set of exhaustive options for an agent, at least one of the options has at least one of nonmoral properties F, G, or H, and
> (2)   Code C prescribes as permissible or obligatory all and only actions having at least one of F, G, or H, in virtue of their having F, G, or H, and
> (3)   either
>> (a)   S has options available at t_1, but lacks any credence that she has such options (and has no credence that there are no such options), or
>> (b)   S assigns some credence to there being actions epistemically available to her as options at t_1, and for each act A that she believes may be epistemically available to her for performance at t_1, S is unsure whether A has F, G, or H.[7]

I intend "being unsure" to cover a wide variety of doxastic states involving less than full confidence or full belief. Thus we can understand "S's being unsure whether A has F, G or H" to cover at least the following kinds of states:

1.   S assigns no credence (that is, has no degree of belief) to A's having F, G, or H (and she does not assign any credence to A's not having F, G, or H);
2.   S assigns no probability (either sharp or imprecise) to A's having F, G, or H (where "assigns no probability to X" means "for any objective, subjective, epistemic probability or chance p that X, S does not believe that X has a probability of p"), and also assigns no probability to A's not having F, G, or H; or
3.   S assigns some probability (or has some credence) less than 1.0 but greater than zero (the probability or credence may be either sharp or imprecise) to A's having F, G, or H (where "assigns some probability less than 1.0 but greater than zero to X" means "for some objective, subjective, epistemic probability or chance p less than 1.0 but greater than zero that X, S believes that x has probability p," and "assigns

---

[7] An agent might be in such an impoverished epistemic situation that she believes she may have options at t_1, but does not have a sufficiently clear idea what these options are to qualify as "believing of act A that it may be an option for her." Definition 9.2 should be expanded to include such cases, although we do not need this complication for our purposes here.

some credence p less than 1.0 but greater than zero to X" means "for some credence p less than 1.0 but greater than zero that X, S has credence p that X");[8] or

4.   S regards the probability of A's having F, G, or H to be indeterminate.[9]

If the agent is unaware that she has options at t_1, then by clause 3(a) she counts as being impeded by the problem of uncertainty. Clause 3(a) is intended to cover cases in which the agent is unaware that she has options at t_1, but not to cover any case in which the agent has credence of zero in her having some options: in this latter case, since she has a relevant but mistaken doxastic state (in effect, disbelief in her having options), she would be subject to the problem of error rather than uncertainty. The kind of case in which the agent is unaware that she has any options at all (perhaps she's never thought about the possibility that she'll be alive and awake at t_1) should not be confused with the kind of case in which the agent thinks she may have options at t_1, but feels her options are morally trivial (tying her left shoe first, or tying her right shoe first). Recall that on my account even morally trivial acts have moral status, since they are deemed permissible by every moral code in virtue of its extension to all possible acts. Thus an agent who believes she has options, but only morally trivial ones, at t_1 is not covered by clause 3(a).

Clause 3(b) addresses the more common situation in which the agent does have at least some credence in her having options. Of the actions she thinks may be options for her, she is unsure—in one of the described ways—about each such supposed option whether it has one of the relevant nonmoral properties (that are in fact right-making according to Code C).[10] For example, she may assign some (but less than full) credence to the proposition that one of the actions in question has one of the relevant nonmoral properties. Her doxastic states as a whole may comprise a mixture of lack of credence (or probability assignments) and less-than-full credences. Indeed, her doxastic states

---

[8] Here I use "probability/credence less than 1.0" to stand in for "assigning a probability less than that necessary for full-on belief." Because of problems arising from the Lottery Paradox, there is much dispute among epistemologists about whether full-on belief can be represented by any probability assignment, although some epistemologists are willing to say, for example, that assigning a probability of 0.95 counts as full-on belief. If some such probability figure is agreed upon, it can be substituted in the description of the third type of doxastic state. For an argument that an agent's beliefs cannot be reduced to her credences, see Buchak (2014).

[9] Definition 9.2 in effect merges the classical decision-theoretical categories of decision-making under risk (probabilities assigned to outcomes) and decision-making under uncertainty (no meaningful probabilities for outcomes). See, for example, Luce and Raiffa (1957), p. 13. Unlike classical decision theorists, I have used the term "uncertainty" to include cases in which the agent assigns no definite probabilities to the outcomes of her actions. I need a term that covers both cases and "uncertainty" seems to be the best equivalent in ordinary English. The definition also incorporates the types of decision problems that arise when an agent assigns imprecise credences or probabilities, or regards the relevant features of the act as indeterminate. For a survey of the state of the literature on imprecise credences, see Joyce (2010). For one approach to the question of decision-making under indeterminacy, see J. Williams (2014).

[10] Suppose the agent believes of *every* act that she thinks may be an option that it has *no chance* of having property F, G, or H. Such an agent does not count under Definition 9.2 as being impeded by the problem of uncertainty. In effect this agent's beliefs entail that she is in a moral dilemma with respect to Code C. She has serious problems in deciding what to do, but I shall not try to resolve this special case.

may even include a full belief about one or more acts that these acts have certain (wrong-making) nonmoral properties, or they may include a credence of zero about some option that it has F, G, or H, but her states may not include a full credence that any one of her supposed options has F, G, or H.

Our previous example provides an illustration. If Celia thinks there is a 60 percent chance taking Route 1 would keep her promise, a 15 percent chance that taking Route 27 would keep her promise, and a 25 percent chance that taking Route 533 would keep her promise, then according to Definition 9.2 her decision is impeded by the problem of uncertainty relative to a code that requires agents to keep their promises.

9.2 Addressing the Problem of Uncertainty

In addressing the problem of uncertainty (now interpreted to include the problem of ignorance), moral theorists have proposed the same three types of approaches that we examined as remedies for the problem of error. Thus an advocate of the Pragmatic approach to the problem of uncertainty holds that the essential role of a moral code is to serve as a decision-guide, usable in the extended sense, to guide moral decisions. This theorist notes that a moral code subject to the problem of uncertainty cannot be used in the extended sense as a decision-guide in cases in which agents are uncertain about the relevant nonmoral properties of their options. Thus if Celia wants to follow Code C, which requires her to keep her promise to her husband, but is uncertain which route would keep the promise, she cannot derive *any* prescription from Code C, much less derive a prescription for the act that would actually comply with Code C.[11] The Pragmatic theorist would reject Code C as unusable, and advocate adoption of an alternative code that would be usable for agents who are hampered by uncertainty. This alternative code might try to solve the problem by including a rule saying "It is obligatory to perform the act that has the highest probability of keeping one's promise." Celia would be able to directly use this revised rule, in the extended sense, in deciding what to do. If she used it, her act would perforce be right according to this new code, whether or not she succeeds in keeping her promise.

By contrast, an advocate of the Austere approach to the problem of uncertainty maintains her position that the essential role of a moral code is to provide a theoretical

---

[11] It is sometimes claimed to the contrary that of course an agent such as Celia can derive a prescription from Code C, for example the prescription to take Route 1 because it has the highest probability of keeping her promise. This is a mistake. Code C does not say "It is obligatory to perform the act that has the highest probability of keeping one's promise"; rather it says, "It is obligatory to keep one's promise." From the high probability that taking Route 1 would conform with C it follows that taking Route 1 has the highest probability of being the act that keeps the promise or fulfills Celia's duty. But this does not entail it *is* her duty to perform this act.

An agent like Celia might accept some epistemic principle that licenses her to believe any proposition to which she assigns a credence of (say) 0.95 or above. If Celia assigned a credence of 0.95 to Route 1 being the road she promised her husband to take, then she could derive, from this credence, her epistemic principle, and Code C the conclusion that she ought to take Route 1. But for cases in which her credence falls below the relevant threshold point, no such conclusion can be derived.

account of what makes actions right and wrong. If the code that does this correctly cannot be used by some decision makers because of their uncertainties, that is a practical problem for them to solve, but it is not a problem showing the code itself is incorrect. In discussing the Austere approach to the problem of error we noted that it can still be claimed (although the Austere theorist would have no interest in this) that the Austere code offers core usability to the user when she labors under false beliefs, even though it does not offer extended usability. However, a code that is subject to the problem of uncertainty cannot even deliver core usability in all cases. If Celia wanted to derive a prescription from Code C, she could not do so if her only relevant beliefs were the less-than-full credences we've ascribed to her. For her, Code C is not usable even in the core sense. So Austere codes are not fully usable even in the core sense, and cannot guarantee autonomy to agents beset with uncertainties about the world. The Austere theorist will not be concerned about this, but those who are attracted by the Austere approach but hoped to show that it is usable in at least the core sense will be disappointed.

Finally, a proponent of the Hybrid approach to the problem of uncertainty argues (as she did in the case of the problem of error) that the best solution is to recognize that a comprehensive moral theory must include two components: a top-tier code providing the correct theoretical account of what makes actions right and wrong, augmented by an appropriate set of lower-tier usable decision-guides that can be applied by any agent making a moral decision, including agents who are beset with uncertainty about the nonmoral features of their actions. Such a comprehensive moral theory would render the top-tier moral code indirectly usable, so long as the lower-tier decision-guides are suitably linked to the top-tier code, and are usable by agents facing uncertainty. For example, a bifurcated Hybrid code might include "It is obligatory to keep one's promises" in the top-tier code, and include "It is obligatory to perform the act that has the highest probability of keeping one's promise" as a lower-tier decision-guide. A Hybrid theorist taking this approach would give up the search for a moral theory that secured universal *direct* extended usability in favor of one that secured universal *indirect* usability in cases of uncertainty.

Most discussions of the epistemic problem for morality tend not to sharply distinguish between the problems of error and uncertainty, and so tend to adopt a single solution to both problems. But we should ask whether it might be advisable to adopt one approach to the problem of error and a different approach to the problem of uncertainty. The feasibility (for guiding decisions) of such a system, in which different solutions are provided for different problems, would depend partly on whether a decision-making agent can determine which epistemic problem she confronts (or at least can believe she faces one problem rather than the other). On the face of things this appears to be possible. In most (although not all) cases the agent knows the content of her own beliefs or credences about the decision that faces her. Of course an agent who is caught in the problem of error is typically not aware that she has any epistemic problem at all, since she typically believes that her (false) beliefs about her options' relevant nonmoral properties are true.[12] However, an agent caught in the problem of error would not judge herself to be subject to the problem of uncertainty, since she has full credence that some option of hers has the relevant properties F, G, or H. Thus she could implement whatever recommendation is made for the problem of error. And an agent who is caught in the problem of uncertainty can typically tell this about herself (at least for cases covered by clause 3(b) in Definition 9.2) because she is aware that she is unsure about the relevant features of her actions. Celia, for example, is very likely aware that she only has less-than-full credences about which of her possible routes would keep her promise (or, more precisely, she would become aware of this if she tried to apply Code C). Thus in trying to solve the problem of uncertainty, we should bear in mind that one possible strategy is to accept one solution to the problem of error and a distinct solution to the problem of uncertainty.

The fact that an agent would not understand herself to be impeded by the problem of uncertainty if she is in the situation addressed by clause 3(a), in which she is totally unaware that she has options available to her at t_1, suggests that it may be a mistake to include this situation as part of the problem of uncertainty. From the point of view of finding a remedy for it, her epistemic situation, in which she is unaware she has options that must be chosen among, is radically unlike the epistemic situation of an agent who thinks she may have options but is unsure what their nonmoral properties are. Proposing a new or a revised decision-guide to the agent suffering from this radical form of uncertainty, or supplementing the account of right and wrong with a usable decision-guide, cannot remedy her situation, since she has insufficient grasp of her situation to apply *any* rule to it. On the other hand, the Austere Response seems to be an adequate solution to this agent's problem, since it can provide her with an excuse for performing the wrong act (at least if her ignorance is non-culpable), does not undermine her autonomy (since she does not believe she has any choice *to* guide by reference to her values), and poses no insurmountable epistemic challenge for the theorist. This is one form of the problem of ignorance that should not be included as a special case of the problem of uncertainty, but rather addressed by the Austere Response, as is the problem of error. In light of this consideration, I shall revise the definition of the problem of uncertainty as follows:

Definition 9.3:   An agent is impeded by the problem of uncertainty relative to moral code C and her possible actions at t_1 if and only if:

(1)   in any suitable set of exhaustive options for an agent, at least one of the options has at least one of nonmoral properties F, G, or H, and

(2)   Code C prescribes as permissible or obligatory all and only actions having at least one of F, G, or H, in virtue of their having F, G, or H, and

---

[12] See Huddleston (2012) for an argument that agents sometimes believe P but also believe that their belief in P is false.

(3)   for at least one possible action A, S assigns some credence (greater than 0) to A's being epistemically available to her as an option for t_1, and for each possible act X that she believes may be an option for her at t_1, S is unsure whether X has F, G, or H.

Armed with this definition of the problem of uncertainty, which now excludes certain forms of ignorance that have been re-categorized within the problem of error, we can begin the hunt for a solution to it.

9.2.1 Feasible joint solutions to the problems of error and uncertainty

Given that theorists have advocated the same three types of approaches both to the problem of error and to the problem of uncertainty, there are nine possible approaches to the two problems together, as set out in Table 9.1, in which a comprehensive approach to both problems is called a "system."

In deciding that none of the Pragmatic or Hybrid approaches to the problem of error are acceptable, we have already rejected systems of types A, B, C, G, H, and I (flagged by the fact that these systems are greyed out in Table 9.1). This leaves only systems of types D, E, and F, in which the Austere approach is adopted for the problem of error. The question, then, is which of the three remaining types of systems is best. Of these, a system of type E adopts the Austere approach to both problems, while systems of types D and F adopt differing approaches to the two problems. Let us assess these three types of systems, beginning with the unitary approach represented by systems of type E.

Table 9.1

System	Problem	Pragmatic approach	Austere approach	Hybrid approach
A	Error	X		
	Uncertainty	X		
B	Error	X		
	Uncertainty		X	
C	Error	X		
	Uncertainty			X
D	Error		X	
	Uncertainty	X		
E	Error		X	
	Uncertainty		X	
F	Error		X	
	Uncertainty			X
G	Error			X
	Uncertainty	X		
H	Error			X
	Uncertainty		X	
I	Error			X
	Uncertainty			X

9.2.2 Evaluation of systems of type E: Austere approaches to both the problem of error and the problem of uncertainty

In a system of type E, the Austere solution is proposed for the problem of error and also for the problem of uncertainty. On this proposal, a given moral code C is identified as the correct theoretical account of right and wrong. It is likely that some agents, in attempting to carry out the prescriptions of C, will choose acts that are wrong, because their beliefs about the morally relevant nonmoral properties of those actions are incorrect. Thus the juror may mistakenly vote for a half million dollar award to the plaintiff, an award which does not fully compensate him for his injury. Agents may have a duty to enhance their nonmoral beliefs as much as possible in order to avoid this sort of mistake, but the inevitable occurrence of some mistakes of this kind is not seen as a reason to reject or revise C itself as the correct theoretical account of right and wrong. In the eyes of friends of the Austere solution, C's role as an account of right and wrong is not cast into question by its failure to adequately guide misinformed agents in their choice of acts. As we saw before, the Austere theorist simply rests with this assertion. However, others may note that the Austere solution nonetheless has important desirable features: such codes protect agents' autonomy, and, when augmented with a suitable account of excusing conditions, enable well-intentioned agents to live a modestly successful moral life.

An advocate of system of type E must also recognize that there are occasions—perhaps many occasions—on which agents do not labor under false beliefs, but nonetheless lack sufficiently comprehensive beliefs to draw any guidance from C at all. In different versions of our stories, the juror may be uncertain which award would justly compensate the plaintiff, and the state governor may be unsure whether raising taxes or cutting spending would maximize utility. Such agents know in the abstract which type of act (for example, fully compensating the plaintiff) would be right according to their code, but they lack the factual beliefs necessary to derive any prescription from the code for any of their concrete alternatives.

A staunch proponent of Austere systems of type E would be unmoved by the plight of these agents. This advocate would emphasize that the preeminent role of a moral code is to provide a theoretical account of what makes acts right and wrong. If people want to use a moral code to decide what to do, and if there are circumstances in which agents can use their knowledge of the world to select an action on grounds that the code deems it to be right, so much the better. But if there are circumstances in which agents' beliefs are so impoverished that they cannot make such a selection, then that only shows that human beings cannot use the moral code in all the ways they would like to. If they want to use such a moral code to guide their decisions, it is incumbent on them, insofar as possible, to enhance their knowledge in ways that will enable them to do so.

Aspects of this System E approach have a great deal of appeal. Certainly it is attractive to think that the correct account of what makes acts right and wrong should not be abandoned or distorted in order to render the code usable by benighted, ignorant, confused, or uncertain agents trying to decide what they should do—just as scientists should not revise their accounts of the fundamental regularities of nature or mathematics just to render "knowledge" of those regularities more easily usable by engineers or computer scientists. The drunk who looks for his lost wallet under the street light because that is where he can see is making a laughable mistake—and Austere theorists say that we would be making an equally laughable mistake to revise our moral theory because doing so would make it easier to use. Nonetheless, the Austere approach to the problem of uncertainty lacks crucial advantages it has as a solution to the problem of error. An *uncertain* agent trying to use a code endorsed by the Austere approach cannot even use the code in the core sense: she is unable to derive any prescription at all from the code. We need not fear that such an agent is condemned to a moral life that is partially unsuccessful, since appropriate excusing conditions may excuse her for wrong actions performed when her uncertainty prevents her from deriving a prescription from her code. But her inability to link the code to any choice about what to do undermines the important form of autonomy that enables her to translate her moral values into a choice of what to do, and she can neither govern her decisions by her moral values nor express those values through her decisions.

If, unlike the Austerity theorist, we take some form of usability seriously, we must conclude that systems of type E have a serious flaw. Although they are adequate for agents facing the problem of error, they fail to provide autonomy to agents facing the problem of uncertainty, since such agents cannot derive any prescription at all from their moral code. We can hope for a better solution.

9.2.3 Evaluation of systems of type D: conjoining Austere solutions to the problem of error with Pragmatic solutions to the problem of uncertainty

In a system of type D, an Austere solution is proposed for the problem of error, but a Pragmatic solution for the problem of uncertainty. On such a proposal, some moral code C (for example, utilitarianism) is identified as the correct account of right and wrong. Since C is an Austere Response to the problem of error, the possibility of error is recognized but accepted: many agents, in trying to make decisions by reference to this code, will be misled by false factual beliefs into deriving prescriptions for the wrong acts. A system of type D espouses the Austere Response in maintaining the correctness of C as an account of right-making characteristics, but also tells agents to employ C as a guide for decisions when they believe of some act that it is prescribed by C. When C is usable for making decisions, it is not required that it be usable in the extended sense, but only that it be usable in the core sense. If agents derive prescriptions for the wrong acts, then the excusing conditions included in the theory shield them from blame.

A system of type D is constructed to address the problem of uncertainty as well as the problem of error. It aims to handle the fact that many agents, in trying to make decisions by reference to C, will sometimes be hamstrung by their uncertainty about any available option whether it has the properties deemed relevant by C. These agents cannot use C itself, even in the core sense, to make any decision. A Pragmatic solution to this situation is offered. It conjoins some new code C* (for example, common-sense morality) to C. Because the Pragmatic theorist maintains that any decision-guide must also function as a theoretical account of right and wrong, and that any theoretical account of right and wrong must also function as a decision-guide, on this type of system the Pragmatic Code C* is deemed to serve both functions. Thus both C and C* serve in these dual roles, dividing the labor between them depending on the epistemic situation of the agent. C serves as a theoretical account and as a decision-guide in cases of both true and false belief, while C* serves as a theoretical account and as a decision-guide in cases in which the agent is uncertain whether any act has the non-moral properties that are relevant to C. Since C is an Austere solution to the problem of error, it is only required to be usable in the core sense, not in the extended sense. But given the commitment of Pragmatic theory to securing extended usability, C* as a Pragmatic solution must be usable in the extended sense. Together the two codes are designed to provide some type of usability for all decisions.

Systems of type D are afflicted with fatal problems. For one thing, the Pragmatic solution to the epistemic problem for morality insists that a single code function *both* as the account of right-making characteristics, and also as a universal decision-guide. A system of type D includes two codes, one of which (C) functions as the account of right-making characteristics and also as a decision-guide for agents enmeshed in the problem of error, while the other of which (C*) functions as the account of right-making characteristics and also as a decision-guide for agents enmeshed in the problem of uncertainty. Thus this kind of system actually offers two different accounts of right-making characteristics plus two distinct decision-guides. It does not appear to be consistent with the guiding spirit of the Pragmatic approach, despite being advertised as incorporating a Pragmatic approach, because its decision-guides (for example, C*) are not necessarily identical with its theoretical accounts of right-making characteristics (for example, C).[13]

Second, insofar as C and C* jointly offer *two* accounts of right and wrong, a system of this type may be vulnerable to fatal inconsistencies. Consider System S1, which is the conjunction of utilitarianism and common-sense morality, the latter of which is often held to be a good guide for decision-making when the agent is unable to use utilitarianism itself:

System S1:

C: An act is right if and only if, and because, it would produce at least as much utility as any other alternative, and

C*:   An act is right if and only if, and because, it is permitted by the rules of common-sense morality.[14]

---

[13] Thanks to an anonymous reader for the Press for pointing this out.

[14] In formulating this and following candidate systems, for brevity's sake I only state norms for rightness, and defer any attempt to make the system comprehensive by including norms for other types of moral status. Stating such a code for "is obligatory" would be complex, since it would have to provide

The idea behind System S1 would be that an agent who believes that some act A would produce at least as much utility as any other alternative ought to follow C by performing A, but if the agent is uncertain which act would produce at least as much utility as any other alternative, he ought to perform the act that C* prescribes. Many moral theorists believe that these particular C and C* often agree in their assessments of individual acts. However, most theorists also believe that the two codes sometimes generate inconsistent assessments. For example, S1 may tell the agent both that A, an act of breaking a promise, is right (according to C), and also that it is not right (according to C*). Since this pair of prescriptions is inconsistent, S1 must be rejected.

But other versions of this strategy might look more promising. Consider another system, which conditionalizes the agent's prescriptions on her doxastic states.

System S2:

C: If and only if, and because, the agent is certain of some act A that it would produce no less utility than any alternative, then the agent would be right to perform A, and

C*:   If and only if, and because, the agent is uncertain of any act that it would produce no less utility than any alternative, and if and only if, and because, the agent is certain of some act that it has F (where acts having F are permitted by the rules of common-sense morality), then the agent would be right to perform the act that he believes to have F.

So long as the agent has a consistent set of doxastic states, System S2 does not run any structural risk of generating inconsistent assessments, since cases in which the two codes, C and C*, issue prescriptions never overlap (for example, C only prescribes an act as right in cases in which the agent has certainty about some act that it would produce no less utility than any alternative, while C* does not prescribe any act as right when the agent is certain about this).

However, System S2 has problems of its own. From the perspective of an Austere theorist, System S2 is unlikely to be acceptable. It ascribes rightness to acts, not in virtue of their actually maximizing utility or their actually having F (and so conforming to the rules of common-sense morality), but rather in virtue of the agent's certainty or uncertainty about these facts. It has swapped out an objectivized theory in favor of a subjectivized theory. The Austere theorist is likely to see this as compromising the account of right and wrong to ensure usability, and would not accept System S2 since it violates a central tenet of the Austere approach.

Worse is the fact that C* does not solve the problem of uncertainty, since there is no guarantee that an agent who is uncertain which act would produce no less utility than any alternative would have either accurate or certain beliefs about any act that it has property F, which makes it permissible according to the rules of common-sense

---

for the case in which an agent is not certain of any act that it is obligatory, but is certain of some act that it is right.

morality. An agent such as the commuter Celia might be uncertain how much utility would be produced by her various options, and equally uncertain which act would keep her promise about which route to take. She can derive no guidance, either in the core or extended sense, from System S2. Because it is incomplete in this manner, S2 fails to solve one of the problems it is intended to solve.

However, this case suggests a different kind of strategy that might enable us to define a more successful system of type D that conjoins the Austere and the Pragmatic approaches. This strategy takes advantage of the fact that some accounts of right and wrong are so closely coordinated with associated decision-guides that the theoretical account of right and wrong can be thought of as a special case of the decision-guide. Such close coordination may make available an alternate technique for avoiding inconsistent prescriptions. The most promising such system may be the following S3:

> **System S3:**
>
> C: An act is right if and only if, and because, it would produce no less utility than any alternative, and
>
> C*:   An act is right if and only if, and because, it would produce no less subjective expected utility than any alternative.

The idea behind System S3 is that if an agent believes some act would produce no less utility than any alternative, then ipso facto that act would produce no less *subjective* expected utility than any alternative, so in such a case C and C* generate identical prescriptions. If the agent doesn't believe of any act that it would produce no less utility than any alternative, the agent's credences will determine which acts produce no less subjective expected utility than any alternative, and he should select his act according to C*. System S3 at least partly escapes the Austere theorist's first objection to System S2, since the account C does not dilute the objectivized version of utilitarianism by subjectivizing it. Moreover, C and C* do generate consistent prescriptions in certain cases, such as the one in which the agent believes correctly that some act A would produce no less utility than any alternative. But these are the favorable cases. In many less favorable cases C and C* would generate inconsistent prescriptions. Suppose keeping a certain promise would produce no less utility than any alternative and so be right according to C. But the agent's credences (even when justified) might entail that *breaking* the promise produces no less subjective expected utility than any alternative, so C* would entail that keeping the promise is not right. In this case the prescription generated by C is inconsistent with the prescription generated by C*. Moreover, in a different promising case, C* might be subject to the problem of error: it might be true that the agent's credences about the possible upshots of his actions entail that *keeping* the promise would produce no less subjective expected utility than any alternative, but also true that the agent (mistakenly) believes that *breaking* the promise would produce no less subjective expected utility than any alternative. This agent can derive a prescription from C*—to break the promise—but this prescription would not be correct.[15] Finally, agents do not always have rich enough credences about the possible upshots of their actions and their probabilities to ground *any* conclusion that one of their options would produce no less subjective expected utility than any alternative. In such a case the agent could not derive a prescription from *either* C or C*. Thus System S3 fails: in commonly occurring epistemic situations it generates inconsistent prescriptions, its decision-guide C* is not always usable in the extended sense as the Pragmatic solution requires, and the system as a whole is not universally usable even in the core sense.

Indeed, there is a more general problem with systems of type D. The ideal Pragmatist demands that the decision-guide C* be universally usable in the extended sense (at least when C itself is not usable). We saw in Chapter 4 that there is only one code that is universally usable: the moral laundry list. We could incorporate this code into a system of type D as follows:

System S4:

C: An act is right if and only if, and because, it would produce no less utility than any alternative, and

C*:   If and only if the agent is uncertain of any act that it would produce no less utility than any alternative, then it would be right for her to perform an act if and only if, and because, it has $F_1, F_2, F_3, \ldots$ or F_n (where $F_1, F_2, F_3, \ldots$ and F_n are the properties of acts prescribed as right by the moral laundry list associated with C).

In System S4 the moral laundry list is constructed in a special way enabling it to prescribe actions described so that an agent knows how to perform each of the prescribed actions, and if he performs such an action, then he performs the act prescribed *both* by C* and by C itself. Thus if the agent believes (correctly or incorrectly) that A would produce no less utility than any alternative, he applies C to his decision. If his belief is correct, C is usable in the extended sense; if his belief is false, C is usable only in the core sense, but this is acceptable for C, which is the Austere component of System S4. If the agent is unsure of any action whether it would produce no less utility than any alternative, he would apply C* in making his decision. C* is constructed in such a way that he can always derive a prescription from it, and that prescription will always be to perform an act that in fact is prescribed as right by C as well. The set of acts prescribed by C* is a proper subset of the acts prescribed by C, since C* only prescribes acts in circumstances where the agent is uncertain, whereas C prescribes acts independently of the agent's doxastic state. Within that subset it appears that C and C* generate consistent prescriptions, since the act prescribed by C* is the very act prescribed by C (although the agent is not in a position to know this except by inference from the general nature of C*). Of course, the agent could be certain about some act A that it would produce no less utility than any alternative, and he could be wrong about this. But in this case C* would not prescribe any action for him, so no inconsistency arises.

---

[15] Of course agents do not always have true beliefs about whether an act would maximize utility, so they may derive a mistaken prescription from C, but this is acceptable for C viewed as the Austere component of System S3, since this component (unlike C*) only requires core usability.

One of the troubling aspects of a system like S4 is that it contains two distinct theoretical accounts of what makes acts right. These accounts are pragmatically co-extensional with each other within the range of the prescriptions of C*, but nonetheless they identify very different right-making properties. Thus on C, an act A is right because it would produce no less utility than any alternative, but according to C* (assuming the agent is uncertain), A is right because it would (say) be donating to Oxfam at t_1. This divergence between the right-making properties should certainly give us pause.

But the fatal problem with a system like S4 is that it relies on a special sort of moral laundry list as its code C*, and we have already seen in Chapter 4 that there is no humanly available way to identify the contents of such a list. System S4 lifts the burden of uncertainty from agents using decision-guide C*, but it places a new and equally crippling epistemic burden on the theorist trying to identify which laundry list is correct (or places it anew on the agent trying to decide which possible laundry list is the correct C*). We might take the *non-ideal* Pragmatic approach to C* and permit C* to fall somewhat short of complete extended usability. But as we saw in Chapter 7, identifying the best, or even a satisfactory, non-ideal list of this type creates far too high an epistemic hurdle for either the theorist or the agent.

This review of ways in which we might hope to construct systems of type D that provide an Austere solution to the problem of error and a Pragmatic solution to the problem of uncertainty is hardly complete. Perhaps someone will devise a system of this type that avoids the kinds of problems we have seen with Systems S1, S2, S3, and S4. But our review strongly suggests that no such system will be satisfactory. Our investigation has revealed that any such system would have to accomplish a number of different tasks: (a) preserve the original Austere theoretical account of right and wrong as Code C, (b) provide a decision-guide C* suitably linked to Code C that provides both theoretical assessments and decision-guiding advice (usable in the extended sense) about actions in cases where the agent's uncertainty prevents his using C itself for guidance, (c) avoid the delivery by C and C* of inconsistent theoretical assessments or inconsistent decision-guiding prescriptions, (d) ideally ensure that the theoretical accounts of right and wrong provided by C and C* identify the same right- and wrong-making properties, and (d) avoid creating a new and insurmountable epistemic challenge to identifying the content of C*. Our review so far has revealed the serious impediments to jointly accomplishing all these tasks, and suggests strongly that no system of type D can coherently accomplish what is needed. Moreover, as I noted at the beginning of this section, a system of type D seems inherently outside the spirit of Pragmatic accounts, even if one could be found that accomplished all these tasks.

It appears, then, that if we start with some moral code C that we believe provides the correct account of right and wrong but is subject to the problems of error and uncertainty, we cannot both preserve C as the correct account of right and wrong and as the best solution to the problem of error, and also adopt a Pragmatic approach in an associated code C* to the difficulties encountered by C because of the problem of uncertainty. Systems of type D which attempt to do this will not afford us the general solution to the problems of error and uncertainty that we are seeking. However, understanding the difficulties they encounter gives us better insight into what we need for a solution to work.

9.2.4 Evaluation of systems of type F: conjoining Austere solutions to the problem of error with Hybrid solutions to the problem of uncertainty

In Chapter 8 we characterized the Hybrid approach to the problem of error as attempting to solve the problem by proposing a two-tier moral system. In this system, the top tier consists in a set of principles, or a code, that provides the correct theoretical account of what makes actions right and wrong. The lower tier consists of a set of decision-guides to be used for actual decision-making. The lower-tier rules must be usable, and their availability must render the top-tier code usable in the indirect sense—so that an agent hoping to do what the top-tier code requires, but hampered by erroneous beliefs about the world, can turn to the lower-tier rules for guidance. Since agents' attempts to apply the top-tier rules would sometimes (because of their error-stricken nonmoral beliefs) lead them astray, the Hybrid solution to the problem of error instructs agents to apply the lower-tier rules rather than top-tier rules.

The systems of type F to be examined in this section conjoin an Austere solution to the problem of error with a Hybrid solution to the problem of uncertainty. This type of system also involves two tiers of rules, and we can see immediately that such a system is closely related to the Hybrid solution described in Chapter 8. The top-tier code is endorsed by the Austere Response as the correct theoretical account of right and wrong. The lower-tier rules are proposed as decision-guides. Clearly, the agent should turn to the lower-tier rules when she is impeded by the problem of uncertainty. But in formulating a system of type F we need to decide which tier the agent should utilize in making a decision when she is vexed by the problem of error. For reasons of theoretical simplicity I will stipulate that the top-tier rules are only to be considered as accounts of right and wrong, not as decision-guides, while the lower-tier rules are to function solely as decision-guides, not as accounts of right and wrong. This implies that one of the lower-tier rules—let us call it "decision-guide DG_0"—must be designed for agents who have all the relevant beliefs necessary to apply the top-tier code to a decision. Thus the semantic content of decision-guide DG_0 mirrors the content of the top-tier code. For example, if the top-tier code stipulates that an act is obligatory if and only if it would maximize utility, DG_0 also stipulates that an act is to be done if it would maximize utility. Of course some agents, in trying to make decisions by reference to DG_0, would be misled by false nonmoral beliefs to derive a prescription for acts that C evaluates as wrong. The System F response to this reaffirms the correctness of C, ideally exhorts agents to improve their factual knowledge to minimize the number of false nonmoral beliefs, and directs agents to use DG_0 as a decision-guide whenever their beliefs allow them to do so. When their relevant beliefs are true, they will successfully derive a prescription to do what C prescribes. When their beliefs are false, they will derive a prescription from DG_0 that (typically) differs from what C prescribes. However, this is not a strike against DG_0, since the prescription that the agent would derive from DG_0 duplicates the prescription the agent would derive from C itself, and we have assumed that C (as an Austere code) provides only core usability, not extended usability. However, all the decision-guides in C* should be usable at least in the core sense, and possibly in the extended sense as well.

The rules in C* are selected because they are both usable and appropriately aligned with the values articulated in C. Notably, the rules of C* are *not* adopted as accounts of what makes actions right and wrong, but only as guides to decisions. This contrasts with the lower-tier codes adopted in systems of type D. As we saw in the previous section, the system of C and C* as a whole needs to avoid generating inconsistencies, both in its evaluations of an action's moral status and in the advice it delivers. In the case of systems of type D, which combine an Austere approach for tier one and a Pragmatic approach for tier two, it is difficult to avoid such inconsistencies, because the code in each tier provides both a theoretical account of right and wrong and a decision-guide. But systems of type F divide up the labor differently, and their structure thus makes it easier for them to avoid this problem.

One way for systems of type F to avoid the inconsistency problem is to construe C and C* as issuing different types of moral assessment. To effect this I temporarily will say that C issues prescriptions that use such normative terms as "ought$_1$," "is right$_1$," and "is wrong$_1$," while C* issues prescriptions that use such normative terms as "ought$_2$," "is right$_2$," and "is wrong$_2$."[16] More will be said about this in Chapter 10. For now we can say that issuance of an evaluation using the "ought$_1$" terminology is meant only to evaluate the act's theoretical moral status. Issuance of an evaluation using the "ought$_2$" terminology is meant only to guide an agent making a decision based on a person's possibly limited or erroneous perspective on her options in that decision—for example, the perspective of an agent trying to decide what to do while uncertain about the nature or upshots of her choices.[17] Here is an example of a system of type F that utilizes this terminology:

System S5:

C: An act is right$_1$ if and only if, and because, it would produce no less utility than any alternative, and
C*:

DG$_0$:   An act is right$_2$ if, and because, it would produce no less utility than any alternative, and

DG$_1$:   An act is right$_2$ if, and because, it would produce no less expected utility than any alternative.

[16]   I adopt this terminology from that suggested by F. Feldman (2012).
[17]   Recall from an earlier discussion that C* should issue evaluations that can be used, not just by agents making decisions, but also by advisors or observers who may wish to evaluate prospective or past actions, including those of another person. However, for simplicity I shall continue to speak as though an "ought$_2$" is directed at agents alone.

This system closely resembles the earlier System S3, which as a system of type D combines the Austere approach to C with the Pragmatic approach to C^*. Since systems of type D are ones in which both C and C^* function as theoretical accounts of right and wrong and as decision-guides, a single normative term ("right") appeared in both C and C^* in System S3. However, in systems of type F, C^* only functions as a decision-guide, so its prescriptions are expressed using the different term "right$_2$," while the prescriptions of C are expressed using "right$_1$." It should be clear at once that systems of type F are structurally able to avoid generating inconsistent prescriptions, precisely because the prescriptions issued by C and C^* use different normative terms and so assign different types of moral status to the acts prescribed.[18] For example, suppose a Federal Reserve Board governor believes that C implies he would be right$_1$ to set interest rates in a manner that will produce no less utility than any alternative strategy. However, he is uncertain whether holding the rates fixed, raising them, or lowering them will have this effect. Using C alone he cannot determine what to do. Nonetheless, if his credences entail that holding the rates fixed is the act that would produce no less expected utility than any alternative, and he is aware of these credences, he can derive from C^* a prescription that it is right$_2$ to hold the rates fixed. If it turns out that C actually prescribes raising the rates rather than holding them fixed, then C implies that the governor's act of holding the rates fixed is not right$_1$, although the assessment of C^* that holding the rates fixed is right$_2$ remains unchanged. In the aftermath, if he looks back on his act with greater knowledge, the governor could say that he did something wrong$_1$ but right$_2$. There is no inconsistency in this pair of judgments, although the governor may well regret that he performed the wrong$_1$ action, even while he feels satisfaction in choosing the act that was best in light of his information.[19]

It is even possible for an agent to believe, *before* he decides what to do, that a single act is wrong$_1$ but also obligatory$_2$. This can occur in the following, now famous, type of case.[20] Since such cases will be important from time to time, I shall call them, after their originator, "*Regan-style cases*."

Strong Medicine: A doctor must choose which type of treatment to use on a seriously ill patient. She believes the following about her choice: if she gives the patient treatment B, the patient will experience moderate improvement. If she gives the patient treatment A, there is a 50 percent chance the patient will be killed,

---

[18] Of course an agent who labors under inconsistent nonmoral beliefs (such as the beliefs that *Act A would produce less utility than some alternative*, and that *Act A would produce more utility than any alternative*) might derive inconsistent prescriptions from a system of this sort, but such inconsistency cannot be traced to a problem in the system itself.

[19] There may still be an inconsistency between the prescription generated by decision-guide DG$_0$ and that generated by decision-guide DG$_1$, at least when we expand the system to include proscriptions for acts that are obligatory$_2$ and wrong$_2$ (there is no inconsistency in the case in the text, since DG$_0$ and DG$_1$ each provide only sufficient conditions for rightness$_2$, and more than one action can be right). This issue will be addressed in Chapter 11.

[20] This kind of case was introduced by Regan (1980), pp. 264–5 and has been discussed by many, including Broome (2013), pp. 37–8; Jackson (1991), pp. 462–3; Kolodny and MacFarlane (2010); Parfit (1988) and (2011), pp. 159–61; and Michael Zimmerman (2008), pp. 12–20 and (2014), p. 29.

and a 50 percent chance he will be completely cured. Treatment C involves a medication that always has the opposite effect of treatment A. If C is used, there is also a 50 percent chance the patient will be killed and a 50 percent chance the patient will be completely cured. If the doctor does nothing (D), the patient will continue to suffer substantially.

Assigning reasonable values to the various possible outcomes, the doctor faces the decision problem presented in Table 9.2.

If the doctor tries to follow System S5, then even in advance of acting, she will believe that act B is wrong$_1$ (since in every circumstance either A or C is better than B) but also that act B is obligatory$_2$ (since its expected value is highest).[21] It may appear paradoxical that it would be obligatory$_2$ for S to do what she knows to be wrong$_1$. But under System S5, there is no technical inconsistency in the doctor's judgments about her possible acts, and C* seems to deliver exactly the correct advice to the doctor.

Introducing the possibility of distinct normative terms in C and C* enables systems of type F to make use of the good idea embodied in systems of type D: building a system in which different codes are dedicated to distinct purposes. It carries the idea further, however, in order to avoid some of the problems that undermine systems of type D.

The potential virtues of a successful system of type F should be clear: such a system enables the correct theoretical account of right and wrong to be indirectly used by epistemically limited agents without needing to compromise its account of right and wrong; it avoids delivering inconsistent guidance or evaluations; it steers clear of inconsistent accounts of which nonmoral properties are right-making and wrong-making; it attains core usability both in cases where the agent has erroneous beliefs and in cases where the agent is uncertain; it provides agents an important form of autonomy by enabling them to connect their values with their choices; and it can promise the modestly successful moral life to all well-intentioned agents, even though they lack perfect information. In order to fulfill these virtues, however, such a system needs to provide agents with guidance no matter what the nature or level of their uncertainty, and to do so in a fashion that doesn't simply transfer the epistemic problem from the

Table 9.2

Act	A kills, C cures (P = 0.5)	C kills, A cures (P = 0.5)	Expected value
A	−1,000	1,000	0
B	500	500	500
C	1,000	−1,000	0
D	−800	−800	−800

[21] Here I'm assuming an understanding of the components of System 5 that cover obligatory$_1$, obligatory$_2$, wrong$_1$, and wrong$_2$ acts.

agent to the theorist (or to the agent acting as theorist). The best systems of type D ran afoul of this last requirement, and we will have to investigate systems of type F further in order to ascertain whether they fulfill their promise or not. We will also have to determine whether the usability generally achievable by the Code C* of a system of type F is extended or merely core usability, although we have already seen that DG_0, at least, can only achieve core usability.

One important question about systems of type F is what the nature is of the rules in Code C*. I have referred to them as *moral* rules, rules that form part of a complete moral system that consists of two tiers of rules. But it is also plausible to view them as principles of *rationality*, suitable for supplementing any account of normative status, whether it is an account of moral status, prudential status, legal status, epistemic status, or other possible types of status. The problem of uncertainty is confronted by agents using all of these types of norms: for example, someone trying to make a prudential decision about how best to invest his retirement funds faces a good deal of uncertainty about what will happen in the financial markets between now and the time he retires. Indeed, such rules as "Maximize subjective expected utility" have been advocated in exactly this guise, as decision principles suitable for guiding any kind of decision made under what I am calling "conditions of uncertainty". Our inquiry into systems of type F is at too early a stage of development to enable us to answer the question of whether the rules of a Hybrid Code C* should be classified as moral rules or more generally as principles of rationality. A convincing answer must await details we have not yet pinned down. The answer will partly depend on the content of the decision-guiding rules. For example, does their content vary with the type of moral code they augment, so that different rules are appropriate for deontological systems than are appropriate for consequentialist systems? And does the content vary when the rules supplement moral codes as compared with (say) prudential codes? The answer will also partly depend on what justifies the decision-guiding rules. Is there some single type of justification that endorses the rules appropriate to each type of normative system? Or does the type of justification itself vary, depending on the type of norm supplemented? The answer may also depend in part on whether there are different constraints for different normative systems on what counts as an appropriate decision-guiding rule. We are not yet in a position to answer these questions. For the time being I shall continue to assume that the decision-guiding rules are indeed moral rules, and part of a larger moral system which also includes the account of right and wrong. But this is a question that must be returned to as our inquiry matures.

9.3 Conclusion

Having concluded in Chapter 8 that the Austere approach is the best response to the problem of error, we turned in this chapter to the problems of ignorance and uncertainty. A careful statement of these problems, and closer inspection, suggested that, with one exception, we should consider the problem of ignorance as a special case of the problem of uncertainty, broadly defined. (The one exception is the kind of radical ignorance that prevents an agent from even realizing she has any options at time t_i; this problem was seen as best handled, like the problem of error, by the Austere Response). We then noted that the response to the problem of uncertainty must be consistent with the preferred Austere Response to the problem of error. Given that theorists have suggested the same three types of approaches—the Austere, Pragmatic, and Hybrid approaches—to the problems of uncertainty and error, we saw that there remain three possible combinations of these approaches to the two problems: conjoining the Austere approach to the problem of error with either the Pragmatic, the Austere, or the Hybrid approach to the problem of uncertainty. This chapter has reviewed these in turn.

Combining the Austere approach to error with an Austere approach to uncertainty avoids certain failings suffered by the other candidates. However, codes endorsed by the Austere approach, which declines to compromise the correct account of right and wrong in order to accommodate agential epistemic weaknesses, offer no guidance to agents hampered by uncertainty. Furthermore, this approach does not offer agents the same autonomy in cases of uncertainty that it offers them in cases of error. These are serious defects.

Combining the Austere approach to error with the Pragmatic approach to uncertainty revealed severe problems. First, it is not clear that it is possible to combine an Austere approach with a genuine Pragmatic approach, given the commitments of the Pragmatic approach. Second, in some cases the proposed system fails to meet the requirement that the lower level C^* account of right and wrong would be endorsed by the Austere approach. Third, in many cases the resulting moral system produces inconsistencies in its theoretical assessments of the moral status of a given act, or in its advice about which act to perform, or in its accounts of right-making properties. In other cases the system fails to furnish decision-guides that are universally usable in the extended sense as required by the Pragmatic approach. In a crucial case (where the decision-guide endorsed by the Pragmatic approach for cases of uncertainty is a version of the moral laundry list) no inconsistency should arise, but we noted again that the moral laundry list is just as epistemically inaccessible to the theorist as the right action is epistemically inaccessible to the uncertain decision maker. Thus this second combination of approaches appears to have fatal flaws.

Finally, we looked at the strategy of combining the Austere approach to error with the Hybrid approach to uncertainty. This approach appears to be the most promising, managing to avoid inconsistent prescriptions on the one hand while potentially delivering full decision-guidance on the other. It remains to be seen whether systems of this type can fulfill this promise without placing an undue epistemic burden on the theorist.

The next chapters will take a closer look at systems which combine the Austere approach to error and the Hybrid approach to uncertainty, and at the concepts I have labeled "ought$_1$" and "ought$_2$," which such systems need to utilize. The term "systems of type F" is an unwieldy one. The type of systems designated by this term combines an Austere approach to the top-tier account of right and wrong, and a Hybrid approach to the second-tier decision-guides. Although there are other types of Hybrid approaches, we need a shorthand label for the type on which we will focus. From now on, I will designate these systems as "Hybrid responses to the problems of error and uncertainty," and use the simple term "Hybrid system" as shorthand.

10

The Hybrid Solution to the Problems of Error and Uncertainty

> To inform a traveler respecting the place of his ultimate destination is not to forbid the use of landmarks and direction-posts on the way.[1]

In Chapter 9 I argued that the most promising solution to the problems of error and uncertainty is what I now call the "Hybrid solution". This solution comprises a two-tier system. In such a system the top-tier Code C functions as a theoretical account of right and wrong. The lower-tier Code C* provides prescriptions geared to an agent's own epistemic grasp of a decision, and functions as the system's decision-guiding response to the problem of error and also to the problem of uncertainty. To avoid inconsistent prescriptions each tier employs different normative terms, which I have temporarily distinguished by the use of different subscripts, such as "ought$_1$" (used by C) and "ought$_2$" (used by C*).

In this chapter we begin to examine this proposed solution in greater depth, working out its details. Since I have already argued that the Austere Response to the problem of error, here embodied in the Hybrid system's top tier, is the most acceptable solution to that problem, the primary focus of our inquiry here will be on whether such a system appropriately handles the problem of uncertainty.[2]

10.1 Criteria of Adequacy for a Hybrid System

We have seen that theorists holding that a moral theory must be usable for making decisions have supported this view by invoking one or more of four general desiderata which a moral theory should fulfill in virtue of its usability: (1) it should be usable even by epistemically limited human beings for making decisions; (2) it should achieve a special form of justice by enabling all moral agents to live a successful moral

---

[1] Mill (1957), p. 31.
[2] Earlier versions of some of the material in this chapter are found in H. Smith (1988), (1989), (1991), and (2010a).

life (now interpreted modestly as a life in which a well-intentioned agent can avoid blameworthiness); (3) its currency should enhance social welfare (and the special goods achievable only through social cooperation and consensus); and (4) its currency should result in a good pattern of actions, that is, actions that conform with the theoretical account of right and wrong. In Chapter 7 we saw that we cannot assume that the best response to the problem of error—the Austere Response— enables a moral code to satisfy the latter two goal-oriented desiderata, that is, enhancing social welfare and producing a better pattern of actions. Since the Hybrid Response to the problems of error and uncertainty incorporates the Austere Response to error, we should now abandon the two goal-oriented desiderata (3) and (4), at least for cases in which agents labor under false beliefs. Perhaps these desiderata can be satisfied by the Hybrid Response's strategy for coping with cases in which agents labor under uncertainty, so we should keep them in mind. However, our findings so far certainly should make us pessimistic about the achievability of these two goals.

Because the Hybrid Response to the problems of error and uncertainty consists of recommending a two-tier system, it's appropriate to introduce further criteria of adequacy for any successful Hybrid system in which a higher-tier Code C provides the account of right and wrong while a lower-tier Code C* provides decision-guidance. Here is a list of such criteria, with brief comments on their rationales:[3]

Criterion A (Consistency):   When Code C and Code C* are paired in a single Hybrid system, their prescriptions should be consistent.

In any given case, both the Code C and the Code C* that are paired under a single Hybrid system should deliver prescriptions for action. As we've seen, these prescriptions must be consistent with each other: it would be unacceptable, for example, for Code C to prescribe act A as obligatory while Code C* prohibits act A as wrong. Since on my proposal a Hybrid system of this type issues prescriptions using different normative terms (such as "obligatory$_1$" and "wrong$_2$"), this type of inconsistency is readily avoided. To avoid further inconsistency when Code C* contains more than one rule, another strategy will be needed, and will be considered in Chapter 11. However, these strategies could be seen as providing only a technical fix to avoid overt inconsistencies. We will need to address the question of how we should view a situation in which, for example, an agent ought$_1$ to do A and ought$_2$ to do not-A.

Criterion B (Moral Adequacy):   Code C* should issue *morally appropriate* guiding prescriptions for an agent who accepts Code C as the correct theoretical account of rightness and wrongness but is hindered by the problem of uncertainty from using C itself to guide her decision. Put differently, an action prescribed by

³ These criteria are a revised version of those offered in H. Smith (2010a), pp. 72–3. A somewhat similar list of criteria is provided by F. Feldman (2012).

234 HYBRID SOLUTION TO ERROR AND UNCERTAINTY

Code C* should be morally reasonable or wise for the agent to choose, relative to a commitment to C and to the agent's imperfect epistemic grasp of the situation.

Code C* needs to be appropriately aligned with Code C in such a way that the prescriptions of C* are morally appropriate given the values embodied in Code C. Of course it would be ideal for Code C* to prescribe, for every agent, exactly the acts prescribed by Code C. But given that Code C* must issue prescriptions to agents impeded by the problem of uncertainty, there is little chance that this ideal will be attainable. For example, there will be cases in which Code C* prescribes an action as obligatory$_2$ even though Code C prohibits it as wrong$_1$. This will be true, for example, in *Strong Medicine*, described in Table 9.2 in Chapter 9, in which the doctor must decide between treatments A, B, C, and D (in which each of A and C have a 50 percent chance of curing the patient but also a 50 percent chance of killing him, while B is certain to moderately improve his condition but will not cure him, and D will leave him untreated to suffer substantially). It is clear to the doctor in advance that giving the patient treatment B would be wrong$_1$. However, since giving the patient treatment B would avoid the risk of death associated with treatments A and C, and would maximize expected value for the patient, it seems like the morally wise or reasonable course of action for the doctor to take. This is the kind of judgment that would be issued by a system satisfying Criterion B.

> **Criterion C (Guidance Adequacy):**   Assuming that Code C provides an exhaustive account of the moral status of all actual and humanly possible actions, then the decision-guiding rule(s) of Code C* should be such that for every occasion for decision, there is an appropriate rule in Code C* which can be directly used by the agent for making a decision on that occasion.

The Hybrid solution seeks to solve the problem of uncertainty by supplementing Code C (the theoretical account of right and wrong) with a Code C* (which provides decision-guides for actual use by agents in light of their grasp of their situations). Supplementing C in this manner allows an agent to use C *indirectly* in deciding what to do. However, this only succeeds if Code C* itself is usable by the agent, despite her epistemic limitations. For now I shall state Criterion C so as to leave open whether it requires Code C* to have full *extended* usability (that is, enables the agent to derive the correct prescription from Code C*) or merely requires C* to have *core* usability (that is, enables the agent to derive a prescription from C*, whether or not the prescription is for the act actually prescribed by C*). We will have to resolve this matter as we explore the Hybrid solution.

> **Criterion D (Normative Adequacy):**   For each plausible theoretic account of right and wrong C, it should be possible to define a C* that would enable every agent affected by the problems of error and uncertainty to apply C indirectly to her decisions through directly applying the decision-guiding rule(s) of C*.

We want the Hybrid solution to work for every plausible theoretical account of right and wrong, not just for some restricted set of such accounts. Criterion D is meant to ensure the breadth of the Hybrid solution's domain.[4]

> **Criterion E (Relation to Blameworthiness):**   The prescriptions (including obliga-
> tions, prohibitions, and permissions) issued by C^* should be appropriate for the role
> of such guidance prescriptions in the correct theory of moral responsibility, and in
> particular appropriate in assessments of whether an agent is blameworthy or credit-
> worthy for her act.[5]

Most theorists agree that the fact an action is prohibited by the theoretical account of right and wrong does not by itself establish that the agent is blameworthy for performing that action. An agent's performing the wrong action does not render him blameworthy if he has an acceptable excuse (such as insanity or non-culpable ignorance) for perform-ing that action. But what if the correct Code C prohibits act A as wrong$_1$, C-appropriate C^* decision-guide also prohibits act A as wrong$_2$, the agent is able to use this decision-guide to ascertain that A is wrong$_2$, does derive a C^*-based proscription not to do act A, but performs A anyway? If the agent accepts Code C and is aware of the relation between C and C^*, then we are likely to conclude the agent is blameworthy for her choice.[6] Thus the decision-guides in Code C^* seem to have an important role in ascertaining an agent's blameworthiness or creditworthiness for her acts. This topic requires further discussion, but in the meantime Criterion E is meant to signal that whatever the proper relationship between blameworthiness and the use of decision-guides, a Hybrid system solution must be consistent with that relationship.[7]

With these criteria in hand to help evaluate Hybrid systems, let us begin our development of the Hybrid Response by reviewing common proposals for which decision-guiding rules should appear in a Code C^*.

10.2 Proposed Decision-Guides for C^*

The two-tier Hybrid solution to the problem of uncertainty has enjoyed a good deal of popularity. Often it is proposed that Code C^* consists of a single decision-guiding rule which will be usable in all cases in which an agent confronts uncertainty about what

---

[4] Some otherwise plausible theoretical accounts of right and wrong may not be compatible with *any* plausible decision-guiding rules for cases of uncertainty. This is arguably a serious fault of these theoretical accounts. See Jackson and Smith (2006) as well as Huemer (2010) for arguments that absolutist non-consequentialist theories (or more generally theories that impose a lexical ordering on their principles) suffer this failing.

[5] Moral theorists standardly view judgments of "blameworthiness" with judgments of "praiseworthiness" as symmetrical. However, this seems a mistake: we do not hold a person to be praiseworthy for merely carrying out his duty unless doing so is especially onerous. Hence I am using the term "creditworthy" for the status an agent achieves for performing the right act for overall good reasons.

[6] There is dispute about whether an agent's blameworthiness depends on her intention to act according to the Code C she believes to be correct, or on her intention to act according to the correct Code C. I shall not try to resolve this issue. See, for example, Arpaly and Schroeder (2014).

[7] See F. Feldman (2012), section 3, for discussion of this issue.

Code C prescribes. Since I have specified that Code C* must contain Decision-Guide DG_0, which mirrors the content of Code C, most of these proposals must be reinterpreted as suggesting that Code C* contains two decision-guiding rules: one that serves agents who have full (if sometimes false) relevant beliefs about their prospective acts, and one that serves agents who are uncertain about the nature and consequences of their prospective acts. Let us call the latter the "primary" decision-guide. Reviewing some of these proposals reveals how inadequate an approach this is for the case of uncertain agents, even leaving aside discussion of Decision-Guide DG_0 until later.

10.2.1 Decision-Guide 1: Perform the act most likely to be right

The first decision-guide that occurs to many people when they consider what it would be wise to do when confronted with uncertainty is the following. I shall state all the proposed decision-guides as prescriptions for what is obligatory$_2$, but in each case parallel rules could be added to address wrongness$_2$ and permissibility$_2$.

Decision-Guide 1:   It is obligatory$_2$ to do what is most likely to be obligatory$_1$.

At first glance this decision-guide seems highly plausible, since how could one go wrong in doing what is most likely to be obligatory$_1$? In fact, however, it violates Criterion B (Moral Adequacy), since in cases with high negative stakes it can prescribe actions that are not morally reasonable for the agent to do relative to the governing Code C. Consider the following case:

Rescue: Tom has been injured and trapped by an avalanche while mountain climbing. The rescue squad has two options for extracting him from his predicament. They can send in a helicopter to lower a line and pull him off the peak, or they can send a rescue team to carry him down by stretcher. The squad's duty (Code C) is to rescue Tom in a manner than minimizes damage to his health and safety. If the stretcher team is sent in, it would take four days before Tom reaches a hospital, and the medic believes that he would suffer frostbite to his injured leg, requiring amputation of a toe. Sending in the helicopter would evacuate him immediately, with no danger of frostbite. However, wind conditions on the mountain are dangerous, and there is a chance that the helicopter's rescue line would break and Tom would plunge to his death. The values (as assessed by the governing Code C) and likelihoods involved in this decision are given in Table 10.1.

Table 10.1

ACT	Line breaks (p = 0.1)	Line holds (p = 0.9)
Helicopter	−1,000	0
Rescue team	−5	−5

There is a probability of 0.9 that the helicopter line will hold, in which case Tom will be rescued from the mountain none the worse for wear (a value of 0). There is a probability of 0.1 that the line will break, in which case Tom will be killed (a value of −1,000). If the rescue team brings him down on a stretcher, his toe will need to be amputated (a value of −5). In this case using the helicopter is the act most likely to be obligatory$_1$, since there is a 90 percent chance that it will be the act that is obligatory$_1$, and only a 10 percent chance that sending the rescue team would be obligatory$_1$. But it seems absurd to most people who think about such cases to recommend that the rescue team ought$_2$ to use the helicopter and run a non-negligible risk of Tom's being killed merely in order to save his toe. Decision-Guide 1 is sensitive only to the probabilities involved in such a case, and not sensitive to the extremity of the costs at stake in each option. For this reason it must be rejected as the sole primary decision-guide for Code C, since it violates Criterion B (Moral Adequacy) with respect to that code (and most others as well).

Moreover, there are cases in which Decision-Guide 1 would violate Criterion C (Guidance Adequacy), since there are cases in which the agent is unable to ascribe probabilities to all the possible outcomes of his actions, and so unable to calculate which action is most likely to be obligatory$_1$. In addition, use of this guide would often be infeasible in cases in which the agent believes there are many options and many possible upshots, with variable values, for each option, and he has insufficient time to compute which option is likely to be best.

10.2.2 Decision-Guide 2: Perform the act that would maximize expected value

Reflection on the moral inadequacy of Decision-Guide 1 for cases such as *Rescue* has led many theorists to advocate the following primary decision-guide:

Decision-Guide 2: It is obligatory$_2$ to perform the act that maximizes expected value (where value is assessed by the governing Code C).

By contrast with Decision-Guide 1, the virtue of Decision-Guide 2 is that it takes into account all the stakes involved in a case (as evaluated by the governing account of right and wrong), not just the probability that a given act might turn out to be the best choice according to Code C. Decision-Guide 2 *weights* the value of each possible outcome by the probability of its occurrence. Thus, in *Rescue*, Decision-Guide 2 would prescribe sending in the rescue team rather than using the helicopter, since the expected value of the former is higher, as shown in Table 10.2.

Table 10.2

ACT	Line breaks (p = 0.1)	Line holds (p = 0.9)	Expected value
Helicopter	−1,000	0	−100
Rescue team	−5	−5	−5

The expected value of using the helicopter is $0.1 \times -1{,}000 \, (= -100)$ plus $0.9 \times 0 \, (= 0)$, or -100. A similar calculation obtains an expected value of -5 for using the rescue team. Since -5 is less bad than -100, using the rescue team maximizes expected value, and is obligatory$_1$ according to Decision-Guide 2.

Some decision theorists have raised credible objections to the moral adequacy of Decision-Guide 2 (for example, on grounds that it does not take proper account of the agent's attitude towards risk, or other global features of her choice).[8] Nonetheless it is widely accepted, and certainly has a great deal to recommend it as a morally sensible recommendation for an agent confronting uncertainty. Thus a strong case can be made that it meets Criterion B (Moral Adequacy). Moreover, for any Code C (whether consequentialist or deontological) that meets certain mathematical conditions regarding the nature of its value prescriptions and the deontic weight of its principles, Decision-Guide 2 appears to be normatively appropriate if the agent's probability estimates are consistent with the probability calculus.[9] Thus it may meet Criterion D (Normative Adequacy) as well as Criterion B. However, it fails to meet Criterion C (Guidance Adequacy).

To see this, it is helpful to recall our definition from Chapter 2 for what is required for an agent to have the ability in the core sense to use a moral principle as a decision-guide:

Definition 2.1.   Ability in the core sense to directly use a moral principle to decide what to do: An agent S is able in the core sense at t_i to directly use moral principle P to decide at t_i what to do at t_j *if and only if:*

(A)   there is some (perhaps complex) feature F such that P prescribes actions that have feature F, in virtue of their having F,

(B)   S believes at t_i of some act-type A that S could perform A (in the epistemic sense) at t_j,

(C)   S believes at t_i that if she performed A at t_j, act A would have F, and

(D)   if and because S believed at t_i that P prescribes actions that have feature F, in virtue of their having F, and if and because S wanted all-things-considered at t_i to derive a prescription from principle P at t_i for an act performable at t_j, then her beliefs together with this desire would lead S to derive a prescription at t_i for A from P in virtue of her belief that it has F.

Decision-Guide 2 prescribes (as obligatory$_2$) actions that would maximize expected value, so feature F, mentioned in clause (A), is "maximizing expected value." The leader of the rescue squad can only use Decision-Guide 2 to decide whether to send in the helicopter or the rescue team if he meets three conditions: (1) he believes that he can

---

[8]   See Buchak (2013).
[9]   See Colyvan and Hájek (2016) for a discussion of cases that fail to meet these requirements and may resist treatment by any decision-guide.

perform each of these two options (in the epistemic sense), (2) he believes of either sending the helicopter or of sending the rescue team that carrying it out would maximize expected value, and (3) it is true that if he believed that Decision-Guide 2 prescribes the action that maximizes expected value, and if he wanted all-things-considered to derive a prescription from Decision-Guide 2, then his beliefs and desires would lead him to derive such a prescription—either for sending the helicopter or for sending the rescue team, depending which option he believes has the relevant property. We can assume the leader satisfies (1). Moreover, he *might* believe *that* one of his options would maximize expected value. But we cannot assume he satisfies (2), that is, believes of one of the options that *it* would maximize expected value. Roughly speaking, to believe this he would have to have assigned probabilities and values to each of the actions and its possible upshots, and then calculated the expected values of both actions on the basis of these assignments.[10] Some agents would indeed have done this, or be able to do it by the time a decision would have to be made. However, there is no reason to think that *every* agent would have done it by the time for a decision. For example, the rescue squad leader may not have assigned any precise probability to any of his options, and he may not be sure exactly what value they have according to Code C. Or even if he has beliefs about these probabilities and values, he may not have calculated (or be able to calculate in a timely fashion) the relevant expected utilities. Thus the leader might not believe of any particular option that it is the one that would maximize expected value. Agents lacking the requisite beliefs would fail to satisfy (2) and also (3). For such agents, Decision-Guide 2 cannot be used for making their decision. I have described *Rescue* as an unusually simple case involving only two possible options, one of which has a certain outcome and the other of which has only two possible outcomes. But a decision about rescuing a stranded climber might more realistically involve twenty or more distinct options (sending the helicopter at different times of the day, with different crews and different apparatus, or sending the rescue team by different routes, or with different combinations of personnel, or calling in additional rescue squads, and so forth), each of which in its turn might have many different possible outcomes, depending on various factors—thus requiring the leader to perform a much more complex calculation. Many decisions are vastly more complex, and clearly exceed what most agents—sometimes any agent—could be expected to calculate with the time and computational resources available, even if we allow such computations to take place at an unconscious level, as I am happy to do.[11] It may sometimes seem to us

---

[10] Of course, it is possible that some trustworthy advisor might simply inform the leader what the expected values of his options are, relieving him of the need to make these calculations. Regrettably, such advisors are thin on the ground for agents making complex decisions.

[11] Lehrer (2009) puts this view succinctly in claiming that "We rely on misleading shortcuts because we lack the computational power to think any other way" (p. 155). For graphic arguments about the difficulties of such reasoning, see Bales, Cohen, and Handfield (2014); Eddy (1982); F. Feldman (2006); Gigerenzer (2008a); and Pollock (2006). Zimmerman (2008) advocates a view he terms "Prospectivism," which requires the agent to maximize expected value. However, he admits that it is not possible for every agent to make a decision by reference to this theory (pp. 43–5). He does not find this a problem, since

that we have decided how to act by quickly calculating which option would maximize expected utility, but in fact we may have appealed to some other decision-guide, such as one restricting the range of options we even consider before we compute their expected utilities.

Precisely how this problem arises depends on how we interpret "expected value" in Decision-Guide 2, and in particular how we interpret the relevant probabilities. For example, on one interpretation, the relevant notion of probability is an objective notion (perhaps the objective frequencies, or the chances, of certain events). Then the problem is that the decision maker is required to have beliefs about these objective probabilities, and of course he may or may not have such beliefs. On another interpretation the relevant notion of probability is a subjective notion (that is, the credence or degree of belief that the agent has for the relevant propositions, such as "The helicopter line will break"). Subjective probabilities are usually explained in terms of the agent's disposition to make bets involving the proposition. However, there is no reason to think that an agent is always certain about his own dispositions to bet, or that he has immediate enough access to the nature of his dispositions to use in making an urgent decision.[12] The leader in *Rescue* has time to think a bit before making his decision, but not all agents have this luxury. An anesthesiologist responding to a patient's plummeting heart rate, or a technician responding to a nuclear power plant emergency, or a mother reacting to a baby's toppling off the sofa, may not have time to query their dispositions in deciding what to do. Moreover, agents' degrees of belief are often incoherent—they violate the probability calculus. From incoherent degrees of belief no rational prescription can reliably be derived. For this reason decision theorists often idealize degrees of belief by assuming the agent's degrees of belief conform to the probability calculus. But of course this is often untrue. And even if an agent wished to ascribe to himself idealized degrees of belief as the basis for his decision, there is no unique way to posit an alteration in his degrees of belief to render them coherent—indeed there are an infinite number of alterations that would do the trick.[13] In any event, we cannot assume that an agent would be able to discern his actual or idealized degrees of belief in time to calculate the expected utilities of his options, or that he would have the computational resources for doing so in any complicated decision problem.[14] Lacking a belief about the expected values of his actions, such an agent fails to satisfy clause (C), and so cannot use Decision-Guide 2, even in the core sense. Decision-Guide 2 fails

his rationale for advocating Prospectivism does not involve attempting to provide a moral theory that would be usable in all cases.

[12] Precisely how we handle this notion of credences as dispositions to bet would depend on whether (using Audi's distinction in (1994)) we consider a subjective probability—interpreted as a disposition to bet—to be a doxastic state that the agent has already formed but needs to retrieve, or a doxastic state that the agent has a disposition to form if the occasion arises.

[13] Pollock (2006), p. 91.

[14] For discussion of the problems associated with using subjective utilities in decision-making, see Pollock (2006), Chapter 6.

Criterion C (Guidance Adequacy) because it cannot be used by every agent on every occasion for decision.

10.2.3 Decision-Guide 3: Try to perform the obligatory act

Some theorists trying to find a primary decision-guide that could be used by any agent facing the problem of uncertainty have steered away from technical notions of probability and proposed the following decision-guide:

Decision-Guide 3:   It is obligatory$_2$ to try to perform the act that would be obligatory$_1$.

Advocates of this guide focus on the fact that the uncertainty facing an agent may present itself to the agent in the form of uncertainty *how* to perform the act required by Code C, or uncertainty *whether* he can perform the act required by Code C. Thus a teenager, out hiking with his father when the father collapses of an apparent heart attack, may believe Code C requires him to perform artificial resuscitation on his father to restore his breathing and heartbeat. However, not having taken a first aid class, the teenager may be uncertain how to perform effective artificial resuscitation. Nonetheless, with no one else available to help, the teenager may conclude that he should follow Decision-Guide 3, and at least *try* to perform artificial resuscitation on his father.[15] And indeed this is often good advice. Unfortunately Decision-Guide 3 also fails Criterion C (Guidance Adequacy), because agents do not always know *how* to try to do what Code C requires. The teenager may know how to try—he might, for example, believe that pressing lightly and repeatedly on his father's chest would count as trying to artificially resuscitate him. But suppose instead of being a teenager, the son is only seven years old. He may have heard there is some procedure called "artificial resuscitation" that could save his father's life in this situation, and in fact he may be strong enough to actually perform it, but not have any idea at all how to try to apply artificial resuscitation. Indeed the young son may not know any way at all he could try to save his father's life, although he may believe there may be some way he could try to save it. The young son doesn't fulfill either clause (C) or clause (D), and so does not have the ability to use Decision-Guide 3, even in the core sense of ability. Like its predecessors, Decision-Guide 3 fails Criterion C (Guidance Adequacy).

Moreover, as Fred Feldman and Derek Parfit point out, sometimes Decision-Guide 3 gives bad moral advice.[16] Consider again *Strong Medicine*, described in Table 9.2 in Chapter 9.

In *Strong Medicine* it is clear to the doctor in advance that either giving the patient treatment A or giving him treatment C would be obligatory$_1$, and that giving the patient treatment B or D would be wrong$_1$. The only way for the doctor to *try* to do what is obligatory$_1$, as Decision-Guide 3 recommends, would be for her to give the

---

[15] Mason (2003); Susan Wolf has suggested it in discussion. Pollock discusses trying in (2006), pp. 152–4, and describes Richard Jeffrey (1965) as suggesting something like Decision-Guide 3.
[16] F. Feldman (2012), p. 155, and Parfit (2011), p. 161.

patient either treatment A or treatment C. However, since both treatments A and C have a 50 percent chance of killing the patient, while giving him treatment B would avoid this risk but improve his condition, treatment B seems like the wisest course of action. But Decision-Guide 3 cannot recommend treatment B, since it does not qualify as trying to do what is obligatory$_1$. Thus it fails Criterion B (Moral Adequacy) as well as Criterion C.[17]

10.2.4 Feldman's Level 2 Decision-Guide

To complete our survey of proposals in which Code C* consists of two decision-guides, DG$_0$ plus a single primary decision-guiding rule which would be usable in all cases in which an agent confronts uncertainty about what Code C prescribes, I will look at two suggestions by theorists who are extremely sensitive to the failings of the previous three decision-guides. The first is a rule proposed by Fred Feldman.[18] Feldman's proposed guide varies somewhat, depending on the content of the governing Code C. However, he argues that a guide with the same basic structure works for many types of theories, including utilitarianism, Rossian deontology, and virtue ethics, and further suggests that it can also be extended to various forms of Kantianism, Rights Theory, and so forth.[19] To streamline our discussion we can focus on his proposed rule for utilitarianism. Feldman advocates what he calls a "Two-Level Theory" with (as his example) act utilitarianism at the first level.[20] On this proposal, principles at the first level generate "ought$_1$" prescriptions, while principles at the second level generate "ought$_2$" prescriptions. This is highly similar to what I am calling the Hybrid solution. The official statement of the theory is as follows:

Feldman's Two-Level Theory:

Level 1: You morally ought$_1$ to perform an act iff it maximizes utility.

Level 2: If you cannot determine what you morally ought$_1$ to do, then you morally ought$_2$ to perform an act if and only if it is an outcome of the Utilitarian Decision Procedure.[21]

Level 2 comprises Feldman's suggestion for the primary decision-guide that appropriately supplements act utilitarianism. We may call it "Feldman's Level 2 Decision-Guide." The meat of the suggestion is embodied in the Utilitarian Decision Procedure, which Feldman characterizes as follows:

Step One: Consider the acts that you take to be your alternatives—described in 'helpful,' 'action-guiding' terms.

---

[17] For an illuminating discussion of trying and a proposal for why it might be wrong$_1$ to try to do what is itself wrong$_1$, see Hanser (2014). Unlike most theorists, Zimmerman (2008) holds that treatments A or C are not obligatory$_1$.

[18] F. Feldman (2012).   [19] F. Feldman (2012), pp. 167ff.   [20] F. Feldman (2012), p. 167.

[21] F. Feldman (2012), p. 166. I have made slight terminological changes in this statement of the theory: Feldman uses "ought1" and "ought2", rather than the subscripts I use for consistency with my own framework.

Step Two: Consider, insofar as your epistemic state permits, what you take to be their values or perhaps just their relative values.

Step Three: If you haven't got useful information about the actual values of your alternatives, then consider how your views about the morality of risk apply to your present situation; and, in light of all this,

Step Four: identify the acts in this particular case that seem most nearly consistent with the general policy of maximizing utility where possible while avoiding things that put people at excessive risk of serious harm; and then,

Step Five: perform one of them.[22]

In footnotes Feldman explains that "Step One does not require the agent to *list* all of her alternatives. There might be millions of them. In many cases it will be sufficient for the agent to consider whole groups of alternatives under suitable general descriptions. For example, suppose an agent has been asked to pick a number between one and one million. There is no need for her to consider picking one, picking two, picking three, etc. Since she will have no epistemic trouble in any case, she can describe her alternatives as a group by saying 'I have to pick a number between one and one million.' This will be sufficiently action guiding."[23] He also notes that "Step Two does not require that the agent consider each individual alternative separately. In the numbers case...she might simply consider that there is no number, n, such that her evidence gives her reason to suppose that picking n will yield more utility than picking any other number."[24] As an example of following such a procedure, he describes a version of *Strong Medicine* in which the doctor avers that what she wants to do is give the patient the utility maximizing treatment, but does not know which that is. She then proceeds to Step Three, recognizes that she feels it would be morally wrong to put the patient at serious risk of death unless doing so is absolutely necessary to save his life. Given this, she throws out all the alternatives that run this risk (giving him treatment A or treatment C), and concludes she ought$_2$ to give him treatment B, which will partly cure him but not risk his death. In a second version of the case the doctor has a different attitude towards risk, and is willing to risk the patient's life in order to cure him completely. Such a doctor might legitimately conclude that she would be wrong$_2$ to give him treatment B, and ought$_2$ to choose at random between treatment A and C.[25] In yet a third version of the case the doctor has no idea about the utility of any of her alternatives, and no views about the extents to which the different treatments would put the patient at risk of serious harm. She may, however, feel that some alternatives are better than others. In that case, the recommendation is that she ought$_2$ to pick at random from among the ones she thinks might be best.[26]

---

[22] F. Feldman (2012), pp. 166–7.   [23] F. Feldman (2012), p. 166.
[24] F. Feldman (2012), p. 166.   [25] F. Feldman (2012), pp. 163–4.
[26] F. Feldman (2012), pp. 164–5. It is not fully clear how this last recommendation follows from Feldman's account of the Utilitarian Decision Procedure.

Reflection on Feldman's Level 2 Decision-Guide suggests that (with some restrictions) it invites each agent to invoke what *she* considers to be the most appropriate decision-guide for act utilitarianism, and then to follow that guide's prescription. If she believes that it is wrong$_2$ to risk a patient's life in order to treat him in a manner that might cure his moderately serious condition, then she ought$_2$ to avoid this course of action. If instead she thinks it is permissible$_2$ for a doctor to place such a patient's life at grave risk in order to cure him, then this is what she ought$_2$ to do. In effect Feldman rejects the idea of a comprehensive moral theory, which as I have described it includes both a theoretical account of right and wrong and also an appropriate decision-guide for an epistemically limited agent to use in applying that theory. Rather than propose a substantive decision-guide, Feldman simply (with a few restrictions) throws utilitarian decision makers on their own devices in trying to ascertain how best to proceed when they are plagued by uncertainty. They should pay attention to risk if they have attitudes and beliefs about risk, and they should keep in mind the importance at Level 1 of maximizing utility, but aside from that they are on their own. This seems especially problematic in Feldman's description of his third type of case, in which the doctor has no beliefs about which alternatives are best according to act utilitarianism and no views about the extents to which the different treatments would put the patient at risk of serious harm. In this case she is supposed to select among the options she thinks are "best." But what is meant by the doctor's believing certain options are "best"? Since she doesn't have any beliefs about which alternatives are best$_1$ according to act utilitarianism, this can only mean she thinks they are best according to the Decision Procedure (that is, "best$_2$"). But to have such a belief she must have some belief about what the Decision Procedure recommends. Without any independent account of what the Decision Procedure recommends, however, Feldman's account of this procedure seems vulnerable to a charge of circularity or emptiness.

Feldman's use of what the agent thinks "best" in this third type of case, and his allowing agents to adopt whatever attitude towards risk appeals to them, suggests that Feldman's solution comes too close to advocating that what an uncertain agent ought$_2$ to do is simply what *she believes she ought$_2$ to do*. He says about the doctor in the third type of case that "Given her very limited information, the best recommendation the Guide can give is just to choose an alternative that, as she sees it, might be among the best available. I think that if [the doctor] follows this advice, she will be in the clear morally. She will have done something permissible$_2$."[27] This suggests that Feldman's fundamental focus is on how agents should make decisions in order to avoid blame-worthiness. It may be true that in the end each agent must make her decision by the decision-guide she believes to be the correct one, and that if she does so and then follows it, she will not be blameworthy. But this doesn't relieve the comprehensive moral theory from the burden of *providing* an appropriate decision-guide. Just as agents want to know whether or not act utilitarianism is the correct theoretical account of right and wrong, so they also want to know what the best decision-guide is, relative

---

[27] F. Feldman (2012), p. 165. Again I have used a subscript instead of Feldman's notation.

to act utilitarianism, when they are uncertain what the nonmoral features of their prospective actions are. They want to know what they ought$_2$ to do, not what they *think* they ought$_2$ to do. Feldman's theory does not genuinely try to answer that question, so it must be rejected on grounds that it fails Criterion C (Moral Adequacy).

Because Feldman's decision-guide is not trying to answer the same question we are asking decision-guides to address, I shall not review the extent to which it is usable by every agent.

10.2.5 Pollock's decision-guide

In *Thinking about Acting: Logical Foundations for Rational Decision Making*, John Pollock notes that "Human beings, and any real cognitive agents, are subject to cognitive resource constraints. They have limited reasoning power, in the form of limited computational capacity and limited computational speed ... An account of how a real agent should make decisions must take account of these limitations."[28] His project is to develop such an account, providing recommendations for what he terms "justified" choices: a choice "that a real [cognitively limited] agent could make given all the reasoning it has performed *up to the present time* and without violating the constraints of rationality."[29] This kind of choice contrasts with what he terms a "warranted" choice, one that "would be justified if the agent could complete all possible relevant reasoning."[30] In his view, real agents, who have finite reasoning powers, are never in a position to make warranted choices. Pollock is also, of course, aware that the information available to an agent (independently of any reasoning process) may itself be limited or deficient, although this factor receives somewhat less attention in his account.[31]

The theory that Pollock proposes has an important limitation: it makes recommendations for situations in which agents have justified beliefs about the relevant probabilities, but it cannot make recommendations for situations in which the agents lack such justified beliefs, and in particular, lack any beliefs at all (including *un*justified beliefs) about the relevant probabilities.[32] Thus the decision-guide it proposes does not apply to situations in which the agent believes that certain options are (or might be) available to her, but does not have any beliefs about the probabilities of these options being available, or any beliefs about how likely the various possible upshots of these options are. Nor does his decision-guide apply to situations in which the agent assigns only imprecise probabilities to relevant occurrences. Hence the decision-guide Pollock advocates fails Criterion C (Guidance Adequacy), since the agent will not be able to apply it in cases in which she lacks the required beliefs about probabilities. However, it is possible that Pollock's decision-guide works well for situations in which the agent does have the relevant beliefs about probabilities, and that his theory could be supplemented by an additional decision-guide for situations in which the agent lacks these beliefs. This would mean that Pollock's solution should actually be seen as a multiple-decision-guide solution for uncertainty, rather than as a solution with

---

[28] Pollock (2006), p. 5.   [29] Pollock (2006), p. 6.   [30] Pollock (2006), p. 6.
[31] Pollock (2006), p. 88.   [32] Pollock (2006), pp. 88 and 111.

a single primary decision-guide. Multiple-decision-guide solutions for uncertainty will be discussed in Chapter 11.

In the meantime, let us examine his solution for situations in which the agent has the relevant justified beliefs about probabilities. Pollock's discussion of the difficulties with finding a decision-guide that works for cognitively limited agents is extremely rich and well worth careful study. For our purposes we can summarize the highlights as follows. First, Pollock concludes that any realistic decision-guide must be applied to plans rather than acts.[33] An act is typically a type of event that would occur over a short interval, such as *raising one's hand* or *pulling the trigger*. But agents cannot, and should not, evaluate potential acts in isolation: instead they should consider them as part of broader plans, which are typically more complex groups or sequences of acts. Often some event that we refer to as an act actually involves carrying out an extended plan by which the agent performs the target "act." Thus one *makes a cup of tea* by implementing a plan that involves picking up the tea kettle, putting it under the tap, turning on the tap, waiting until the kettle has filled sufficiently, turning off the tap, placing the kettle on the stove, turning on the stove, and so forth.[34] It is natural to suppose that a plan is rational if and only if carrying out that plan would maximize value. (Here I will assume that "value" or "utility" are whatever is endorsed by the theoretical account of right and wrong. Although Pollock is not primarily interested in *moral* decision-making, this assumption does not seem to be inconsistent with his broad view about value and utility.[35]) However, Pollock argues that calculating which plan would maximize value is impossible, partly because there are infinitely many "local" plans, so it would be impossible for a cognitively limited agent to survey all the possibilities, and partly because rival plans can have different lengths (for example, I might want to compare the plan involved in making a cup of tea versus the plan involved in calling my father, another option I might be considering, and these might take different lengths of time).[36] In principle we could finesse this problem by trying to calculate the expected value of what Pollock calls "universal plans" (that is, detailed conditional plans for the entire remainder of the agent's life). Pollock rightly rejects this possibility as not a remedy available to limited agents, who have neither the time nor the computational capacity to compare the infinitely many alternatives that such extended plans would involve.[37]

Pollock's conclusion is that we must abandon optimality, and instead seek a plan that is "good enough." Then, if more information becomes available, we should abandon that plan in favor of a better one.[38] Local plans are to be merged into the agent's "master plan" since whether or not a more local plan is worthwhile depends on its relation to larger-scaled plans the agent may already have adopted.[39] An agent's master plan is the result of merging into one larger plan all the plans the agent has adopted but not yet

---

[33] Pollock (2006), pp. 17–18 and Chapters 9 and 10.   [34] Pollock (2006), p. 178.

[35] Pollock (2006), p. 23. However, Pollock does distinguish between "expected value" and "expected utility" (p. 159). This is a technicality that should not affect the issues examined in the text.

[36] Pollock (2006), pp. 181–2.   [37] Pollock (2006), pp. 172–3.

[38] Pollock (2006), pp. 167 and 187.   [39] Pollock (2006), p. 167.

executed. As such it is larger than a merely local plan, but significantly smaller than a Universal Plan.[40] Although master plans have expected utilities, and so in principle could be compared, in fact doing so is beyond any real agent's computational capacities.[41] In the end Pollock recommends the following:

Pollock's Decision-Guide:

A.   It is rational to make a change C to the master plan M if and only if the marginal expected utility of C is positive, that is, if and only if the expected utility of adopting the change C to the master plan is greater than the expected utility of the master plan left unchanged.

B.   It is rational to perform an action if and only if it is prescribed by a rationally adopted master plan.[42]

A master plan is adopted rationally "if and only if it is the result of incremental updating in accordance with" clause A.[43] The rough idea encapsulated in Pollock's decision-guide can be illustrated by the following example. Suppose your master plan involves grocery shopping this afternoon. It now occurs to you that you might supplement this plan with an additional local plan: on the way to the supermarket, stop off at the post office in order to buy stamps. Your contemplated local plan has a good feature: you're almost out of stamps, and will need more stamps within the next day or two. On the other hand, if you add buying stamps to your master plan, there may be a long line at the post office, so that you may arrive at the supermarket later in the afternoon, when the selection of fresh produce may be less good. You weigh these up, and draw a conclusion (taking into account the various probabilities of being able to go to the post office tomorrow, of there being a long line at the post office today, of the available produce being less fresh, etc.) as to whether your master plan plus the proposed local plan has higher expected utility than your master plan without this amendment. If adding the local plan would improve the expected utility of the master plan, it is rational to adopt it. Pollock describes rational decision makers as "evolutionary planners," who replace their plans with better plans as they are found. Rational planners do not seek to produce optimal plans, but rather to update their plans whenever improvements are found.[44] Because the agent only has to compare two options (the expected utility of an unchanged master plan, and the expected utility of the master plan supplemented by the proposed local plan), the proposed decision problem appears reasonably tractable.

There is much in this picture that is highly attractive. Two main questions confront the proposal: (1) is every agent capable of applying Pollock's decision-guide—that is, does it satisfy Criterion C (Guidance Adequacy), and (2) is the moral advice it gives normatively acceptable—that is, does it satisfy Criterion B (Moral Adequacy)? In addressing the first question, we should recall that, as Pollock notes, his decision-guide

---

[40] Pollock (2006), Chapter 10, section 7.
[41] Pollock (2006), pp. 186–7.   [42] Pollock (2006), pp. 188–9.
[43] Pollock (2006), p. 189.   [44] Pollock (2006), p. 190.

cannot be used by any agent who does not have any beliefs about the probabilities of the possible outcomes of his various possible options, or who assigns imprecise probabilities to relevant occurrences.[45] Thus it is not universally usable, as Criterion C requires. However, we agreed previously that Pollock could simply advocate use of some different decision-guide for such cases, thus abandoning any claim to have a single primary decision-guide for all occasions, but maintaining his claim that his decision-guide is appropriate and feasible for the kinds of cases it is designed to cover.

But is it really feasible for every agent (even those equipped with suitable beliefs about probabilities) to apply Pollock's decision-guide? In Chapter 11 Pollock addresses this question explicitly and argues that applying his decision-guide, which at first glance appears to require outrageously complicated computations of probabilities, in fact can be reduced by a process he calls "direct inference" to "simple probabilities that are easily computed by a resource bounded agent."[46] To illustrate this he spells out the reasoning that would be required of an agent who is practicing shooting at a firearm target range with the goal of hitting the target. In order to do this the agent must load the gun, aim the gun, and pull the trigger. His decision how to proceed is complicated by the fact that there is a warning light over the target that glows red when it is not safe to shoot, and turns green when it is safe to shoot. The agent needs to construct a "nonlinear" plan, building in various conditionals about what to do under which conditions, about how to proceed (a nonlinear plan leaves open the order in which some of the elements must be performed).[47]

After spelling out all the complexities that constructing such a plan and calculating its expected utilities would involve, Pollock shows how estimating its expected utility can be reduced to a much simpler calculation. However, this "simple" calculation itself takes up two thirds of a book page to spell out, and there are twenty-one different probabilities to be summed.[48] While it may be true, as Pollock claims, that such a computation is manageable for some resource limited agents, it seems far from true that *every* agent who possesses the requisite probability assignments could perform this calculation, especially in the time available—particularly if the agent has no paper, pencil, or computer to assist him. A sportsman at a target range equipped with a hand-held calculator is one thing, but a policeman, facing a possibly armed suspect, who has to make a snap decision about firing with a structure similar to that of the sportsman's decision is quite another. Thus I must conclude that valiant as Pollock's effort is to find a decision-guide for cognitively limited agents, it nonetheless fails Criterion C (Guidance Adequacy), and so falls short of what we need, even for the limited set of agents for which it is designed.[49]

---

[45] Pollock (2006), p. 88. Pollock requires these beliefs to be *justified* beliefs. This adds to the strain on the decision maker.

[46] Pollock (2006), Chapter 11 and p. 210. On direct inference, see sections 4.1 and 4.2 in Chapter 7.

[47] Pollock (2006), pp. 204 and 199.   [48] Pollock (2006), p. 210.

[49] In fairness, early in his book Pollock argues that humans can represent both numbers and expected values by using analog representations rather than precise mathematical ones, thus rendering certain kinds

Let us turn to the second question identified above: assuming that an agent is capable of applying Pollock's decision-guide, is the moral advice the guide gives normatively acceptable—that is, does it satisfy Criterion B (Moral Adequacy)? Recall that Pollock recommends an action as rational if and only if it is prescribed by a rationally adopted master plan, and deems making a change C to a master plan to be rational if and only if the expected utility of adopting the change C to the master plan is greater than the expected utility of the master plan left unchanged. Notably, the prescription for making a change to a master plan does not require that the change be the *best* change available, but only that its effect be positive relative to the unsupplemented master plan. This leaves it open that a rational action might be one prescribed by a supplemented master plan whose expected utility is exceeded by some—indeed by every—alternative supplemented master plan. The altered master plan merely needs to be "good enough," that is, to produce more expected utility than the unaltered master plan. Pollock notes the similarity between his decision-guide and the "satisficing" decision-guide advocated originally by Herbert Simon.[50] However, Pollock maintains that there is a distinction between the two, since Simon's concept of satisficing involves establishing a threshold value and accepting any plan that achieves that threshold, even if it becomes clear that some other plan would have even more value.[51] Pollock says that he only recommends accepting a plan as "good enough" so long as one's information doesn't support the conclusion that some alternative plan is better. If new information becomes available that identifies a better plan, then the better plan should supplant the original one.[52]

This comes across as a somewhat mixed message. If a plan seen to produce higher expected utility on the basis of new information must be adopted, and the old plan abandoned, then it appears that an action is only prescribed if it is recommended by the adjusted master plan that has the *highest* expected utility on the basis of the agent's information at the time the action is prescribed. It is difficult to see how this counts as recommending either an action or a master plan as merely "good enough" rather than as the optimal plan (relative to the agent's current information). This seems especially clear in a case where you initially believe you have multiple competing options. Consider your decision whether to stop off at the post office on your way to the supermarket. You might consider several alternative such detours, only one of which can be adopted: stopping at the post office, stopping at the dry cleaners, and stopping at the pharmacy. How would you use Pollock's proposal to make a decision? One way to do so would be

---

of otherwise intractable computation problems much more feasible (see Pollock 2006, pp 30–5). It is unclear, however, how this insight could be applied to the present computational problem.

   Pollock does not consider how costly in terms of time or opportunity costs it might be to carry out his procedure.

   [50] Simon (1955).

   [51] A host of problems for various versions of "satisficing" are described by Bradley (2006). Since Pollock is careful to specify the "baseline" against which the proposed local plan would be judged, his theory avoids some of these problems.

   [52] Pollock (2006), p. 187.

to consider your current master plan as supplemented by a trip to the post office, as alternatively supplemented by a trip to the dry cleaners, and as alternatively supplemented by a trip to the pharmacy. After comparing the expected utility of each supplemented master plan, you would then select the best. This looks just like calculating which option would maximize expected utility, a process Pollock is trying to avoid. Another way to carry out Pollock's proposal would be to pick one of these options at random, say adding the trip to the post office, and then calculate whether adding the post office trip would produce more expected utility than simply going to the supermarket. If it would, you would add the post office trip to your master plan. You would not then consider the trips to the dry cleaners and the pharmacy, because those trips could not be added on to your (newly expanded) master plan. But this method seems counterproductive, since it means consciously disregarding two of your alternative revised master plans, even though one you don't consider (for example, going to the dry cleaner) could actually be your best option—one you cannot now even consider, since your decision to first consider the post office trip takes the dry cleaner trip off the table.

Pollock seems to have in mind a process in which you simply make use of whatever information you have ready to hand. However, you also face a decision whether or not to acquire more information. This decision is itself a decision, and so apparently needs to be chosen on the basis of Pollock's decision-guide. This would make the original decision problem much less tractable, and would be subject to the same questions as I have just raised about the original decision, since there are often alternative ways to acquire more information. Of course Pollock could avoid this by ruling that the decision whether to seek more information is not a candidate for application of his decision-guide, and simply need not be done. But this seems an extreme position to take (especially for an epistemologist!), and leaves the decision maker captive to the winds of whatever information happens to come his way, rather than being an active seeker of information. In itself this seems problematic, even though its acceptance would reduce the amount of work and computation needed to solve decision problems not involving the search for more information. Finally, although it is clear from Pollock's description how one might reason in deciding whether or not to add a local plan to an existing master plan, it is far from clear how one gets started, when no master plan as yet exists, and so does not provide a base to which one compares a proposed change.

Our main worry, however, is that even Pollock's proposed decision-guide is sufficiently cognitively demanding that it could not be used by every agent, even those equipped to calculate probabilities.

10.3 Conclusion: Rejection of Hybrid Systems with a Single Primary Decision-Guide

We have now considered five Hybrid proposals identifying a single rule to be used for every decision under uncertainty:

Decision-Guide 1:   It is obligatory$_2$ to do what is most likely to be obligatory$_1$.

Decision-Guide 2:   It is obligatory$_2$ to perform the act that maximizes expected value (where value is assessed by the governing Code C).

Decision-Guide 3:   It is obligatory$_2$ to try to perform the act that would be obligatory$_1$.

Feldman's Level 2 Decision-Guide: If you cannot determine what you morally ought$_1$ to do, then you morally ought$_2$ to perform an act if and only if it is an outcome of the Utilitarian Decision Procedure.

Pollock's Decision-Guide:

A.   It is rational to make a change C to the master plan M if and only if the marginal expected utility of C is positive, that is, if and only if the expected utility of adopting the change C to the master plan is greater than the expected utility of the master plan left unchanged.

B.   It is rational to perform an action if and only if it is prescribed by a rationally adopted master plan.

Most of these proposed guides have some normative attractiveness—it appears as though they would be wise to follow in at least some circumstances, although we also saw that several of the guides would provide poor advice in other circumstances. However, each is proposed as a primary guide to be used in *every* circumstance, and we have seen that for each of the guides (with the exception of Feldman's Decision-Guide, for which we did not assess the usability) there are circumstances in which it is not actually usable. Each fails Criterion (C) (Guidance Adequacy).

We could of course try to find some alternative single primary decision-guide to serve as our Code C* in the Hybrid Response to the problem of uncertainty. However, reflection about the failures of these five candidates suggests that no single rule is ever going to do the job required. Instead what we need is a Hybrid system that recognizes *multiple* decision-guides in Code C* in addition to DG$_0$. Each of these rules would be usable by some subset of decision makers; taken together, they would provide a broad enough range of options that they could afford guidance to all decision makers.[53] I have already argued (in Chapter 9) that the decision-guides must include Decision-Guide DG$_0$, which semantically mirrors the content of Code C, the governing theoretical account of right and wrong. Thus any lower-tier code C* must perforce contain at least two decision-guides, Decision-Guide DG$_0$, which guides agents possessing all

---

[53] An alternative would be to adopt a Hybrid system with a single decision-guide for uncertainty, but add another level for a decision-guide to steer agents seeking to use the first decision-guide. Thus a system consisting of act utilitarianism as the account of right and wrong (Code C), and Decision-Guide 1 ("It is obligatory$_2$ to do what is most likely to be obligatory$_1$," as the single rule addressing uncertainty in Code C*, would have a third tier consisting of a decision-guide for Decision-Guide 1 for agents uncertain how to apply Guide 1. Such a guide might state "It is obligatory$_3$ to do what is most likely to be obligatory$_2$," or "It is obligatory$_3$ to try to perform the act that would be obligatory$_2$." Since guides with this kind of content were shown not to be usable by every agent, it seems highly unlikely that inserting them as guides in a third tier would effectively rescue the single guide approach.

the beliefs relevant to applying Code C (some of which may be false), and at least one additional decision-guide which guides agents facing uncertainty who cannot apply DG_0. The five candidate systems we have just assessed propose a single guide for cases of uncertainty. As we've seen, they are inadequate for the task of providing guidance for every decision maker, no matter how deep her uncertainty. A Hybrid system offering multiple decision-guides for uncertainty seems far better positioned to discharge this task. In Chapter 11 we will explore how a system containing multiple guides for uncertainty might be constructed.

11

Multiple-Rule Hybrid Solutions to the Problems of Error and Uncertainty

> Whatever we adopt as the fundamental principle of morality, we require subordinate principles to apply it by.[1]

Having concluded in the last chapter that Hybrid codes offering a sole primary principle to guide decision-making in the face of uncertainty are inadequate, let us turn to a consideration of Hybrid codes containing multiple decision-guides for cases of uncertainty.

11.1 Multiple-Rule Decision-Guiding Codes

The suggestion that the theoretical account of right and wrong should be supplemented by multiple decision-guides is not a novel one. Mill, for example, in claiming that we require subordinate principles to apply the fundamental principle of morality, mentions murder and theft as types of actions which would be regarded as prohibited by a well-informed utilitarianism.[2] Mill's proposal to supplement the account of right and wrong with multiple decision-guides, each focused on a different field of action, is a natural one. Versions of this strategy, more detailed than Mill's proposal, have been offered by a number of theorists, including R. M. Hare, Portmore, and co-authors Michael S. Moore and Heidi M. Hurd.[3] For example, Moore and Hurd describe "mini-maxims"

---

[1] Mill (1957), p. 32.

[2] Mill (1957), p. 32. There is dispute among Mill scholars about whether Mill viewed these "principles" as decision-guides in a Hybrid system, or whether he was advocating a form of rule utilitarianism. Since the distinction was unavailable at the time he wrote, this question is probably unanswerable. Sidgwick could also be interpreted as proposing a Hybrid system in which utilitarianism provides the theoretical account of right and wrong, while common-sense morality provides associated decision-guides, especially useful to the common person. See Sidgwick (1907).

[3] Hare (1981), especially Part I; Portmore (2011), section 1.4; and Moore and Hurd (2011), pp. 96–148. In many such proposals the lower-tier decision-guides are offered as solutions to a number of distinct problems, including but not limited to the epistemic problems confronting decision makers. Here I consider

such as "Don't play with matches; don't run along a poolside; look both ways before crossing a street...never shake an infant, even in good-natured fun; always face the handle of a hot pan towards the back of the stove; always wear a seatbelt, and always ensure that those who travel with you do the same; carry scissors with their handles facing forward; never point a gun at another person, even if you think it is unloaded," and so forth.[4] In their view, these mini-maxims (some of which concern self-regarding action, and some of which concern action affecting others) are well known to all, or at least to almost all, since parents drill such rules into their children in the hope that behavior required by the rules will become "automatic" or "routine," and we learn additional rules as we grow older.[5] In their view these rules are *epistemic* mini-maxims, designed not to provide accounts of what features make actions right or wrong (carrying scissors with the point forward is not inherently wrong), but rather to guide our decisions in cases where information may be lacking, hasty judgments are required, or a bulwark is needed against one's own worst tendencies.[6] In our conception, they view the mini-maxims as components of C*, not as components of Code C. Moore and Hurd concede, with regret, that there are arenas for decision-making that as yet have not acquired any such helpful maxims.[7]

Philosophers are not the only theorists who have offered multi-rule versions of the Hybrid approach that propose distinct decision-guides for different fields of action. Psychologists and economists have also pursued this strategy.[8] For example, the psychologist Gerd Gigerenzer and his collaborators have argued that we rely on a battery of "heuristics" (such as "Don't break ranks" and "If there is a default, do nothing about it") that epistemically challenged people commonly use when making moral decisions.[9] Although Gigerenzer is optimistic that these heuristics often provide excellent guidance,

---

only their role as responses to the epistemic problems. For an insightful discussion about two-tier systems, see Star (2011).

[4] Moore and Hurd (2011), p. 186.

[5] Moore and Hurd (2011), p. 186. Matt Richtel (2015) provides an interesting account of the development of new mini-maxims as social needs change.

[6] Moore and Hurd (2011), p. 190.

[7] Moore and Hurd (2011), p. 191, where they state "Notice that there really is no well-worn rule of thumb that, if followed, would ensure that one would never inadvertently forget a sleeping child in a hot car. There is no obvious rule that will save one from inadvertently leaving a pot to boil over, or ice upon a sidewalk, or a bottle of prescription pills within reach of a suicidal teenager."

It is important to note that mini-maxims of this sort can have several functions. The function with which we're here concerned is that of guiding action when full information is lacking. But mini-maxims can also be used, especially when prudential considerations loom largest, as a tool for inculcating useful habits so that the agent will do what is (usually) best when she acts without thinking. For example, one of the houses in which I lived had external doors that automatically locked whenever one left and closed the door behind one. To avoid inadvertently locking myself out, I cultivated the habit of always taking a key with me when I left the house, even in cases where I was fully alert to the potential danger of being locked out but knew there was someone in the house who could unlock the door for me if needed. By taking the key I was solidifying a habit I thought would be useful when, at some future time, I acted without thought.

[8] An example of a decision theorist who takes this line is Resnik (1987), who says (p. 40) that "I would also conjecture that we will ultimately conclude that no rule is always the rational one to use but rather that different rules are appropriate to different situations."

[9] Gigerenzer and Goldstein (1999), Gigerenzer (2008a), and other works.

other theorists, such as Tversky, Kahneman, and Sunstein, express concern that they can often lead us astray.[10] Sunstein, for example, speculates that many of our moral judgments are driven by the following heuristics, which can work well in many contexts but deliver bad recommendations in others: "Do not knowingly cause a human death"; "People should not be permitted to engage in moral wrongdoing for a fee"; "Punish, and do not reward, betrayals of trust"; "Do not tamper with nature"; and "Do not kill an innocent person, even if this is necessary to save others."[11]

In many of these proposals there is little or no potential overlap among the proposed decision-guides: they typically guide behavior in distinct fields of action. Thus each of Moore and Hurd's mini-maxims focuses on a different arena of conduct, such as handling matches, behavior near a swimming pool, and playing with or disciplining infants. Since each such guide is designed to address a different type of situation in which a decision needs to be made, the guides themselves are typically not rivals, and there is no need to establish any priority among them for cases of conflicting advice. However, there is another version of the Hybrid approach, discussed by decision theorists as well as by philosophers, that proposes multiple decision-guides. These decision-guides are all-purpose, in the sense that they are designed to be used in any field of action, whether the agent is handling guns, babies, or scissors. But they are explicitly designed to be usable by agents *with different amounts of information or different computational capacities.*[12] As we've seen, even agents facing identical circumstances may vary in their epistemic grasp of their situations: some are perfectly informed about the nonmoral nature and consequences of their proposed actions; others have complete but false beliefs; others have a full set of probability assignments for the outcomes of their actions; some have a full set of probability assignments but no capacity or time to carry out further computations using those assignments; still others believe only that certain actions might be available to them, or that those actions might have certain outcomes, although they cannot assign probabilities to any of these possibilities, and so forth. One all-purpose decision-guide could be usable by the agents in one type of epistemic situation, while different and epistemically less demanding all-purpose decision-guides could be usable by other agents in other types of epistemic situations. Thus decision theorists often recommend that an agent with complete value and probability assignments should follow the recommendation to maximize expected

---

[10] Tversky and Kahneman (1974); Kahneman, Slovic, and Tversky (1982); Kahneman and Tversky (2000); and Sunstein (2005) and (2008).

[11] Sunstein (2005), pp. 536, 537, 539, and 541.

[12] The canonical discussion by Luce and Raiffa (1957) explores which decision rules should be used by agents making decisions under different epistemic situations (see especially Chapters 1, 2, and 13). Rawls (1971) famously also discusses the different epistemic situations that would differentially call for use of the maximin rule or the rule of maximizing expected value (p. 154). A more recent example is provided by J. Williams (2014). In this article he explores several decision-guides (such as "Caprice" and "Randomize") that might be employed by a decision maker who can assign only indeterminate probabilities to the outcomes of his options. Another recent example is found in Grant and Quiggin (2013) and (2015), in which a "precautionary principle" is proposed as the best decision rule for agents who possess only partial awareness of the set of circumstances in which their actions will take place.

value, while they sometimes recommend that an agent who can assign no probability to the outcomes of her possible actions should comply with the "maximin" policy,[13] that is, choose an action of which the worst possible outcome is no worse than the worst possible outcome of any alternative option. Since an agent who has complete value and probability assignments could follow either the recommendation to maximize expected value or the recommendation to select the maximin action, these decision-guides are sometimes rivals, in the sense that they make different recommendations in the same choice situation. Thus some priority must be established for which one to use when both are available.

A concrete mini-maxim (such as "Never point a gun at another person") could be usable by an agent who would not be able to use the most epistemically demanding all-purpose decision-guides recommended by decision theorists for cases of uncertainty, and might be superior to less demanding all-purpose guides. Hence it appears that the most promising Hybrid theory will utilize both of these two kinds of decision-guides in order to provide to any agent at least one attractive decision-guide that is usable by her. In such a system, the lower-tier Code C* will proffer an extensive array of decision-guides, some of which are concretely tailored to the nature of the action (*Never shake an infant; Never point a gun at another person*), while others are more explicitly tailored for the epistemic situation of the agent (*Perform the action that would maximize expected happiness*). It is the availability of *all* of these guides that potentially makes it possible for Code C* to offer guidance to every agent; no single decision-guide alone needs to be usable by every agent.

11.2 Avoiding Inconsistent Prescriptions

Because a multi-rule Hybrid system of the sort we are considering contains multiple rules, more than one of which may be applicable to a given decision problem, and more than one of which may be usable by a given agent in light of her beliefs, the system needs to recognize a hierarchy among these rules, so that it can recommend the appropriate one for the agent to employ. A rule stands higher in this hierarchy when it is deontically better than one standing lower. Consider an agent who wants to follow act utilitarianism in deciding whether to pass a slow moving vehicle on a two-lane highway, and who is uncertain how great her chance is of successfully passing without causing an accident. She might be able to employ any of the following decision-guides: 1. *Never perform an act that has less expected utility than some alternative act*; 2. *Never perform an act which is likely to produce less happiness than some alternative*; 3. *Never perform an act whose worst possible outcome would produce less happiness than the worst possible outcome of some alternative*; 4. *Never add a local plan to your master plan unless doing so would produce greater expected utility than doing nothing*; and 5. *Never kill an innocent person*. An adequate Hybrid version of act utilitarianism would recommend one of these

---

[13] Also called the "minimax" policy or strategy.

decision-guides as the best one to apply (or recommend some subset of guides equally good and no worse than the others). There is no point, of course, in such a system recommending a decision that the agent's epistemic situation would prevent her from using, such as 0. *Never perform an act that has less utility than some alternative act.* Thus we should conclude that an appropriate Hybrid system would recommend (roughly) that the agent perform an act that is recommended by the decision-guide, usable by her, that stands higher in the hierarchy than any alternative decision-guide usable by her. Whether or not one decision-guide is better, or higher, than another is *not* a function of whether the first is usable and the second is not. The usability of rival guides by a given agent determines whether it is a candidate for use; it does not determine how it ranks compared to other guides. Position in the hierarchy is a function of a guide's deontic superiority. The nature of the standard that determines deontic superiority will be addressed in due course.

To formulate this a bit more precisely, we need to employ suitable terminology. In Chapter 10 I temporarily introduced the normative terms "$ought_1$" and "$ought_2$," where the theoretical account of right and wrong delivers prescriptions phrased in terms of "$ought_1$" and the decision-guide delivers prescriptions phrased in terms of "$ought_2$." However, we now need to abandon this terminology. Not only is it cumbersome, but we can now see that in a multi-rule system the decision-guides must use one term for their recommendations, while a *different* term must be used for the system's recommendation to perform the act recommended by the highest usable decision-guide. These terms must enable the system to avoid three possible problems with inconsistency. The first problem would be that the prescription of Code C might be inconsistent with the prescription of Code C* (for example, Code C might recommend act A while Code C* recommends incompatible act B). The second problem would be that the recommendations of the different decision-guides might be inconsistent with each other (for example, Decision-Guide 1 might prescribe act A, while Decision-Guide 2 prescribes act B). Finally, the recommendation of a decision-guide that is usable, but not the highest usable guide, might be inconsistent with the final recommendation of Code C*, the decision-guiding system as a whole. The recommendation of any decision-guide is in a sense only provisional, having actual clout only when that decision-guide is in fact the highest one usable by the agent (or is no lower than any alternative usable guide).[14] To avoid these possible inconsistencies, I will adopt the following conventions. The prescriptions of the theoretical account of right and wrong (Code C) will be stated in terms of what is "objectively" obligatory, right, or wrong. The recommendations of

---

[14] If an act A is prescribed by DG_2, but a different act is prescribed by DG_3, and DG_2 is ranked higher than DG_3 but DG_3 is the highest usable decision-guide for the agent, then the prescription of DG_2 has no actual clout or moral residue. Similarly if both DG_2 and DG_3 are usable by the agent and prescribe different acts, then there is no moral residue from the fact that B is prescribed by the lower DG_3. A prescription leaves a "moral residue" if, when breached, it generates other moral recommendations that have either prima facie or all-things-considered force, such as a recommendation that the agent apologize for not complying with the original prescription.

any individual decision-guide will be stated in terms of what is "choice-mandated," "choice-worthy," or "choice-prohibited." These latter recommendations will be understood as somewhat analogous in force to "prima facie" duties in the sense that there is no contradiction in a single act A being both choice-mandated by one decision-guide and choice-prohibited by another decision-guide. Finally, the overall prescription of the Code C*, the decision-guiding tier of the system, will be stated in terms of what is "subjectively" obligatory, right, or wrong.[15] Hybrid moral theories will be stated using these terms.

11.3   Sample Hybrid Multi-Decision-Guide Systems

Given these new conventions, a Hybrid system in which act utilitarianism provides the theoretical account of right and wrong might appear something like the following system. This system, like the Rossian one that follows, are truncated versions of the entire theories, since they include only partial lists of decision-guides, and only include principles governing one form of moral status (either rightness or obligatoriness). The Hybrid Rossian system is further truncated in only including decision-guides for the prima facie duty of keeping a promise. The full systems would include principles governing obligation, rightness, and wrongness, and, in the case of the Rossian system, decision-guides for every type of prima facie duty. Both systems incorporate the equivalent of Decision-Guide$_0$, which mirrors the semantic content of the theoretical account of right and wrong. Notice that some of the decision-guides incorporated into this system are ones reviewed in our earlier discussion of single-rule Hybrid systems. These may not have been adequate when intended to serve as the *sole* primary decision-guide for all agents, but they may be perfectly appropriate as guides for agents who are able to use them even though they cannot use any better guide. Although I have specified that the decision-guides must be ordered in a hierarchy, the ordering of guides in the following two moral codes does not purport to reflect such a hierarchy, but simply to set them out as a list.

1. Hybrid act utilitarianism

Code C: An act is objectively right if and only if it would produce no less happiness than any alternative act.

Code C*:   Relative to Code C and to the credences of agent S, an act A is subjectively right for S to perform if and only if it is prescribed as choice-worthy by a

---

[15] Some moral theorists have argued that all we need is the concept of "objective" moral status and the concept of "blameworthiness," since we can carry out all the work for which the concept of "subjective" moral status is needed by saying things like "His action was objectively wrong, but he non-culpably believed it was objectively right and so was not blameworthy for it." This strategy might work for cases in which the agent suffers from the problem of error, but does not work for agents who suffer from the problem of uncertainty, since we need to be able to phrase a moral recommendation to these agents despite their uncertainty. A separate concept of subjective moral status is needed for such cases.

decision-guide, usable by S, that is no lower in the hierarchy of choice-worthiness decision-guides than any other choice-worthiness decision-guide usable by S and appropriate to Code C.[16]

Decision-guides:

0. An act that would produce no less happiness than any alternative act is choice-worthy.

1. An act that would produce no less expected happiness than any alternative act is choice-worthy.

2. An act which is at least as likely as any alternative to produce no less happiness than any alternative is choice-worthy.

3. An act whose worst possible outcome would produce no less happiness than the worst possible outcome of any alternative act is choice-worthy.

4. An act prescribed by a local plan is choice-worthy if adding the local plan to the agent's master plan would produce no less expected happiness than not adding it.

5. An act is choice-worthy if it would produce at least the satisfactory amount of happiness.

6. It is choice-worthy never to kill an innocent person.

7. It is choice-worthy never to take the property of another person without her consent.

8. It is choice-worthy never to shake an infant.

9. It is choice-worthy never to carry scissors point first.

10. Unless you are in the military or the police, it is choice-worthy never to point a gun at another person.

.

.

.

N. Every act is choice-worthy.

A Hybrid system in which Ross's deontological principles serve as the theoretical account of right and wrong might appear as follows. Again, this is a truncated version of the full theory. Here, to highlight important differences between recommendations

---

[16] For ease of reading I have deleted the temporal indices that must be included in a full statement of Code C*. Thus the full statement would read:

Code C*:   Relative to Code C and to the credences of agent S, an act A is subjectively right at time t_i for S to perform at time t_j if and only if it is prescribed as choice-worthy by a decision-guide, usable by S at time t_i, that is no lower in the hierarchy of choice-worthiness decision-guides than any other choice-worthiness decision-guide usable by S at time t_i and appropriate to Code C.

In this and subsequent formulations we should understand a decision-guide's being "no lower than any other" as encompassing situations in which DG_x and DG_y are equally ranked in the relevant hierarchy, situations in which they are ranked on a par with each other (in the sense of Chang (2002)), and situations in which the ranking of DG_x and DG_y relative to each other is indeterminate, but each is ranked higher than any other (usable) decision-guide.

for the right act and those for the obligatory act, I phrase the system in terms of what is obligatory, not in terms of what is right.

2. Hybrid Rossian deontology

Code C: An act is objectively obligatory all-things-considered if and only if its net balance of prima facie rightness over prima facie wrongness is greater than the net balance of prima facie rightness over prima facie wrongness of any alternative act.

Principles of prima facie obligation:

1.   It is prima facie obligatory to keep a promise.
2.   It is prima facie obligatory to compensate another person for wronging that person in the past.
3.   It is prima facie obligatory to return services freely rendered by another person.
4.   It is prima facie obligatory to distribute happiness in accord with the merits of the persons concerned.
5.   It is prima facie obligatory to benefit others.
6.   It is prima facie obligatory to improve one's own virtue or intelligence.
7.   It is prima facie obligatory not to harm others.

Code C*:   Relative to Code C and to the credences of agent S, an act A is subjectively obligatory all-things-considered for S to perform if and only if either (a) it is prescribed as choice-mandated by the highest choice-mandating decision-guide, usable by S, that is appropriate to C, or (b) it is prescribed as choice-mandated by every choice-mandating decision-guide, usable by S, that is appropriate to C, and that is no lower in the hierarchy of choice-mandating decision-guides than any other decision-guide usable by S and appropriate to Code C.[17]

A.   Decision-guides for all-things-considered obligatoriness:

0.   An act is choice-mandated if it would have a larger net balance of prima facie rightness over prima facie wrongness than the net balance of prima facie rightness over prima facie wrongness of any alternative act.
1.   An act is choice-mandated if it maximizes expected deontic weight.
2.   An act is choice-mandated if it fulfills more prima facie duties than any alternative act.

.
.
.

B.   Decision-guides for prima facie obligatoriness:

1.   Promises
a.   If you must choose between performing act A or performing act B, act A is choice-mandated if you promised to do A rather than promised to do B.

---

[17] Here again I eliminate the temporal indices required in the full statement of Code C*.

b.   If you are uncertain whether you promised to do A or promised to do B, Act A is choice-mandated if the expected deontic weight of A is greater than the expected deontic weight of doing B.

c.   Act A is choice-mandated if A is most likely to be the act you promised.

.

.

.

Since the statement of the basic clause of Code C* is long and cumbersome, for brevity I shall sometimes state it using only its subclause (a).

Ross himself never addressed in detail the question of how best to proceed in cases where you are uncertain what the nonmoral character, and therefore the prima facie moral status, of your options would be, so these are merely suggestions for decision-guides that a Rossian might find congenial. For overall obligation, and for each type of prima facie obligation in a Rossian Hybrid system, there will be a multitude of decision-guides designed to address a given type of uncertainty or a more specialized field of action.

The restriction in these examples of a Code C* that (for example) the relevant decision-guide is "no lower in the hierarchy of *choice-worthiness* decision-guides than any other choice-worthiness decision-guide" is meant to ensure that the ranking of decision-guides is determined only by their ranking relative to decision-guides in the same class: choice-worthiness guides are ranked relative only to other choice-worthiness guides, choice-mandating guides are ranked relative only to choice-mandating guides, and so forth. For brevity in subsequent discussion I shall sometimes omit these qualifiers. I shall assume that the recommendation of the highest positive decision-guide (a choice-mandating or choice-worthiness guide) overrides the recommendation in the same case by the highest negative guide (a choice-prohibiting guide). Knowing that an act is proscribed by the highest negative guide—for example that it would fail to maximize happiness—still doesn't give an agent any guidance about which act she *should* perform. Thus, if the highest negative decision-guide evaluates act A as choice-prohibited, while the highest positive decision-guide evaluates act A as choice-worthy, act A is subjectively permissible for the agent. Similarly, if act A is evaluated as choice-mandated by the most highly-ranked decision-guide of its class, this outweighs the evaluation of B (but not A) as choice-worthy by the most highly-ranked decision-guide of its class. These assumptions will be revisited in section 11.5.

Some of the decision-guides listed in Hybrid act utilitarianism may seem a bit odd. It sounds strange to include decision-guides stating that it is choice-worthy never to kill an innocent person, or never to shake an infant, since these acts would usually be viewed as choice-mandated, not merely choice-worthy. However, the acts they prescribe would necessarily be choice-worthy as well as choice-mandated, so I've included them in the list to illustrate the fact that the list of decision-guides includes mini-maxims as well as the all-purpose guides.

In the case of Hybrid act utilitarianism I've added a bottom-most Decision-Guide N that prescribes as choice-worthy any act available to the agent. If an act utilitarian agent is bedeviled by such uncertainty about the nonmoral features of her possible acts that she can apply no higher guide to her decision, then it seems morally reasonable for her to simply choose an act at random. Since it is not possible for her to apply one of the higher decision-guides, or to identify any moral ground to prefer one act over another, then every option has equal subjective status. Because the stated component of the Rossian Hybrid system is phrased in terms of the agent's obligations and decision-guides recommending actions as choice-mandated, it does not include a lowest decision-guide prescribing any act as morally choice-worthy. However, the component of the Rossian system spelling out what is subjectively right in terms of decision-guides recommending acts as choice-worthy would include such a last resort decision-guide.

Note that the Code C* in Hybrid act utilitarianism and that in Hybrid Rossian deontology imply that the subjective status of an act does not depend on the agent's *actual reasons* for performing the act. In the case where the last resort N is the highest usable guide, this means that whatever the uncertainty-bedeviled agent does, for whatever reason, counts as subjectively right. Hence, at least in these theories, for every agent there is a subjectively right act, no matter how deep the agent's uncertainty about the nonmoral features of her options, so long as there is some act she can perform.[18] If there is no act the agent can perform, but she believes there is such an act, she nonetheless has the ability in the core sense to use her moral principle to guide her choice of action, even though that choice may not issue in any actual action.[19]

It's worth remarking that an agent who cannot apply any decision-guide superior to Decision-Guide N might quite rationally decide to choose the action that is best according to some other normative principle, such as prudence or legality. Since all of her options are morally choice-worthy according to Decision-Guide N, she may just as well try to satisfy some additional legitimate normative concern.[20]

Let's examine some implications of adopting our new terminology. One implication, as we can see from these two moral theories, is that an action's subjective moral status (unlike its objective moral status) is relative to a particular agent and time, since a decision-guide that is usable by one agent may not be usable by another epistemically less favored agent, or usable by the same agent at another time. Which act counts as subjectively right or obligatory is not only relativized to a particular agent and time, but also relativized to a particular Code C—to some account of objective moral status. What is subjectively obligatory for an agent to do relative to the Rossian deontological

---

[18]   When the account of what is subjectively right is developed in Chapter 13, I retract this statement.

[19]   In other types of Hybrid moral theories, it's possible that some or all decision-guides would prescribe acts that must be done from a certain intention or with a certain reason (although it's unclear how tenable it is to include instructions about acting from a certain reason in a decision-guide). This may have negative implications for how broadly usable such theories are.

[20]   This is also a point at which an agent may invoke considerations arising from her belief that some alternative moral theory may be superior to act utilitarianism. However, for purposes of this book we are setting aside the problem of how to deal with such normative uncertainties.

theory may well be different from what it is subjectively obligatory for that same agent to do relative to utilitarianism. This is what we would expect. But we could also define what it is *absolutely* subjectively obligatory for an agent to do, which would be the subjectively obligatory action relative to the *correct* theory of objective obligation.

My proposed convention for distinguishing the recommendations of any Code C from those of its associated Code C* mirrors a standard distinction often invoked by philosophers, in discussing the problems of error or uncertainty, between acts that are objectively right and those that are subjectively right. The standard distinction is sometimes explained as differentiating a type of moral status that depends on the nonmoral facts of the situation (not including the agent's beliefs about the situation), versus a type of moral status that depends on the agent's beliefs about the nonmoral facts of the situation. However, according to some theoretical accounts of what makes actions right or wrong, the agent's beliefs can themselves be one feature of the act that makes it objectively right or wrong. Thus some philosophers hold that it is wrong to kill an innocent person, and also wrong *in the same way* (although possibly less wrong) to knowingly risk killing an innocent person. The wrongness of knowingly risking killing an innocent person depends on facts about the agent's beliefs about the probability of harm, just as the wrongness of actually killing an innocent person depends on the non-mental facts such as the act's causing the death of the victim.[21] Other philosophers believe that it is wrong to tell a lie, where telling a lie involves (roughly) asserting what the agent believes to be a falsehood with the intention of deceiving her audience. To perform an act of lying requires the agent to have two beliefs: the belief that her assertion is false, and the belief that her assertion may deceive her audience. Since I don't wish to rule out theoretical accounts in which an agent's beliefs at least partly determine whether her action is objectively right or wrong, we must understand the "objective" moral status of an act as simply the moral status accorded it by a Code C, the theoretical account of right and wrong in a Hybrid system.[22]

Similarly, we should understand the subjective moral status of an act as simply the moral status ascribed to it by a Code C*, the decision-guiding tier of a Hybrid system. We can express this in formal Definition 11.1.

Definition 11.1.   Subjective moral status: The **subjective moral status of an act** is the moral status ascribed to it by a Code C*, the decision-guiding tier of a Hybrid system.

Note that while the decision-guides in Code C* may themselves recommend actions in virtue of certain of the agent's beliefs or other mental states, they may also recommend actions in virtue of features of the action not involving the agent's mental states.[23]

---

[21] On some accounts of "risking," risking killing a person involves taking an objective chance of killing the other person. Here I am using the subjective account of risking, which involves the agent's taking what he believes (perhaps mistakenly) to be a chance of killing the other person.

[22] See H. Smith (2010a) and Sepielli (2012), pp. 47–8.

[23] Thanks to Andrew Sepielli for pressing me on this point.

Rossian Decision-Guide B.1.b (*If you are uncertain whether you promised to do A or promised to do B, act A is choice-mandated if the expected deontic weight of A is greater than the expected deontic weight of doing B*) makes reference to the agent's estimation of likelihoods.[24] By contrast, Rossian Decision-Guide A.2 (*An act is choice-mandated if it fulfills more prima facie duties than any alternative act*) and Utilitarian Decision-Guide 6 (*It is choice-worthy never to kill an innocent person*) make no reference to what the agent believes.

It's important to understand that the all-things-considered recommendation of a Code C* does not recommend the action the agent *believes to be prescribed by the highest usable decision-guide*—rather it recommends the action that *is* prescribed by the highest usable decision-guide. This means there is an important element of objectivity to an act's subjective moral status, since an agent might be mistaken about this status. On the other hand, whether or not a given decision-guide is *usable* is partly a function of what the agent believes (or is a function of the agent's credences). Thus, for a decision-guide to be usable by an agent, that agent must believe of some act-type A that she could perform A, and must believe that if she performed A it would have the feature F designated by the decision-guide as making the action choice-worthy. Hence there is an element of subjectivity, as well as an element of objectivity, in the recommendations of any Code C*.[25]

These statements of Code C* examples are provisional, since we will have occasion to revise them yet again in Chapter 13. However, for now we can usefully continue to use the formulations of the Code C* employed here.

Finally, let me emphasize the difference between what I called "subjectivizing" moral principles in Chapter 4, and my current proposal that any Code C* recommends an action as subjectively right. We can now see that Chapter 4's subjectivizing moral principles (such as those suggested by Prichard and Ross) are actually advocated as what I am now calling theoretical accounts of *objective* right and wrong (that is, as a Code C) in which the feature of the act that makes it objectively right or wrong is the fact that the agent has certain beliefs about the act and its circumstances. Such a subjectivizing principle might say, for example, "An act is objectively wrong if the agent believes it would violate a promise." By contrast, a Code C* in a Hybrid system does not claim to

---

[24] Again I am interpreting these decision-guides as referring to the agent's subjective estimates of the relevant probabilities. There are alternative versions that interpret these decision-guides as referring to the objective probabilities of the events in question, in which case there is no reference to the agent's beliefs.

[25] Parfit (2011), p. 150, distinguishes between what he calls the "fact-relative" and the "belief-relative" sense of right and wrong. These senses are similar to what I am calling an action's "objective" and "subjective" moral status. Unfortunately Parfit's definition of the belief-relative sense of right and wrong misfires. He says that "some act of ours would be... *wrong* in the *belief-relative* sense just when this act would be wrong in the ordinary sense if our beliefs about these facts were true" (p. 150). Apparently Parfit's "ordinary sense" of "wrong" entails that the act is wrong and that we (or the agent) believe it to be wrong (p. 150). Although Parfit's definition of the "belief-relative" sense of wrong nicely handles cases in which the agent has *false* nonmoral beliefs about the act, it cannot properly handle cases in which the agent is *uncertain* about what nonmoral features the act has, since there is no usable sense here of what would be true if the agent's probabilistic beliefs were true. Characterizing the belief-relative sense of right and wrong is regrettably far more complex than Parfit's formulation countenances.

provide a theoretical account of what makes acts objectively right or wrong, but instead merely claims to provide guidance for making decisions to agents who may be unable to directly apply the governing theoretical account. Thus subjectivizing principles on the one hand, and Code C* and decision-guides on the other hand, occupy very different roles in a comprehensive moral theory. And only the former invariably phrase their recommendations in terms of what the agent believes about her possible actions.

Since Decision-Guide A.0 in the Rossian theory (for example) mirrors the content of the account C of objective obligation, there will be cases in which the act that is objectively obligatory for an agent is also subjectively obligatory. Prominent among these cases are ones in which the agent has sufficient true beliefs to derive a prescription from Decision-Guide A.0, so that Decision-Guide A.0, as the highest usable decision-guide, dictates which act is subjectively obligatory, and that act is also objectively right. (Of course, there are also cases in which by good luck the action prescribed by one of the lower decision-guides is identical to the one prescribed by the account of objective obligation.) But we must also recognize that the act prescribed by the highest usable decision-guide will sometimes be different from the one prescribed by the governing Code C. For example, it may be the case that donating to Oxfam would produce the greatest happiness, but donating to CARE would produce the greatest expected happiness, and the highest decision-guide usable by the agent is a decision-guide recommending performance of the act that would produce the greatest expected happiness. Moreover, there will be many cases in which the agent has false beliefs about which act is prescribed by a given decision-guide. For example, within the Hybrid Rossian theory, Decision-Guide A.2 prescribes an act as choice-mandated if it fulfills more prima facie duties than any alternative act. The agent might falsely believe that A would fulfill more prima facie duties than any alternative, and so derive a prescription for A. But in fact some alternative act B may fulfill more prima facie duties than any alternative, and the agent is mistaken in thinking that A is prescribed by Decision-Guide A.2. Thus a decision-guide such as A.2 may be usable in the core sense by the agent, but not usable in the extended sense.

11.4 Interpolated Decision-Guides

It is worthwhile pointing out two additional possible developments of multi-rule Hybrid codes. Consider the following portion of the version of Hybrid act utilitarianism stated above:

1. Hybrid act utilitarianism

Code C: An act is objectively right if and only if it would produce no less happiness than any alternative act.

Code C*:   Relative to Code C and to the credences of agent S, an act A is subjectively right for S to perform if and only if it is prescribed as choice-worthy by a decision-guide, usable by S, that is no lower in the hierarchy of choice-worthiness decision-guides than any other choice-worthiness decision-guide usable by S and appropriate to Code C.

Decision-guides:

0.   An act that would produce no less happiness than any alternative act is choice-worthy.

1.   An act that would produce no less expected happiness than any alternative act is choice-worthy.

2.   An act which is at least as likely as any alternative to produce no less happiness than any alternative is choice-worthy.

3.   An act whose worst possible outcome would produce no less happiness than the worst possible outcome of any alternative act is choice-worthy.

4.   An act prescribed by a local plan is choice-worthy if adding the local plan to the agent's master plan would produce no less expected happiness than not adding it.

5.   An act is choice-worthy if it would produce at least the satisfactory amount of happiness.

Imagine an agent Tina who wants to guide her action by act utilitarianism, isn't sure which action would produce no less happiness than any alternative act, and so turns to decision-guides lower than Decision-Guide 0. She thinks act A might satisfy Decision-Guide 1 ("An act that would produce no less expected happiness than any alternative act is choice-worthy"), but she is uncertain about this. She doesn't have any idea which act would satisfy Decision-Guides 2–4, but believes act B would satisfy Decision-Guide 5 ("An act is choice-worthy if it would produce at least the satisfactory amount of happiness"). She also recognizes that Decision-Guide 5 is much lower ranked than Decision-Guide 1. Since she is uncertain of any act (including act A) whether it satisfies Decision-Guide 1, and has no clue which acts might satisfy Guides 2–4, Decision-Guide 5 appears to be the highest usable decision-guide for her. This would imply that act B is the subjectively right act for her. But what if she believes there is a 90 percent chance that act A satisfies Decision-Guide 1? (This might happen if she is unable, at least in the time available, to calculate precisely the expected happiness of all her options, but estimates, or is informed on good authority, that there's a 90 percent chance A would produce no less expected happiness than any alternative act.) Should she really disregard act A and perform act B instead? This doesn't seem rational. What it suggests is that the list of decision-guides should include additional "interpolated" guides such as the guide "An act that has a greater chance than any other of producing at least as much expected happiness as any alternative act is choice-worthy" in the list of appropriate decision-guides. This guide would be ranked somewhere between Decision-Guide 1 and Decision-Guide 5. Similar intermediate guides on the same model should also be introduced, such as "If act A's worst possible outcome is likely to produce at least as much happiness as the worst possible outcome of any alternative act, then act A is choice-worthy." Cases in which the agent has only "fuzzy" probability estimates regarding her actions' properties can similarly be handled by appropriately worded decision-guides.

Although Decision-Guide 1 isn't the highest usable decision-guide for Tina, the decision-guide advising her that "An act is choice-worthy that has a greater chance than any other of producing at least as much expected happiness as any alternative act" is usable by her (in virtue of her beliefs about act A), and it may be the highest-ranked usable decision-guide. So by interpolating decision-guides that take into account uncertainties of this kind that may afflict agents, the Hybrid solution can not only provide a greater number of agents with usable decision-guides, but can also avoid issuing counterintuitive advice to agents such as Tina.[26]

For the second, and related, potential development of multi-rule Hybrid codes, consider another agent Regina, who also wants to be guided by act utilitarianism. Regina, too, isn't sure which actions would produce at least as much happiness as any alternative act. She thinks act A might satisfy Decision-Guide 1, but she is uncertain whether she can actually perform act A. She doesn't have any idea which act would satisfy Decision-Guides 2–4, but believes act B would satisfy Decision-Guide 5, and believes she can perform act B. However, she also recognizes that Decision-Guide 5 is much lower ranked than Decision-Guide 1. It appears we have to say that act B is the subjectively right act for Regina to perform—even though she might believe there is a 90 percent chance she can perform act A. Here, too, we can take advantage of the newly interpolated decision-guides. If Regina thinks there is a 90 percent chance she can perform act A, she must believe there is some other act she can perform—*trying to perform act A*—that has at least a 90 percent chance of resulting in her performing act A. This act (let us call it "act C") is one she can perform, and it is prescribed by the decision-guide advising her that "An act is choice-worthy that has a greater chance than any other of producing at least as much expected happiness as any alternative act." This decision-guide is usable by her, even though Decision-Guide 1 is not. So the subjectively right act for her is act C (trying to perform act A), not act A or act B. This too seems like the reasonable recommendation for Regina to follow.

11.5 A Profusion of Normative Act-Evaluations

Some theorists have argued against the view that several distinct moral "oughts" apply to an agent trying to decide what to do on a particular occasion. I have framed the Hybrid theory so that it involves more than one "ought" applying to a given agent, and these prescriptions may not always coincide. For example, an act A might be objectively obligatory but subjectively wrong for the agent. The theorists in question find this aspect of the Hybrid theory disturbing. The concern of these theorists is that

---

[26] This proposal raises the possibility that the hierarchy of decision-guides may be a dense ordering, in the sense that for every decision-guide DG_x and DG_y, where DG_x is lower in the hierarchy than DG_y, there is a DG_z higher than DG_x and lower than DG_y. This could be problematic, but I shall not attempt to address it.

to admit several potentially conflicting prescriptions of this sort leaves the agent without a univocal answer to the question of what she ought to do, and so does not solve her practical problem.[27]

The Hybrid theory I have sketched can lead to "conflicting" act-evaluations of this type. However, I cannot see this as a difficulty in itself. Just as a 4′ 3″ child can be both tall (relative to his classmates) and short (relative to his siblings), so too an action can be both objectively obligatory but subjectively wrong. These latter evaluations play different roles, so their conflict is not in itself troublesome. The only serious problem would arise if either Code C or Code C* in the system generates contradictory prescriptions *using the same type of evaluative term*. For example, Code C might evaluate an act A as both objectively right and objectively wrong. However, unless Code C in this system contains some disguised contradiction, in which case it has a fatal flaw as a theoretical account, this should not happen at the Code C level. Nonetheless a parallel phenomenon can happen at the Code C* level, and these are the kinds of cases that give pause to theorists who are concerned with a "plurality of 'oughts'" and their impact on an agent's *practical* problem. If a Code C* generates a recommendation for the agent to perform act A, and also generates a recommendation for the agent not to perform act A, then the agent is left without clear univocal advice, and this would be a genuine matter of concern. Although the theorists who object to a plurality of "oughts" envision this as occurring in a Hybrid system because the evaluation generated by Code C can differ from that generated by Code C*, it actually arises in a different and more pointed manner within Code C* itself. Even so, the occasions on which it can happen are rare.

Let us focus on the unusual kind of case in which this can happen. The salient example is provided by Regan-style cases. For instance, in *Strong Medicine*, introduced in Chapter 9, the doctor is in the unusual position of believing both that she would be objectively wrong to use treatment B (which would produce moderate improvement in the patient's condition), but also that she is subjectively obligated to use B. As I have described Hybrid systems, what this means is that the doctor believes that a DG_0 in Code C* prescribes act B as choice-prohibited, while a different DG_1 in Code C* prescribes act B as choice-mandated. The practical conflict occurs at *this* level, where she is told by Code C* both to do B and also not to do B. However, conflicts of this sort among the recommendations of various decision-guides are again not a problem in themselves, since a given agent may be able to use several different decision-guides that generate different advice. As I characterized them, the recommendations of these guides only have moral clout when they issue from the highest guide the agent is able to use. The physician is able to use both the DG_0 and the DG_1, so the question is which one is highest and therefore prevails. In section 11.3 of this chapter I said that the rankings of decision-guides only rank them relative to the same class of guides (for example, a decision-guide that prescribes acts as choice-worthy is only ranked

---

[27] A prominent example of this objection is raised by Zimmerman (2008), pp. 7–8.

relative to other decision-guides prescribing acts as choice-worthy). In cases where there is a conflict between decision-guides from two different classes, I stated that the recommendation of the highest *positive* decision-guide (a choice-mandating or choice-worthiness guide) overrides any recommendation in the same case by the highest *negative* guide (a choice-prohibiting guide). That assumption bears fruit in Regan-style cases. Since knowing that an act is proscribed by the highest negative guide doesn't give an agent any guidance about which act she *should* perform, and she must do something, she must turn for ultimate advice to the highest-ranked usable positive guide. In this instance that guide is DG_1, which tells her to maximize expected value, which in this case means using treatment B on the patient. This is the prescription she should follow, even though she also knows that this act is prohibited by the highest-ranked negative decision-guide she can use. Contrary to past assumptions, then, Regan-style cases don't give rise to troublesome conflicts between objective evaluations and subjective evaluations. Instead they give rise to potentially troublesome conflicts between positive and negative decision-guides. We have to resolve such conflicts in order to determine which act is subjectively right for the agent, and the way to do so that conforms to the judgment of every theorist about Regan-style cases is to give the highest-ranked positive decision-guide priority over the highest-ranked negative decision-guide. The physician is thus told that her using treatment B is subjectively right.[28] Just as we have to resolve conflicts between the advice of two decision-guides that issue differing choice-mandated prescriptions, so we have to resolve conflicts between positive and negative decision-guides that issue differing prescriptions. What I have outlined is the obvious way to do so.

Of course at some later time, when more information has become available, an agent can come to believe that some act A was objectively right even though, relative to her beliefs at the time of action, it was subjectively wrong. Thus the doctor in *Strong Medicine* might discover after the fact that giving the patient treatment A would have completely cured him. She may have a certain kind of regret that, in view of its being subjectively wrong, she chose not to perform that action. At the same time she can recognize that she made the best choice possible relative to her information at the time she had to decide, and from that perspective she will not regret her choice. The availability of these two types of action assessment enables her to have a more nuanced view of her action's moral merits and demerits, and her own merits and demerits as a decision maker, than would be possible without them.[29]

---

[28] In (2014) Zimmerman maintains that any acceptable decision-guide must prescribe exactly the same actions that are prescribed by the account of objective moral status, or at least be justifiably thought to do so by the decision maker (pp. 100–7). This seems to me far too strong a requirement. DG_1, which tells the utilitarian agent to act so as to maximize expected utility, is an excellent decision-guide relative to act utilitarianism, even though an agent following it will justifiably believe that the act it recommends will sometimes fail to maximize utility.

[29] This fact is recognized by many ordinary people. For example, Stephen Farrell, a British reporter who was kidnapped by the Taliban while pursuing a story about an alleged bombing in northern Afghanistan, was rescued four days later at the cost of the lives of his interpreter, a British paratrooper, an Afghan

How best to interpret ordinary uses of "ought" to accommodate the apparent need for several different kinds of "oughts" is a matter hotly debated by philosophers of language.[30] I shall not attempt to enter this technical debate, but rather to describe the tools I think we need to effectively address the question of using moral theories for guiding decisions. These tools may or may not correspond to ordinary uses of normative language, which themselves may reflect people's confusion on some of these issues.

11.6 How Usable Must the Decision-Guides Be?

As we saw in section 11.2, an agent can suffer from the problems of nonmoral error and uncertainty with respect to a moral theory's decision-guides, just as she can suffer from these problems with respect to the first-tier principles of Code C. Thus an agent, because she is mistaken about which act is most likely to be the one she promised to perform, might mistakenly believe that act A is choice-mandated by Decision-Guide B.1.c in the Rossian Hybrid theory, which prescribes A as choice-mandated if it is most likely to be the act she promised. For this agent Decision-Guide B.1.c is usable in the core sense but not the extended sense. Similarly, if the agent is uncertain which act is most likely to be the one she promised, she is unable to use Decision-Guide B.1.c even in the core sense. The problem of uncertainty with respect to a decision-guide is solved by Code C*'s provision of additional decision-guides that can be used even when a given guide, such as B.1.c, cannot. But the problem of error remains.

Having concluded that the problem of error for principles of objective moral status is best dealt with by the Austere solution, we have reason to think the problem of error for decision-guides is best dealt with in the same manner, by rejecting the demand for extended usability in decision-guides. A demand for extended usability would interpret Code C* so that the "highest usable" decision-guide is one that is usable not only in the core sense but also the extended sense. In Chapter 8 we concluded that Austere theories were correct to reject the demand for usability in the extended sense for accounts of what makes actions right or wrong in cases involving the problem of error. The specific arguments in favor of the Austere solution to the problem of error for objective moral principles may not carry over wholesale to the realm of

woman and others, including Taliban fighters. Afterwards Farrell told a reporter, "[I]...was comfortable with the decision to go [on the mission]...[but] I am distraught that a reporting mission which was intended to find out if avoidable deaths had been caused, led, through a catastrophic series of events, to more deaths...No one can know in advance which calculated risks they take will work out well, and which will go wrong. I will have to live with the consequences of my actions." See Hoyt (2009). But not everyone is capable of understanding both perspectives on a decision. As reported by Leonhardt (2006), Robert Rubin and his co-author Jacob Weisberg wrote in Rubin's memoir *In an Uncertain World* that "Unfortunately, Washington—the political process and the media—judges decisions based solely on outcomes, not on the quality of the decision making."

[30] For discussion, see Dowell (2012) and (2013), Kolodny and MacFarlane (2010), MacFarlane (2014), and Schroeder (2011). Any such discussion must address not only the kinds of moral evaluations an agent might make, but also those that might be made by the agent's advisors and by observers having no possibility of interaction with the agent.

decision-guides. Nonetheless it is hard to see how to make workable a Code C* that requires decision-guides to be usable in the extended sense. An agent who is subject to the problem of error with respect to some decision-guide DG_x will perforce not realize that she cannot use DG_x in the extended sense. She will have no way, barring guidance from a better-informed advisor, to identify the correct decision-guide to use. Such advisors are often not available. Of course the last resort guide, which prescribes every action as choice-worthy, is usable by every moral agent, no matter how impoverished the agent's nonmoral information. Thus an agent, seeking certainty that she is using a decision-guide which she cannot err in using, might turn to the last resort guide. But the Hybrid approach aims to provide agents with better advice than recommending that they choose an action at random whenever they are uncertain which action has the nonmoral features required for objective moral rightness. We should conclude that the decision-guides representing that "better advice" are ones that are not always usable in the extended sense.

Without arguing for this in greater detail here, I shall henceforth assume that we should require the decision-guide that determines whether or not an action is subjectively right or obligatory to be usable in the core sense, but not in the extended sense.[31] This means that an agent can be mistaken about an action's subjective status: the act can be subjectively wrong even though the agent believes it to be subjectively right, or it can be subjectively right even though the agent believes it is not.

11.7 A New Opening for the Pragmatic Approach?

At this point one can envision the Pragmatic theorist as saying "Thank you for your exposition of the Hybrid approach! I can now see how to formulate my own Pragmatic theory to escape all the problems that have been raised for it. What I can do is take the successful Hybrid theory, discard its top tier, and elevate its constellation of second-tier decision-guides into first-tier principles that serve both to define what the right-making characteristics are and to provide practical action guidance. There will be no need to supplement these principles with any independent second-tier decision-guides. This structure will leave me, not with a unitary account of right and wrong, but with a multi-principle account. On this new account the right act for an agent is the act prescribed by the highest (appropriate) principle usable by that agent. We no longer need to differentiate objective from subjective rightness of an action; there is just one form of rightness. And for each agent there will be some principle of (simple) rightness that is usable by that agent, no matter how deep her ignorance or uncertainty about the actual circumstances and consequences of the act." This Pragmatic theorist is inspired by our account of a Hybrid theory to propose a version of what I earlier called a "Splintered Pragmatic" approach. The current version mirrors in certain important

---

[31] The argument in this section raises issues about the agent's knowledge of which decision-guide is the correct one for her to use. We will return to these issues in Chapters 12 and 13.

respects the Hybrid theory and aims to provide a solution to both the problem of error and the problem of uncertainty. To my knowledge no actual Pragmatic theorist has proposed such a theory, but it may seem like a tempting alternative to any Pragmatic theorist who grasps the advantages offered by the Hybrid theory but wishes to preserve his central tenet that the same moral principle must serve both a theoretical and a practical function.

Let's see what such a theory would look like, using Hybrid act utilitarianism as the model. Evidently this new-fangled Pragmatic theorist has something like the following in mind for a theory inspired by act utilitarian concerns.

1. Pragmatic Splintered act utilitarianism

Code C: An act A is right for agent S to perform if and only if it is prescribed as permissible by an injunction, usable by S, that is no lower in the hierarchy of injunctions than any other injunction usable by S and appropriate to Code C.

Injunctions:

0.   An act that would produce no less happiness than any alternative act is enjoined as permissible.

1.   An act that would produce no less expected happiness than any alternative act is enjoined as permissible.

2.   An act which is at least as likely as any alternative to produce no less happiness than any alternative is enjoined as permissible.

3.   An act whose worst possible outcome would produce no less happiness than the worst possible outcome of any alternative act is enjoined as permissible.

4.   An act prescribed by a local plan is enjoined as permissible if adding the local plan to the agent's master plan would produce no less expected happiness than not adding it.

5.   An act is enjoined as permissible if it would produce at least the satisfactory amount of happiness.

6.   It is enjoined as permissible never to kill an innocent person.

7.   It is enjoined as permissible never to take the property of another person without her consent.

8.   It is enjoined as permissible never to shake an infant.

9.   It is enjoined as permissible never to carry scissors point first.

10.   Unless you are in the military or the police, it is enjoined as permissible to never point a gun at another person.

.

.

.

N.   Every act is enjoined as permissible.

In stating this new Pragmatic theory I've replaced the term "decision-guide" with the term "injunction," since within the context of this theory the norms in question are intended to govern the moral status of actions in addition to functioning as decision-guides. For the same reason I've replaced the terms "choice-worthy" and "choice-mandated" with such terms as "enjoined as permissible." But what do these new terms mean in the context of the Splintered Pragmatic theory? They don't mean "prescribed as permissible," since an act might be enjoined by an injunction without being the act enjoined by the highest usable injunction, and only an act enjoined by the highest usable injunction qualifies under Code C as truly permissible. Here again, as in the case of the Hybrid theory, we'll have to say that the normative status assigned by these injunctions to an action is merely provisional, and has no moral significance (and no moral residue) unless the injunction in question is the highest usable one.

Unfortunately for the Pragmatic theory, the new Splintered version fails to meet the distinctive Pragmatic demand that principles of moral status be universally usable in the extended sense by every agent. Earlier in this chapter I argued that the Hybrid approach cannot require that the decision-guide that determines an act's subjective status be usable in the extended sense. A Pragmatic theorist who insists that a "usable" injunction must mean an injunction "usable in the extended sense" would run into the very same difficulties that led to the rejection of a parallel requirement in the case of Hybrid theories. It appears, then, that the Splintered Pragmatic theory, whatever its other virtues, would insist only at its peril on maintaining the core demand of the Pragmatic theorist that a moral theory's theoretical account of right and wrong be usable in the full extended sense.

There is another pressing issue for this type of Pragmatic theory. In the original statement of Hybrid act utilitarianism, Code C* states that relative to Code C and to the credences of agent S, an act A is subjectively right for S to perform if and only if it is prescribed as choice-worthy by a decision-guide, usable by S, that is no lower in the hierarchy of choice-worthiness decision-guides than any other choice-worthiness decision-guide usable by S and appropriate to Code C. The hierarchy of decision-guides in Code C* does not include every conceivable decision-guide: it includes only those *appropriate to Code C*. A standard is implicitly invoked that determines which decision-guides are appropriate, and further determines which decision-guides rank higher than others in the hierarchy. In later chapters we will look more closely at what the content of this standard is. But clearly the standard evaluates candidate decision-guides by reference to Code C itself. A decision-guide that is appropriate to a Rossian Hybrid theory is not necessarily appropriate to Hybrid act utilitarianism, and vice versa. Identifying a suitable standard of this sort for Hybrid theories will not necessarily be easy. But at least it is clear that the job of the standard is to assess decision-guides with respect to the governing account of objective right and wrong. This is what provides an important unity to the moral theory as a whole, and underlies the rationale for which decision-guides are to be included and how they are to be ranked. The decision-guides are not mere appendages independent of the account of right and wrong, but instead are importantly justified by reference to it.

This particular justificatory structure is not available in the new Splintered Pragmatic theory. So far it simply consists of a Code C that instructs the agent to perform an action prescribed by one of a list of highly varied injunctions which themselves are not unified by any central theme or master principle. It is difficult to imagine, without smuggling back in an illicit Code C# higher than Code C, what qualifies one injunction for inclusion and another for exclusion from the list, or what rationale justifies the rank-ordering of injunctions within the list. This seems to me potentially a devastating flaw in the proposed Splintered Pragmatic theory.

The Pragmatic theorist is not wholly without resources to address this problem. For example, if he has a utilitarian bent, he might claim that the individual injunctions are justified and rank-ordered by their effects on welfare when used: the highest-ranked injunctions have the most salutary effect, while lower-ranked injunctions have less salutary effects. It's not fully clear how to work out the details of such an appeal to effects on welfare. Should we consider the effects on welfare of (say) Injunction 1 by considering what effect it would have if all agents tried to employ it? Or should we consider the effects on welfare if it were used only by those agents able to use it? However this idea might be filled in, carrying it out would clearly impose an insurmountable epistemic burden on the theorist (or agent) trying to establish the rank-ordering of different candidate injunctions. He would have to know far more about the nonmoral facts, including facts about how agents would act when trying to apply the candidate decision-guides, than an agent merely trying to figure out what act is best to do in his particular circumstances. This strategy seems doomed by the same kinds of epistemic barriers that we've now seen many times.[32]

Even if the appeal to effects on welfare might attract a Pragmatic theorist with a utilitarian bent, clearly it wouldn't be appropriate for a Pragmatic theorist with a deonto-logical bent. He would not find it appropriate to justify the inclusion of injunctions, or their rank-ordering, merely by appealing to their effects on welfare. But this deontologically inclined Pragmatic theorist might try a different approach. He might argue that, as we've seen already, any non-ideal Pragmatic theorist must acknowledge that the deontic merit of his theory can be assessed by comparing the content and assigned weights of the principles in his theory to those of what I called the "deontically perfect code" in Chapter 6. The deontically perfect code may fall short in terms of its usability, but in purely deontic terms it cannot be surpassed: the perfect code is the

---

[32] Our earlier consideration of Splintered Pragmatic approaches, in Chapter 4, examined them as responses to the problem of error alone, and noted that no agent suffering from the problem of error would be in a position to believe what principle within a Splintered theory she ought to use, since she would not believe herself to be caught in the problem of error.

The new Splintered Pragmatic theorist might respond to the problem raised in the text by arguing that neither he nor the agent need to be able to identify the injunction that *would have* the best effects on welfare. Instead they could merely aim to identify the injunction that *is likely to have* the best effects on welfare. But this tactic simply amounts to permitting the agent and theorist, when doing meta-ethics, to appeal to decision-guides in a covert Hybrid theory to guide their choices of the subjectively right injunction. If it is acceptable for them to appeal to decision-guides in selecting injunctions, it should also be acceptable for the agent to appeal to a decision-guide when trying to decide what action is subjectively right to perform.

one the Pragmatic theorist would make universally usable if he could do so by waving a magic wand. Since there is no such wand, the Pragmatic theorist is willing to accept reduction in deontic merit of his theory in order to achieve greater usability. At this juncture the deontologically inclined advocate of the Splintered Pragmatic theory might say that for his theory the deontically perfect code serves a role somewhat similar to that of the first-tier Code C in a Hybrid theory. The standard for evaluating injunctions of the Splintered Pragmatic theory would judge their appropriateness relative to the deontically perfect code. Even though the deontically perfect code does not provide the account of objective moral status, and so does not qualify as a Code C in the sense of a true Hybrid theory, nonetheless it provides the master principle that unifies the multitude of injunctions, and helps provide the rationale for why these, rather than other candidates, are the correct injunctions.

This is a possible strategy on the part of the advocate for this type of Splintered Pragmatic theory. But at this point it seems to me he has won a battle but lost the war: there is no longer any significant distinction between his Splintered Pragmatic theory and a full-fledged Hybrid theory. Although the advocate of the Splintered Pragmatic theory may decline to describe the deontically perfect code as providing the theoretical account of objective moral status, in fact it is hard to see how else to understand what its function is. My conclusion is that a Splintered Pragmatic theory cannot take this sort of inspiration from the Hybrid theory without losing its soul as a distinctive approach to the problems of error and uncertainty. And we've already seen that the Splintered approach cannot secure the Pragmatist's Holy Grail: a theory of right and wrong that is usable in both the core and the extended sense by every agent.

11.8 Conclusion

I have now outlined my proposal for a Hybrid solution to the problems of error and uncertainty. Such a system can only provide guidance to the broadest possible range of agents if it incorporates numerous decision-guides in its decision-guiding tier Code C*. Whether or not a given decision-guide is usable by a given agent depends on that agent's epistemic situation. Only by including a multiplicity of decision-guides, variously usable by agents with differing epistemic grasps on their situation, can such a system offer guidance to every agent, no matter how excellent or impoverished or faulty the agent's epistemic grasp of her situation, or how limited her computational powers for manipulating her information. These decision-guides are arranged in a hierarchy which prioritizes on deontic grounds the guides that are best to use in cases where an agent can use more than one guide in deriving a prescription. The system includes a theoretical account of right and wrong (Code C) that prescribes acts as objectively obligatory, together with a general decision-guiding principle (Code C*) that prescribes as subjectively obligatory the act recommended as choice-mandated by the decision-guide, usable in the core sense by the agent, that is higher in the hierarchy of choice-mandating decision-guides than any other decision-guide usable by the agent and appropriate to Code C.

But this is only a sketch of the proposed Hybrid solution. Important questions remain to be addressed. Does the proposal satisfy the four desiderata that theorists seeking usability in a moral theory require? Does it satisfy the criteria of adequacy set out in section 10.1 of Chapter 10? What standard determines the appropriateness and rank-ordering of decision-guides relative to a given theoretical account of objective moral status? What decision process must an agent be able to go through in order to count as "indirectly" using Code C, via utilizing some decision-guide from Code C*, to make her decision? Does the Hybrid solution itself still require too much knowledge on the part of the decision maker? There are other major issues to be settled as well. In Chapter 12 we will begin addressing these questions.

12

Developing the Hybrid Solution

Our Science is a drop, our ignorance a sea.[1]

Chapters 9, 10, and 11 sketched the major outlines of the Hybrid solution to the problems of error and uncertainty. According to this solution, a comprehensive moral theory must have two tiers. The top-tier code consists of the theoretical account of what makes actions right and wrong. The lower-tier code consists of the recommendation to follow the prescription of the highest usable decision-guide from an array of decision-guides designed to enable any decision maker, however impoverished her nonmoral information, to make a decision. To do so, she uses the theoretical account indirectly by applying an appropriate lower-tier decision-guide to her choice. Thus act utilitarianism, as an account of what makes actions right and wrong, would be supplemented by a variety of appropriate decision-guides such as "An act that has greater expected utility than any alternative act is choice-mandated" and "An act which is more likely than any alternative to produce the greatest amount of happiness is choice-mandated." The moral theory is designed so that agents whose uncertainty prevents them from applying the theoretical account of right and wrong will be able to apply at least one of these other decision-guides in order to make a decision appropriate to the values of act utilitarianism.[2]

But important details of this solution remain to be worked out, and questions about its adequacy remain to be answered. Work on these tasks will begin in this chapter. Because carrying out these tasks is complex, the work will stretch into Chapter 13. As we shall see, devising an acceptable version of the Hybrid solution is not the walk in a park that many of its advocates have supposed.

---

[1] James (1895), p. 17.
[2] In cases in which the agent believes of some act that it has the right-making feature required by the top-tier code, then she can make a decision either by reference to the top-tier code (in which case she directly applies the top-tier code), or by reference to Decision-Guide 0, which mirrors the content of the theoretical account of right and wrong but recommends the act as choice-worthy (in which case the agent applies the top-tier code indirectly). In cases in which the decision-guide used by the agent does not mirror the content of the theoretical account of right and wrong, the agent can apply the theoretical account of right and wrong only indirectly.

12.1   Indirect Use of a Top-Tier Code or Principle

At various points I have described an agent facing uncertainty who applies one of the lower-tier decision-guides in making a decision as "indirectly" applying the top-tier code (or one of its principles). But what is required for this to be true?

12.1.1   Indirect inferences

Suppose Ned, who believes that some act A would have greater expected utility than any other option available to him, applies the expected utility rule to his decision, and so derives a prescription to perform act A. Does Ned thereby count as applying act utilitarianism indirectly in making his decision? From the information I have provided so far, we cannot conclude that Ned is indirectly applying act utilitarianism as a theory of objective moral status. Ned might believe, for example, that the expected utility rule just *is* the objective account of right and wrong—he might be following Zimmerman's "Prospectivism" rather than act utilitarianism.[3] In this case he would correctly understand himself to be *directly* applying his top-tier code, not indirectly applying act utilitarianism. Or suppose instead he applies a rule requiring him not to say something that will probably deceive his audience. Since this rule might be an appropriate decision-guide either for act utilitarianism or for a Rossian deontological theory, from the information given we cannot infer *which* theoretical account of right and wrong he is attempting to indirectly follow merely from the fact that he utilizes this decision-guide to make his decision.

Clearly, for an agent to use a decision-guide as a way of indirectly applying a given theoretical account of right and wrong, the agent must have some appropriate belief about the relationship between the decision-guide and the theoretical account, and must employ the decision-guide because of that relationship. Consider an agent Jason who believes act utilitarianism to be the correct theoretical account of objective right and wrong, believes the expected utility rule to be the highest appropriate decision-guide relative to act utilitarianism that he can presently use, and chooses to derive a prescription from the expected utility rule in order to do what is subjectively right relative to act utilitarianism. In this scenario Jason certainly counts as a clear-cut case of "indirectly" applying act utilitarianism in deciding what to do.[4]

---

[3] Zimmerman (2008). If Ned formulates his prescription carefully, for example as "Act A would be subjectively obligatory," then we would know he is not attempting to follow Prospectivism, which would issue a prescription that A is objectively obligatory (in my terms, not in Zimmerman's terms). But most agents will not formulate their derived prescriptions in such precise terms.

[4] Broome (2014) argues that following a rule in reasoning does not necessarily require an agent to *believe* that she ought to follow that rule. On his account, although sometimes an agent might believe she ought to follow a certain rule, on most occasions to follow a rule is rather to manifest a disposition to behave in a particular way, and for this behavior to seem right to the agent, which itself simply involves having a disposition to be ready to accept correction (p. 632). Even if Broome's account is correct, there is an important difference between the disposition of Jack, who is directly following Prospectivism, and the disposition of Jason, who is indirectly following act utilitarianism, in each case by following the rule to maximize expected utility. This difference would have to be spelled out. Those who find Broome's view on

But must we require *any* agent who counts as indirectly applying a theoretical account of right and wrong to go through an inferential process like Jason's? Part of the issue here has to do with what concepts or terms are available to the agent. In this book I have introduced and defined various technical concepts, such as the concept of a two-tier code, the concepts of objective and subjective rightness, and the concepts of an option being choice-mandated, choice-worthy, or choice-forbidden. Ideally readers of this book will come to possess these concepts. But these concepts are certainly not included in the conceptual repertoire of the ordinary layperson, and still less in the repertoire of those children and cognitively impaired agents who nonetheless qualify as moral decision makers. In fact we need not require an agent to have or deploy these technical concepts in order to qualify as applying her moral theory indirectly. Thus consider the reasoning used by Sharon, who wants to do what act utilitarianism requires of her. She thinks "The right thing for me to do is to act in a way that would produce the most happiness, but I'm uncertain which of my options would do this. Given my uncertainty, it appears that the most reasonable thing for me to do, relative to my moral theory, is to perform the act that seems most likely to produce the greatest happiness." Sharon thinks in terms of what is "most reasonable relative to my moral theory," but it appears that her thought process should count as indirectly applying act utilitarianism in her decision. We need not require her to deploy the technical concepts or the terminology I have used in formulating the Hybrid solution. Her concepts and thought process are close enough. From Sharon's case we can see that what qualifies as indirect use of a moral theory should be understood with a good deal of flexibility: there is a broad range of thought patterns by which an agent counts as indirectly using an account of right and wrong to guide her decision via some intermediate decision-guide.

Reflection on these cases suggests how we might define what it is to be able to use a moral code indirectly in making a decision. In Chapter 11 I argued that an agent, in deciding how to act in a given situation, must derive a *positive* prescription—that is, a prescription for what would be subjectively right or subjectively obligatory for her to perform. It is not enough for her to derive a prescription for what it would be subjectively wrong for her to perform, since that leaves her in the position of knowing[5] what she ought to avoid but not what it would be acceptable or required for her to do. Thus

---

this question attractive can substitute the agent's having a special kind of disposition for what I shall describe as "the agent's having a belief that such-and-such a rule is the highest appropriate decision rule relative to the governing moral theory." What I am arguing is that something special of this sort must be present for the agent to count as indirectly applying the moral theory. An agent who is uncertain whether a certain rule is an appropriate decision-guide for her moral theory is (in Broome's terms) someone who lacks the relevant disposition. The dispositions in question must have a cognitive basis: we're not talking here about mere nerve- and muscle-based dispositions, such as might underlie one's disposition to kick when the doctor taps one's knee.

[5] Here, and elsewhere, for reasons of style I will use the term "know" to mean simply "believe," rather than to have a true belief that meets all the conditions for knowledge.

ability to use a moral code to make a decision must involve having the ability to derive a prescription for an act that is subjectively right or subjectively obligatory. Given this, we need to define the indirect usability of a moral code in terms of the indirect usability of its positive principles for subjective rightness and subjective obligation. We can start with definitions of indirect ability to use objective principles of rightness and obligation to guide a decision.

> **Definition 12.1. Ability to indirectly use an objective principle of moral rightness in the core sense to decide what to do:** An agent S who is uncertain at t_i which of the acts she could perform (in the epistemic sense) is prescribed by P, a principle of objective rightness, is able at t_i to indirectly use principle P in the core sense to decide at t_i what to do at t_j *if and only if*:
>
> (A) S believes at t_i of some act A that S could perform A (in the epistemic sense) at t_j;[6]
> (B) There is some decision-guide DG_x such that
>
> > (1) DG_x is directly usable in the core sense by S to decide at t_i what to do at t_j,
> > (2) DG_x is no lower in the hierarchy of choice-worthiness decision-guides than any other choice-worthiness decision-guide usable by S and appropriate to Code C, and
> > (3) DG_x prescribes at least one act as choice-worthy for S at t_j;[7] and
>
> (C) If and because S wanted all-things-considered to use principle P indirectly for guidance at t_i for an act performable at t_j, and if and because she believed of some DG_y (not necessarily identical to DG_x) that there is no higher-ranked choice-worthiness decision-guide (relative to P) usable by her at t_i, then
>
> > (1)   she would come to believe of act A that it is prescribed as choice-worthy for performance at t_j by DG_y, and
> > (2)   her beliefs[8] together with this desire would lead S at t_i to derive a prescription for A as subjectively right for her relative to P.

The definition for ability to indirectly use an objective principle of moral obligation is similar:

> **Definition 12.2. Ability to indirectly use an objective principle of moral obligation in the core sense to decide what to do:** An agent S who is uncertain at t_i which of the acts she could perform (in the epistemic sense) is prescribed by P, a principle of objective obligation, is able at t_i to indirectly use principle P in the core sense to decide at t_i what to do at t_j *if and only if*:

---

[6] Technically this clause should be stated in terms of "act-type A" rather than "act A." To simplify exposition I will henceforth use "act A."

[7] For full accuracy this definition would need a further clause B.4 to accommodate the situation in which one highest-level decision-guide prescribes an act as choice-worthy while another decision-guide of equal rank prescribes an act as choice-worthy or as choice-mandated.

[8] We should understand "her beliefs" in this and subsequent definitions to refer to the beliefs described in previous clauses of this definition, but for brevity I will not state this qualification.

(A)   S believes at t_i of some act A that S could perform A (in the epistemic sense) at t_j;
(B)   There is some decision-guide DG_x such that
    (1) DG_x is directly usable in the core sense by S to decide at t_i what to do at t_j,
    (2) DG_x is the highest choice-mandating decision-guide usable by S and appropriate to Code C, and
    (3) DG_x prescribes an act as choice-mandated for S at t_j;[9] and
(C)   If and because S wanted all-things-considered to use principle P indirectly for guidance at t_i for an act performable at t_j, and if and because she believed of some DG_y (not necessarily identical to DG_x) that it is the highest-ranked choice-mandating decision-guide (relative to P) usable by her at t_i, then
    (1)   she would come to believe of act A that it is prescribed as choice-mandated for performance at t_j by DG_y, and
    (2)   her beliefs together with this desire would lead S at t_i to derive a prescription for A as subjectively obligatory for her relative to P.

Definitions 12.1 and 12.2 merge a requirement (in clause B) that there be an appropriate positive decision-guide that is directly usable by the agent, together with a requirement (in clause C) that if the agent wanted to be guided by the objective principle, she would derive a prescription from some decision-guide that she believes to be the most appropriate one relative to that principle. Given the problems we saw with Feldman's single-principle version of the Hybrid solution, we need to include clause B to ensure that it is not just the case that the agent believes of some decision-guide that it provides suitable guidance as a way of applying her objective moral principle, but also that there be such a decision-guide, even though the agent uses a different one.

Using these definitions we can now propose a definition for what it is to have the indirect ability to use an objective moral code to decide what to do.

Definition 12.3.   Ability to indirectly use an objective moral code in the core sense to decide what to do: An agent S is able at t_i to indirectly use objective Code C in the core sense to decide at t_i what to do at t_j *if and only if* S is able at t_i to indirectly use one of Code C's principles of objective rightness or objective obligation in the core sense to decide at t_i what to do at t_j.

Applying this definition to Jason and Sharon, we can see that each agent qualifies under Definition 12.3 as having the ability to use act utilitarianism indirectly, since it is true for each agent that (a) he or she wants to use act utilitarianism in determining what to do, (b) there is some choice-mandating decision-guide (for Jason, the guide prescribing the act that would maximize expected utility, and for Sharon, the guide prescribing

---

[9] For full accuracy this definition would need a further clause B.4 to accommodate the situation in which more than one positive decision-guide of equal rank (and higher than any alternative decision-guide) each prescribe the same act as choice-mandated.

the act most likely to produce the most happiness) that is the highest such decision-guide usable by that agent, (c) he or she believes (using his or her own terminology) of some decision-guide that there is no higher-ranked choice-mandating decision-guide usable for this decision, (d) he or she believes of some performable act that it is prescribed by this decision-guide, and (e) if and because the agent has these beliefs and desires, he or she derives a prescription for an action as subjectively obligatory (or has the equivalent beliefs in the agent's own terminology). If an agent has the ability to use act utilitarianism directly, then she also qualifies as having the ability to use it indirectly, because she would be in a position to indirectly derive a prescription from act utilitarianism by invoking Decision-Guide 0, which mirrors the content of act utilitarianism itself.

Definitions 12.1 and 12.2 give an account of ability to indirectly use a moral principle *in the core sense* to guide a decision. This means that S counts as having the ability to indirectly apply P in the core sense even if she is mistaken about her ability to perform A, or mistaken in believing that act A is prescribed as choice-worthy (or choice-mandated) by a decision-guide than which there is no higher-ranked guide usable by her. This parallels our earlier Definition 2.1 of an agent's ability in the core sense to directly apply a moral principle. According to Definition 2.1, an agent has this ability even if she would be mistaken in believing of some act that she could perform it, or mistaken in believing that the principle actually prescribes that act. As we saw in section 11.6 of Chapter 11, just as an act can fail to be objectively obligatory even though the agent believes it is objectively obligatory, so too an action can fail to be subjectively obligatory even though the agent believes it is subjectively obligatory. An agent who believes, erroneously, that her objective moral principle prescribes act A, still qualifies as able—in the core sense—to use her moral principle directly to guide her decision. Similarly, an agent who believes, erroneously, that there is no higher decision-guide usable by her than the one she uses in deriving a prescription for act A, and who therefore concludes that it is subjectively right for her to perform A, still qualifies as someone who is able—in the core sense—to indirectly use her objective moral principle.

Note that Definitions 12.1 and 12.2 do not require the agent to have a belief that some action is prescribed as choice-worthy (or choice-mandated) for performance by the highest-ranked decision-guide (relative to P) usable by her at t_i *before* she sets out to derive a prescription indirectly from P. It's possible that she would only come to have the relevant belief after she forms the desire to derive such a prescription and begins considering the matter. Using a principle indirectly to make a decision appears to be a several-step process that takes more time than simply using a principle directly to make a decision. For this reason in each of these definitions clause C.1 is stated in terms of what the agent *would come* to believe, rather than in terms of what she *does* believe.

Slight alterations in Definitions 12.1, 12.2, and 12.3 would provide definitions of an agent's ability to indirectly use a principle in the extended sense. These alterations would chiefly involve stipulating that the agent's relevant beliefs are true. However, since I have argued in Chapter 11 that we cannot hope to find moral principles that are usable by every agent in the extended sense, I will not take the opportunity to spell out such definitions in detail.

Definitions 12.1 and 12.2 state the matter in our terminology, but as we saw in the case of Sharon, agents may represent the matter to themselves using different terminology or concepts. Note also an important difference between these definitions of ability to use a principle indirectly and our original Definitions 2.1 and 2.4 of what is required for an agent to have the ability (in either the core or the extended sense) to *directly* use a moral principle to guide a decision. According to Definitions 2.1 and 2.4, an agent can have the ability to directly use a moral principle P without having any moral beliefs, and in particular without believing that principle P is correct or even being aware of principle P. Thus, according to Definitions 2.1 and 2.4, an agent can have the ability to directly use the Ten Commandments in making a decision even though the agent believes the Commandments are an erroneous account of right and wrong, or even though, having been raised as a Buddhist, the agent may be completely unaware of the Commandments. However, the new Definitions 12.1, 12.2, and 12.3 entail, through clause C, that an agent can apply a moral principle indirectly only if she has (or would come to have in her reasoning process) certain moral beliefs. It is still the case that the agent need not believe that the relevant Code C is correct. But Definition 12.1 implies (for example) that she must believe (or come to believe) about the act in question that it is prescribed as choice-worthy for performance at t_j by a decision-guide than which there is no higher-ranked choice-worthiness guide (relative to P) usable by her at t_i. Her salient moral belief is the belief that there is no higher-ranked usable decision-guide than the one from which she derives the prescription. Whether or not it is appropriate to require an agent to have such a moral belief, in order to have the ability to use an objective principle P indirectly, is a question to which we'll return in section 12.2.

12.1.2 Beliefs based on the advice of others

It's worthwhile pausing briefly to consider agents whose inferential decision-making processes involve complicating factors. Consider another agent, Yuri, who wants to do what is right according to act utilitarianism but is uncertain which act this is. Yuri follows the guidance of some moral advisor, who simply tells him that given his uncertainty about what act utilitarianism requires him to do, and his desire to comply with it, it would be right for him to perform act A. Yuri takes the sage's advice and does A. Should Yuri count as indirectly using act utilitarianism to make his decision?

This depends on the further details of the case. If Yuri interprets the advisor to mean "Act A is the act that is objectively right according to act utilitarianism," then Yuri may be seeing the advisor's suggestion as compelling evidence that A is objectively right. In this case Yuri comes to believe that A is objectively right, and counts as directly using act utilitarianism to make his decision (or as indirectly using it, via Decision-Guide 0).

If instead Yuri interprets the advisor to mean "A is choice-worthy according to the highest-ranked decision-guide, relative to act utilitarianism, usable by you (Yuri)," then Yuri may be seeing the advisor's suggestion as compelling evidence that A is subjectively right for him. In this case Yuri comes to believe that A is subjectively right for him. But suppose Yuri has no idea what particular decision-guide prescribes A: he just knows that the advisor tells him that A is prescribed by the highest-ranked decision-guide that he can use. Then Yuri doesn't count according to Definition 12.1 as having the ability to use act utilitarianism indirectly to derive a prescription, since he doesn't satisfy clause C. It's false of him that "If and because he wanted all-things-considered to use principle P indirectly for guidance at t_i for an act performable at t_j, and if and because he believed of some DG_y (not necessarily identical to DG_x) that there is no higher-ranked choice-worthiness decision-guide (relative to P) usable by him at t_i, then (1) he would come to believe of act A that it is prescribed as choice-worthy for performance at t_j by DG_y, and (2) his beliefs together with this desire would lead him at t_i to derive a prescription for A as subjectively right for him relative to P." Yuri doesn't have the relevant belief about any DG_y (even though he believes there is some such DG_y). Nonetheless, it seems as though, by virtue of the existence of a usable decision-guide and by virtue of the advice of his advisor, he should be counted as having the ability to use act utilitarianism indirectly. What seems crucial is that if he wanted to make a decision appropriate for act utilitarianism, he would come to believe of a particular act that it is subjectively right according to act utilitarianism. He doesn't need to have beliefs about all the details that might make this true.[10]

To secure this we can reject Definition 12.1 and instead adopt the slightly less demanding Definition 12.1.1:

Definition 12.1.1.   Ability to indirectly use an objective principle of moral rightness in the core sense to decide what to do: An agent S who is uncertain at t_i which of the acts she could perform (in the epistemic sense) is prescribed by P, a principle of objective rightness, is nonetheless able at t_i to indirectly use principle P in the core sense to decide at t_i what to do at t_j *if and only if*:

(A)   S believes at t_i of some act A that S could perform A (in the epistemic sense) at t_j;

(B)   There is some decision-guide DG_x such that

  (1) DG_x is directly usable in the core sense by S to decide at t_i what to do at t_j,

---

[10] This position may seem inconsistent with the position I took in section 2.3 of Chapter 2. There I argued that Randy, who is told by a moral sage that the Categorical Imperative prescribes act A, does not qualify under Definition 2.1 as having the ability to use the Categorical Imperative directly, because he has no idea what the content of the Categorical Imperative is, and in particular has no belief that act A would have the relevant property of *being in accord with a maxim that the agent could at the same time will that it become a universal law*. However, we can now see that Randy has the ability to use the Categorical Imperative *indirectly*, since he can reason from it to a prescription for act A via a decision-guide "It is choice-worthy to act on the advice of a moral sage." Yuri only qualifies as having the ability to use utilitarianism indirectly because there is some decision-guide he could use directly to derive a prescription. However, he is not required to know what the content of this decision-guide is. The beliefs that are required shift when we shift from direct to indirect use of a principle.

(2)   DG$_x$ is no lower in the hierarchy of choice-worthiness decision-guides than any other choice-worthiness decision-guide usable by S and appropriate to Code C, and

(3)   DG$_x$ prescribes at least one act as choice-worthy for S at t$_j$; and

(C)   If and because S wanted all-things-considered to use principle P indirectly for guidance at t$_i$ for an act performable at t$_j$, then

(1)   she would come to believe of act A that it is prescribed as choice-worthy for performance at t$_j$ by a decision-guide than which there is no higher choice-worthiness guide (relative to P) usable by her at t$_j$; and

(2)   her beliefs together with this desire would lead S at t$_i$ to derive a prescription for A as subjectively right for her relative to P.

According to this definition Yuri, in the scenario in question, counts as having the ability to indirectly use act utilitarianism as an indirect guide, since he would infer that act A is subjectively right for him, even though he has no inkling about the content of the decision-guide that prescribes it. Definition 2.1.1 still requires that there be a usable decision-guide that prescribes a choice-worthy act for the agent, and that the agent believe this. He need not, however, correctly identify this decision-guide, or know what its content is.

A similar emendation would produce the parallel less-demanding Definition 12.2.1 for moral obligation.

Definition 12.2.1.   Ability to indirectly use an objective principle of moral obligation in the core sense to decide what to do: An agent S who is uncertain at t$_i$ which of the acts she could perform (in the epistemic sense) is prescribed by P, a principle of objective rightness, is nonetheless able at t$_i$ to indirectly use principle P in the core sense to decide at t$_i$ what to do at t$_j$ *if and only if:*

(A)   S believes at t$_i$ of some act A that S could perform A (in the epistemic sense) at t$_j$;

(B)   There is some decision-guide DG$_x$ such that

(1)   DG$_x$ is directly usable in the core sense by S to decide at t$_i$ what to do at t$_j$,

(2)   DG$_x$ is the highest choice-mandating decision-guide usable by S and appropriate to Code C, and

(3)   DG$_x$ prescribes an act as choice-mandated for S at t$_j$; and

(C)   If and because S wanted all-things-considered to use principle P indirectly for guidance at t$_i$ for an act performable at t$_j$, then

(1)   she would come to believe of act A that it is prescribed as choice-mandated for performance at t$_j$ by the highest choice-mandating decision-guide (relative to P) usable by her at t$_j$; and

(2)   her beliefs together with this desire would lead S at t$_i$ to derive a prescription for A as subjectively obligatory for her relative to P.

We've looked at two different accounts on how Yuri might interpret his advisor's statement that it would be right for him to perform act A. A third possibility is that Yuri interprets the advisor to mean "A is deemed choice-worthy by the highest-ranked decision-guide, relative to act utilitarianism, usable by me (the advisor)." Yuri must decide what to do with this information. It might be reasonable for Yuri to think that A's being choice-worthy according to the highest decision-guide usable by the advisor provides evidence that A is likely to be objectively right.[11] But he still needs a decision-guide to derive a prescription from the fact that A is likely to be objectively right. Perhaps he uses this evidence to apply the decision-guide "An act which is at least as likely as any alternative to produce no less happiness than any alternative is choice-worthy," and conclude from this that A is subjectively right. But there is also the possibility that he uses a hitherto unremarked decision-guide that says "An act that is recommended by a knowledgeable advisor is choice-worthy." Indeed, in the two previous interpretations of Yuri's case (in the first of which Yuri interprets the advisor as recommending the act as objectively right, and in the second of which he interprets the advisor as recommending the act as subjectively right for Yuri), I described Yuri as simply accepting the advisor's testimony as compelling evidence and acting directly on this evidence. But alternatively he could view the advisor's testimony as less-than-compelling evidence which only partially supports the view that act A is objectively or subjectively right. In these alternative cases he would still need to invoke a decision-guide, since he thinks there's some chance the evidence from the advisor's recommendation may not be correct. In these alternative cases, Yuri could also derive a prescription by invoking the new decision-guide saying that moral advice from knowledgeable advisors is choice-worthy. In any of the cases in which Yuri's thought process involves invoking this new decision-guide as the highest-ranked one that is usable by him, he counts under Definition 12.1.1 as indirectly using act utilitarianism.

12.1.3 Unconscious beliefs

Another complicating factor is the nature of the beliefs that are required in the agent's inferential process. According to Definition 12.1.1 (ability to use a principle of objective rightness indirectly in the core sense) and its cousins, an agent has the ability to use a moral principle indirectly only if she has certain nonmoral beliefs, such as the belief that an act A is one she could perform. Similarly earlier Definitions 2.1 and 2.4 (definitions of the ability to directly use a moral principle) require an agent to have certain nonmoral beliefs about her prospective actions. I raised the question in Chapter 2 whether these beliefs can be unconscious or need to be conscious. There I suggested that unconscious beliefs should be allowed, so long as they would play the appropriate causal role in the agent's deriving a prescription from the principle if she wanted to derive one. Although I don't wish to take a definitive stand on this

---

[11] There is yet another possibility: Yuri might interpret the advisor's statement as evidence that A is likely to be subjectively right (not objectively right). This kind of case will be examined later.

issue, the same considerations suggest that we should also say that a process of deriving a prescription from a moral principle should count as indirectly deriving a prescription from the principle even if the agent's relevant nonmoral beliefs are unconscious.

Definition 12.1.1 and its cousins also imply that the agent has the ability to use a moral principle indirectly only if she has (or would come to have) a certain *moral* belief, for example the belief about a certain act that it is prescribed as choice-worthy for performance at t_j by a decision-guide than which there is no higher-ranked guide (relative to P) usable by her at t_i. Does an agent satisfy these definitions if the relevant moral belief is unconscious? Again, although I don't wish to take a definitive stand on this issue, one can imagine cases in which it would be highly plausible to count an agent having merely unconscious moral beliefs as indirectly applying the governing theory of right and wrong. Suppose, for example, that Crystal believes in a deontological theory much like Ross's, in which there are multiple principles of prima facie moral status, one of which prohibits breaking promises and another of which requires compensating others for wronging them. Crystal realizes that in driving through a crowded parking lot she may have scraped another person's car, and also thinks that if she stops to investigate, she may be late in submitting a promised report to her boss. Crystal is faced with a situation in which she must choose between (a) stopping to investigate, which is likely to involve breaking a promise but also likely to lead to compensating someone if she has wronged that person, and (b) not stopping to investigate, which is likely to involve keeping an important promise but also somewhat likely to lead to failing to compensate someone she may have wronged. She consciously believes that failing to compensate another driver is worse than breaking her promise. She also has several unconscious beliefs: that in cases of uncertainty it is wisest to do what is most likely to be right, and that stopping to investigate is most likely to be right. Without any reasoning of which she is consciously aware, she promptly concludes she should stop to investigate whether she scraped the other car. If she carries out an unconscious reasoning process that carries her from her avowed moral theory via her unconscious moral beliefs to the conclusion she should stop to investigate, I find it highly plausible that we should count her as indirectly applying her moral theory. Many cases of moral reasoning in the face of uncertainty probably have much this character, and I shall assume that we may characterize these agents as indirectly applying their moral theories.

Of course in many cases this train of reasoning will have become compressed through habit, just as decision-making about the standard maneuvers involved in driving a car becomes compressed through habit. A novice driver of a manual shift car may originally go through a process involving a series of conscious thoughts: "A tight curve is coming up. With my right foot I should press the brake pedal. Then with my left foot I should apply the clutch, and then downshift as the car slows down." But as the driver becomes more used to driving the car, he will perform these maneuvers out of habit, without any conscious thought about their appropriateness. Similarly it seems quite possible that "novice" moral agents applying a theoretical account of right and wrong in cases of uncertainty may start out with a conscious train of thought involving rehearsal of the moral theory, conscious consideration of which decision-guide would be most appropriate in the current circumstances and whether it is usable, and finally conscious derivation of a prescription for action from the selected decision-guide. However, as such agents repeatedly encounter certain types of situations and utilize the same decision-guides over and over, this thought process may become so compressed that it becomes unconscious. Indeed it seems likely that the separate steps involved in the process disappear altogether in such repetitive uncertainty cases, and experienced agents simply go directly from an awareness of certain moral issues to decisions about what to do.[12] But so long as this ingrained process arises from the right history, it seems appropriate to count such agents as indirectly applying their moral theory, via what they regard as an appropriate decision-guide, to their choices.

A choice emanating from a set of unconscious beliefs is one about which questions can often be raised. Suppose an employee reports her co-worker as stealing company property. Did the employee choose to report her co-worker for theft of company property because she believes stealing is wrong, or did she report the co-worker because she is jealous of his professional success and hopes to derail his career? It may be difficult, or impossible, for outsiders or even for the agent herself to know what actually motivated her action. Perhaps both motives played a role. But the difficulty of pinning down what actually happened shouldn't undermine the appropriateness of counting actions which genuinely arise from moral commitments as decisions guided directly or indirectly by the agent's moral theory.

12.2 A Deeper Look at Beliefs about the Highest Usable Decision-Guide

In section 12.1.1 I described a case in which the agent Jason believes the expected utility rule to be the highest appropriate decision-guide, relative to act utilitarianism, that he can presently use, and from it derives a prescription for action. But clearly agents who have such beliefs can be mistaken. Moreover, agents can be uncertain which decision-guide is highest. Let us look at these situations in turn.

12.2.1 False beliefs about the highest usable decision-guide

Consider Carol, also an act utilitarian, who explicitly formulates and derives a prescription for an act A from the decision-guide recommending that she perform an act which is at least as likely as any alternative to produce no less happiness than any alternative act. Carol believes this decision-guide is the highest one she can use.

---

[12] See Kruglanski and Gigerenzer (2011). For a report of an action which seems to embody this phenomenon, see Goodman and Santora (2013). In this article the action of a plumber who rescued a woman from an out-of-control taxi about to hit her is described as follows: "Before [the plumber] could even stop to think, he swept [the woman] out of the way. 'I came over, and I grabbed one girl,' he said. 'It just happened too fast.'"

Suppose Carol makes a mistake in deriving her prescription for act A. Were we correct to accept a definition for indirectly using a moral principle in the core sense that implies Carol indirectly uses act utilitarianism in the core sense in deciding what to do? Or should we reject this definition as unhelpful, because she selects an act that is not recommended for her?

Carol's mistake might have arisen from either or both of two kinds of false belief. Suppose she has compared the expected utility rule and the at-least-as-likely-to-produce-no-less-happiness rule in the past, and concluded erroneously that the second of these rules is superior to the first. Then she has a straightforwardly false *moral* belief—she is mistaken about the relative merits of these two decision-guides. Alternatively we can imagine that Carol has a false nonmoral belief—the false belief that act A is no less likely than any alternative to produce no less happiness than her alternatives. Recall our statement in Hybrid act utilitarianism of Code C* in Chapter 11:

> **Code C*:**   Relative to Code C and to the credences of agent S, an act A is subjectively right for S to perform if and only if it is prescribed as choice-worthy by a decision-guide, usable by S, that is no lower in the hierarchy of choice-worthiness decision-guides than any other choice-worthiness decision-guide usable by S and appropriate to Code C.

This definition implies that the act Carol chooses, act A, is not subjectively right. Either the decision-guide she employs is not the highest-ranked one she was able to use, or the act she chooses is not prescribed by the decision-guide she employs. Thus Carol does what is subjectively wrong (unless she's lucky). Nonetheless Definition 12.1.1 implies that Carol indirectly uses act utilitarianism in the core sense to guide her choice. I think we are correct to accept a definition of "indirect use" that has this implication.

One piece of evidence for this arises from the fact that there is a close, albeit complicated, connection between subjective rightness and blameworthiness. That connection seems to be appropriately maintained by the implication of Definition 12.1.1 in Carol's case. If her mistake about the relative merits of the two decision-guides is non-culpable, or in the alternative case her mistaken belief that A is choice-worthy according to her selected decision-guide is non-culpable, then we should conclude (other things being equal) that Carol is not to blame for performing an act that is subjectively wrong. She non-culpably believed that it was subjectively right (or had an equivalent belief expressed in her terms), and chose it for that reason, so we should not blame her for acting as she did, even if her act is subjectively wrong (as well as objectively wrong).

Assessing Carol as able to use her moral theory indirectly in the core sense (despite her false beliefs) parallels our assessment of an agent as able to use a moral theory directly in the core sense, despite her false beliefs. Such an agent can derive a prescription (possibly an erroneous one) from the moral theory, and similarly Carol can indirectly derive a prescription (possibly an erroneous one) from her moral theory. Just as the definition of using a moral theory directly in the extended sense addressed agents with false beliefs about what actions are prescribed by their moral theory, so a definition (not stated) of using a moral theory indirectly in the extended sense would address agents who have the relevant false beliefs. Agents with false beliefs, such as Carol, may qualify as able to use the theory indirectly in the core sense, although not in the extended sense. In any contexts where true beliefs seem important, we could utilize the concept of ability to use a theory in the extended sense. However, for assessing agents' blameworthiness and creditworthiness, ability in the core sense seems to be the appropriate concept.

12.2.2 Uncertainty about the highest usable decision-guide

Consider another scenario. Suppose Damien, like Crystal, has accepted a Ross-like deontological theory. He promised his wife to do a family errand on the way home, but can't remember whether he promised to pick up the dry cleaning or buy new diapers. He can't contact his wife, and doesn't have time to do both errands. He considers what decision-guide is best to follow in such a situation, and considers two possible rules:

(a) When you are uncertain whether you promised to do A or promised to do B and can't do both, doing A is choice-mandated if the expected deontic value of A is greater than the expected deontic value of doing B.

(b) When you are uncertain whether you promised to do A or promised to do B and can't do both, and you think doing A is most likely to be what you promised, A is choice-mandated.

Damien believes that one of these decision-guides is superior to the other, but is uncertain which is superior. He also believes that decision-guide (a) mandates buying the diapers, but that decision-guide (b) mandates picking up the dry cleaning, and he further believes he could do what each of these decision-guides recommends. What should he do?

It's important to distinguish Damien's case as just described, in which he is uncertain which decision-guide is highest, from a different kind of case, in which Damien believes (say) that decision-guide (a) is highest but is uncertain what concrete act is recommended by decision-guide (a). The remedy for this latter kind of case is for Damien to reject decision-guide (a) as unusable and instead invoke some alternative decision-guide that he can use. If Damien isn't certain what act is recommended by decision-guide (a), then that decision-guide *is not usable by him*. The subjectively right act for him is the one recommended by the highest *usable* decision-guide, not the act recommended by the highest guide. He needs to abandon decision-guide (a), and turn to the highest guide he can actually use. The multi-rule Hybrid solution's technique for dealing with this situation is one of its great advantages.

But what should we say about the original Damien case, in which he is uncertain whether decision-guide (a) or (b) is higher in the hierarchy? Damien's uncertainty could have either of two sources. The first possible source of Damien's uncertainty is uncertainty which decision-guide satisfies the relevant standard for assessing guides. Suppose he believes, for example, that the correct decision-guide is the one that would be used by a virtuous agent, but is uncertain whether the virtuous agent would use decision-guide (a) or (b). This form of uncertainty is a form of moral uncertainty, since Damien is uncertain which decision-guide is best, although it arises because Damien suffers from *non*moral uncertainty—he is uncertain which decision-guide would be used by the virtuous agent. Similarly, if Damien believes that the correct decision-guide is the one most likely to bring about the largest number of objectively right acts over the long run but isn't sure which decision-guide has this property, he may suffer from nonmoral uncertainty about which decision-guide meets this standard. But his nonmoral uncertainty generates a moral uncertainty about which decision-guide is best.

The second possible source of uncertainty is lack of certainty about what normative standard should be used in ranking decision-guides. Damien might be uncertain, for example, whether to rank decision-guides in terms of their likelihood to bring about the largest number of objectively right acts over the long run, or in terms of their being the decision-guide that would be used by a virtuous agent. This kind of uncertainty is a straightforward form of moral uncertainty. Damien may know what standard to use in judging the objective moral status of individual actions, but he isn't sure what standard to use in judging the relative normative status of decision-guides.

Recall our working definition of ability to indirectly use a principle of moral obligation:

Definition 12.2.1.   Ability to indirectly use an objective principle of moral obligation in the core sense to decide what to do: An agent S who is uncertain at t_i which of the acts she could perform (in the epistemic sense) is prescribed by P, a principle of objective rightness, is nonetheless able at t_i to indirectly use principle P in the core sense to decide at t_i what to do at t_j *if and only if*:

(A)   S believes at t_i of some act A that S could perform A (in the epistemic sense) at t_j;
(B)   There is some decision-guide DG_x such that
    (1) DG_x is directly usable in the core sense by S to decide at t_i what to do at t_j,
    (2) DG_x is the highest choice-mandating decision-guide usable by S and appropriate to Code C, and
    (3) DG_x prescribes an act as choice-mandated for S at t_j; and
(C)   If and because S wanted all-things-considered to use principle P indirectly for guidance at t_i for an act performable at t_j, then
    (1)   she would come to believe of act A that it is prescribed as choice-mandated for performance at t_j by the highest choice-mandating decision-guide (relative to P) usable by her at t_i; and
    (2)   her beliefs together with this desire would lead S at t_i to derive a prescription for A as subjectively obligatory for her relative to P.

Whether Damien's uncertainty arises from uncertainty which decision-guide is ranked highest by the relevant standard, or from his uncertainty about how to assess decision-guides, Damien does not qualify under this definition as able to indirectly use his moral principle in the core sense as a decision principle. He fails to satisfy clause C, since even though he wants to use his Rossian moral theory indirectly, his uncertainty renders both clause C.1 and clause C.2 false. Since the concept of subjective moral status was introduced to make moral theories indirectly usable by all agents, the fact that someone in Damien's position is unable to use his moral theory indirectly—even though the comprehensive form of a deontological code would include a vast array of decision-guides tailored to all the forms of nonmoral uncertainty agents may face—appears to be a severe setback to the Hybrid solution.

If some decision-guides are better than others—that is, are more highly ranked on deontic grounds—there must be some evaluative standard according to which a decision-guide is appropriate to a governing account of right and wrong, and according to which one guide is better than another relative to that account. Without trying to state at this point what the content of this standard is, we can recognize that agents may be uncertain what its content is: they may have no idea how to evaluate guides, or they may have some ideas about ways to evaluate guides, but be uncertain what the correct way is. (They may also have false beliefs about this, as we recognized in the case of Carol in section 12.2.1. However, false beliefs are not a problem for such an agent's ability in the core sense to indirectly apply a moral code to her decision, since this sense does not require true beliefs. Such an agent can derive a prescription from a decision-guide, even when she is mistaken that this decision-guide is superior to some other that is also directly usable by her.) Similarly, agents may be certain what the content of the relevant evaluative standard is, but be uncertain which decision-guide satisfies it. Writing on "moral ignorance" normally focuses on ignorance (or uncertainty) about which principle of objective rightness is correct, but the agents I have just described also suffer from forms of moral ignorance or uncertainty—in their case the uncertainty concerns the correct standard for evaluating decision-guides, or concerns which decision-guide is best according to the relevant standard.

Let's focus on the first type of case in which Damien is uncertain whether decision-guide (a) or (b) is correct because he's uncertain which guide satisfies the relevant standard. Just as the agent who is uncertain whether utilitarianism or Kantianism is correct cannot derive a prescription for action without some strategy for dealing with this kind of normative uncertainty, so Damien can't derive a prescription for action without some strategy for dealing with this new kind of normative uncertainty. Normative uncertainty at the level of decision-guides may be a more tractable problem than normative uncertainty about which of two rival accounts of right and wrong is correct. At least uncertainty of the kind Damien faces is uncertainty within a single framework of objective values, so the issue of comparing values (or deontic weights) across two theoretical frameworks may not arise. I argued in Chapter 3 that we should recognize that moral uncertainty whether a given moral theory is correct does not impede an agent's ability to make a decision using that theory directly, so long as it is true that if the agent wanted to make a decision using that theory, he would be able to derive a prescription from it.[13] Here we need to make a choice: does this form of uncertainty about which decision-guide is best prevent the indirect use of a governing moral code to make a decision? If so, then Damien is indeed unable to indirectly use his moral code, and Definitions 12.1.1 and 12.2.1 of indirect usability can stand. If not, we need to show why, and perhaps to find new definitions for indirect usability. In addressing this problem I will canvass three possible approaches to it. We need to assess the advantages and drawbacks of each of these approaches.

A. FIRST APPROACH: AS A CONDITION FOR INDIRECT USABILITY, DO NOT REQUIRE AN AGENT TO HAVE MORAL BELIEFS ABOUT WHICH DECISION-GUIDE IS CORRECT

The first approach to solving the problem that agents may be uncertain which decision-guide is best rejects the high bar set by a requirement that a moral principle qualifies as indirectly usable only if the agent has a belief about which decision-guide is best. Let us call this the "Low Bar" approach, since it sets a low bar for an agent's counting as having the ability to indirectly use a moral principle. There are substantial considerations in favor of this approach. To not require moral beliefs about the ranking of decision-guides is to treat moral uncertainty in the context of indirect usability in the same way we treated moral uncertainty in the context of direct usability—as no impediment to a principle's usability. It is true that in his actual circumstances Damien can't derive a prescription, even indirectly, from his moral principle, because he is uncertain what decision-guide is best for him to use in order to do so. But it is also true that *if* Damien believed that (say) decision-guide (a) were the highest usable decision-guide, he *would* derive a prescription indirectly from his moral principle by connecting it with the prescription he would derive from decision-guide (a). On this view it's sufficient that Damien would derive a prescription if he had the requisite normative information. One could argue that the truth of this counterfactual is sufficient to show the moral principle is indirectly usable for Damien. All that is required is that the agent has the requisite *non-normative* information. The vast array of decision-guides is constructed so that virtually any amount of non-normative information, however sparse or erroneous, will be sufficient.

Perhaps one way to conceptualize the Low Bar view is to recognize that a genuinely comprehensive moral code includes a multiplicity of different components: an account of what makes acts objectively right or wrong, an account of what makes acts subjectively right or wrong, a set of appropriate decision-guides that determine an act's choice-worthiness and so its subjective moral status, and also a standard for ranking the decision-guides relative to the account of objective moral status. When faced with nonmoral

---

[13] Note the difference between asking whether uncertainty whether Kantianism is correct impedes an agent's ability to *make a moral decision*, versus asking whether uncertainty whether Kantianism is correct impedes an agent's ability to *derive a prescription from Kantianism*. It is the latter question on which we are focused.

uncertainty, one can need beliefs about many or all of these components of a moral code in order to actually derive prescriptions for action, either directly or indirectly, from that code.[14] But it's coherent to claim that ability to use a moral code for guidance should not depend on having any of this information, either information about the content or status of the accounts of objective and subjective rightness, or information about the content and status of possible decision-guides that form part of the comprehensive theory, or information about the standards for assessing decision-guides. On this view, it's sufficient that one would derive a prescription *if* one had the requisite normative information and motivation.

If we accepted the view that an agent counts as having the ability to indirectly use a moral principle even though she may be uncertain which decision-guides are appropriate or most highly ranked, we would need to revise the definition of indirect usability along the following lines:

(Low Bar) Definition 12.2.2.   Ability to indirectly use an objective principle of moral obligation in the core sense to decide what to do: An agent S who is uncertain at t_i which of the acts she could perform (in the epistemic sense) is prescribed by P, a principle of objective obligation, is nonetheless able at t_i to indirectly use principle P in the core sense to decide at t_i what to do at t_j *if and only if*:

(A)   S believes at t_i of some act A that S could perform A (in the epistemic sense) at t_j;

(B)   There is some decision-guide DG_x such that

(1) DG_x is directly usable in the core sense by S to decide at t_i what to do at t_j,

(2) DG_x is the highest choice-mandating decision-guide usable by S and appropriate to Code C, and

(3) DG_x prescribes an act as choice-mandated for S at t_j; and

(C)   If and because S wanted all-things-considered to use principle P indirectly for guidance at t_i for an act performable at t_j, then

(1)   *if and because* she would come to believe of act A that it is prescribed as choice-mandated for performance at t_j by the highest choice-mandating decision-guide (relative to P) usable by her at t_i; then

(2)   her beliefs together with this desire would lead S at t_i to derive a prescription for A as subjectively obligatory for her relative to P.

---

[14] Some theorists might prefer to say that such an agent has a normative belief, but not a moral belief, about the status of the decision-guides. They might base this on the claim that the ranking of decision-guides is a matter of their rationality (relative to the governing moral theory) rather than their moral status. They view decision-guides as principles of rationality, rather than as moral principles. Since we still don't have enough information about the content or justification of the decision-guides to determine whether they are best viewed as principles of rationality or moral principles, we need to leave this question open. In the meantime, I will continue referring to them as moral principles. However, if they are instead principles of rationality, they could not be viewed as components of a comprehensive moral theory, but rather as components of a generic theory of normativity. In that case, accepting that an agent can have the ability to apply a comprehensive moral theory even though she lacks knowledge of the correctness of that moral theory would not automatically entail accepting that an agent can have the ability to apply the moral theory even though she lacks knowledge of the principles of rationality.

Both Definition 12.2.1 and Low Bar Definition 12.2.2 are definitions of core usability for a principle of moral obligation; they do not require true beliefs on the part of the agent. The only difference between the two definitions is the phrase "if and because" at the beginning of clause C.1 in the Low Bar definition. This implies that the agent counts as having the ability to use P indirectly, even though the agent might lack the moral beliefs necessary to reason from P to a prescription for action. All that is required is that *if* she had these beliefs, she would so reason. By contrast clause C.1 in the Expanded Moral Theory definition states that the agent *would* come to believe act A is prescribed if she wanted to use P.

According to Definition 12.2.2, Damien qualifies as able to use his moral theory indirectly in deciding what to do, even though he is uncertain whether decision-guide (a) or (b) is correct. Let's assume that decision-guide (a) ("When you are uncertain whether you promised to do A or promised to do B and can't do both, doing A is choice-mandated if the expected deontic value of A is greater than the expected deontic value of doing B") is the highest usable guide for Damien. It is true that if Damien wanted to use his Rossian theory indirectly, and if he believed of buying diapers that it is choice-mandated by the highest usable decision-guide, then he would derive a prescription for buying diapers as the subjectively obligatory act. Hence he qualifies under Definition 12.2.2 as able to indirectly use his moral code—even though in fact he is uncertain whether (a) is the highest usable guide.

By revising the definition of indirect usability in this way, we could accommodate an agent's uncertainty about which usable decision-guide is the most highly-ranked one. However, I think the Low Bar approach makes it far too easy for a moral principle to qualify as indirectly usable. Virtually any moral principle (so long as it is provided with decision-guides that are usable by the agent) will qualify as indirectly usable by virtually any agent, no matter how uncertain he is about the relevant ranking of the usable decision-guides. But just as it might be extremely difficult for an agent to ascertain the nonmoral facts necessary to directly apply a moral theory, so too it might be extremely difficult for him to ascertain which of the available and usable decision-guides is ranked highest, and thus extremely difficult for him to actually put his moral principle to indirect use in making a decision. His normative uncertainty about decision-guides seems to bar his way to *indirectly* using the moral principle in just the way that his nonmoral uncertainty barred his way to *directly* using the moral principle. While it is true that *if* he believed some decision-guide to be the best one, he would indirectly apply his moral theory by means of using that decision-guide, so too it is true that *if* he had the relevant nonmoral belief (for example, the belief that he promised to buy diapers), he would directly apply his moral theory to decide what to do. We don't take the latter fact to show that his moral theory is directly usable, and for similar reasons we shouldn't take the former fact to show that it is indirectly usable. The fact that there is some usable decision-guide that would be the best one for Damien to use is no genuine help to him as a decision maker, and seems to me hardly to satisfy our goal of solving the problem of uncertainty for moral codes.

Thus adopting the Low Bar view does not appear to provide a truly satisfactory solution to the problem of uncertainty. It would be better to avoid adopting this "solution" if we can find a workable solution that nonetheless requires the agent to have relevant credences about the ranking of available decision-guides.

B. SECOND APPROACH: AS A CONDITION FOR INDIRECT USABILITY, REQUIRE AN AGENT TO HAVE CREDENCES ABOUT WHICH DECISION-GUIDE IS CORRECT

An advocate of the second approach to solving the problem of the agent's uncertainty about the ranking of decision-guides dismisses the first approach as, in effect, conceding defeat. She insists that an agent only qualifies as having the ability to use a moral principle indirectly if the agent believes there is a suitable connection between the moral principle and an identifiable decision-guide that the agent can use. Thus the second approach rejects the Low Bar definition of ability to indirectly use a moral principle. It seeks definitions of the ability to indirectly use an objective moral principle that, like Definitions 12.1.1 (moral rightness) and 12.2.1 (moral obligation), require the agent to have credences regarding an appropriate link between the moral principle and a usable decision-guide. An advocate of this approach argues that our project can find inspiration in our earlier solution to the problem of nonmoral ignorance. That solution involved expanding a moral theory to include not merely an account of right and wrong, but also decision-guides usable by epistemically challenged agents. The job of these decision-guides is to provide tools within the moral theory that compensate for agents' lack of adequate nonmoral information. Using the same technique, we can find a solution to the problem of uncertainty about the moral status of those decision-guides by realizing that a *truly* complete moral theory must also include a whole new level of guides to assist agents impeded by this further type of uncertainty. The job of these new guides is to provide tools that compensate for agents' lack of adequate *moral* information about the first level decision-guides. This second approach, unlike the first, requires the agent to have relevant credences about the ranking of decision-guides. It aims to accommodate credences of this sort that fall short of full belief in a way that enables their agents to make decisions by expanding the resources within a comprehensive moral theory. Let us call this the "Expanded Moral Theory" approach. This approach attempts to define a *truly* comprehensive theory that is equipped to address uncertainty on the part of an agent about certain components of the theory itself,[15] not just address uncertainty about the nonmoral features of the prospective acts.

Building the truly comprehensive moral theory proceeds by analogy with the strategy for introducing decision-guides. We can think of the latter strategy as follows. We start with Code C, which prescribes acts as objectively right or wrong. This can be represented visually in Figure 12.1, in which the solid downward pointing arrow represents "prescribes."

---

[15] These components do not include Code C itself, the theoretical account of objective right and wrong.

Code C

Acts (objectively obligatory, right, or wrong)

Figure 12.1

When an agent is uncertain what features her available acts have, in order to make a decision she needs to substitute a more usable prescriptive guide for Code C. No single guide will do the job for all agents, so Code C needs to be supplemented with a group of such decision-guides. These in turn prescribe acts as choice-worthy.[16] This is shown in Figure 12.2.

Although we haven't said a great deal about it, clearly there is some normative standard that determines the appropriateness and rank-order of the decision-guides relative to Code C. Let us call this *Standard S₁*. It evaluates the objective ranking of decision-guides. Of course, which standard is appropriate may vary from theory to theory. The appropriate standard within a comprehensive utilitarian theory, for example, may be different from the appropriate standard within a comprehensive pluralist deontological theory. To fix ideas let's formulate this standard as follows:

Standard S₁: A decision-guide is objectively appropriate for Code C if and only if it has feature K, and it is objectively better relative to Code C than another decision-guide of the same class if and only if it has more K than the other guide.

One decision-guide is "of the same class" as another if they each recommend actions as choice-worthy, or each recommend actions as choice-mandated, or each recommend actions as choice-prohibited. Here "K" simply stands in for whatever feature of a decision-guide is deemed by Standard S₁ to affect the evaluation of decision-guides. Although I have stated Standard S₁ in terms of "more K than any other decision-guide," it is possible that it may take some quite different, non-maximizing, form. Standard S₁ is merely a stand-in for whatever standard is correct. According to it, if one guide has more K than another, the first is better than the second. An example of K might be "when the guide is adopted it produces acts that are right according to Code C," interpreted so that a decision-guide whose adoption leads to the performance of more

Decision-guides

Acts (choice-worthy)

Figure 12.2

---

[16] Or prescribe acts as choice-mandated or choice-prohibited. For brevity here and in subsequent formulations I shall not include this qualification.

Standard S_1

Decision-guides (ranking)

Acts (choice-worthy)

Figure 12.3

objectively right acts is objectively better, according to Standard S_1, than one whose adoption leads to fewer such acts.

Part of our theory's expanded structure can now be represented in Figure 12.3, in which the broken arrow represents "evaluates," while the solid arrow continues to represent "prescribes."

This figure depicts Standard S_1 evaluating decision-guides, which in turn prescribe acts as choice-worthy. In Chapter 11 we stated the relevant portion of Code C* for act utilitarianism as follows:

> **Code C*:**   Relative to Code C and to the credences of agent S, an act A is subjectively right for S to perform if and only if it is prescribed as choice-worthy by a decision-guide, usable by S, that is no lower in the hierarchy of choice-worthiness decision-guides than any other choice-worthiness decision-guide usable by S and appropriate to Code C.

Invoking Standard S_1 (and for simplicity ignoring issues about ties among decision-guides) we can now fill out this account of subjective rightness by saying that, within this form of act utilitarianism, an act is subjectively right just in case it is prescribed as choice-worthy by the decision-guide evaluated by Standard S_1 as objectively best among those that are usable by the agent.

As we've seen, the decision-guides objectively appropriate to act utilitarianism—that is, those that satisfy Standard S_1—might include the following examples. To shorten exposition, these are limited to those prescribing acts as choice-worthy. Only a small number of sample decision-guides are stated, here ranked from top to bottom as Standard S_1 might rank them. For brevity only the more abstract general-purpose decision-guides rather than the less abstract mini-maxims are included. However, we should not forget that the mini-maxims may be part of the arsenal of a comprehensive theory.

- Decision-guide DG_0: An act that would produce no less utility than any alternative is choice-worthy.
- Decision-guide DG_1: An act that would produce no less expected utility than any alternative is choice-worthy.
- Decision-guide DG_2: An act that is at least as likely as any alternative to produce no less utility than any alternative is choice-worthy.

- Decision-guide DG_3: An act whose worst possible outcome would produce no less utility than the worst possible outcome of any alternative is choice-worthy.
- Decision-guide DG_4: An act that would produce a satisfactory amount of utility is choice-worthy . . .
- Decision-guide DG_n: Every act is choice-worthy.

We can now restate the problem we're attempting to solve by describing it as arising from the fact that an agent such as Damien can be uncertain which usable decision-guide is evaluated as objectively best by Standard S_1. Such an agent needs to substitute *a more usable prescriptive guide in place of Standard S_1* (just as an agent, whose uncertainty which act would maximize utility makes her unable to apply Code C, needs to substitute a more usable prescriptive guide in place of Code C). For the same reasons that no single decision-guide can be substituted for Code C, no single guide will adequately substitute for Standard S_1. It follows that Standard S_1 needs to be supplemented with a group of such guides. To distinguish these guides from the original decision-guides (which prescribe acts), let us call the new guides "precepts." The precepts prescribe *decision-guides* as choice-worthy (or choice-mandated, or choice-prohibited). This is represented in Figure 12.4.

Of course, some precepts will be usable by a given agent while others will not. This means we should now say that a decision-guide is *subjectively* right if and only if it is prescribed as choice-worthy by the precept evaluated as objectively best among the precepts of the same class that are usable by the agent. Moreover, it seems clear that an *action* should count as subjectively right if it is prescribed by a decision-guide that is subjectively right. If an agent cannot identify the objectively right act, or even the act prescribed by the objectively best usable decision-guide, then her advisable course is to perform an action prescribed by the subjectively right decision-guide.

What is the content of these precepts? Here's a list of precepts that might be used in Truly Comprehensive Act Utilitarianism. Like Standard S_1 for which they substitute, these particular examples prescribe a decision-guide in view of its possession of K. However, just as decision-guides are more flexible than Code C in the appeal they make to the production of utility, so these precepts are more flexible than Standard S_1 in the appeal they make to the possession of K (and some precepts might not appeal to K at all, just as some decision-guides for act utilitarianism might not appeal to utility).

Precepts

Decision-guides (choice-worthy)

Acts (choice-worthy)

Figure 12.4

I have used precepts that mirror the content of the decision-guides themselves, but it's quite possible that their content would be rather different.

- Precept PRE_0: A decision-guide that has no less K than any other decision-guide is choice-worthy.
- Precept PRE_1: A decision-guide that has no less expected K than any alternative decision-guide is choice-worthy.
- Precept PRE_2: A decision-guide that is at least as likely as any alternative to possess no less K than any other decision-guide is choice-worthy.
- Precept PRE_3: A decision-guide whose worst possible outcome would possess no less K than the worst possible outcome of any other decision-guide is choice-worthy.
- Precept PRE_4: A decision-guide that possesses a satisfactory amount of K is choice-worthy...
- Precept PRE_n: Every decision-guide is choice-worthy.

To see how this expanded system works, consider a utilitarian agent Martha who wants to decide whether to donate a spare $50 to Oxfam or to Feeding America. She is uncertain which of these donations would produce the greatest utility, so she cannot directly derive a prescription from her Code C (or from DG_0). She is able to use either decision-guide DG_2 or DG_3 to select a subjectively right act, but (like Damien) is uncertain which of these guides is ranked objectively highest. In light of this, she needs to turn to precepts in order to select a subjectively right decision-guide. Suppose she understands PRE_3 to be the highest-ranked precept she can use, and suppose further that she would derive a prescription from PRE_3 for decision-guide DG_2. For her the act prescribed by DG_2 is then subjectively right. A parallel situation may hold for Damien, who wants to use a Rossian system rather than a utilitarian one.

It looks as though expanding Comprehensive Act Utilitarianism to include precepts for selecting subjectively right decision-guides is an important step towards equipping the moral theory to solve the problem faced by agents who are uncertain which decision-guide is best. However, we can see immediately that agents may be uncertain, not just about which decision-guide is best, but also about which precept is objectively best according to the standard for evaluating precepts. Let's call this *Standard S₂*, and state it as follows. As before, "feature M" simply stands in for whatever feature is deemed to make one precept better than another, and Standard S_2 may not take the maximizing form utilized here.

Standard S_2:   A precept is objectively appropriate for Code C if and only if it has feature M, and it is objectively better relative to Code C than another precept of the same class if and only if it has more M than the other guide.[17]

The relation between Standard S_2, precepts, decision-guides, and acts is depicted in Figure 12.5.

---

[17] Again, two precepts are "of the same class" if they both prescribe decision-guides as choice-mandated, or both prescribe decision-guides as choice-worthy, or both prescribe decision-guides as choice-prohibited.

Standard S_2

Precepts (ranking)

Decision-guides (choice-worthy)

Acts (choice-worthy)

Figure 12.5

In an expanded variant on Martha's case, she might be uncertain about which act maximizes utility, uncertain about which decision-guide is ranked objectively highest by Standard S_1, and also uncertain about which precept is ranked objectively highest by Standard S_2. The comprehensive moral theory needs to be augmented still further to equip agents facing uncertainty at this higher level. An agent who is uncertain what precept satisfies Standard S_2 needs to substitute a more usable prescriptive guide in place of Standard S_2. Just as no single decision-guide can be substituted for Code C or for Standard S_1, no single guide will adequately substitute for Standard S_2, so Standard S_2 needs to be supplemented with a group of such guides. To distinguish them from the original decision-guides and from precepts, we can call them "maxims." The maxims prescribe *precepts* as choice-worthy (or choice-mandated, or choice-prohibited). This can be represented in Figure 12.6.

Since not every maxim will be usable by every agent, we can say that a precept is subjectively right if and only if it is prescribed as choice-worthy by the maxim evaluated as objectively best among maxims of the same class that are usable by the agent. As before, it seems clear that an action should qualify as subjectively right if it is prescribed by a decision-guide that is prescribed as choice-worthy by a subjectively right precept.

Maxims

Precepts (choice-worthy)

Figure 12.6

A list of suitable maxims could include the following.

- Maxim MAX_0: A precept that has no less M than any other precept is choice-worthy.
- Maxim MAX_1: A precept whose use has no less expected M than any alternative precept is choice-worthy.

- Maxim MAX$_2$: A precept that is at least as likely as any alternative to possess no less M than any other precept is choice-worthy.
- Maxim MAX$_3$: A precept whose worst possible outcome would possess no less M than the worst possible outcome of any alternative is choice-worthy.
- Maxim MAX$_4$: A precept that possesses a satisfactory amount of M is choice-worthy…
- Maxim MAX$_n$: Every precept is choice-worthy.

Of course the maxims are also evaluated by a standard, which we can call *Standard S_3*. It might be stated as follows:

Standard S_3:   A maxim is objectively appropriate for Code C if and only if it has feature N, and it is objectively better relative to Code C than another maxim of the same class if and only if it has more N than the other maxim.

The relation between Standard S_3, maxims, precepts, decision-guides, and acts is depicted in Figure 12.7.

But just as an agent might be uncertain what precept is objectively best according to Standard S_2, so an agent might be uncertain which maxim is objectively best according to Standard S_3. The comprehensive moral theory needs to be augmented still further to equip agents facing uncertainty at this additional level. An agent who is uncertain what precept satisfies Standard S_3 needs to substitute a more usable prescriptive guide in place of Standard S_3. No single guide will adequately substitute for Standard S_3, so Standard S_3 too needs to be supplemented with a group of such guides. We can call guides at this level "counsels." The counsels prescribe *maxims* as choice-worthy. This is represented in Figure 12.8, which depicts the built-out theory as developed so far.

Figure 12.7

Counsels

Maxims (choice-worthy)

Precepts (choice-worthy)

Decision-guides (choice-worthy)

Acts (choice-worthy)

Figure 12.8

We could state possible counsels, as we have stated possible maxims, precepts, and so forth. However, it should now be clear where this line of thought is going. Since an agent might be uncertain which counsel is objectively best according to the relevant standard, that agent will need to substitute a more usable prescriptive guide in place of the standard for counsels. It is clear, then, that the built-out theory we have seen so far is only a portion of a theory capable of addressing all the levels of normative uncertainty that an agent might confront. We are looking at the possibility of an indefinite series of levels in the truly comprehensive theory, each level designed to enable agents make a decision despite their uncertainty about the adjacent level. For any given agent, however, she only needs to have beliefs about guides at the level she needs to resolve her uncertainty. Thus an agent who is certain which decision-guides are objectively best might never need to have beliefs about her theory's precepts, maxims, counsels, and so forth. However, the levels we have developed so far provide the recipe for how to extend the theory still further as necessary.

Gathering this all together, we can spell out the components of the expanded version of act utilitarianism as follows. Since the theory could include indefinitely many levels, this represents only a portion of the full theory (and, for brevity, includes only the norms covering rightness, not those covering obligation or wrongness).

1. **Truly Comprehensive Act Utilitarianism**
    A. **Principle action-evaluating norms**
        Code C: An act is objectively right if and only if it would produce no less utility than any alternative act.
        Code C*:   Relative to Code C and to the credences of agent S, an act A is subjectively right for S to perform if and only if it is prescribed as choice-worthy by a decision-guide, usable by S, that is no lower in the

hierarchy of choice-worthiness decision-guides than any other choice-worthiness decision-guide usable by S and appropriate to Code C.

B.   **Guide-evaluating norms**

Standard S_1:   A decision-guide is objectively appropriate for Code C if and only if it has feature K, and it is objectively better relative to Code C than another decision-guide of the same class if and only if it has more K than the other guide. [Precepts substitute for Standard S_1 in cases of uncertainty about the evaluations of S_1; being prescribed by the objectively highest usable precept makes a decision-guide subjectively right.]

Standard S_2:   A precept is objectively appropriate for Code C if and only if it has feature M, and it is objectively better relative to Code C than another precept of the same class if and only if it has more M than the other guide. [Maxims substitute for Standard S_2 in cases of uncertainty about the evaluations of S_2; being prescribed by the objectively highest usable maxim makes a precept subjectively right.]

Standard S_3:   A maxim is objectively appropriate for Code C if and only if it has feature N, and it is objectively better relative to Code C than another maxim of the same class if and only if it has more N than the other maxim. [Counsels substitute for Standard S_3 in cases of uncertainty about the evaluations of S_3; being prescribed by the objectively highest usable counsel makes a maxim subjectively right.]…

C.   **Guides**

Decision-guides

- Decision-guide DG_0: An act that would produce no less utility than any alternative is choice-worthy.
- Decision-guide DG_1: An act that would produce no less expected utility than any alternative is choice-worthy.
- Decision-guide DG_2: An act that is at least as likely as any alternative to produce no less utility than any alternative is choice-worthy.
- Decision-guide DG_3: An act whose worst possible outcome would produce no less utility than the worst possible outcome of any alternative is choice-worthy.
- Decision-guide DG_4: An act that would produce a satisfactory amount of utility is choice-worthy…
- Decision-guide DG_n: Every act is choice-worthy.

Precepts

- Precept PRE_0: A decision-guide that has no less K than any other decision-guide is choice-worthy.
- Precept PRE_1: A decision-guide that has no less expected K than any alternative decision-guide is choice-worthy.

- Precept PRE_2: A decision-guide that is at least as likely as any alternative to possess no less K than any other decision-guide is choice-worthy.
- Precept PRE_3: A decision-guide whose worst possible outcome would possess no less K than the worst possible outcome of any other decision-guide is choice-worthy.
- Precept PRE_4: A decision-guide that possesses a satisfactory amount of K is choice-worthy...
- Precept PRE_n: Every decision-guide is choice-worthy.

Maxims

- Maxim MAX_0: A precept that has no less M than any other precept is choice-worthy.
- Maxim MAX_1: A precept whose use has no less expected M than any alternative precept is choice-worthy.
- Maxim MAX_2: A precept that is at least as likely as any alternative to possess no less M than any other precept is choice-worthy.
- Maxim MAX_3: A precept whose worst possible outcome would possess no less M than the worst possible outcome of any alternative is choice-worthy.
- Maxim MAX_4: A precept that possesses a satisfactory amount of M is choice-worthy...
- Maxim MAX_n: Every precept is choice-worthy.

This is an example of the components of a truly comprehensive moral theory, a theory required to make it possible for agents to decide what to do when they are uncertain about the nonmoral nature of their options, or are afflicted by moral uncertainty about which decision-guide (or higher-level guide) is objectively best. A similar structure could be described for a truly comprehensive Rossian Hybrid theory.

The next step for the Expanded Moral Theory approach to solving agents' moral uncertainties is to see how the definition of ability to indirectly use a moral theory can be applied when the extensive resources of a truly comprehensive moral theory are available. That will be the first task of the next chapter.

12.3 The Second Form of Uncertainty about which Decision-Guide is Best

At this point we need to revisit an issue I raised briefly when introducing the case of Damien in section 12.2.2. Damien accepts a Ross-like deontological theory. He promised his wife to do a family errand on the way home, but can't remember whether he promised to pick up the dry cleaning or buy new diapers. He considers what decision-guide is best to follow in such a situation, believes of two guides that one is superior to the other, but is uncertain which is the superior one.

Up until this point we have been exploring how a moral theory can address uncertainty about the ranking of decision-guides when it arises from uncertainty about which decision-guide satisfies the relevant standard for assessing guides. We assumed Damien had no uncertainty about which standard is relevant. But we also briefly noted a second possible source for uncertainty about which decision-guide is superior: lack of certainty about what normative standard should be used in ranking decision-guides. Damien might be uncertain, for example, whether to rank decision-guides in terms of their likelihood to bring about the largest number of objectively right acts over the long run, or in terms of their being the decision-guide that would be used by a virtuous agent. This is a straightforward form of moral uncertainty. Damien may know what standard to use in judging the objective moral status of individual actions, but he isn't sure what standard to use in judging the objective normative status of decision-guides. Clearly, similar problems could arise for the higher-level standards S_2, S_3, and so forth as well.

It is not obvious that the solution we have developed to address an agent's uncertainty about which decision-guide is ranked highest by a known relevant standard also correctly addresses an agent's uncertainty about which standard is in fact relevant. This leaves an important gap in our treatment.

I view the issue of how to deal with this second type of uncertainty as still an open question waiting to be answered. One tempting possibility, of course, is that it could be addressed, like the form of uncertainty we have principally dealt with in this chapter, by adding layers of "guides" to the moral theory. My instinct, however, is to think that this would be a mistake. It would not be appropriate, for example, to address an agent's uncertainty about whether Ross's theory is the correct moral theory by adding some kind of decision-guide to Ross's theory itself. The question falls outside the moral theory about which the agent is uncertain. But the standards we have recognized (S_1, S_2, S_3, and so forth) as being part of the moral theory, are, just like Code C itself, norms governing the objective moral status of the items they evaluate. For example, Code C evaluates whether actions are objectively right, while Standard S_1 evaluates whether decision-guides are objectively right. The chief strategy that we have developed for dealing with uncertainty about nonmoral facts involves introducing a norm which supplements a norm of objective rightness by identifying which items are subjectively right relative to the norm of objective rightness. But this takes as fixed the norm of objective rightness. If an agent is uncertain which standard is correct for evaluating the objective rightness of decision-guides, his situation seems most analogous to the situation of an agent who is uncertain which Code C is correct. We need to reach outside the moral theory itself to advise this agent. The solution cannot be a component of the comprehensive moral theory itself.

If I'm correct about this, then stating a definition of indirect usability so as to deal in different ways with these two different forms of moral uncertainty about the ranking of decision-guides is far from a simple task. In view of my tentativeness about how to handle the second type of uncertainty, and in view of the likely complexity of this task, I shall not attempt to revise Definitions 12.2.1 and 12.2.2 (or any of their successors) to handle the second type of uncertainty in the manner I provisionally judge to be most appropriate. Nor shall I address the issue further. However, I will retain my background assumption that uncertainty about rankings that arises from uncertainty about which standard is correct should not render the agent unable to indirectly use her moral code, any more than uncertainty whether the code itself is correct renders her unable to use it.

12.4 Summary

In this chapter we have extended the development of the Hybrid approach to the problems of error and uncertainty. We began by looking at how to define the concept of an agent's ability to indirectly use an objective moral theory by selecting an action that is prescribed by a decision-guide appropriate to the theory. I discussed how such a definition should best handle agents who act on the advice of other agents, agents whose decisions involve unconscious beliefs, and agents who have false beliefs about which decision-guide is most appropriate. I argued that the appropriate concept of "indirect usability" is a concept of "indirect core usability," which does not require agents' beliefs about which decision-guide is best to be true. However, our first definitions of ability to indirectly use a moral theory (Definitions 12.1, 12.2, 12.3, 12.1.1, and 12.2.1) imply that an agent lacks this ability if she is uncertain which decision-guide is the best one for her to use. Since this situation is likely to occur, we saw that the Hybrid approach needs to address it.

I stated that I would describe three solutions to this issue. The first solution is the Low Bar approach, reflected in Definition 12.2.2, which rejects the demand that an agent must believe of some decision-guide that it is the highest-ranked guide that is usable for her, substituting the weaker demand that it merely be true of the agent that if she had such a belief and suitable motivation, she would derive a prescription from the governing moral theory via a decision-guide. I argued that the Low Bar approach makes it too easy for an agent to count as having the ability to indirectly use a moral theory's Code C even though she doesn't believe of any act that it fulfills that Code C, and even though she is uncertain which decision-guide would be the best usable one. In light of this we turned to a second approach, which involves retaining definitions of indirect usability closer in spirit to Definitions 12.1.1 and 12.2.1, and expanding the moral theory to include more levels of guides to assist decision-making when an agent suffers from uncertainty at higher levels than the original mere uncertainty about which act complies with Code C. Our investigation of the Expanded Moral Theory approach continues in Chapter 13.

13

Assessing the Hybrid Solution

...the mind boggles at the complexity.[1]

The core idea behind the Hybrid solution to the problem of uncertainty is that an objective moral principle qualifies as usable by an agent if the agent can use it, either by directly deducing a prescription from it, or by indirectly deriving a prescription from a decision-guide appropriate to that objective principle.[2] This solution advocates supplementing a theoretical account of what makes actions objectively right and wrong with an array of decision-guides that are appropriate for agents to use in deriving prescriptions indirectly from the theoretical account when they cannot derive a prescription directly from the account itself. In Chapter 12 we described an agent who indirectly applies a moral principle as someone who believes that her decision-guide is appropriate to use in connection with the principle. Thus it appears that a certain type of moral belief is necessary for an agent to use a moral principle indirectly: she should believe that the prescription she derives comes from the best decision-guide, relative to that principle, that she can use. Although many agents will be able to identify a decision-guide they believe has this property, other agents will be uncertain which decision-guide is best. According to our first Definitions 12.1, 12.2, 12.3, 12.1.1, and 12.2.1 of "ability to use a moral principle indirectly," those who are uncertain would not count as having the ability to use the moral principle indirectly. This would be a serious blow to the Hybrid solution, which attempts to make moral principles usable, at least indirectly, by every agent no matter how much uncertainty she labors under.

I said there are three approaches to rescuing the Hybrid solution from this problem. The first, the Low Bar approach, holds that just as an agent does not need to believe a given moral principle is correct to qualify as able to use it *directly*, so the agent does not need to believe of any decision-guide that it is best in order to qualify as having the ability to use its governing principle *indirectly*. To capture this sense of indirect usability, we introduced a revised definition, Low Bar Definition 12.2.2 of indirect usability. I argued,

---

[1] Keeney and Raiffa (1993), p. 17.

[2] In addition, according to Definition 12.2.1, the agent can indirectly use a moral principle P if the agent derives a prescription for an act that the agent believes is subjectively right relative to P, even though he himself does not derive this from an intermediate decision-guide.

however, that the Low Bar approach throws in the towel too soon, and that we should look for another approach that retains the requirement that the agent have some credence in the appropriateness of the decision-guide as a condition for indirect usability. We began this quest with the second approach to the problem: the Expanded Moral Theory view. This approach extends the original Hybrid solution by recognizing yet more components to the truly comprehensive moral theory—higher-level guides designed to allow an agent who is uncertain which decision-guide is objectively best to nonetheless select an action as the wisest one to perform relative to the moral theory. Such a truly comprehensive theory includes not just principles of objective and subjective rightness and decision-guides, but also precepts, maxims, and counsels, each designed to issue prescriptions for agents who suffer from some uncertainty arising at a lower level in the theory. A model comprehensive version of act utilitarianism was spelled out at the end of Chapter 12, along with the note that there is no principled limitation to the number of levels of guides it may contain.

Let us turn, now, to an assessment of whether the truly comprehensive moral theory genuinely enables any agent, no matter how deep her uncertainty, to use her moral theory indirectly.

13.1 Filling out the Expanded Moral Theory Approach

13.1.1 The decision-mandated act

In Truly Comprehensive Act Utilitarianism, only three types of norms directly ascribe moral status to actions: Code C, Code C*, and the various decision-guides. For example, Code C prescribes an act as objectively obligatory, Code C* prescribes it as subjectively obligatory, and the various decision-guides prescribe acts as choice-mandated or choice-worthy. Higher-level norms directly ascribe moral status, not to acts, but rather to decision-guides, precepts, maxims, and so forth. Nonetheless it is clear that prescriptions for actions are indirectly derivable from the higher-level norms such as Standard S_1. Standard S_1 directly evaluates certain decision-guides for their objective deontic standing, and those decision-guides directly prescribe actions as choice-mandated (or choice-worthy, or choice-forbidden). The action prescribed by the highest usable such decision-guide is subjectively obligatory. Thus Standard S_1 can be understood as *remotely* prescribing an act that is deemed choice-mandated by the objectively mandatory decision-guide.[3] Similarly, higher-level Standard S_2 directly evaluates certain precepts for their objective standing, those precepts directly prescribe certain decision-guides as choice-mandated (or choice-worthy, or choice-forbidden),

---

[3] Note that the terminology here can be slightly confusing. The "objectively *best*" decision-guide is the one that is deontically best (whether or not it is usable by the agent), whereas the "objectively *obligatory*" decision-guide is the one that is the deontically best decision-guide *that is usable by the agent*. Of course, since the actual prescription depends on the usability of the decision-guide, Standard S_1 does not all by itself prescribe an action.

and those decision-guides directly prescribe actions as choice-mandated (or choice-worthy, or choice-forbidden). The highest usable decision-guide prescribed by the objectively obligatory precept is itself subjectively obligatory. The action prescribed by the subjectively obligatory decision-guide can then be understood as subjectively obligatory (although it does not fit our official Definition 11.1 of "subjectively moral status"). Thus Standard S_2 too can be understood as remotely prescribing an act that is deemed choice-mandated by the subjectively obligatory decision-guide. Similarly, prescriptions for actions as subjectively obligatory are remotely prescribed—albeit through several links in a chain—by Standard S_3 and by its higher-level successors.

This feature of the comprehensive code implies that a number of agents may encounter decision situations in which several different acts are prescribed as subjectively obligatory: one act may be prescribed by the objectively obligatory decision-guide, a different act may be prescribed by the subjectively obligatory decision-guide, perhaps a third act is prescribed by the decision-guide prescribed by the subjectively obligatory precept, and so forth. To see this, consider an example in which utilitarian Martha has to decide whether to donate a spare \$50 to Oxfam, Feeding America, or CARE. She is uncertain which of these donations would produce the greatest utility. The objectively most highly-ranked decision-guide she can use is decision-guide DG_1, which states that an act that would produce the most expected utility is choice-mandated. She believes that donating to Oxfam would produce more expected utility than any alternative, so donating to Oxfam is subjectively obligatory for her. She could also use decision-guide DG_3, which states that an act whose worst possible outcome would produce more utility than the worst possible outcome of any alternative is choice-mandated. Suppose that giving to CARE would satisfy DG_3 but donating to Oxfam would not (although donating to Oxfam has the highest expected utility, its worst possible outcome would produce less utility than the worst possible outcome of giving to CARE). Thus donating to CARE is deemed choice-mandated by DG_3, while donating to Oxfam is deemed choice-mandated by the objectively higher DG_1.

Let us add further details to Martha's situation. Although Martha can use DG_1, let us assume she can't use Standard S_1 to evaluate the relative rankings of DG_1 and DG_3, so she is unsure which decision-guide is best, and so unsure which act is subjectively obligatory by our earlier official Definition 11.1. However, she can invoke a precept to tell her what to do in view of this uncertainty. Suppose that the objectively most highly-ranked usable precept for her is Precept PRE_2, which says that a decision-guide that possesses more K than any other decision-guide is choice-mandated. Suppose that decision-guide DG_3 (but not DG_1) satisfies PRE_2, so decision-guide DG_3 is subjectively obligatory for Martha to use.[4] Then DG_1 is not subjectively obligatory for her to use, even though it is selected by Standard S_1 as objectively obligatory. Thus donating to

---

[4] Recall that Precept PRE_2 is usable by Martha so long as she believes of some decision-guide that it has the property required by PRE_2. Her belief doesn't have to be correct; she could misidentify which decision-guide has this property. In this case her belief could be true.

CARE is directly deemed choice-mandated by DG_3 and remotely deemed choice-mandated by PRE_2, while giving to Oxfam is directly deemed choice-mandated by the objectively right decision-guide DG_1, but not remotely choice-mandated by PRE_2. In short, two rival acts—donating to Oxfam and donating to CARE—both are prescribed as choice-mandated and subjectively obligatory for Martha by Truly Comprehensive Act Utilitarianism. Donating to Oxfam is deemed choice-mandated by the objectively obligatory decision-guide, while donating to CARE is deemed choice-mandated by the subjectively obligatory decision-guide. This creates a dilemma: we need to identify which of these two choice-mandated acts is overall best for Martha to perform relative to her own credences. And we need to avoid recommending to Martha the subjectively obligatory act, as defined in Definition 11.1, in a case like this one in which she cannot make use of this recommendation (even though it emerges from the highest usable decision-guide) because her higher-level uncertainty leaves her uncertain which act is subjectively obligatory.

To do so we can introduce a new concept of "decision-mandatoriness" to be characterized in Definition 13.1 (which I envision as extended to include clauses similarly defining its cousins "decision-worthiness" and "decision-proscribed"). This definition makes use of the fact that a comprehensive moral theory provides us with an implicit hierarchy of the moral status of various decision-guides. What I will call the *highest* decision-guide in this hierarchy is the objectively obligatory decision-guide, while the second highest is the subjectively obligatory decision-guide. The third highest is the decision-guide prescribed by the subjectively obligatory precept; below that is the decision-guide remotely prescribed by the subjectively obligatory maxim; below that is the decision-guide remotely prescribed by the subjectively obligatory counsel; and so forth. Recall that for a decision-guide to qualify as either objectively or subjectively obligatory, it must be one the agent can use (see Code C* and Standard S_1). Clearly it is better for an agent to use a decision-guide that occurs higher in the moral status hierarchy just defined than to use one that occurs lower down.[5] Moreover, relative to her beliefs about the situation, it is better for her to use a decision-guide that is believed by her to fall in a rank in the hierarchy that is higher than the rank she accords to any rival decision-guide. This enables us to introduce an act's *decision-mandatoriness* in Definition 13.1.

Definition 13.1.   Decision-mandatoriness in the core sense: An act A is decision-mandatory (relative to a principle P of objective obligation) in the core sense at time t_i for agent S to perform at t_j if and only if:

(a)   S believes at t_i of A that S could perform A (in the epistemic sense) at t_j; and either

---

[5] Notice again the possibility for confusion here. A decision-guide that is prescribed at a higher level in the *moral status hierarchy* is better than one that is prescribed at a lower level in this hierarchy. Similarly a decision-guide that is deontically better than another decision-guide (according to Standard S_1) is *higher* in the *hierarchy of deontic value* than one that is deontically worse.

(b)   S believes of A that it is objectively obligatory according to P,[6] or

(c)   S is uncertain which act is prescribed as objectively obligatory according to P, but S believes of A that it is prescribed as choice-mandated by a decision-guide that is objectively obligatory,[7] or

(d)   S is uncertain which act is prescribed as objectively obligatory according to P, and S is uncertain which act is prescribed as choice-mandated by a decision-guide that is objectively obligatory; but S believes of A that it is prescribed as choice-mandated by a decision-guide that is subjectively obligatory, or

(e)   S is uncertain which act is prescribed as objectively obligatory according to P, uncertain which act is prescribed as choice-mandated by a decision-guide that is objectively obligatory, and uncertain which act is prescribed as choice-mandated by a decision-guide that is subjectively obligatory; but S believes of A that it is prescribed as choice-mandated by a decision-guide that is prescribed as choice-mandated by a precept that is subjectively obligatory, or

(f)   S is uncertain which act is prescribed as objectively obligatory according to P, uncertain which act is prescribed as choice-mandated by a decision-guide that is objectively obligatory, uncertain which act is prescribed as choice-mandated by a decision-guide that is subjectively obligatory, and uncertain which act is prescribed as choice-mandated by a decision-guide that is prescribed as choice-mandated by a precept that is subjectively obligatory; but S believes of A that it is prescribed as choice-mandated by a decision-guide that is prescribed as choice-mandated by a precept that is prescribed as choice-mandated by a maxim that is subjectively obligatory, or...

I shall view this definition as also including parallel clauses, here unstated, defining decision-worthiness and decision-prohibitedness in the core sense.

In effect Definition 13.1 handles the possibility of two or more acts being deemed choice-mandated for an agent by decision-guides endorsed at different levels in the comprehensive theory by giving priority to the prescription issued by the principle of objective rightness itself, or failing that, the prescription issued by the usable decision-guide that, given the agent's beliefs, is highest in the moral status hierarchy described above. Many acts may be choice-mandated for the agent according to the moral theory, but an act that qualifies as decision-mandated according to Definition 13.1 takes precedence over other choice-mandated acts that therefore fail to qualify as decision-mandated. The decision-mandated act is the one to be chosen. In cases where the

---

[6]   For completeness this clause should read "S believes of A either that is it objectively obligatory according to P, or that it is prescribed by DG_0 for P as choice-mandated." However, to simplify exposition I will suppress the clause referring to DG_0.

[7]   The long form of the definition would spell out details I have suppressed for ease of reading. Thus the long form of clause (b) would say "S believes of A that it is prescribed as choice-mandated by a decision-guide that is objectively obligatory relative to P for S at t_i." Similar details would appear in the long form of each of the other clauses.

agent is uncertain which act is prescribed by the governing moral principle, the decision-mandatoriness of an act A arises from the agent's belief that some decision-guide DG_x deems A to be choice-mandated, her belief that DG_x has a certain moral status relative to C, and her failure to believe about any act that it is deemed to be choice-mandated by a decision-guide that has higher moral status relative to C than the status of DG_x.

To be crystal clear, we should highlight the fact that although the decision-mandatoriness of an act depends on the agent's having certain credences, it does not depend on the agent's credences *about* the act's decision-mandatoriness. There is no circularity here, or lapse into the form of subjectivism that makes the moral status of an act depend on the agent's belief that it has that moral status.

To see how Definition 13.1 works in practice, consider Adele, who accepts a deontological theory that requires her to compensate others for injuries she has caused. She believes that she injured Adam, and that his injury would be fully compensated by a payment of $1,000. She further believes that her objective theory prescribes providing Adam with $1,000 so paying him $1,000 is decision-mandated for her by clause (b) of Definition 13.1. This case shows how the act believed by the agent to be objectively obligatory counts as decision-mandated under this definition. Note that I have adapted the concept of "core usability" for the definition of "decision-mandatoriness in the core sense." This means that providing Adam with $1,000 is decision-mandated for Adele even if her relevant beliefs are mistaken: her beliefs that she injured Adam or that the injury would be compensated by a payment of $1,000 may be false, and her belief that providing him with $1,000 is objectively obligatory may be false (perhaps he is unreachable so that she can't actually provide him with $1,000, or her theory instructs her to provide him with more than $1,000). Indeed, in the spirit of core usability, we should interpret Definition 13.1 so that it does not even require that act A be an act that the agent can perform; it can be a "merely possible" but not actually performable act. So long as she believes she can perform it, a "merely possible" act would count as decision-mandated. This seems correct, since an agent may deliberate about whether to perform a certain type of act, and needs guidance in this deliberation, even though her belief that she can perform it turns out to be false. We could construct a parallel definition for "decision-worthy in the extended sense" that requires true beliefs, but since this is not a notion we will need, I will not do so here.

Adele does not suffer from the problem of uncertainty about which act is objectively obligatory. But consider the case of Martha, the utilitarian who is uncertain which donation would produce the greatest utility. Suppose, in Case 1, a variant on the original Martha case, that she believes that DG_1 prescribes giving to Oxfam and that DG_3 prescribes giving to CARE, and she also believes that DG_1 is ranked higher than DG_3, and indeed is objectively obligatory for her to use, given her uncertainty about which act is objectively best. Then giving to Oxfam is decision-mandated for her according to clause (c) of Definition 13.1.

Consider a Case 2 involving Martha. In this case she is uncertain which of these decision-guides is objectively best. (She believes each of these decision-guides is usable, but is uncertain which is most highly ranked.) However, suppose she believes that decision-guide DG_3 is *subjectively* obligatory for her to use. Then giving to CARE is decision-mandated for her according to clause (d) of Definition 13.1. Note that Definition 13.1 is deliberately stated to imply that in neither Case 1 nor Case 2 are there two competing decision-mandated acts for Martha. In Case 1 clause (c) is satisfied, so giving to Oxfam is decision-mandated, but by virtue of clause (c)'s being satisfied, neither clause (d) nor any lower clause is satisfied, so giving to CARE is not decision-mandated. In Case 2 clause (d) is satisfied but clause (c) is not, so giving to CARE is decision-mandated but giving to Oxfam is not. In general an agent who satisfies a given clause in Definition 13.1 does not satisfy any lower or higher clause, so the problem of conflicting recommendations from different clauses for two alternative acts does not arise. (Of course in the case of decision-worthiness, it may sometimes happen that two alternative acts are equally good according to a single clause—each act is deemed choice-worthy but not choice-mandated by the highest-ranked decision-guide at that level, or each act is deemed choice-worthy or choice-mandated by two decision-guides that are themselves equally ranked. This is not a problem, since both of these acts are genuinely equally decision-worthy. It may also sometimes happen that an agent has contradictory beliefs that generate conflicting prescriptions. But in such a case the problem arises from the agent's contradictory beliefs, and should not be seen as a problem with the comprehensive moral theory itself.)

There could be an even more sophisticated version of Martha in a Case 3. In this case she is uncertain which decision-guide is objectively obligatory and also uncertain which decision-guide is subjectively obligatory, but she does believe that (say) decision-guide DG_4 is evaluated as choice-mandated by a precept that is subjectively obligatory, and that DG_4 prescribes donating to Feeding America. According to clause (e) of Definition 13.1, donating to Feeding America is the decision-mandated act for this highly sophisticated Martha.

We can ask how Definition 13.1 deals with a situation in which the agent does not fully believe of some act that she can perform it, although she has some credence that she can. Clause (a) of Definition 13.1 requires for an act A to be decision-mandated that the agent believes that she could perform A (in the epistemic sense). But what if an agent thinks of acts A, B, and C as "possible" options, but has a credence of only 0.8 that she can perform A, which she identifies as the morally best option if she can perform it? In such a case her options need to be reconceptualized: for her the options that might be decision-mandated are "trying to perform A," act B, and act C. Thus the genuine candidates for decision-mandatoriness of a military leader trying to protect his troops from an enemy assault may not be "Destroy the enemy attackers," "Call in air support," and "Surrender," but rather "Try to destroy the enemy attackers," "Call in air support," and "Surrender." "Trying to perform act A" may well be prescribed as choice-mandated by some decision-guide appropriate to account C, and be the best of the three alternatives, even though the agent has no certainty that he will succeed in actually doing A. Since the leader does believe that he can try to destroy the enemy attackers, this act (rather than "Destroy the enemy attackers") may be the decision-mandated act for him.

Several features of decision-mandatoriness in the core sense are worth remarking. First, because the truly comprehensive moral theory has an infinite number of levels, the definition of decision-mandatoriness must also have an infinite number of clauses. However, in itself this does not seem to be a pernicious form of infinite extension. Since any given clause is only needed to determine which act is decision-mandated for an agent in light of that agent's actual beliefs and uncertainties, the only levels that are needed are those that address some actual agent's levels of beliefs and uncertainties. Although the construction of Truly Comprehensive Act Utilitarianism provides a model from which we could extract an algorithm for constructing any clause at any level that is needed, there is no need to construct these unless an agent exists who has more levels of beliefs and uncertainties than those described in stated higher levels. It is unlikely that any agent exists who has the beliefs and uncertainties described in clause (e), much less that an agent exists who has even more sophisticated beliefs and uncertainties, so the capacity of Definition 13.1 to be extended indefinitely does not appear to be a serious concern.

In this connection we should expect that for most agents the decision-mandated act will be the one identified by clause (c) in Definition 13.1, that is, the act the agent believes to be prescribed as choice-mandated by the objectively obligatory decision-guide. The truly comprehensive moral theory will contain a great variety of decision-guides, sufficiently many and various so that for any agent, no matter how uncertain she is about the nonmoral properties of her prospective acts, there is some decision-guide that she can use to select an act.

This is reinforced by the fact that if all else fails, in the case of decision-worthiness (but not decision-mandatoriness) decision-guide DG_n recommends as choice-worthy any act that could be chosen at random. This can arise when the agent considers a list of decision-guides that she believes are appropriate candidates for using to evaluate actions, believes that each of these is more highly ranked than DG_n, but is unable to use any of these guides. For example, Cindy might believe that DG_2 and DG_4 are appropriate for evaluating acts' choice-worthiness, but have no idea which act satisfies either of these guides. She does believe, however, that the lowest-ranked guide appropriate for determining acts' choice-worthiness is DG_n, and she believes of some act A that it is deemed choice-worthy by DG_n. She isn't aware of any other decision-guides. She believes that A is prescribed as choice-worthy by a decision-guide that is objectively right, so act A is decision-worthy for her. Of course, if Cindy believes that some act B has a greater than 60 percent chance of producing no less expected utility than any alternative, then she could invoke an interpolated decision-guide $DG_{1.5}$, and act B will turn out to be decision-worthy for her. But if her credences don't support invoking any such intermediate decision-guide, then she can fall back on DG_n and choose any act at random as decision-worthy. She need not progress to any lower level in Definition 13.1, and it is clause (c) rather than clause (d) or any lower-level clause that determines what is decision-worthy for her. Lower clauses do not need to be invoked to address the case of such agents. This fact provides additional evidence for the view that the infinitely extension of clauses of Definition 13.1 is not necessarily a genuine problem.

It appears, then, that a comprehensive moral theory offers agents a generous array of resources for guiding their decisions even in the face of their uncertainties. Any agent who is aware of this may well have beliefs about what act is prescribed by the objectively obligatory or right decision-guide.

Although Definition 13.1 describes agents as having certain beliefs and certain kinds of uncertainties, here again it does not seem necessary that an agent's beliefs be phrased using precisely my terminology or my concepts. Recall Sharon, who wants to do what act utilitarianism requires of her. She thinks "The best thing for me to do is to act in a way that would produce the most happiness, but I'm uncertain which of my options would do this. Given my uncertainty, it appears that the most reasonable thing for me to do, relative to my moral theory, is to perform the act that seems most likely to produce the most happiness." Although Sharon doesn't use the terminology of "choice-mandated" or "decision-guide," she should surely count as someone who satisfies clause (c) of Definition 13.1, and the act that seems to her most likely to produce the most happiness should count as decision-mandated for her relative to act utilitarianism.

We can now see that we need to reframe the recommendation of a moral theory's Code C*. In Chapter 12 our earlier formulation of Code C* (for example, within Truly Comprehensive Act Utilitarianism) stated that an act A is subjectively right for S to perform if and only if it is prescribed as choice-worthy by a decision-guide, usable by S, that is no lower in the hierarchy of choice-worthiness decision-guides than any other choice-worthiness decision-guide usable by S and appropriate to Code C. But we can now see that some agents' uncertainties about the ranking of decision-guides will make them unable to follow the advice to perform the subjectively right action so defined. These agents should instead perform the *decision-worthy* action. Thus Code C* should be restated. To mark this change I will label this as Code**, and in line with our recent cases, phrase it in terms of subjective obligatoriness rather than subjective rightness.

>   **Code C**:**   Relative to an account C of objective obligation, an act A is subjectively obligatory at time t_i for agent S to perform at t_j if and only if A is decision-mandated (relative to C) in the core sense at time t_i for S to perform at t_j.[8]

Code C** incorporates, via clause (c) of Definition 13.1 of decision-mandatoriness, the previous recommendation to perform the action that is prescribed as choice-mandated

---

[8] This formulation includes the appropriate temporal indices, unlike the more abbreviated previous formulations of Code C*.

by the objectively right decision-guide, but it also incorporates recommendations for actions which qualify as decision-mandated by virtue of different clauses in Definition 13.1.

Of course, the full statement of Code C** would include parallel clauses for the subjectively right and the subjectively wrong action, as well as this clause covering the subjectively obligatory action. Notice that Code C** is very general; it can serve not only as a component of Truly Comprehensive Act Utilitarianism, but also as a general definition of an act's being subjectively obligatory, stated in Definition 13.1.1, which replaces earlier Definition 11.1.

Definition 13.1.1.   Subjective obligation: Relative to an account C of objective obligation, an act A is subjectively obligatory at time t_i for agent S to perform at t_j if and only if A is decision-mandated (relative to C) in the core sense at time t_i for S to perform at t_j.

Introducing the concept of decision-mandatoriness through Definition 13.1, and replacing Code C* with Code C**, which defines subjective obligation in terms of decision-mandatoriness, moves the Expanded Moral Theory view an important step forward: it provides the concept we need to define ability to use a moral theory indirectly in a way that can accommodate, not only agents' uncertainties about the non-moral properties of their prospective acts, but also their uncertainties about the moral properties of the decision-guides that may prescribe these acts.

We now need to consider whether we can propose a revised definition for "ability to indirectly use a moral theory" which, together with Definition 13.1 and the resources of truly comprehensive moral theories (including their versions of Code C**), makes it true that every plausible moral theory is such that every agent, no matter the depth of her uncertainty, can use that moral theory either directly or indirectly to guide her decision. If we can find a definition that has this upshot, we will have established that the Expanded Moral Theory view succeeds in solving the problem of agents' uncertainties about which of their possible decision-guides is best.

13.1.2 Redefining indirect usability

Our inquiry in this chapter was launched by the question of whether a moral code might be indirectly usable by an agent like Damien who can use each of two decision-guides, but is uncertain which decision-guide is superior. We hope to find a morally demanding account of indirect usability that (unlike Low Bar Definition 12.2.2) requires the agent to have appropriate credences about the moral status of available decision-guides. The availability of Definition 13.1 of decision-mandatoriness in the core sense suggests Definition 13.2, a new account of indirect usability modeled on Definitions 12.1.1 and 12.2.1.

Definition 13.2.   Ability to indirectly use a moral principle in the core sense to decide what to do: An agent S who is uncertain at t_i which of the acts she could perform (in the epistemic sense) at t_j is prescribed by P (a principle of objective moral obligation or rightness) is nonetheless able to indirectly use P in the core sense at t_i to decide at t_i what to do at t_j *if and only if*:

(A)   S believes at t_i of some act A that S could perform A (in the epistemic sense) at t_j;

(B)   There is some act X (not necessarily identical to A) that is decision-mandated or decision-worthy in the core sense for S at t_i, and

(C)   if and because S wanted all-things-considered to use principle P for guidance at t_i for an act performable at t_j, she would then come to believe about act A (in time to choose A for time t_j) that it is decision-mandated or decision-worthy in the core sense for her, relative to P.

For an agent to satisfy Definition 13.2, she must have several relevant normative beliefs. (Henceforward to avoid switching back and forth I shall phrase most examples in terms of "decision-mandatoriness," but the reader should understand that my remarks implicitly include cases of "decision-worthiness" as well.) For example, for there to be an act that is decision-mandated for her, she must have one of the beliefs specified by the clauses in the definition of "decision-mandatoriness": for example, she might believe of act X that it is prescribed as choice-mandated by a decision-guide that is objectively obligatory. Clause (C) stipulates that it must also be true of her that she would come to believe about A that is it decision-mandated for her. In short, she must come to believe there is a suitable normative link between her objective principle P and her selected act A. However, consonant with our approach to definitions of ability and to Definition 13.1 of decision-mandatoriness in the core sense, Definition 13.2 provides an account of ability in the core sense, which does not require the agent's beliefs to be true, or even require that any act A is genuinely performable by her.[9]

If A is decision-worthy but not decision-mandated, there may be some other act that is also decision-worthy. For example, the agent may believe of some other act that it is also deemed choice-worthy by the same decision-guide that evaluates A as choice-worthy, or may believe that A is deemed choice-worthy by some other decision-guide that is no lower in the deontic hierarchy of same-class decision-guides. Thus the agent's ability to indirectly derive a prescription for act A from P may render P indirectly usable, and yet the agent might not choose to do A even if she wanted all-things-considered to use P for guidance, because (for example) she might choose some other equally decision-worthy act. Hence Definition 13.2 can't require that S choose to perform A. But for P to count as indirectly usable, it needs to be the case that she would come to believe of at least one act that it is decision-mandated or decision-worthy.

To see how Definition 13.2 works in practice, recall Martha in Case 1. In this case Martha is uncertain which donation would produce the greatest utility. She believes

---

[9]   Again, in the spirit of core usability, we should interpret clause (B) in Definition 13.2, like Definition 13.1, so that it does not require that there is an actually performable act about which the agent has certain beliefs.

that DG_1 prescribes giving to Oxfam and that DG_3 prescribes giving to CARE, and she also believes that DG_1 is ranked higher than DG_3, and indeed is objectively obligatory for her to use. Then giving to Oxfam is decision-mandated for her according to clause (c) of Definition 13.1, and she also counts as believing that giving to Oxfam is decision-mandated. According to Definition 13.2, Martha qualifies straightforwardly as having the ability to use utilitarianism indirectly as a decision-guide. Martha's impediment to using utilitarianism to directly guide her decision is her uncertainty about which action would produce more utility than any alternative act, and her comprehensive theory provides a remedy for this impediment. Each comprehensive moral theory should contain an extensive number of decision-guides, each tailored to different kinds of nonmoral uncertainty that might impede decision makers. Thus most decision makers, like Martha in Case 1, will have the ability to use a given moral theory indirectly by virtue of their coming to believe, if they wanted to use that theory, of some act that it is decision-mandated or decision-worthy under clause (c) of Definition 13.1 (where they may conceptualize the status of this act using their terms, not necessarily using my terms). Note that according to Definition 13.2, Martha counts as having the ability to indirectly use utilitarianism, even though she may never have heard of utilitarianism, and even though she may not currently believe that DG_1 is the objectively highest-ranked decision-guide she can use. All that is required is that she would come in a timely way to have the relevant belief about some decision-guide if she wanted to use utilitarianism for guidance.

However, we were impelled to introduce the notion of "decision-mandated" in order to accommodate the situation of agents who, unlike Martha in Case 1, are impeded in using their moral theory for guidance, not merely by uncertainty about the nonmoral properties of their acts, but also by their uncertainty about which decision-guide is best (or even uncertainty about whether any decision-guide is objectively appropriate for their moral theory at all). These are the agents who, like Damien, must choose an act by descending to decision-mandatoriness as fixed by clause (d) or even some lower-level clause.

To see how Definition 13.2 helps in the case of Damien, let's recall his situation. Damien accepts a deontological theory. He promised his wife to do a family errand on the way home, but can't remember whether he promised to pick up the dry cleaning or promised to buy new diapers. Considering which decision-guide is best to follow in such a situation, he contemplates two possible rules:

(a)   When you are uncertain whether you promised to do A or promised to do B, doing A is choice-mandated if the expected deontic value of A is greater than the expected deontic value of doing B.

(b)   When you are uncertain whether you promised to do A or promised to do B, and you think A is most likely to be the one you promised, A is choice-mandated.

Damien believes that one of these decision-guides is objectively superior to the other, but is uncertain which is superior. He believes that decision-guide (a) mandates buying the diapers, while decision-guide (b) mandates picking up the dry cleaning, and he also believes he could do what each of these decision-guides recommends. Since Damien is uncertain which of these decision-guides is objectively superior, the original Definition 12.1 of "indirect use" implies that he is unable to apply his moral code indirectly, since he doesn't believe of any act that it is prescribed by the objectively highest-ranked decision-guide. However, the new Definition 13.2 implies that he can use his moral code indirectly so long as he believes of some act that it is decision-mandated. Suppose Damien believes that the objectively highest *precept* he can use prescribes decision-guide (a) in cases where he is uncertain which decision-guide is objectively best. (Perhaps this precept prescribes a decision-guide whose worst possible outcome would be better than the worst possible outcome of any other decision-guide.) Decision-guide (a) is then subjectively obligatory for him. The act it prescribes, buying the diapers, counts as decision-mandated under clause (d), which is satisfied when the agent, although uncertain which act is prescribed as choice-mandated by a decision-guide that is objectively obligatory, nonetheless believes of some act (in this case, buying diapers) that it is prescribed as choice-mandated by a decision-guide that is subjectively obligatory. Suppose, as is consistent with this story, that if Damien wanted all-things-considered to use his deontological theory for guidance at t_i for an act performable at t_j, he would then come to believe that buying diapers is decision-mandated in the core sense for him, relative to the theory and to his credences at t_i about the relation between buying diapers and his deontological theory. In this case Damien's deontological theory counts as indirectly usable by him under Definition 13.2. Moreover, if we apply this definition to agents who have moral uncertainties at even higher levels (such as the more sophisticated Marthas in Cases 2 and 3), it is easy to see that they, too, could qualify as having the ability to use their moral theory indirectly. Thus the new definition of indirect usability enables us to surmount the problem that confronted the earlier Definition 12.1: we have found a definition for "indirect usability" that can count an agent as having the ability to indirectly use this moral theory even though he is uncertain which decision-guide is objectively best. And unlike Definition 12.2.2, which implemented the Low Bar view, our new definition makes demands on certain ones of Damien's moral beliefs. It requires that the agent have morally relevant beliefs about the connection between the recommended act and the governing moral theory.

The revised Definition 13.2 then appears to be a promising approach to our search for a suitably morally demanding account of ability to indirectly use one's moral theory for guidance.

13.1.3 Issues for Definition 13.2 of ability to indirectly use a moral theory for guidance

Despite the promise of Definition 13.2, it faces serious problems. In this section I'll describe the problem I have found most surprising and perhaps most troubling.

Suppose act utilitarianism is the moral theory under review. An agent Timothy is uncertain which of his prospective acts is objectively obligatory according to act utilitarianism. However, a possible decision-guide for him would be an analog to the moral laundry list: in this case a "laundry list decision-guide," suitably coordinated with act utilitarianism, that prescribes as choice-mandated a series of actions, each for a different time, each described in terms that render the action one the agent has the epistemic ability to perform, and each such that it would produce more utility than any alternative action. Such a decision-guide might consist of a prescription to donate $25 to Oxfam at t_1, a prescription to write a letter to his elderly mother at t_2, a prescription to read background material for the town council meeting at t_3, and so forth. Having attached the label "DG_0" to the decision-guide that semantically mirrors his Code C by telling Timothy to act so as to produce more utility than any other action, we could label the new coordinated laundry list decision-guide "DG_{00}." In the actual world its prescriptions would be co-extensive with those of DG_0, as well as with the prescriptions of act utilitarianism itself. But unlike the case with DG_0, Timothy has the ability to use DG_{00}. It's worthwhile spelling this out. Recall Definition 2.1:

Definition 2.1.   Ability in the core sense to directly use a moral principle to decide what to do: An agent S is able in the core sense at t_i to directly use moral principle P to decide at t_i what to do at t_j *if and only if*:

(A)   there is some (perhaps complex) feature F such that P prescribes actions that have feature F, in virtue of their having F,

(B)   S believes at t_i of some act-type A that S could perform A (in the epistemic sense) at t_j,

(C)   S believes at t_i that if she performed A at t_j, act A would have F, and

(D)   if and because S believed at t_i that P prescribes actions that have feature F, in virtue of their having F, and if and because S wanted all-things-considered at t_i to derive a prescription from principle P at t_i for an act performable at t_j, then her beliefs together with this desire would lead S to derive a prescription at t_i for A from P in virtue of her belief that it has F.

Here the question is whether Timothy has the ability in this sense to use a principle consisting of the prescriptions "Donate $25 to Oxfam at t_1, write a letter to your elderly mother at t_2, read background material for the town council meeting at t_3,..." to decide what to do. This list, which spells out DG_{00}, prescribes actions having certain features (being a case of donating $25 to Oxfam at t_1 and so forth). Timothy believes that he could perform each of these acts (in the epistemic sense), and also believes that if he performed it, it would have the feature prescribed by the principle.[10] And it is true of him that if and because he believed that "Donate $25 to Oxfam at t_1, write a letter to

---

[10]   All that is actually required is that Timothy be able at time t_1 to perform the first of the prescribed acts, and that he would acquire the ability to perform each of the prescribed acts at its proper time.

your elderly mother at t_2, read background material for the town council meeting at t_3, . . ." prescribes actions having the relevant features, and if and because he wanted all-things-considered to derive a prescription for an act performable at t_j, then his beliefs together with this desire would lead him to derive a prescription to donate $25 to Oxfam from his principle in virtue of his belief that this act has the prescribed property. Timothy can use DG_{00} on this occasion, even though he cannot use act utilitarianism itself.

There's certainly a strong case to be made that DG_{00} is the objectively obligatory decision-guide for Timothy, since it is directly usable and tells him in every case to do exactly the act that utilitarianism identifies as objectively obligatory. What decision-guide could possibly do better?

Of course, since Timothy is uncertain which acts utilitarianism itself prescribes as objectively obligatory, he will hardly believe of the correct list that it is in fact DG_{00}, or believe that it is the objectively obligatory decision-guide, or believe that donating to Oxfam, the act DG_{00} recommends for t_1, is decision-mandated. Does this mean that Timothy is unable to use utilitarianism indirectly to guide his decision? If so, this would be a terrible blow for Definition 13.2 and the Expanded Moral Theory solution, since for every possible moral theory there will be an associated DG_{00}—a laundry list decision-guide—that arguably would be objectively obligatory (or right) for any agent, and yet which no agent faced with the problem of uncertainty would be in a position to identify as objectively obligatory.

If Timothy is suitably informed about the possibility of laundry list decision-guides, he will believe there is some list that qualifies as DG_{00} and so is objectively obligatory, and that it prescribes some act as choice-mandated. Believing that DG_{00} is objectively obligatory, he will deny that any other decision-guide is objectively obligatory, or (more accurately) he will be uncertain whether any other decision-guide is objectively obligatory, since he will have no way to tell whether any other decision-guide delivers the same prescriptions as DG_{00}. It seems, then, that because Timothy is unable to identify the content and prescriptions of DG_{00}, he won't believe of any act that *it* is choice-mandated according to the objectively obligatory decision-guide.

Of course, the fact that Timothy doesn't believe of any act that it is choice-mandated according to the objectively obligatory decision-guide doesn't entail that no act is decision-mandated for Timothy, or that he is unable to use his moral theory indirectly. It is true that the act prescribed by DG_{00} is not (in virtue of this) decision-mandated for him, since according to clause (c) of Definition 13.1 an act A is only decision-mandated for an agent if he believes of A that it is prescribed as choice-mandated by a decision-guide that is objectively obligatory. Given Timothy's uncertainties, there is no act of which it is true that Timothy believes it is prescribed by DG_{00}, which he holds to be the objectively obligatory decision-guide. However, there could be some act that is decision-mandated for Timothy in virtue of his satisfying lower clause (d), which states that an act A is decision-mandated for agent S if S is uncertain which act is prescribed as choice-mandated by a decision-guide that is objectively obligatory, but

S believes of A that it is prescribed as choice-mandated by a decision-guide that is subjectively obligatory.

According to Truly Comprehensive Act Utilitarianism, a directly usable decision-guide DG_x is subjectively obligatory for agent S if and only if DG_x is prescribed as choice-mandated by the objectively obligatory precept, that is, the highest-ranked precept that is appropriate to Code C and that is directly usable by S for a decision about which decision-guide to use. Suppose that although Timothy can't identify any list of prescriptions as the guide DG_{00}, it is true that he could use DG_4, which prescribes performing an act that would produce a satisfactory amount of utility. He believes that donating to CARE would produce a satisfactory amount of utility. He doesn't (fully) believe that this act is prescribed by DG_{00}, but he believes there is a 55 percent chance it is prescribed by DG_{00}, and more generally that there is a 55 percent chance that the acts prescribed by DG_4 are identical to the acts prescribed by DG_{00}. (He could infer this from his belief that there is a 55 percent chance that the acts prescribed by DG_4 are objectively obligatory according to utilitarianism, since DG_{00} prescribes the very same acts as those prescribed by utilitarianism.) Suppose Timothy also believes that this feature means that DG_4 satisfies Precept PRE_4, which prescribes as choice-mandated any decision-guide that would produce a satisfactory amount of K (where "a satisfactory amount of K" is "a greater than 50 percent chance of prescribing the act that is prescribed by the objectively obligatory decision-guide"). Precept PRE_4, if it is the highest precept that Timothy can use, is the objectively obligatory precept for selecting subjectively obligatory decision-guides. This may suggest that he can view DG_4, which he believes PRE_4 selects, as subjectively obligatory. If so, then it appears that he would qualify as able to use his moral theory indirectly under clause (d) of Definition 13.1. He fails to satisfy clauses (a)–(c), but he does satisfy clause (d), which stipulates that an act A is decision-mandated if the agent is uncertain which act is prescribed as choice-mandated by a decision-guide that is objectively obligatory but the agent believes of A that it is prescribed as choice-worthy by a decision-guide that is subjectively obligatory.

Unfortunately, the sophisticated Timothy will realize that Precept PRE_4 can't be the highest precept he can use, because there will be another superior but still usable precept: Precept PRE_{00}, the laundry list guide for selecting subjectively obligatory decision-guides. Recall that a directly usable decision-guide DG_x is subjectively obligatory at time t_i for agent S to apply at t_i if and only if DG_x is prescribed as choice-mandated for t_i by the objectively obligatory precept, where the objectively obligatory precept has no less M than any other precept that is appropriate to Code C and that is directly usable by S for a decision at t_i about which decision-guide to use at t_i. What is feature M that the objectively obligatory precept must have no less of than any rival usable precept? Arguably, a usable precept that prescribes a decision-guide that prescribes exactly the same acts that Code C prescribes has no less of feature M than any rival usable precept. PRE_{00}, which prescribes DG_{00}, has this feature. PRE_{00} might read "The highest usable decision-guide is DG_{00}, which prescribes donating $25 to Oxfam at t_1, writing a letter to your elderly mother at t_2, reading background material for the town council meeting at t_3, ..." Like DG_{00}, PRE_{00} is usable by Timothy, because if he believed it selected the right decision-guide, he could pick out and then use the list of act prescriptions mentioned in PRE_{00} as the content of the appropriate decision-guide DG_{00}. No usable decision-guide could be better than DG_{00}, and for the same reason, no precept could be better than PRE_{00}. Of course, Timothy is not in a position to identify the content of PRE_{00}, but being sophisticated he nonetheless believes that its content is such that he could use it to select the best decision-guide, and that he could not do better than to use PRE_{00}.[11]

This doesn't mean he believes of any decision-guide that it is prescribed by PRE_{00}. His earlier uncertainty now stands in the way of identifying which decision-guide is actually prescribed by PRE_{00}. Since he's uncertain which decision-guide PRE_{00} recommends, clause (d) doesn't identify the decision-mandated act for him. Instead it would have to be identified by the next lower clause in Definition 13.1, clause (e), which says an act A is decision-mandated if the agent is uncertain which act is prescribed as choice-mandated by a decision-guide that is objectively obligatory, and also uncertain which act is prescribed as choice-mandated by a decision-guide that is subjectively obligatory, but nonetheless the agent believes of A that it is prescribed as choice-mandated by a decision-guide that is prescribed as choice-mandated by a precept that is subjectively obligatory. A precept is subjectively obligatory if and only if it is prescribed as choice-mandated by the objectively obligatory maxim. But once again, all-too-sophisticated Timothy could realize that the objectively obligatory maxim is Maxim MAX_{00}, the laundry list guide for selecting subjectively obligatory precepts. Not having any idea what the exact content of MAX_{00} is, of course he doesn't believe of any precept that it is prescribed by MAX_{00}. So the decision-mandated act can't be picked out by clause (e) either. Indeed, if Timothy has a full grasp of Comprehensive Utilitarianism, it appears that there is no clause of Definition 13.1 that succeeds in identifying a decision-mandated act for him. If he's sufficiently well-informed about the structure of Comprehensive Utilitarianism and the requirements of Definition 13.1, then Timothy himself will realize that this problem continues to crop up at every successive level in Definition 13.1 of decision-mandatoriness. Given this realization, *there is no act that is decision-mandated for him.*[12] And given this fact together with his sophisticated understanding of the system, he fails clause (C) of Definition 13.2 of indirect usability: it is false that if he wanted all-things-considered to use act utilitarianism for guidance, he would then come to believe of some performable act that it is

[11] Precept PRE_{00} is a single item list, unlike DG_{00}, which contains a very long list of act prescriptions. But because PRE_{00} inherits some of DG_{00}'s characteristics, it seems appropriate to refer to it also as a laundry list guide.

[12] Note that this is consistent with my earlier assertion that a well-equipped truly comprehensive moral theory would have, for every agent, a decision-guide that is usable by that agent. In Timothy's case DG_{00} itself is usable, and many other decision-guides could be as well, such as DG_1, which prescribes an act that would produce no less expected utility than any alternative is choice-worthy, or DG_n, which says that any act is choice-worthy.

decision-mandated in the core sense for him. There is no way for him to indirectly use his moral theory to decide what to do.

Of course Timothy might make a mistake at some level and not realize that the laundry list guide at that level is the objectively obligatory guide. For example, he might be uncertain which act is prescribed as choice-mandated by a decision-guide that is objectively obligatory, but believe of donating to Oxfam that it is prescribed as choice-mandated by decision-guide DG_3, which he (mistakenly) believes is subjectively obligatory because it is prescribed by the objectively obligatory precept. In this situation, donating to Oxfam would count as decision-mandated for him according to clause (d) of Definition 13.1. He would then also count as having the indirect ability to use his moral theory because he would believe of donating to Oxfam that it is decision-mandated. But we don't want to advocate, as a solution to the problem of agents' uncertainty about the moral status of decision-guides, a system whose success *depends* on agents having mistaken beliefs about the moral status of their various guides. A successful core solution should work whether the agent has true or false beliefs about the relative merits of rival guides. Since there is no decision-mandated act for Timothy in the original story, he cannot both have true beliefs and also have the ability to use his code indirectly.

It might be hoped that Timothy could be extricated from this situation by the availability of the last resort decision-guide—DG_n—which tells him that an act that could be selected at random is choice-worthy. Sadly, the availability of DG_n is no help. It identifies the decision-worthy act only if it is the highest usable decision-guide of its class available to Timothy. But DG_n is not the highest usable decision-guide—instead DG_{00} has that honor. And since Timothy believes this, even though he may be aware of DG_n, he knows it should not be used to select which act to perform.[13]

What Timothy's case shows is that the Expanded Moral Theory approach to the problem of agents' uncertainties about the best decision-guides does not fully solve this problem, since it leaves sophisticated agents such as Timothy unable to indirectly use their moral theories. The kind of solution we're looking for should both make it the case that some act is the subjectively obligatory act for the agent, given her uncertainties about the nonmoral facts and the moral facts about which guides are best, and also make it possible for the agent to indirectly use the extended moral theory in selecting a subjectively obligatory act (even if inaccurately). The Expanded Moral Theory solution attempts to achieve this by introducing the truly comprehensive moral theory and the notion of the "decision-mandated act," and by using Definition 13.2 as the account of an agent's ability to indirectly use a moral theory in terms of her belief about what act is decision-mandated for her. Whereas previously the usability of moral theories ran aground on agents who are under-informed about the world, we can see that the Expanded Moral Theory solution runs aground on sophisticated agents who have

---

[13] Also note that there is no counterpart to DG_n for decision-mandated acts (rather than decision-worthy acts).

some uncertainty about the world, but otherwise are too well-informed about the structure of the truly comprehensive theory, and so realize that for them there is no decision-mandated or decision-worthy act. We need to look further for a better solution.[14]

13.2   Third Approach: As a Condition for Indirect Usability, Require an Agent to Have Credences about Which Decision-Guide is Correct, and Make this Possible by Constraining the Standard for Guides

The third approach to securing indirect usability in the face of agents' uncertainties about decision-guides is one that, like the Expanded Moral Theory approach, takes advantage of the truly comprehensive moral theory and also requires the agent to have beliefs about which guides are best. However, it places constraints on which standards determine the deontic rank-ordering of decision-guides (and of higher-level guides, such as precepts and maxims). So far relatively little has been said about the content of these standards. But at this point one might plausibly suggest that we have been too lax about the allowable content of these standards. If we constrain the content of these standards, problems such as Timothy's may disappear. Let us call this third approach the "Constrained Standards Hybrid" approach.

One tempting idea along these lines would propose that the standard by which decision-guides are ranked should take into account how easy it is for human beings to learn and remember the guides.[15] Since DG_{00} is simply an extremely long list of descriptions of individual actions, it is clear that no agent would be able to learn or remember DG_{00}. If we require decision-guides to be learnable, DG_{00} would not qualify after all as an appropriate or highly-ranked decision-guide, thus eliminating the type of problem faced by Timothy.

This is an attractive idea. However, reflection suggests that it mislocates the importance of features such as human learnability and memorability. Possession of these kinds of features does not seem to be a factor that makes a given decision-guide objectively better: the more easily learned or memorized decision-guide does not necessarily pick out morally better actions. Rather possession of such features seems to make a decision-guide the best one *for an agent to learn and memorize* at a time prior to her decision, so that she has a decision-guide ready to hand when the occasion for decision arrives and the decision must be made immediately.[16] If the agent has memorized the

---

[14] The argument of this section was briefly suggested in Chapter 8, section 8.1.2, in which the laundry list was considered as a decision-guide for a non-ideal Hybrid approach to the problem of error.

[15] Developed in detail, this proposal would probably have to stipulate that the rank of a given decision-guide depends on how learnable it is on a specific occasion by a specific agent.

[16] By the same token, it also may make the decision-guide the best one for an advisor to teach a moral learner.

decision-guide, then when the time for decision arrives, the memorized decision-guide may spring to the agent's mind, and if she has the requisite nonmoral information, she will be able to utilize it in indirectly using her moral theory for guidance. But this fact does not make the *content* of this decision-guide superior to the content of other guides.

We can see continuity between the thought that the standard for decision-guides should be sensitive to their learnability and the thought that which decision-guide an agent should use must reflect factors such as how time-consuming or how costly it would be to use. There is clearly a sense in which an agent who has a choice between using DG_x and DG_y, where using DG_x would require more expensive resources than using DG_y, has at least a prima facie reason to use the "cheaper" DG_y instead. But this does not mean that DG_y is in itself a better guide; it just makes it a better one to use on this occasion. Similarly the fact that DG_w is more easily learned than DG_z may make it the one the agent should learn for future use, but it does not make DG_w deontically better in itself than DG_z. These kinds of practical factors should play no role in the objective rankings of decision-guides.

Here is a second and more promising Constrained Standards thesis proposed by Andy Egan.[17] According to this suggestion, a decision-guide's objective deontic status should be *modally robust*: its appropriateness and ranking as a decision-guide relative to its governing moral theory should be the same in reasonably near-by possible worlds as its appropriateness and ranking are in the actual world. Thus consider act utilitarianism. If decision-guide DG_1 (which states that an act that would produce more expected utility than any alternative is choice-mandated) is appropriate for utilitarianism in the actual world, it should also be appropriate for utilitarianism in every reasonably near-by possible world. And if DG_1 is ranked higher relative to utilitarianism than DG_2 (which states that an act that is most likely to produce the most utility is choice-mandated) in the actual world, it should also be ranked higher in the sphere of reasonably near-by possible worlds.

Of course the *usability* of a given decision-guide will vary from world to world, depending on the agent's beliefs and abilities. Timothy might be able to use DG_1 in our world, but unable to use it in other possible worlds. As we have seen, this implies that which decision-guide is objectively obligatory for an agent will also vary from world to world, since the objective status of a guide depends on its usability by the agent in question. So DG_1 could be the objectively obligatory decision-guide for Timothy in his actual circumstances, but some other guide, such as DG_2, would be the objectively obligatory guide in a world in which Timothy can't use DG_1. But the objective obligatoriness of a given decision-guide depends not just on its usability, but also on its ranking in the deontic hierarchy of decision-guides. And this ranking is what should be modally robust.

---

[17] Personal communications, August 29, 2014 and January 28, 2015.

By the same reasoning, just as the appropriateness and rankings of decision-guides should be modally robust, so too the rankings of upper-level guides, such as precepts and maxims should be modally robust. To require that the relative rankings of decision-guides, precepts, maxims, and so forth be modally robust in this way is analogous to the requirement, accepted by many moral philosophers, that the correct theoretical account of right and wrong be correct in every reasonably near-by possible world.[18] One can see modal robustness as a requirement on *all* the norms in a comprehensive normative system. These norms are evaluated by different standards: Standard S_1 evaluates decision-guides; Standard S_2 evaluates precepts; Standard S_3 evaluates maxims, and so forth. But the standards evaluating these different guides should maintain the relative rankings of the guides they evaluate in every reasonably near-by possible world, and indeed the standards themselves should be appropriate to the governing theory in every reasonably near-by possible world.[19]

The point for now is that while DG_0 is modally robust in this sense (no rival decision-guide is ever ranked above it), the laundry list decision-guide DG_{00} is not. For Timothy in the original case, DG_{00} is a list of individualized prescriptions such as *donate \$25 to Oxfam at t_1, write a letter to your elderly mother at t_2, and read background material for the town council meeting at t_3*. In the actual world these actions are the ones that would maximize utility; this fact makes this particular list the highest-ranked decision-guide (setting aside the modal robustness constraint) for Timothy in this world.[20] But in a slightly different world, these particular actions would not maximize utility: perhaps, under slightly different conditions, it would maximize utility for Timothy to instead donate to CARE, spend time with a home-bound neighbor, and garner support for a proposal to block a planned big box store in his township. Thus in the slightly different world, the list comprised of prescriptions to donate to Oxfam, write a letter to his elderly mother, and read background material for the town council meeting would not be the correct DG_{00}. As Egan points out, the original DG_{00} could in principle be converted to a modally robust decision-guide by filling out the description of each prescribed action so that it describes not just the action narrowly conceived, but also the entire state of the world. But if Timothy can only determine whether or not to perform an act if he has beliefs about the entire state of the world,

---

[18] Many moral philosophers would want a stronger version of this requirement, namely that the appropriateness and relative rankings of a set of decision-guides, relative to a given moral theory, be invariant across *all* possible worlds. See, for example, Cohen (2003). Others reject any requirement of this sort. See Anderson (2015).

[19] We need to be careful in stating this requirement. Several norms (for example, the principle of objective rightness and the decision-guides) in a comprehensive moral theory directly evaluate *acts*. The evaluations of acts by these norms of course will not be invariant across possible worlds. For example, although Martha's giving to Oxfam may maximize utility in one possible world, her giving to CARE would maximize utility in a close-by possible world. But the status and relative rankings of the norms themselves should be invariant across near-by possible worlds.

[20] More accurately, DG_0 and DG_{00} are equally highly-ranked, since they each prescribe all and only acts that would maximize utility. Our previous discussion suggested that DG_{00} rather than DG_0 is objectively obligatory for Timothy in this world because he can use it, whereas he cannot use DG_0.

then there is no way in which the resulting modally robust DG_{00} would be usable by him. The epistemic problem it would pose would be far worse than that posed by utilitarianism itself. To maintain its usability, the act descriptions in his DG_{00} must be simple and epistemically non-demanding enough that he could actually use them to decide what to do, and no modally robust expanded version of DG_{00} satisfies that requirement. Thus if we require the relative rankings of decision-guides to be modally robust, DG_{00} no longer qualifies as the objective obligatory decision-guide for Timothy. If it no longer qualifies, then we have restored the possibility that there is some decision-mandated act for him. We can retain Definition 13.2 as our definition of ability to indirectly use a moral principle, and according to it, act utilitarianism is a moral theory Timothy could indirectly use (if, for example, he believes that act A is decision-mandated for him, having ruled out DG_{00} as an unacceptable decision-guide).[21]

But what decision-guides would satisfy the demand for modal robustness? In general, any decision-guide for which the rationale is that adherence to the decision-guide would tend to result in compliance with the governing Code C is one that is *not* modally robust across possible worlds in which the physical, social, and psychological facts are different. Thus the requirement that decision-guides be modally robust eliminates in one fell swoop, not only DG_{00}, but also entire swaths of decision-guides whose justification depends on highly variable nonmoral facts in the actual world.

It appears, then, that the most promising decision-guides satisfying the demand for modal robustness are ones whose justification depends on metaphysical, mathematical, or semantic necessities, or more generally those whose justification does not depend on the precise possible world that the agent finds herself in. Fortunately there are arguments favoring certain decision-guides that rely on these kinds of justification. For example, DG_1, which prescribes maximizing expected utility, is often justified on the ground that it is the only decision-guide that is consistent with certain intuitively obvious axioms governing preference orderings and probability assignments.[22] It is also

---

[21] This raises the question of whether some similar demand might be made of the original moral laundry list, introduced in Chapter 4, and discussed again in Chapter 6, as an ideal or non-ideal account of what makes actions objectively right or wrong. Should it, too, as a normative theory, be required to be modally robust, that is, true in all reasonably near-by possible worlds? As we noted in Chapter 4, it is clear that any moral laundry list that contains prescriptions for individual actions that are actually usable by epistemically limited agents will not be true in all reasonably near-by possible worlds, so it would fail the demand for modal robustness. Proponents of the Pragmatic solution must reject any requirement that the correct moral theory be correct in all near-by possible worlds, since which principles are usable will vary from world to world. Thus my reason for rejecting laundry list decision-guides here would not be available to the Pragmatic theorist. Many theorists would see this as a major defect in Pragmatic theories. The discussion of whether a Hybrid solution to the problem of error could incorporate the moral laundry list in effect envisions the laundry list as the moral theory's Code C*, and rejects this proposal on grounds that no agent (or advisor) would have the epistemic capacity to identify the content of this Code C*. This argument is closely related to the one deployed in the current chapter.

[22] The canonical presentation of this argument for objective probabilities is in Luce and Raiffa (1957), Chapter 2, while its counterpart for subjective probabilities is in Savage (1954). An updated summary discussion is provided by Briggs (2014). As Briggs points out, various theorists have challenged this argument. See Lara Buchak's defense of "risk-weighted expected utility" as superior to DG_1 in Buchak (2013). See also Portmore (2011), pp. 20–2.

sometimes justified on mathematical grounds which show that according to the Law of Large Numbers following this decision-guide will (very roughly speaking) result in the best results over the long run.[23] And it is sometimes justified by arguing that, for mathematical reasons, it protects the agent from being "Dutch Booked"—having a series of bets made against her that would result in her losing money (or utility) over the long run.[24] These kinds of arguments have both advocates and detractors. Nonetheless, arguments of these kinds, if successful, seem on the right track to showing that DG_1's status as appropriate to utilitarianism is modally robust, and perhaps to showing that it is most highly ranked (after DG_0 itself).

Unfortunately DG_1 is only one decision-guide, and as we have seen, a moral theory needs to be supplemented by more than one or two decision-guides if it is to be indirectly usable by every moral agent. DG_1 itself can only be applied by agents who have a good deal of information and, typically, the time as well as the cognitive capacity to perform complex calculations. So decision-guides requiring less information are needed. In debates about "bounded rationality" decision theorists have long debated about other possible decision-guides, such as DG_2, DG_3, and DG_4, which are less epistemically taxing on agents. Nonetheless there is as yet no consensus about which of these is deontically appropriate, much less a consensus about how they should be rank-ordered for agents suffering from progressively more serious epistemic limitations. Nor do we have compelling suggestions about which decision-guides would be appropriate, within our constraint, for agents unable to use any of those commonly discussed by decision theorists. Thus if we adopt the Constrained Standards approach, which for indirect usability requires agents to believe that a decision-guide is the best one available among those that she can use, and which seeks to make this possible by restricting suitable decision-guides to those which can be justified by reference to metaphysical, mathematical, or semantic necessity, we face a daunting shortage of decision-guides that have been shown to be appropriate and whose rank in the hierarchy of decision-guides is established. Moreover, decision-guides that are appropriate for normative theories with uni-dimensional accounts of value (such as standard act utilitarianism) have been worked out in much more detail than have decision-guides for normative theories displaying other structures, such as those with multi-dimensional accounts of value. And of course, decision-guides for deontological theories have received almost no attention. Clearly, much work remains to be done by decision theorists to fill out the promise of the Constrained Standards approach. Nonetheless, this approach enables us to dismiss the particular problem facing Timothy because it eliminates decision-guide laundry lists such as DG_{00} that fail the test of modal robustness.

If we accept the constraint of modal robustness, one question is how we should understand the role of the mini-maxims, which in fact people often rely on in making

---

[23] Somewhat more precisely, in the finite long run, the average value associated with a repeated gamble is overwhelmingly likely to be close to its expected value (Briggs (2014)). Of course many situations calling for decision are not part of a series of repeated gambles.

[24] See, for example, Vineberg (2011).

their decisions. The most natural argument for the appropriateness (and relative ranking) of mini-maxims relies on the empirical assumption that they issue prescriptions which fairly closely match those of the governing moral principle in their relatively narrow field of action, even though they fail to duplicate these prescriptions exactly. If this claim is true for a given mini-maxim, then it may be sufficiently modally robust to satisfy the Constrained Standards approach. Take, for example, the mini-maxim "Never shake an infant." This maxim only provides good advice (relative to an object-ive moral principle such as "Never harm an innocent person") in a world in which the developing brains of young infants are vulnerable to injury from severe shaking. There are certainly some possible worlds in which infants' brains are not vulnerable to this type of injury. But it seems plausible that in all the close-by possible worlds, they are vulnerable to being harmed by this kind of treatment. Thus it is arguable that this mini-maxim is sufficiently modally robust to pass the Constrained Standards approach. To settle this question would require us to determine how close a possible world must be in order to qualify as "reasonably near-by" for purposes of moral theory, a task I shall not undertake here.

An agent who is considering whether or not to shake an infant does not need to be certain about precisely which possible world he occupies in order to believe it is appro-priate to follow the mini-maxim "Never shake an infant." Nonetheless he needs to have some beliefs about the nature of his world, and in particular to believe that there is a good probability that shaking the infant will injure her (or at least to believe that reputable authorities advise one never to shake an infant, even if he doesn't have any concrete idea what medical facts support this advice). This is the kind of information that many people acquire as they mature and become better informed about the world. If the agent believes it's appropriate to follow a decision-guide saying "It's choice-prohibited to do anything with a significant probability of injuring an infant," and if he believes that shaking the infant has a significant probability of injuring her, then he may be using the mini-maxim, not as a decision-guide per se, but rather as a piece of *epistemic* information that enables him to apply his actual decision-guide.

We should remember that Definition 13.2 of indirect usability does not require that the agent's belief that a given act is decision-worthy be correct. Thus consider an agent who believes that a given mini-maxim (such as "Never shake an infant") is a suitable decision-guide. Suppose further that she is wrong about this: her mini-maxim is not sufficiently modally robust to qualify as a decision-guide. Nonetheless she uses it to derive a prescription not to shake an infant as a decision-worthy (indeed mandated) act. Although she is mistaken that this mini-maxim qualifies as a decision-guide, she nonetheless counts as indirectly using her moral principle ("Never harm an innocent person"). So even when agents use mini-maxims that fail to meet the modal robustness standard for decision-guides, they nonetheless succeed in indirectly using their moral principle in the core sense.

The upshot: our third approach to the problem of agents' uncertainty about which decision-guides are best—the Constrained Standards approach—avoids one of the main hazards encountered by the Expanded Moral Theory, namely the possibility that there will be no decision-worthy act at all for sophisticated agents such as Timothy who understand all too well the structure of the truly comprehensive moral theory. The Constrained Standards approach utilizes the truly comprehensive moral code, adopts Definition 13.1 of decision-worthiness in the core sense, and retains Definition 13.2 of ability to use a moral principle in the core sense as a decision-guide. But it restricts admissible decision-guides (and other higher-level accessory guides) to those that are modally robust in the sense explained. By utilizing all these tools it provides a way for a moral code to qualify as indirectly usable by agents who are uncertain which acts are directly prescribed by the moral code itself, while retaining the demand that an agent only qualifies as able to indirectly use a moral code if she believes of some decision-guide that it is best for her to use relative to that moral code. On this approach even Timothy, who has an unusually sophisticated understanding of the structure of the truly comprehensive moral theory, can be in a position to use utilitarianism indirectly, since DG_{00} is not admissible as a decision-guide, and he can use another guide such as DG_4 to identify the decision-mandated act.

13.3   The Status of Decision-Guides

In Chapter 9, and again in Chapter 12, I raised the question of whether decision-guides should be considered (as I have been doing) as *moral* rules that form part of a complete moral system, or should instead be considered as principles of rationality, suitable for supplementing any account of practical normative status, including not only accounts of moral status, but also accounts of prudential status, legal status, the epistemic status of beliefs, and so forth. Now that we've seen the truly comprehensive moral theory, we can see that the same question can be raised about the higher-level guides in the comprehensive moral theory such as precepts, maxims, and counsels. In these earlier chapters I said it was too early to try to settle the question about the status of these guides, since we lacked any account of the content or justification of these various guides. Adopting the Constrained Standards approach moves us closer to having such an account, since it says that a guide should be modally robust in the sense that its appropriateness and ranking as a guide relative to its governing moral theory should be the same in reasonably near-by possible worlds as its appropriateness and ranking are in the actual world. We have mentioned at least one plausible decision-guide, DG_1, which prescribes maximizing expected value (although some deontologists and even consequentialists view this guide as inappropriate relative to their theory of objective rightness). But we have no clear view about what lower-ranked decision-guides might be appropriate for agents unable to apply DG_1. It's also true that we've articulated standards for evaluating and ranking the various guides. For example, we described Standard S_1 as saying that a decision-guide is appropriate for Code C if and only if it has feature K, and it is better relative to Code C than another decision-guide of the same class if and only if it has more K than the other guide. However, we introduced this standard (and its counterparts for higher-level guides) as merely a stand-in for whatever standard is actually appropriate; we made no attempt to determine what "feature K" is, and we noted that even the maximizing character of Standard S_1 may not reflect the actual nature of the appropriate standard. So the question is whether knowing that the appropriateness and ranking of a guide must be invariant in reasonably near-by possible worlds tells us enough to determine whether the guides should be viewed as principles of rationality or as narrower principles of morality which might vary from moral theory to moral theory, or might vary between moral theories and other accounts of normative status.

I suspect that the requirement of modal robustness tends to tip the balance in favor of these guides' being broad principles of rationality incorporating parameters that could accommodate different kinds of values. However, I think the question may still be open: it remains possible that the standard by which decision-guides are evaluated relative to some moral theories is unique to those theories, and is not appropriate for the evaluation of decision-guides relative to other moral theories, or relative to other kinds of normativity. This could imply that guides appropriate for one context are inappropriate for another. For this reason I shall continue to view the guides at various levels as components of the comprehensive moral theory itself. As I remarked in Chapter 12, what position we finally take on this issue has implications for what kind of information is required for an agent to qualify as having the ability to indirectly apply her moral theory. For example, if the agent correctly views her moral theory as simply constituted by its Code C account of objective rightness, but understands that applying this account in cases of uncertainty requires her to deploy certain principles of rational decision-making, then her ability to indirectly use her moral theory will depend on her beliefs about which principles of rationality are available and appropriate for her to use. If these principles of rationality can supplement any moral theory, it may be easier for moral agents to use any given moral theory, since once they have learned the principles of rationality and their broad applicability they will be in a position to believe these principles are appropriate to any moral theory, and can employ them (assuming they have the appropriate nonmoral information) in the context of whichever normative theory they wish to use.

13.4 Limitations of the Constrained Standards Approach

Even though the Constrained Standards approach handles Timothy's case in a satisfactory manner, it still has limits. Other types of cases loom as ones in which the agent—even with the help of the truly comprehensive moral theory—cannot indirectly use her guiding moral principle to make a decision. Let us canvass some examples of apparent and actual problems. Doubtless there are others as well.

13.4.1 Agents' credences short of full belief that a decision-guide is objectively right

The first apparent problem arises in the following kind of case. Suppose Eric wants to use objective principle P for guidance but isn't certain which decision-guide is objectively right. However, he believes that there is a 70 percent chance that (say) DG_3 is objectively right, and also believes that DG_3 prescribes some act A as choice-worthy.

Definition 13.2 for indirect usability requires that the agent believe of some act that it is decision-worthy, so it may appear that Eric does not have the requisite belief. However, he may believe that the *subjectively* right decision-guide prescribes an act as choice-worthy if there's at least a 70 percent chance that it is prescribed as choice-worthy by the objectively right decision-guide. An agent such as Eric would be able to apply his moral theory indirectly by virtue of believing act A is decision-worthy according to clause (d) of the definition of decision-worthiness. So mere uncertainty which decision-guide is objectively right does not necessarily stand in the way of the agent's being able to indirectly apply his moral code. Agents with this type of uncertainty are not a problem for Definition 13.2 so long as they have an appropriate belief about decision-guides endorsed at a higher level.

13.4.2 Moral nihilism about decision-guides

The second problem is raised by the fact that there may be agents who have a special type of false belief that renders them unable to indirectly use their moral theory. Consider an agent Jean who believes that Ross's pluralism is the correct moral theory, but who denies that there are any decision-guides (or guides at higher levels) that are appropriate for Ross's theory. Jean admits the truth of Ross's Code C but is a nihilist about other guides and norms in the truly comprehensive Rossian theory.[25] If Jean wants to apply Ross's theory to some decision, and is uncertain which of her options would maximize the net balance of prima facie rightness over prima facie wrongness, then it is false she would come to believe of any act that it is decision-worthy for her, or even that it is morally appropriate for her in some other sense.

I don't think the Hybrid theory provides any remedy for Jean's problem, but I also think this shouldn't be considered a serious flaw in the Hybrid theory. If the only way to dig a hole in the ground is to use a shovel, and the agent who needs to dig the hole declines the shovel offered to her, then there is nothing more that can be done to help her aside from convincing her to use the shovel. Her problem does not show that the shovel itself is inadequate to the task. Similarly, if the only way to indirectly use a moral theory is to employ decision-guides, and the agent who needs to use a moral theory declines the decision-guides the theory offers her, then there is nothing more the theory can do to help her. Her problem does not show that the comprehensive theory or its decision-guides are themselves inadequate to the task.[26]

---

[25] This possibility was pointed out to me by Andy Egan (private communication, August 29, 2014).

[26] We should also note that this case involves the problem of error, not the problem of uncertainty.

13.4.3 Uncertainty all the way down

The third and more serious problem is the agent who is uncertain all the way down. Consider Amber, who is uncertain which decision-guide is objectively right, uncertain which decision-guide is subjectively right, uncertain which decision-guide is prescribed as choice-worthy by a precept that is subjectively right, uncertain which decision-guide that is prescribed as choice-worthy by a precept that is prescribed as choice-worthy by a maxim that is subjectively right, and so forth, for each of the indefinitely many clauses of Definition 13.1 of "decision-worthiness." Let's assume Amber has a full grasp of the notion of decision-worthiness as defined in Definition 13.1, and believes that it is the correct account of which actions are morally appropriate to perform, relative to her moral theory and to her credences at t_i about herself and about her actions' relations to that theory. However, given her pervasive uncertainty, there is no act that is decision-worthy for her, since each of the descending clauses of Definition 13.1 is false of her. And, since she believes this, she is unable to use her moral theory even indirectly.

An agent who is uncertain which decision-guide is objectively right might still have an act that is decision-worthy, because she might believe of some decision-guide that it is subjectively right. So mere uncertainty which decision-guide is objectively right does not itself stand in the way of the agent's being able to indirectly apply her moral code. But we are now examining a more pernicious case of uncertainty, in which the agent does not believe of any decision-guide that it's either objectively or subjectively right, and does not believe anything of this sort *at any level*. She's just completely at sea about which decision-guide is best to use. Perhaps such agents would be rare. But for them there is no decision-worthy act, and Definition 13.2 counts them as unable to indirectly use their moral principles.

The last resort decision-guide DG_n is not necessarily of any help to an agent like Amber. Even if she realizes that DG_n prescribes any performable act as choice-worthy, she may still be able to identify several rival and usable decision-guides that she views as possibly superior to DG_n. In that case she would remain uncertain whether decision-guide DG_n is the objectively highest-ranked decision-guide usable by her at its level. Hence the availability of DG_n does not remedy her uncertainty about which decision-guide is objectively right. Unlike Eric from section 13.4.1, however, Amber is also uncertain which of several available decision-guides is subjectively right (for example, if she's aware of last resort PRE_n but also aware of several other precepts that might be superior to PRE_n). Hence she can't appeal to the notion of the subjectively right decision-guide, or to the last resort decision-guide at this level. Similar things may be true at all the lower levels. In this case, it is a combination of full knowledge of the appropriateness of Definition 13.1, plus uncertainty about which decision is objectively right, subjectively right, and so on, that renders her unable to indirectly guide her decision by reference to her moral code. Here again, I see no remedy for her problem given our current definitions. But in this case the lack of any remedy seems to be deficiency in the moral theory, not in the agent.

13.4.4 Uncertainty about one's own beliefs

A similar problem can crop up for an agent who is uncertain what his or her own beliefs are. Suppose, for example, that Harry isn't sure which act would maximize utility, but wants to use utilitarianism for indirect guidance. He can do so if there is some act he believes to be decision-worthy for him. For an act to be decision-worthy for him according to Definition 13.1, it must be true that he believes of some act that it is prescribed as choice-worthy by some level of guide appropriate to utilitarianism. So for him to believe that some act is decision-worthy, he must believe *that he has a certain type of belief*—the belief of some act that it is prescribed as choice-worthy by some level of guide appropriate to utilitarianism. However, as we've seen before, agents may not be certain whether they have any given belief. For example, Harry may be unsure whether or not he believes of any act A that it is prescribed as choice-worthy by a decision-guide that is objectively right. But he may also be uncertain whether or not he believes of any act A that it is prescribed as choice-worthy by a subjectively right decision-guide, and indeed unsure whether he believes of any act that it is prescribed as choice-worthy by any other top-rated guides mentioned in the clauses of Definition 13.1. If he is unsure about his beliefs at each level, then no act counts as decision-worthy for him.

13.4.5 Impoverished awareness of what decision-guides are available

Consider an agent Maggie who is aware of decision-guides DG_2 and DG_3, but is unable to use either of them (and is aware of that fact). She is not aware of any alternative decision-guide—including DG_n. She could, of course, use DG_n, but not being aware of it, she does not believe of any act that it is decision-worthy in virtue of being deemed choice-worthy by DG_n. Maggie might be aware of certain precepts that endorse decision-guides as choice-worthy, and she might even believe that the highest usable such precept endorses DG_2 as choice-worthy. However, this doesn't help her, since she is unable to use DG_2. Even if she is aware of guides at yet higher levels in her theory, this doesn't help her, since she isn't able to use any of the first level decision-guides of which she is aware, even if she believes they are endorsed indirectly by some higher-level standard.

It appears that for Maggie there is no act that is decision-worthy, since her situation doesn't satisfy any of the clauses of Definition 13.1. Moreover, if she is aware of the definition of "decision-worthiness," it also appears that she fails to qualify under Definition 13.2 as having the ability to indirectly apply her moral theory, since she will not believe of any act that it is decision-worthy.

13.4.6 Strategies for remedying these problems

A defender of the Constrained Standards version of the Hybrid approach might try to address the problems of uncertainty all the way down, uncertainty about one's own beliefs, and impoverished awareness of the available decision-guides in several different ways. She might add new norms to the truly comprehensive moral code, or introduce a new concept, say of an act's being "subjectively decision-worthy." Possibly these strategies could be carried out. However, my instinct is that the truly comprehensive theory is already more than complicated enough, and that adding further layers would simply make it more complex but not necessarily more useful to those agents whose minds are already boggled by the current complexity. But we can also see a deeper problem with this strategy. In effect the truly comprehensive version of the Hybrid theory attempts to remedy agents' uncertainties by adding new components to the comprehensive moral theory, components that an agent can use to decide what to do when uncertain about lower layers in the theory. However, these new layers simply open new elements about which agents can also be uncertain, thus creating new problems as the price for solving the original one. The approach of adding more layers to the moral theory appears doomed to fall short of our goal of rendering any moral theory usable by any agent, however deep her uncertainty.

Instead it might appear that we could better address the problem by recognizing a simplified version of the Constrained Standards solution. What we have done so far is describe a theory which implies that, for most if not all agents who have profound uncertainties, there is nonetheless an act which is morally most appropriate for them to perform despite their uncertainties. This is the act that is decision-mandated (or decision-worthy) for them. If they believe of some act that it is decision-mandated, then they can link their governing moral theory to that act as the most appropriate one to perform, given their epistemic circumstances. Since the definition of "decision-mandated" is a definition of decision-mandatoriness in the core sense, and Definition 13.2 of "ability to indirectly use a moral principle to decide what to do" is a definition of ability in the core sense, agents qualify as having this ability even though their relevant beliefs are false. Thus they may have the ability to use their moral theory indirectly, even though they are mistaken that they can perform the act in question, or mistaken that it is prescribed by an objectively obligatory decision-guide, and so forth. What this suggests is that we could count an agent as having this ability even though her beliefs about the act and its relation to the moral theory are *significantly off-base*—not just off-base about some detail—and so don't closely reflect what our definitions require. We might, then, introduce a more lenient definition of ability to use a moral theory indirectly that can be stated as follows:

(Lenient) Definition 13.2.1.   Ability to indirectly use a moral principle in the core sense to decide what to do: An agent S who is uncertain at t_i which of the acts she could perform (in the epistemic sense) at t_j is prescribed by P (a principle of objective moral obligation or rightness) is nonetheless able to indirectly use P in the core sense at t_i to decide at t_i what to do at t_j *if and only if:*

(A)   S believes at t_i of some act A that S could perform A (in the epistemic sense) at t_j; and
(B)   if and because S wanted all-things-considered to use principle P for guidance at t_i for an act performable at t_j, she would then come to believe about A that it is morally appropriate to perform A, relative to P and to her credences at t_i about herself and about A's relation to P.

An agent could satisfy this definition even if she has only a foggy or wildly inaccurate notion of what is required for an action to be "morally appropriate." In effect this might be the situation of our earlier agent Sharon, who wants to do what act utilitarianism requires of her. She thinks "The best thing for me to do is to act in a way that would produce the most happiness, but I'm uncertain which of my options would do this. Given my uncertainty, it appears that the most reasonable thing for me to do, relative to my moral theory, is to perform the act that seems most likely to produce the most happiness." We said before that the act of Sharon's that seems to her most likely to produce the most happiness should count as the decision-mandated act for her, and also said that it appears Sharon is able to use utilitarianism indirectly to decide what to do. We can now see that Lenient Definition 13.2.1 more transparently implies she has this ability. Even an agent who is unsure whether or not act A is decision-mandated in the core sense for her, relative to P (or uncertain whether she believes that it is), may still come to believe that A is morally appropriate for her to perform, if she can deploy some other way to select an act that doesn't require her to be certain whether A is decision-mandated. However, Lenient Definition 13.2.1 does require that she selects the act in the belief that it is morally appropriate for her, relative to P and to her credences at t_i about herself and about A's relation to P. She can't simply select A in light of some other belief, such as the belief that A would be prudent for her, or the belief that it would be morally appropriate relative to some other governing moral theory.

Adopting Lenient Definition 13.2.1 would constitute a happy move in the direction of simplicity. One of the potential criticisms of the Hybrid solution, as I have developed it, is that it attempts to remedy agents' uncertainties about the world in which they act, and their uncertainties about certain features of their moral theory, by expanding the moral theory, adding additional layers of norms—norms that (given our rejection of the Low Bar approach) inevitably pose yet another epistemic hurdle for decision makers to surmount. If agents already struggle with uncertainty about their world or their moral theory, why should we expect that they will have the relevant beliefs about an even more complicated version of the moral theory? One answer to this criticism is that it isn't in fact unrealistic to think that many moral agents genuinely do have beliefs about the contents of a more complicated moral theory that enables them to make decisions despite their uncertainty. Many moral agents do have beliefs about which decision-guides are best for them to use when they are uncertain about the nonmoral features of their actions: they believe it would be appropriate to perform the act that is most likely to be right, or the act that would maximize expected value, or an act that is sufficiently likely to be right. For such agents to qualify (according to Definition 13.2) as able to use their moral theory indirectly, these beliefs need not be correct. For most agents the issue stops here: they have not asked themselves how likely it is that these decision-guides are correct, so they do not need to have beliefs about how best to make a decision if they are uncertain which decision-guide is correct. Thus the complexity of the moral theory beyond the level of decision-guides need never play a role in these agents' deliberations. However, for those who do suffer from higher levels of uncertainty,

Lenient Definition 13.2.1 counts them as able to use their moral theory indirectly so long as they have the relatively simple thought that a given action is morally appropriate relative to the moral theory and to their credences at t_i about themselves and about the act's relation to the moral theory. They do not need to fill out this thought by any detailed awareness of exactly what makes the act appropriate in this way. They do not need any awareness of the actual structure of the Hybrid moral theory. This is a very attractive feature of Lenient Definition 13.2.1. An agent who is uncertain all the way down about applying the truly comprehensive moral theory, or who is uncertain all the way down about the beliefs required by the truly comprehensive moral theory, or who has impoverished beliefs about which decision-guides are available to her, might nonetheless qualify as able to use her moral theory indirectly if she utilizes some other way to envision an appropriate connection between her moral theory and one of the acts available to her.

We have to recognize, however, that not every such agent may conceive of some way to do this. In Amber's case, for example, she is not only uncertain all the way down, but accepts the notion of decision-mandatoriness as defined in Definition 13.1, and believes that it is the correct account of which actions are morally appropriate to perform, relative to her moral theory and to her credences at t_i about herself and about her actions' relations to that theory. For her there is no decision-mandated or subjectively obligatory act, and moreover it is highly unlikely that she would qualify as being able to apply her moral theory in virtue of satisfying Lenient Definition 13.2.1, since she would reject any rival account of what makes an action morally appropriate for her. So accepting Lenient Definition 13.2.1 is no guarantee that every agent will be able to indirectly use her moral theory to make a decision.

Even though invoking Lenient Definition 13.2.1 may expand the number of agents who are able to apply their moral theories, nonetheless there is a serious problem with this lenient approach. Under Lenient Definition 13.2.1 an agent could qualify as someone who has the ability to indirectly use her moral principle to make her decision even though there is no defined decision-mandated (or subjectively obligatory) act for her to perform. Consider, for example, a Rossian agent Daria who is uncertain all the way down, but who nonetheless picks act A in the thought that it is morally appropriate for her relative to P and to her credences (perhaps she rejects our definitions of an act's being "decision-mandated" and "subjectively obligatory" and accepts some alternative definitions in their stead). According to Definition 13.2.1 she qualifies as able to indirectly use P. But given her uncertainties, no act actually qualifies as the decision-mandated or subjectively obligatory for her. Thus her ability to indirectly use her moral theory is unmoored from any underlying fact about there being any act which actually is most appropriate for her to perform, relative to P and to her credences.

If we adopt Lenient Definition 13.2.1, more agents will qualify as able to indirectly use their moral principle. This is a significant advantage, since it appears that agents such as Daria (who is uncertain all the way down, but who would nonetheless pick an action as morally appropriate) are ones who, like Sharon, should count as making a decision we can recognize as appropriate. If the beliefs (and lack of beliefs) of such an agent are non-culpable, then even in a situation in which the agent performs an act A that is both objectively wrong according to P and not decision-worthy, the fact that she performed it in the belief that A is morally appropriate relative to P and to her credences should mean that she is not blameworthy for performing A.

Nonetheless it's troubling that adopting Lenient Definition 13.2.1 would imply that in certain cases the multi-principle Hybrid approach can suffer from the same defect that we criticized in Feldman's single-principle approach. In these cases Lenient Definition 13.2.1 leaves agents to their own devices if they suffer from certain kinds of epistemic limitations, since the theory itself has no way to pick out what act is really most appropriate for them to select. In the case of Feldman's single-principle approach this defect afflicts every decision. In the case of Lenient Definition 13.2.1 it only arises in the relatively rare cases in which the agent satisfies Lenient Definition 13.2.1 but not Definition 13.2. Because of this deficiency I view Definition 13.2 as providing the primary definition of ability to indirectly use a moral principle, but nonetheless proffer Lenient Definition 13.2.1 as providing a sufficient condition for a weaker but still useful sense of ability to indirectly use a moral principle, a definition that some theorists may prefer to use.

13.4.7 Upshot

Doubtless there are other possible kinds of cases, as well, in which the Constrained Standards version of the Hybrid solution would fail to identify a decision-mandated act, or would fail to render a moral code indirectly usable by a given agent. It is always possible that some further developments of the theory might overcome these problems. But I am not sanguine. It appears to me that the theory I have presented is the best available version of the Hybrid theory, and I have difficulty seeing how it could be improved in ways that would render it invulnerable to the kinds of problems we have canvassed already (or to their successors). If this pessimism is correct, then the Hybrid solution fails in two ways to make moral codes usable, directly or indirectly, by every agent: there are some cases (such as that of Amber and Harry) in which there is no decision-mandated or subjectively obligatory act and in which there is no way for the agent to indirectly apply her moral theory; and there are other cases (such as that of Daria) in which there is no defined decision-mandatory or subjectively obligatory act for the agent to perform although the agent is able under Lenient Definition 13.2.1 to apply her moral theory. These cases may be unusual, but we have not found a way to preclude them.

The Hybrid solution remains the best answer to the problems of error and uncertainty even though it cannot wholly solve the epistemic limitations that agents confront. As we've seen, the Hybrid solution makes no pretense of trying to solve the problem of error. The kinds of uncertainties (as contrasted with false beliefs) that defeat the Hybrid solution may be relatively rare, especially among unsophisticated agents. A Hybrid theory's inclusion of a myriad of decision-guides, each tailored to a different epistemic limitation, enables it to provide guidance to a vast number of decision makers, unlike solutions that rely on one principle or guide to address all the possible epistemic limitations. There may be no complete solution. Recognizing that a comprehensive moral theory contains a vast array of resources that compensate for agents' uncertainties about the world and about morality goes a significant distance towards accomplishing this aim, but in the end it cannot overcome every kind of informational impoverishment. Those agents whose epistemic limitations leave them with no way to directly or indirectly apply their adopted moral theory in a given situation suffer from erosion in their autonomy in this situation. For their sakes we can only hope that the number of these situations is not large.

We should, however, recall that an agent's autonomy is only reduced if she is unable to apply the moral theory she has actually adopted. The fact that some other moral theory—one in which she has no interest—would not be usable by her does not affect her autonomy. Having adopted a moral theory, agents are likely to develop views about which decision-guides are suitable for indirect use of that theory when they are uncertain about the circumstances in which they want to apply it. This means many agents will come to most of their decisions already equipped with a list of what they regard as suitable decision-guides, so the actual impact on individuals' autonomy may not be large.

13.5 Is the Constrained Standards Hybrid Approach itself too Epistemically Demanding?

We now have a fairly clear picture of the Constrained Standards Hybrid approach to solving the epistemic problem for morality—its strengths and weaknesses, as well as its overall structure. It's true that substantial details of the approach remain to be filled in, most pressingly the content of the standards for evaluating guides, and the content of the various guides themselves. However, I have reasonable hope that the overall framework of the approach has been described sufficiently to steer the future work required to develop these important features of the theory.

One of the chief strengths of the approach, the fact that it enables many uncertain agents to nonetheless guide their choices by their chosen moral theory, arises in part from the structure of a comprehensive moral theory, which includes additional components that arm decision makers with the tools to make decisions despite their uncertainty. But it's a fair question whether this structure is in itself one of the weaknesses of the approach. The structure I have described is, in its full development, an elaborate edifice. Its complexity at least rivals the complexity of Kant's Categorical Imperative, and may well be even more conceptually difficult to grasp. Doesn't this fact leave the approach vulnerable to the charge that it has alleviated the problem of uncertainty at the level of the agent (who must choose how to act when she is uncertain about the nonmoral features of her prospective actions), only to create greater uncertainty at the level of the meta-ethicist (who may be unsure about the overall structure and content of the higher-level norms and guides)? In other words, doesn't it fall into the same trap as the ideal and non-ideal Pragmatic approaches, which I rejected on the ground that they only "solve" the epistemic problem by shifting it from the agent trying to decide how to act to the meta-ethicist trying to decide which account of right and wrong is correct?

This is a legitimate and indeed natural question. I would make several replies. First, the various Pragmatic approaches were rejected because they shifted the *very same epistemic problem*—a problem about ascertaining what nonmoral features prospective actions have—from the level of the agent to the level of the meta-ethicist. For example, the most promising Ideal Pragmatic approach to the problem of error is the moral laundry list. But just as the agent plagued by false beliefs about the world cannot identify the correct act according to a standard moral theory, so the meta-ethicist doesn't have sufficient knowledge about the world to identify which laundry list is correct. Parallel problems undermine the Non-Ideal Pragmatic solution to the problem of error and both the Ideal and Non-Ideal Pragmatic solutions to the problem of uncertainty. The purported advances made by Pragmatic solutions are fundamentally illusory because they only relocate the problem of lack of knowledge about the world to another level.

However, the Constrained Standards Hybrid approach, unlike the Pragmatic approach, does not simply shift a given problem from one level to another. Instead, it solves the problem at the level of the agent, but at the price of creating a different kind of problem at the level of the meta-ethicist. Because the standards for evaluating guides must be modally robust, the difficulty in identifying them does not have its source in any lack of knowledge about the world, unlike the original difficulty encountered by the agent. Mastering the Hybrid approach, or mastering any particular Constrained Standards moral theory, does not require mastery of nonmoral facts. So if the Constrained Standards Hybrid approach is subject to criticism as being epistemically demanding, it is not the same criticism that I leveled at the Pragmatic approach.

In Chapter 3 I differentiated the problem of moral ignorance and uncertainty from the problem of nonmoral ignorance and uncertainty, and said that this book would focus only on solving the latter. So it might appear I could simply decline to address any problem raised by the conceptual complexity of the Constrained Standards approach on the ground that it involves epistemic limitations about moral matters, not about nonmoral matters, and thus is beyond the scope of the book. However, the situation is not that simple. As we've seen in Chapters 12 and 13, providing an agent with a Constrained Standards Hybrid solution to her uncertainty about nonmoral matters requires giving her the equipment, in the form of decision-guides, to apply her moral theory indirectly. This "equipment" is part of the comprehensive moral theory, so if she lacks this moral information she will be unable to solve her nonmoral uncertainty. Thus the problem of moral uncertainty (at a certain level) and the problem of nonmoral uncertainty are inextricably intertwined.

However, we must keep in mind that in order to solve her problem of nonmoral certainty, the agent does not by any means need a full grasp of the complexities of the Constrained Standards Approach. Most agents who want to use a given moral theory can proceed quite successfully with only a grasp of the theory itself (its Code C), together with the idea that in cases of uncertainty they can apply the theory indirectly by utilizing appropriate decision-guides, such as ones recommending that they choose the action most likely to be right, or the action that would minimize the possible harm, or (for more sophisticated agents) the action that would maximize expected value. They don't need to think about the elaborate structure that supports this procedure. Deeper thinkers may ask why this is the best way to proceed, or may ask what makes one of these decision-guides better than another. These are the agents who will have occasion to explore the upper reaches of the Constrained Standards approach. But such agents will be in the tiny minority, and we can hope they have the intellectual resources to work out and understand the approach. In any event, the approach does not require that their beliefs about this structure be correct. There is reason to think these explorers will be assisted by the fact that the guides and standards appropriate for one moral theory will be very similar to those appropriate for every other moral theory, so (for example) work done by utilitarian thinkers can benefit deontological thinkers as well. But for most agents no such enterprise is required.

This contrasts with the "problem-shifting" issue afflicting the Pragmatic approach, in which almost every agent in almost every uncertain decision is blocked by the fact that no one has been able to work out what the content of the correct moral theory is, since no one has the requisite empirical information. This is a far more serious weakness in the Pragmatic approach.

All things considered, then, I conclude that the "problem-shifting" criticism of the Constrained Standards approach is not nearly as serious as it may appear at first glance.

13.6 Conclusion

This chapter concludes my development of the Hybrid solution to the problems of error and uncertainty. We can understand the Constrained Standards version of the Hybrid solution as consisting of the following chief components:

(1)   the truly comprehensive version of each moral theory, comprising

    (a)   an account of what makes actions objectively right and wrong (Code C),

    (b)   an account of what makes actions subjectively obligatory or right in terms of their decision-mandatoriness or decision-worthiness (Code C**),

    (c)   a set of standards to evaluate decision-guiding norms at the required levels (Standards S_1, S_2, S_3, and so forth),

    (d)   sets of decision-guiding norms at ascending levels (decision-guides, precepts, maxims, counsels, and so forth);

(2)   the requirement that the appropriateness and rankings of the guides be modally robust relative to the moral theory in question;

(3)   Definition 13.1 for an action's being decision-mandatory, decision-worthy, or decision-prohibited in the core sense;

(4)   Definition 13.2 and (possibly) Lenient Definition 13.2.1 for ability to indirectly use a moral principle in the core sense as a decision-guide.

The Constrained Standards Hybrid solution requires agents, in order to qualify as able to indirectly use their moral theory, to have beliefs about the appropriateness of some action relative to that theory and to their credences about their situation. It implicitly incorporates the Austere solution to the problem of error, since it provides a theoretical account of the objective right-making features of actions that countenances erroneous beliefs that agents might have about the nonmoral features of their prospective acts.

At various points I have argued that the solution to the problems of error and uncertainty should meet several criteria. In concluding Chapter 14 I will revisit those criteria to assess the extent to which the Constrained Standards version of the Hybrid solution meets those criteria, and how it compares overall with its main rivals, the Austere and Pragmatic solutions.

14

Conclusion

Ethics is supposed to serve as a moral compass.[1]

In Chapter 1 I described two primary tasks for a morality's tool for evaluating actions, its theory of right conduct. The first task is a theoretical one: to explain the moral status of actions by providing an account of the features that make actions right or wrong. The second task is a practical one: to assist agents in choosing which actions to perform and which not.[2] Some theorists hold that a moral theory must accord equal priority to both these tasks, while other theorists privilege one of the tasks over the other, or even view a moral theory as charged with only one of these tasks. This book has conducted an extended examination of the questions of whether, how, and why, a moral theory might carry out the practical task of action guidance. The questions are pressing ones, because human agents are subject to two salient epistemic impediments to using traditional moral theories to make decisions: they suffer from the problem of error when their false beliefs about the nonmoral aspects of the world can result in their deriving erroneous prescriptions from their moral theory, and they suffer from the problem of uncertainty when their uncertainty about the nonmoral aspects of the world results in their inability to derive any prescription at all from their moral theory.

The first project of the book, carried out in Chapter 2, was to spell out what is required for a moral principle to be usable for decision-making. Careful examination of this concept revealed the importance of differentiating "core" from "extended" usability of a moral principle. In Chapter 3 I then turned to the question of why it might be required that a moral theory must be usable in either of these senses. Four rationales are prominent among those that have been offered for this Usability Demand. These rationales claim, respectively, that a moral theory should offer practical guidance because (1) the primary or even sole aim of a theory of right action is to be usable by moral agents for making decisions; (2) such a theory must achieve a special form of justice by enabling all moral agents to live a successful moral life; (3) the theory's

---

[1] Rhodes (2015).
[2] Although we have focused on the use of moral theories by epistemically limited decision makers, we should not forget that theories of right conduct perform other tasks as well: for example, they are used by observers to evaluate the conduct of others or themselves in the past. Such evaluators struggle with the same epistemic limitations that can cripple decision makers.

currency should enhance social welfare (or the special goods achievable only through social cooperation and consensus); and (4) the theory's currency should result in an ideal pattern of actions, that is, actions that conform with the theoretical account of right and wrong. It is claimed that these achievements can only be obtained by a moral theory that is genuinely usable for guiding action.

Chapter 3 continued by examining three dominant responses to the claim that a moral theory must be capable of providing action guidance. The first response I called the "Pragmatic approach." It holds that the theoretical function of morality cannot be isolated from its practical or regulative function, in the sense that one crucial test of a moral principle's theoretical correctness just *is* its practical usability by the limited human beings who will actually employ it. For advocates of this first approach, the content of a moral theory is constrained by its regulative role; any moral theory that fails to fulfill this role must be rejected. The second response I called the "Austere approach." It denies that a moral theory should be judged by how well it carries out the practical task, holding instead that the only role to be played by an account of right action is the theoretical role of explaining what features make actions right or wrong. For advocates of the Austere approach, a moral principle's practical usability, or lack thereof, is no test of its adequacy or inadequacy as a theoretical account of right and wrong. The third response I called the "Hybrid approach." It rejects both extremes, and instead attempts to blend the best parts of the Austere approach and the Pragmatic approach in a manner that pays allegiance both to the view that the correctness of a moral principle is not affected by its practical usability, and also to the view that moral principles must be usable for making decisions. The Hybrid approach attempts to achieve these goals by two stratagems. First, it divides the moral theory into two tiers: one tier provides the theoretical account of objective moral status, while a second tier provides suitable practical guidance for those hoping to comply with the prescriptions of the first tier. Second, the Hybrid approach introduces the concept of "indirectly" applying a moral theory. According to this approach, an agent counts as indirectly using a first-tier theoretical account of right and wrong when she appropriately utilizes the second tier's rules to guide her actions. According to this approach, the Usability Demand is satisfied by indirect as well as by direct usability.

To ascertain which of these three approaches is best, we separated the problem of error from the problem of uncertainty, examining first how the three approaches deal with the problem of error. Chapters 4–7 examined the Pragmatic approach to this problem.

Ideal versions of the Pragmatic approach aim to provide a moral theory that can be used without error by every moral agent—no matter how cognitively limited—on every occasion for decision. We quickly saw, however, that standard proposals for theories often advertised as meeting the goal of usability, such as simple deontological codes and the subjectivizing theories of Prichard and Ross, fall significantly short of satisfying the ideal version of the goal, since agents frequently make mistakes about the deontological features of actions, and indeed make mistakes about their own beliefs. The radical objectivizing theory that successfully meets this goal—the moral laundry list—only achieves universal usability by dint of shifting the problem of error from the level of normative theory to the level of meta-ethical theory. Hence the apparent victory it procures over agents' epistemic limitations is fundamentally illusory. Furthermore, as I argued in Chapter 5, subjectivizing codes violate the requirement that an acceptable moral theory must provide a satisfactory account of our duty to acquire information before deciding how to act.

Having found no viable ideal Pragmatic solution to the problem of error, we next examined non-ideal Pragmatic approaches. These approaches weaken the demand to provide universally usable moral codes to a less taxing demand to provide codes that are merely highly usable, more usable than standard moral theories. A complex argument in Chapters 6 and 7 showed that even these non-ideal Pragmatic approaches to the problem of error fail to achieve their goal. A major portion of these chapters was devoted to working out, in a way not previously attempted, exactly what a non-ideal Pragmatic theorist should seek in a moral code. I began by arguing that "bare usability" is not what the Pragmatic theorist needs by way of usability in a moral code. Instead the theorist should focus on a code's extended usability *value*—a value that depends on two features of the code: the deontic merit of its principles, and how usable its principles are. We discovered, however, that the epistemic challenge of securing even high usability value in a code is insurmountable. We also saw that the logic of the non-ideal Pragmatic position drives it back to the ideal Pragmatic position, which we had already dismissed as suffering fatal epistemic costs at the meta-ethical level. Moreover, we found that even codes with high usability values fail, other things being equal, to necessarily promote three of the four rationales claimed for highly usable moral codes: achievement of the special form of justice, enhancement of welfare and social consensus, and production of a better pattern of actions. Finally, we concluded that even if non-ideal Pragmatic solutions to the Usability Demand avoided being driven back to the ideal Pragmatic position, and were epistemically attainable, nonetheless they would typically come at a high price: the price of accepting an undesirable decrease in the deontic merit of the best code, since deontic merit must often be significantly compromised in order to attain increased usability. Thus (even setting aside the problem that the non-ideal Pragmatic solution merges back into the Ideal solution with all its problems) at most the non-ideal Pragmatic solution can achieve a limited version of the conceptual advantage of usability, but the epistemic costs of such a solution place it far beyond our reach, it cannot be guaranteed to satisfy three of the four rationales for usability, and the deontic price may be higher than we want to accept.

Given that the Pragmatic approach to the problem of error displays such deficiencies, I turned in Chapter 8 to a consideration of the Hybrid and Austere approaches to this problem, beginning with the Hybrid approach. Hybrid approaches endorse moral theories that involve two tiers, an upper-tier Code C (the theoretical account) and a lower-tier Code C* (the practical decision-guiding component). In an ideal Hybrid solution, the acts an agent would perform if she attempted to follow the lower-tier rules of Code C* would be the very same acts prescribed by the upper-tier principles of Code C. Unfortunately, we saw that the only discoverable Code C* that meets this standard is the moral laundry list, now reconfigured as a decision-guide. However, no agent afflicted with the problem of error is in a position to know what the content of the appropriate laundry list decision-guide would be. Nor is there likely to be any advisor or theorist who would know infallibly what the content of this decision-guide would be. Once again, the original epistemic challenge has simply been shifted to the meta-ethical level but not surmounted. In short the ideal Hybrid solution collapses, for much the same reason that the ideal Pragmatic solution collapses.

This conclusion led me to consider the non-ideal Hybrid approach to the problem of error, which attempts to find a two-tier code in which the lower-level tier would merely secure high, although not perfect, usability. Such a theory would retain a deontically pure theoretical account of right-making characteristics while supplementing this with a practical Code C* that improves (even if it does not perfect) agents' ability to link their theory with their choices. However, our examination of this proposal revealed that it, like its predecessors, is too epistemically demanding on agents and theorists. Moreover, we observed that the standard for determining the better of any two decision-guides actually drives the non-ideal Hybrid theorist back into ideal Hybrid theory, and forces her to accept the laundry list decision-guide as the best possible guide. Since this guide presents an insuperable epistemic problem, non-ideal Hybrid theory turns out to be the same dead end that ideal Hybrid theory is.

Moving on to the Austere approach to the problem of error, we found that it is distinctly more promising. According to the Austere approach, a moral code's practical usability, or lack thereof, is no sign of its adequacy or inadequacy as a theoretical account of right and wrong. Purely theoretical considerations govern the determination of which moral code is correct. Thus the Austere approach rejects the Usability Demand. Those persuaded by the Austere approach's refusal to dumb down its account of right and wrong to accommodate human limitations, but who still care about usability, may be attracted by the fact that an Austere theory can nonetheless incorporate a normative requirement that agents improve their knowledge as much as is appropriate before making a moral decision (Chapter 5 explored what the content of such a requirement should be), thus increasing the theory's usability. Of equal importance, the Austere approach can claim to provide an important form of autonomy for agents who, suffering from the problem of error, nonetheless can use their moral code in the *core* sense. The Austere approach enables such agents to make decisions in the light of their values, and so does not leave them rudderless when choosing how to act. Austere theories provide this form of autonomy to any agent who believes of some act that it complies with her moral theory, even if her belief is false. Such an agent has access to a principled way to determine what conduct to engage in. Her choice, if not her action, is suitably shaped by her values. Thus, although Austere theorists themselves may have no interest in this, those who feel the force of the Usability Demand may find that Austere theories offer a fair amount of usability.

Moreover, the Austere approach can secure a variant on the special form of justice required in the second rationale. At this point I argued that the most defensible conception of the special form of justice required of a moral theory is a modest one that requires every agent to have the opportunity to lead a successful moral life *in the sense that* a properly motivated agent can always avoid blameworthiness for her acts, even though she sometimes, through faulty beliefs, performs an act that is wrong. This form of justice is attainable in cases of error by any moral theory exemplifying the Austere approach so long as it has a suitable account of excusing conditions under which agents are not to blame for morally wrong acts done from ignorance (or from non-culpable ignorance).

Finally, the Austere approach can claim that it shields the theoretical account of right-making characteristics from distortions arising from attempts to impose pragmatic constraints on that account. Despite the fact that the Austere approach itself rejects the importance of usability in a moral code, nonetheless in cases involving the problem of error it manages to preserve the purity of its theoretical account while securing both core usability (and its attendant form of autonomy) and a modest version of the special form of justice that can be demanded of morality. For those who care about usability, these are no small achievements. However, I argued that the Austere approach cannot be credited with necessarily enhancing social welfare or guaranteeing an ideal pattern of actions, so it fails to satisfy the third and fourth (goal-oriented) rationales for usability.

The upshot of these investigations is that neither the Pragmatic nor Hybrid approach provides an adequate solution to the problem of error. The Austere solution appears to provide an acceptable solution to at least this problem, even though it, like the other two approaches, cannot claim to satisfy the goal-oriented rationales for seeking usability in a moral code. With this result in hand, we turned our focus to the problem of uncertainty. Chapter 9 began by developing a detailed understanding of what is encompassed by the problem of uncertainty. We then sought a moral system capable of jointly addressing the problem of error and the problem of uncertainty.

Given that the Austere approach to the problem of error is the most successful, there are only three types of moral systems that might accomplish this task: a system that offers the Austere solution to both problems, a system that offers the Austere solution to the problem of error but a Pragmatic solution to the problem of uncertainty, and a system that offers the Austere solution to the problem of error but a Hybrid solution to the problem of uncertainty. The first of these types of systems was readily found to be unacceptable to anyone who cares about usability, since the Austere solution to the problem of error can provide no guidance at all to an agent facing the problem of uncertainty. Such an agent is unable to use her moral code, even in the core sense, to make a decision. Hence in cases of uncertainty she cannot even achieve the form of autonomy we described as arising from core usability.

Turning to systems that join the Austere solution to the problem of error with the Pragmatic solution to the problem of uncertainty, I found no way to maintain the central commitments of both the Austere and Pragmatic approaches and at the same time to provide a suitable set of decision-guides for uncertain agents, avoid inconsistent theoretical assessments or inconsistent decision-guiding prescriptions, and avoid new and insurmountable epistemic challenges to the decision-guiding component of the system. This combination of approaches is simply not viable.

This leaves, as the remaining contenders, systems involving the Austere approach to the problem of error and a Hybrid approach to the problem of uncertainty. Such a system can avoid inconsistent prescriptions by recognizing that a moral theory involves two separate codes. The upper-tier Code C only concerns theoretical assessments of right and wrong, and issues prescriptions using one set of evaluative terms (temporarily represented by "ought$_1$," "right$_1$," and "wrong$_1$"). Lower-tier Code C*, which is only concerned with practical decision-guiding advice, consists of decision-guides that appropriately link the theoretical account of right and wrong with reasonable recommendations about what to do when one is uncertain what the circumstances and outcomes of one's actions might be. Code C* issues prescriptions using a different set of evaluative terms (temporarily represented by "ought$_2$," "right$_2$," and "wrong$_2$"). Using different sets of evaluative terms allows such a system to avoid inconsistent prescriptions while maintaining an uncompromised Austere account of what makes actions right and wrong. It also offers decision-guides capable of issuing advice to agents whether they are ensnared by the problem of error or the problem of uncertainty. In offering such guides it supports agents' autonomy by enabling them to connect their values with their choices, and (equipped with a suitable theory of excuses) it can promise the modestly successful moral life to all well-motivated agents, even though they lack perfect information.

However, such a system cannot guarantee that an otherwise attractive moral theory will satisfy the two goal-oriented desiderata for a moral code, since it cannot claim necessarily to enhance social welfare (or social cooperation) or to produce an ideal pattern of actions. I argued that we need to abandon these goal-oriented rationales. An agent directly using her moral theory may be tripped up by false beliefs about her world so that her pattern of action fails to enhance social welfare or conform to the requirements of the theoretical account of right and wrong. And even an agent faced with uncertainty who follows the very best advice genuinely available to her will inevitably fail on occasion to perform the right action according to Code C. Only good luck would result in her pattern of actions conforming in every case to the moral theory, and luck, by its very nature, cannot be guaranteed. It follows that there can be no reason to expect that the actions of an agent successfully using a Hybrid theory's decision-guides will necessarily maximize welfare, or secure the benefits of social cooperation, even if perfect conformity to the theory itself would have done that. Proponents of usability should therefore discard goal-oriented rationales (3) and (4). We have seen no realistic way to satisfy these rationales, and it may have been a mistake to suppose that we could, or that we ought to try.

Having argued that a Hybrid system involving the Austere account of the principles in Code C is the best approach to the problems of error and uncertainty, I began in

Chapter 10 to investigate these systems more closely. Chapter 10 reviewed selected attempts to build a Hybrid system by offering a single decision-making principle as the system's Code C*. We saw that such systems all fall short, primarily because they fail to provide guidance to many agents. Consequently, in Chapter 11 we turned to multi-rule Hybrid systems which offer an extensive array of decision-guiding rules with the view to providing for each agent attempting to indirectly apply the system's Code C at least one usable rule on each occasion for decision. The decision-guiding rules are hierarchically organized in terms of their deontic superiority; agents are advised to employ the highest-ranked rule they can use. Provision of a rule that any agent can use is guaranteed by the fact that the hierarchy of decision-guides terminates in a bottom-most Decision-Guide N which simply prescribes as choice-worthy any available action. An agent who is so uncertain about the nonmoral features of her choice (or so beleaguered by other cognitive limitations) that she can use none of the higher-ranked decision-guides can, as a last resort, turn to this rule for guidance.

Chapter 12 was then dedicated to further development and exploration of the system that I now termed the "Hybrid" solution to both the problems of error and uncertainty. Part of this project involved resolving how this solution should deal with cases in which the agent suffers not only from *nonmoral* error or uncertainty about the circumstances and consequences of her action, but also from *moral* error or uncertainty about which decision-guides are appropriate to her Code C, and how they should be rank-ordered relative to each other. Addressing the problem of this sort of moral error, I argued that we should accept, as the relevant notion of ability to indirectly use a Code C, core rather than extended ability. Hence ability to indirectly use Code C does not require the agent to have true beliefs about which decision-guide is best for her to use.

In Chapters 12 and 13 I then considered three ways in which the Hybrid solution could address the problem of moral uncertainty. The first, the Low Bar approach, makes no demands on an agent's beliefs about which usable decision-guide is ranked highest. All it requires is the truth of the counterfactual that *if* an agent believed of the guide that is highest-ranked (or tied for highest) that it is ranked highest (or tied for highest), then she would derive a prescription for action from it. She is not required to actually believe this of any decision-guide. Thus an agent's moral uncertainty is no bar to her ability to indirectly use her Code C on the Low Bar approach. However, in Chapter 12 I rejected the Low Bar approach as unsatisfactory, because it makes it all too easy for a moral principle to qualify as indirectly usable.

Next, also in Chapter 12, I introduced the Expanded Moral Theory approach, the second way in which the Hybrid solution might respond to the problem of moral uncertainty. The Expanded Theory approach comes to the rescue of the morally uncertain agent by adding new elements to the moral theory itself. The Hybrid approach already incorporated a hierarchy of decision-guides for agents facing nonmoral uncertainty about actions, but the Expanded Moral Theory approach supplements those guides with a variety of additional components, including higher-level guides (such as precepts, maxims, and counsels) intended to assist an agent who faces moral uncertainty about the rank-ordering of decision-guides on the various tiers. Thus, for example, a theory embodying the Expanded Moral Theory approach includes precepts advising the agent which decision-guide to use when she is uncertain which decision-guide is ranked highest but does have credences concerning the *likelihoods* that various decision-guides are ranked highest.

Chapter 13 continued to refine the Expanded Moral Theory. As we saw in Chapter 11, Code C* advises an agent to perform as subjectively right the act prescribed as choice-worthy by the agent's highest usable decision-guide, but this was shown to be insufficient to guide an agent who is uncertain what her highest usable decision-guide is. Such an agent could nonetheless believe that a given decision-guide is subjectively right because it is prescribed by the objectively highest usable precept, or could believe that a decision-guide is prescribed by a precept that is subjectively right. To accommodate the prescriptions for agents that become possible when this is recognized, Chapter 13 introduced the new concept of decision-worthiness to help agents choose an act in such cases. It then reformulated Code C* as Code C**, which advises an agent to perform as subjectively right the decision-worthy action. A new definition for a Code C's indirect usability was formulated in terms of the agent's belief about some act that it is decision-worthy, rather than, as earlier, in terms of her belief about some act that it is prescribed as choice-worthy by the highest usable decision-guide. This definition of indirect usability, unlike the Low Bar approach, requires an agent to have an appropriate belief about which decision-guide is best for her to use. She is enabled to meet this requirement because of the additional resources that have been added to a comprehensive moral theory. The revised definition of "indirect usability" substantially expands the numbers of agents who are able to employ a chosen moral theory to guide their decisions.

However, Chapter 13 also showed that the Expanded Moral Theory approach, despite these refinements, fails to enable *all* uncertain agents to indirectly use their Code C. There remain some agents who are uncertain about which act they should perform to adhere to their Code C, and who further do not believe of any identifiable decision-guide that it is the best one available to them, because they know that there always exists an even better (though unidentifiable) "moral laundry list" among the decision-guides of Code C**. These agents will recognize that there is no decision-worthy act available to them and therefore will not count as able to indirectly use their Code C. This led me to build on the Expanded Moral Theory approach to develop the third and final approach to the problem of moral uncertainty: the Constrained Standards approach.

The Constrained Standards approach subscribes to a definition of indirect usability that (like the Expanded Moral Theory approach) requires agents to possess appropriate credences about which decision-guide is best for them to use. The approach seeks to ensure that all agents will have the necessary credences by placing constraints on which standards determine the deontic rank-ordering of decision-guides (and of higher-level guides, such as precepts and maxims. One promising constraint for doing this work is the requirement that decision-guides must be modally robust relative to their moral theory: their appropriateness and relative ranking must remain invariant in all near-by possible worlds. Because the moral laundry list is not modally robust in this way, it is ruled out as a decision-guide, and thus the Constrained Standards approach is inoculated against the problem arising from the possibility of a moral laundry list decision-guide that proved fatal for the Extended Moral Theory approach.

Despite this success, Chapter 13 noted that, even on the Constrained Standards approach, there remain some agents in special or unusual circumstances who are unable to use their moral theory, even indirectly. I offered a way to return at least some such agents to the realm of usability, namely by resorting to a more lenient definition (Lenient Definition 13.2.1) of the ability to indirectly use a moral principle that is nonetheless still in keeping within the spirit of the Constrained Standards approach. Although I did not adopt this more lenient definition as a default component of the Constrained Standards approach, I presented it so that those who would like to avail themselves of its advantages may do so. Even so, there are a few possible agents in special situations who would be unable to apply their moral theory, even according to this lenient standard for usability.

I have argued that the solution to the problems of error and uncertainty should meet several criteria. At various points in the book, I have revisited those criteria in order to assess the extent to which the various approaches satisfy them. Now I will turn to this task in a more systematic way in order to display more precisely the extent to which the Constrained Standard version of the Hybrid approach meets or falls short of these criteria.

To do this it is useful to introduce the idea of a moral theory that *successfully* embodies the Constrained Standards Hybrid moral theory approach, calling such a moral theory a "Constrained Standards Hybrid theory" or "CSH theory" for short. To assess the degree to which the Constrained Standard version of the Hybrid approach meets or falls short of our criteria, we should focus exclusively on CSH moral theories. A CSH theory includes all the elements of a truly comprehensive moral theory: a Code C account of what makes actions objectively right or wrong, a Code C** account of what makes actions subjectively right or wrong in terms of their decision-worthiness, a set of standards to evaluate decision-guiding norms at each level, and sets of decision-guiding norms at as many ascending levels as are needed (decision-guides, precepts, maxims, counsels, and so forth). The CSH moral theory meets the requirement that the appropriateness and rankings of the guides be modally robust relative to the moral theory in question, and its concepts satisfy Definition 13.1 for an action's being decision-mandatory in the core sense, as well as Definition 13.2 and (potentially) Lenient Definition 13.2.1 for ability to indirectly use a moral principle in the core sense as a decision-guide. Furthermore, to count as successful, such a moral theory's Code C** must be appropriate relative to its Code C, its standards for evaluating the decision-guiding norms must be appropriate relative to its Code C, and the decision-guiding norms must meet those standards and be modally robust. Moreover, the norms must be as extensive as possible, enabling as many agents as possible to use them in deciding how to act.[3] Many moral theories do not qualify as CSH theories because as yet they lack some necessary component or possess some inappropriate component given the theory's Code C.

According to the four rationales that have been offered for the Usability Demand, a moral theory should offer practical guidance because (1) the primary or even sole aim of a theory of right action is to be usable by moral agents for making decisions; (2) such a theory must achieve a special form of justice by enabling all moral agents to live a successful moral life; (3) the theory's currency should enhance social welfare (or the special goods achievable only through social cooperation and consensus); or (4) the theory's currency should result in an ideal pattern of actions, that is, actions that conform with the theoretical account of right and wrong.

Of the original four rationales, we concluded that a CSH theory cannot be guaranteed to satisfy rationales (3) and (4), the goal-oriented rationales, and indeed may often fall significantly short of satisfying them. There can be no guarantee that, other things being equal, adoption of a CSH theory will promote social welfare or an ideal pattern of action. This leaves the two conceptual rationales, the requirements that (1) a moral theory should be usable even by epistemically limited human beings for making decisions, and that (2) currency of the moral theory should achieve a special form of justice under the most defensible interpretation of this concept, by enabling all moral agents to live a modestly successful moral life. Although the promise of a CSH theory to meet these rationales appears to be substantial, Chapter 13 conceded that such a theory cannot be guaranteed to fully meet requirement (1), that is, be usable, even indirectly, by *every* human being, no matter how pervasive her uncertainty. However, it appears that a CSH theory, with all its resources for guiding agents struggling with various degrees and levels of uncertainty, both about the nonmoral world and about sub-components of the moral theory, can be expected to provide more indirect usability than any other type of theory, at least without sacrificing other desiderata. And the potentially wide array of these resources in the form of various levels of guides for decisions suggests that this job will be good indeed. Unfortunately, only a few of these decision-guides have yet been developed, justified, and ranked relative to each other.

By the same token a CSH theory satisfies, to a great extent if not completely, what we might identify as a fifth conceptual rationale for seeking a usable moral theory (perhaps really a recasting of the first rationale), namely the rationale requiring that a moral theory secure a form of autonomy for agents that enables them to guide their decisions by reference to their values. As discussed in Chapter 13, a CSH moral theory enables an agent to make decisions in light of her beliefs about the objective moral status of her actions, even when those beliefs are false. And to the greatest extent possible,

---

[3] Note I am not requiring that the theory's Code C itself be morally correct.

it enables an agent who is uncertain about the objective moral status of her actions to make a decision despite her uncertainty, because she can apply her theory indirectly by appealing to its decision-guides. Such agents are thus equipped with a compass in their endeavors to make decisions that are appropriate to their moral values.

What about requirement (2), that currency of the moral theory should achieve a special form of justice by enabling all moral agents to live a modestly successful moral life (that is, a life in which a well-intentioned agent can avoid blameworthiness)? If we regard an agent as blameless, despite the fact that she does something wrong, so long as she acted either in the belief that what she did was objectively right, or in the belief that what she did was subjectively right, or in the more general belief that what she did was morally appropriate relative to her moral theory and her credences about herself and about her act's relationship to her moral theory, then the Hybrid solution is consistent with this, since it can require that CSH moral theory incorporate such a position about the circumstances under which agents are blameless.[4] Indeed, a CSH moral theory could expand on this by incorporating a clause excusing agents who must decide how to act even though they cannot use their moral theory, even indirectly, to derive a prescription for action. The detailed content of such a clause should be explored, but one plausible candidate would be a clause stipulating simply that a person is excused from blameworthiness if she acts from the (perhaps reasonable) belief that she cannot derive any prescription for action from her moral theory. An appropriate clause of this sort is fully consistent with the Constrained Standards Hybrid approach, and together with the clauses described above setting out conditions for non-culpability, would provide the backbone for an appropriate account of blameworthiness within a CSH moral theory. Thus a CSH moral theory can secure the special form of justice for moral agents, since it equips them with a comprehensive moral theory and a set of concepts that enable them to use that theory, either directly or indirectly, for most of their decisions, and it can incorporate a suitable account of the conditions under which agents are blameless for any wrongful acts. Well-intentioned agents trying to follow such a moral theory can live a modestly successful moral life.

In addition to the four general rationales for requiring a moral theory to be usable for making decisions even in cases of error and uncertainty, of which CSH theories meet Rationale (2) and come as close as seems possible to satisfactorily meeting Rationale (1), I adopted five criteria for evaluating specifically Hybrid solutions to the problem of uncertainty. These were originally stated in Chapter 10. Since we have replaced Code C* of the original formulations of Hybrid theories with Code C**, and have also made certain other changes, these criteria need to be restated as follows (to mark these changes I label them Criterion A*, Criterion B*, and so forth):

Criterion A* (**Consistency**): When a Code C and a Code C** are paired in a single CSH moral theory, their prescriptions should be consistent.

---

[4] For some alternative views about what renders agents blameless, see note 6 to the subsequent discussion of Criterion E*.

Criterion B* (**Moral Adequacy**): The guiding prescriptions issued by Code C** in a CSH moral theory for an agent who accepts the theory's Code C as the correct theoretical account of rightness and wrongness should be morally appropriate for that Code C. Put differently, an action prescribed by Code C** should be morally reasonable or wise for the agent to choose, relative to a commitment to C and to the agent's epistemic grasp of the situation.

Criterion C* (**Guidance Adequacy**): Assuming that Code C in a CSH moral theory provides an exhaustive account of the moral status of all actual and humanly possible actions, then the decision-guiding rule(s) of the theory's Code C** should be such that for every agent and every occasion for decision, there is an appropriate rule in Code C** which can be directly used by the agent for making a decision on that occasion.

Criterion D* (**Normative Adequacy**): For each plausible theoretic account of right and wrong C, it should be possible to define a C** that would enable every agent affected by the problems of error and uncertainty to apply C indirectly to each of her decisions through directly applying the decision-guiding rule(s) of C**.

Criterion E* (**Relation to Blameworthiness**): A CSH moral theory should evaluate an agent as not blameworthy for performing an action if she performs it because she accepts the moral theory, and believes (or reasonably believes) that the action is prescribed as subjectively or objectively right or obligatory by either Code C or Code C** of the theory. Such evaluations should be independently plausible, given our background concept of what makes agents blameworthy for their actions.

It appears that the Hybrid solution and CSH moral theories come as close to satisfying these criteria as it is possible to come.

The first criterion, Criterion A* (Consistency) requires that when a Code C (encompassing the principles of objective moral status) and a Code C** (the overarching principle of subjective moral status) are paired in a single CSH moral theory, their prescriptions should be consistent. This is met by CSH moral theories, since in such theories Code C and Code C** issue prescriptions utilizing different evaluative terms. For example, Code C prescribes actions as objectively right, while Code C** prescribes actions as subjectively right. The subjective rightness of an action depends on its being decision-worthy. Direct prescriptions for actions derived from decision-guides are prescriptions for those actions as choice-worthy rather than either objectively or subjectively right, so it is impossible for the decision-guides' prescriptions to be inconsistent with those of either Code C or Code C**, or with prescriptions for actions as decision-worthy. These terms have all been chosen to avoid any technically inconsistent prescriptions. Of course a single act might be (for example) both objectively right and subjectively wrong, or vice versa. But this is what the structure of the comprehensive theory should permit, just as the structure of a Rossian-type deontic theory should allow an action to be both prima facie right but all-things-considered wrong.

The second criterion, Criterion B* (Moral Adequacy), requires that the guiding prescriptions issued by Code C** in a CSH moral theory for an agent who accepts the theory's Code C as the correct theoretical account of rightness and wrongness should be morally appropriate for that Code C. According to this criterion, an action prescribed by Code C** should be morally reasonable or wise for the agent to choose, relative to a commitment to C and to the agent's epistemic grasp of the situation, which may include false or uncertain beliefs about nonmoral aspects of her situation, or false or uncertain beliefs about the components of the moral theory beyond Code C itself. A comprehensive Constrained Standards Hybrid moral theory includes Standards S_1, S_2, and so forth. The job of these standards is to determine which guides are appropriate relative to C. Suitable standards will guarantee that the prescriptions issued by the moral theory's Code C** are indeed morally appropriate relative to its Code C. Thus any genuine comprehensive CSH moral theory will meet Criterion B*.

The real question here is whether any genuine CSH moral theory—that is, a moral theory that *successfully* embodies the Constrained Standards Hybrid approach—actually exists or can be constructed. I have not proved that any CSH exists, much less that a normatively attractive one exists. I have only described what features such a theory must have. We are familiar, of course, with many plausible proposals for the content of Code C. However, our assurance that a CSH theory exists depends on our finding the correct standards for evaluating decision-guides within any proposed theory, and on our identifying suitable arrays of decision-guides for that theory. I have not argued for any particular set of standards, or for any particular sets of decision-guides. Until the case for particular standards and decision-guides has successfully been made, we cannot be certain that a genuine CSH theory exists. A great deal of theoretical work remains to be done before we will have reached this point. However, I am hopeful that now the task has been described, this work will be accomplished over time.

The third criterion, Criterion C* (Guidance Adequacy), requires that the decision-guiding rule(s) in the Code C** of a CSH moral theory be such that for every agent and every occasion for decision-making, there is an appropriate decision-guiding rule which can be directly used by the agent to make a decision on that occasion. Any CSH moral theory meets this demand, given the availability of many decision-guides, and given that the last resort decision-guide for subjective rightness tells the agent that any action is choice-worthy. Presumably every moral agent could at least directly follow this last resort guide.[5] We should not be misled by this, however, since this criterion by itself is too weak to procure universal usability: although for each agent and each occasion for decision there is a decision-guide that the agent can directly use, nonetheless it may not be possible for the agent to use Code C indirectly by appealing to this directly usable decision-guide (since the agent may not have the relevant belief about how

[5] The hierarchy of decision-guides for subjective obligation does not include a similar last resort decision-guide. However, an agent who cannot determine which decision-guide for subjective obligation is ranked highest can then turn to decision-guides for subjective rightness.

this decision-guide is ranked relative to others). Or there may be no decision-worthy act for that agent. To better capture the Usability Demand, we need to strengthen this criterion as follows:

> **Criterion C**** **(Guidance Adequacy):** Assuming that Code C in a CSH moral theory provides an exhaustive account of the moral status of all actual and humanly possible actions, then it should be possible, for every agent and every occasion for decision-making, to use Code C directly or indirectly to make a decision about what to do on that occasion.

As we have seen, any CSH moral theory goes a very long way towards meeting Criterion C** (especially if we invoke Lenient Definition 13.2.1 of indirect usability), since every CSH moral theory is equipped with a multiplicity of guides at various levels, tailored to different epistemic situations of various possible agents. Each level of guides that issues prescriptions regarding "choice-worthiness" includes a last resort guide similar to the last resort Decision-Guide N, which states that every available action is choice-worthy. Criterion C** could be interpreted as demanding that each Code C be usable in both the core and the extended sense. However, I argued that usability in the core sense is sufficient, and is in fact the most that could be justifiably demanded of a moral theory. Nonetheless, we also saw that even a CSH moral theory may not be able to meet this demand fully, since there may be agents whose uncertainties cannot be circumvented by any decision-making resource the theory can provide. Perhaps these cases are few and far between, but they are certainly possible. Sadly, there seems no effective solution on the horizon to fully vanquish this problem.

The fourth criterion, Criterion D* (Normative Adequacy), although its statement is quite similar to that of Criterion C**, has a different focus. It requires that the Hybrid solution be highly general: it should provide, *for each plausible theoretic account of right and wrong* (or Code C), an associated Code C** that would enable every agent affected by the problem of uncertainty to apply C indirectly to her decisions through directly applying the decision-guiding rule(s) of C**. The emphasis is on the adaptability of the Hybrid solution to each plausible moral theory. I have characterized the Constrained Standards Hybrid approach in such a way that it should be possible, for every plausible account of objective right and wrong, to define for it an appropriate supplementary account of subjective right and wrong and of decision-worthiness. For many traditional accounts of right and wrong, especially deontological ones, this work remains to be done, primarily at the level of standards and the concrete decision-guides (since Code C** as a general principle may be the same for all theories). However, we can hope that there is no theoretical bar to carrying out this task. Insofar as a theoretical account of objective right and wrong does not lend itself to supplementation by an appropriate Code C** and an extensive array of attendant decision-guides, anyone committed to some version of the Usability Demand should view the account as deserving of suspicion. Uncertainty about one's circumstances afflicts every agent, and the Usability Demand requires each moral theory to be able to accommodate these uncertainties so far as possible through supplementation by a suitable Code C**. Once again, however, we must note that CSH theories are not capable of being used by every agent on every occasion, even though that is the aspiration.

The fifth criterion, Criterion E* (Relation to Blameworthiness) requires a CSH moral theory to evaluate an agent as not blameworthy for performing an action if she performs it because she accepts the moral theory, and (perhaps reasonably) believes that the action is prescribed as subjectively or objectively right or obligatory by either Code C or C** of the theory. It further stipulates that such ascriptions of blamelessness should be independently plausible, given our background concept of what makes agents blameworthy for their actions. In discussing whether a CSH moral theory meets the desideratum of enabling all moral agents to live a modestly successful moral life (that is, a life in which a well-intentioned agent can avoid blameworthiness), we saw that such a theory can satisfy this demand, partly because any CSH moral theory is usable by most moral agents, however deep their uncertainties, and partly because (as we detailed above) such theories can readily incorporate an account of excuses that shields agents from blameworthiness in appropriate cases even though their (perhaps reasonable) relevant beliefs are mistaken or lead them to perform actions that are objectively wrong (at least if those beliefs are non-culpable).[6]

Thus a CSH moral theory—one that successfully embodies the Constrained Standards Hybrid approach—satisfies Criteria A* and E*. With luck and enough theoretical work we can hope to identify such a theory, which will then satisfy Criterion B*. Such a moral theory only falls short of satisfying Criteria C** and D* because there can be no assurance that the theory will provide guidance to every moral agent, no matter how pervasive her epistemic limitations. However, any CSH theory provides a great deal of guidance to most cognitively limited agents.

We found no alternative approach to the problems of error and uncertainty to be superior to the Constrained Standards Hybrid approach. The Hybrid approach surpasses the Pragmatic approach because it protects what we have theoretical grounds to regard as the correct theory of objective rightness and wrongness while making that theory as usable as possible, and accomplishes this without shifting the epistemic

---

[6] Recall that whether or not blameworthiness depends on the reasonableness of an agent's mistaken beliefs is a debatable question. I am in the minority arguing that even unreasonable beliefs can excuse wrongdoing, but do not rely on that assumption in this book. (See Smith (1983), (2011), and (2016).) Those who uphold the "reasonable belief" standard will interpret the above claim so that it requires the beliefs or credences in question to be reasonable ones.

This is often stated as a sufficient condition for blamelessness. Some theorists would deny that acting in the (perhaps reasonable) belief that one's act is morally right is sufficient for an agent to be blameless. On these views an agent can be blameworthy for an act she believes to be morally right if she is mistaken (even reasonably mistaken) about the moral status of the act. See Harman (2011). Such theorists would want to revise Criterion E* to accommodate this view. Other theorists contend that blameworthiness should be tied to beliefs about certain nonmoral properties of acts (such as "helping a person in need of assistance"); beliefs about the moral status of the act are irrelevant. Theorists advocating this latter position would need to expand their list of the relevant nonmoral properties to include ones (such as "helping a person *who is likely* to be in need of assistance") referring to the agent's uncertainty. See Arpaly (2003) and Arpaly and Schroeder (2014).

problem from one level of the theory to another. The Hybrid approach is superior to the Austere approach to uncertainty because, unlike that solution, it successfully renders the account of right and wrong indirectly usable by agents suffering from uncertainty. Given these successes, it is hard to see what better solution there could be, even though the Constrained Standards Hybrid solution falls slightly short of rendering every moral theory indirectly usable by each agent, no matter how epistemically challenged.

Arriving at this assessment has been a long haul. I conclude that we should embrace the Hybrid solution as the best available remedy for the epistemic problem in ethics. Our future efforts should be directed toward developing its still missing pieces: the standards for evaluating decision-guides at each level, and a full array of decision-guides, precepts, maxims, and so forth, capable of providing moral guidance to as many agents as possible, however profound their epistemic limitations.[7]

---

[7] I am grateful to Eli Shupe for assistance with this chapter.

Appendix
List of Principles and Definitions

Note: when definitions or principles are stated only informally in the text, this Appendix may state them slightly differently to make the intended meaning clear when the surrounding textual context is absent.

Chapter 2: Using Moral Principles to Guide Decisions

- The **Usability Demand** is the requirement that an acceptable moral principle must be usable for guiding decisions.
- **Definition 2.1. Ability in the core sense to directly use a moral principle to decide what to do:** An agent S is able in the core sense at t_i to directly use moral principle P to decide at t_i what to do at t_j *if and only if*:
  - (A) there is some (perhaps complex) feature F such that P prescribes actions that have feature F, in virtue of their having F,
  - (B) S believes at t_i of some act-type A that S could perform A (in the epistemic sense) at t_j,
  - (C) S believes at t_i that if she performed A at t_j, act A would have F, and
  - (D) if and because S believed at t_i that P prescribes actions that have feature F, in virtue of their having F, and if and because S wanted all-things-considered at t_i to derive a prescription from principle P at t_i for an act performable at t_j, then her beliefs together with this desire would lead S to derive a prescription at t_i for A from P in virtue of her belief that it has F. (p. 16)
- **Definition 2.2. Core usability as an action-guide:** A moral principle P is directly usable in the **core** sense by an agent S to decide at t_i what to do at t_j *if and only if* S is able in the core sense at t_i to directly use principle P as a guide to decide at t_i what to do at t_j. (p. 18)
- **Definition 2.3. Epistemic ability to perform an act:** S has the epistemic ability at t_i to perform act A at t_j *if and only if*:
  - (A) there is a basic act-type A* which S truly believes at t_i to be a basic act-type for her at t_j,
  - (B) S truly believes at t_i that she is (or will be) in standard conditions with respect to A* at t_j, and
  - (C) either
    - (1) S truly believes at t_i that A* = A, or
    - (2) S truly believes at t_i that there is a set of conditions C* obtaining at t_j such that her doing A* would generate her doing A at t_j. (p. 19)
- **Definition 2.4. Ability in the extended sense to directly use a moral principle to decide what to do:** An agent S is able in the extended sense at t_i to directly use moral principle P to decide at t_i what to do at t_j *if and only if*:
  - (A) there is some (perhaps complex) feature F such that P prescribes actions that have feature F, in virtue of their having F,

(B) S *truly* believes at t_i of some act-type A that she could perform A (in the epistemic sense) at t_j,

(C) S *truly* believes at t_i that if she performed A at t_j, act A would have F, and

(D) if and because S believed at t_i that P prescribes actions that have feature F, in virtue of their having F, and if and because S wanted all-things-considered at t_i to derive a prescription from principle P at t_i for an act performable at t_j, then her beliefs together with this desire would lead S to derive a prescription at t_i for A from P in virtue of her belief that it has F. (p. 21)

- **Definition 2.5. Extended usability as an action-guide:** A moral principle P is directly usable in the **extended** sense by an agent S to decide at t_i what to do at t_j *if and only if* S is able in the extended sense at t_i to directly use principle P as a guide to decide at t_i what to do at t_j. (p. 22)

- Informal definition of **ability to use a principle in the core sense**: an agent is able to directly use a principle in the core sense for deciding what to do just in case he would directly derive a prescription for action from the principle if he wanted all-things-considered to do so.

- Informal definition of **ability to use a principle in the extended sense**: an agent is able to directly use a principle in the extended sense for deciding what to do just in case he would directly derive a prescription for action from the principle if he wanted all-things-considered to do so, and the action for which he would derive a prescription is one that he would be able to perform and that would conform to the principle.

Chapter 3: Impediments to Usability: Error, Ignorance, and Uncertainty

- The **theoretical domain** of a moral principle includes all the actual and possible acts to which it ascribes deontic status (where "deontic status" would include any of the types of moral status specially ascribable to acts, such as being right, obligatory, wrong, permissible, just, unjust, and supererogatory, or being prima facie right and obligatory).

- The **practical domain** of a principle includes all the actual and possible acts with respect to which the principle can be used by the act's potential agent for guiding decisions (including decisions based on an assessment of the act as morally permissible).

- A principle is **universally usable** if its practical domain matches its theoretical domain exactly. Such a principle could be used for making a decision, not necessarily with respect to *every* action, but with respect to every action that it evaluates.

- A principle is **unintelligible** by an agent if the agent is, by reason of her cognitive limitations, unable to understand the principle in question: to grasp some of its crucial concepts (whether these are evaluative, formal, or empirical), or to comprehend the overall structure of the principle.

- The **problem of error regarding nonmoral facts** afflicts an agent who can derive a prescription for action from his or her moral principle, but some nonmoral factual premise the agent would invoke, in order to derive a prescription for an act, is false.

- The **problem of uncertainty about nonmoral facts** arises when an agent is beleaguered by uncertainty regarding the nonmoral facts necessary for deriving a prescription from the principle in question, uncertainty that prevents her from deriving any prescription directly from the principle.

- The **problem of ignorance about nonmoral facts** arises when an agent lacks any belief at all about whether act A has or fails to have morally relevant feature F, or lacks any belief about whether some act A is one she could or couldn't perform.

- The **problem of computational constraints** arises when an agent possesses enough lower-level factual beliefs to calculate what act is prescribed by her principle, but she is unable (either in general, or in this case, or within the time available) to take the necessary cognitive steps to make the calculation and so identify this act.

- The **problem of moral error** arises when an agent, in appealing to a moral principle to guide her decision, appeals to a principle that is incorrect.

- The **problems of moral uncertainty and ignorance** arise when an agent is uncertain which moral principle is correct, or lacks any belief at all about which moral principle is correct.

- The problem **of meta-moral uncertainty** arises when an agent believes of the correct moral principle that it is correct, but is uncertain how to justify her belief in its correctness, or uncertain whether this belief is justified.

- The **problem of meta-moral error** arises when an agent believes that such-and-such is a valid justification for her moral view, but she is wrong about this.

- The **Pragmatic Response** to the problems of error and uncertainty holds that the theoretical function of morality cannot be isolated from its practical or regulative function, in the sense that one crucial test of a moral principle's theoretical correctness just *is* its practical usability by the epistemically limited human beings who will actually employ it. On this view an ethical theory is a theory to be used in guiding our choices and actions.

- The **Austere Response** to the problems of error and uncertainty holds a moral principle provides an explanatory theory: it tells us which acts are right and wrong, and tells us why they are right or wrong—what features make these acts have the status they do. On this view a moral principle's practical usability, or lack thereof, is no test of its adequacy or inadequacy as a theoretical account of right and wrong.

- The **Hybrid Response** to the problems of error and uncertainty claims that the correct response involves blending the best parts of the Austere Response and the Pragmatic Response in a manner that pays allegiance to the view that the truth of a moral principle should not be affected by its practical usability, but also pays allegiance to the view that one task for moral principles is to be used for making decisions. It achieves these goals by a division of labor within the theory, and by introducing the concept of "indirectly" applying a moral theory. According to the Hybrid Response, which principle is the correct theoretical account of right and wrong is determined without any reference to the practical usability of such a principle. This account is supplemented with second-level rules to be used in making decisions by human beings operating under constraints of information and computation. Because the function of these rules is to help us make decisions, it is a test of their adequacy that they be usable as decision-guides. However, the supplementary rules do not provide an account of the features that actually make acts right and wrong. Instead they *link* the account of right and wrong with advisable decisions.

- Rationales for the Usability Demand:
  Conceptual rationales:
    (1) The concept of morality, or the point of morality, requires that moral principles be usable for action-guiding purposes.
    (2) A moral code must be usable in order to satisfy the demand of a special form of justice, which requires that everyone should have the opportunity to live a successful moral life.
  Goal-oriented rationales:
    (3) A moral code must be usable in order to serve its function of enhancing social welfare, or facilitating cooperative social endeavors and enabling citizens to organize their plans for the long-term future.
    (4) A moral code must be usable in order to serve its function of producing the best possible pattern of actions, where what makes an action fit into the best pattern of actions is specified by the theoretical criteria provided by the morality itself.

Chapter 4: Pragmatic Responses to the Problem of Error

- The "pure" variant of the Pragmatic approach to the problem of error denies the normative significance of any principle of moral conduct that is subject to the problem of error.
- The "concessive" variant of the Pragmatic approach to the problem of error restricts "action-guiding" terms—such as "ought," "right," and "wrong"—to acts prescribed or prohibited by moral principles that are not subject to the problem of error. It concedes, however, that it may be acceptable to evaluate an act as "best" or "fortunate" if it would be prescribed by the error-prone moral theory from which the Pragmatic theory is derived.
- The "Uniform Pragmatic Response" to the problem of error holds that a moral code or principle which is affected by the problem of error on even one occasion must be rejected in favor of some alternative uniform code or principle that is universally usable in the extended sense, that is, usable without error by every agent on each occasion for decision-making.
- The "Splintered Pragmatic Response" to the problem of error holds that if a moral code or principle is affected by the problem of error on one occasion, then it must be rejected as incorrect (both as a theoretical account of what makes acts right and wrong and also as a decision-guide for that occasion) *for that agent on that occasion*. However, the original code or principle may be correct for any occasion on which it is *not* vulnerable to the problem of error. On the Splintered view, there will be many correct moral principles covering the same field of action, but (because agents vary in their susceptibility to the problem of error) no one principle will be correct for all agents or even for the same agent on similar occasions.
- A **moral laundry list code** consists of a list of many highly specific descriptions of the actions to be performed or avoided, descriptions that are tailored to what each agent accurately believes about his options. Such a code would be error-proof in a very strong sense, since it would be universally usable in the extended sense.
- A "subjectivized" moral code is a code that prescribes actions in virtue of the agent's internal mental attitudes towards those actions.

- A **belief is self-intimating** just in case it is true that if we have that belief, we believe that we have that belief.
- An individual is **infallible with respect to her beliefs** just in case it is true that if she believes she has a certain belief, then she does have that belief.

Chapter 5: A Further Disadvantage of Subjectivized Moral Codes

- An **objective moral code** is a code in which the agent's obligations depend on objective facts about the world, not on what the agent believes about the world.
- P_{E1}. One has a prima facie duty to act in ways that maximize the number of true beliefs and minimize the number of false beliefs.
- P_{E2}. One has a prima facie duty to act in ways that lead to knowledge.
- P_{E3}. One has a prima facie duty to act in ways that lead to justified cognitive attitudes.
- P_{E4}. One has a prima facie duty to act in ways that will lead to accurate and comprehensive beliefs.
- A **deontic duty to gather information is a free-standing duty** just in case it is not defined or justified in terms of the consequences of gathering information for the agent's subsequent choice.
- P_{M1}. One has a prima facie duty to consider the circumstances as fully as one can.
- P_{M2}. One has a prima facie duty to investigate the circumstances relevant to an upcoming duty until either (a) one must act because time has run out, or (b) one has reached the point where no further consideration would enable one to judge better of the circumstances relevant to the duty.
- P_{M3}. One has a great variety of prima facie obligations to inform oneself about matters relevant to the moral permissibility of one's future conduct, such as an obligation to look out for other people when one is out walking.
- P_{E5}. For any proposition P, time t, and person S, if P is less than certain for S at t, then S has a prima facie duty at t to gather additional evidence concerning P.
- P_{E6}. If S is unjustified in believing P, then S has a prima facie duty to gather additional evidence regarding P.
- P_{E7}. S has a prima facie duty to gather additional evidence regarding P if (a) P is important, or (b) there is a strong likelihood of S's gaining additional evidence, or (c) the evidence that S would gain would conflict with S's current evidence.
- P_{E8}. One has prima facie duties to be inquisitive, attentive, careful and thorough in inquiry, open-minded, and fair-minded.
- P_{E9}. One has a prima facie duty to use one's cognitive faculties carefully and in appropriate ways, where the standards of "appropriateness" are implicit in community practices.
- A **deontic duty to gather information is a derivative duty** just in case the fact that it is a duty derives from the subsequent duties it would lead the agent to satisfy.
- The **deontic weight of an act** expresses the weight, or stringency, of the duty to perform (or not to perform) an act of that type (or, in other terminology, the force of the moral reason to perform or not to perform that action). Prohibitions and permissions, as well as obligations, have deontic weights.

- P_{OD}: An agent has an objective derivative prima facie duty to acquire information if and only if doing so would lead the agent subsequently to produce the maximum possible amount of deontic weight (typically through his carrying out the various deontic duties that would later be incumbent on him). (p. 103)
- P_{SD}: An agent has a derivative prima facie subjectivized duty to do what he believes is acquiring information if and only if he believes that doing what he believes is gathering information would lead him subsequently to produce the maximum amount of deontic weight (typically through his doing what he then believes to be carrying out the various deontic duties that would then be incumbent on him). (p. 107)
- Code C:
    (1) When an agent believes she has been tasked to lay off employees in light of a financial retrenchment, the agent ought prima facie either to
        (a) do what she believes to be laying off an employee if she believes that person to be the least productive employee, or
        (b) do what she believes to be laying off the most recently hired employee if she does not believe of any employee that he or she is the least productive employee.
    (2) When an agent believes she has the opportunity to gather information relevant to a subsequent duty, then the agent ought prima facie to do what she believes to be gathering relevant information before fulfilling her subsequent duties if and only if she believes that doing so would subsequently lead her to produce the maximum amount of deontic weight.
- Code C_1:
    (1) When an agent reasonably believes she has been tasked to lay off employees in light of a financial retrenchment, the agent prima facie ought either to
        (a) do what she reasonably believes to be laying off an employee if she reasonably believes that person to be the least productive employee, or
        (b) do what she reasonably believes to be laying off the most recently hired employee if she does not reasonably believe of any employee that he or she is the least productive employee.
    (2) When an agent reasonably believes she has the opportunity to gather information relevant to a subsequent duty, then the agent ought prima facie to do what she reasonably believes to be gathering relevant information before fulfilling her subsequent duties if and only if she reasonably believes that doing so would subsequently lead her to produce the maximum amount of deontic weight.
- Code C_2:
    (1) When an agent has been tasked to lay off employees in light of a financial retrenchment, the agent prima facie ought either to
        (a) lay off an employee if that person is the least productive employee, or
        (b) lay off the most recently hired employee among those who are tied for least productive if there is no unique least productive employee.
    (2) When an agent has the opportunity to gather information relevant to a subsequent duty, then the agent ought prima facie to gather relevant information before fulfilling her subsequent duties if and only if doing so would subsequently lead her to produce the maximum amount of deontic weight.

Chapter 6: Non-Ideal Pragmatic Responses to the Problem of Error

- **Standard 6.1.** If moral Code X has higher extended usability than moral Code Y, then, other things being equal, X is better than Y. (p. 127)
- A **feature of a moral code has "positive valence"** just in case the code's having that feature is always relevant to its overall acceptability, and it always contributes positively towards the code's being more acceptable than a code that lacks that feature.
- The **P/T ratio of a moral principle** (for Practical domain/Theoretical domain) is the ratio between the principle's extended practical domain and its theoretical domain (in other words, the ratio between the number of occasions on which agents could use the principle without error and the number of acts to which the principle ascribes moral status).
- **Definition 6.1. Comparative extended usability for codes:** Code X is more usable (in the extended sense) than Code Y if and only if there are *more occasions* on which agents can use Code X without error to select their potential actions than there are such occasions for Code Y. (p. 130)
- A code has an **"exhaustive theoretical domain"** just in case it ascribes moral status to every actual and humanly possible action.
- A **moral code's "bare usability"** is the number of occasions on which a code can be used without error to derive a prescription.
- **Definition 6.2. Code-weighted extended usability of a moral code:** The code-weighted extended usability of a code equals the sum of the occasions on which it is usable in the extended sense, each weighted by the deontic importance of those occasions as determined by the code in question. (p. 134)
- **Standard 6.2.** If the code-weighted extended usability of moral Code X is greater than the code-weighted extended usability of moral Code Y, then, other things being equal, X is better than Y. (p. 134)
- Principle P1: "It is permissible to lie only when doing so will violate important rights."
- Principle P2: "It is permissible to lie to anyone except members of one's family."
- Principle P3: "It is obligatory to keep a promise unless it has been elicited by deceit."
- A **"deontically perfect code"** (or, for short, a **"perfect code"**) is a code that has all the deontically correct features, whether or not it is widely usable. The deontically correct features include the content of the code's principles, and the weight or importance the code assigns to its various principles.
- The **content merit of a code** rises or falls as the content of its principles resembles or diverges from the content of the perfect code's principles.
- The **weight merit of a code** rises or falls as the weight it ascribes to its principles resembles or diverges from the weight ascribed to them by the perfect code.
- A code's **"usability value"** is a function of two factors: its deontic merit, and how usable its principles are.
- The **"content"** of a code is the set of acts the code prescribes (in the relevant possible worlds).
- The **deontic merit of a code** depends on two factors: its *content merit* and its *weight merit*. The *content merit* of the code rises or falls as the content of its principles resembles or diverges from the content of the perfect code's principles. The *weight merit* of a code rises or falls as the weight it ascribes to its principles resembles or diverges from the weight ascribed to them by the perfect code.

- The **deontic merit of a principle** depends on both its content and its code-assigned importance, each as assessed in comparison to the content of the relevant perfect principle and the importance assigned by the perfect code to that principle.
- A **corrupt moral principle** is one that prescribes or permits actions that are *thoroughly wrong* as assessed by the perfect code.
- Principle P4: "It is obligatory to keep every promise."
- **Criterion 6.1:** If Principles P and Q have the same content merit, and P's weight merit is greater than that of Q, then P has higher deontic merit. (p. 140)
- **Criterion 6.2:** If Principles P and Q have the same weight merit, and P's content merit is greater than that of Q, then P has higher deontic merit. (p. 141)
- Principle P5: "The only promises it is obligatory to keep are promises to one's friends and family."
- Principle P6: "It is obligatory to pay what one owes in taxes."
- Principle P7: "It is obligatory not to cut into movie queues."
- Principle P17: "It is obligatory to offer your seat on public transportation to elderly persons."
- Principle P18: "It is obligatory not to tell a lie unless doing so is necessary in order to protect important rights."
- **Definition 6.3. Usability weight of a principle:** The usability weight of a principle is the deontic merit of the principle multiplied by the weight assigned to that principle by the perfect code. (p. 149)
- **Criterion 6.3:** If Principles P and Q have the same extended usability, and P has higher usability weight than Q, then P has higher usability value than Q. (p. 150)
- **Criterion 6.4:** If Principles P and Q have the same usability weight, and P is more usable in the extended sense than Q, then P has higher usability value than Q. (p. 150)
- **Criterion 6.5:** If Principle P has higher usability weight than Principle Q, there is some possible level at which Q's extended usability could exceed P's extended usability such that Q would have greater usability value than P. (p. 150)
- **Formula 6.1:** The extended usability value of principle P = P's usability weight × P's extended usability (or $UV_p = UW_p \times EU_p$). (p. 150)
- Principle 19: "It is permissible to break a promise if it has been elicited by fraud."
- Principle P20: "It is permissible to break a promise if it has been elicited by coercion."
- **Definition 6.4. Comparative extended usability of a principle:** Principle P is more usable (in the extended sense) than Principle Q if and only if the P/T ratio of Principle P is greater than the P/T ratio of Principle Q. (p. 152)
- **Definition 6.5. Extended usability value of a code:** The extended usability value of a code equals the average extended usability value of the code's principles. (p. 154)
- **Standard 6.3.** If the extended usability value of moral Code X is higher than the extended usability value of moral Code Y, then, other things being equal, X is better than Y. (p. 154)

Chapter 7: Assessing Non-Ideal Pragmatic Responses to the Problem of Error

- Principle P: "It is obligatory to offer your seat on public transportation to people on crutches."
- Principle P*: "It is obligatory to open the door for people on crutches."
- **Definition 7.1. Usability value of an action relative to Code C:** The usability value of act A, relative to Code C, is the usability value of the principle in Code C that prescribes A

(or, if A is prescribed by more than one principle in C, the combined usability values of those principles). (p. 175)

- **Definition 7.2. Relatively better pattern of action:** One pattern of actions is better, relative to Code C, than another pattern of actions is, relative to Code C*, if and only if the actions comprising the first pattern have a higher total usability value relative to Code C than the total usability value relative to Code C* of the actions comprising the second pattern. (p. 175)
- Principle P26: "It is obligatory to always tell the truth."
- The **non-ideal Splintered Pragmatic Response to the problem of error** maintains that there are many moral codes, each devised for some set of agents and occasions for decision, and each such that it has high (but not necessarily perfect) usability value for that set of agents and decisions.

Chapter 8: Hybrid and Austere Responses to the Problem of Error

- In a two-tier Hybrid system the **top tier** consists in a set of principles, or code (labeled "Code C") that provides the correct theoretical account of what makes actions right and wrong.
- In a two-tier Hybrid system the **lower tier** consists of a set of decision-guides (labeled "Code C*") that are to be used for actual decision-making.
- In an **ideal Hybrid approach**, the lower-tier rules—encoded in C*—are so constructed that agents who attempt to apply these rules would actually do what the top-tier code C prescribes.
- Hybrid systems incorporate a **division of moral labor**: Code C serves a different function (providing the correct theoretical account of what makes actions right and wrong) from the function (guiding decision-making) served by Code C*.
- Code C and C* may be **pragmatically co-extensional** in the special sense that the acts the agent would perform if she attempted to follow C* are the acts actually prescribed by C.
- A **non-ideal Hybrid approach** incorporates a decision-guide C* that merely secures high, but not perfect, indirect usability for C.
- **Standard 8.1.** Decision-guiding Code C* is a better decision-guiding second-tier code for theoretical account C than decision-guiding Code C# if and only if C* has higher Code C-weighted usability than does C#. (p. 188)
- A principle secures an agent's **autonomy** (with respect to that principle) if the principle is usable in the core sense by that agent: adopting such a principle enables her to translate her moral values into her choice of what to do.
- The **"strong" conception of a successful moral life** is the conception of a life in which the agent never does wrong and is never blameworthy for any of her actions.
- The **"modest" conception of the successful moral life** is the conception of a life in which, although the agent may sometimes act wrongly in striving to do right, nonetheless she is never blameworthy for any of her actions. When her actions fall short of what morality requires, there is always some factor that excuses her for any infraction.
- Principle P6*: "It is obligatory to pay what one calculates that one owes in taxes, plus 1 percent."

Chapter 9: The Problems of Ignorance and Uncertainty

- **Definition 9.1:** An agent is impeded by the problem of ignorance relative to moral code C and her possible actions at t_1 if and only if:
  - (1) In any suitable set of exhaustive options for an agent, at least one of the options has at least one of nonmoral properties F, G, or H; and
  - (2) Code C prescribes as permissible or obligatory all and only actions having at least one of F, G, or H, in virtue of their having F, G, or H, and
  - (3) either
    - (a) S has options available for performance at t_1, but lacks the belief she has such options (and does not believe there are no such options), or
    - (b) S believes there are actions that may be epistemically available to her as options for performance at t_1, and for each act A that the agent believes may be epistemically available to her for performance at t_1, she lacks any belief that act A would have F, G, or H. (p. 209)
- A principle or code prescribes actions *positively* when it prescribes them as either permissible or obligatory.
- **Definition 9.2:** An agent is impeded by the problem of uncertainty relative to moral code C and her possible actions at t_1 if and only if:
  - (1) In any suitable set of exhaustive options for an agent, at least one of the options has at least one of nonmoral properties F, G, or H; and
  - (2) Code C prescribes as permissible or obligatory all and only actions having at least one of F, G, or H, in virtue of their having F, G, or H, and
  - (3) either
    - (a) S has options available at t_1, but lacks any credence that she has such options (and has no credence that there are no such options), or
    - (b) S assigns some credence to there being actions epistemically available to her as options at t_1, and for each act A that she believes may be epistemically available to her for performance at t_1, S is unsure whether A has F, G, or H. (pp. 212–13)
- "S's being unsure whether A has F, G, or H" covers at least the following kinds of states:
  1. S assigns no credence (that is, has no degree of belief) to A's having F, G, or H (and she does not assign any credence to A's not having F, G, or H);
  2. S assigns no probability (either sharp or imprecise) to A's having F, G, or H (where "assigns no probability to X" means "for any objective, subjective, epistemic probability or chance p that X, S does not believe that X has p"), and also assigns no probability to A's not having F, G, or H; or
  3. S assigns some probability (or has some credence) less than 1.0 but greater than zero (the probability or credence may be either sharp or imprecise) to A's having F, G, or H (where "assigns some probability less than 1.0 but greater than zero to X" means "for some objective, subjective, epistemic probability or chance p less than 1.0 but greater than zero that X, S believes that x has p," and "assigns some credence p less than 1.0 but greater than zero to X" means "for some credence p less than 1.0 but greater than zero that X, S has credence p that X"); or
  4. S regards the probability of A's having F, G, or H to be indeterminate.

- **Definition 9.3:** An agent is impeded by the problem of uncertainty relative to moral code C and her possible actions at t_1 if and only if:
  - (1) In any suitable set of exhaustive options for an agent, at least one of the options has at least one of nonmoral properties F, G, or H; and
  - (2) Code C prescribes as permissible or obligatory all and only actions having at least one of F, G, or H, in virtue of their having F, G, or H, and
  - (3) For at least one possible action X, S assigns some credence to X's being epistemically available to her as an option for t_1, and for each possible act X that she believes may be an option for her at t_1, S is unsure whether X has F, G, or H. (pp. 216–17)
- In a **system of type E**, the Austere solution is proposed for the problem of error and also for the problem of uncertainty.
- In a **system of type D**, an Austere solution is proposed for the problem of error, but a Pragmatic solution for the problem of uncertainty.
- **System S1:**

  C: An act is right if and only if, and because, it would produce at least as much utility as any other alternative, and

  C*: An act is right if and only if, and because, it is permitted by the rules of common-sense morality.

- **System S2:**

  C: If and only if, and because, the agent is certain of some act A that it would produce no less utility than any alternative, then the agent would be right to perform A; and

  C*: If and only if, and because, the agent is uncertain of any act that it would produce no less utility than any alternative, and if and only if, and because, the agent is certain of some act that it has F (where acts having F are permitted by the rules of common-sense morality), then the agent would be right to perform the act that he believes to have F.

- **System S3:**

  C: An act is right if and only if, and because, it would produce no less utility than any alternative, and

  C*: An act is right if and only if, and because, it would produce no less subjective expected utility than any alternative.

- **System S4:**

  C: An act is right if and only if, and because, it would produce no less utility than any alternative, and

  C*: If and only if the agent is uncertain of any act that it would produce no less utility than any alternative, then it would be obligatory for her to perform an act if and only if, and because, it has F_1, F_2, $F_3 \ldots$ or F_n (where F_1, F_2, $F_3 \ldots$ and F_n are the properties of acts prescribed as right by the moral laundry list associated with C).

- A **system of type F** conjoins an Austere solution to the problem of error with a Hybrid solution to the problem of uncertainty.
- **Decision-Guide DG_0** is designed for agents who have all the relevant beliefs necessary to apply the top-tier code to a decision; its semantic content mirrors the content of the top-tier code.

- An evaluation using the "ought$_1$" terminology is meant only to evaluate the act's theoretical moral status. Issuance of an evaluation using the "ought$_2$" terminology is meant only to guide an agent making a decision based on a person's possibly limited or erroneous perspective on her options in that decision.
- System S5:

  C: An act is right$_1$ if and only if, and because, it would produce no less utility than any alternative, and

  C*:

  DG$_0$:   An act is right$_2$ if, and because, it would produce no less utility than any alternative, and

  DG$_1$:   An act is right$_2$ if, and because, it would produce no less expected utility than any alternative.

- "Regan-style cases" are cases in which one act is known by the agent to be objectively wrong, but is also known by the agent to be the act that would maximize expected value.

Chapter 10: The Hybrid Solution to the Problems of Error and Uncertainty

- **Criterion A (Consistency):** When Code C and Code C* are paired in a single Hybrid system, their prescriptions should be consistent. (p. 233)
- **Criterion B (Moral Adequacy):** Code C* should issue *morally appropriate* guiding prescriptions for an agent who accepts Code C as the correct theoretical account of rightness and wrongness but is hindered by the problem of uncertainty from using C itself to guide her decision. Put differently, an action prescribed by Code C* should be morally reasonable or wise for the agent to choose, relative to a commitment to C and to the agent's imperfect epistemic grasp of the situation. (pp. 233–4)
- **Criterion C (Guidance Adequacy):** Assuming that Code C provides an exhaustive account of the moral status of all actual and humanly possible actions, then the decision-guiding rule(s) of Code C* should be such that for every occasion for decision, there is an appropriate rule in Code C* which can be directly used by the agent for making a decision on that occasion. (p. 234)
- **Criterion D (Normative Adequacy):** For each plausible theoretic account of right and wrong C, it should be possible to define a C* that would enable every agent affected by the problems of error and uncertainty to apply C indirectly to her decisions through directly applying the decision-guiding rule(s) of C*. (p. 234)
- **Criterion E (Relation to Blameworthiness):** The prescriptions (including obligations, prohibitions, and permissions) issued by C* should be appropriate for the role of such guidance prescriptions in the correct theory of moral responsibility, and in particular appropriate in assessments of whether an agent is blameworthy or creditworthy for her act. (p. 235)
- **Decision-Guide 1:** It is obligatory$_2$ to do what is most likely to be obligatory$_1$.
- **Decision-Guide 2:** It is obligatory$_2$ to perform the act that maximizes expected value (where value is assessed by the governing Code C).
- **Decision-Guide 3:** It is obligatory$_2$ to try to perform the act that would be obligatory$_1$.
- **Feldman's Two-Level Theory:**

Level 1:   You morally ought$_1$ to perform an act iff it maximizes utility.

Level 2:   If you cannot determine what you morally ought$_1$ to do, then you morally ought$_2$ to perform an act if and only if it is an outcome of the Utilitarian Decision Procedure.

Step One: Consider the acts that you take to be your alternatives—described in 'helpful,' 'action-guiding' terms.

Step Two: Consider, insofar as your epistemic state permits, what you take to be their values or perhaps just their relative values.

Step Three: If you haven't got useful information about the actual values of your alternatives, then consider how your views about the morality of risk apply to your present situation; and, in light of all this,

Step Four: identify the acts in this particular case that seem most nearly consistent with the general policy of maximizing utility where possible while avoiding things that put people at excessive risk of serious harm; and then

Step Five: perform one of them.

- **Pollock's Decision-Guide:**
  A. It is rational to make a change C to the master plan M if and only if the marginal expected utility of C is positive, that is, if and only if the expected utility of adopting the change C to the master plan is greater than the expected utility of the master plan left unchanged.
  B. It is rational to perform an action if and only if it is prescribed by a rationally adopted master plan.

Chapter 11: Multiple-Rule Hybrid Solutions to the Problems of Error and Uncertainty

- A rule is a **mini-maxim** if it is designed, not to provide an account of what features make actions right or wrong, but rather to guide our decisions in cases where information may be lacking.
- A **decision-guide is all-purpose** if it is designed to be used in any field of action.
- The prescriptions of the theoretical account of right and wrong (Code C) are stated in terms of what is **"objectively" obligatory, right, or wrong.**
- The overall prescription of Code C*, the decision-guiding tier of the system, is stated in terms of what is **"subjectively" obligatory, right, or wrong.**
- The recommendations of an individual decision-guide are stated in terms of what is **"choice-mandated," "choice-worthy," or "choice-prohibited."**
- An act is **absolutely subjectively obligatory** just in case it is the subjectively obligatory act relative to the correct theory of objective obligation.
- **Hybrid act utilitarianism**

Code C: An act is objectively right if and only if it would produce no less happiness than any alternative act.

Code C*:   Relative to Code C and to the credences of agent S, an act A is subjectively right for S to perform if and only if it is prescribed as choice-worthy by a decision-guide, usable by S, that is no lower in the hierarchy of choice-worthiness decision-guides than any other choice-worthiness decision-guide usable by S and appropriate to Code C.

Decision-guides:

0. An act that would produce no less happiness than any alternative act is choice-worthy.

1. An act that would produce no less expected happiness than any alternative act is choice-worthy.

2. An act which is at least as likely as any alternative to produce no less happiness than any alternative is choice-worthy.

3. An act whose worst possible outcome would produce no less happiness than the worst possible outcome of any alternative act is choice-worthy.

4. An act prescribed by a local plan is choice-worthy if adding the local plan to the agent's master plan would produce no less expected happiness than not adding it.

5. An act is choice-worthy if it would produce at least the satisfactory amount of happiness.

6. It is choice-worthy never to kill an innocent person.

7. It is choice-worthy never to take the property of another person without her consent.

8. It is choice-worthy never to shake an infant.

9. It is choice-worthy never to carry scissors point first.

10. Unless you are in the military or the police, it is choice-worthy to never point a gun at another person.

.

.

.

N. Every act is choice-worthy.

- The full statement of Code C*, including temporal indices, reads:

Code C*: Relative to Code C and to the credences of agent S, an act A is subjectively right at time t_i for S to perform at time t_j if and only if it is prescribed as choice-worthy by a decision-guide, usable by S at time t_i, that is no lower in the hierarchy of choice-worthiness decision-guides than any other choice-worthiness decision-guide usable by S at time t_i and appropriate to Code C.

- **Hybrid Rossian deontology**

Code C: An act is objectively obligatory all-things-considered if and only if its net balance of prima facie rightness over prima facie wrongness is greater than the net balance of prima facie rightness over prima facie wrongness of any alternative act.

Principles of prima facie obligation:

1. It is prima facie obligatory to keep a promise.

2. It is prima facie obligatory to compensate another person for wronging that person in the past.

3. It is prima facie obligatory to return services freely rendered by another person.

4. It is prima facie obligatory to distribute happiness in accord with the merits of the persons concerned.

5. It is prima facie obligatory to benefit others.

6. It is prima facie obligatory to improve one's own virtue or intelligence.

7. It is prima facie obligatory not to harm others.

Code C*: Relative to Code C and to the credences of agent S, an act A is subjectively obligatory all-things-considered for S to perform if and only if either (a) it is prescribed as choice-mandated by the highest choice-mandating decision-guide, usable by S, that is appropriate to C, or (b) it is prescribed as choice-mandated by every choice-mandating decision-guide, usable by S, that is appropriate to C, and that is no lower in the hierarchy of choice-mandating decision-guides than any other decision-guide usable by S and appropriate to Code C.

    A.   Decision-guides for all-things-considered obligatoriness:

        0.   An act is choice-mandated if it would have a larger net balance of prima facie rightness over prima facie wrongness than the net balance of prima facie rightness over prima facie wrongness of any alternative act.

        1.   An act is choice-mandated if it maximizes expected deontic weight.

        2.   An act is choice-mandated if it fulfills more prima facie duties than any alternative act.

        .

        .

        .

    B.   Decision-guides for prima facie wrongness:

        1.   Promises

           a.   If you must choose between performing act A or performing act B, act A is choice-mandated if you promised to do A rather than promised to do B.

           b.   If you are uncertain whether you promised to do A or promised to do B, act A is choice-mandated if the expected deontic weight of A is greater than the expected deontic weight of doing B.

           c.   Act A is choice-mandated if A is most likely to be the act you promised.

        .

        .

        .

- The **last resort decision-guide** (DG_n) prescribes every action as choice-worthy.
- The **objective moral status of an act** is the moral status accorded it by a Code C, the theoretical account of right and wrong in a Hybrid system.
- The **subjective moral status of an act** is the moral status ascribed to it by a Code C*, the decision-guiding tier of a Hybrid system.
- **Definition 11.1. Subjective moral status:** The **subjective moral status of an act** is the moral status ascribed to it by a Code C*, the decision-guiding tier of a Hybrid system. (p. 263)
- An "interpolated" decision-guide resides in the decision-guide hierarchy between two other guides, the higher of which prescribes acts having feature F, and the lower of which prescribes acts having feature G. The interpolated guide prescribes an action that has a chance greater than 0 but less than 1.0 of having F.
- **Pragmatic Splintered act utilitarianism**

Code C: An act A is objectively right for agent S to perform if and only if it is prescribed as permissible by an injunction, usable by S, that is no lower in the hierarchy of injunctions than any other injunction usable by S and appropriate to Code C.

Injunctions:

0.   An act that would produce no less happiness than any alternative act is enjoined as permissible.

1.   An act that would produce no less expected happiness than any alternative act is enjoined as permissible.

2.   An act which is at least as likely as any alternative to produce no less happiness than any alternative is enjoined as permissible.

3.   An act whose worst possible outcome would produce no less happiness than the worst possible outcome of any alternative act is enjoined as permissible.

4.   An act prescribed by a local plan is enjoined as permissible if adding the local plan to the agent's master plan would produce no less expected happiness than not adding it.

5.   An act is enjoined as permissible if it would produce at least the satisfactory amount of happiness.

6.   It is enjoined as permissible never to kill an innocent person.

7.   It is enjoined as permissible never to take the property of another person without her consent.

8.   It is enjoined as permissible never to shake an infant.

9.   It is enjoined as permissible never to carry scissors point first.

10.   Unless you are in the military or the police, it is enjoined as permissible to never point a gun at another person.

.

.

.

N.   Every act is enjoined as permissible.

• An "injunction" is an individual principle within a Splintered Pragmatic theory that enjoins acts as obligatory, right, permissible, or wrong.

Chapter 12: Developing the Hybrid Solution

• Definition 12.1. Ability to indirectly use an objective principle of moral rightness in the core sense to decide what to do: An agent S who is uncertain at t_i which of the acts she could perform (in the epistemic sense) is prescribed by P, a principle of objective rightness, is able at t_i to indirectly use principle P in the core sense to decide at t_i what to do at t_j *if and only if*:

(A)   S believes at t_i of some act A that S could perform A (in the epistemic sense) at t_j;

(B)   There is some decision-guide DG_x such that

(1) DG_x is directly usable in the core sense by S to decide at t_i what to do at t_j,

(2) DG_x is no lower in the hierarchy of choice-worthiness decision-guides than any other choice-worthiness decision-guide usable by S and appropriate to Code C, and

(3) DG_x prescribes at least one act as choice-worthy for S at t_j; and

(C)   If and because S wanted all-things-considered to use principle P indirectly for guidance at t_i for an act performable at t_j, and if and because she believed of some DG_y (not necessarily identical to DG_x) that there is no higher-ranked choice-worthiness decision-guide (relative to P) usable by her at t_i, then

(1) she would come to believe of act A that it is prescribed as choice-worthy for performance at t_j by DG_y, and

(2) her beliefs together with this desire would lead S at t_i to derive a prescription for A as subjectively right for her relative to P. (p. 280)

- **Definition 12.2. Ability to indirectly use an objective principle of moral obligation in the core sense to decide what to do:** An agent S who is uncertain at t_i which of the acts she could perform (in the epistemic sense) is prescribed by P, a principle of objective obligation, is able at t_i to indirectly use principle P in the core sense to decide at t_i what to do at t_j *if and only if:*

(A) S believes at t_i of some act A that S could perform A (in the epistemic sense) at t_j;

(B) There is some decision-guide DG_x such that

  (1) DG_x is directly usable in the core sense by S to decide at t_i what to do at t_j,

  (2) DG_x is the highest choice-mandating decision-guide usable by S and appropriate to Code C, and

  (3) DG_x prescribes an act as choice-mandated for S at t_j; and

(C) If and because S wanted all-things-considered to use principle P indirectly for guidance at t_i for an act performable at t_j, and if and because she believed of some DG_y (not necessarily identical to DG_x) that it is the highest-ranked choice-mandating decision-guide (relative to P) usable by her at t_i, then

  (1) she would come to believe of act A that it is prescribed as choice-mandated for performance at t_j by DG_y, and

  (2) her beliefs together with this desire would lead S at t_i to derive a prescription for A as subjectively obligatory for her relative to P. (pp. 280–1)

- **Definition 12.3. Ability to indirectly use an objective moral code in the core sense to decide what to do:** An agent S is able at t_i to indirectly use objective Code C in the core sense to decide at t_i what to do at t_j *if and only if* S is able at t_i to indirectly use one of Code C's principles of objective rightness or objective obligation in the core sense to decide at t_i what to do at t_j. (p. 281)

- **Definition 12.1.1. Ability to indirectly use an objective principle of moral rightness in the core sense to decide what to do:** An agent S who is uncertain at t_i which of the acts she could perform (in the epistemic sense) is prescribed by P, a principle of objective rightness, is nonetheless able at t_i to indirectly use principle P in the core sense to decide at t_i what to do at t_j *if and only if:*

(A) S believes at t_i of some act A that S could perform A (in the epistemic sense) at t_j;

(B) There is some decision-guide DG_x such that

  (1) DG_x is directly usable in the core sense by S to decide at t_i what to do at t_j,

  (2) DG_x is no lower in the hierarchy of choice-worthiness decision-guides than any other choice-worthiness decision-guide usable by S and appropriate to Code C, and

  (3) DG_x prescribes at least one act as choice-worthy for S at t_j; and

(C) If and because S wanted all-things-considered to use principle P indirectly for guidance at t_i for an act performable at t_j, then

  (1) she would come to believe of act A that it is prescribed as choice-worthy for performance at t_j by a decision-guide than which there is no higher choice-worthiness guide (relative to P) usable by her at t_i; and

  (2) her beliefs together with this desire would lead S at t_i to derive a prescription for A as subjectively right for her relative to P. (p. 284)

- **Definition 12.2.1. Ability to indirectly use an objective principle of moral obligation in the core sense to decide what to do:** An agent S who is uncertain at t_i which of the acts she could perform (in the epistemic sense) is prescribed by P, a principle of objective rightness, is nonetheless able at t_i to indirectly use principle P in the core sense to decide at t_i what to do at t_j *if and only if*:
  - (A) S believes at t_i of some act A that S could perform A (in the epistemic sense) at t_j;
  - (B) There is some decision-guide DG_x such that
    - (1) DG_x is directly usable in the core sense by S to decide at t_i what to do at t_j,
    - (2) DG_x is the highest choice-mandating decision-guide usable by S and appropriate to Code C, and
    - (3) DG_x prescribes an act as choice-mandated for S at t_j; and
  - (C) If and because S wanted all-things-considered to use principle P indirectly for guidance at t_i for an act performable at t_j, then
    - (1) she would come to believe of act A that it is prescribed as choice-mandated for performance at t_j by the highest choice-mandating decision-guide (relative to P) usable by her at t_i; and
    - (2) her beliefs together with this desire would lead S at t_i to derive a prescription for A as subjectively obligatory for her relative to P. (p. 285)
- The **Low Bar approach:** As a condition for indirect usability, do not require an agent to have moral beliefs about which decision-guide is correct.

(Low Bar) Definition 12.2.2. Ability to indirectly use an objective principle of moral obligation in the core sense to decide what to do: An agent S who is uncertain at t_i which of the acts she could perform (in the epistemic sense) is prescribed by P, a principle of objective obligation, is nonetheless able at t_i to indirectly use principle P in the core sense to decide at t_i what to do at t_j *if and only if*:
  - (A) S believes at t_i of some act A that S could perform A (in the epistemic sense) at t_j;
  - (B) There is some decision-guide DG_x such that
    - (1) DG_x is directly usable in the core sense by S to decide at t_i what to do at t_j,
    - (2) DG_x is the highest choice-mandating decision-guide usable by S and appropriate to Code C, and
    - (3) DG_x prescribes an act as choice-mandated for S at t_j; and
  - (C) If and because S wanted all-things-considered to use principle P indirectly for guidance at t_i for an act performable at t_j, then
    - (1) if and because she would come to believe of act A that it is prescribed as choice-mandated for performance at t_j by the highest choice-mandating decision-guide (relative to P) usable by her at t_i; then
    - (2) her beliefs together with this desire would lead S at t_i to derive a prescription for A as subjectively obligatory for her relative to P. (p. 294)
- The **"Expanded Moral Theory" approach:** As a condition for indirect usability, require an agent to have credences about which decision-guide is best for her to use, and expand the *truly* complete moral theory to include a whole new level of guides to assist agents impeded by uncertainty about the ranking of decision-guides.
- **Standard S_1:** A decision-guide is objectively appropriate for Code C if and only if it has feature K, and it is objectively better relative to Code C than another decision-guide of the same class if and only if it has more K than the other guide. (p. 297)

- **Two decision-guides are "of the same class"** just in case they each recommend actions as choice-worthy, or each recommend actions as choice-mandated, or each recommend actions as choice-prohibited.
- In Hybrid act utilitarianism, **an act is subjectively right** just in case it is prescribed as choice-worthy by the decision-guide evaluated by Standard S_1 as objectively best among those that are usable by the agent.
- Some **decision-guides that may be objectively appropriate to act utilitarianism:**
  - Decision-guide DG_0: An act that would produce no less utility than any alternative is choice-worthy.
  - Decision-guide DG_1: An act that would produce no less expected utility than any alternative is choice-worthy.
  - Decision-guide DG_2: An act that is at least as likely as any alternative to produce no less utility than any alternative is choice-worthy.
  - Decision-guide DG_3: An act whose worst possible outcome would produce no less utility than the worst possible outcome of any alternative is choice-worthy.
  - Decision-guide DG_4: An act that would produce a satisfactory amount of utility is choice-worthy...
  - Decision-guide DG_n: Every act is choice-worthy.
- A **precept prescribes decision-guides** as choice-worthy, choice-mandated, or choice-prohibited.
- A **decision-guide is subjectively right** if and only if it is prescribed as choice-worthy by the precept evaluated as objectively best among the precepts of the same class that are usable by the agent.
- Some **precepts** that might be appropriate for Truly Comprehensive Act Utilitarianism:
  - Precept PRE_0: A decision-guide that has no less K than any other decision-guide is choice-worthy.
  - Precept PRE_1: A decision-guide that has no less expected K than any alternative decision-guide is choice-worthy.
  - Precept PRE_2: A decision-guide that is at least as likely as any alternative to possess no less K than any other decision-guide is choice-worthy.
  - Precept PRE_3: A decision-guide whose worst possible outcome would possess no less K than the worst possible outcome of any other decision-guide is choice-worthy.
  - Precept PRE_4: A decision-guide that possesses a satisfactory amount of K is choice-worthy...
  - Precept PRE_n: Every decision-guide is choice-worthy.
- **Standard S_2:** A precept is objectively appropriate for Code C if and only if it has feature M, and it is objectively better relative to Code C than another precept of the same class if and only if it has more M than the other guide. (p. 300)
- A **maxim prescribes precepts** as choice-worthy, choice-mandated, or choice-prohibited.
- Some **maxims** that might be appropriate for Truly Comprehensive Act Utilitarianism:
  - Maxim MAX_0: A precept that has no less M than any other precept is choice-worthy.
  - Maxim MAX_1: A precept that has no less expected M than any alternative precept is choice-worthy.
  - Maxim MAX_2: A precept that is at least as likely as any alternative to possess no less M than any other precept is choice-worthy.

- Maxim MAX_3: A precept whose worst possible outcome would possess no less M than the worst possible outcome of any alternative is choice-worthy.
- Maxim MAX_4: A precept that possesses a satisfactory amount of M is choice-worthy...
- Maxim MAX_n: Every precept is choice-worthy.
- **Standard S_3:** A maxim is objectively appropriate for Code C if and only if it has feature N, and it is objectively better relative to Code C than another maxim of the same class if and only if it has more N than the other maxim. (p. 302)
- A **counsel prescribes maxims** as choice-worthy, choice-mandated, or choice-prohibited.
- Truly Comprehensive Act Utilitarianism
  A. Principle action-evaluating norms

  Code C: An act is objectively right if and only if it would produce no less utility than any alternative act.

  Code C*:   Relative to Code C and to the credences of agent S, an act A is subjectively right for S to perform if and only if it is prescribed as choice-worthy by a decision-guide, usable by S, that is no lower in the hierarchy of choice-worthiness decision-guides than any other choice-worthiness decision-guide usable by S and appropriate to Code C.

  B. Guide-evaluating norms

  Standard S_1:   A decision-guide is objectively appropriate for Code C if and only if it has feature K, and it is objectively better relative to Code C than another decision-guide of the same class if and only if it has more K than the other guide. [Precepts substitute for Standard S_1 in cases of uncertainty about the evaluations of S_1; being prescribed by the objectively highest usable precept makes a decision-guide subjectively right.]

  Standard S_2:   A precept is objectively appropriate for Code C if and only if it has feature M, and it is objectively better relative to Code C than another precept of the same class if and only if it has more M than the other guide. [Maxims substitute for Standard S_2 in cases of uncertainty about the evaluations of S_2; being prescribed by the objectively highest usable maxim makes a precept subjectively right.]

  Standard S_3:   A maxim is objectively appropriate for Code C if and only if it has feature N, and it is objectively better relative to Code C than another maxim of the same class if and only if it has more N than the other maxim. [Counsels substitute for Standard S_3 in cases of uncertainty about the evaluations of S_3; being prescribed by the objectively highest usable counsel makes a maxim subjectively right.]

  C. Guides
  Decision-guides
- Decision-guide DG_0: An act that would produce no less utility than any alternative is choice-worthy.
- Decision-guide DG_1: An act that would produce no less expected utility than any alternative is choice-worthy.
- Decision-guide DG_2: An act that is at least as likely as any alternative to produce no less utility than any alternative is choice-worthy.
- Decision-guide DG_3: An act whose worst possible outcome would produce no less utility than the worst possible outcome of any alternative is choice-worthy.
- Decision-guide DG_4: An act that would produce a satisfactory amount of utility is choice-worthy...
- Decision-guide DG_n: Every act is choice-worthy.

Precepts

- Precept PRE_0: A decision-guide that has no less K than any other decision-guide is choice-worthy.
- Precept PRE_1: A decision-guide that has no less expected K than any alternative decision-guide is choice-worthy.
- Precept PRE_2: A decision-guide that is at least as likely as any alternative to possess no less K than any other decision-guide is choice-worthy.
- Precept PRE_3: A decision-guide whose worst possible outcome would possess no less K than the worst possible outcome of any other decision-guide is choice-worthy.
- Precept PRE_4: A decision-guide that possesses a satisfactory amount of K is choice-worthy…
- Precept PRE_n: Every decision-guide is choice-worthy.

Maxims

- Maxim MAX_0: A precept that has no less M than any other precept is choice-worthy.
- Maxim MAX_1: A precept whose use has no less expected M than any alternative precept is choice-worthy.
- Maxim MAX_2: A precept that is at least as likely as any alternative to possess no less M than any other precept is choice-worthy.
- Maxim MAX_3: A precept whose worst possible outcome would possess no less M than the worst possible outcome of any alternative is choice-worthy.
- Maxim MAX_4: A precept that possesses a satisfactory amount of M is choice-worthy…
- Maxim MAX_n: Every precept is choice-worthy.

Chapter 13: Assessing the Hybrid Solution

- **Standard S_1** (which directly evaluates decision-guides for their objective deontic standing) **remotely prescribes the act** that is deemed choice-worthy by the objectively right decision-guide.
- The **moral status hierarchy of decision-guides**: the highest decision-guide in this hierarchy is the objectively right decision-guide, while the second highest is the subjectively right decision-guide. The next highest is the decision-guide prescribed by the subjectively right precept; below that is the decision-guide remotely prescribed by the subjectively right maxim; below that is the decision-guide remotely prescribed by the subjectively right counsel; and so forth.
- **Definition 13.1. Decision-mandatoriness in the core sense:** An act A is decision-mandatory (relative to a principle P of objective obligation) in the core sense at time t_i for agent S to perform at t_j if and only if:
  (a) S believes at t_i of A that S could perform A (in the epistemic sense) at t_j; and either
  (b) S believes of A that it is objectively obligatory according to P, or
  (c) S is uncertain which act is prescribed as objectively obligatory according to P, but S believes of A that it is prescribed as choice-mandated by a decision-guide that is objectively obligatory, or
  (d) S is uncertain which act is prescribed as objectively obligatory according to P, and S is uncertain which act is prescribed as choice-mandated by a decision-guide that is objectively obligatory; but S believes of A that it is prescribed as choice-mandated by a decision-guide that is subjectively obligatory, or

(e) S is uncertain which act is prescribed as objectively obligatory according to P, uncertain which act is prescribed as choice-mandated by a decision-guide that is objectively obligatory, and uncertain which act is prescribed as choice-mandated by a decision-guide that is subjectively obligatory; but S believes of A that it is prescribed as choice-mandated by a decision-guide that is prescribed as choice-mandated by a precept that is subjectively obligatory, or

(f) S is uncertain which act is prescribed as objectively obligatory according to P, uncertain which act is prescribed as choice-mandated by a decision-guide that is objectively obligatory, uncertain which act is prescribed as choice-mandated by a decision-guide that is subjectively obligatory, and uncertain which act is prescribed as choice-mandated by a decision-guide that is prescribed as choice-mandated by a precept that is subjectively obligatory; but S believes of A that it is prescribed as choice-mandated by a decision-guide that is prescribed as choice-mandated by a precept that is prescribed as choice-mandated by a maxim that is subjectively obligatory, or…(pp. 311–12)

- **Code C****: Relative to an account C of objective obligation, an act A is subjectively obligatory at time t_i for agent S to perform at t_j if and only if A is decision-mandated (relative to C) in the core sense at time t_i for S to perform at t_j.
- Code C** serves as a **general definition of an act's being subjectively right**.
- **Definition 13.2. Ability to indirectly use a moral principle in the core sense to decide what to do:** An agent S who is uncertain at t_i which of the acts she could perform (in the epistemic sense) at t_j is prescribed by P (a principle of objective moral obligation or rightness) is nonetheless able to indirectly use P in the core sense at t_i to decide at t_i what to do at t_j *if and only if*:
  (A) S believes at t_i of some act A that S could perform A (in the epistemic sense) at t_j;
  (B) There is some act X (not necessarily identical to A) that is decision-mandated or decision-worthy in the core sense for S at t_i, and
  (C) if and because S wanted all-things-considered to use principle P for guidance at t_i for an act performable at t_j, she would then come to believe about act A (in time to choose A for time t_j) that it is decision-mandated or decision-worthy in the core sense for her, relative to P. (pp. 317–18)
- A **laundry list decision-guide** prescribes as choice-worthy a series of actions, each for a different time, each described in terms that render the action one the agent has the epistemic ability to perform, and each such that it is prescribed by the associated theoretical account of what makes actions right or wrong.
- The **Constrained Standards approach** requires the agent to have beliefs about which guides are best, and also places constraints on which standards determine the deontic rank-ordering of decision-guides (and of higher-level guides, such as precepts, maxims, and so forth).
- A **decision-guide's objective deontic status is modally robust** just in case its appropriateness and ranking as a decision-guide relative to its governing moral theory is the same in reasonably near-by possible worlds as its appropriateness and ranking are in the actual world.
- **(Lenient) Definition 13.2.1. Ability to indirectly use a moral principle in the core sense to decide what to do:** An agent S who is uncertain at t_i which of the acts she could perform

(in the epistemic sense) at t_j is prescribed by P (a principle of objective moral obligation or rightness) is nonetheless able to indirectly use P in the core sense at t_i to decide at t_i what to do at t_j *if and only if*:

(A) S believes at t_i of some act A that S could perform A (in the epistemic sense) at t_j; and

(B) if and because S wanted all-things-considered to use principle P for guidance at t_i for an act performable at t_j, she would then come to believe about A that it is morally appropriate to perform A, relative to P and to her credences at t_i about herself and about A's relation to P. (p. 337)

- The **Constrained Standards version of the Hybrid solution** consists of the following chief components:

  (1) the truly comprehensive version of each moral theory, comprising

   (a) an account of what makes actions objectively right and wrong (Code C),

   (b) an account of what makes actions subjectively obligatory or right in terms of their decision-mandatoriness or decision-worthiness (Code C**),

   (c) a set of standards to evaluate decision-guiding norms at the required levels (Standards S_1, S_2, S_3, and so forth),

   (d) sets of decision-guiding norms at ascending levels (decision-guides, precepts, maxims, counsels, and so forth);

  (2) the requirement that the appropriateness and rankings of the guides be modally robust relative to the moral theory in question;

  (3) Definition 13.1 for an action's being decision-mandatory, decision-worthy, or decision-prohibited in the core sense;

  (4) Definition 13.2 and (possibly) Lenient Definition 13.2.1 for ability to indirectly use a moral principle in the core sense as a decision-guide.

Chapter 14: Conclusion

A "Constrained Standards Hybrid theory" (or "CSH theory" for short) is a moral theory that *successfully* embodies the Constrained Standards Hybrid moral theory approach. Such a theory includes all the elements of a truly comprehensive moral theory: a Code C account of what makes actions objectively right or wrong, a Code C** account of what makes actions subjectively right or wrong in terms of their decision-worthiness, a set of standards to evaluate decision-guiding norms at each level, and sets of decision-guiding norms at as many ascending levels as are needed (decision-guides, precepts, maxims, counsels, and so forth). The CSH moral theory meets the requirement that the appropriateness and rankings of the guides be modally robust relative to the moral theory in question, and its concepts satisfy Definition 13.1 for an action's being decision-mandatory in the core sense, as well as Definition 13.2 and (potentially) Lenient Definition 13.2.1 for ability to indirectly use a moral principle in the core sense as a decision-guide. Furthermore, to count as successful, such a moral theory's Code C** must be appropriate relative to its Code C, its standards for evaluating the decision-guiding norms must be appropriate relative to its Code C, and the decision-guiding norms must meet those standards and be modally robust. Moreover, the norms must be as extensive as possible, enabling as many agents as possible to use them in deciding how to act.

- **Criterion A* (Consistency):** When a Code C and a Code C** are paired in a single CSH moral theory, their prescriptions should be consistent. (p. 355)

- **Criterion B* (Moral Adequacy):** The guiding prescriptions issued by Code C** in a CSH moral theory for an agent who accepts the theory's Code C as the correct theoretical account of rightness and wrongness should be morally appropriate for that Code C. Put differently, an action prescribed by Code C** should be morally reasonable or wise for the agent to choose, relative to a commitment to C and to the agent's epistemic grasp of the situation. (p. 356)

- **Criterion C* (Guidance Adequacy):** Assuming that Code C in a CSH moral theory provides an exhaustive account of the moral status of all actual and humanly possible actions, then the decision-guiding rule(s) of the theory's Code C* should be such that for every agent and every occasion for decision, there is an appropriate rule in Code C* which can be directly used by the agent for making a decision on that occasion. (p. 356)

- **Criterion D* (Normative Adequacy):** For each plausible theoretic account of right and wrong C, it should be possible to define a C** that would enable every agent affected by the problems of error and uncertainty to apply C indirectly to each of her decisions through directly applying the decision-guiding rule(s) of C**. (p. 356)

- **Criterion E* (Relation to Blameworthiness):** A CSH moral theory should evaluate an agent as not blameworthy for performing an action if she performs it because she accepts the moral theory, and believes (or reasonably believes) that the action is prescribed as subjectively or objectively right or obligatory by either Code C or Code C** of the theory. Such evaluations should be independently plausible, given our background concept of what makes agents blameworthy for their actions. (p. 356)

- **Criterion C**(Guidance Adequacy):** Assuming that Code C in a CSH moral theory provides an exhaustive account of the moral status of all actual and humanly possible actions, then it should be possible, for every agent and every occasion for decision-making, to use Code C directly or indirectly to make a decision about what to do on that occasion. (p. 358)

References

Adams, R. M. 1976. Motive Utilitarianism. *Journal of Philosophy* 73(14): 467–81.

Alston, William. 1971. Varieties of Privileged Access. *American Philosophical Quarterly* 8(3): 223–41.

Anderson, Elizabeth. 1996. Reasons, Attitudes, and Values: Replies to Sturgeon and Piper. *Ethics* 106: 538–54.

Anderson, Elizabeth. 2015. Moral Bias and Corrective Practices: A Pragmatist Perspective. *Proceedings and Addresses of the American Philosophical Association* 89: 21–47.

Andric, Vuko. 2013. The Case of the Miners. *Journal of Ethics and Social Philosophy* (January): 1–8. <http://www.jesp.org> (accessed December 20, 2015).

Aristotle. 1941. *The Nicomachean Ethics*. In *The Basic Works of Aristotle*, ed. Richard McKeon, 935–1112. New York: Random House.

Arpaly, Nomy. 2003. *Unprincipled Virtue*. Oxford: Oxford University Press.

Arpaly, Nomy, and Timothy Schroeder. 2014. *In Praise of Desire*. Oxford: Oxford University Press.

Audi, Robert. 1994. Dispositional Beliefs and Dispositions to Believe. *Noûs* 28(4): 419–34.

Axtell, Guy. 2011. Recovering Responsibility. *Logos and Episteme* 2(3): 429–54.

Axtell, Guy, and Philip Olsen. 2009. Three Independent Factors in Epistemology. *Contemporary Pragmatism* 6(2): 89–109.

Baehr, Jason. 2011. *The Inquiring Mind*. Oxford: Oxford University Press.

Baier, Kurt. 1965. *The Moral Point of View*. Abridged edn. New York: Random House.

Bales, Adam, Daniel Cohen, and Toby Handfield. 2014. Decision Theory for Agents with Incomplete Preferences. *Australasian Journal of Philosophy* 92(3): 453–70.

Bales, Eugene. 1971. Act-Utilitarianism: Account of Right-Making Characteristics or Decision-Making Procedure? *American Philosophical Quarterly* 8(3): 257–65.

Barry, Christian. 2005. Applying the Contribution Principle. *Metaphilosophy* 36(1–2): 210–27.

Bennett, Jonathan. 1995. *The Act Itself*. Oxford: Clarendon Press.

Bentham, Jeremy. 1949. Introduction to the Principles of Morals and Legislation. In *The English Philosophers from Bacon to Mill*, ed. E. A. Burtt. New York: Modern Library.

Bergstrom, Lars. 1966. *The Alternatives and Consequences of Actions*. Stockholm: Almqvist & Wiksell.

Berkeley, George. 1929. Passive Obedience or the Christian Doctrine of Not Resisting the Supreme Power, Proved and Vindicated upon the Principles of the Law of Nature. In *Berkeley: Selections*, ed. Mary W. Calkins. New York: Scribner's.

Berker, Selim. 2013. Epistemic Teleology and the Separateness of Propositions. *The Philosophical Review* 122(3): 337–93.

Bradley, Ben. 2006. Against Satisficing Consequentialism. *Utilitas* 18(2): 97–108.

Brandt, Richard. 1963. Towards a Credible Form of Utilitarianism. In *Morality and the Language of Conduct*, ed. Hector-Neri Castañeda and George Nakhnikian, 107–43. Detroit: Wayne State University Press.

Brandt, Richard. 1979. *A Theory of the Good and the Right*. Oxford: Clarendon Press.

Briggs, Rachel. 2014. Normative Theories of Rational Choice: Expected Utility. *The Stanford Encyclopedia of Philosophy*. Fall edn., ed. Edward N. Zalta. <http://plato.stanford.edu/archives/fall2014/entries/rationality-normative-utility/> (accessed December 15, 2015).

Brink, David. 1986. Utilitarian Morality and the Personal Point of View. *Journal of Philosophy* 83(8): 417–38.

Brink, David. 1989. *Moral Realism and the Foundations of Ethics*. New York: Cambridge University Press.

Brooks, David. 2012. The Moral Diet. *The New York Times* (June 7). <http://www.nytimes.com/2012/06/08/opinion/brooks-the-moral-diet.html> (accessed June 9, 2012).

Brooks, David. 2015. Learning from Mistakes. *The New York Times* (May 19). <http://www.nytimes.com/2015/05/19/opinion/david-brooks-learning-from-mistakes.html?_r=0> (accessed December 22, 2015).

Broome, John. 1991. *Weighing Goods*. Oxford: Blackwell.

Broome, John. 2013. *Rationality through Reasoning*. Malden, MA: Wiley-Blackwell.

Broome, John. 2014. Normativity in Reasoning. *Pacific Philosophical Quarterly* 95: 622–33.

Buchak, Lara. 2013. *Risk and Rationality*. Oxford: Oxford University Press.

Buchak, Lara. 2014. Belief, Credence, and Norms. *Philosophical Studies* 169(2): 285–311.

Buss, Sarah. 2014. Personal Autonomy. *The Stanford Encyclopedia of Philosophy*. Winter edn., ed. Edward N. Zalta. <http://plato.stanford.edu/archives/win2014/entries/personal-autonomy/> (accessed December 15, 2015).

Carlson, Erik. 1995. *Consequentialism Reconsidered*. Dordrecht: Kluwer Academic Publishers.

Carlson, Erik. 2002. Deliberation, Foreknowledge, and Morality as a Guide to Action. *Erkenntnis* 57(1): 71–89.

Cartwright, Nancy. 1983. *How the Laws of Physics Lie*. New York: Oxford University Press.

Cartwright, Nancy. 1989. *Nature's Capacities and their Measurements*. New York: Oxford University Press.

Castañeda, Hector-Neri. 1974. *The Structure of Morality*. Springfield, IL: Charles D. Thomas.

Chang, Ruth. 2002. *Making Comparisons Count*. New York: Routledge.

Chappell, Richard Yetter. 2012. Fittingness: The Sole Normative Primitive. *Philosophical Quarterly* 62(249): 684–704.

Chignell, Andrew. 2013. The Ethics of Belief. *The Stanford Encyclopedia of Philosophy*. Spring edn., ed. Edward N. Zalta. <http://plato.stanford.edu/archives/spr2013/entries/ethics-belief/> (accessed December 15, 2015).

Christman, John. 2015. Autonomy in Moral and Political Philosophy. *The Stanford Encyclopedia of Philosophy*. Spring edn., ed. Edward N. Zalta. <http://plato.stanford.edu/archives/spr2015/entries/autonomy-moral/> (accessed December 15, 2015).

Churchland, P. M. 1996. The Neural Representation of the Social World. In *Mind and Morals*, ed. L. May, M. Friedman, and A. Clark, 91–108. Cambridge, MA: MIT Press.

Clark, Andy. 2000. Word and Action: Reconciling Rules and Know-How in Moral Cognition. *Canadian Journal of Philosophy* 30 (Supp. Vol. 26): 267–89.

Clifford, W. K. 1999 (originally published 1877). The Ethics of Belief. In *The Ethics of Belief and Other Essays*, ed. T. Madigan, 70–96. Reprint, Amherst, MA: Prometheus.

Code, Lorraine. 1987. *Epistemic Responsibility*. Hanover, NH: University Press of New England.

Cohen, G. A. 2003. Facts and Principles. *Philosophy and Public Affairs* 31: 211–45.

Cohen, G. A. 2008. *Rescuing Justice and Equality*. Cambridge, MA: Harvard University Press.

Cohen, Jonathan, and Craig Callendar. 2009. A Better Best System Account of Lawhood. *Philosophical Studies* 145(1): 1–34.

Colyvan, Mark, and Alan Hájek. 2016. Making Do without Expectations. *Mind* 125(499): 829–57.

Conee, Earl. 2000. The Moral Value of Promises. *The Philosophical Review* 109(3): 411–22.

Conee, Earl, and R. Feldman. 2004. *Evidentialism*. Oxford: Oxford University Press.

Dancy, Jonathan. 2004. *Ethics Without Principles*. Oxford: Clarendon Press.

Dancy, Jonathan. 2013. Moral Particularism. *The Stanford Encyclopedia of Philosophy*. Fall edn., ed. Edward N. Zalta. <http://plato.stanford.edu/archives/fall2013/entries/moral-particularism/> (accessed November 2, 2017).

De Lazari-Radek, Katarzyna, and Peter Singer. 2014. *The Point of View of the Universe: Sidgwick and Contemporary Ethics*. Oxford: Oxford University Press.

Dennett, Daniel. 1986. The Moral First Aid Manual. The Tanner Lectures on Human Values, delivered at the University of Michigan, November 7 and 8. <https://tannerlectures.utah.edu/lecture-library.php#d> (accessed July 15, 2011).

DeRose, Keith. 2000. Ought We to Follow Our Evidence? *Philosophy and Phenomenological Research* 60(3): 697–706.

Dhami, Mandeep K. 2001. Bailing and Jailing the Fast and Frugal Way: An Application of Social Judgment Theory and Simple Heuristics to English Magistrates' Remand Decisions. PhD dissertation, City University, London.

Dhami, Mandeep K. 2003. Psychological Models of Professional Decision-Making. *Psychological Science* 14: 175–80.

Dhami Mandeep K., and Peter Ayton. 2001. Bailing and Jailing the Fast and Frugal Way. *Journal of Behavioral Decision-Making* 14: 141–68.

Donagan, Alan. 1977. *Theory of Morality*. Chicago: University of Chicago Press.

Dougherty, Trent. 2012. Reducing Responsibility: An Evidentialist Account of Epistemic Blame. *European Journal of Philosophy* 20(4): 534–47.

Dowell, Janice. 2012. Contextualist Solutions to Three Puzzles about Practical Conditionals. *Oxford Studies in Metaethics* 7, ed. Russ Shafer-Landau, 271–303. Oxford: Oxford University Press.

Dowell, Janice. 2013. Flexible Contextualism about Deontic Modals: A Puzzle about Information-Sensitivity. *Inquiry* 56(2–3): 149–78.

Dreier, Jamie. 1993. Structures of Normative Theories. *The Monist* 76(1): 22–40.

Dreier, Jamie. 2011. In Defense of Consequentializing. In *Oxford Studies in Normative Ethics* 1, ed. Mark Timmons, 97–119. Oxford: Oxford University Press.

Dreyfus, H., and S. Dreyfus. 1990. What Is Morality? A Phenomenological Account of the Development of Ethical Expertise. In *Universalism vs. Communitarianism: Contemporary Debates in Ethics*, ed. D. Rasmussen, 237–64. Cambridge, MA: MIT Press.

Driver, Julia. 2000. Moral and Epistemic Virtue. In *Knowledge, Belief, and Character*, ed. Guy Axtell, 124–33. Lanham, MD: Rowman & Littlefield.

Driver, Julia. 2003. The Conflation of Moral and Epistemic Virtue. In *Moral and Epistemic Virtues*, ed. Michael Brady and Duncan Pritchard, 101–16. Malden, MA: Blackwell Publishing.

Driver, Julia. 2012. *Consequentialism*. New York: Routledge.

Dwyer, Sue. 2009. Moral Dumbfounding and the Linguistic Analogy: Implications for the Study of Moral Judgment. *Mind & Language* 24(3): 274–96.

Eddy, David M. 1982. Probabilistic Reasoning in Clinical Medicine: Problems and Opportunities. In *Judgment under Uncertainty: Heuristics and Biases*, ed. Daniel Kahneman, Paul Slovic, and Amos Tversky, 249–67. Cambridge: Cambridge University Press.

Enoch, David. 2010. The Epistemological Challenge to Metanormative Realism: How Best to Understand It, and How to Cope with It. *Philosophical Studies* 148(3): 413–38.

Evans, Jonathan St. B. T., and Keith Frankish, eds. 2009. *In Two Minds: Dual Processes and Beyond*. Oxford: Oxford University Press.

Ewing, A. C. 1939. A Suggested Non-Naturalistic Analysis of Good. *Mind*, New Series 48(189): 1–22.

Ewing, A. C. 1947. *The Definition of Good*. New York: Macmillan.

Fantl, J., and M. McGrath. 2009. *Knowledge in an Uncertain World*. New York: Oxford University Press.

Feldman, Fred. 1980. The Principle of Moral Harmony. *Journal of Philosophy* 89(4): 166–79.

Feldman, Fred. 2006. Actual Utility, the Objection from Impracticality, and the Move to Expected Utility. *Philosophical Studies* 129(1): 49–79.

Feldman, Fred. 2012. True and Useful: On the Structure of a Two Level Normative Theory. *Utilitas* 24(2): 151–71.

Feldman, Richard. 2000. The Ethics of Belief. *Philosophy and Phenomenological Research* 60(3): 667–95.

Feldman, Richard. 2002. Epistemological Duties. In *The Oxford Handbook of Epistemology*, ed. Paul K. Moser, 362–84. Oxford: Oxford University Press.

Flanagan, Owen. 1991. *Varieties of Moral Personality*. Cambridge, MA: Harvard University Press.

Flanagan, Owen. 1996. Ethics Naturalized. In *Mind and Morals*, ed. L. May, M. Friedman, and A. Clark, 19–44. Cambridge, MA: MIT Press.

Foley, Richard. 2010. Epistemological Self-Profile. In *A Companion to Epistemology*, 2nd edn., ed. Jonathan Dancy, Ernest Sosa, and Matthias Steup, 134–9. Malden, MA: Blackwell Publishing.

Franklin-Hall, Andrew. 2013. On Becoming an Adult: Autonomy and the Moral Relevance of Life's Stages. *Philosophical Quarterly* 63(251): 223–47.

Gardner, John. 2004. The Wrongdoing that Gets Results. In *Philosophical Perspectives* 18: *Ethics*, ed. John Hawthorne and Dean W. Zimmerman, 53–88. Malden, MA: Wiley-Blackwell.

Geach, P. T. 1977. *The Virtues*. Cambridge: Cambridge University Press.

Gert, Bernard. 2004. *Common Morality: Deciding What to Do*. Oxford: Oxford University Press.

Gibbard, Allan. 1990. *Wise Choices, Apt Feelings*. Cambridge, MA: Harvard University Press.

Gigerenzer, Gerd. 2000. *Adaptive Thinking*. Oxford: Oxford University Press.

Gigerenzer, Gerd. 2008a. Moral Intuition = Fast and Frugal Heuristics? In *Moral Psychology* 2: *The Cognitive Science of Morality*, ed. Walter Sinnott-Armstrong, 1–26. Cambridge, MA: MIT Press.

Gigerenzer, Gerd. 2008b. Reply to Comments. In *Moral Psychology* 2: *The Cognitive Science of Morality*, ed. Walter Sinnott-Armstrong, 41–6. Cambridge, MA: MIT Press.

Gigerenzer, Gerd, and Daniel G. Goldstein. 1999. Betting on One Good Reason: The Take the Best Heuristic. In *Simple Heuristics that Make Us Smart*, ed. Gerd Gigerenzer, Peter M. Todd, and the ABC Research Group, 75–96. New York: Oxford University Press.

Godfrey-Smith, P. 2009. Models and Fictions in Science. *Philosophical Studies* 143(1): 101–17.

Goldman, Alvin I. 1970. *A Theory of Human Action*. Englewood Cliffs, NJ: Prentice-Hall.

Goldman, Alvin I. 1978. Epistemics: The Regulative Theory of Cognition. *Journal of Philosophy* 75(10): 509–23.

Goldman, Holly S. 1974. David Lyons on Utilitarian Generalization. *Philosophical Studies* 26(2): 77–94.

Goldman, Holly S. 1976. Dated Rightness and Moral Imperfection. *The Philosophical Review* 85(4): 449–87.

Goldman, Holly S. 1978. Doing the Best One Can. In *Values and Morals*, ed. A. I. Goldman and J. Kim, 186–214. Dordrecht: Reidel.

Goodin, Robert. 2009. Demandingness as a Virtue. *Journal of Ethics* 13(1): 1–13.

Goodman, David J., and Marc Santora. 2013. Cabby Had Violations Before Crash in Midtown. *The New York Times* (August 21). <http://www.nytimes.com/2013/08/22/nyregion/after-a-taxi-hits-a-woman-a-crowd-scrambles-to-help.html> (accessed June 12, 2014).

Graham, Peter. 2010. In Defense of Objectivism about Moral Obligation. *Ethics* 121(1): 88–115.

Grant, Simon, and John Quiggin. 2013. Bounded Awareness, Heuristics and the Precautionary Principle. *Journal of Economic Behavior and Organization* 93: 17–31.

Grant, Simon, and John Quiggin. 2015. A Preference Model for Choice Subject to Surprise. *Theory and Decision* 79(2): 167–80.

Greene, Joshua D. 2008. The Secret Joke of Kant's Soul. In *Moral Psychology* 3: *The Neuroscience of Morality*, ed. Walter Sinnott-Armstrong, 35–80. Cambridge, MA: MIT Press.

Griffin, James. 1996. *Value Judgment: Improving Our Ethical Beliefs*. Oxford: Clarendon Press.

Gruzalski, Bart. 1981. Foreseeable Consequence Utilitarianism. *Australasian Journal of Philosophy* 59(2): 163–76.

Guerrero, Alexander A. 2007. Don't Know, Don't Kill: Moral Ignorance, Culpability, and Caution. *Philosophical Studies* 136(1): 59–98.

Gustafsson, Johan E., and Olle Torpman. 2014. In Defence of my Favourite Theory. *Pacific Philosophical Quarterly* 95(2): 159–74.

Haack, Susan. 2001. The Ethics of Belief Reconsidered. In *Knowledge, Truth, and Duty*, ed. Matthias Steup, 21–34. Oxford: Oxford University Press.

Haidt, Jonathan. 2001. The Emotional Dog and its Rational Tail: A Social Intuitionist Approach to Moral Judgment. *Psychological Review* 108(4): 814–34.

Hajek, Alan. 2003. What Conditional Probability Could Not Be. *Synthese* 137(3): 273–323.

Haji, Ishtiyaque. 1998. *Moral Appraisability*. Oxford: Oxford University Press.

Hall, Richard J., and Charles R. Johnson. 1998. The Epistemic Duty to Seek More Evidence. *American Philosophical Quarterly* 35(2): 129–40.

Hanser, Matthew. 2014. Acting Wrongly by Trying. In *Oxford Studies in Normative Ethics* 4, ed. Mark Timmons, 135–58. Oxford: Oxford University Press.

Hardin, Russell. 1988. *Morality within the Limits of Reason*. Chicago: University of Chicago Press.

Hare, R. M. 1965. *Freedom and Reason*. Oxford: Oxford University Press.

Hare, R. M. 1981. *Moral Thinking*. Oxford: Clarendon Press.

Harman, Elizabeth. 2011. Does Moral Ignorance Exculpate? *Ratio* 24(4): 443–68.

Haslett, D. W. 1984. Is Allowing Someone to Die the Same as Murder? *Social Theory and Practice* 10: 81–95.

Hauser, Marc. 2006. *Moral Minds: How Nature Designed Our Universal Sense of Right and Wrong*. New York: Ecco/HarperCollins.

Hawthorne, John, and Jason Stanley. 2008. Knowledge and Action. *Journal of Philosophy* 105(10): 571–90.

Henig, Robin Marantz. 2015. Death by Robot. *The New York Times Magazine* (January 9). <http://www.nytimes.com/2015/01/11/magazine/death-by-robot.html?_r=0> (accessed January 26, 2015).

Hindriks, Frank A. 2004. A Modest Solution to the Problem of Rule-Following. *Philosophical Studies* 121(1): 65–98.

Hodgson, D. H. 1967. *Consequences of Utilitarianism: A Study in Normative Ethics and Legal Theory*. Oxford: Clarendon Press.

Hooker, Brad. 2000. *Ideal Code, Real World*. Oxford: Clarendon Press.

Horwich, Paul. 1982. *Probability and Evidence*. Cambridge: Cambridge University Press.

Howard-Snyder, Frances. 1997. The Rejection of Objective Consequentialism. *Utilitas* 9(2): 241–8.

Hoyt, Clark. 2009. Calculations of War: Which Risk is Reasonable? *The New York Times* (September 19). <http://www.nytimes.com/2009/09/20/opinion/20pubed.html?_r=0> (accessed July 1, 2015).

Hubbard, Ben. 2016. Saudi Enforcer Shares Doubts, and Pays Price. *The New York Times* (July 11), p. A6.

Huddleston, Andrew. 2012. Naughty Beliefs. *Philosophical Studies* 160(2): 209–22.

Hudson, James L. 1989. Subjectivization in Ethics. *American Philosophical Quarterly* 26(3): 221–9.

Huemer, Michael. 2010. Lexical Priority and the Problem of Risk. *Pacific Philosophical Quarterly* 91(3): 332–51.

Humberstone, I. L. 1983. The Background of Circumstances. *Pacific Philosophical Quarterly* 64(1): 19–34.

Hurka, Thomas. 2010. Asymmetries in Value. *Noûs* 44(2): 199–223.

Jackson, Frank. 1991. Decision-Theoretic Consequentialism and the Nearest and Dearest Objection. *Ethics* 101(3): 461–82.

Jackson, Frank, and Robert Pargetter. 1986. Oughts, Options, and Actualism. *The Philosophical Review* 95(2): 233–55.

Jackson, Frank, and Michael Smith. 2006. Absolutist Moral Theories and Uncertainty. *Journal of Philosophy* 103(6): 267–83.

James, William. 1895. Is Life Worth Living? *International Journal of Ethics* 6(1): 1–24.

Jeffrey, Richard. 1965. *The Logic of Decision*. New York: McGraw-Hill.

Joyce, James. 2010. A Defense of Imprecise Credences in Inference and Decision Making. *Philosophical Perspectives* 24, *Epistemology*: 281–323.

Kagan, Shelly. 1988. The Additive Fallacy. *Ethics* 99(1): 5–31.

Kagan, Shelly. 1989. *The Limits of Morality*. Oxford: Clarendon Press.

Kagan, Shelly. 1992. The Structure of Normative Ethics. *Philosophical Perspectives* 6: 223–42.

Kagan, Shelly. 2005. The Geometry of Desert. The Lindley Lecture, University of Kansas.

Kahneman, Daniel. 2011. *Thinking, Fast and Slow*. New York: Farrar, Straus & Giroux.

Kahneman, Daniel, Paul Slovic, and Amos Tversky, eds. 1982. *Judgment under Uncertainty*. Cambridge: Cambridge University Press.

Kahneman, Daniel, and Amos Tversky, eds. 2000. *Choices, Values, and Frames*. Cambridge: Cambridge University Press.

Kant, Immanuel. 1949. On the Supposed Right to Lie. In *Critique of Practical Reason and Other Writings in Moral Philosophy*, ed. and trans. Lewis White Beck, 346–50. Chicago: University of Chicago Press.

Kant, Immanuel. 1956. *Critique of Practical Reason*. Indianapolis: Bobbs-Merrill.

Kant, Immanuel. 1959. *Foundations of the Metaphysics of Morals*. Indianapolis: Bobbs-Merrill.

Keeney, Ralph L. and Howard Raiffa. 1993. *Decisions with Multiple Objectives: Preferences and Value Trade-Offs*. Cambridge: Cambridge University Press.

King, Matt, and Peter Carruthers. 2012. Moral Responsibility and Consciousness. *Journal of Moral Philosophy* 9: 200–28.

Kivy, Peter. 1992. Oh, Boy! You Too! Aesthetic Emotivism Reexamined. In *The Philosophy of A. J. Ayer*. The Library of Living Philosophers, vol. XXI, ed. L. E. Hahn. La Salle, IL: Open Court.

Kolodny, Niko, and John MacFarlane. 2010. Ifs and Oughts. *Journal of Philosophy* 107(3): 115–43.

Kornblith, Hilary. 1983. Justified Belief and Epistemically Responsible Action. *The Philosophical Review* 92(1): 33–48.

Kriegel, Uriah. 2007. Self-Consciousness: Essential Indexicals and De Se Thought (Section B). *The Internet Encyclopedia of Philosophy*, ed. James Fieser and Bradley Dowden. <http://www.iep.utm.edu/self-con> (accessed December 20, 2015).

Kripke, Saul. 1982. *Wittgenstein on Rules and Private Language*. Oxford: Blackwell.

Kruglanski, Arie W., and Gerd Gigerenzer. 2011. Intuitive and Deliberate Judgments are Based on Common Principles. *Psychological Review* 118(1): 97–109.

Kudo, Timothy. 2015. How We Learned to Kill. *The New York Times Sunday Review* (March 1), p. 4.

Lang, Gerald. 2004. A Dilemma for Objective Act-Utilitarianism. *Politics, Philosophy & Economics* 3(2): 221–39.

Lehrer, Jonah. 2009. *How We Decide*. Boston: Houghton Mifflin Harcourt.

Lenman, James. 2000. Consequentialism and Cluelessness. *Philosophy and Public Affairs* 29(4): 342–70.

Leonhardt, David. 2006. This Fed Chief May Yet Get a Honeymoon. *The New York Times* (August 23), p. C1.

Lessig, Lawrence. 1999. *Code and other Laws of Cyberspace*. New York: Basic Books.

Levi, Isaac. 1986. *Hard Choices: Decision Making Under Unresolved Conflict*. Cambridge: Cambridge University Press.

Levy, Neil. 2014. *Consciousness and Moral Responsibility*. Oxford: Oxford University Press.

Lockhart, Ted. 2000. *Moral Uncertainty and Its Consequences*. New York: Oxford University Press.

Luce, R. Duncan, and Howard Raiffa. 1957. *Games and Decisions*. New York: John Wiley and Sons.

Lyons, David. 1965. *Forms and Limits of Utilitarianism*. Oxford: Clarendon Press.

McAlpine, Kate. 2015. Mayday Machine. *Michigan Today* (January 21). <http://michigantoday.umich.edu/mayday-machine/> (accessed January 27, 2015).

MacAskill, William. 2016. Normative Uncertainty as a Voting Problem. *Mind* 125(500): 967–1004.

McConnell, Terrance. 1988. Ross on Duty and Ignorance. *History of Philosophy Quarterly* 5(1): 79–95.

McConnell, Terrance. 2010. Moral Dilemmas. *The Stanford Encyclopedia of Philosophy.* Summer edn., ed. Edward N. Zalta. <http://plato.stanford.edu/archives/sum2010/entries/moral-dilemmas/> (accessed December 19, 2015).

MacFarlane, John. 2014. *Assessment Sensitivity.* Oxford: Oxford University Press.

Machery, Edouard. 2009. *Doing Without Concepts.* New York: Oxford University Press.

McKeever, Sean, and Michael Ridge. 2006. *Principled Ethics.* Oxford: Clarendon Press.

Mackie, John L. 1977. *Ethics: Inventing Right and Wrong.* New York: Penguin.

McKinnon, Christine. 2003. Knowing Cognitive Selves. In *Intellectual Virtue: Perspectives from Ethics and Epistemology*, ed. Michael DePaul and Linda Zagzebski, 227–54. Oxford: Clarendon Press.

McLeod, Carolyn. 2005. How to Distinguish Autonomy from Integrity. *Canadian Journal of Philosophy* 35(1): 107–33.

McMullin, Ernan. 1985. Galilean Idealization. *Studies in History and Philosophy of Sciences* 16: 247–73.

Maier, John. 2011. Abilities. *The Stanford Encyclopedia of Philosophy.* Fall edn., ed. Edward N. Zalta. <http://plato.stanford.edu/archives/fall2011/entries/abilities/> (accessed December 19, 2015).

Mason, Elinor. 2003. Consequentialism and the 'Ought Implies Can' Principle. *American Philosophical Quarterly* 40(4): 319–31.

Mikhail, J. 2007. Universal Moral Grammar: Theory, Evidence, and the Future. *Trends in Cognitive Sciences* 11(4): 143–52.

Mill, John Stuart. 1957. *Utilitarianism.* Indianapolis: Bobbs-Merrill.

Miller, Richard B. 2009. Actual Rule Utilitarianism. *Journal of Philosophy* 106(1): 5–28.

Monmarquet, James. 1993. *Epistemic Virtue and Doxastic Responsibility.* Landham, MD: Rowman & Littlefield.

Moore, G. E. 1965. *Ethics.* New York: Oxford University Press.

Moore, G. E. 1993. *Principia Ethica.* Cambridge: Cambridge University Press.

Moore, Michael S., and Heidi Hurd. 2011. Punishing the Stupid, Clumsy, Selfish, and Weak: The Culpability of Negligence. *Criminal Law and Philosophy* 5: 96–148.

Mulgan, T. 2001. *The Demands of Consequentialism.* Oxford: Oxford University Press.

Murphy, L. 2000. *Moral Demands in Nonideal Theory.* New York: Oxford University Press.

Murphy, Mark. 2008. Theological Voluntarism. *The Stanford Encyclopedia of Philosophy.* Fall edn., ed. Edward N. Zalta. <http://plato.stanford.edu/archives/fall2008/entries/voluntarism-theological/> (accessed December 20, 2015).

Narveson, Jan. 1967. *Morality and Utility.* Baltimore, MD: Johns Hopkins University Press.

Nell, Onora. 1975. *Acting on Principle.* New York: Columbia University Press.

Nesbitt, Winston. 1995. Is Killing No Worse than Letting Die? *Journal of Applied Philosophy* 12(1): 101–5.

Nickerson, Raymond. 2008. *Aspects of Rationality.* New York: Taylor & Francis.

Nisbett, Richard E., David H. Krantz, Christopher Jepson, and Geoffrey Fong. 1982. Improving Inductive Inference. In *Judgment under Uncertainty: Heuristics and Biases*, ed. Daniel Kahneman, Paul Slovic, and Amos Tversky, 445–59. Cambridge: Cambridge University Press.

Norton, John D. 2008. Ignorance and Indifference. *Philosophy of Science* 75(1): 45–68.

Nottelmann, Nikolaj. 2007. *Blameworthy Belief: A Study in Epistemic Deontologism.* Dordrecht: Springer.

Nozick, Robert. 1974. *Anarchy, State, and Utopia.* New York: Basic Books.

Oddie, Graham, and Peter Menzies. 1992. An Objectivist's Guide to Subjective Value. *Ethics* 102(3): 512–33.

O'Neil, Onora. 1996. *Towards Justice and Virtue.* Cambridge: Cambridge University Press.

Parfit, Derek. 1984. *Reasons and Persons.* Oxford: Clarendon Press.

Parfit, Derek. 1988. What We Together Do. Unpublished manuscript.

Parfit, Derek. 2011. *On What Matters*, Vol. 1. Oxford: Oxford University Press.

Parker, Tom. 2008. *Rules of Thumb.* New York: Workman Publishing.

Parks, Tim. 2013. The Greatest Intellectual Diary of Italian Literature. *The New York Review* 40(15): 28–30.

Peacocke, Christopher. 1999. *Being Known.* Oxford: Clarendon Press.

Pettit, Philip. 2003. Consequentialism. In *Consequentialism*, ed. Stephen Darwall, 95–107. Malden, MA: Blackwell Publishing.

Pettit, Philip, and Geoffrey Brennan. 1986. Restrictive Consequentialism. *Australasian Journal of Philosophy* 64(4): 438–55.

Piller, Christian. 2007. Ewing's Problem. *European Journal of Analytic Philosophy* 3: 43–65.

Pogge, Thomas. 1990. The Effects of Prevalent Moral Conceptions. *Social Research* 57(3): 649–63.

Pollack, Andrew. 1982. Computerizing Nuclear Plants. *The New York Times* (August 12), p. 32.

Pollock, John L. 2006. *Thinking about Acting: Logical Foundations for Rational Decision Making.* Oxford: Oxford University Press.

Portmore, Douglas. 2011. *Commonsense Consequentialism.* Oxford: Oxford University Press.

Prichard, H. A. 1968. Duty and Ignorance of Fact. In H. A. Prichard, *Moral Obligation and Duty and Interest*, 18–39. Oxford: Oxford University Press.

Putoto, Josephine R. 2012. The NCAA's Brave New World. *The Chronicle of Higher Education* (July 25). <http://chronicle.com/article/The-NCAAs-Brave-New-World/133115/?cid=at&utm_source=at&utm_medium=en> (accessed July 25, 2012).

Quenqua, Douglas. 2015. Facebook Knows You Better than Anyone Else. *The New York Times* (January 20), p. D4.

Quinton, Anthony. 1973. *Utilitarian Ethics.* Dordrecht: Springer.

Railton, Peter. 1984. Alienation, Consequentialism, and the Demands of Morality. *Philosophy and Public Affairs* 13(2): 134–71.

Railton, Peter. 2014. The Affective Dog and its Rational Tale: Intuition and Attunement. *Ethics* 124(4): 813–59.

Rawls, John. 1971. *A Theory of Justice.* Cambridge, MA: Harvard University Press.

Rawls, John. 1980. Kantian Constructivism in Moral Theory. *Journal of Philosophy* 77(9): 515–72.

Regan, Donald. 1980. *Utilitarianism and Co-operation.* Oxford: Clarendon Press.

Resnik, Michael D. 1987. *Choices: An Introduction to Decision Theory.* Minneapolis: University of Minnesota Press.

Rhodes, Rosamond. 2015. Good and Not So Good Medical Ethics. *Journal of Medical Ethics* 41(1): 71–4.

Richtel, Matt. 2015. A Culture of Nagging Helps California Save Water. *The New York Times* (October 12). <http://www.nytimes.com/2015/10/13/science/a-culture-of-nagging-helps-california-save-water.html> (accessed October 17, 2015).

Roberts, Robert C., and W. Jay Wood. 2007. *Intellectual Virtues: An Essay in Regulative Epistemology*. Oxford: Clarendon Press.

Roeder, Erica, and Gilbert Harman. 2010. Linguistics and Moral Theory. In *The Moral Psychology Handbook*, ed. John Doris and the Moral Psychology Research Group, 272–95. Oxford: Oxford University Press.

Rosen, Gideon. 2002. Culpability and Ignorance. *Proceedings of the Aristotelian Society* 108: 61–84.

Rosen, Gideon. 2004. Skepticism about Moral Responsibility. *Philosophical Perspectives* 18(1): 295–313.

Ross, Jacob. 2006. Rejecting Ethical Deflationism. *Ethics* 116(4): 742–68.

Ross, Jacob. 2012. Rationality, Normativity, and Commitment. In *Oxford Studies in Metaethics* 7, ed. Russ Shafer-Landau, 138–81. Oxford: Oxford University Press.

Ross, Lee, and Richard E. Nisbett. 2011. *The Person and the Situation*, 2nd edn. London: Pinter & Martin.

Ross, W. D. 1930. *The Right and the Good*. Oxford: Clarendon Press.

Ross, W. D. 1939. *Foundations of Ethics*. Oxford: Clarendon Press.

Russell, Bertrand. 1910. The Elements of Ethics. In *Readings in Ethical Theory*, 2nd edn., ed. Wilfrid Sellars and John Hospers, 10–15. Reprint, New York: Appleton-Century-Crofts, 1970.

Savage, Leonard J. 1954. *The Foundations of Statistics*, 2nd revised edn. New York: Dover Publications.

Scanlon, T. M. 1998. *What We Owe to Each Other*. Cambridge, MA: Belknap Press of Harvard University Press.

Scanlon, T. M. 2008. *Moral Dimensions: Permissibility, Meaning, Blame*. Cambridge, MA: Harvard University Press.

Schaffer, Amanda. 2006. A President Felled by an Assassin and 1880's Medical Care. *The New York Times* (July 27), pp. F5–6.

Schapiro, Tamar. 1999. What is a Child? *Ethics* 109(4): 715–38.

Scheffler, Samuel. 1982. *The Rejection of Consequentialism*. Oxford: Clarendon Press.

Scheffler, Samuel. 1992. *Human Morality*. New York: Oxford University Press.

Schroeder, Mark. 2011. Oughts, Agents, and Actions. *The Philosophical Review* 120(1): 1–41.

Sepielli, Andrew. 2009. What to Do When You Don't Know What to Do. In *Oxford Studies in Metaethics* 4, ed. Russ Shafer-Landau, 5–28. Oxford: Oxford University Press.

Sepielli, Andrew. 2012. Subjective Normativity and Action Guidance. In *Oxford Studies in Normative Ethics* 2, ed. Mark Timmons, 45–73. Oxford: Oxford University Press.

Sepielli, Andrew. 2013. Moral Uncertainty and the Principle of Equity among Moral Theories. *Philosophy and Phenomenological Research* 86(3): 580–9.

Shanker, Thom, and Matt Richtel. 2011. In the New Military, Data Overload Can Be Deadly. *The New York Times* (January 7), pp. A1–6.

Shaw, William. 1999. *Contemporary Ethics: Taking Account of Utilitarianism*. Malden, MA: Blackwell Publishing.

Shaw, William. 2007. The Consequentialist Perspective. In *Ethical Theory*, ed. Russ Shafer-Landau, 463–7. Malden, MA: Blackwell Publishing.

Shepherd, Joshua. 2015. Scientific Challenges to Free Will and Moral Responsibility. *Philosophy Compass* 10(3): 197–207.

Sher, George. 2009. *Who Knew?* Oxford: Oxford University Press.

Sher, George. 2014. *Equality for Inegalitarians.* Cambridge: Cambridge University Press.

Sidgwick, Henry. 1907. *The Methods of Ethics*, 7th edn. Chicago: University of Chicago Press.

Simon, Herbert. 1955. A Behavioral Model of Rational Choice. *Quarterly Journal of Economics* 69(1): 99–118.

Singer, Peter. 1972. Famine, Affluence, and Morality. *Philosophy and Public Affairs* 1(3): 229–43.

Singer, Peter. 1979. *Practical Ethics.* Cambridge: Cambridge University Press.

Sinnott-Armstrong, Walter. 1988. *Moral Dilemmas.* Oxford: Basil Blackwell.

Slemrod, Joel. 2007. Cheating Ourselves: The Economics of Tax Evasion. *Journal of Economic Perspectives* 21(1): 25–48.

Smart, J. J. C. 1973. An Outline of a System of Utilitarian Ethics. In J. J. C. Smart and Bernard Williams, *Utilitarianism: For and Against*, 1–74. Cambridge: Cambridge University Press.

Smith, Holly M. 1983. Culpable Ignorance. *The Philosophical Review* 92(4): 543–71.

Smith, Holly M. 1988. Making Moral Decisions. *Noûs* 22(1): 89–108.

Smith, Holly M. 1989. Two-Tier Moral Codes. *Social Philosophy and Policy* 7(1): 112–32.

Smith, Holly M. 1991. Deciding How to Decide: Is There a Regress Problem? In *Essays in the Foundations of Decision Theory*, ed. Michael Bacharach and Susan Hurley, 194–219. Oxford: Basil Blackwell.

Smith, Holly M. 1997. A Paradox of Promising. *The Philosophical Review* 106(2): 153–96.

Smith, Holly M. 2010a. Subjective Rightness. *Social Philosophy and Policy* 27(2): 64–110.

Smith, Holly M. 2010b. Measuring the Consequences of Rules. *Utilitas* 22(4): 413–33.

Smith, Holly M. 2011. The Moral Clout of Reasonable Beliefs. In *Oxford Studies in Normative Ethics* 1, ed. Mark Timmons, 1–25. Oxford: Oxford University Press.

Smith, Holly M. 2012. Using Moral Principles to Guide Decisions. *Philosophical Issues* 22(1): 369–86.

Smith, Holly M. 2014. The Subjective Moral Duty to Inform Oneself before Acting. *Ethics* 125(1): 1–28.

Smith, Holly M. 2016. Tracing Cases of Culpable Ignorance. In *Perspectives on Ignorance from Moral and Social Philosophy*, ed. Rik Peels, 95–119. New York: Routledge.

Sorensen, Roy. 1995. Unknowable Obligations. *Utilitas* 7(2): 247–71.

Sosa, David. 1993. Consequences of Consequentialism. *Mind*, New Series 102(405): 101–22.

Sosa, Ernest. 2014. Knowledge and Time: Kripke's Dogmatism Paradox and the Ethics of Belief. In *The Ethics of Belief: Individual and Social*, ed. Jonathan Matheson and Rico Vitz, 77–88. Oxford: Oxford University Press.

Span, Paula. 2015. A Prescription for Confusion: When to Take All Those Pills. *The New York Times* (December 22), p. D5.

Spencer, Herbert. 1851. *Social Statics.* London: John Chapman.

Stanley, Jason. 2005. *Knowledge and Practical Interests.* New York: Oxford University Press.

Star, Daniel. 2011. Two Levels of Moral Thinking. *Oxford Studies in Normative Ethics* 1: 75–96.

Sunstein, Cass. 2005. Moral Heuristics. *Behavior and Brain Sciences* 28(4): 531–73.

Sunstein, Cass. 2008. Fast, Frugal, and (Sometimes) Wrong. In *Moral Psychology 2, The Cognitive Science of Morality: Intuition and Diversity*, ed. Walter Sinnott-Armstrong, 27–30. Cambridge, MA: MIT Press.

Sverdlik, Steven. 2011. *Motive & Rightness*. Oxford: Oxford University Press.

Tadros, Victor. 2011. *The Ends of Harm*. Oxford: Oxford University Press.

Talbott, William J. 2005. *Which Rights Should Be Universal?* Oxford: Oxford University Press.

Talbott, William J. 2010. *Human Rights and Human Well-Being*. Oxford: Oxford University Press.

Temkin, Larry. 2012. *Rethinking the Good*. Oxford: Oxford University Press.

Thomson, Judith Jarvis. 1971. A Defense of Abortion. *Philosophy and Public Affairs* 1(1): 47–66.

Thomson, Judith Jarvis. 1990. *The Realm of Rights*. Cambridge, MA: Harvard University Press.

Timmons, Mark. 2002. *Moral Theory: An Introduction*. Lanham, MD: Rowman & Littlefield.

Toulmin, Stephen. 1950. *The Place of Reason in Ethics*. New York: Cambridge University Press.

Turri, John, and Peter Blouw. 2015. Excuse Validation: Study in Rule-Breaking. *Philosophical Studies* 172(3): 615–34.

Tversky, Amos, and Daniel Kahneman. 1974. Judgment under Uncertainty: Heuristics and Biases. *Science* 185(4157): 1124–31.

Unger, P. 1996. *Living High and Letting Die*. New York: Oxford University Press.

Van Someren Greve, Rob. 2014. The Value of Practical Usefulness. *Philosophical Studies* 168(1): 167–77.

Van Woudenberg, Rene. 2009. Ignorance and Force: Two Excusing Conditions for False Beliefs. *American Philosophical Quarterly* 46(4): 373–86.

Varner, Gary E. 2012. *Personhood, Ethics, and Animal Cognition: Situating Animals in Hare's Two-Level Utilitarianism*. New York: Oxford University Press.

Väyrynen, Pekka. 2006. Ethical Theories and Moral Guidance. *Utilitas* 18(3): 291–309.

Vineberg, Susan. 2011. Dutch Book Arguments. *The Stanford Encyclopedia of Philosophy*. Summer edn., ed. Edward N. Zalta. <http://plato.stanford.edu/archives/sum2011/entries/dutch-book/> (accessed December 20, 2015).

Wallace, R. Jay. 2011. "Ought," Reasons, and Vice: A Comment on Judith Jarvis Thomson's "Normativity." *Philosophical Studies* 154(3): 451–63.

Wallach, Wendell, and Colin Allen. 2009. *Moral Machines*. Oxford: Oxford University Press.

Warnock, C. J. 1971. *The Object of Morality*. London: Methuen.

Weisberg, Michael. 2007. Three Kinds of Idealization. *Journal of Philosophy* 114(12): 639–59.

Wiland, Eric. 2005. Monkeys, Typewriters, and Objective Consequentialism. *Ratio* 18(3): 352–60.

Williams, Bernard. 1973. Morality and the Emotions. In *Problems of the Self*. Cambridge: Cambridge University Press.

Williams, Bernard. 1976. Moral Luck. *Proceedings of the Aristotelian Society*, Supp. Vol. 50: 115–35.

Williams, Bernard. 1981. Moral Luck. In *Moral Luck: Philosophical Papers 1973–1980*, 20–39. Cambridge: Cambridge University Press.

Williams, Evan. 2013. Promoting Value As Such. *Philosophy and Phenomenological Research* 87(2): 392–416.

Williams, J. Robert G. 2014. Decision-Making under Indeterminacy. *Philosophers' Imprint* 14(4): 1–34. <http://www.philosophersimprint.org/014004/> (accessed December 19, 2015).

Williams, Michael. 2008. Responsibility and Reliability. *Philosophical Papers* 37(1): 1–27.

Williamson, Timothy. 2000. *Knowledge and Its Limits*. Oxford: Oxford University Press.

Williamson, Timothy. 2008. Why Epistemology Cannot be Operationalized. In *Epistemology: New Essays*, ed. Quentin Smith, 277–300. Oxford: Oxford University Press.

Wolf, Susan. 1990. *Freedom within Reason*. New York: Oxford University Press.

Zagzebski, Linda. 1996. *Virtues of the Mind*. Cambridge: Cambridge University Press.

Zimmerman, Michael J. 2006. Is Moral Obligation Objective or Subjective? *Utilitas* 18(4): 329–61.

Zimmerman, Michael J. 2008. *Living with Uncertainty*. Cambridge: Cambridge University Press.

Zimmerman, Michael J. 2014. *Ignorance and Moral Obligation*. Oxford: Oxford University Press.

Index of Names

General Index

Names of formal criteria, definitions, formulas, principles of recurring importance, and standards appear in italic. Names of tables and figures appear in bold.

Hybrid Response to epistemic problem in
morality (*cont.*)
need to establish priority among
decision-guides 256–8
non-ideal Hybrid system 187
posits deontically perfect code as top-tier
code 188
Standard 8.1 188
sample Hybrid systems 258–61
whether requires a single or multiple
decision-guides 235, 250–2, 275–6
see also Constrained Standards Hybrid
(C.S.H.) approach; counsels;
decision-guides; maxims; precepts
Hybrid Rossian deontology 258, 260–1;
see also Rossian deontological system;
deontologism
Hybrid solution, *see* Hybrid Response to
epistemic problem in morality

ideal and non-ideal moral theory 5
ignorance, nonmoral:
distinction between ignorance and
uncertainty 211
relevant definitions of 208–10
Definition 9.1 209
subsuming problem of ignorance under
problem of uncertainty 41–2, 211
see also epistemic impediments to using
morality to make decisions
immediately helpful description of an action 15,
18–20
information, interpretation of 43
injunction, as used in Splintered Pragmatic act
utilitarianism 272–3

justice, special form of 55–6, 165;
see also Usability Demand, conceptual
rationales for; successful moral life

Kantianism 37, 192n17, 242
knowledge as true belief 159n3

Low Bar approach, *see* usability of a moral
principle or theory/code

maxims 301
examples of 301–2
standard for objective evaluation of 302
Standard S₃ 302
uncertainty about objective standard for
maxims 306
miners' case, *see* Regan-style cases
mini-maxims 253–5, 261, 330–1
modal robustness 327–30
moral code, *see* moral theory (or code)
moral laundry list 70–7, 162, 185, 189

as practical decision-guide 185, 189, 321, 328
as theoretical account of right and wrong
70–7, 126
not modally robust as a decision-guide 328–9
moral dilemmas 12–13 n5
moral principle:
combine content and weight merit of principle
into deontic merit, how to 140–1
Criterion 6.1 140
Criterion 6.2 141
content merit of principle 137–9, 140–2, 144
content value of principle 141–2
corrupt 136, 142, 145, 146–7
deontic merit of principle 139, 140–1
extended practical domain of error- proof
principle 128
failure of agent to follow principle or
code 166, 175–6
imperfect but not corrupt principle
139–40, 145–6
importance of principle 137, 139, 142, 144
mental representation of principle 28–30
practical domain of principle 34, 128
principles vs. considerations in moral
theorizing 7–8, 28–30
semantic content of principle 138
theoretical domain of principle 33
traditional moral principles 36–7, 156
usability value of principle 149–53, 156–7
Criterion 6.3 150
Criterion 6.4 150
Criterion 6.5 150
Formula 6.1 156
usability value of principle, epistemic
challenge of ascertaining 159–61
usability weight of principle 149
Definition 6.3 149
way of expressing principle affects
usability 169
weight merit of principle 137–8, 140–6
moral status hierarchy of decision-guides 311;
see also hierarchy of deontic value
moral system 1, 182, 215, 217
foundations of 9
moral system of type D 219
moral system of type E 218
moral system of type F 225
moral system of type F, merits of 228–9
moral system of type F, relabeled "Hybrid
response to problems of error and
uncertainty" 231
moral systems of types A, B, C, G, H,
and I 217
moral system, two-tier 182–4
criteria of adequacy for 233–5;
see also Hybrid Response to epistemic
problem in morality